# AMERICAN CERAMICS

# AMERICAN CERAMICS

## THE COLLECTION OF EVERSON MUSEUM OF ART

EDITED BY BARBARA PERRY

RIZZOLI, NEW YORK

EVERSON MUSEUM OF ART, SYRACUSE

First published in the United States of America in 1989 by
RIZZOLI INTERNATIONAL PUBLICATIONS, INC.
597 Fifth Avenue, New York, NY 10017

Library of Congress Cataloging-in-Publication Data
Everson Museum of Art.
American ceramics : the collection of Everson Museum of Art/
edited by Barbara Perry.
Bibliography: p.
Includes index.
ISBN 0-8478-1025-9     ISBN 0-8478-1026-7 (pbk.)
1. Pottery, American—Catalogs. 2. Pottery—New York (State)—
Syracuse—Catalogs. 3. Porcelain, American—Catalogs. 4. Porcelain—
New York (State)—Syracuse—Catalogs. 5. Everson Museum of Art—
Catalogs.   I. Perry, Barbara. II. Title.
NK4005.E94 1989     738'.0973'074014—dc19     88-31282

Front jacket: detail from Adrian Saxe, *Untitled*, 1980 (entry 502)
Back jacket: Waylande Gregory, *Europa*, 1938 (entry 166)
Frontispiece: Adelaide Robineau, *Scarab Vase*, 1910 (entry 109)

All photography is by Courtney Frisse, except #421 by Jamey Stillings
and #475 courtesy Willard Gallery, New York

Designed by Steven Schoenfelder
Set in type by Rainsford Type, Danbury, Connecticut
Printed and bound in Japan

# CONTENTS

Everson Museum gratefully acknowledges the generous support
of the following contributors who have made this catalogue possible:

The Annie Laurie Aitken Charitable Trust

Mrs. Edward F. Beadel

Mr. and Mrs. Richard P. Davis

Everson Museum Members' Council

Mr. and Mrs. Alfred J. Flanagan

Joan and Edward Green

Mr. and Mrs. John S. Hancock

Mr. John F. Marsellus

Dorothy and Marshall M. Reisman

Dorothy and Robert Riester

Benjamin and Hedwig Sulzle Foundation, Inc.

Mrs. Hedwig Sulzle

Mr. Robert J. Theis, Sr., former Chairman

and President of Syracuse China

Grace M. Witting

Anonymous

This catalogue was supported in part by a grant
from the National Endowment for the Arts, a federal agency.

# FOREWORD

## THE STATUS OF CERAMICS

In the United States, as in almost any other country, the history of ceramics spans more years than its history as a nation, its history of painting, sculpture, furniture, or architecture. Still it is perhaps the least explored of these fields and given little attention in most general histories of art. This is due, we can presume, to confusion with the position of ceramics in the supposed hierarchy of art and its chronic omission from most art-historical education. This is a glaring fault since ceramics is the most universal of art forms, perhaps the most ancient and in some cultures the most quintessential, as in Greece, China, Japan, Peru, and Mexico. While usefulness, utility, and wear are considered aesthetic virtues in the appreciation of ceramics in some cultures, as in Japan, for instance; in others these same qualities are considered liabilities, as in England or France. The same contrariness of cultural attitude applies to ceramics's fragility, although its permanence on the other hand makes its presence one of the earliest signs of civilization on earth. Many issues such as these must be considered when determining why we know so little about ceramic art history.

My personal experience was not exceptional. Until I came to the Everson in 1974 I knew little about the history of ceramics. I had the good fortune, however, of coming from California where ceramics were emerging in the many university art departments and in the ubiquitous art fairs of the late sixties and early seventies. I also made the acquaintance of Beatrice Wood in Santa Barbara, whose iridescent vases and bowls I thought among the most beautiful objects I had ever seen and whose clay figures were so unusually gay and witty one begged to know more about this versatile artist's background. Besides this, my child-hood exposure to the ceramics displayed to advantage alongside the painting and sculpture in the Cleveland Museum of Art's annual May shows, gave me an inkling of the importance of ceramics as art. Again, in California, through an intense interest in Pre-Columbian art I learned that most of that culture's extant art history dealt with ceramics. At the Everson, it quickly became apparent as I surveyed the collections for the first time, that there was a resource in these ceramics, unique in content and extent, which could be feasibly added to without an immense financial challenge. This resource, of which the museum had been justly proud, would also eventually make it very famous. In addition, as a bonus, I welcomed the opportunity to learn in my new post about a relatively unexplored area of art. A brief visit to the gallery of Warren E. Cox (author of *The Book of Pottery and Porcelain*) in New York, just before he died, greatly impressed me with the encyclopedic knowledge of ceramics possible in one great afficionado's lifetime.

By 1974, besides the large collection of Adelaide Alsop Robineau's works—said by one of my mentors, Henry Hawley, Curator of Decorative Arts at the Cleveland Museum of Art, to be the greatest American to have created works of art in porcelain—the Everson had a large collection of pieces mostly garnered from the Ceramic National exhibitions and representing works dating from 1932 to 1968. These were usually on view in the Robineau Gallery, a gallery especially designed for the display of ceramics in the new I. M. Pei building, and endowed by the Robineau family. The museum also had the Cloud Wampler Collection of oriental art (mostly Chinese ceramics), the Lake Collection (English eighteenth- and nineteenth-century ceramics), the Davison Collection of early nineteenth-century American stoneware and slipware housed at the Onondaga Historical Association, and a small collection of Southwest American Indian pottery acquired in the late 1930s. A number of South American ceramics and also some Scandinavian works were included as a result of the Ceramic Nationals that traveled abroad in the early 1940s. Thus the mission for collecting seemed obvious to me: with the support of the Accession and Exhibitions Committee, our mandate was to build up the American ceramics collection focusing on the twentieth century but pushing back in time as well for the sake of depth to the nineteenth century and beyond. Furthermore, we were to encourage gifts and occasionally purchase representative works from as many of the world's ceramic cultures as feasible, in order to provide further context and breadth for the study of American ceramics.

Since then we have pursued collecting and the organization of exhibitions, accompanied by publications, with a certain amount of consistency and determination. When I first arrived in Syracuse, Margie Hughto, artist and professor of ceramics at Syracuse University, proposed a project called "New Works in Clay," which entailed inviting well-known artists in other media (painters and sculptors of the Abstract Expressionist school) to come to Syracuse to produce ceramics under her staff's technical supervision and to showcase the results in a series of exhibitions. This resulted in three shows from which eventually the Everson acquired works by Helen Frankenthaler, Anthony Caro, Jules Olitski, Kenneth Noland, and Friedel Dzubas, among others. The idea of the project was controversial (why didn't we invite potters to do paintings?) but because of the apparent identity crisis the ceramics world seemed to be undergoing at the time, it was felt that something should be done to get the attention of the "art-world" and essentially break down the barrier caused by a certain disdain for the medium of clay. As an antidote to our concentration of East Coast Formalists, we organized in 1978, with the co-curatorship of Judy Schwartz, "Nine West Coast Clay Sculptors," a prelude, in a way, to a later show at the Whitney Museum in New York, which brought great attention to the clay artists we had earlier recognized.

After an admittedly experimental phase of our ceramic enterprises under Hughto's direction, it seemed obvious that what was badly lacking in the field was an historical review of American ceramics from the beginning to the present day. No ceramics surveys existed, no exhibitions had covered this area of art in any comprehensive way. As we began discussing plans for an ambitious historical survey exhibition, Margie Hughto (now Adjunct Curator of Ceramics at Everson) and I had the good fortune to meet Garth Clark, visiting from England, and invited him to give a series of lectures concerning modern European ceramics. Clark, one of the few people with a formal education in the history of ceramics, went on to found the Institute for Ceramic Art History, which held its first conference in Syracuse. He later opened galleries in Los Angeles and New York and became a prime mover in the ceramic art market as well as the author of a number of new books. It quickly became apparent that we had a scholarly and willing collaborator in Garth Clark and thus he joined our efforts to produce the exhibition and groundbreaking publication, *A Century of Ceramics in the United States, 1878–1978*, in 1979. The exhibition was a great success and traveled to six other museums including the Cooper Hewitt in New York and the Renwick in Washington, D.C. In Washington it was commemorated by a special party given at the Vice-President's house by Vice-President and Mrs. Walter Mondale, a great supporter of the arts, and her-

self a potter.

Following the "Century show," we continued to concern ourselves with documenting the past, and in 1981, under the aegis of Curator Peg Weiss and Guest Curator Martin Eideleberg, we organized "The Porcelains of Adelaide Alsop Robineau" and published a definitive catalogue with Syracuse University Press.

Also in 1981, under Curator Ross Anderson, a small but definitive exhibition and catalogue on *The Ceramic Art of William Grueby* was produced. In 1983, Adjunct Curator of Ceramics Barbara Perry and Ross Anderson organized and published *The Diversions of Keramos, American Clay Sculpture 1925–1950*, another close and unprecedented look at an era of ceramics in which the Everson's collections are especially strong. In 1986, a banner year, Dr. Barbara Perry became full-time Curator of Ceramics, and the renovation of a large portion of the first floor of the Everson created the Syracuse China Center for the Study of American Ceramics, supported by the Canadian Pacific Corporation, U.S. With floor to ceiling cases and pedestals, the entire collection of ceramics became accessible to the public for the first time in a study/storage environment.

In 1986 the Ceramic National was revived with "American Ceramics Now," which opened in conjunction with the twentieth meeting of the National Council on Education in the Ceramic Arts, held in Syracuse. The exhibition was judged by three authorities in the field of contemporary art—only one of whom could be considered a specialist in ceramics—chosen for their broader perspectives and to emphasize our interest in the art of ceramics, rather than the craft per se. The desire to revive this traditional Everson event seemed justified even though many ceramists had had stunning success in entering the art market and although many galleries showed American ceramics now as an accepted art form. Even so, such bellwethers of contemporary art as the Whitney and Corcoran biennials rarely, if ever, show ceramics. There still seemed to be a need for a national stage upon which new talent

could emerge without the constraints and limitations of the commercial art gallery system.

The Everson's collections have grown dramatically since 1974 because of the generosity of many individual donors, artists, trustees, and National Endowment for the Arts grants. An endowment gift for the purchase of ceramics in 1986 by Mr. and Mrs. Robert Riester of Cazenovia, New York, has helped the Museum significantly enhance both its contemporary holdings and its collection of early twentieth-century art pottery.

The Everson was founded in 1896 by George Fiske Comfort as the Syracuse Museum of Fine Arts. It acquired its first ceramics in 1916 under Director Fernando Carter, a painter, when it bought thirty-two pieces of Robineau's porcelains. Syracuse at that time was not only the home of Adelaide Alsop Robineau, the great master of porcelain, and her publication *Keramic Studio*, but also the home of Gustave Stickley, the renowned maker of arts and crafts furniture, and a number of architects including Ward Wellington Ward, who designed houses in the arts and crafts idiom. The museum's name was changed in the 1950s after a local heiress, Helen Everson, died and left funds to build a new museum building using her family name. I. M. Pei was selected as the architect (his first museum commission) and the present award-winning structure opened in 1968.

While the American ceramics collection certainly gives the Everson a unique claim to fame, it is not a museum of ceramics as the Corning Museum is a museum of glass. The Everson's collection of American painting and sculpture is outstanding and its smaller collections of prints and drawings, photography, African sculpture, and Chinese and Japanese art make it a general museum of art. It is in this context of art that the Everson views its ceramics collection, not as decorative art, not as design, not as craft.

Nor has it divided, within the ceramic medium, sculpture from vessel forms, since from the most ancient times figures were as prevalent as vessels in clay. While the

Arts and Crafts movement of the nineteenth century promoted the virtues of good design and good craft with many fine results, its holdover philosophy has developed to this day in a quagmire of semantic confusion and perhaps by now irrelevant categorization of the arts. The art of ceramics has its own history as does the art of painting and architecture. It is just that its history has rarely been broadly illustrated. We hope this book and other more recent publications will help rectify that condition.

It would be a great tribute to one of my most admired predecessors, Anna Wetherill Olmsted (director from 1931 to 1959), who so single-handedly carried the torch for American ceramics in the thirties, forties, and fifties, if the collection that she assembled with meager funds, each year acquir-

ing prize-winners from the Ceramic Nationals, became the key to greater recognition for the art of ceramics in general. Her foresight and will-power managed to orchestrate a special role for the modest-sized Everson, enabling it to make a contribution unequaled elsewhere in this country.

I remember a journalist interviewing me in my office in order to write a review of the recently opened Syracuse China Center for the Study of American Ceramics rather ingenuously asking how I could consider ceramics as art. In response I pointed to two recent, prized acquisitions—one, an American Tonalist painting circa 1885 hanging over my desk by J. Francis Murphy, and the other a Rookwood vase circa 1890 standing on a table nearby signed A. Valentien. I asked her which she consid-

ered more beautiful. She liked them both very much fortunately, but told me she could not decide which one she liked best—they were equally attractive objects to her.

Ceramics as an art form no longer need take refuge in the craft category which for so long (since the Arts and Crafts movement at the turn of the century) celebrated it, but also down the road, by prolonged emphasis on the word "craft" instead of the word "arts," somewhat minimized its potential for appreciation as art in America. Now, the saga of American ceramics can be followed aesthetically in this book's cogent words and descriptive pictures as well as in the galleries of the Everson in Syracuse.

Ronald A. Kuchta
Director

# ACKNOWLEDGMENTS

This catalogue was compiled with the assistance of many people. Amy Schwartzott, research assistant, was indispensable throughout this whole project, as was Rosemarie Romano, Everson's librarian and archivist. Carole Burke was a most agreeable typist and helped in innumerable other ways. Marlene Hamann, Lynn Gobol, Patricia Shapiro, and Deborah Freeman helped with descriptions. Michele Bosley of the Fulton Historical Society provided information on the Hart family of potters. The expertise and patience of photographer Courtney Frisse helped to make this undertaking less demanding than it might have been, and Sarah Burns was a patient and discriminating editor. Their contributions are all gratefully acknowledged.

Barbara Perry

Syracuse China Corporation can trace its history back to a stoneware pottery established by Williams Farrar in Syracuse in 1856. By 1888 the company was producing fine porcelain, such as the Imperial Geddo ware pictured here. They also made specialty items, such as the Herbert Hoover mug, and developed a sturdy china body for everyday dinnerware. The company now makes fine commercial dinnerware.

# PREFACE

Clay vessels and figures have been formed by nearly every culture since the beginning of civilization. These objects, made of the very earth itself, were not only utilitarian, but also often ritualistic or created purely for aesthetic purposes. The ceramics collection of Everson Museum contains objects of each of these types, and ranges in scope from vessels and sculpture of the second millennium B.C. to the present, from ancient China and Greece to present day Africa and the United States. The focus, however, is on American ceramics, including those of ancient pre-Columbian America to utilitarian wares of the nineteenth century and the exquisite and often revolutionary art works of the United States today. Over half of the American collection is made up of works from the twentieth century.

The earliest American objects—pots and jars from the ancient Southwest—date from about 850 A.D. through the late Pueblo eras. A few examples from other early cultures are also included, and though this is the smallest section of the collection, it is slowly being expanded. With the coming of the Europeans more and more types of ceramic vessels were introduced to this country, and examples of products of early American potteries make up the next grouping in the collection. These wares are mostly utilitarian, but also illustrate that even when function was of paramount importance, the creative instinct found expression. We admire the simple floral decorations on early salt-glazed wares and the whimsical animals produced during the nineteenth century.

The art potteries of the late nineteenth and early twentieth centuries are represented in the collection by primary examples from major producers and their finest decorators. This era established a basis for the attitudes and objects which were to come to the fore in the following years. The art pottery movement laid the groundwork for the establishment of an American ceramic tradition.

The following decades, up to mid-century, saw the emergence of particular characteristics which might at last be identified as peculiar to ceramics produced by Americans. And during the last forty years these characteristics have become more fully defined, most particularly in the works of those artists who were involved in and who have benefited from the "revolution" in American ceramics that took place after the Second World War.

Today American ceramics, once a stepchild of other cultures, is strong enough to not only stand alone, but also to influence many of those other cultures on which it once depended.

Barbara Perry
Curator of Ceramics

## NOTES TO THE CATALOGUE:

All the exhibitions mentioned in the catalogue were held at Everson Museum of Art, Syracuse, New York (which was the Syracuse Museum of Fine Arts until 1959), unless otherwise noted.

The exhibition list following certain entries includes those exhibitions not already mentioned in the entry.

Dimensions: D.= Depth; Diam.= Diameter; H. = Height; L. = Length; W. = Width

The titles of the Ceramic National Exhibitions have been abbreviated in the entries; they are listed in full in the bibliography.

# ANCIENT AMERICAN CERAMICS

## BARBARA PERRY

The inhabitants of America before the arrival of Columbus were as varied as the land in which they lived. Their distinctive cultures derived from their environment and the demands it placed on them for survival. They gradually grew beyond subsistence level, and their established patterns and customs gave them singular identities, which were expressed in their rituals, community organization, and their art. One of our major sources of information on these early people is their pottery, which is often exceedingly fine, both in form and decoration.

Pottery was made from the forested regions of the Northeast to the tropical areas of Florida. The moundbuilders of Ohio and the Mississippi area, and the southwestern people all made vessels—and often ritual figures—from clay. Their objects were for daily use, as seed jars, water carriers, and cooking pots, and included mugs, bowls, and ladles. Some of the existing pottery is undecorated, but much of it bears designs indicating the special functions of these particular vessels. Sometimes they might simply be more elaborate, utilitarian objects, perhaps used for serving food. Others were obviously for ritual purposes, and some were burial vessels.

### THE HOHOKAM

One of the earliest of these ancient American cultures was that of the Hohokam people in the Gila and Salt valleys of Arizona. The area is very dry, and the Hohokam developed an ingenious and detailed system of irrigation, digging miles of canals to channel the precious water to their villages. They had courts for ball games similar to those of the Maya and other Central American peoples and built flattened mounds for ceremonial use.

The Hohokam made clay figurines, usually female nudes, probably for religious purposes. Since the wheel was unknown in ancient America prior to the arrival of the Europeans, the Hohokam formed their vessels with coils. They were shaped with paddles and anvils, which were tapped along the outside of the damp clay body against a stone or shard held along the inside wall. In this way the Hohokam could achieve thin-walled vessels. They painted their pottery with red designs, usually on a buff ground (entry 5). The vessels produced by this culture were used for carrying and storing water, food, and seeds; for cooking; and for ritual purposes. The Hohokam, unlike their Anasazi neighbors to the north and east, also made tripod vessels and incense burners, the latter often in the shape of animals.

### THE ANASAZI

The ancient people known as the Anasazi lived in northern Arizona and New Mexico. They were fine basket makers and probably first began to make pottery by molding clay around or inside a basket for a sturdier container. Accidentally dropped in a fire, these may have become their first pottery vessels. Or these people may have been introduced to pottery by neighboring cultures, perhaps the Hohokam.

Whether adapted from basketry or learned from neighbors, the Anasazi vessels were made by the coil method and fired in a reducing atmosphere. The coils of clay were pinched together and then smoothed with a piece of gourd or a stone. The clay turned gray-white when fired. Black decorations were added, using vegetable or mineral materials—minerals left a darker impression on the surface of the clay. An early method of construction using very thin coils which were then pinched in a rhythmical fashion around the vessel produced jars with extraordinarily textured surfaces, almost corrugated. These corrugations are often surprisingly evenly spaced and thin, resulting in a ribbed effect, as in the Salado bell-mouthed jar in the Everson collection (entry 1).

Forms were determined by function. Ollas, or water jars, were large, full-bodied vessels with narrow necks used for storage within the home and probably held corn, beans, and such foodstuffs, as well as water. Seed jars were small bowls with wide shoulders and relatively small mouths (entry 4). Ladles were of various sizes and had handles ranging from round to oval in cross section, and sometimes had a furrow down the center (entry 2). Some vessels were made to resemble gourds, with curved handles representing the necks or vines. Cooking pots were large-bodied with wide mouths. Serving bowls were wide, and often decorated. Bowls and mugs were often used in funerary rites.

Though much ancient American pottery was of the black-on-white variety, the Anasazi also made red-on-orange ware and later, polychrome wares with white, black, and red as the main colors. These required a different method of firing, which the Anasazi may have learned from neighboring people. Serving bowls and ceremonial vessels were decorated with linear designs and hatching as well as solid black areas. The earliest objects were decorated with heavy black lines, but later, as the decoration became more involved, lines became thinner. Triangles, stepped triangles, serrated bands, frets, checkerboard designs, and spirals were also used.

As the Anasazi population grew and their various settlements became larger, each developed its own particular style of pottery with features which distinguished it from other settlements, yet all preserved the same underlying characteristics. The descendants of these ancient people are the present day Pueblos, who carry on the pottery-making traditions of their ancestors.

## THE MIMBRES VALLEY

Some of the finest pottery produced in ancient North America was made by the people of the Mogollon culture who lived in the Mimbres valley of New Mexico. The Mogollon people had a tradition of pottery that may have originated in Mexico and they, too, made their pots by coiling clay and then scraping the walls of the vessels to a smooth, finished surface suitable for decorating. First red-on-white styles appeared, then the familiar black-on-white wares were produced.

Mogollon wares produced during the Mimbres period, that is, in the eleventh and twelfth centuries, were exceedingly fine. These vessels were decorated with crisp geometric designs and also realistic images of humans and animals, including bats, turtles, insects, frogs, and rabbits. Sometimes the figures made up a scene, such as a hunt or a ceremony. The form of the vessel determined whether the decoration would be figural or geometric. The bowl, in fact, seems to have been treated primarily as a canvas upon which to paint. Form and decoration were invariably united, each dependent upon the other.

During later periods geometric designs were often enclosed within a structuring outline, usually a band at the rim and another lower down to give the center a frame. Both interiors and exteriors were decorated. The space enclosed by the frames was subdivided further, but the unity of the whole was never lost. Combinations of hatching and black and white areas were used.

Since the Mimbres potter was more intent on decoration than form, the shapes tend to be simple and similar to those of neighboring cultures. They made ollas, bowls, seed jars, mugs, and canteens, as well as effigies of birds and animals. Rare fragments of human effigies have also been found. Early Mimbres vessels had textured surfaces, including the corrugated type, like other Mogollon vessels.

Mimbres pots had religious significance as well. Burial sites always contain finely decorated vessels, usually bowls, which have been ritually broken by punching a hole in the bottom. This seems to have been done at the grave site, since often the broken piece will be found close by. The significance of this ritual is not known with certainty, although it has been suggested that the holes were either to let the spirit escape or the result of a symbolic "killing" at the burial site. A small bowl in the Everson collection illustrates this ritual use (entry 5) although the hole does not appear in the photograph.

## THE MISSISSIPPI VALLEY

In the Southeast and central areas of the continent there existed a complex culture referred to as Mississippian. It lasted from about 800 A.D. until the arrival of the Europeans. These people lived in large towns or villages and were great farmers, intensively cultivating the lands around them. Their culture was theocratic; ritual and ceremony, with the attendant need for vessels and objects of adornment, played important roles. The Caddoan culture in Arkansas, and other Mississippian cultures, created vessels that were unpainted, with incised or modeled decoration, some abstract, some figural. The Caddoans produced clay sculptural figures as well as pottery. Incising was a common form of decoration, and often was extremely refined, particularly in ceremonial vessels. Both figural and geometric motifs were used. Of particular interest are bowls with the head and tail of a bird or animal modeled into the rim; the body of the vessel then represented the body of the animal (entry 7). Such effigy vessels were often covered with finely incised decorative motifs.

These ancient cultures produced pottery of an incredible beauty with only the basic ingredients of pottery making: clay, water, mineral or vegetable coloring, and of course, fire. The harshness of the environment in many cases precluded the possibilities of much further technical innovation. But the number of objects found indicates a vital interest in pottery making and the intricate decorative motifs tell us much about the aesthetic sensibilities of these innovative and complex people.

1

**1 Salado**

*Jar,* 850–1150 A.D.
Earthenware
H. 13½, Diam. 13 in.
(33.75 × 32.5 cm.)
Marks: none
Gift of Mr. and Mrs. Jonathan
Holstein  P.C. 81.51.13

Large earthenware olla-like (or water storage) jar. The bulbous body tapers to a flared mouth. The modeled exterior surface creates a corrugated effect, except at the rim, which is smooth. The brown clay has been left unglazed. The corrugations were created by the fingers of the potter as the coils were pinched together.

The people of the Salado culture lived and farmed in the Salt River Valley in what is now central Arizona, where they built complex houses in cliff-side caves.

2

## 2 Anasazi

*Clockwise, beginning at left*:
*Ladle,* 950–1100 A.D.
Earthenware
H. 2¼, L. 10½, Diam. 6 in. (5.6 ×
26.25 × 15 cm.)
Marks: none
Gift of Mr. and Mrs. Jonathan
Holstein   P.C. 81.85.6

Large earthenware ladle with pointed cylindrical handle decorated in a
black stripe design. The bowl interior has a black geometric design
on the sides and a gray bottom. Fire

clouds mark the gray exterior.

The straight line, often repeated
to create hatching, is the most basic
element of decoration in early Anasazi pottery. Here, hatched elements have been combined with flat
black areas, typical of the Pueblo II
phase of the Anasazi culture.

*Ladle,* 950–1100 A.D.
Earthenware
H. 1¾, L. 6½, Diam. 3½ in.
(4.3 × 16.25 × 8.75 cm.)

Marks: none
Gift of Mr. and Mrs. Jonathan
Holstein   P.C. 81.85.8

Earthenware ladle from the Pueblo
II phase with extended cylindrical
handle decorated with black linear
designs. The bowl interior is covered
in an intricate step pattern in black.
The body of the piece is gray.

*Ladle,* 1100–1125 A.D.
Earthenware
H. 1¾, L. 6¾, Diam. 3¼ in. (4.3 ×
16.8 × 8.1 cm.)
Marks: none

Gift of Mr. and Mrs. Jonathan
Holstein   P.C. 81.85.7

Earthenware ladle, black-on-white
with allover square-at-center pattern. There is a deep trough or
groove running the full length of the
handle.

This dipper is from the Pueblo III
phase of the Anasazi culture, Mesa
Verde type. The ancient potters used
solid, grooved, or hollow handles on
their ladles. The design on the interior is typical of this period.

3

**3 Anasazi**

*Four Mile Polychrome Olla,* n.d.
Earthenware
H. 9, Diam. 12 in. (22.5 × 30 cm.)
Marks: none
Gift of Mr. and Mrs. Jonathan
Holstein    P.C. 85.82.1

Flattened, ovoid earthenware vessel
with wide, raised cylindrical neck
and mouth. A large, black, geometric
design covers the vessel; faint white
outlines remain on the orange-brown
body.

This large, reconstructed storage
jar is of an extraordinarily sensitive
shape, with a full body and slightly
curved neck. Black-on-red ware first
appeared in Basket Maker III, and
reached its highest level in Pueblo I.

4

**4 Anasazi**

*Clockwise, beginning at left*:
*Seed Storage Jar,* 1000–1200 A.D.
Earthenware
H. 4¾, Diam. 6½ in.
(11.8 × 16.25 cm.)
Marks: none
Gift of Mr. and Mrs. Jonathan
Holstein   P.C. 81.85.3

Round, bulbous earthenware seed jar with circular mouth. There are four holes at the top—two sets of two on opposite sides. Black linear and step designs, angled vertically, surround the orange body of the jar.

This seed jar from the early Pueblo III phase has a full body and a combination of stepped and broad straight lines that seem to hug the shape of the vessel. The holes along the rim may have had ritual significance, or they may simply have al-

lowed the jar to be hung by a leather cord.

*Pitcher with Handle,* 1085–1200 A.D.
Earthenware
H. 9, W. 6¾ in. (22.5 × 16.8 cm.)
Marks: none
Gift of Mr. and Mrs. Jonathan
Holstein   P.C. 81.85.5

Ovoid earthenware pitcher with bulges at midsection. The applied band handle tapers to a small mouth at the top. Diamond shapes with checkered designs cover the sides of the vessel. A large fire cloud patch is at the back.

During Pueblo II phase, pitchers were commonly made. There was usually only a slight demarcation between body and neck, as illustrated

by this reconstructed example. The ovoid shape evolved from the gourd.

*Bowl,* 1150–1400 A.D.
Earthenware
H. 5, Diam. 10¼ in.
(12.5 × 25.6 cm.)
Marks: none
Gift of Mr. and Mrs. Jonathan
Holstein   P.C. 81.85.2

This large, round, gray earthenware bowl has flaring sides and an undecorated exterior. The interior has two decorative bands with alternating geometric and stripe designs near the black rim.

In these early wares, the surface was coated with a smooth slip and the design brushed on in black. The patterns were symbolic in origin, such as the step pattern which represented rain clouds. But the signif-

icance of these symbols seems to have been gradually lost or altered for purely aesthetic reasons.

*Miniature Canteen,* 1085–1200 A.D.
Earthenware
H. 5⅝, Diam. 6 in. (14 × 15 cm.)
Marks: none
Gift of Mr. and Mrs. Jonathan
Holstein   P.C. 81.85.4

Bulbous earthenware canteen with raised cylindrical neck. Two round loop handles rise from the shoulder. A black step pattern covers the gray body. Fire clouds appear on the base.

Fire clouds, which result from the firing process, are accidental and have no ritual significance.

5 *Clockwise, beginning at left:*

**Tonto Basin Region**

*Bowl,* c. 1050 A.D.
Earthenware
H. 3, Diam. 8 in. (7.5 × 20 cm.)
Marks: none
Gift of Mr. and Mrs. Kenneth
Siebel, Jr.   P.C. 84.51.26

Round earthenware bowl with flared rim. The exterior is brown and white overall. Two brown bands surround the bowl on the interior near the rim. There is a checkerboard design at the center, with step and geometric designs overall, in brown on white.

**Sikyatki**

*Bowl,* 1250–1400 A.D.
Earthenware
H. 4½, Diam. 12 in. (11.25 × 30 cm.)
Marks: none
Gift of Mr. and Mrs. Kenneth
Siebel, Jr.   P.C. 84.51.10

Hemispherical earthenware bowl. The body is of an iron-bearing clay which turns ochre or orange upon firing. Brown rectangular designs surround the rim. A light brown band surrounds the bowl beneath the rim on the exterior. A light brown bird design covers the interior.

Birds were a favorite subject of Sikyatki decorators. The brown-on-ochre stands out among the black and white wares of the Anasazi or Mimbres cultures.

The bird depicted in the center of this large bowl appears to have been pierced by an arrow.

**Hohokam**

*Flare Rimmed Jug,* 1100–1200 A.D.
Earthenware
H. 4¾, Diam. 4 in. (11.8 × 10 cm.)
Marks: none
Gift of Mr. and Mrs. Kenneth
Siebel, Jr.   P.C. 84.51.3

The body of this squat, bulbous jug tapers to a wide, flaring mouth. A geometric step design covers the white body of the vessel.

The Hohokam people painted their pottery with red designs, often intricate, as in this piece. Though the Hohokam culture had begun to decline by the time this jug was made (during the Sakaton phase), it fits the hand snugly, pointing to the skill of the potter.

**Hohokam**

*Bowl,* n.d.
Earthenware
H. 4, Diam. 9¼ in. (10 × 23.1 cm.)
Marks: none
Gift of Mr. and Mrs. Kenneth
Siebel, Jr.   P.C. 84.51.25

Rounded bowl with wide, flared rim. The interior is covered with a linear design composed of straight and wavy lines dividing the bowl equally into quadrants. Four circular designs surround the area near the rim.

Hohokam decorators often used tension-producing motifs which made their pottery lively and vigorous. Here, chevrons with one wavy and one straight line are created with spontaneous brushwork.

**Mogollon**

*Bowl,* 900–1100 A.D.
Earthenware
H. 3¾, Diam. 9 in. (9.3 × 22.5 cm)
Marks: none
Gift of Mr. and Mrs. Kenneth
Siebel, Jr.   P.C. 84.51.12

Hemispherical earthenware bowl with a polished black interior and an unglazed red earthenware exterior. A smooth band surrounds the rim area, in contrast to the raised textured surface below.

This carefully formed, corrugated bowl has a fire cloud on the exterior rim. The narrow coil maintains a uniform width and the pinched corrugations are exceedingly even, a superlative example of this technique.

**Mimbres**

*Bowl,* c. 1100 A.D.
Earthenware
H. 3½, Diam. 7¼ in.
(8.75 × 18.1 cm.)
Marks: none
Gift of Mr. and Mrs. Kenneth
Siebel, Jr.   P.C. 84.51.17

Rounded earthenware bowl. The exterior is unglazed with fire clouds. The interior is off-white with a brown linear and step design.

The people of New Mexico's Mimbres Valley decorated their bowls with complex geometric designs as well as stylized images of humans and animals. Their vessels were often buried with the dead, and, as in this one, have holes punched in the bottom. However, the significance of this ritual is not known with certainty.

Here, the artist has divided the bowl into four sections, with the curved, rotational fan shape imparting a sense of movement to the design.

6 *Clockwise, beginning at left:*

**Mimbres**
*Bowl,* c. 1000 A.D.
Earthenware
H. 4, Diam. 9 in. (10 × 22.5 cm.)
Marks: none
Gift of Mr. and Mrs. Kenneth
Siebel, Jr.   P.C. 84.51.27

Hemispherical earthenware bowl.
The exterior and the rim are orange,
with many fire clouds. The interior
is decorated with a black geometric
design integrating triangular forms
and grids on a white background.

The design areas on this bowl were
outlined with a black line before
being filled in, as was common practice with Mimbres potters. The solid
black shapes here create a lively ambiguity between positive and negative areas.

**Anasazi**
*St. John's Polychrome Bowl,*
c. 1100 A.D.
Earthenware
H. 5½, Diam. 11½ in.
(13.75 × 28.75 cm.)
Marks: none
Gift of Mr. and Mrs. Jonathan
Holstein   P.C. 81.85.14

Large, hemispherical earthenware
bowl. The interior is decorated with
black step designs on an orange
background. The exterior has a geometric motif in white over black and
orange.

St. John's polychrome is a red
ware that has white or cream decoration in addition to the black. It is
from the Pueblo II phase of the Anasazi culture.

**Jedditto**
*Bowl,* 1325–1600 A.D.
Earthenware
H. 3¾, Diam. 7½ in.
(9.3 × 18.75 cm.)
Marks: none
Gift of Mr. and Mrs. Jonathan
Holstein   P.C. 81.51.11

Hemispherical earthenware bowl. A
brown step design on a white base
surrounds the bowl. The off-white
interior has a band at midpoint. A
central geometric motif is contained
in a circle on the bottom.

**Gila**
*Bowl,* 1250–1400 A.D.
Earthenware
H. 5½, Diam. 10¾ in.
(13.75 × 26.8 cm.)
Marks: none

Gift of Mr. and Mrs. Jonathan
Holstein   P.C. 81.85.10

Large, hemispherical earthenware
bowl. The undecorated orange exterior and rim have fire clouds. A
black band encircles the center, with
black linear designs on the white
interior.

**Gila**
*Bowl,* 1250–1400 A.D.
Earthenware
H. 3, Diam. 5¾ in. (7.5 × 14.3 cm.)
Marks: none
Gift of Mr. and Mrs. Jonathan
Holstein   P.C. 81.51.9

Small, hemispherical earthenware
bowl with red-brown exterior and
rim. The interior has black linear
step designs and geometric patterns
in black on a white background.

7

7 *Clockwise, beginning at left:*
**Mississippian**
*Bowl,* n.d.
Earthenware
H. 4, Diam. 7½ in. (10 × 18.75 cm.)
Marks: none
Gift of Mr. and Mrs. Kenneth
Siebel, Jr.   P.C. 84.51.15

Rounded earthenware bowl with flared rim at the mouth. Modeling on the rim creates a textured surface, while linear incising covers the body. The bowl is unglazed.

The Mississippian culture was complex and highly organized. Evidence shows that their pottery was traded as far as South Dakota.

**Caddoan**
*Jar with Birds,* n.d.
Earthenware
H. 7½, Diam. 6¾ in. (18.75 × 16.8 cm.)
Marks: none
Gift of Mr. and Mrs. Kenneth
Siebel, Jr.   P.C. 84.51.19

Bulbous earthenware jar tapering to a cylindrical neck. The unglazed brown body is incised with a bird motif and abstract geometric designs beginning at the shoulder and extending over the entire body.

**Caddoan**
*Jar,* n.d.
Earthenware
H. 7¼, Diam. 6¾ in. (18.1 × 16.8 cm.)
Marks: none
Gift of Mr. and Mrs. Kenneth
Siebel, Jr.   P.C. 84.51.18

Rounded earthenware jar with round lobed neck and mouth. Modeled areas with rough linear incisings surround the neck. Fire clouds cover the surface.

This Caddoan jar is finely formed, but the incising about the neck is less fully realized. The four lobes at the rim are reminiscent of ancient Iroquois pottery.

**Mississippian**
*Bowl,* n.d.
Earthenware
H. 4, W. 7½ in. (10 × 18.75 cm.)
Marks: none
Gift of Mr. and Mrs. Kenneth
Siebel, Jr.   P.C. 84.51.14

Rounded earthenware bowl of unglazed, gray clay. The area surrounding the rim is modeled with a raised design. Two incised arrows point to a modeled avian head on one end of the bowl. Opposite is a wide, flattened form which represents the tail of the bird.

Such effigy vessels were common among the Mississippian people. Both birds and animals were used, and often the body was decorated with a finely incised design.

# AMERICAN CERAMICS
# 1700 – 1880

## PART 1: EARLY POTTERY AND PORCELAIN
## WILLIAM C. KETCHUM, JR.

Potters were among the first skilled artisans to arrive on the shores of North America. The English ceramist Philip Drinker had arrived in Charlestown, Massachusetts by 1635, and the Dutch "pottmaker" Dirck Claesen was already established in Manhattan before 1655. These men brought with them skills learned in their native lands, which they were immediately able to put to good use in the colonies where ceramic vessels were in short supply. Pottery was fragile and, in larger forms such as storage jars and crocks, bulky. Moreover, utilitarian pieces—those used for the storage and serving of food—did not bring a high price. As a result precious shipboard space was allocated to other, more valuable goods.

To a great extent, this situation dictated the development of the American pottery industry. Throughout the colonies in the earliest years, and at a much later date in frontier communities, the potter found a ready market for his goods, no matter how crude they might be. As late as 1814 Norman L. Judd of Rome, New York, then a rough, new town on the Western Turnpike, remarked that "ware here is ready cash . . ." (Spargo, *Potters and Potteries of Bennington*, Boston, 1926). Yet, scarcely forty years later his customers had turned to tin, glass, and mass-produced factory ceramics.

This rise and gradual decline of local potteries mirrored similar developments in England and Europe, and craftsmen from those areas played a major role in the American scene. In the first place, most potters who worked in this country were either trained in Europe or by those only a generation or two removed from that tradition. As late as 1875, a statistical analysis of the New York State census revealed that of the state's 367 potters, thirty percent were German born, twenty-three percent from England, and only forty-one percent native. Given such figures it is hardly surprising that American wares resemble in technique and decoration those made in other lands.

On the other hand, nothing remained the same here. Potters and their pottery changed under the effect of the new environment and the new freedom, resulting in forms and, particularly, decoration which may be said to be uniquely American, such as the so-called "flint enamel" glaze developed at Bennington, Vermont by Christopher Webber Fenton.

Moreover, there is a fairly clear progression in technique and organization from the earliest potteries and their wares to those which were later established. Initial production throughout the country was of redware, a low-fired ceramic produced from the same earth employed in brickmaking. Since this was available throughout the United States, potters simply settled near a local vein of clay, which could be burned in easily constructed brick or stone kilns.

However, inherent problems and limitations of this material, such as the fragility of the work produced and the toxicity of the lead glazes employed, led craftsmen in some areas to use stoneware clays, which could be fired to a much harder, more durable body. But because these earths were not available everywhere, initial production was limited to regions of New York, New Jersey, the Carolinas, and Pennsylvania where suitable deposits were located. Artisans in other areas—such as New England, which is totally lacking in stoneware clay—were forced to import their raw materials. This expense, coupled with the need for bigger, more sophisticated ovens to fire a ware requiring substantially higher maturation temperatures, led to larger shops,

producing more goods, often with the financial backing of local businessmen.

There were also clays, found primarily in New Jersey, Pennsylvania, and Ohio, which could be used in the production of yellow-bodied ceramics. The ductility of this material lent itself to casting, and by the 1830s sizable factories were established for the production of molded yellowwares, primarily kitchen utensils such as mixing bowls and baking pans.

Application of a brown, tortoiseshell-like glaze to this yellow body resulted in Rockingham, a finish which had been developed in England in the late eighteenth century. The American variation was made in many places including Maryland, Ohio, and New Jersey, but in the public mind it is most closely associated with Bennington, Vermont.

Also available in New Jersey, the Carolinas, and Ohio were clays firing to a white, earthen body, and these were used as early as the 1770s by John Bartlam of Charleston, South Carolina in the manufacture of Queensware, a thin-bodied, cream-colored pottery. However, it was not until the mid-nineteenth century that successful mass production was initiated.

Porcelain, a translucent ceramic composed of kaolin, flint, and feldspar, was made by André Duché in Savannah, Georgia around 1739, but this and later attempts by Bonnin and Morris of Philadelphia in the 1770s were unsuccessful. It was not until the middle of the nineteenth century that American porcelain manufacturing was established on a firm footing.

Of all these ceramics, the only ones widely manufactured today are various white earthenwares, such as the ironstone china from which most of us eat, and porcelain, which is inexpensive enough to be in relatively common use. Redware, stoneware, yellowware, and Rockingham, which were replaced in popularity by more durable, cheaper materials such as tin and glass, are still made but in limited quantity and by methods having little in common with those employed by the early potters.

## Redware

Redware was the quintessential pioneer ceramic. Usually made in one- or two-man shops from Maine to California, it was designed to answer the basic needs of an isolated and often rural society, with the artisan usually selling his goods within ten to twenty miles of his studio. As a consequence most redware is unmarked, though there are exceptions such as the many pieces impressed with names of members of the Bell family of Waynesboro, Pennsylvania and of Alvin Wilcox of West Bloomfield, New York.

The potter threw his wares on a wheel or shaped them, as with pie plates and platters, over a wooden drape mold. Hollow ware—jugs and jars—were traditionally ovoid in form, gradually becoming more straight-sided as the nineteenth century advanced, a pattern which may also be seen in the later stoneware.

Since the red clay body was porous even after firing, it was given a clear, lead glaze which enhanced the red to brown body color. The addition of metallic oxides such as copper, iron, or manganese, produced several bright colors employed in decoration.

In New England and Pennsylvania this might range from simple black manganese splotches on the red clay ground to elaborate calligraphic writing and designs produced in light clay on a darker body by use of a tool termed a slip cup. Abstract geometric patterns were most common, but personalized messages—"Mary's Dish," "Clams & Oysters," "Pony Up The Cash," "New York City"—appeared as well on many vessels.

Potters in other areas, such as Galena, Illinois and the Shenandoah Valley of Virginia produced pieces that were daubed with several different colors—white, green, yellow, brown, red, and black—to create a bright panorama. Even in these seemingly random patterns, however, could be seen European influences—the tortoiseshell-colored English Whieldon ware or the multicolored redwares of Scandinavia. Such decoration, however, was relatively uncommon. Most potters, for reasons of time and expense, simply dipped their pieces in clear, lead glaze and placed them in the oven for firing.

The wares the potters made were amazingly consistent from place to place and time to time. Jugs for water, whiskey, vinegar, and cider and jars for the storage of everything from sweetmeats to oysters, plums, and tomatoes were by far the most common. Pitchers, mugs, and cups (termed porringers in the earlier period and used for soup as well as tea or coffee), pear-shaped flasks to carry whiskey to the fields or workshop, plates, platters, bowls, milk pans, cake molds, bottles, water coolers, inkwells, and milk churns were among the basic, but less often seen, forms. And, by the late 1800s every redware potter still in business turned out flowerpots and the tile used in draining farm fields.

There were also, however, many less common objects; among these were manganese-decorated washboards (in wooden frames), coin banks, often in the form of fruit such as apples or oranges, door stops and mantel ornaments shaped to resemble dogs or lions and based on contemporary English Staffordshire figures, tubes for candle molds, poultry waterers, teapots, and such basic necessities as bedpans, spittoons, and chamber pots.

The redware maker thrived where there was no competition from better quality, less fragile ceramics or from other materials that served the same purpose more efficiently. Already battered by just accusations that the lead glaze was poisonous, the redware maker gradually lost the market to stoneware and imported ceramics. By the 1860s a wide variety of redware was being made only in isolated areas such as sections of the South and the Mormon settlements of Utah. By 1900 only the flowerpot makers remained in business.

## Stoneware

Stoneware was being manufactured in New York and Philadelphia in the 1730s and in Boston, under the guidance of Grace Parker, in the following decade. Its advantages, as opposed to redware, were substantial. Almost steel hard and impervious to water, this durable body did not require glazing. However, for the sake of appearances (unglazed stoneware looks a bit like cement), it was given a glass-like salt glaze.

Forms were usually wheel-thrown and limited in comparison to the variations of redware. Storage vessels—jugs, jars, and the later, straight-sided crocks—made up the bulk of the output. Also commonly seen were pitchers, inkwells, churns, water coolers, spittoons, and flowerpots. Although seen occasionally, pie plates, milk pans, harvest jugs, bowls, flasks, cups, whiskey stills, poultry waterers, and vinegar measures were much rarer.

Decoration was also less varied than that found on redware. The high temperatures at which salt-glazed stoneware was fired destroyed all coloring matter except cobalt blue and manganese brown, and the former was by far the more popular. Initially, blue was used to fill floral or other pictorial decoration scratched into the clay before firing, or impressed on the surface with a cookie cutter-like device. By the early 1800s, though, free-hand cobalt decoration had become customary; and with the increasing popularity of calligraphic writing in the second half of the nineteenth century, a group of decorators emerged who could create interesting and elaborate designs—houses, dogs, horses, human figures, and entire pastoral scenes—on the salt-glazed pieces.

The work done during this period, roughly 1850 to 1890, reflects a major change in the potter's traditional role as decorator. In the redware shops and in early stoneware factories decoration was done by the same person who shaped the ware. Talent seems to have been of little concern. In the second half of the nineteenth century decorating became a specialty, often handled by women or children who had been trained in calligraphy. Moreover, the remarkable uniformity of design from Maine to Ohio indicates that either some decorators traveled or that motifs were copied with great fidelity.

However, such decoration was not universal. Midwestern and southwestern kilns, many of which were not established until after 1870, seldom used blue. Their wares, frequently covered with an opaque white Bristol glaze, were either undecorated or embellished only with a small, stenciled logo. Though popular in western Pennsylvania and West Virginia, stenciling was never customary in New England and New York.

Southern stoneware kilns employed both incising and blue decoration in the late eighteenth and early nineteenth centuries (at a time when New England potters were migrating into the area), but by the middle of the last century ware made in the South was usually covered with a brownish yellow alkaline glaze referred to rather aptly as "tobacco spit."

Because of the cost of both raw materials and shipment of the heavy ware, the stoneware trade was always closely associated with water transportation. The first kilns were located near clay sources and often by the ocean or rivers. As canals were built during the 1830s, the kilns followed the new waterways—up the Erie Canal in New York, or along the Delaware & Hudson Canal in Pennsylvania. Later, in the western states, railroads shipped the products.

Ultimately, it was these transportation routes that did in the less efficient kilns and traditional wheel-based potteries, enabling more modern, mechanized factories in Ohio and New Jersey to ship cheaply-made, molded goods throughout the country. By 1900 most of the traditional potteries were gone, except in the South where they lingered until Prohibition put an end to the need for whiskey jugs.

## YELLOWWARE

Ambiguous references to yellowware production appeared in Massachusetts and New York in the eighteenth century and in Philadelphia in the very early 1800s; however, the first well-documented manufac-

turer was David Henderson of Jersey City, New Jersey whose American Pottery Manufacturing Company was in business by 1829.

Henderson's output was not that different from the wares later made in the great yellowware producing centers of East Liverpool and Cincinnati, Ohio; Philadelphia, Pennsylvania; Baltimore, Maryland; and Trenton, New Jersey. Because the clay was both easily cast and heat-resistant, molded household wares rather than storage vessels were made. These included a variety of mixing bowls—some with pouring lips— milk pans, pitchers, pie plates, bean pots, ovoid or oblong baking and serving dishes, pudding molds, custard cups, rolling pins, cups and mugs, coffee pots, platters, salts, mustard pots, and pepper shakers.

All these pieces were characterized by clay bodies in some shade of yellow, covered with a clear, alkaline glaze. Decoration, if present, consisted of embossing or bands of colored slip running horizontally around the vessel.

The greatest production period for yellowware extended from the 1860s, by which time more than a dozen large factories were concentrated in East Liverpool alone, to the 1930s. The ware is still made today but not in great quantity, having been largely replaced by white earthenware and modern, heat-resistant bakeware.

## ROCKINGHAM & FLINT GLAZE

With the addition of a splashed or dripped brown glaze, yellowware becomes Rockingham—an important product of the mid- to late nineteenth-century factories in Vermont, Ohio, and Maryland. Like yellowware, Rockingham was cast in molds, usually reflecting the Gothic- or Rococo-revival styles of the Victorian period. Complex, embossed decorations were customary on elaborate and often fanciful forms: whiskey flasks resembling books, bottles in the form of top-hatted coachmen, cow-shaped creamers, and mantel ornaments in the guise of cows, deer, lions, and dogs.

There were also many practical objects, the most common of which were pitchers, various flowerpots, spittoons, and teapots.

Also frequently seen were pie plates, mixing bowls and serving or baking dishes, custard cups, cake molds, pipkins, shaving mugs, soap dishes, pitcher and bowl sets, vases, door knobs, foot warmers, bed pans, and chamber pots. Much rarer were candlesticks, picture frames, coffee pots, elaborate Gothic water filters, and even foot baths.

These wares were manufactured in large factories such as that of Edwin and William Bennett in Baltimore (entry 39), various concerns in East Liverpool, Ohio, Trenton, New Jersey, and Bennington, Vermont.

The Bennington firm, known as the United States Pottery Company (entries 56–58), was in business only from 1853 to 1858; however, during that relatively brief period it turned out so much Rockingham in such great variety (much of it marked) that the misnomer "Bennington Ware" is often applied by collectors to any brown-glazed yellowware.

It was also at Bennington in 1849 that Christopher Fenton patented his flint enamel process, which involved sprinkling metallic oxides over wet Rockingham glaze. In the course of firing, these oxides melted, resulting in streaks of green, blue, and red against the brown background (entry 44).

It should also be noted that many eastern potteries produced during the nineteenth century a pseudo-Rockingham consisting of a solid brown glaze over a stoneware body. Among the makers of such ware were factories at Lyons and Geddes (now Syracuse), New York.

## WHITE EARTHENWARE

Though made in limited quantity since the eighteenth century, white-bodied earthenwares were not firmly established in this country until after the Civil War. At that time large factories began to emerge in Trenton, Baltimore, East Liverpool, Syracuse, and Brooklyn. Their major product was ironstone or "Hotel" china, a high-fired, dense, and hard-bodied ware which was given a clear, alkaline glaze.

Cast in molds and used for tablewares and household necessities such as bathroom sets, ironstone proved durable and popular. It continues to be used today. Unlike other earlier wares, it was also usually marked with an inkstamp or impression making possible the identification of various manufacturers' products.

Other more attractive wares using the same body included spongeware and majolica. The former was a heavy ironstone body (sometimes, also stone or yellowware) which was daubed in blue, green, brown, red, yellow, or various combinations of these. A product of the late nineteenth and early twentieth centuries, spongeware consisted primarily of simple pitchers, bowls, custard cups, casseroles, cuspidors, and storage cannisters, with the occasional odd piece such as a water cooler, trivet, teapot, creamer, or gravy boat.

Though it often appears crude and handmade, spongeware was a cast, factory product. Large quantities of marked ware were produced by Minnesota's Red Wing Union Stoneware Company, the Globe Pottery of East Liverpool (entry 47), the Western Stoneware Company of Monmouth, Illinois, and the Bennett works in Baltimore.

Much more delicate in feeling and appearance was majolica, which in this country consisted generally of an elaborately molded (pitchers in the form of cabbages or owls and leaf-shaped serving dishes were not uncommon!), cream-colored body covered with a multitude of bright glazes. Tablewares and vases were the major products. Best known of American producers is Griffen, Smith, and Hill of Phoenixville, Pennsylvania (entries 51 and 52), makers in the late nineteenth century of the well-known Etruscan majolica. Other manufacturers included the Bennett factory of Baltimore and the Morley firm of East Liverpool (entry 53).

## PORCELAIN

The complexity of porcelain manufacture, the high costs involved, difficulty in finding native materials, and the necessity for a large number of skilled craftsmen combined with the "dumping" of low-priced goods by English firms to keep the American industry in check until the middle of the nineteenth century. By 1844 there were two major firms in Brooklyn—Charles Cartlidge and Company and William Boch and Brothers. The former failed in 1856, but the latter, under a successor, Thomas C. Smith, continued as the Union Porcelain Works into the twentieth century. Another important, if short-lived, producer was the United States Pottery of Bennington, Vermont (entries 56–58), best known for its unglazed or Parian wares.

By the 1860s other firms in East Liverpool, Trenton, and Syracuse had entered the field, and the passing of favorable tariff laws late in the century assured continuation of the business. While most companies confined themselves to tablewares, some undertook the making of elaborate porcelain statuary. Among the best known of these are examples designed for the Union Porcelain Works by Karl Müller, the work of Ott & Brewer at Trenton, and the innumerable small bisque figures, after English examples, produced at Bennington.

These pieces, though, bore little relationship in appearance or technique to the simple utilitarian wares which for over three hundred years were turned out by American potters. These practical wares, with their straight-forward, functional forms and native materials, both served the emerging nation and typified its craftsmanship. By studying these early utilitarian ceramics, we can learn much of the potter's trade and the general role of the craftsman in the development of the American community.

# PART 2:
# EARLY POTTERS OF SYRACUSE
# AND ONONDAGA COUNTY
# RICHARD CASE

The simple pieces of New York State stoneware that have survived from the nineteenth century—some plain, some with attempts at decoration—reflect the times and personalities of their makers. On a practical level, they also reflect the needs of a community for sturdy storage vessels—pots for making sauerkraut and pickles, pans for milk, crocks for preserving meats, and bottles for beer and ginger ale. They were made not as works of art but as utilitarian containers for the basic needs of life—for food and drink. Each has a story to tell.

Today, as we search for the names of their creators, we learn more of the history of our communities. We learn of settlement patterns and the origins of our own ancestors, the histories of businesses, transportation, and the use of raw materials. We learn of the demand for goods and services and how the early entrepreneurs responded to those demands. The potter took a place among the providers.

Central New York's first potters were New Englanders and European immigrants who joined the westward movement. They set up their kilns and at first fired the fragile redware they shaped from local clay. In time, some moved on, deeper into the "frontier." Those who stayed produced a household line of ware from stoneware clay, most of it brought into New York from New Jersey by canal boat.

They made bricks, flowerpots, drain tiles, and clay pipes. Some artisans worked alone, or with the help of family members; others, such as the early Oneida County pot maker Dwight Graves, were also farmers.

Potteries were established in many of the urban centers of early New York by 1800. Pottery historian William Ketchum listed the names of more than 1,400 potters and pottery owners active in New York State from the seventeenth to twentieth centuries. But by the end of the nineteenth century, most of them were out of business.

William Cooper, the squire who founded the village of Cooperstown, wrote in about 1806 of his new community on Otsego Lake: "The manufacture of leather, wool, fur hats and common earthenware are all flourishing..." (Cooper, *A Guide in the Wilderness*, Dublin, 1810).

The earliest reference to a potter in Onondaga County located to date is in the advertisement taken by Ezra Morehouse in *The Manlius Times* of 1 May 1813 for a bluing business. He mentioned his shop was "at the Old Pottery, about half a mile west of Manlius village."

We do not have the name of that early potter. He may have been Amos Russell, who lived in Manlius in 1810. His daughter married Madison Woodruff, who later opened his own pottery at Cortland.

## SYRACUSE'S FIRST POTTER

Amos Russell is credited by historians with being Syracuse's first potter. In the 1820s he set up business on Water Street, east of the Erie Canal basin (on the block east of the present Erie Canal Museum).

In his recollections of early Syracuse, *Reminiscences of Syracuse*, written in 1856, Timothy C. Cheney spotted Amos Russell's shop and mentioned that the "old man" lived in a small frame house a little south of his pottery. Cheney said Russell made "jars, jugs, mugs, milk pans and all other articles commonly made at such establishments." M. C. Hand, writing in 1889, called Russell the community's first potter.

"At one time a large quantity of pottery of rough quality was manufactured here and shipped to different points on the line of the canal," he reported in *Masters and Stone Printers*.

We know of no examples of Russell's work that have survived. He certainly was a redware potter, at least at the start. An 1830 entry in the account book of Kasson and Heermans store preserved at the Onondaga Historical Association listed Russell as a customer for "red lead."

Communities developed along waterways; Syracuse, at the junction of the Erie and Oswego canals, was no exception. The canal became the easiest and cheapest way of transporting the product of the potter and other pioneer business people to market. Russell probably sold ware out of his shop and perhaps in a peddler's wagon. Later, if he changed from redware to stoneware, he could have drawn on the canal as a source of clay from New Jersey.

The Clark family operated successful potteries at Athens, Lyons, and Mt. Morris, New York (entries 17 and 18). The canals—the Erie and the Genesee Valley— were put to good use. The Clarks owned two boats. Horse and wagon were carried on the boat and the pots and jugs were sold, or traded for other goods, through the streets of the towns along the waterways.

The Clark potteries reflect the strong family ties in some of the companies. Businesses prospered into second and third generations of the same family. Apprentices trained with a family master potter, then moved their skills to another city and perhaps opened their own shops.

The presence of water—the Erie Canal— and local clay, coupled with the prospering new salt industry, made the village of Geddes a promising place for a New England potter to establish his own works.

Geddes, named for its early benefactor, the surveyor and saltmaker James Geddes, developed at the bend of the canal just west of the village of Syracuse. It was incorporated in 1832. In 1886 it would become part of Syracuse, which was by then a city. At one time close to one thousand people lived in Geddes—this included several families listed in census records with the male members as potters.

## GEDDES POTTERIES

Geddes, Baldwinsville, and Jordan were the centers of potting in Onondaga County in the nineteenth century. Geddes was the most active of the three and had a lasting tradition of creating ceramics in the community. The line of potting which began in the village in the 1840s continues today at the Syracuse China Corporation.

The first maker of ceramics in Geddes was a "practical potter" from Vermont named Williams H. Farrar (entries 19–21 and 41–43). In 1839 he came with his wife to live in the village of Geddes. He bought a lot on West Genesee Street in 1841 (near the present Milton Avenue), where he built the pottery which was operated continuously on the site until 1887, when it was destroyed by fire.

In October 1850 *The Syracusan* newspaper published an item on W. H. Farrar and Company, commenting on the "most perfect ware of every description" made there on Genesee Street "from clay brought from Amboy, N.J." The writer noted: "We were surprised to hear the amount of business done at this establishment; many thousands of dollars of ware is sold in this city annually."

Farrar's pottery seems to have both thrived and failed at various points in its history. The potter himself was involved in several businesses at Geddes, including a grocery store. He sold the Genesee property—a house, shop, and kiln—to Joseph Shepard, Jr., in 1857.

The next owner of the original Geddes pottery was Charles E. Pharis (entry 27); and in 1866 Charles E. Hubbell and Denison Chesebro became the proprietors (entries 25 and 26). In 1883 the business was leased to Geddes Stoneware Company.

The *Syracuse Standard's* account of the fire that wiped out the landmark on 28 August 1887 provides one of the handful of descriptions we have of the potteries of Geddes. The reporter called the pottery "as old as Geddes itself and the home of the first industry established in that village."

The building was composed of several parts, which had been added over the years. It was forty feet wide by one hundred feet long. The two-story section closest to the street housed the pottery proper and drying room. The kiln was located twenty feet behind the building. Behind the kiln was a storage room, which held twenty cords of wood at the time of the fire.

Few original documents have come down to us from the fascinating Williams Farrar. (The Onondaga Historical Association has an 1849 receipt for "12 spittons [sic] sold to Onon Co. 1849 by W. H. Farrar & Co." for $7.50.) Presumably, however, the premier potter of Geddes would have approved of the "Rules for Making & Burning Stoneware" written down about 1835 by Nathan Clark, a colleague in the Green County village of Athens.

Clark potteries thrived at Athens from 1805 until 1900, most of that time under family ownership.

Nathan Clark's instructions give us a rare look at the craft in the potter's own words:

1st. Let the wheelman be careful to have every piece run exactly true on the wheel. Make them of a kind precisely of same height & width. Have the same turned [by the] light hands [of a man] finisher. Shape, smooth inside & outside, the bottom a suitable thickness and good top.
2nd. Let it be handsomely handled & smoothly polished in proper season [sequence].
3rd. Let the ware when dry be carefully set in [——] in this last washed and blued [lined inside with Albany slip, decorated outside].
4th. Let the plate be well made. Kiln cleaned out and mended in complete order for setting.
5th. Care must be taken to set the course [of pottery] straight—one piece exactly over another.
6th. Have your wood in good order. Raise your fire progressively, neither too fast nor too slow. Examine well and understand the management of your kiln so as to have all parts alike. Be careful not to throw your wood in the [fire] too soon or do any other act that may have a tendency to retard the heat. When fit to glaze have your salt dry. Scatter it well in every part of your kiln. During this act you must keep a full and clear blaze so as to accelerate the glazing and give the

ware a bright gloss. Stop it perfectly tight in and in six days you may draw good kiln of ware.

It is likely the potters of Geddes produced many a "good kiln of ware" in much the same way. And likely too the potter's handful of rock salt "well scattered" into the kiln to fix the glaze was brought in from the nearby salt fields along the south shore of Onondaga Lake.

Williams Farrar produced a range of wares during his career at Geddes. He began throwing simple redware, and by the end of his business career he was processing sophisticated Rockingham. He grew professionally as American ceramics grew in complexity, and tastes and needs of the marketplace changed.

This potter's life as a merchant was as varied as his production. The Geddes entrepreneur's tracks have not been fully documented. He may have left the community briefly to help set up a pottery in South Carolina. In 1856 Farrar was back at Geddes, at a new location on West Fayette Street, the future site of the Onondaga Pottery Company.

Farrar's first business at this place was called Geddes Rockingham Pottery (entries 41–43). His buildings would form the basis of the potteries which followed him on this lot overlooking the Erie Canal and the city of Syracuse.

An article in the *Syracuse Courier* of May 1858 introduced the new Geddes businessman to the community again. The item was titled "Geddes Rockingham Pottery:"

Mr. Smith Craine, a beautiful designer and painter of signs in this city, furnished a few days since a number of beautiful ornamental signs designated to call attention to the establishment of Mr. W. H. Farrar of Geddes, where the gentleman has established an extensive Pottery for the manufacture of that beautiful ware known as the Rockingham Ware.

His pottery is located on the west side of the Erie Canal, at the above village about 1 1/2 miles from this city. Besides the above, he is also manufacturing flint, enamelled and yellow ware, comprising such articles as pitchers, sealing cans and spittons [sic] in imitation of shells.

Mr. Farrar has manufactured stoneware with

real success for many years. This Rockingham ware is a new thing in this part of the country and is fast becoming into general use. Some specimens of this ware were exhibited by him at our Merchant's Fair last winter, which were high complimented.

Success to this new enterprise. It will add another link to the already extensive chain of Syracuse manufactories.

Farrar carried the business line to the modern Syracuse China Corporation. His Geddes Rockingham works was sold to Empire Pottery Company. Empire, which produced a line of "white ware" for table use, was reorganized as Onondaga Pottery Company in 1871. Farrar died in 1876.

The new company, like its predecessors, faced a struggle. It was helped along by the manufacture of a white granite ware, which was started in 1873. At the end of four years, "the company actually showed a profit," according to a company history of Onondaga Pottery.

Next was the development of a high-fired semi-vitreous ware in 1885. One year later this product was replaced by a high-fired china with the guarantee that the glaze would not craze or crackle. This was described as the first time American-made tableware carried such a warranty.

The company history, published in 1960, provided this assessment of the young pottery's success:

Although Onondaga Pottery Co.'s product now required other clay components than those available locally, two other factors in the Syracuse area favored success.

In the first place, the Erie Canal was readily available and provided economical transportation for materials and supplies needed by the plant, as well as for shipment of finished product.

Secondly, a great tide of immigrants was pouring in from Europe. Many of these newcomers traveled up the waterways of the Northeast and followed the Erie Canal to Syracuse. Thus a desirable labor supply seemed assured for the future.

One of these immigrants was James Pass, an English potter and amateur chemist. It was this innovator who developed the product that came to be known as Syracuse China. Pass's dinnerware won the "High Award Medal" at the World Columbian Exposition in 1893. Prosperity brought changes to the old pottery lot on Fayette Street. A new plant was built there in 1880, six years before Geddes was absorbed into the boundaries of Syracuse. The company remained there until 1971, when operations were consolidated at the Court Street plant site, which had opened in 1921. The name of the company was changed to Syracuse China in 1966.

Williams Farrar's Rockingham pottery on West Fayette had an unusual business symbol. It was a large water pitcher, attached to the ridge pole of the building. When a new plant rose on the site, the same pitcher was given a perch on the highest roof peak of the Fayette plant. Later, when the potters moved all operations to the Court Street plant, a new home was provided the pitcher where it remains today; at the top of the pole outside the main building of the Syracuse China Corporation.

8

*8 From left to right:*

**Unknown potter**

*Redware Crock,* 1800–1870
Earthenware
H. 8, Diam. 6 in. (20 × 15 cm.)
Marks: none
Gift of Mrs. William J. Davison
P.C. 41.372.20

Tall storage vessel with sides sloping
in from high shoulders to short neck.
The rim flares slightly, and the interior
of the mouth has a narrow rim. The

sides below the shoulder taper to a
shaped base. A clear, lead glaze, accented with patches of green under
brown streaks, covers the exterior.

**Unknown potter**

*Connecticut Slipware Plate,* before
1800
Earthenware
H. ¾, Diam. 7¾ in. (1.8 × 19.3 cm.)
Marks: three short parallel lines in-
cised on back

Gift of Mrs. William J. Davison
P.C. 41.372.7

Circular, brown earthenware plate
with low, curving sides and coggled
rim. The interior is covered in dark
brown slip, with a light slip decoration of a wavy line between two
straight lines, which extends around
the plate. The underside and rim are
unglazed.

**Unknown potter**

New England
*Slipware Crock,* 18th century
Earthenware
H. 8½, Diam. 5¾ in. (21.25 ×
14.3 cm.)
Marks: none
Gift of Mrs. William J. Davison
P.C. 41.372.12

Cylindrical, red earthenware crock
with angular shoulder and flaring rim.
An incised line just above the bottom
defines the base. Mottled brown
gloss glaze is used overall.

This is a preserving jar and would
have been used to keep foodstuffs.

**9 Unknown potter**

*Pennsylvania Slipware Plate,* before
1800
Earthenware
H. 1½, Diam. 12 in. (3.75 × 30 cm.)
Marks: none
Gift of Mrs. William J. Davison
P.C. 41.372.13

Circular baking dish of red earthenware. Yellow curvilinear and zigzag-
ging lines decorate the interior. Its
sides curve gently outward to a coggled rim.

Early slip-decorated redware is
seldom marked, and was produced
in quantity. Yellow slip (clay of a
cream-like consistency) was trailed
across the surface with a slip-cup.

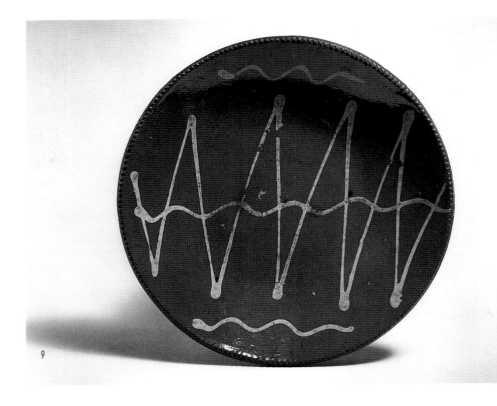

9

10

10 **Unknown potter**

*Pennsylvania Slipware Bowl,* 18th
century
Earthenware
H. 2⅛, Diam. 12¾ in.
(5.3 × 31.9 cm.)
Marks: none
Gift of Mr. and Mrs. John S.
Hancock   P.C. 78.10.2

Shallow, buff clay bowl with wide
everted rim and pale yellow gloss
glaze. The bowl is decorated on the
inner sides with two wavy lines and
four pairs of blue swimming swans
with brown beaks. A brown dot pattern decorates the inner edge, and a
blue zigzag runs along the outer rim.

This large and exceptionally fine
bowl has a trailed slip decoration;
the swan motif adds a charming
detail.

11

11 *Clockwise, beginning at left:*

**Unknown potter**
*Slipware Flask,* 1780–1840
Earthenware
H. 6½, W. 3½, D. 2½ in. (16.25 × 8.75 × 6.25 cm.)
Marks: none
Gift of Mrs. William J. Davison
P.C. 41.372.18

Flattened, red earthenware bottle with high shoulder, short neck, and thickly shaped mouth. Below the shoulder, the sides slope to a small, unglazed base. Clear lead glaze coats the upper and middle portions of the flask.

Flasks such as this were used by travelers. The flattened sides allowed them to be carried in pockets more comfortably.

**Unknown potter**
*Redware Flask,* 1780–1840
Earthenware
H. 7, W. 3½, D. 2¾ in. (17.5 × 8.75 × 6.8 cm.)
Marks: none
Gift of Mrs. William J. Davison
P.C. 41.372.21

Flattened, red earthenware vessel with high shoulder, short neck, and oval base. It has a lead glaze overall except the lower inch of the flask, which is unglazed.

The unglazed lower section of this flask is the part held by the potter when it was turned upside down and dipped in the glaze.

**Unknown potter**
*Redware Cake/Jelly Mold,* 1800–1850
Earthenware
H. 3½, Diam. 9 in. (8.75 × 22.5 cm.)
Marks: none
Gift of Mrs. William J. Davison
P.C. 41.372.24

Circular, red earthenware "Turk's head" mold with central, slightly fluted, cone projection. Fifteen fluted channels spiral in a counter-clock-wise direction. The mold is covered in a gloss glaze.

The fluting caused these molds to resemble Turkish turbans, hence the name "Turk's head" or "Turk's cap" mold.

**Unknown potter**
*Redware Porringer,* 1750–1850
Earthenware
H. 3, W. 6½ in. (7.5 × 16.25 cm.)
Marks: none
Gift of Mrs. William J. Davison
P.C. 41.372.16

Short, wide cup with sides sloping gently to a plain rim. Three lines are incised just above the plain base. Splashes of black manganese deco-rate the exterior glaze but the inte-rior glaze is plain. A ribbed, ear-shaped handle is attached directly below the rim and above the base.

Shaped like a large cup, porringers were usually used for serving soups.

**Unknown potter**
*Pennsylvania Slipware Bottle,* 19th century

Earthenware
H. 4, Diam. 3 in. (10 × 7.5 cm.)
Marks: none
Gift of Mrs. William J. Davison
P.C. 41.372.19

Flattened, squat redware bottle with wide, low belly, tapering shoulders, short neck, and double rim. A thick, deep brown glaze covers the upper three quarters of this vessel.

**Unknown potter**
*Bank,* c. 1825
Earthenware
H. 4, Diam. 3½ in. (10 × 8.75 cm.)
Marks: none
Gift of Mrs. William J. Davison

P.C. 41.372.2

Small, redware bank with gently sloping sides and button like finial. Its shoulder is encircled by one in-cised line and pierced by the hori-zontal coin slot. A clear. lead glaze with areas of black has been applied to the exterior.

12 **Unknown potter**
*Pennsylvania Slipware Plate,* late 18th century
Earthenware
H. 1½, Diam. 10 in. (3.75 × 25 cm.)
Marks: none
Gift of Mrs. William J. Davison
P.C. 41.372.17

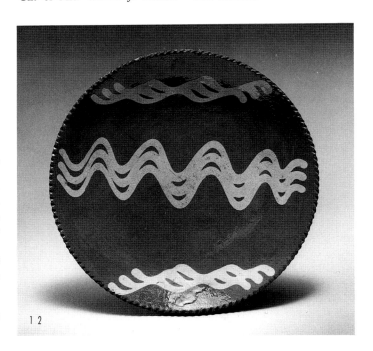

12

13

Shallow, circular baking dish of red earthenware. The interior is decorated with three sets of slip-trailed wavy lines. The sides curve gently to a coggled rim. The underside is unglazed.

**13 Unknown potter**
Boston, Massachusetts
*Jug*, c. 1804
Stoneware
H. 14¼, Diam. 10 in. (35.6 × 25 cm.)
Marks: *2 Boston* stamped at neck
Gift of Ronald A. Kuchta
P.C. 87.100.5

Ovoid, salt-glazed stoneware jug. The form bulges at the shoulder, then tapers to a narrow neck with ridges surrounding it. A single, brown handle with brown mottling is attached at the shoulder and mouth.

Early jugs were ovoid in form. After about 1840 they became more straight-sided.

## 14 Unknown pottery

*Bottle,* 1850–1900
Stoneware
H. 8, Diam. 3¼ in. (20 × 8.1 cm.)
Marks: *O.C. Wilson/Oneida Valley*
impressed on shoulder
Gift of Mrs. William J. Davison
P.C. 41.372.15

Cylindrical stoneware bottle with high, rounded shoulder, thick, rounded rim and plain base. The name of the retailer for whom the bottle was ordered is impressed on its shoulder. Bottles such as these held beer, ale, or root beer.

## 15 Unknown potter

Charlestown, Massachusetts
*Jug,* 1805–1810
Stoneware
H. 14½, Diam. 10¼ in. (36.25 × 25.6 cm.)
Marks: *Charlestown* stamped on neck at shoulder, with three hearts impressed. Label on bottom reads: *225ᶠ30*
Gift of Ronald A. Kuchta
P.C. 87.100.6

Ovoid, salt-glazed stoneware jug with bulging shoulder tapering to short neck and mouth. Two handles are applied close to the neck at the shoulder. Ridges surround the vessel below the neck.

## THOMAS D. CHOLLAR POTTERY 1839–1849 Cortland, New York

Thomas D. Chollar and Joseph Darby were already running a pottery in Homer, New York when they purchased the Mason and Russell pottery in Cortland, New York in 1839. Upon the retirement of Joseph Darby, Thomas Chollar continued to operate the Cortland branch (the Homer establishment had been closed in 1844) until 1849, when he sold it to Madison Woodruff.

## 16 Thomas D. Chollar Pottery

*Jug,* c. 1845
Stoneware
H. 13, Diam. 9½ in.
(32.5 × 23.75 cm.)
Marks: *Thomas D. Chollar/Cortland*
stamped at top
Gift of Mr. and Mrs. Victor Cole
P.C. 81.83.6

Ovoid, salt-glazed stoneware jug with short neck and rimmed mouth. An applied, band handle stretches

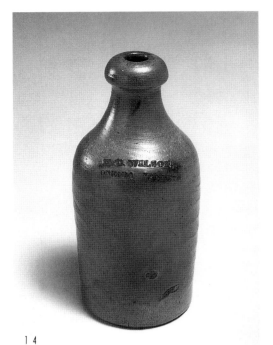

14

15

16

17

18

from the neck to the shoulder, which is decorated with a blue-brushed, swirl design. The stamp at the top is also brushed over in blue. The ovoid shape of this jug is typical of those made before the 1840s and fifties.

## CLARK FAMILY POTTERIES
### c. 1822–1892
### Athens and Lyons, New York

After establishing a pottery business in Athens, New York, Nathan Clark expanded his interests and organized potteries in villages along the Erie Canal, manning them with apprentices trained at his Athens shop. One of these branches was established in Lyons, New York about 1822, and in 1826 Clark hired Thompson Har-

rington to manage the plant. The operation continued until 1852, when Harrington assumed ownership as the Clark family divested itself of some of its potteries.

Nathan Clark, Jr., assumed ownership of the Athens pottery in 1843. By that time the pottery was a large business venture, owning barges and other vessels for transporting both raw materials and finished products. Nathan Clark, Jr., died in 1891, when the pottery passed to his son, Nathan E. Clark. It was sold in 1892.

### 17 Nathan Clark and Company
Lyons, New York
*Jug,* 1826–1852
Stoneware

H. 14, Diam. 9½ in. (35 × 23.75 cm.)
Marks: *N Clark & Co/Lyons* stamped on shoulder
Gift of Mr. and Mrs. Victor Cole
P.C. 81.83.7

Two-gallon, salt-glazed stoneware jug. The ovoid shape bulges at the center, then tapers at the base and neck. The rimmed mouth is encircled by an incised band. A thick, strap handle is applied at the neck and shoulder. A number two is brushed on beneath the pottery stamp.

The large numbers stamped or brushed on the shoulders of many jugs indicated the standard volume of the vessels in gallon sizes. Such

numbers also often appear on the sides of crocks.

### 18 Nathan Clark, Jr.
Athens, New York
*Crock,* 1843–1889
Stoneware
H. 10¼, Diam. 11¼ in. (25.6 × 28.1 cm.)
Marks: *N. CLARK JR. ATHENS N.Y.* in circle, surrounding large *3* impressed in blue near top
Gift of Richard G. Case
P.C. 88.17.2

Cylindrical, salt-glazed stoneware crock with thick rim and two inverted C-shaped handles at sides. A blue floral design is on one side.

19

## W. H. FARRAR AND COMPANY
## 1841–1857
## Geddes, New York

In 1841 Williams Farrar, a Vermont potter, established a pottery in Geddes, New York, a village which would eventually become part of the city of Syracuse. The area had developed into a major stoneware pro-

ducing center, situated as it was along the Erie Canal, which allowed easy transport of New Jersey clays and distribution of finished wares. Farrar produced earthenware at first, but by 1850 had expanded to include salt-glazed stoneware, fire bricks, and beer bottles. In 1857 Farrar sold the manufactory to Joseph Shepard and the following year opened a new

20

### 20 W. H. Farrar and Company

*Jug,* 1841–1857
Stoneware
H. 16, Diam. 9¼ in. (40 × 23.1 cm.)
Marks: *W. H. FARRAR & CO./ GEDDES, N.Y.* stamped on shoulder
Museum purchase P.C. 86.19

Tall stoneware jug with high shoulder. The sides curve in to a narrow neck with a thick, shaped rim. A handle is attached at the rim and shoulder. Below the shoulder, the sides taper to a plain base. The front of the jug is decorated with a design in blue and the number three appears directly below.

The decoration on this jug is quite unusual. It may be a quilt design or a game board. The diagonal line across the bottom may indicate a misdirected stroke of the drip cup, or perhaps the decoration was left unfinished.

### 21 W. H. Farrar and Company

*Jug,* 1841–1857
Stoneware
H. 12½, Diam. 7¼ in. (31.25 × 18.1 cm.)
Marks: *W. H. FARRAR & CO./ GEDDES, N.Y.* stamped on shoulder
Gift of Mr. and Mrs. Victor Cole
P. C. 81.83.10

Salt-glazed, ovoid, one-gallon stoneware jug. The straight sides taper at the shoulder to a narrow neck and thickly banded mouth. A strap handle stretches from the mouth to the shoulder. A blue floral motif decorates the center of the body.

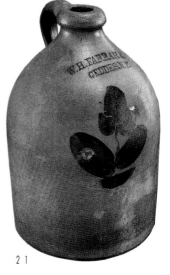

2 1

pottery at another Geddes location. Here he concentrated on the production of Rockingham and yellowware.

In 1868 this second Farrar pottery, the Geddes Rockingham Pottery (entries 41–43), was purchased by Charles W. Coykendall & Company, who changed the name to the Empire Pottery. The emphasis now turned to tableware rather than the coarser utilitarian stoneware products. In July 1871 the firm became the Onondaga Pottery Company

which first made ironstone ware, then fine china (entry 91). This pottery still exists, now known as Syracuse China Corporation (entries 253, 254, 540, 541, and page 10), one of the world's largest manufacturers of fine commercial dinnerware, and the only one of the nineteenth-century New York potteries to survive.

### 19 W. H. Farrar and Company

*Jug,* 1841–1857
Stoneware
H. 18¼, Diam. 11½ in. (45.6 × 28.75 cm.)

Marks: *W. H. FARRAR & CO./ GEDDES N.Y.* stamped on shoulder
Gift of Mrs. William J. Davison
P.C. 41.372.28

Salt-glazed, buff stoneware jug with straight sides and sloping shoulder. An applied, strap handle reaches from the rim to the shoulder. A graceful motif of three blue tulips with foliage in blue is brushed on the front. The number five is also brushed in blue on either side of the center tulip.

## HART FAMILY POTTERIES
## 1832–1892
## Upstate New York

The Hart family was involved in a number of upstate potteries for many generations. Samuel and his brother James established the initial manufactory in Oswego Falls, now Fulton, New York, in 1832. In 1840 James sold his interest to Samuel and established his own pottery in Sherburne, New York. James's son Charles joined with his uncle Samuel in establishing another pottery in Ogdensburg, New York, in 1850.

In 1858, James, apparently in poor health, retired and Charles returned to Sherburne to operate that manufactory, selling his Ogdensburg interest to his younger brother William.

The Fulton pottery continued in operation under Samuel's descendants until 1892 when it was destroyed by fire.

22

**22 Attributed to Samuel Hart Pottery**
Fulton, New York
*Preserve Jar,* 1861
Stoneware
H. 4¼, Diam. 3½ in.
(10.6 × 8.75 cm.)
Marks: *Mary Hart/Fulton/1861* incised on front
Gift of Mrs. William J. Davison
P.C. 41.372.4

Small, ovoid preserve jar of buff stoneware with a gently tapered neck and flaring rim. Two incised lines appear one-quarter inch below the rim and two wavy lines, with a straight incised line in between, encircle the jar at the shoulder. The jar is covered in dark brown glossy glaze.

This jar, used to store spices or preserves, was undoubtedly made at the Samuel Hart Pottery in Fulton, New York. Samuel had a daughter named Mary, for whom this little jar was probably intended.

23

24

### 23 William H. Hart and Company

Ogdensburg, New York
*Jug*, 1860–1861
Stoneware
H. 14, Diam. 9¼ in. (35 × 23.1 cm.)
Marks: *W. H. Hart and Co./Ogdensburg, NY/2* stamped at shoulder in blue
Gift of Mr. and Mrs. Victor Cole
P.C. 81.83.5

Salt-glazed stoneware jug with straight, cylindrical sides tapering to a long neck. An incised band surrounds the neck. A wide, strap handle extends from the neck to the shoulder.

The stamp *W. H. Hart and Co.* indicates that this jug was made between 1860 and 1861, when William H. Hart had a brief partnership with Hiram Davis.

### 24 Charles Hart and Son

Sherburne, New York
*Jug*, 1866–1885
Stoneware
H. 13¼, Diam. 9¼ in. (33.1 × 23.1.)
Marks: *C. Hart & Son/Sherburne/2* impressed at neck
Gift of Richard G. Case
P.C. 88.17.1

Salt-glazed, ovoid stoneware jug tapering to thick, banded rim. A thick, curved handle is applied at the shoulder. A floral design is brushed on the body in blue.

Charles Hart operated the Sherburne pottery with his son Nahum from 1866 until 1885, when Charles died.

### HUBBELL AND CHESEBRO
### c. 1867–1884
### Geddes, New York

Charles E. Hubbell and Denison Chesebro had purchased the Charles Pharis Pottery in Geddes, New York by 1867. They continued making utilitarian stoneware and later introduced stoneware beer bottles into their line. The firm was reorganized in 1884 when Chesebro retired, and the name was changed to Geddes Pottery, which operated until shortly after 1887.

Charles Hubbell was one of the initial investors in Onondaga Pottery Company (now Syracuse China Corporation) and eventually became president of that company.

25

### 25 Hubbell and Chesebro

*Jug*, 1869
Stoneware
H. 18¼, Diam. 12½ in. (45.7 × 31.25 cm.)
Marks: *Hubbell & Chesebro/Geddes N.Y.* impressed on shoulder

Gift of Mr. and Mrs. Joseph Caldwell III   P.C. 85.59

Tall, salt-glazed stoneware jug with high shoulder. The sides curve in above the shoulder to a small, slightly molded rim. Handles are attached at the rim and upper shoulder. A blue slip butterfly-like design is framed by four number five motifs. The date 1869 is brushed in blue at center bottom.

This is an unusually fine jug as it has clear, carefully applied slip-trailed decoration and is dated.

**26** *From left to right:*

**Hubbell and Chesebro**

*Crock,* 1867–1884
Stoneware
H. 9, Diam. 10 in. (22.5 × 25 cm.)
Marks: *Hubbell & Chesebro/Geddes NY* stamped at top
Gift of Mr. and Mrs. Victor Cole
P.C. 81.83.3

Salt-glazed stoneware crock. The round, wide shape has a rimmed mouth and two applied band handles on the sides. The company name is stamped at the top in blue with a brushed number two and slip-trailed decoration on the front.

**Hubbell and Chesebro**

*Churn,* 1869
Stoneware
H. 19¼, Diam. 13 in. (48.1 × 32.5 cm.)
Marks: *Hubbell & Chesebro /Geddes N.Y.* stamped on shoulder
Gift of Mrs. William J. Davison
P.C. 41.372.27.3

Tall, cylindrical, salt-glazed stoneware churn with a wide rim at the mouth and a lip. A brown flat cover

with a flared opening fits inside the top. Since the lid does not fit securely, it may not be the original cover. Thick **C**-shaped handles are applied on the shoulder. The company name and a large number six are stamped at the shoulder with an intricate floral design brushed on in blue.

**Unknown pottery**

Geddes, New York
*Jug,* 19th century
Stoneware
H. 14¼, Diam. 8½ in. (35.6 × 21.25 cm.)
Marks: *Geddes N.Y.* stamped at neck
Gift of Mr. and Mrs. Victor Cole
P.C. 81.83.9

Two-gallon, rounded, salt-glazed stoneware jug with applied handle at the shoulder. A large number two and a simple floral design are brushed on in blue.

## CHARLES E. PHARIS AND COMPANY
### c. 1864–1867
### Geddes, New York

Charles E. Pharis had acquired the Joseph Shepard pottery in Geddes, New York by 1864, but by 1867 the pottery had been transferred to Charles E. Hubbell and Denison S. Chesebro. Since the pottery was under the management of Pharis for such a short time, these objects are rarer than other Onondaga County wares.

**27** **Charles E. Pharis and Company**

*Jug,* 1864–1867
Stoneware
H. 11, Diam. 7 in. (27.5 × 17.5 cm.)
Marks: *C. E. Pharis & Co. / Geddes N.Y.* stamped at shoulder in blue
Gift of Mr. and Mrs. Victor Cole
P.C. 81.83.11

Salt-glazed stoneware jug with straight, cylindrical base and curving shoulder. The rimmed mouth has a band, and an applied handle stretches from the neck to the shoulder. Abstract brush work appears on the body.

## JOHN REMMEY III
### 1765–c. 1835
### New York, New York

John Remmey III was the grandson of an early Manhattan potter who came from Germany in 1735. This first John Remmey set up a pottery near the present City Hall in New York. It was operated by his son, John II, after his death, and then by his grandson, John III, who changed the location to a site on Cross Street and turned the pottery into a prosperous business. John Remmey III fought in the War of 1812, served as city alderman, and was also known as a scholar for his extensive library. He eventually lost the pottery as a result of a misguided financial venture. His brothers, however, continued the family tradition and operated potteries in Philadelphia and Baltimore.

27

29

### 28 John Remmey III
*Eva Jar,* c. 1795
Stoneware
H. 11½, Diam. 6½ in. (28.75 × 16.25 cm.)
Marks: none
Museum purchase with funds from the Dorothy and Robert Riester Ceramic Fund   P.C. 88.38

Tall, straight-sided stoneware jar with flat shoulder, short neck, and wide, flat rim. The upper half bulges slightly, and the rim is uneven. A swag decoration is incised and brushed at the top; the word *Eva* is brushed to the left of the decoration.

This early stoneware jar was used for "putting down" or preserving food. The wide rim allowed a string to be tied around it and thus secure a cloth covering over the mouth.

28

### NORMAN AND ARDEN SEYMOUR
### 1815–1849
### Rome, New York

Colonel Arden Seymour established a pottery in Rome, New York in 1815. Seymour was not a potter himself, but employed craftsmen who produced first earthenware pieces, then upon the opening of the Erie Canal in the 1820s, salt-glazed stoneware with New Jersey clay. A relative, Norman Seymour, joined the firm during the stoneware period. Wares marked *N & A Seymour* are rare.

### 29 Norman and Arden Seymour
*Crock,* 1825–1849
Stoneware
H. 13½, Diam. 12½ in. (33.75 × 31.25 cm.)
Marks: *N & A Seymour/Rome* impressed on shoulder
Gift of Mr. and Mrs. Victor Cole
P.C. 81.83.4

Tall, ovoid vessel with high, flared rim. Two incised lines accent the shoulders at the point where two bilateral lug handles are applied.

30

### 30 Unknown pottery

*Jug*, 1860–1865
Stoneware
H. 13, Diam. 10 in. (32.5 × 25 cm.)
Marks: *SEARLES AND CO./SELL
ALL DESCRIPTIONS/OF GOODS
VERY CHEAP/ELLISBURGH, NY*
impressed on front
Gift of Mr. and Mrs. Newell
Rossman   P.C. 86.68

Ovoid, salt-glazed stoneware jug
with shoulders tapering to a rimmed
mouth. A thick handle curves from
the neck to the body. Brush decoration and a number two appear on
the front, below the impressed
inscription.

The unusual inscription on this jug
refers to the firm for whom the jug
was made, rather than the pottery
that produced it.

### 31 Unknown pottery

*Bottle*, 19th century
Stoneware
H. 9½, Diam. 4¼ in. (23.75 ×
10.6 cm.)
Marks: *AVERY N LORD* impressed
in blue at shoulder
Gift of Richard G. Case
P.C. 88.7.14

Salt-glazed, cylindrical, tan stone-

ware bottle with straight sides, tapering shoulder, and thick band rim.
Blue glaze drips over the inscription
onto the bottle's side.

### JOHN C. WAELDE
### c. 1851–1880
### North Bay, New York

John C. Waelde, from Wittenburg,
Germany, arrived in North Bay, New
York, a community on the east shore
of Oneida Lake, in 1851. He produced salt-glazed stoneware until his
death, sometime between 1876 and
1880, when the pottery ceased
operations.

### 32 John C. Waelde

*Jug*, 1851–1880
Stoneware
H. 13½, Diam. 8¾ in. (33.75 ×
21.8 cm.)
Marks: *J. C. Waelde/North Bay* im-
pressed on shoulder
Gift of Mr. and Mrs. Victor Cole
P.C. 81.83.8

Tall, salt-glazed stoneware jug with
sloping shoulder and thick lip. A
large floral and foliage motif is
brushed in blue on the front. A strap
handle extends from the lip to the
shoulder.

31

32

33

## NOAH WHITE AND SONS
## 1838–1909
## Utica, New York

Noah White came to Utica, New York from Vermont in 1828. Already trained as a potter, he worked in various potteries until 1838, when he purchased his own business. In 1849 his two sons, Nicholas and William, joined the firm, which became Noah White and Sons. In 1856 William went west and the firm became N. A. White and Son. Noah died in

1865. The business continued in the White family until the retirement of Charles N. White in 1909. At this time the firm was called the Charles N. White Clay Products Company, was highly mechanized, and produced stoneware, a variety of bricks, tiles, and Rockingham and cream ware.

The stoneware marked "N. A. White & Son" is prized for its intense cobalt blue decoration. The pottery manufactured its own coloring and its process was a closely guarded secret.[1]

1. Barbara Franco, *White's Utica Pottery.* (Utica, New York: Munson Williams Proctor Institute, exhibition catalogue, 1969), unpaginated.

### 33 N. A. White and Son
*Crock with Bird*, 1863–1865
Stoneware
H. 10, Diam. 7 in. (25 × 17.5 cm.)
Marks: *WHITES UTICA* impressed on shoulder

Gift of Richard G. Case   P.C. 88.6

Cylindrical stoneware crock curving at shoulder to a narrow, raised mouth with extended lip. Two inverted slab handles are applied on either side. An incised line encircles the vessel below the company name impressed on the shoulder. A cobalt blue linear representation of a parrot decorates the body.

White's pottery in Utica is noted for the graceful bird motifs trailed in cobalt on the sides of their pieces.

34

35

36

### 34 Noah White

*Cream Crock,* 1838–1849
Stoneware
H. 10, Diam. 10 in. (25 × 25 cm.)
Marks: *N. White Utica* on shoulder
Gift of Barbara and Norman
Perry   P.C. 86.11

Salt-glazed stoneware cream crock.
The body tapers slightly at the shoulder then flares to a wide mouth. An
incised band surrounds the crock at
the shoulder where two **C**-shaped
handles are applied. A freely decorated blue design is brushed on the
front with casual blue dashes beneath both handles.

### 35 N. A. White and Son

*Crock,* 1863–1865
Stoneware
H. 7½, Diam. 8½ in.
(17.5 × 21.25 cm.)
Marks: *WHITES UTICA N.Y.* impressed near top
Gift of Richard G. Case
P.C. 88.17.3

Short, salt-glazed stoneware crock. A
thick rim surrounds the mouth, with
two **C**-shaped handles at the sides.
An incised ridge surrounds the form
at handle level. A blue linear design
decorates the front.

### A. O. WHITTEMORE POTTERY
c. 1862–1893
Havana, New York

Albert O. Whittemore was operating
a pottery in Havana (now Montour
Falls) by 1862. It burned down in
1893.

### 36 A. O. Whittemore Pottery

*Crock with Lid,* 1862–1893
Stoneware
H. 11, Diam. 9½ in.
(27.5 × 23.75 cm.)
Marks: *A. O. Whittemore/Havana,
N.Y./2* impressed on shoulder
Gift of Mr. and Mrs. Victor Cole
P.C. 81.83.2a, b

Squat, straight-sided, salt-glazed
stoneware crock with sloping shoulder and shaped rim. Bilateral lug
handles are applied on the shoulder.
There is a blue floral design on the
front, beneath the mark. The crock
has a flat lid with a button-like knob.

## 37 Unknown pottery

*Mug*, c. 1812
Stoneware
H. 4½, W. 4½ in.
(11.25 × 11.25 cm.)
Marks: *J. Schue* incised on side
Gift of Mrs. William J. Davison
P.C. 41.372.14

Barrel-shaped mug with three grooves incised around the body. A thick, ear-shaped handle is attached just below the rim and below the center. The name J. Schue, scratched through the reddish-brown slip, may refer to the mug's owner. Tradition has it that this mug was carried during the War of 1812.

## 38 Unknown pottery

*Rebecca at the Well Teapot*, c. 1855
Stoneware
H. 7, W. 6 in. (17.5 × 15 cm.)
Marks: none
Gift of Mrs. William J. Davison
P.C. 41.372.10

Rockingham teapot with foot ring, tapering sides, and rim at mouth. A molded, biblical motif of Rebecca at the Well appears on two sides. The slightly curved spout has three narrow, horizontal bands at midpoint. The C-shaped handle is opposite. The domed lid has a pointed finial and a molded scallop motif around the sides.

Rebecca at the Well was a popular motif on teapots made in the United States during the second half of the nineteenth century. They were first produced here by E. & W. Bennett in Baltimore, designed by Charles Coxon from a design created earlier in England by Samuel Alcock and Company. The teapot in the Everson collection, however, is unlike the Bennett piece as it has a palm tree flanking the scene on the right and a broad-leafed tree on the left. The modeling on the Everson piece is also shallow.

3 7

3 8

3 9

## E. & W. BENNETT
## c. 1848–1890
## Baltimore, Maryland

In 1846 Edwin Bennett moved from Pittsburgh, where his family had operated a pottery since 1839, to Baltimore, where he opened his own manufactory and produced primarily Rockingham pieces. His brother William became a partner in 1848. Charles Coxon was employed as a modeler and a number of narrative pitchers and teapots were produced by him.

## 39 E. & W. Bennett

*From left to right*:
Charles Coxon, modeler
*Hound-handled Pitcher*, 1851
Stoneware
H. 8½, W. 8½ in.
(21.25 × 21.25 cm.)
Marks: none
Gift of Mrs. William J. Davison
P.C. 41.372.25

Squat, low-bellied pitcher with flaring mouth and druid-head spout. The handle is in the form of a hound, paws and head resting on the rim; the hind feet are attached just above the waist. One side is embossed with running deer and a rabbit; a hawk and wild boar are on the other. The pitcher is covered in Rockingham glaze.

*Toby Shaving Mug*, c. 1850
Earthenware
H. 4, W. 5½ in. (10 × 13.75 cm.)

Marks: none
Gift of Mrs. William J. Davison
P.C. 41.372.11

A squat, seated man appears in relief on each side of this Rockingham mug. An ear-shaped handle with an embossed branch design is attached at the rim and just above the base. A vertical sprig of foliage in relief is found on the opposite side. Half of the wide mouth is closed.

## JOHN DARROW AND SONS
### 1845–1876
### Baldwinsville, New York

A pottery was established a few miles north of Baldwinsville, New York in 1845 by John Darrow. Three years later Darrow moved his works to a spot south of the village where a bank of red clay had been discovered. Soon after, he took his sons, Lansing and Edwin, into the business, and in 1852 they began to manufacture stoneware from Amboy clay brought up the Erie Canal. The manufactory closed in 1876.

### 40 John Darrow and Sons

*Small Pitcher,* 1852–1876
Stoneware
H. 4½, W. 5 in. (11.25 × 12.5 cm.)
Marks: *AMELIA* stamped just below handle
Gift of Mrs. William J. Davison
P.C. 41.372.1

Pear-shaped pitcher with low, wide waist. The shoulder is marked with a wave pattern between two straight lines. The rim, with a short spout, flares out slightly from the short neck.

40

An ear-shaped handle is attached at the rim and waist. Brown glaze covers both the interior and exterior.

## GEDDES ROCKINGHAM POTTERY
### W. H. Farrar and Company
### 1858–1868
### Geddes, New York

After selling his first Geddes pottery in 1858, Williams Farrar opened a new one where he produced Rockingham and yellowware. This pottery is still in operation today as the Syracuse China Corporation.

### 41 W. H. Farrar and Company

*Pair of Spaniels,* 1857–1868
Stoneware
H. 9½, W. 6¾, D. 4½ in. (23.75 × 16.8 × 11.25 cm.)
Marks: *W. H. FARRAR & CO.* impressed on bottom of figure at right
Gift of Mrs. William J. Davison
P.C. 41.372.9a, b

Two stoneware spaniels sitting on their haunches with eyes open, heads erect and turned to the side. The embossed collars have locks with chains

41

42

which curve down and over the dogs' backs.

Spaniels such as these were made by many American and English potteries, though the American products are much less common. Marked American pieces are rare. These two spaniels are a pair, but stand in opposite directions. An unusual indentation under the front forelegs indicates that the dogs may have been intended for some specific use or may originally have been joined together.

Though these brown-glazed objects produced in the Farrar pottery are usually referred to as Rockingham, they do not have the gloss of a true Rockingham glaze.

## 42 Attributed to Geddes Rockingham Pottery

*Pitcher*, c. 1858
Stoneware

H. 10½, W. 7½ in.
(26.25 × 18.75 cm.)
Marks: none
Gift of Mr. and Mrs. Joseph Caldwell III   P.C. 87.101

Footed stoneware spatter pitcher with eight sectioned, flat sides, applied handle, and sieve mouth. The form is slip-cast, and covered with a Rockingham-type glaze. A design of grapes, vines, and leaves in high re-

lief decorates the pitcher. A leaf design in relief covers the handle as well.

This cast pitcher was probably made at Williams Farrar's Geddes Rockingham Pottery. The glaze used by Farrar was not a true Rockingham glaze.

## 43 Geddes Rockingham Pottery

*Lion Inkwell,* 1858–1868
Stoneware
H. 2½, L. 4¾, W. 1½ in. (6.25 ×
11.8 × 3.75 cm.)
Marks: none
Gift of Mrs. William J. Davison
P.C. 41.372.8

Reclining lion with a hole in the
back, on a thin, rectangular base.
The hair and facial details are defined by modeling. The lion is covered in brown Albany slip.

Lion inkwells were popular and
were made in many American potteries during the nineteenth century.
They were also imported from
England.

## LYMAN, FENTON AND COMPANY
## 1849–1853
## Bennington, Vermont

Christopher Webber Fenton went
into partnership with his brother-in-
law Julius Norton in the Norton family pottery in Bennington, Vermont,
about 1845. The pottery produced
functional stoneware items, and after
Fenton's association, some Rockingham wares. The partnership was
short-lived, however, and in 1847
Fenton started his own business
where he produced not only Rockingham, but also porcelain wares.
The firm became known as Lyman,
Fenton and Company in 1849, with
Alanson P. Lyman a partner. Daniel
Greatback, an English designer, was
responsible for many of the unique
forms produced by the company in
Rockingham and flint enamel. In 1853
the pottery was incorporated under
the name United States Pottery
Company (entries 56–58). The pottery closed in 1858.

Both the Norton and Fenton potteries produced Rockingham, yellow, and white ware but only the
Fenton manufactory made parian
ware and flint enamel articles.

44 *From left to right*:
**Lyman, Fenton and Company**
*Tulip and Heart Milk Pitcher,*
1849–1853
Stoneware
H. 8, W. 8 in. (20 × 20 cm.)
Marks: *Lyman Fenton & Co./Fen-
ton's/Enamel/1849/Bennington, Vt.*
impressed on bottom
Gift of Mrs. William J. Davison
P.C. 41.372.23

4 3

Octagonally-shaped pitcher of buff
stoneware with a wide, low belly on
a pronounced foot. The scalloped
rim flares to form a curved pouring
lip. The body has eight panels, with
a small molded heart at the top of
each rib—hence the "tulip and
heart" pattern. The pitcher is covered in brown flint enamel.

The curved handle has been extensively repaired; the original handle
was angular.

### Attributed to Lyman, Fenton and Company

*Rockingham Cuspidor,* c. 1850
Stoneware
H. 3½, Diam. 9½ in.
(8.75 × 23.8 cm.)

Marks: none
Gift of Mr. and Mrs. Bronson
Quackenbush   P.C. 77.105.957

Squat, bulbous cuspidor with buff
stoneware body covered in Rockingham glaze. A raised decoration of
twelve seashells rings the top. Gadrooning decorates the center section
which slopes down to a hole. There
is a triangular drainage hole on the
side.

This type of "shell cuspidor" was
made by a number of companies in
the east during the later half of the
nineteenth century. This one is identical to the Lyman and Fenton example in Richard Carter Barret's
*Bennington Pottery and Porcelain*
(New York: Bonanza Books, 1958,

plate 186 B), except for the glaze.

### Unknown pottery

Bennington, Vermont
*Cow Creamer,* c. 1850
Stoneware
H. 5½, W. 7, D. 3½ in. (13.75 ×
17.5 × 8.75 cm.)
Marks: *N* impressed on bottom
Gift of Mrs. William J. Davison
P.C. 41.372.5

Stoneware creamer in the shape of a
standing cow, with an oval base. The
open, well-defined eyes, crescent-
shaped nostrils, and clearly defined
ribs and neck-folds indicate that this
piece was made in Bennington. The
cover for the hole on the back is
missing. The yellow body is covered

4 4

in a brown glaze.

The letter *N* impressed on the bottom could indicate that this creamer was produced by J. and E. Norton, but Lyman, Fenton and Company also produced these popular creamers.

**Lyman, Fenton and Company**
*Toby Pitcher,* 1849–1853
Stoneware
H. 7, W. 5 in. (17.5 × 12.5 cm.)
Marks: *Lyman, Fenton & Company, Bennington, Vt. Patented 1849* stamped on bottom
Gift of Mrs. William J. Davison
P.C. 41.372.3

Male figure sitting on a round base with a concave bottom. His right arm is tucked into his coat and the entire figure is embossed with details. The spout and rim take the shape of a hat, and the grapevine handle with raised decoration is attached to the back of the hat and lower portion of the figure. The entire piece is covered with a Rockingham glaze.

The Museum also owns a duplicate of this piece, P.C. 41.372.6.

**45 Lyman, Fenton and Company**
*Washbowl and Pitcher,* 1849–1853
Stoneware

Bowl: H. 4½, Diam. 14 in. (11.25 × 35 cm.). Pitcher: H. 12, W. 9 in. (30 × 22.5 cm.)
Marks: Bowl: *Lyman, Fenton & Co.* stamped on bottom. Pitcher: none.
Gift of Mrs. William J. Davison
P.C. 41.372.22a, b

Twelve-sided, scalloped, rib pattern bowl with flaring rim and deep, round foot. The top edge of the rim has three molded lines. Flint enamel in browns, with flecks of blue, covers the piece.

The tall octagonal pitcher has a wide foot, tapering sides, and D-shaped handle. The mouth flares out to form a wide pouring lip. A molded ring is at the neck. The pitcher is covered in flint enamel in browns.

This handsome set is a fine example of the flint enamel process patented by Christopher Fenton, founder of the company, in 1849.

**46 Unknown pottery**
*Rockingham Spaniel,* 1840–1890
Stoneware
H. 6¾, W. 5, D. 3¼ in. (16.8 × 12.5 × 8.1 cm.)
Marks: none
Gift of Mr. and Mrs. Bronson Quackenbush  P.C. 77.105.939

4 6

Spaniel dog of buff stoneware covered in a Rockingham glaze. The dog sits on its haunches, tail curled forward, collar about its neck. These spaniel figurines were popular in America during the nineteenth century and are usually unmarked.

47

### GLOBE POTTERY COMPANY
### 1888–c. 1905
### East Liverpool, Ohio

The Globe Pottery Company of East Liverpool, Ohio was incorporated in 1888, but it had functioned as Frederick, Shenkle, Allen and Company since 1881. The firm made toilet ware, dinnerware, and hotel ware. It eventually consolidated with other firms to form the East Liverpool Potteries Company.

### 47 Globe Pottery Company

*Pitcher,* c. 1897
Stoneware
H. 7¼, W. 5 in. (18.1 × 12.5 cm.)
Marks: Globe Pottery stamp imprinted twice: globe surrounded by *Globe Pottery/Company/East Liverpool, Ohio,* all within a circle
Museum purchase   P.C. 85.67

Buff stoneware pitcher with tapered sides and a raised, narrow band at the mouth. The angular handle has shallow grooves down the spine. The pitcher is spattered overall with dark brown and blue glazes.

### 48 Unknown pottery

*Spongeware Bowl,* c. 1900
Stoneware
H. 5⅞, Diam. 11¼ in. (14.6 × 28.1 cm.)
Marks: none
Gift of Courtney A. Spore
P.C. 85.80.2

Circular stoneware mixing bowl with raised, rectangular panels radiating from the base around the exterior. The exterior is decorated with blue and rust sponging.

As the name implies, spongeware was decorated by dabbing color on the surface with a sponge. Blue and rust were commonly used colors. Most spongeware dates from the last decades of the nineteenth century.

### 49 Unknown pottery

*Molded Pitcher,* c. 1880
Stoneware
H. 8⅝, W. 7¾ in. (21.5 × 19.3 cm.)
Marks: *SC* [or *SO?*] impressed on bottom
Museum purchase   P.C. 85.68

Graceful, pear-shaped body with very low foot and curved lip. The

48

49

branch handle extends around the body from the top, creating a relief decoration of leaves and hazel nuts.

### 50 Unknown pottery

*Majolica Pitcher,* c. 1880
Earthenware
H. 4⅞, W. 4 in. (12.1 × 10 cm.)
Marks: none
Gift of Michael Dietz    P.C. 85.64

A trio of vertical green leaves is the primary motif on this slender ochre pitcher. Graceful curving leaves also entwine its base and form its handle. Varying shades of lavender tint the interior.

5 0

51

## GRIFFEN, SMITH, AND HILL
## 1880–1890
## Phoenixville, Pennsylvania

"Etruscan majolica" was produced by Griffen, Smith, and Hill of Phoenixville, Pennsylvania. The pottery was originally established as the Phoenix Pottery, Kaolin, and Fire Brick Company in 1867. The manufacture of the Etruscan line, a majolica with an extremely thin body, began in 1880, a year after it had been acquired by new management, and continued until 1890, when much of the manufactory was destroyed by fire.

The pottery produced a wide range of objects, including leaf-and flower-shaped plates and dishes, pitchers, coffee and tea pots, bowls and other hollow vessels, covered boxes, and comports with dolphin-shaped feet, for which they were well known.

Of all American majolica, Etruscan is among the most highly prized because of its sensitive forms and delicate coloring. In some instances, molds were made from natural objects, as seen in the dishes in the form of a leaf.

51 **Griffen, Smith, and Hill**
*Shell and Seaweed Cup, Saucer, and Pitcher,* 1880–1890
Earthenware
Cup: H. 2¼, W. 4¼ in. (5.6 × 10.6 cm.). Saucer: H. ⅞, Diam. 6 ⅛ in. (2.1 × 15.3 cm.). Pitcher: H. 5¾, W. 9 in. (14.3 × 22.5 cm.)
Marks: Etruscan majolica monogram impressed on bottom of saucer and pitcher
Museum purchase   P.C. 87.36a, b, and 85.69

Etruscan majolica cup, saucer, and pitcher. A repeated, raised pattern of shells and seaweed decorates the body of each piece. Tiny scallops line the rims. The cup and pitcher have twisted branch-shaped handles in brown and green. The exteriors are covered in light pink, green, blue, and violet glazes; the interiors of the cup and pitcher are glossy pink. The shell and seaweed pattern is one of the company's finest.

**52** *From left to right*:

**Unknown pottery**

*Majolica Pitcher,* n.d.
Earthenware
H. 7½, W. 7¼ in. (18.8 × 18.1 cm.)
Marks: *LM* in black script under the glaze on the bottom
Gift of Mr. and Mrs. Edward F. Beadel   P.C. 82.25.3

Oval majolica pitcher with twisted vine handle extending into apple blossom tendrils that reach around the body. A fern motif is at the bottom of each side. Green, magenta, and yellow glazes are used against a gray-white back ground on the exterior. The interior is in turquoise gloss glaze.

This pitcher may have been produced in Ohio. The mark is quite like that of Lillie Mitchell, who worked at Weller Pottery in Zanesville, Ohio.

**Griffen, Smith, and Hill**

*Majolica Leaf Dish,* 1880–1890
Earthenware
H. 2, W. 9¼ in. (5 × 23.1 cm.)
Marks: *G.S.H.* impressed on bottom
Museum purchase   P.C. 85.54

Single oval leaf form, gently fluted, forms the body of this dish. The surface has a naturalistic texture and the colors are green, gold, and pink. The underside is green.

**Unknown pottery**

*Majolica Plate,* c. 1881
Earthenware
H. 1, Diam. 8½ in. (2.5 × 21.25 cm.)
Marks: *33* impressed on bottom
Museum purchase   P.C. 85.53

Round majolica plate with raised leaf and branch pattern in greens, yellow-green, and brown tones.

53

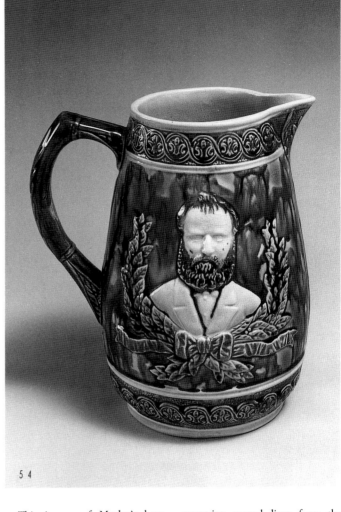

54

## GEORGE MORLEY'S MAJOLICA
## c. 1870–1890
## East Liverpool, Ohio

George Morley was a skilled English potter who settled in East Liverpool, Ohio. He produced majolica in both East Liverpool and Wellsville. Morley retired from his pottery in 1890 and served as mayor of East Liverpool for the following six years.

### 53 George Morley's Majolica

*Majolica Pitcher in the Form of an Owl,* c. 1880
Earthenware
H. 9¾, W. 6¼ in. (24.3 × 15.6 cm.)
Marks: none
Gift of Mrs. Donald Giancola
P.C. 87.59

Majolica pitcher in owl form with modeled decoration detailing facial features and plumage. The owl's head is at the mouth of the pitcher. The handle is created by a modeled, interwoven stem design with a flower at the top. The exterior of the pitcher is green with a red flower, the interior is light pink.

This is one of Morley's best-known pitchers, and with its color and high relief, is relatively rare today.

### 54 Unknown pottery

*Garfield Pitcher,* c. 1881
Earthenware
H. 9¾, W. 8½ in. (24.3 × 21.25 cm.)
Marks: none
Museum purchase   P.C. 85.52

Two relief portrait busts of President Garfield embellish this commemorative majolica pitcher. A semicircular laurel wreath frames each portrait. A similar leaf pattern extends down the handle's spine. Intersecting curved lines form the border design near the base and rim. Brown, gold, green, and rose color its exterior while light lilac tints the interior.

The human figure or head was a rare subject in American majolica, though it was often used in England. This rare pitcher has exceptionally fine coloring.

### 55 Unknown Pottery

*Majolica Pitcher,* c. 1877
Earthenware
H. 7, W. 6¼ in. (17.5 × 15.6 cm.)
Marks: *2* in black script on bottom
Museum purchase   P.C. 86.17

Molded majolica pitcher with flat, full moon body, decorated with begonia leaves and a branch handle.

On one side of the body an eagle with spread wings is depicted holding a rabbit, while on the opposite side an identical eagle holds a bird. Turquoise, gray, brown, green, and yellow glazes are on the exterior, lavender is on the interior. This is a rare majolica pitcher.

56

## UNITED STATES POTTERY COMPANY
## 1853–1858
### Bennington, Vermont

In 1853 Lyman, Fenton and Company incorporated and became the United States Pottery. Known especially for their flint-enamel process, which they patented, and for their Rockingham wares, the pottery also produced porcelain parian ware and figurines.

Parian ware, so-called because it originally was made to imitate marble from the Cycladic island of Paros, was first made in America by Christopher Fenton.

*56 Clockwise, beginning at left:*
### Unknown pottery
*Figurine,* 19th century
Porcelain
H. 7½, W. 3½ in. (18.75 × 8.75 cm.)
Marks: none
Gift of Edgar de N. Mayhew
P.C. 86.42.7

White bisque porcelain figure of a young woman with basket of fish on a circular base.

Such figurines were very popular in the United States during the nineteenth century and were produced by many potteries both here and in England. Many were imported.

### Attributed to Lyman, Fenton and Company
*Vase,* 1847–1853
Porcelain
H. 8¾, Diam. 3¾ in.
(21.8 × 9.3 cm.)
Marks: none
Gift of Edgar de N. Mayhew
P.C. 86.42.3

Graceful amphora-shaped vase of white porcelain. A raised pattern of foliage extends upward from the base and smaller stylized leaves reoccur at the shoulder and edge of neck. The vase's midsection is blue, and narrow blue lines extend up the neck.

Colored porcelain, mainly blue and white, was made at Bennington, and was also imported from England during this period.

### Unknown pottery
*Parian Vase,* 19th century
Porcelain
H. 6½, Diam. 3¾ in.
(16.25 × 9.3 cm.)
Marks: none
Gift of Edgar de N. Mayhew
P.C. 86.42.4

Pear-shaped vase of unglazed white porcelain. Three clusters of grapes with tendrils and leaves are applied to the vase's tall, wide neck. A raised design of small blossoms and larger leaves extends around the vase's lower body. The neck flares outward to create a cupped mouth.

57

**United States Pottery Company**
*Parian Vase,* 1853–1858
Porcelain
H. 5¼, Diam. 2¼ in.
(13.1 × 5.6 cm.)
Marks: none
Gift of Edgar de N. Mayhew
P.C. 86.42.5

A slender, elegant hand grasps this vase adorned with a slightly raised pattern of flowers and foliage. A lace design accents the bottom of the vase and leaf edges form its slightly flared mouth.

**Unknown pottery**
*Parian Bust,* late 19th century
Porcelain
H. 4½, W. 5, D. 3½ in. (11.25 × 12.5 × 8.75 cm.)
Marks: none
Gift of Edgar de N. Mayhew
P.C. 86.42.1

Porcelain bust of young woman with head tilted toward her right shoulder. Her mouth and eyes are slightly open and swirling locks of hair fall over her left shoulder. Three rose-buds adorn her hair and a single bud graces her bodice. A second flower has been lost from her right shoulder.

**United States Pottery Company**
*Lidded Box,* c. 1853
Porcelain
H. 2⅜, L. 4⅞, D. 3 in. (5.9 × 12.1 × 7.5 cm.)
Marks: none
Gift of Edgar de N. Mayhew
P.C. 86.42.6a, b

Lidded box of bisque porcelain, elongated quatrefoil shape. A band of stylized blossoms extends around the box. An identical pattern covers the lid and a cluster of grapes with tendrils is applied to its center.

Boxes of this design are illustrated in Richard Carter Barret's *Bennington Pottery and Porcelain* (New York: Bonanza Books, 1958, plate 325 E, F, and G).

**United States Pottery Company**
*Miniature Parian Pitcher,* c. 1853
Porcelain
H. 3¼, W. 2⅜ in. (8.1 × 6.5 cm.)
Marks: none
Gift of Edgar de N. Mayhew
P.C. 86.42.2

A raised pattern of flowers and arabesques covers the squat body and slightly flared neck of this white

5 8

bisque pitcher.

This miniature pitcher is illustrated in Richard Carter Barret's *Bennington Pottery and Porcelain* (New York: Bonanza Books, 1958, plate 442 B).

**57 United States Pottery Company**
*Parian Vase,* 1853–1858
Porcelain
H. 7, Diam. 3¾ in. (17.5 × 9.3 cm.)
Marks: none
Gift of Mr. and Mrs. Bronson Quackenbush   P.C. 77.105.1067

Elongated, pear-shaped vase of bisque porcelain with splayed foot.

The long neck flares outward towards the scalloped mouth. A Moorish, raised design encircles the neck and lower body. Gadrooning on the neck extends to the body. Two applied clusters of grapes with tendrils and leaves are on opposite sides of the neck.

The piece is unmarked, like much parian ware produced in America. A similar piece, using the same form for the body, is listed in Richard Carter Barret's *Bennington Pottery and Porcelain* (New York: Bonanza Books, 1958, plate 252 A).

**58 United States Pottery Company**
*Parian Vase,* 1853–1858
Porcelain
H. 12, Diam. 6 in. (30 × 15 cm.)
Marks: none
Gift of Ronald A. Kuchta
P.C. 87.102

Footed, pear-shaped parian ware vase. The bulbous porcelain body tapers to a slightly flared mouth. The grape and leaf decoration on front and back of vase are in high relief. "Twig" handles with leaves are applied to the sides of the pitcher. A low relief leaf design with veining and mottling of surface between the leaves is in the background.

# ART POTTERY
# 1880 – 1920

## ULYSSES G. DIETZ

The Arts and Crafts movement as it developed in America had an irreversible effect on the decorative arts that is still very much in evidence today. All phases of the "minor arts" were touched: metalware, textile, woodworking, glass, and ceramics. It is this last area, ceramics, that in its heyday was the most fertile source for expression of the arts and crafts ideal, an ideal that has left the most profound mark on the subsequent development of the medium.

Art pottery grew out of the self-conscious application of "high art" values and techniques to the "low art" medium of household vessels. It was a notion born of Victorian idealism, romantic hindsight, and fear of industry; yet it did not rise phoenix-like from the ashes of some dead tradition. The art pottery movement was the rebellious offspring of a European ceramic heritage which can be traced back to the Renaissance. This rebellious child challenged the accepted ceramic truths of its day, only to become in turn the bemused parent, challenged by its own progeny: studio pottery and industrial artware. The people who created art pottery in America from 1880 to 1920 were figuratively (*and* sometimes literally) the mothers and fathers of the studio potters of the twentieth century, as well as of the industrial designers who have so greatly influenced the commercial ceramics world.

If the art pottery movement was in some ways doomed from its inception by the impossibility of maintaining the proper "creative tension" between the artist and the businessman,[1] it is also true that the art pottery era was a necessary phase in the creation of both the studio potter and the industrial ceramics designer. Art pottery was the historic bridge between traditional ceramics and contemporary ceramics. It grew

in a period of intellectual and technological ferment, and dwindled when its role was obsolete. It left behind a polarized ceramics world with art and industry in opposing camps; yet each camp played a vital role in the ongoing development of the applied arts. The art pottery movement raised art out of an industry, and created an industry sensitive to art.

The artistic tradition in ceramics was certainly nothing new in 1880. The great French potter Palissy had broken the art/pottery barrier in the sixteenth century and was considered an heroic figure to nineteenth-century artists. Similarly, the masterful, tin-glazed earthenwares of sixteenth-century Italy, with their skillful painting and complex iconography, were "art pottery" in their own right. By the early eighteenth century, artist J. G. Herold was creating chinoiserie scenes for the porcelains at Meissen, and J. J. Kaendler was celebrated for his sculptural work in porcelain at the Dresden factory. But these men were professional artists, not potters. Their status in Dresden placed them above the artisans who actually fabricated the objects and did the minor decorative elements. They managed the artistic side of the factories, leaving the physical part of potting and body development to the laborers and technicians. There was no idea at Meissen that the potter could also be seen as an artist.

English pottery traditions followed this pattern as well. In the mid-eighteenth century various enterprising engravers produced genre scenes for the newly invented transfer-printing method of decorating blank ceramic wares. This technique was developed by John Sadler of Liverpool, and his own designs often bore his signature, as did the engraved decorative scenes of

Richard Abbey and Thomas Rothwell.

Fine, hand-painted work on creamware was also a major part of English ceramic decoration. Capitalizing on his vastly successful ivory-colored pottery, Josiah Wedgwood employed anonymous, yet clearly professional, artists to complete the 1,244 different English landscapes on the famous "Frog Service," completed for Catherine the Great of Russia in 1774. Some painters of English porcelains did sign their work, such as John Pennington, who painted a Worcester service for the Duke of Clarence in 1792. But most porcelain decorators remained unknown, as with the many finely decorated botanical wares produced at the Chelsea works during the Rococo period. The division seen here is, oddly enough, not unlike that of some art potteries a century later. Professional—even famous—artists were hired to paint and sculpt for a pottery (Wedgwood hired William Blake, John Flaxman, Joshua Reynolds, and George Stubbs), while anonymous decorators usually completed these artists' designs on the actual ceramic objects. The decorative designer, such as Blake or Flaxman, and the decorative laborer were separated and each enjoyed a very different status. The decorative designer was seen as an artist, the person who actually decorated the object was relegated to the position of mere artisan. The same parallel existed in nineteenth-century sculpture studios where the artist produced the maquette, but anonymous craftsmen actually carved the finished marbles. The potters themselves and the chemist/technicians were part of yet another division of the complex ceramics production system. This division of labor was the rule in European ceramics houses right through the 1870s when art pottery first made its debut. The art pottery ethos would take Josiah Wedgwood, Joshua Reynolds, and the anonymous ceramics operative and create from them a single individual: the artist/potter—who worked in a pottery to create pieces of both commercial and aesthetic value—from whom the studio potter—who produced objects to fulfill an artistic impulse, regardless of public approval—would emerge in the twentieth century.

The artist/potter concept—an artist who actually manipulated the clay and did the glaze work—was a rarity before the later nineteenth century (although Palissy probably approached it). Paul Donhauser has noted that the purely decorative slipware and sgraffito plates produced in eighteenth-century Pennsylvania and New Jersey were one manifestation of a sort of proto-studio pottery. Similarly, the eccentrically decorated redware cups by George Richardson and other potters of seventeenth-century Wrotham, England, seem to be folk forerunners of the artist/potter instinct.[2] Both show personalized design and a focus on the aesthetic impact over mere functional concerns, as well as a unity between the designer and the creator.

The professional artist tradition in American pottery first came from England. Daniel Greatbach, who achieved fame as. a designer-modeler in New Jersey's Henderson pottery and at Bennington, Vermont, was imported from Wedgwood in the late 1820s.[3] His role was the direct forerunner of the "staff designer" for industrial artware firms, since the output of the potteries for which he worked was largely utility wares. But he was also one of the first "professional" pottery men in America, one of a long line of designers with English roots who would play major roles in the development of American art pottery and industrial artware well into the twentieth century.

The art pottery movement itself grew out of a burgeoning dissatisfaction in England with the physical and aesthetic quality of mass-produced consumer goods. Artistically sensitive industrial design was virtually nonexistent, a fact first made painfully clear to the British at the Crystal Palace Exhi-

bition of 1851. The French products showed better design and manufacture, which must have aggravated the English no end.[4]

From this awareness grew the focus of the Aesthetic Reform movement in England: to combat commercial design degeneration, create high-quality goods for a middle-class market, and to improve the lot of the worker. Carrying on John Ruskin's medievalized ideals, William Morris and his circle were not only concerned about shoddy products, but about the wretched conditions under which factory employees worked—the two great evils of the industrial marketplace. The reformers envisioned a pre-industrial, machine-free ethic, which embodied a sense of social conscience as well as an aesthetic renaissance.[5] The result would be more beautiful, better made objects, and happier, healthier lives for the artisan class. As W. H. Taylor, the founder of the Ruskin Pottery, put it: "life without industry is guilt and industry without art is brutality."[6]

By the time Morris had founded his arts and crafts decorating studio in 1861, the ideals of the Arts and Crafts movement were firmly rooted in the British mind.[7] To the medieval influence of the Ruskinian school had been added another element: the Orient. With the reopening of Japan by Commander Perry in the 1850s, oriental objects began to enter the western market. The skilled craftsmanship and careful design evident in Japanese goods, especially ceramics, served as a further inspiration to the aesthetic reformers, as did the fantasy-like pre-industrial culture that produced those objects. Japanese art shops sprang up in London and Paris in the 1860s, at first exhibiting goods made for the Japanese household, and later showing things specially designed for export to the west. The Japanese attention to line, color, and ornament, as well as its exotic decorative elements and flat asymmetrical composition, enthralled Europeans with their novelty.

It was this social and aesthetic background against which the first art pottery studios and art design schools in England were created. The South Kensington

School in London was the first school to address the profession of design in relation to industry. Its earliest contemporary American parallels were the Massachusetts Normal Art School, the Rhode Island School of Design, and the Cincinnati School of Art.[8] Simultaneously, art pottery studios were being formed by the major British ceramics establishments—Doulton in 1866 and Minton in 1871. William de Morgan set up an independent studio for art pottery in the 1860s, prefiguring the smaller scale art potteries in the United States.[9] The major difference in these American "art potteries" from their eighteenth- and early nineteenth-century counterparts was the increased prestige and power granted to the decorators as artists. Professional artist-decorators and potters began to play a more important role in the studio, and they rose above the level of mere artisan. Although professional artist-designers were still in evidence, their elevation above and separation from the decorators and potters was not as distinct as in the past.[10]

An ironic aspect of this burgeoning art pottery world was that embodied by Christopher Dresser, a designer and theorist who actually ran an art pottery from 1879 to 1882.[11] Unlike Ruskin and Morris, Dresser was fascinated by the idea that good design could be the way to "tame" the machine, and to create a world where machine-made objects would be beautiful *and* well made.[12] While Morris's circle wanted to retreat from reality, Dresser looked ahead to the positive aspects of the machine age, a forerunner of those in the ceramics world who wanted to design beautiful pottery forms for affordable mass-reproduction. It was this division between the handcraft ideal and the production line ideal that eventually helped bring about the demise of the art pottery movement.

## THE BEGINNINGS IN AMERICA

Just as the Crystal Palace Exhibition helped trigger the Arts and Crafts movement in England, so the fairs in the New World helped bring art pottery to America. Maria Nichols and Mary Louise Mc-

Laughlin had already begun their china-painting experiments at the Cincinnati School of Art by 1872, and they were well aware of the philosophies of Morris and the aesthetic reformers in England.[13] However, it was the Centennial Exposition of 1876 in Philadelphia that first gave Americans a significant opportunity to see the products of the English and Continental art potteries alongside their own new work. Nichols and McLaughlin of Cincinnati displayed their wares at the Centennial, as did the Robertson clan of Chelsea, Massachusetts. More importantly, Americans saw the French "barbotine" (underglaze slip-painted) ceramics as well as the novel and exotic Japanese artwares. Ernest Chaplet had developed the barbotine technique at the Haviland works, and it was this that got the American art pottery ball rolling.[14]

America never got as deeply embroiled in the guilty-conscience side of the Arts and Crafts movement as the British did. The major moral thrust in the United States was the profit-versus-beauty debate. America's ceramics industry was far less technically advanced than Europe's in 1876, and it was the artistic and technological development of ceramics that became a driving force in art pottery. Oscar Wilde had chided America, saying "your people love art, but do not sufficiently honor the handicraftsman."[15] It was a new obsession with the craftsman, rather than guilt over the miserable factory worker, that lent a lighter touch to the arts and crafts in America. This, combined with less rigid social barriers between America's economic classes, more than likely made the art pottery ideal more attainable here than in England. It may also have helped make that ideal less economically viable, for the emphasis on artistic integrity over commercial production methods ultimately was the undoing of most American art potteries.

Fairs continued to influence American art pottery. Mary Louise McLaughlin displayed her newly-developed "Cincinnati Limoges" at the Paris World's Fair of 1878—the first major step in Cincinnati's celebrity.[16] It was the ceramics at the New Orleans Cotton Exposition of 1884 that inspired Mary G. Sheerer to found what would eventually become the Newcomb Pottery.[17] In the 1889 Paris fair Rookwood won a gold medal, and was further spurred on to glory by developing a highly-skilled painting technique made possible by one of their decorators, Laura Fry. William Grueby of Boston, inspired by Delaherche and Chaplet's mat glazes at the 1893 World's Columbian Exposition in Chicago, went on to perfect his own award-winning satin glazes by 1898. The year 1893 also marked a major display of American artwares in Chicago, as did the Paris fair of 1900 and the Louisiana Purchase Exposition at St. Louis in 1904. The "see and be seen" effect of the great fairs provided American potters with both new aesthetic and technological ideas and gave them a chance to show off their own efforts and win recognition world-wide.

The respect for evident handcraft and simplicity in the American art pottery world by 1900 was in part a rejection of the visual excesses of the aesthetic movement's ornate Japanism, but also an increasing nationalism on the part of American arts and crafts practitioners. Inspired by European ceramics, American potters nonetheless wanted to create objects which spoke of American taste. David Hanks has posited that the angularity of Japanism, stripped of the complex ornamental overlay of the 1870s and 1880s, was adopted for the "prairie-school" look of Stickley and Frank Lloyd Wright.[18] Similarly, simplification of forms and ornament as well as nationalistic instincts were very much a part of the Colonial revival in America, with its political and aesthetic ramifications.[19] The less elaborate oriental ceramics, collected and studied by Americans after 1876, suited the new homespun-colonial mindset nicely. Through classical oriental forms and restrained decoration, the orientalism of the Centennial was reshaped to fit the Beaux-Arts conservatism of 1900. A striking example of this was Charles Lang Freer's patronage of Mary Chase Perry Stratton and her Pewabic Pottery (entry 92). Her simple forms and brilliant, subtle glazes suited Freer's love of oriental art, and her work holds a unique place in his Beaux-Arts gallery in Washington, D.C.[20]

Nationalism, in the form of regionalism, was very much a theme in art pottery throughout its heyday. Cincinnati had created its own style of art pottery and spawned a legion of regional imitators in Ohio. Even when European influence was clear, American potters adapted techniques and styles to their own purposes. William Grueby's work was clearly inspired by Delaherche in France, but Grueby's forms and glazes are uniquely his own (entries 78–80). Even Artus Van Briggle, whose French study made him more directly aligned with the Art Nouveau than Grueby, ultimately created a pottery which was more suited to American tastes (entries 132–137).[21] His interest in native American Indian forms paralleled that of Louis Comfort Tiffany, whose own organic Art Nouveau pottery is said to have its roots as much in American molded wares of the 1840s as in French work of the turn of the century.[22] The Clifton Art Pottery of Newark, New Jersey also offered a line of Indian ware based on prehistoric native American forms and using native New Jersey red clays.[23] This line accompanied a classical oriental line, glazed with subtle metallic greens with crystalline textures. Both the subdued oriental wares and the esoteric Indian forms were ideally suited to the Colonial revival and arts and crafts ideologies.

Susan Frackleton used local Wisconsin stoneware for her unique Milwaukee artwares and the Fulper Pottery of Flemington, New Jersey, adapted the gray New Jersey stoneware (used for its salt-glazed storage vessels since 1815) to its line of Vase Kraft wares in 1910, dressing up the local clay with elegant oriental forms and exotic glazes (entries 73–77).[24] The Arequipa pottery used native California clays, and native fuels for its kiln, while Henry C. Mercer at his quirky Moravian Pottery in Doylestown, Pennsylvania, favored the coarse local red clay in his effort to achieve the rough-hewn medieval effects he desired (entries 85 and 86).[25] Newcomb used both local clays and Louisiana imagery in its famous artware, consciously striving for a uniquely Southern pottery (entries 87 and 88). Charles Hyten created his marbled Niloak Mission ware in classic Chinese shapes using native Arkansas clays (entry 89), while William J. Walley of West Sterling, Massachusetts, adopted a studio potter's penchant for local clay and glaze materials, which he used with ancient Chinese and Korean forms during the 1910s.[26]

Although certainly economic considerations entered into the use of local clays for art potteries, the custom was by no means universal among the many potteries across the country, and clearly native pride in the use of regional materials was a significant factor.

## THE GOALS OF AMERICAN ART POTTERY

While not as guilt-ridden perhaps as the British arts and crafts mentality, the American art pottery movement did strive for "improvement" on a number of levels. A primary goal for art pottery was creative freedom and artistic professionalism. The love of handcraft and the idea of ceramics transcending its lowly artistic position inspired the American potteries. It was English sculptor-modelers like Daniel Greatbach in the 1830s and 1840s and Isaac Broome in the 1870s who first were brought to America to lend their professional artistic skills to the American pottery industry. Edward Lycett, from the Spode factory, was among the first professional china painters to teach his skills in the United States, and to link the concept of china painting with the higher arts.[27] John Low hired a sculptor, Arthur Osborne, to make "plastic sketches" for the J. & J. G. Low Art Tile Works in Chelsea, Massachusetts, and thus elevate fireplace tiles from their basic function.[28] Even before the Rookwood pottery started, two subsequently major artist-decorators, Albert Valentien and John Rettig, were teaching china painting *and* watercolor at the Cincinnati School of Art.[29]

This constant connection between china painting and fine art was part of the vision of the early art potters. Paired with this was the desire—inspired by British concern for

factory workers—to infuse pride back into the creation of an object, to make the decorators feel they were producing something important. Art potteries also freed the china painter from the constraints of relying on commercially (and usually foreign) made blanks, which limited their artistic creativity. As the English defined art pottery, it was to be the result of an individual's artistry, or that of a cooperative group of individuals.[30]

Artistic freedom varied widely in American potteries, as it did in Europe. At one extreme was the Chelsea Keramic Art Works, where the quest for aesthetic excellence and complete experimental freedom ultimately undermined the viability of the pottery (entry 64).[31] At Rookwood and Newcomb artistic freedom was somewhat "forced" on the artists to prevent duplication of designs, thus making creativity a happy requirement for the decorators. In these more middle-of-the-road systems, aesthetic expression blended with commercial concerns to make a viable, moderately priced product that did not hamper the artists. Here lay the rebellion against mass-produced goods that had no artistic soul. In this sort of pottery the artists signed their work, and at least at Rookwood, were paid according to their importance to the firm.[32]

On the most controlled end of the spectrum, the "artists," who might or might not initial their work, based their decoration on planned patterns produced by the owner/designers, and had little real freedom, except in the practice of their technical skills. Grueby, Marblehead, Tiffany, Paul Revere, Buffalo, and Arequipa all operated under this sort of system, with the "artists" serving more as operatives than as creative designers. This set-up was not, except for the handcraft element, much different from the ceramics factory system. The decorators worked in a smaller scale pottery, they were treated very well, and did not suffer as the true industrial ceramics workers supposedly did.

As an example of this system's variance one can compare the work of Frederick Walrath (entry 138) with that of the Mar-

blehead Pottery (entry 84)—whose wares are technically and stylistically quite similar. Walrath's wares are one-man creations, from the body design to the glaze formulations and firing effects. Marblehead's are in fact also one-man creations, as the shape, clay, and designs all came from the mind of Arthur E. Baggs, who owned the pottery. However, Baggs's ideas were carried out by potters, kiln-men, and decorators in the Marblehead studio, while Walrath did all his work himself. Both styles fall easily into the art pottery definition, and yet each expresses the divergence among the different potteries, revealing the basic polarity that would finally rend the movement in two. Walrath's descendants would be the studio potters, and Marblehead's would be the industrial artware firms (although Baggs himself would become a studio potter).

The nineteenth century saw the birth of a therapeutic craft notion, something that only affected ceramics slightly. Arthur Baggs initially set up the Marblehead Pottery as part of a sanatorium for "nervously worn-out" patients. Clearly the nature of the medium did not lend itself to overwrought people, and this therapeutic phase of the Marblehead Pottery passed quickly. More successful was the Arequipa Pottery in Fairfax, California, which used pottery as a therapeutic training for convalescing female tuberculosis patients. Because there was no emotional strain involved with the patients' care, pottery decoration apparently worked well as a therapy. Frederick Hurten Rhead's short-lived Halcyon Art Pottery in California was also tangentially connected with a "regenerative sanatorium," but this seems to have been more of a self-help cooperative than a hospital-like setting.[33]

## WOMEN IN ART POTTERY

One underlying theme in many of the art potteries was the education of women, although this too encompassed a diversity of philosophies. The art pottery studio established by the Minton works in 1871 had focused on "educated women of good social position," because china painting was something a lady could do without "loss of dignity."[34] By Rookwood's inception in 1880 china painting was being touted as a "promising field for the lucrative employment of women."[35] But beneath this lurked another precious Victorian concept, that *ladies* were by definition "cultured," and that china painting was something women could do which was both practical and ladylike. The vast number of amateur women china painters in Cincinnati in the 1870s attests to this. By connection, then, pottery decoration was seen as a way of protecting those women who *had* to work from losing their status as ladies through the brutality of menial labor or factory work.

If Rookwood began as a club for well-heeled Cincinnati socialites, it soon became a place of employment for professional-yet-genteel working women. Similarly, Newcomb was created as a training-ground and a job source for college-educated women who had learned a craft "which would allow them to make an honorable living." The New York Society of Decorative Arts supported this notion, as did the American Woman's League of St. Louis, which was behind the ill-fated University City experiment of 1909 and 1910.[36] The "Saturday Evening Girls" of Boston's Paul Revere Pottery were "nice" immigrant girls from the North End; china decoration was their route to Americanization as well as gentility and salvation from the factories—a concept of the Arts and Crafts movement tied in with a Colonial revival one.[37]

Not all pottery figures were so career-oriented, and ironically it was Ellsworth Woodward, head of the Newcomb Pottery, who seems to have seen art pottery training more ideally as an extension of natural wife and motherhood skills than as a career path.[38]

This sort of dichotomy in the view of women's roles in the pottery world would figure significantly in the participation of women throughout the movement's lifespan. It was, in the end, the educational institutions, born of the art pottery movement, which would free women from the china-painting prison in which Victorian custom had placed them.

There is no question that women played a vast and vital role in the art pottery movement, but it is also true that their power and influence has been greatly exaggerated because of some major historical exceptions. It is a startling fact that in virtually every case the role of men and women in American art pottery can be very clearly divided: women were china painters and decorators and men were chemists and potters. It was the breakdown of this sexual barrier and the fusion of the artist with the potter that allowed for the rise of the studio potter of the twentieth century.

Many of the men who were important in American art pottery came from pottery traditions of long duration. Many also combined ceramic interests with professional art training. Isaac Broome and Daniel Greatbach, both noted earlier, were long-time pottery professionals, although their training was in the fine arts as well. Edward Lycett, who taught china painting, was also an expert in clay body composition and ceramic technique. It is this combination of artistic training and practical pottery acumen which typifies the major male art pottery figures in America. The scientific knowledge required for glaze and clay chemistry, as well as the physical stamina needed for throwing and firing, were seen as masculine attributes in the nineteenth century. Frederick Hurten Rhead (Rhead Pottery, Santa Barbara) came from an English pottery family, as did his sometime colleague William Jervis (Jervis Pottery, Oyster Bay), a theoretician on ceramic chemistry. John G. Low got his ceramic start at the Chelsea Keramic Art Works, which he added to his academic training as a painter before starting his own tile works in 1878. He hired the British sculptor Arthur Osborne and the glaze chemist George Robertson to complete the picture.[39]

William Long of the Lonhuda and Clifton Potteries, was a painter and a chemist, as was Cadmon Robertson, who came to J. S. Taft and Company to create bodies and glazes for their Hampshire Pottery artware line (entries 81 and 82). The famous Robertson clan of Chelsea and Dedham were all chemist/potters, as was Charles Hyten of the Niloak Pottery and William

Hill Fulper of New Jersey's Fulper Pottery. Artus Van Briggle started as an artist-trained china painter at Rookwood, becoming a chemist/potter later on before founding his Colorado pottery in 1901.

The self-styled eccentricity of George Ohr of Biloxi, Mississippi (entries 59 and 60), diverted attention from a skilled ceramic chemist and an unparalleled potter, who was truly a studio potter before his time. In this way, Ohr was not unlike Theophilus Brouwer, trained as an artist, whose Middle Lane Pottery in the Hamptons of Long Island was as avant-garde as any in its day.[40] Both William Walley, an early studio potter in New England, and R. Guy Cowan, a major producer of fine industrial artwares (entries 66 and 67), were sons of the East Liverpool, Ohio pottery community, and specialized in glazes and bodies.[41]

The great Charles F. Binns, an English ceramist who all but founded American studio pottery, put his ceramics background into the founding of the New York School of Clayworking and Ceramics at Alfred University in 1900, the second such school in America. Binns trained other important chemist/potters such as Guy Cowan, Arthur Baggs, Paul Cox, and Frederick Walrath. Finally, Charles Volkmar and his son Leon got their hands-on experience at the Haviland Limoges factories, learning china painting as well as clay chemistry before returning to the United States to start their own art potteries.[42]

The women who became major forces in American art pottery were exceptions—and important ones—to the male-ruled pottery world. At the beginning, in England, the art pottery classes run by Minton might have been aimed at genteel lady decorators, but the directors felt behooved to bring in male potters from the Stoke-on-Trent works to lend a "professional atmosphere" to the studio.[43] The idea that women might actually be a motivating force in the ceramics industry was not taken at all seriously, despite the acknowledged goal of women's vocational training.[44] It is of special note that, even at Alfred's ceramics program, by 1910 the five female graduates had their degrees in ceramic art and design, while the nine male graduates received theirs in ceramic engineering and technology.[45] The Ohio State ceramics program wouldn't even accept women into its classes, as Mary Sheerer would find out. The role of the woman in art pottery was, ultimately, seen as a "decorative" one.

At Arequipa, the female patients did the glazing and decorating, while men did the heavy work of potting and firing. The director, Albert Solon, provided the designs.[46] This was true at Grueby's pottery, where trained women followed George Kendrick's designs in applying the clay filets to the male-thrown pots.[47] All of the female artists at Grueby were anonymous, save for Ruth Erikson, whose initials do appear on some major pieces. Arthur Baggs controlled the designs at Marblehead, using English potters and kiln-men, and both men and women as decorators (entry 84). The Saturday Evening Girls in Boston followed the designs prepared for them and used blanks thrown by and fired by English-born potters (entry 127). It apparently was the Paul Revere Pottery's intent to train some of the girls in ceramic technology, but it is not clear to what extent this ever occurred.[48] Even at the Pauline Pottery, established and run by Pauline Jacobus between 1883 and 1898, Jacobus let men do the ceramic work while she designed and did the decorative work.[49]

Rookwood, though similarly divided by sex in respect to potting and painting, was a pottery where the women and the men shared equal creative freedom in the decoration of the wares (entries 115–124). Rookwood was in many ways the most completely realized American art pottery, and the importance its women artists enjoyed is part of what has made it legendary. And yet, when push came to shove, men still claimed ascendancy. When William Watts Taylor reorganized the pricing of the pottery based on the pay scale of the decorators, it was Albert Valentien, William McDonald, and Matthew Daly who were the highest paid and whose work was the most costly.[50]

It was the male potters who made the technical breakthroughs and won individual recognition. Artus Van Briggle developed the matte glaze lines and was sent to Paris to study; he later attained fame with his own pottery. Stanley Burt created the silky transparent "vellum" glaze which won the pottery prizes in St. Louis in 1904.[51] If Maria Nichols herself dabbled in the technical side of things early on, it was only with the guidance of a male ceramist. In fact, Laura Fry, who developed the air-powered atomizer for the slip painting which made Rookwood famous, was practically the only woman who made a major technical breakthrough for Rookwood, and that in the realm of decoration.[52]

Rookwood has historically been seen as a "woman's pottery" because of the importance of Maria Longworth Nichols's role in its development. She was the archetypal china-painting society lady, who embraced the Japanism and creative freedom of the Aesthetic Reform movement. In the 1880s the birth of her brainchild attracted a lot of attention in the press, and her role as entrepreneur was played up because of its novelty.[53] Her own work was exuberant, ambitious, and naive. Like the hundreds of other genteel hobbyists in the midwest in the 1880s, Nichols took classes in china painting, but she never truly became a professional decorator, nor achieved the artistic skills that the career women at Rookwood attained.[54] Had it not been for Nichols's money, and her foresight in creating and supporting her pet pottery in the early years, her name might well have slipped into obscurity. In fact, it was William Watts Taylor who made Rookwood into a real business after 1883 and who eventually bought control of the firm in 1890 from Nichols, after her marriage to Bellamy Storer. Once Maria Storer's interests had turned more to her new husband's political career, her focus on the pottery lessened, and she returned to her more "natural" role as hobbyist and patron. Despite her genuine love for Rookwood, Storer never really knew what it was to be a woman worker in the art pottery world.

On the other hand, Mary G. Sheerer, who masterminded the Newcomb Pottery in New Orleans (entries 87 and 88), was a figure of vast importance in her pottery's life. She also suffered all the trials of a professional pottery woman. It was Mary Sheerer who began the china-painting course at Tulane's Sophie Newcomb College in 1894. Once the Newcomb Pottery was underway in 1895, she supervised the decorators and designed patterns for the products. But Sheerer was equally concerned with the technical side of the pottery—fretting over the glazes and the bodies despite her lack of ceramics training.[55]

Perhaps the greatest irony of Newcomb was that Mary Sheerer's rightful role was largely usurped by men. A women's pottery at a women's school, Newcomb was nonetheless run by a man, Ellsworth Woodward. The potting was mostly done by Joseph Meyer, who had an Alsatian pottery family behind him. Furthermore, Woodward's goals were not as favorable as one might think. As Jessie Poesch has written, his view was more that pottery training enhanced a woman's natural domestic instincts. He was not really interested in making ceramics artists at Newcomb, but simply in creating workers who did what *he* felt best for the pottery. Paul E. Cox, called in from Alfred University to oversee the technical side of the potting process, shared his views. As Poesch succinctly puts it: "Women were fit to be designers, but men would remain in charge of the technical and physical side of the production."[56]

How galling it must have been for Sheerer that, when attempting to take steps to learn ceramic technology, she was thwarted at every move. Ohio State would not accept women into its ceramics courses, and when she applied to Charles Binns for summer courses at Alfred, Mr. Woodward would not let her go under pretext of needing her close at hand. Having been initially pushed aside by Cox in technical matters, her attempts to learn more were squelched.[57] When in 1921 Woodward sought to replace the dying Frederick Walrath with a Binns student, he balked at the offer of a female student, as he was not convinced that any woman could handle the arduous work required—unless, of course, she was a "masculine type."[58] Beyond all of this, it seems that Cox and Meyer both treated Sheerer with a rather superior attitude, as if they resented her pretension to technical knowledge when she should have been keeping her place in the decorating studio.[59] Coupled with the meagre pay doled out to Newcomb's women,[60] and despite her genuine friendship with Woodward and their long association, Mary Sheerer must have felt the frustration acutely.

When women broke out of the role set for them in the art pottery world, it was the exception, not the rule. One such exception was the Overbeck Pottery of Cambridge, Indiana (established 1911). The four Overbeck sisters ran the operation virtually alone. Three of the sisters were classic china painters and handled the more delicate glazing and decorating chores. The fourth sister, Elizabeth, having studied with Binns at Alfred, did the clay chemistry, the throwing, and the firing for her sisters. She apparently adopted the "masculine type" role envisioned by Ellsworth Woodward and achieved "male" status in a family-run operation.[61]

Susan Frackleton was also a china painter who made the crossover to artist/potter. Her unique stoneware pottery and her independence may have been due to the fact that she was the daughter of a brickmaker. In sharing the ceramic lineage of other American pottery men, she managed to shake the genteel shackles of china painting and take an active role in developing a pottery.[62]

Mary Louise McLaughlin became a ceramist through her quest for a workable porcelain body. Dissatisfied by the world of china painting, she set out to create an art pottery that was truly "hers," and thus in fact became an early studio potter with her Losanti porcelains. Unlike her onetime ally Maria Nichols Storer, McLaughlin's ceramics hobby became a career. Also unlike Storer, McLaughlin's finances did not allow her dream to survive.

Mary Chase Perry Stratton and Adelaide Robineau are perhaps the two most truly important exceptions to the rule of the female china painter (entries 92 and 94–114). Again, because of their fame and success, their place as "typical" pottery women has been exaggerated, obscuring the uniqueness of their triumphs. Both Stratton and Robineau started out as artists and china painters, and moved on to become artist/potters. Both studied with Charles Binns, learning to share his love for classical oriental beauty and devotion to perfection. Both had actively supportive husbands who were not threatened by the "masculine" role their wives took in their pottery work. And both, in retrospect, were far more "typical" of twentieth-century studio potters than nineteenth-century art potters. They were academically trained as potters, they both taught later on in their lives, and neither made as much money in ceramics as their worldwide honors might suggest. Stratton's successful Pewabic Pottery relied on its famous tiles for financial solvency, while she continued her studio work for intellectual patrons like Charles Lang Freer.[63] Robineau attempted to supplement her income with crystalline-glazed doorknobs, and ultimately turned to full-time teaching.[64] And yet both women achieved more personal glory in their lifetimes, and have claim to more real historical importance today, than any other women in the art pottery movement. In this fact lies the great irony of the movement and the role women played in its development, for when Adelaide Robineau and Mary Perry Stratton left behind the world of the subservient decorator and dilettante china painter, they left behind most of their own sex as well.

## THE ECONOMICS OF ART POTTERY

Since one of the basic tenets of the arts and crafts ethos was to make art available to the average person, it follows that production cost and affordability were of central importance. On the other hand, handcraft involved labor and training costs as well as production overhead. Art and the marketplace were not readily compatible concepts, and art potteries learned that truth early on. If the art pottery was doomed from the start, it is because the ideal of an artistically-elevated cooperative pottery that espoused handcraft practice, paid its artists well, and was also a viable business venture, presented a very difficult goal. What happened was that the potters either became chemists or designers for commercial pottery firms in the long run; or became academics who taught ceramics and made studio wares "on the side." The art potteries that survived invariably had less artistic commercial wares which subsidized the more intellectual (and expensive) artwares. In times of economic stress, artwares were the first luxuries to be dropped by the middle class, and potteries without industrial lines were helpless.

Hugh Robertson was so obsessed with his oriental glaze research that his Chelsea studio failed in 1889. Not until he recreated it as the Dedham Pottery in 1895 with a popular line of crackled dinnerwares did it succeed at all on a financial level (entries 68–71). John Low's Art Tile Works finally collapsed in 1907 because of its "inability to maintain high artistic standards in the face of low-priced imports." Artistic standards could not hold when confronted with the marketplace.

William Morris's English decorating firm never realized his dream of making "art for all," since only the well-to-do could afford Morris, Marshall, Faulkner & Company's costly handmade objects.[65] In America, where Elbert Hubbard's Roycrofters produced a more "plebian" arts and crafts line aimed at the middle class, the middle class's pocketbook had great power over the life of any art pottery.[66]

In England, the subsidizing of art pottery by large commercial firms such as Minton and Doulton allowed freedom for artistic quality.[67] In America it was similar means that subsidized successful art pottery lines. In the 1880s, William Taylor clamped down on the exotic Japanism of Rookwood's output in order to create a line that was more commercial, if less individualistic.[68] Even Maria Nichols herself had experimented with transfer-printing as a means of cost-cutting mass-production as early as 1881. Over the years, Rookwood was bailed out more than once with Longworth money. Rookwood did produce a large line of mass-produced porcelains and molded artwares. These not only subsidized the artist-painted pieces, but created a standard for "designed" industrial or production wares which fulfilled Christopher Dresser's predictions and prefigured later high-design industrial artware firms.

Rookwood's sometime imitator, J. B. Owens of Zanesville, Ohio, subsidized its artware line with gas logs, jardinieres, and spittoons. Roseville, another Ohio pottery (entries 125 and 126), eventually abandoned signed artware completely for a hugely successful (and much underrated) line of mass-produced pottery. Both the Weller and Buffalo potteries followed a similar course (entries 61, 62, 139 and 140). The Fulper Pottery managed to produce its artware in large quantity and still retain quality because it relied on form and glaze rather than on decoration (entries 73–77). Its financial success is largely due to this blend of art and industry (but has also resulted in its being sneered at by contemporary collectors who see it as too commercial).

Charles and Leon Volkmar made studio-like artware in their Metuchen, New Jersey kilns, yet made money on their popular architectural tile lines. In this way William Grueby also supported his famous and expensive hand-made goods, until he, too, failed in 1919, selling the tile formulae to a commercial tile firm in New Jersey. The Paul Revere Pottery, despite its popularity, never was financially stable, and even with the constant financial support of Mrs. James Storrow, finally collapsed in 1942.

Many smaller, shorter-lived firms folded owing to the inability to create the happy mix of art and commerce which was central to the art pottery. Among these were the Alberhill, Arc-en-Ciel, Niloak, Stockton, Tiffany, and Matt Morgan potteries.

The "proto-studio potters" of the late nineteenth century were solitary figures in an economically hostile world. America had only just begun to take its painters and sculptors seriously in the mid-nineteenth century, and the affluent middle class was

far from ready to accept the artist/potter who did not care about popular taste. Mary Louise McLaughlin's Losanti wares represented true artistic experiment, and while certainly within the realm of late Victorian taste, they never were popular enough to pay off. McLaughlin eventually gave up her quest for the perfect porcelain body and turned to other pursuits.

Neither Theophilus Brouwer nor William Walley got rich *or* famous from their adventurous pottery work, yet each pursued his studio-like enterprise with a creative vision akin to the avant-garde ceramists who followed the second World War. "One man's ideas, one man's work," Walley's dictum, applies equally to both, and just as well to George E. Ohr, whose public demeanor and fairly successful flowerpot business did not bring acclaim to his artware; he achieved only marginal notoriety in his lifetime. Only a few scholars, like Edwin Atlee Barber, even approached understanding Ohr's talent.

As noted previously, Mary Perry Stratton and Adelaide Robineau achieved fame through their artware, but not fortune. Though neither ever knew poverty, their money came from sources other than their studio ceramics. Robineau in fact took a step into the modern world in 1921 by leaving commercial concerns behind and accepting a post at Syracuse University teaching ceramics.[69] This, coupled with her fortuitous alliance with the Syracuse Museum of Fine Arts (now Everson Museum), secured her financially and also created a "survival model," which would serve future generations of studio potters. Stratton, although commercially successful with her Pewabic tiles, remained always a studio potter and taught as well at Wayne State in Michigan.

Robineau's teacher and mentor, Charles Binns, was that rarest of all American potters—one who had *never* tried to run an art pottery for profit. Binns, called to Alfred University directly from Royal Worcester in 1900, lived his whole American career as a teacher/artist/chemist/potter. He deplored the profit motive and sought excellence in clay above all concerns.[70] As the

first noncommercial purist, he was also the first to realize that the true art in ceramic work could have no tie to popular taste or commercial reality, any more than could the arts of painting and sculpture. Likewise it was he who seems to have first acknowledged the competence of women as artist/potters, and so by his philosophy and teaching has paved the way for the women potters of the twentieth century. Alfred was the second clayworking school in America, and became the benchmark for those that followed. Binns's work, like Robineau's, with its classical form and elegant glazes, forms a link between the aesthetic ideals of the nineteenth century and the creative ideals of the twentieth.

Arthur Baggs also moved from the commercial world to the academic/artist world, teaching at the Cleveland School of Art and Ohio State, while producing highly praised studio pieces on his own. Leon Volkmar left his father's business to form the Durant Kilns in 1910, which were essentially a studio pottery. He also taught at Columbia, the University of Cincinnati, the Pratt Institute, and founded the ceramics department at the Pennsylvania School of Industrial Arts.[71] Frederick Walrath taught ceramics at the Mechanics Institute in Rochester, where he produced elegant studio ware in the arts and crafts taste.[72] He reversed the pattern somewhat by going to Newcomb to run their technical affairs until his untimely death in 1921.

Artus Van Briggle, Guy Cowan, and Frederick Rhead all took another path. Van Briggle, driven west by tuberculosis, adopted a modified production-line system for making limited edition artwares—not unlike some of Rookwood's best production goods—which after his death became an industrial artware operation, still running today. Guy Cowan also looked to the idea of production pieces, which by virtue of excellent design and carefully worked out glazing, would achieve a quality beyond merely industrial products and still survive in a competitive market. Finally, Frederick Rhead, who sought the art pottery ideal from coast to coast, settled in at the Homer Laughlin China Company in Newell, West

Virginia, where he designed the most celebrated line of commercial ceramics in America in the 1930s, Fiesta Ware.

So the struggle to create art pottery in America resulted instead in the creation of two complete spheres of ceramic thought. It gave ceramists the self-respect and public recognition to pursue careers as artists, while teaching the public to appreciate ceramics as more than just household goods. It taught ceramists the potential for good

design in mass production, proving that the machine age was not of necessity an age devoid of beauty. It established a foundation for the professional teaching of ceramic technology and technique, so that a tradition of ceramics professionals would continue to develop. And the art pottery movement gave women a first (albeit rather distant) vision of artistic and professional freedom, beyond the strictures of Victorian custom.

Ultimately the art pottery movement foiled itself, because it made potters think like artists, and it made the middle-class public want more than pots for their money. The economic reality of a middle-class market and the artistic hopes of young ceramics professionals were never fated to blend, but the attempt to do so, which began in America in the 1880s, was a catalyst that created a whole new world for clay and its disciples.

# NOTES

1. See Paul Evans, *Art Pottery of the United States* (New York: Charles Scribner's Sons, 1974), 2.
2. Paul S. Donhauser, *History of American Ceramics, The Studio Potter* (Dubuque, Iowa: Kendall/Hunt, 1978), 2.
3. Ibid., 5.
4. Jessie Poesch, *Newcomb Pottery, An Enterprise for Southern Women, 1895–1940* (Exton, Pennsylvania: Schiffer Publishing Company, 1984), 9.
5. Charles Spencer, ed., *The Aesthetic Movement, 1869–1890* (New York: St. Martin's Press, 1973), 8.
6. A. W. Coysh, *British Art Pottery, 1870–1940* (Rutland, Vermont: C. E. Tuttle, 1976), 79.
7. Spencer, 11.
8. Poesch, 9.
9. See Coysh, 11–26, for listing of various art potteries in England.
10. Coysh, 16.
11. Coysh, 55. This was the Linthorpe Pottery in Yorkshire.
12. Spencer, 12.
13. Martin Eidelberg, "Art Pottery," in Robert Judson Clark, ed., *The Arts and Crafts Movement in America, 1876–1916* (Princeton: Princeton University Press, 1972), 119.
14. Ibid., 119.
15. Robert Judson Clark, ed., *The Arts and Crafts Movement in America, 1876–1916* (Princeton: Princeton University Press, 1972), 9.
16. Eidelberg, 119.
17. Poesch, 9.
18. David Hanks, "Chicago and the Midwest," in Robert Judson Clark, ed., *The Arts and Crafts Movement in America, 1876–1916* (Princeton: Princeton University Press, 1972), 59.

19. Clark, 13.
20. See Lillian Myers Pear, *The Pewabic Pottery, A History of Its Product and Its People* (Des Moines, Iowa: Wallace-Homestead Book Company, 1976).
21. Garth Clark and Margie Hughto, *A Century of Ceramics in the United States, 1878–1978* (New York: E. P. Dutton with Everson Museum of Art, 1979), 20.
22. Clark, 13 and Clark and Hughto, 45.
23. Evans, 59 and Ulysses G. Dietz, *The Newark Museum Collection of American Art Pottery* (Newark, New Jersey: The Newark Museum, 1984), 32.
24. Evans, 105, 110.
25. Evans, 17, 18 and Clark, 180.
26. Evans, 316.
27. Donhauser, 11.
28. Eidelberg, 127.
29. Evans, 66.
30. Coysh, 7 and Donhauser, 12.
31. Evans, 50.
32. Herbert Peck, *The Book of Rookwood Pottery* (New York: Bonanza Books, 1968), 51.
33. Evans, 125.
34. Coysh, 26.
35. Peck, 4.
36. Eidelberg, 173.
37. Ibid., 180 and Evans, 213.
38. Poesch, 68.
39. Evans, 151.
40. Ibid., 173.
41. Ibid., 69, 316.
42. Ibid., 307.
43. Coysh, 26.
44. Poesch, 6.
45. Ibid., 56.
46. Evans, 19.

47. Eidelberg, 136.
48. Evans, 213, 214.
49. Ibid., 218.
50. Peck, 51.
51. Ibid., 52, 73.
52. Eidelberg, 119.
53. Peck, 40.
54. A pair of monumental, Japanesque vases produced in 1883 are known showing this naiveté on Maria Nichols's part. One, in the Everson Museum (see entry 115) is attributed to Albert Valentien, a trained professional. The other, in the collection of The Newark Museum, attributed to Maria Nichols, is much "looser" in its brushwork and less skilled in its drawing.
55. Evans, 182.
56. Poesch, 56, 68, 69.
57. Ibid., 53, 56.
58. Ibid., 72.
59. Ibid., 70.
60. Ibid., 52.
61. Evans, 203.
62. Ibid., 105.
63. Evans, 225–227.
64. Ibid., 246 and Peg Weiss, ed., *Adelaide Alsop Robineau, Glory in Porcelain* (Syracuse: Syracuse University Press, 1981), 18, 22.
65. Spencer, 11–12.
66. Clark, 45.
67. Coysch, 11.
68. Clark and Hughto, 9.
69. Ibid., 246 and Weiss, 31, 32.
70. Donhauser, 65, 66.
71. Eidelberg, 180 and Evans, 93.
72. See Dietz, 122, 123.

59

60

## BILOXI ART POTTERY
### c. 1882–1910
### Biloxi, Mississippi

George E. Ohr and the Biloxi Art Pottery are synonymous. One of the finest art potters in the United States, Ohr learned his craft from Joseph Meyer, a family friend who worked at Newcomb College Pottery. After a two-year tour of American potteries Ohr returned to Biloxi to set up his own business. His first pottery burned down in 1893 but was soon rebuilt. Ohr was able to throw extraordinarily thin forms and then glaze them with unique mottled, tortoiseshell, or metallic glazes. Ohr's handling of the clay was unexpectedly gestural and expressionistic, quite unlike the carefully controlled and "fussy" methods of other Victorian ceramists. As a result, his best work was not really understood or appreciated by his contemporaries. His eccentric behavior, perhaps calculated to attract attention to his

work, earned him the title of "The Mad Potter of Biloxi," although Ohr himself felt he was a genius. Ahead of his time and unrecognized by his contemporaries, Ohr hoarded his best work and in 1909 packed away thousands of pieces and closed his pottery. After his death in 1918, Ohr's family sold some of the pieces, but retained the remainder in storage. The artist was largely forgotten until the cache was sold as one lot to an antique dealer in 1972.

### 59 Biloxi Art Pottery
George Ohr
*Vase,* n.d.
Earthenware
H. 6¾, Diam. 3¼ in.
(16.9 × 8.1 cm.)
Marks: *G.E. OHR/Biloxi, Miss.* stamped on bottom
Museum purchase    P.C. 76.60

This earthenware vase is wheel-thrown and altered. The cylindrical form flares slightly outward at the base and there is a clockwise twist in the

midsection. The top curves slightly inward to form a wide mouth. The glossy glaze, blue at the top and green at the bottom, runs in streaks which expose the buff color of the body in places.

Ohr was such a genius at the wheel that his pieces are of an incredible thinness and always take full advantage of the characteristics of the clay. In fact, Ohr emphasizes these characteristics and as a result, his work is descriptive of both the medium and the process.

The freely altered form of this vase illustrates Ohr's expressionist tendencies which made him a precursor of the later Abstract Expressionist movement of the 1950s. But his adventuresome nature and individual style, in which he completely rejected the classic European attention to perfection of form, are typical of American artists in general, and place him in the mainstream of American art, although he was an enigma during his own time.

Exhibitions: "Biloxi Art Pottery of George E. Ohr," Mississippi State Historical Museum, Jackson, 1978; "A Century of Ceramics in the United States, 1878–1978," 1979

### 60 Biloxi Art Pottery
George Ohr
*Bicycle Pitcher,* n.d.
Earthenware
H. 14½, W. 7¼ in. (36.25 × 18 cm.)
Marks: *G.E. Ohr/Biloxi, Miss.* impressed on bottom
Gift of David Rudd in memory of Terry Rudd   P.C. 88.15

Footed, cylindrical pitcher with thick, applied, C-shaped handle, and rim curving to a pouring lip. A woman in period dress on a bicycle is depicted in relief on both sides. The pitcher is dark blue with ochre, red, and green flowing glazes.

This is an example of the molded wares produced by Ohr at his Biloxi pottery.

## BUFFALO POTTERY
### 1901–1956
### Buffalo, New York

Buffalo Pottery was organized as an adjunct of the Larkin Soap Company. Larkin gave coupons that could be redeemed for premiums, which included pottery items. Though chartered in 1901, the pottery did not go into actual production until 1903. Buffalo was the first American firm to manufacture Blue Willow, and the first pottery in the world to be operated entirely by electricity. From the beginning until the 1940s the pottery dated almost all the pieces it produced. In 1956 the pottery became Buffalo China, Inc.

The company made semi-vitreous wares until 1915, when it began to manufacture vitrified bodies which were marked "Buffalo China" rather than "Buffalo Pottery."

### 61 Buffalo Pottery

*Covered Pitcher,* 1910
Stoneware
H. 5¾, W. 6½ in. (14.4 × 16.25 cm.)
Marks: Buffalo pottery stamp on bottom: figure of buffalo, the words *semi-vitreous* above, *Buffalo Pottery/1910* below, in blue
Gift of Leonard Fried
P.C. 81.23.3a, b

Straight-sided pitcher with slight foot, high shoulder, and broad neck with wide spout. A **C**-shaped handle is applied at the neck and lower half of the body. The pitcher is decorated with a transfer design (decalcomania) in Blue Willow pattern with a border around the neck and outer edge of the handle. The top is flat, with indented handle, and extends over the spout.

This pitcher is listed as no. 53 in the 1905 Buffalo Pottery booklet. In 1905 Buffalo Pottery produced an underglaze blue that equaled imported wares in the Blue Willow pattern and this became their most popular line.

### 62 Buffalo Pottery

*Bowl,* 1910–1912
Stoneware
H. 3⅜, Diam 9⅛ in. (9 × 22.8 cm.)
Marks: Roycroft symbol on outer body, Buffalo pottery stamp on bottom: figure of buffalo with the words *semi-vitreous* above, *Buffalo Pottery* below
Museum purchase   P.C. 86.54

6 1

6 2

Low, wide bowl with angular, inward sloping sides. The Roycroft symbol is on the front, with a band of green and rust around the rim. This bowl is part of the service made for the Roycroft Inn in East Aurora, New York.

## BYRDCLIFFE POTTERY
### c. 1903–1928
### Woodstock, New York

Ralph Radcliffe Whitehead founded Byrdcliffe, an arts and crafts colony, in 1902 in Woodstock, New York. Here, in an idyllic rural setting, craftsmen could work surrounded by companions who held similar ideas and who produced finely crafted pieces. Courses were offered in drawing, painting, decorative design, and woodcarving. Furniture, textiles, pottery, and metal-work were produced, but because of extensive handcrafting the pieces were expensive and marketing was difficult. Furniture was produced only until 1905, and other crafts were continued only by individual craftsmen in their own studios at Byrdcliffe.

Whitehead and his wife, Jane Byrd McCall, continued to work at Byrdcliffe but Whitehead's associate in the establishment of the colony, Hervey White, left to establish his own artists' colony, the Maverick, near Woodstock. Thus began a tradition which lasts even to this day, making the Woodstock area one of the oldest centers for the arts in this country.

### 63 Byrdcliffe Pottery
Zulma Parker Steele
*Vase,* c. 1928
Earthenware (Zedware)
H. 8½, Diam. 7¼ in.
(21.25 × 18.1 cm.)
Marks: *Z* with slash across center incised on bottom
Gift of Mr. Joseph I. Lubin in honor of Syracuse University Vice Chancellor Newell Rossman   P.C. 81.16.2

Heavily potted, ovoid vase of buff earthenware with brush decoration in blue and accents of ochre, covered in a transparent glossy glaze.

Zulma Steele came to Byrdcliffe in the early years of its founding and remained in Woodstock for the rest of her life, though she traveled extensively. Up until World War I, when she went to France with the Red Cross, her work had been mainly in furniture-making, specializing in the carved, decorative panels which were incorporated into chests and cabinets produced at the colony. After the War she turned to pottery, using a kick wheel and local clay. She used decorative motifs inspired by local flowers and plants. She called her pottery Zedware.

6 3

### CHELSEA POTTERY, U.S.
### 1891–1895
### Chelsea, Massachusetts

Hugh C. Robertson, who had been associated with the Chelsea Keramic Art Works, was persuaded by a group of investors to reopen that defunct pottery. This was accomplished in 1891, and the new manufactory was known as the Chelsea Pottery, U.S. Production continued at this site until 1895 when the pottery was moved to Dedham, Massachusetts, after which it was known as Dedham Pottery (entries 68–71). It was at Chelsea that Robertson perfected the crackle glaze for which Chelsea and Dedham are so well known.

### 64 Chelsea Pottery, U.S.
*Whale* (or *Dolphin*) *Plate,* 1891–1895
Earthenware
H. 1¼, Diam. 8¾ in. (3 × 21.9 cm.)
Marks: *CPUS* in a clover leaf impressed on back. *E* on face, just below ledge, in blue
Gift of Albert E. Simonson in memory of Priscilla Lord Simonson P.C. 62.45.2

White earthenware plate with sloping rim and gray crackle glaze. A border design of ten dolphins and stylized waves is molded and painted in blue. The letter *E* appears in one wave on the inner edge of the border. Two blue bands run parallel along the edge of the plate and the well.

Exhibitions: "A Century of Ceramics in the United States, 1878–1978," 1979

64

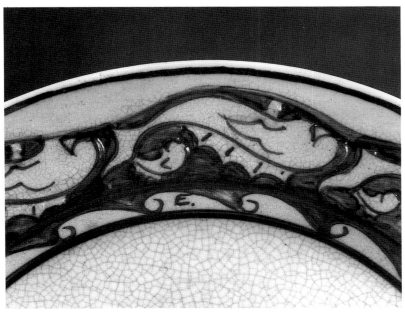

65

## CLEWELL METAL ART
### 1906-1965
### Canton, Ohio

Charles Walter Clewell was a metal worker, not a ceramist. Throughout his life he was involved with the process of applying a thin metal skin to the body of a ceramic form in an effort to simulate metal work. He purchased bisque blanks from such firms as Weller; Owens; and Knowles, Taylor and Knowles, never creating the clay bodies himself. He developed techniques that not only caused the metal to adhere to the clay, but allowed a certain amount of oxidation to take place, producing various colorations of the surfaces.

Clewell always worked alone and never taught his techniques to others.[1]

---

1. Paul Evans, *Art Pottery of the United States* (New York: Feingold and Lewis, 1987), 58.

### 65 Clewell Metal Art

*Vase,* n.d.
Stoneware body with metal surface
H. 13½, Diam. 5 in.
(33.75 × 12.5 cm.)
Marks: *Clewell 254* incised on base
Gift of the Social Art Club
P.C. 86.7

Tall, baluster-shaped vase with flared foot and neck. The exterior, bottom, and most of the interior are covered in a variegated green metallic skin which shows pale green oxidation in spots. An interior chip reveals a reddish stoneware body.

## COWAN POTTERY STUDIO
### 1920-1931
### Rocky River, Ohio

R. Guy Cowan came from a family of potters in East Liverpool, Ohio, and by the time he went to the New York State School of Clayworking and Ceramics at Alfred he already had experience in working with clay. After completing his studies at Alfred under the direction of Charles F. Binns, Cowan accepted a teaching position at East Technical High School in Cleveland, Ohio and in 1912 opened his own studio in Lakewood, a Cleveland suburb. Here he produced functional pottery and tiles of redware.

The pottery closed when Cowan served in World War I.

In 1920 Cowan opened a new studio in Rocky River, Ohio and replaced the redware with high-fired porcelain, producing both commercial wares and art pottery.

Cowan employed a number of fine designers and decorators, including Waylande Gregory, Viktor Schreckengost, Edris Eckhardt, A. Drexel Jacobson, Walter Sinz, Thelma Frazier Winter, and Russell Barnett Aitken.

Ceramic sculptures were produced in limited editions, some requiring as many as fifteen molds and ten hours of firing time. Commercial items included vases, bowls, candlesticks, compotes, and candy dishes. These were marketed in fine stores from coast to coast. When a limited edition had been completed the molds were destroyed.

In 1927 a special line called Lakeware was developed to satisfy a demand for inexpensive flower containers, but the wares were far inferior to the regular Cowan products and contributed to future financial difficulties.

As the Great Depression struck in 1929, the pottery attempted reorganization but went into receivership in 1930. Since the 1931 catalogue had already been produced the studio was allowed to remain open for one year to make use of materials already in stock. During this period the young artists working for Cowan had free rein and produced some highly creative work.

Probably the finest and best known design produced at Cowan was Viktor Schreckengost's *Jazz Bowl*; initially designed for Eleanor Roosevelt, it became a limited edition piece in two sizes. The bowl, with its New York City theme, was done in sgrafitto technique with black slip and Egyptian blue glaze. Others were produced in green as well. The smaller sizes were in relief.

After the close of the pottery in 1931, Cowan worked for Onondaga Pottery (Syracuse China Corporation) and became a member of the Board of Trustees of the Syracuse Museum of Fine Arts, now Everson Museum of Art.

66

**66 Cowan Pottery Studio**

*Vases,* 1924
Porcelain
Left: H. 7½, Diam. 2½ in. (18.8 ×
6.25 cm.) Right: H. 4, Diam. 8½ in.
(10 × 21.25 cm.)
Marks: Cowan mark stamped in
black on bottom of each, *552* on bot-
tom of piece at left, *573A* on bottom
of piece at right
Left: Gift of Edris Eckhardt
P.C. 79.20
Right: Gift of Ronald A. Kuchta
P.C. 84.19

Two porcelain vases — one tall and
tapering, the other flaring widely to
create a bowl-like mouth. Both are
covered in a larkspur blue luster
glaze.

Edris Eckhardt, donor of the piece
at the left, worked at the Cowan pottery while she was a student at the
Cleveland Institute of Art.

**67 Cowan Pottery Studio**

A. Drexel Jacobson
*Antinaeus,* c. 1928
Porcelain
H. 13½, W. 3½, D. 5½ in. (33.75
× 8.75 × 13.75 cm.)
Marks: Cowan mark impressed on
upper left back of base, and *Z* im-
pressed on upper right back of base
Gift of Justin Beauchat   P.C. 77.64

Molded, black-glazed porcelain
head in Art Deco style with long
neck on high rectangular base.

The name Antinaeus is probably
a corruption of Antinous, the chief
suitor of Penelope, wife of Odysseus.
He was killed by Odysseus upon his
return from Troy. The subject was a
popular one early in the century.

67

68

## DEDHAM POTTERY
### 1895–1943
### Dedham, Massachusetts

Dedham Pottery grew out of the Chelsea Pottery which had opened in Chelsea, Massachusetts in 1891. The pottery moved to Dedham in 1893 (production began in 1895) and the name was changed to avoid confusion with English Chelsea potteries. Hugh Robertson was director and while still at the Chelsea location he perfected the crackle glaze for which Dedham was to become famous. Combined with blue decoration, the crackle glaze was used to produce over fifty patterns of tableware using both floral and animal motifs. All designs were free-hand, no stencils or decalcomania were used.

Initially, forms were mold-made, with the designs raised. The decorator had only to follow the outline of the form with a brush. But this technique proved unsatisfactory, both aesthetically and technically, and by 1895 it was discontinued and the molds were smoothed. However, on some of the molds a hint of the raised design remained and can be traced on some pieces. In some cases a motif different from the one painted in blue can be traced.

Though the crackle ware has been most thoroughly identified with Dedham, the pottery also produced other wares, such as flambés and "volcanic ware." The pottery closed in 1943.

### 68 Dedham Pottery

*Clockwise, beginning with top left:*
*Iris and Leaf Plate,* after 1928
Earthenware
H. 1¼, Diam. 8½ in. (3 × 21.25 cm.)
Marks: Dedham rabbit, registered, imprinted in blue
Gift of Albert E. Simonson in memory of Priscilla Lord Simonson
P.C. 62.45.4

White earthenware plate with gently sloping ledge and gray crackle glaze. The ledge is decorated in blue with seven irises connected by a pattern of leaves.

Exhibitions: "A Century of Ceramics in the United States, 1878–1978," 1979

*Tortoise Plate,* 1896–1928
Earthenware
H. 1, Diam. 8½ in. (2.5 × 21.25 cm.)
Marks: Dedham rabbit imprinted in blue, and a foreshortened rabbit impressed
Gift of Albert E. Simonson in memory of Priscilla Lord Simonson
P.C. 62.45.1

White earthenware plate with gently sloping ledge and crackle glaze. The ledge is decorated in blue with five pairs of tortoises facing counterclockwise in gray.

*Flower and Leaf Plate,* 1896–1928
Earthenware
H. 1, Diam. 8½ in. (2.5 × 21.25 cm.)
Marks: Dedham rabbit imprinted in blue
Gift of Albert E. Simonson in memory of Priscilla Lord Simonson
P.C. 62.45.3

White earthenware plate with sloping ledge and gray crackle glaze. The ledge is decorated with a flower and leaf design and two narrow blue bands at the edge of the well.

Exhibitions: "A Century of Ceramics in the United States, 1878–1978," 1979

*Fruit and Leaf Plate,* 1896–1928
Earthenware
H. 1, Diam. 8½ in. (2.5 × 21.25 cm.)
Marks: Dedham Pottery mark imprinted on bottom

Gift of Albert E. Simonson in memory of Priscilla Lord Simonson
P.C. 62.45.5

White earthenware plate with gently sloping ledge and gray crackle glaze. Two thin lines define the inner border, which is decorated with blue leaves, outlined fruit, and linear arabesques.

*Plate with Grapes,* 1904–1928
Maud Davenport, decorator
Earthenware
H. 1, Diam. 8½ in. (2.5 × 21.3 cm.)
Marks: Dedham rabbit imprinted in blue. *O* hidden in design on upper ledge of plate is the mark of decorator Maud Davenport
Gift of Albert E. Simonson in memory of Priscilla Lord Simonson
P.C. 62.45.8

White earthenware plate with gray crackle glaze. The ledge is decorated with a slightly raised, blue grape motif. A narrow blue band rings the outer edge of the ledge, another is on the inner edge and two more are on the well.

**69 Dedham Pottery**

Joseph L. Smith, designer
*Rabbit Bowl,* 1896–1928
Earthenware
H. 3, Diam. 12½ in. (7.5 × 31.3 cm.)
Marks: Dedham rabbit imprinted in blue, and a foreshortened rabbit impressed
Gift of Mr. and Mrs. John S. Hancock  P.C. 78.10.1

Gray clay body with gray crackle glaze. A rabbit and brussel sprout motif is painted in blue on the wide, everted lip. Two thin bands define the inner edge of the border. The bowl is slightly warped.

Exhibitions: "A Century of Ceramics in the United States, 1878–1978," 1979

**70 Dedham Pottery**

*Crab Plate,* 1896–1928
Earthenware
H. 1½, Diam. 8¾ in.
(3.75 × 21.9 cm.)
Marks: Dedham rabbit imprinted in blue
Gift of Albert E. Simonson in memory of Priscilla Lord Simonson
P.C. 62.45.6

White earthenware plate with sloping ledge and gray crackle glaze. A large blue crab is painted on one half; a blue linear pattern suggesting waves is freely brushed on the ledge opposite. A narrow blue band surrounds the edge.

Exhibitions: "A Century of Ceramics in the United States, 1878–1978," 1979

**71 Dedham Pottery**

*Azalea Plate,* after 1929
Earthenware
H. 1, Diam. 6¼ in. (2.5 × 15.6 cm.)
Marks: Dedham rabbit, registered, imprinted, and two foreshortened rabbits impressed
Gift of Albert E. Simonson in memory of Priscilla Lord Simonson
P.C. 62.45.7

Small, white earthenware plate with sloping ledge and gray crackle glaze. The ledge is painted dark blue with the azalea motif left in reserve. Two narrow blue bands surround the edge of the well.

69

70

71

72

## FAIENCE MANUFACTURING COMPANY
### 1880–1892
### Greenpoint, New York

This Brooklyn factory produced for the most part decorative objects with ornamentation modeled in very low relief and painted under the glaze. Gilding was often used. Edward Lycett, who joined the firm in 1884, was their most important decorator.

### 72 Faience Manufacturing Company

Attributed to Edward Lycett
*Vase,* 1884–1892
Porcelain
H. 10¼, Diam. 5¾ in.
(25.6 × 14.3 cm.)
Marks: entwined monogram of company stamped on bottom
Museum purchase with funds from the Dorothy and Robert Riester Ceramic Fund   P.C. 86.9.5

Bottle-shaped vase of white earthenware. A finely detailed scene of a bird in an oak tree, and a dragonfly and butterfly extends from the body up its long, tubular neck. Delicate gilded outlines and acorns reflect the strong interest in oriental design.

## FULPER POTTERY COMPANY
### 1899–1955
### Flemington, New Jersey

The Fulper Pottery had been established for some years before its line of artware was first produced. In 1814 Samuel Hill opened a pottery, which in 1860 was sold to Abram Fulper. Later Fulper's sons operated the business as G. W. Fulper and Brothers and then as Fulper Brothers. The firm was incorporated early in 1899 as the Fulper Pottery Company.

Initially the firm made crocks, filters, and cooking utensils, but in 1909 an art pottery line called Vase Kraft was added. This included vases, bowls, candlesticks, bookends, jardinieres, coffee sets, tiles, and other items in hundreds of glazes in gloss, matte, luster and crystalline finishes. The most prestigious glaze line was the "famille rose," developed by W. H. Fulper, Jr., who considered it a rediscovery of an ancient Chinese secret; thus the glaze was used on oriental shapes.

In 1928 William H. Fulper died, and in the same year a new plant was opened in Trenton, New Jersey. The following year the main plant at Flemington was completely destroyed by fire, including a large stock of artware and many of the firm's records. In 1930 J. Martin Stangl, who had been superintendent of the pottery since 1911, acquired the firm. After 1935 emphasis was placed on the production of a dinnerware under the Stangl name, and later figurines and gift ware were made. In 1955 the pottery formally became the Stangl Pottery Company. Martin Stangl died in 1972.

### 73 Fulper Pottery Company

*Vase,* 1900–1915
Stoneware
H. 10⅜, W. 5¾ in.
(25.9 × 14.4 cm.)
Marks: *Fulper* within a vertical rectangle imprinted on bottom
Museum purchase   P.C. 77.50

Buff stoneware, beaker-shaped vase with trumpet-shaped mouth, altered to create four curved lips. Blue flambé glaze on the top half runs down over the rose matte glaze. The interior is in blue flambé.

### 74 Fulper Pottery Company

*Vase,* c. 1915
Stoneware
H. 11¾, Diam. 9¾ in.
(29.4 × 24.4 cm.)
Marks: *Fulper* within vertical rectangle imprinted on bottom (central portion obliterated); Fulper sticker, partially removed, also on bottom.
Gift of Mr. Joseph I. Lubin in honor of Syracuse University Vice Chancellor Newell W. Rossman
P.C. 81.16.1

Ovoid vase or neck amphora, with foot and short wide neck. The two handles, attached at neck and shoulder, have four nobs each. The gray stoneware body is covered in an iridescent green glaze.

Fulper often used classic Greek forms, sometimes adding imaginative handles. Persian, Egyptian, and oriental shapes were also used. Fulper is known and admired especially for fine glazes with rich, unique coloring.

### 75 Fulper Pottery Company

*Handled Vase,* 1915–1920
Stoneware
H. 6, Diam. 6 in. (15 × 15 cm.)
Marks: raised vertical Fulper mark on bottom

73

7 4

7 5

7 6

7 7

Gift of the Social Art Club
P.C. 86.5

Bulbous vase with sloping shoulder, short neck, everted lip, and slight foot. The curved handles are attached at the lip and shoulder. The buff stoneware body is covered with medium blue crystalline glaze. The crystallization is denser at the lip and lower body.

## 76 Fulper Pottery Company

*Handled Vase,* c. 1923
Stoneware
H. 9½, Diam. 7 in.
(23.8 × 17.5 cm.)
Marks: raised vertical Fulper mark on bottom
Gift of the Social Art Club
P.C. 86.6

Art Deco vase in buff stoneware. The squat form has a low shoulder tapering into the neck. Two angular handles are attached at the mouth and just above the shoulder. The vase is covered in olive and brown flambé glaze.

This vase appears as number 572B in a Fulper catalogue of 1923. Its price was $7.50.

## 77 Fulper Pottery Company

*Three-handled Vase,* c. 1920
Stoneware
H. 6½, Diam. 8¼ in.
(16.3 × 20.6 cm.)

Marks: incised vertical Fulper mark on bottom
Museum purchase with funds from the Dorothy and Robert Riester Ceramic Fund. P.C. 86.9.6

Squat, globular stoneware vase with foot and short neck. Three loop handles are attached at the neck and shoulder. Green crystalline glaze covers the vase.

## GRUEBY-FAIENCE COMPANY AND GRUEBY POTTERY
### 1897–1921
**Boston, Massachusetts**

The Grueby-Faience Company began operations in 1894 to produce glazed bricks, tiles and architectural terracotta, and a limited amount of art pottery. In 1897 the firm incorporated and expanded the art pottery operation.

William Henry Grueby, the founder and general manager, was responsible for the development of the glazes for which the company became so well known. All the artware was thrown and emphasis was placed on integrity of form and contour rather than on decoration or elaborate ornamentation. The influence of Auguste Delaherche is widely recognized. Most of the modeling and decoration at Grueby was done by young women students from Boston art schools. Nature themes—mainly flowers and leaves—were used, each created individually, without patterns or stamps. The decorator applied thin rolls of clay to the damp vessel, smoothing it on one side and modeling it on the other to create the edges of the stems, leaves, or flowers of the design. The pieces were bisque-fired, then matte-glazed. Grueby was widely known for his glazes, especially the overwhelmingly successful watermelon rind glaze, which was his most popular and frequently imitated.

In 1899 the Grueby Faience designation (now without the hyphen) was used for the architectural faience, and the Grueby Pottery name applied to the artware. In 1907 the Grueby Pottery Company was incorporated as a separate entity, with Grueby as president. In 1909, however, Grueby Faience went into receivership and Grueby regrouped under the name Grueby Faience and Tile Company, producing architectural wares using his own glazes. In 1911 Grueby Pottery produced its last artware. Grueby Faience and Tile survived a fire in 1913, when the pottery was rebuilt and production resumed. In 1919 the firm was sold to the C. Pardee Works of Perth Amboy, New Jersey where the works were moved in 1921. William Grueby died in New York in 1925.

78

79

### 78 Grueby Pottery
*Monumental Vase,* c. 1900
Earthenware
H. 22, Diam. 9½ in. (55 × 23.8 cm.)
Marks: *Grueby Pottery Co., Boston, U.S.A.* encircling lotus flower impressed on bottom. Triangle in green glaze loosely brushed on bottom
Museum purchase   P.C. 82.42

Elongated, pear-shaped vase of light buff earthenware. The body of the vase is enwrapped with long, strap-like leaves. Ten tri-petaled, yellow-green blossoms rising on stems encircle the flared mouth. Green watermelon rind glaze is on both the inside and outside.

This vase is a fine example of the matte green glaze developed by

80

Grueby which was to eventually bear his name. When it first appeared, this glaze was an important factor in determining the direction of the art pottery movement in the United States, for it became a popular alternative to the more traditional glitter of the high gloss glazes used by Rookwood and others. Inspired by the French, this matte glaze has a vibrancy and depth that sets it apart from the dead European matte glazes in use at the time.

## 79 Grueby-Faience Company
*Vase,* 1898–1899
Earthenware
H. 10, Diam 9 in. (25 × 22.5 cm.)
Marks: *Grueby Faience Co., Boston. U.S.A.* encircling lotus flower impressed on bottom
Museum purchase   P.C. 77.48

Squat, bulbous form with broad cylindrical neck. The throwing spirals created by the hands of the potter give a grooved effect to the entire form. The vase is covered in matte green glaze.

## 80 Grueby Pottery
*Vase,* c. 1900
Earthenware
H. 12½, Diam. 8½ in. (31.25 × 21.25 cm.)
Marks: *Grueby Pottery Co. Boston. U.S.A.* encircling lotus flower impressed on bottom. *8* impressed on bottom
Museum purchase with funds from the Dorothy and Robert Riester Ceramic Fund.   P.C. 86.9.2

Double-lobed, wide-mouthed vase of light buff earthenware covered in matte green "Grueby" glaze.

Organic vegetal forms are a basic part of the Grueby repertoire and reflect the interest in nature at the turn of the century and a few years earlier. The heavy potting and thick matte glazes are indicative of contemporary trends toward handcraftsmanship and away from Victorian delicacy and slickness.

8 1

## HAMPSHIRE POTTERY
## 1871–1923
## Keene, New Hampshire

The Hampshire Pottery was established in 1871 by James Scholly Taft and his uncle James Burnap. It originally produced utilitarian wares but in 1882 a new kiln was added to produce art pottery. Rookwood Standard and Royal Worcester type wares were produced, often decorated with transfer designs. There were several decorators working at Hampshire, however, who produced individually decorated pieces, which they signed with their names or initials.

Cadmon Robertson, brother-in-law of James Taft (and no relation to the Robertsons of Chelsea) became a chemist at the pottery in 1904, then was appointed superintendent. He was responsible for the variety of matte glazes for which the pottery has been known. Robertson died in 1914 and production ceased later that year. Taft sold the pottery in 1916 to George M. Morton, who revived the most popular shapes and colors of the Hampshire line. After the First World War Morton expanded production to include common hotel china and floor tiles, but increased competition forced the closing of the pottery in 1923.

8 2

**81 Hampshire Pottery**
Cadmon Robertson
*Bowl,* c. 1910
Earthenware
H. 3, Diam 10 in. (7.5 × 25 cm.)
Marks: *Hampshire Pottery, 57, M* within an *O* incised on bottom
Museum purchase   P.C. 76.61

Broad, shallow bowl of white earthenware with sides curving inward to form a wide mouth. A raised water lily motif decorates the bowl, which is covered in dark green matte glaze.

The *M* within a circle mark indicates that this piece was designed by Cadmon Robertson in tribute to his wife Emoretta.[1]

[1]Paul Evans. *Art Pottery of the United States* (New York: Charles Scribner's Sons, 1974), 132.

**82 Hampshire Pottery**
*Vase,* n.d.
Earthenware
H. 5⅞, W. 5¾ in. (14.6 × 14.4 cm.)
Marks: *HAMPSHIRE* impressed on bottom, barely legible
Gift of Mr. Richard Barons
P.C. 84.43

Flattened, bottle-shaped vase with matte green glaze. Two sling-like handles are attached to the neck; the top handle ends in a modeled mask at the point where it joins the neck.

83

## JONATHAN SCOTT HARTLEY
### 1845–1912
### New York, New York

Jonathan Scott Hartley was born and educated in Albany, New York. He studied in New York with Erastus D. Palmer, and at the age of twenty-one went to England, where he studied for three years at the Royal Academy. He won a silver medal at the Academy in 1869, then studied for a year in Germany. After traveling to Paris and Rome he returned to New York where he established a studio. He was married in 1888 to

Helen Inness, daughter of the painter George Inness. He was one of the founders of the Salmagundi Club, which met in his New York studio.

Hartley produced a number of monumental sculptures, notably *Miles Morgan*, now in Springfield, Massachusetts; *Alfred the Great* in New York City; and the Daguerre monument in Washington, D.C. He received much publicity because of his small sculpture called *The Whirlwind*, a lively Art Nouveau creation that may have been a source for some

Cowan figures of the 1920s. But Hartley was known during his lifetime mainly for his portrait busts.

### 83 Jonathan Scott Hartley
*The Sunflower,* 1878
Earthenware
H. 24, W. 9¼, D. 9¼ in. (60 × 23.1 × 23.1 cm.)
Marks: *The Sunflower/J. S. Hartley Sc N.Y./Copyright 1878* incised on left side of base
Gift of Georgia Kells   P.C. 87.4

Earthenware bust of a young girl depicted as a sunflower. The sunflower

leaves wrap her shoulders and a large blossom adorns her head like a cap. The girl has long, wavy hair and a dream-like look. The bust rests on a flared, rectangular base.

The sunflower was used extensively as a decorative motif in the Aesthetic movement, and its personification in terracotta as a demure young girl caught in reverie embodies the romantic obsession with nature characteristic of this period.

8 4

## MARBLEHEAD POTTERY
### 1904–1936
### Marblehead, Massachusetts

Marblehead Pottery began in 1904 as a therapeutic craft shop for convalescents, but the pottery, under the direction of Arthur E. Baggs, became so successful that it soon separated from the medical facility and operated independently until it closed in 1936.

Baggs had been a student of Charles F. Binns at Alfred and by 1915 he assumed ownership of the Marblehead plant. Baggs worked part of the time at Marblehead, where he took charge of technical and artistic matters, and taught the remainder of the time, first in New York, then at the Cleveland Institute of Art; he finally assumed a professorship of Ceramic Arts at Ohio State University. Baggs continued his association with Ohio State until his death in 1947.

By 1908 Marblehead produced vases, jardinieres, lamps, and tiles, all with the traditional Marblehead matte glazes. In 1912 a line of faience ware was added, including teapots, luncheon and dinner sets, as well as children's ware.

Molds were used for only a few articles of the artware; most pieces were individually thrown. The designs were created by Baggs himself or under his direction; the forms and decoration were simple and restrained.

## 84 Marblehead Pottery

*Clockwise, beginning at left:*
*Vase,* n.d.
Earthenware
H. 6⅜, Diam. 5½ in.
(15.9 × 13.8 cm.)
Marks: Marblehead stamp barely legible on bottom
Museum purchase    P.C. 84.14.8

The earthenware body of this vase is ovoid with a slightly flared lip and a brown matte glaze.

*Vase,* n.d.
Earthenware
H. 7⅞, Diam. 4⅜ in.
(19.6 × 10.9 cm.)
Marks: Marblehead stamp on bottom, and torn oval Marblehead sticker on bottom
Museum purchase    P.C. 84.14.9

Tall, tapered, cylindrical vase with brown earthenware body, everted lip, and turned-in base. Soft lilac-blue matte glaze is on the exterior with a lighter tone inside.

*Vase,* n.d.
Earthenware
H. 3¼, Diam. 5¼ in.
(8.1 × 13.1 cm.)
Marks: Marblehead stamp on bottom
Museum purchase    P.C. 84.14.7

The dark, red-brown earthenware body of this vase is covered by a dark blue matte glaze. It has a globular shape with a wide mouth.

*Vase,* c. 1915
Earthenware
H. 4½, Diam. 4⅛ in.
(11.3 × 10.3 cm.)
Marks: Marblehead stamp on bottom
Museum purchase    P.C. 84.14.4

Red earthenware cylindrical vase with narrow shoulder and gray matte glaze. This piece, and the others in the collection, are illustrative of the restrained, classic forms produced at Marblehead.

*Flower Holder,* n.d.
Earthenware
Vase: H. 1¾, Diam. 3½ in. (4.4 × 8.75 cm.). Insert: H. 1, Diam. 1¾ in. (2.5 × 4.4 cm.)
Marks: Vase: Marblehead stamp on bottom. Insert: unmarked
P.C. 84.14.5a, b

This small, broad-based, bowl-like vase has a dark red-brown earthenware body and rich dark blue matte glaze on the outside. The inside has a lighter blue glossy glaze. The insert is cylindrical with two niches on the bottom which create two feet, and three holes on the top. It is glazed with the same matte dark blue as the exterior of the vase.

*Vase,* n.d.
Earthenware
H. 3⅜, Diam. 2¼ in. (8.4 × 5.6 cm.)
Marks: Marblehead stamp on bottom, barely legible
Museum purchase    P.C. 84.14.6

Small tapered vase, no lip, covered in mottled yellow and ochre matte glaze.

## MORAVIAN POTTERY AND TILE WORKS
### 1898–Present
### Doylestown, Pennsylvania

One of the most successful potteries of the Arts and Crafts era was, surprisingly, established and operated by a man with no formal training in either the art or technology of ceramics. Henry Chapman Mercer, an independently wealthy archaeologist, became fascinated with ceramics through his interest in pre-industrial Pennsylvania history. He set about learning how to handle clay from local folk potters and eventually established his pottery in a mission-style cloister which he designed and had built of poured concrete, using tiles set into the walls and kiln stacks for decoration. It still stands, now restored and revived as a functioning pottery which produces reproductions of Mercer's original designs (entries 437 and 438).

Everything was hand-produced. Mercer devised ways of pressing relief tiles and limited his glazes so that he was able to compete successfully with larger mechanized tile producers. Moravian tiles were used on the floors of Fenway Court (now the Isabella Stewart Gardner Museum in Boston), in the Pennsylvania State Capitol building at Harrisburg, and in buildings designed by many leading architects of the Arts and Crafts movement, including Stanford White, Julia Morgan, and Ward Wellington Ward.

## 85 Moravian Pottery and Tile Works

Henry Chapman Mercer, designer
*Clockwise, beginning with top left:*
*City of God Tile,* 1913
Earthenware
H. 5½, W. 5½, D. ¾ in. (13.75 × 13.75 × 1.8 cm.)
Marks: *PS.46/4* in pencil on back
Museum purchase    P.C. 86.20.4

Red earthenware tile in buff and blue glazes with a raised design of an ancient city (Jerusalem) behind a crenelated wall and river. The raised inscription reads "FLUMINIS IMPETUS FLUMINIS" and "LAETIFICAT CIV/TATEM DEI" (The Force of the River Gives Joy to the City of God).

*Lotus Tile,* 1898
Earthenware
H. 6⅝, W. 5⅝, D. ¾ in. (16.5 × 14 × 1.8 cm.)
Marks: *Moravian* and cypher stamped on reverse
Museum purchase   P.C. 86.20.2

Red earthenware tile covered in brown mottled glaze, with a raised design of a lotus blossom and leaves topping a column. Unrecognizable motifs decorate the lower corners.

One of Mercer's design sources was old cast-iron stove plates he had collected in the Pennsylvania German area of Bucks County. He not only used the iconographic motifs, but also incorporated architectural elements—columns, canopies, arches—from the stone plates onto his tiles. Here, the column and half-arches serve as a support and frame for the lotus blossom.

This rare tile was a dealer's sample.

*Pisces Tile,* 1914
Earthenware
H. 5¾, W. 5¾, D. ¾ in. (14.3 × 14.3 × 1.8 cm.)
Marks: none
Museum purchase   P.C. 86.20.6

Red earthenware tile with two fish within a circle carved and incised in the center. The fish curve to create a semblance of the Yin-and-Yang motif. The background of the circle is dark green.

This is a unique tile which Cleota Reed has noted was made after a design for a stained glass medallion by D'Ascenzo of Philadelphia. It was left over from a fireplace installed in a Ward Wellington Ward house in Syracuse, New York.

*Aries Tile,* 1913
Earthenware
H. 4, W. 4, D. ½ in. (10 × 10 × 1.25 cm.)
Marks: none

Museum purchase   P.C. 86.20.3

Red earthenware tile with a raised design of a ram within a quatrefoil within a diamond. Stylized tulips are in each corner. The motifs are in blue and buff glazes.

Mercer drew his inspiration from a wide range of sources: the Bible, history, folk lore, literature, and, in this case, astrology.

*Tulip Tile,* 1913
Earthenware
H. 2⅝, W. 2⅝, D. ¾ in. (6.5 × 6.5 × 1.8 cm.)
Marks: none
Museum purchase   P.C. 86.20.1

Small tile of red earthenware with incised stylized tulip in blue glaze.

The tulip motif has its source in the iconography of Pennsylvania German folk art. Mercer's conventional tiles, both plain and relief, were hand-rolled or hand-pressed and hand-glazed. No two were ever

precisely alike. This tile came from a 1914 house at 111 Clairmont Street in Syracuse, New York, designed by Ward Wellington Ward for George Fairchild.

*Swan and Tower Tile,* 1901
Earthenware
H. 3¾, W. 3¾, D. ½ in. (9.3 × 9.3 × 1.25 cm.)
Marks: none
Museum purchase   P.C. 86.20.5

Red earthenware tile in blue and buff glaze, with raised motif of swan and tower above water, surrounded by border with inscription which reads: "FLUMINISIM/PETUSLETI/FICATCIVIT/ATEMDEI" (The Force of the River Gives Joy to the City of God).

**86 Moravian Pottery and Tile Works**
Henry Chapman Mercer
*Clockwise, beginning with top left:*
*Montezuma,* 1913
Earthenware
H. 11½, W. 14¼, D. 1¾ in.
(28.75 × 35.6 × 4.3 cm.)
Marks: none
Museum purchase   P.C. 86.20.8

Eighteen piece, baroque-style tile arrangement depicting Montezuma holding a scepter and sitting on a throne. To the right are two bowls of fruit and a fruit tree in which a large bird sits eating a piece of fruit. "MONTEZUMA" in raised letters appears to the left of the figure. The scene is flanked on each side by a classic column, and a border of tile pieces encloses three sides.

This group, set in cement, is part of the series of scenes of the New World which Mercer created to be used as fireplace surrounds and borders.

*Norum Bega,* 1913
Earthenware
H. 14, W. 12, D. 1¾ in. (35 × 30 × 4.3 cm.)

Marks: *MR* cypher on extreme right balustrade
Museum purchase   P.C. 86.20.7

Brocade-style tile assemblage consisting of nineteen pieces set in cement. The scene depicts a vision of the New World, with two Indian figures, each wearing a cloak, feathered headdress, necklace, and holding an arrow. One half-figure stands before a balustrade, another sits. Architectural structures appear on the left. "NORUM BEGA," a name for the New World found on early maps, appears in raised letters at the top left. The remaining pieces create a border for the scene and a running border for the whole fireplace surround of which this scene was a part.

Mercer was an admirer of Columbus and used his discovery of America, and the New World itself, as a theme for much of his work. He created modular tile panels, with over seventy-five subjects, which could be ordered by the running foot for use as fireplace surrounds, borders, and friezes.

This particular panel was found unmounted and was set in cement by Cleota Reed, who has noted that Mercer's source for many of these scenes, including this one, was a publication, *Narrative and Critical History of America* by Justin Windsor, which reproduced sixteenth-century woodcuts depicting the voyages of Columbus and the discovery and exploration of America.

*The Fountain of Youth,* 1913
Earthenware
H. 16, W. 13, D. 1¾ in. (40 × 32.5 × 4.3 cm.)
Marks: *MR* cypher on fountain
Museum purchase   P.C. 86.20.9

A baroque-style tile assemblage of twenty-five pieces set in cement. A fountain spilling water is flanked by two figures, one of whom points to the fountain, the other holds aloft a bowl. The figures are flanked by palm trees bearing fruit. The border encloses a group and also relates it to the remaining sections of the fireplace surround of which this was a part.

The three New World tiles in the Everson collection came from a house in Syracuse, New York and were reset in cement at the Moravian Pottery.

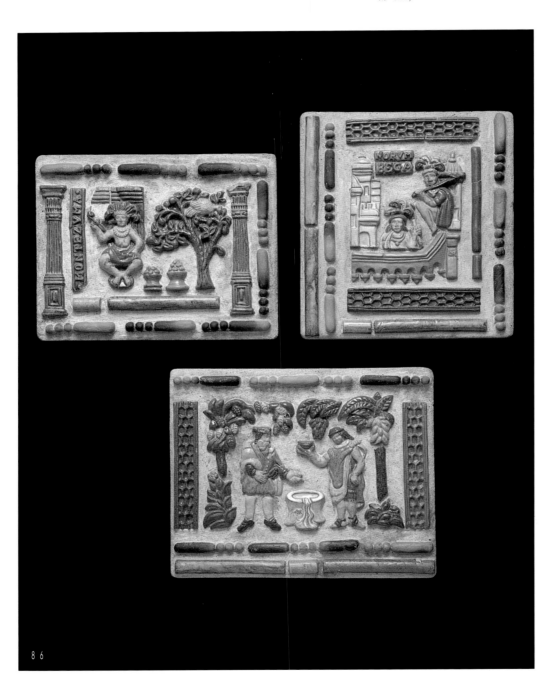

86

## NEWCOMB POTTERY
### 1895–1940
### New Orleans, Louisiana

Newcomb Pottery was established in 1895 in conjunction with Newcomb College, the women's division of Tulane University. Ellsworth Woodward was general manager and Mary G. Sheerer supervised the women. Sheerer had studied at the Cincinnati Art Academy and the Newcomb Pottery was patterned after the Rookwood Pottery. Potters and ceramists were hired to throw the forms which the young women students decorated, but as production increased women were hired as decorators on a permanent basis.

In the early years underglaze decoration was used with a high gloss finish. In 1911 Paul E. Cox developed a matte glaze which could be used over the same underglaze colors.

In 1918 the pottery was moved to the Art Building and became an educational studio where undergraduates could produce individual pieces from start to finish and learn more varied techniques. Thus there was less emphasis on the commercial venture. In 1930 production of the familiar matte ware ended and Woodward retired the following year. A limited number of pieces continued to be produced under the name of "The Newcomb Guild" into the 1940s but the finest wares were those produced in the earlier years up until about 1930.

### 87 Newcomb Pottery

Esther Huger Elliot, decorator
*Lily Vase,* 1902
Earthenware
H. 16⅜, Diam. 8½ in.
(40.9 × 21.25 cm.)
Marks: *124 E.H.E. N* within a *C* painted on bottom in blue
Museum purchase   P.C. 86.9.1

Buff earthenware vase, tall cylindrical form with short raised neck. The body is decorated with three pairs of lilies; each pair has a bud on a single stem. The arrangement of leaves creates a vertical, linear motif around the body of the vase. A horizontal line encompasses the vase one inch from the bottom. The decoration is all in tones of blue, with a gloss glaze overall.

Esther Elliot was a student or pottery worker at Newcomb from 1890 to 1891 and from 1896 to 1905, except for 1899.[1]

8 7

*An Enterprise for Southern Women.* Exhibition catalogue (Exton, Pennsylvania: Schiffer Publishing, Ltd., 1984), 99.

1. Jessie Poesch. *Newcomb Pottery:*

88

89

### 88 Newcomb Pottery

Henrietta Bailey, decorator
Joseph Meyer, potter
*Vase,* c. 1905
Earthenware
H. 6, Diam. 2¾ in. (15 × 6.9 cm.)
Marks: NC monogram and *HB* incised and stained blue. *HD59* painted in blue, *262* stamped in clay, *C* and *40* incised in clay, and *JM* incised, all on bottom
Museum purchase   P.C. 77.52

Tapered, cylindrical vase rising to a slight shoulder and narrow neck. The buff earthenware body is covered by a matte glaze with a scene of trees with hanging moss in shades of blue which give a hazy effect. The interior is covered with clear matte glaze.

The *HB* mark incised on the bottom refers to the decorator, Henrietta Bailey, who was with Newcomb from 1902 to 1915. *JM* is the mark of potter Joseph F. Meyer, who threw most of the vases produced by the pottery. The NC monogram is that of Newcomb College.

### NILOAK POTTERY
### 1909–1944
### Benton, Arkansas

The Niloak Pottery produced two lines of wares: Mission ware, of which each piece was hand-thrown and unique, and Hywood, a less expensively produced line of cast ware. Mission ware has a body composed of various colors of specially treated clays which, when worked on the wheel, swirled together to create a marbleized effect. The forms were classic and most were unglazed in order to emphasize the unusual technique, though some early pieces were glazed. Interiors were sometimes glazed, as well.

### 89 Niloak Pottery

*Vase,* n.d.
Earthenware
H. 12, Diam. 7 in. (30 × 17.5 cm.)
Marks: *Niloak* in "art lettering," sticker from Biggs Art Shop, Hot Springs, Arkansas, on bottom
Gift of the Social Art Club
P.C. 86.8

Marbled earthenware body in shades of blue, brown, and buff. The tapered cylindrical form has an abrupt shoulder and rolled lip.

This Mission vase is a classic example of the wares produced at Niloak until about 1942.

## OHIO POTTERY COMPANY
### 1900–1923
### Zanesville, Ohio

The Ohio Pottery Company grew out of the Radford Pottery, established in Zanesville, Ohio by Albert Radford, who had emigrated from England in 1882. The Ohio Pottery Company produced dinnerware and, for a short time, art pottery under the name Petroscan. The company was reorganized in 1923 and became the Fraunfelter China Company, which produced a chinaware so sturdy that it was used by Admiral Richard Byrd on his expedition to the South Pole.[1]

1. Roy Gillespie, of the Muskingum County Historical Society, provided the information on Ohio Pottery Company and Petroscan.

90

### 90 Ohio Pottery Company
*Bowl*, 1922–1923
Stoneware
H. 2¾, Diam. 8⅜ in.
(6.8 × 20.9 cm.)
Marks: *Petroscan / The Ohio Pottery Company / Zanesville, Ohio / 1001 / waterproof* stamped in black on the bottom
Gift of Mr. Richard Barons
P.C. 86.92

Stoneware bowl, short cylindrical lower section flaring outward and upward to create a wide mouth. A medium blue gloss glaze with a thin flame effect around the mouth runs in thin rivulets down the sides, both inside and out.

The glaze on this piece is reminiscent of Fulper, but not as fine.

This is a rare piece. Petroscan production began about 1922. The Ohio Pottery Company became Fraunfelter China Company in 1923. Thus pieces bearing this mark were made for only about a year or so.

## ONONDAGA POTTERY COMPANY
### 1871–1966
### Syracuse, New York

Onondaga Pottery Company had its roots in a small enterprise established by Williams H. Farrar to produce utilitarian, salt-glazed, stoneware vessels in Geddes, New York, now a part of the city of Syracuse. The Farrar pottery (entries 19–21, 41–43), which also made Rockingham ware, became Empire Pottery Company which, in turn, became Onondaga Pottery in 1871. Onondaga Pottery produced white ware for table use, and in 1886 began making porcelain. The products of this company were designated "Syracuse China," which became such a widely accepted name that in 1966 Onondaga Pottery officially became Syracuse China Corporation (entries 253, 254, 540, 541, and page 10).

## CHITTENANGO POTTERY COMPANY
### 1897–c. 1900
### Chittenango, New York

Chittenango Pottery began operations in 1897 and was situated on the Erie Canal in Chittenango, New York, near Syracuse.

91 *Left to right:*

### Onondaga Pottery Company
*Imperial Geddo Bonbon Dish*, 1888
Porcelain
H. 1¾, W. 7, L. 7 in. (4.3 × 17.5 × 17.5 cm.)
Marks: dragon-like figure with *Imperial Geddo* stamped on back and the letter *O* stamped in gold.
Museum purchase   P.C. 86.61

Triangular porcelain dish with low sides curving upward, ending in a ruffled edge, which is trimmed in gold. The flower and vine motif in gold and gray meanders on the inside.

The Imperial Geddo body was developed by James Pass, and his initials are stamped on many of these pieces.

### Chittenango Pottery Company
*Footed Serving Dish,* c. 1900
Porcelain
H. 2¼, W. 6, L. 8½ in. (5.6 × 15 × 21.25 cm.)
Marks: *C.P. CO./CHITTENANGO, N.Y./CHINA*
Gift of Mr. and Mrs. Victor Cole
P.C. 86.28

Low, four-footed dish in ovoid quatrefoil shape. The white body has a molded, branch-like design on the exterior; a gold branch motif is painted on the interior and covered in a clear gloss glaze. Touches of gold are on the feet and the crimped rim.

91

92

## PEWABIC POTTERY
### 1903–1961, reopened 1968
### Detroit, Michigan

Mary Chase Perry Stratton (1867–1961), the founder and driving force of Pewabic Pottery, began her involvement with ceramics during the china-painting movement. Determined to work in clay, she established a studio-workshop where she began experiments in clay bodies and glazes. This ultimately evolved into Pewabic Pottery. Early production pieces included pitchers, vases, teapots, mugs, and candlesticks, as well as tiles and lamps.

These pieces were all hand-thrown, using a high-fire clay developed at the pottery. Then gloss, matte, luster, iridescent, and flow glazes were skillfully applied.

Tile production became the mainstay of the pottery and commissions were received from architects to dec-orate churches and public buildings, among which were St. Paul's Cathedral in Detroit, the Cathedral of St. John the Divine in New York, and the Shrine of the Immaculate Conception in Washington, D.C.

The pottery was given to Michigan State University in 1966 and in 1981 the ownership was turned over to the Pewabic Society, a non-profit organization formed in 1979 to preserve the pottery. It is now a museum, gallery, and ceramic art learning center. The production of site-specific architectural tiles has been resumed.

### 92 Pewabic Pottery

Mary Chase Perry Stratton
*Monumental Vase,* n.d.
Earthenware
H. 25, Diam. 14½ in.
(62.5 × 36.25 cm.)
Marks: none
Anonymous gift    T.N. 132

Tall, earthenware vase with spade form and tapered base flaring to a wide body. The high shoulder tapers to an extended neck with a flared mouth. Gold, deep blue, and pinkish luster glazes create a serene Impressionist-like coloring.

Pewabic was noted especially for its iridescent glazes, especially its Egyptian Blue (or Persian Blue). The glaze on this piece in the Everson Collection has been attributed to Mary Chase Perry Stratton.

## RAINBOW POTTERY
### c. 1932–1942
### Sanford, North Carolina

Rainbow Pottery was established by A. R. Cole in a log cabin in Sanford, North Carolina in the early 1930s. Cole, who was born near Ashgrove, North Carolina, was a descendant of English potters from Staffordshire who had settled in the area. The sign before his pottery proclaimed: "Rainbow Pottery/Stop and See It Made." In the early 1940s Cole changed the name of the works to A. R. Cole Pottery. After his death in 1972, his daughters Celia and Neolia continued in the business, the ninth generation to work as potters. They changed the name to Cole Pottery and still produce hand-made wares today.

### 93 Rainbow Pottery

*Vase,* c. 1940
Stoneware
H. 3¾, Diam. 5⅜ in. (9.3 × 13.4 cm.)
Marks: *RAINBOW POTTERY, Sanford, N.C. HAND MADE* stamped on bottom in black
Gift of Nancy Farr Fulmer
P.C. 78.34.11

Broad baluster form with foot, very short neck, and wide lip. The buff clay is covered in a green speckle glossy glaze.

94

95

## ADELAIDE ALSOP ROBINEAU
## 1865–1929
## Syracuse, New York

Adelaide Beers Alsop was born in 1865 in Middletown, Connecticut. Soon after, her family moved to Moorhead, Minnesota, and Adelaide attended school at St. Mary's Hall in Faribault. She later returned there to teach porcelain painting. The Alsop family moved to Syracuse for a brief time, and Adelaide then went to New York, where she studied painting with William Merritt Chase. She exhibited twice in the annual exhibitions of the National Academy, but returned to china painting in order to have a steady income.

While in Minnesota, Adelaide met Samuel Robineau, a Parisian, and they were married in 1899. Robineau, too, was interested in ceramics and had a collection of oriental wares. Together they formed Keramic Studio Publishing Company, and produced the immensely influential magazine *Keramic Studio*, which would become the most important design source for china painters and a source of income for the Robineaus.

In 1901 the Robineaus moved to Syracuse, where they built a home and studio, and where Adelaide continued to edit and publish *Keramic Studio*. By this time she had tired of painting on blanks produced by others, and had determined to create her own porcelain forms. She published a translation of Taxile Doat's explanation of the methods of *grand feu* ceramics and enrolled for a summer course under Charles Binns at Alfred University. Her husband provided constant support and encouragement, and helped her fire her kilns.

Initially, Adelaide had planned to establish a production pottery, marketing functional objects such as doorknobs and drawer pulls. But she soon abandoned this idea and turned solely to her own work. She worked mainly in porcelain, but also produced some stoneware pieces. She experimented widely with glazes, achieving the elusive oxblood *flammé*, and exquisite crystallines in blue, ivory, green, lilac, and gold. Her decorative techniques included excising, carving, inlays, and modeling.

In 1904 her work was shown at the St. Louis Exposition and in 1911 her *Scarab Vase* won a grand prize at the Turin International Exposition. In 1912 she exhibited at the Paris Salon and the Musée des Arts Décoratifs. She was also recognized by the Art Institute of Chicago and arts and crafts societies in Boston and Detroit. In 1915 she won a Grand Prix at the Panama-Pacific International Exposition and two years later she received an honorary doctorate of the ceramic sciences from Syracuse University, where she taught from 1920 to 1928. Robineau's students produced stoneware under the name of Threshold pottery at Syracuse University.

In 1910 Robineau was invited to join the University City Pottery, where she worked with Taxile Doat until the venture failed and she returned to Syracuse.

Her work was sold at Tiffany's and at Macbeth Gallery in New York. In 1916 the Syracuse Museum of Fine Arts (now Everson Museum of Art) purchased thirty-two pieces of her porcelains, and in 1930, a year after her death, added forty-four more, including the *Scarab Vase*. Samuel Robineau donated her cinerary urn at the same time. The museum now owns eighty-two pieces of Robineau porcelain.

Adelaide Robineau is one of America's most important studio potters. She was a pioneer in the use of porcelain and created unique and exquisite glazes. She combined an incredible technical virtuosity with an equally singular aesthetic sensibility.

### 94 Adelaide Robineau
*Painted Bowl,* 1897
Porcelain
H. 3½, Diam. 10 in. (8.75 × 25 cm.)
Marks: *Adelaide Alsop 1897* inscribed on bottom
Museum purchase   P.C. 85.66

Squat, round, footed bowl with four-lobed rim. Two **C**-shaped handles are attached with lions' heads at the points of juncture with the rim. A painted decoration of Fiji chrysanthemums covers the body. The interior is painted in purple luster.

This bowl is an example of Robineau's china painting, done before she began to produce her own forms. The blank is unidentified and is probably European.

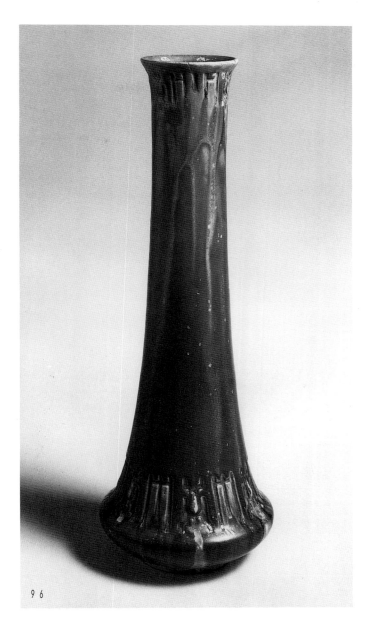

9 6

### 95 Adelaide Robineau
*Vase,* 1905
Porcelain
H. 7, Diam. 4 in. (17.5 × 10 cm.)
Marks: conjoined *AR* in a circle incised; *230* and *5* excised—both on bottom
Museum purchase   P.C. 16.4.24

Ovoid porcelain vase covered in blue crystalline glaze, with six incised vertical lines which divide the body into six panels. It originally had a knobbed lid.

Exhibitions: Turin Exposition, Turin, Italy, 1911

### 96 Adelaide Robineau
*Vase,* before 1917
Porcelain
H. 12, Diam. 4 in. (30 × 10 cm.)
Marks: conjoined *AR* in a circle excised; *506* incised—both on bottom
Museum purchase   P.C. 16.4.32

Footed porcelain vase with squat, circular base, which tapers to a long, cylindrical neck with a slight flaring at the top. The incised design surrounding the vessel near the base depicts scarabs amidst a linear geometric design. Further incising is at the mouth in an insect-like design. Tan and brown matte glaze with blue and tan streaks cover the vase.

97

**97** **Adelaide Robineau**
*Vase,* 1905
Porcelain
H. 8½, Diam. 3 in. (21 × 7.5 cm.)
Marks: conjoined *AR* in a circle excised on bottom
Museum purchase    P.C. 16.4.26

Heart-shaped porcelain vase with cylindrical, tapering neck. The vase sits within the attached, three-footed circular base with incised band. The vase is covered with a light blue crystalline glaze overall and light blue glaze at the rim.

98

**98 Adelaide Robineau**

*Viking Ship Vase,* 1905
Porcelain
H. 7¼ in., Diam. 2¾ in. (18.1 ×
6.8 cm.)
Marks: conjoined *AR* in a circle ex-
cised; *570* incised–all on bottom of
vase. On inside of base: incised cy-
pher of conjoined AR in a rectangle
Museum purchase
P.C. 16.41.1 a, b

Tapered, cylindrical porcelain vase
with high shoulder rising gently to a
short neck. The vase sits on a reticulated ring base. A decoration of Viking ships is excised on the upper
half of the vase and around the base.
Blue, green, and brown matte and
semi-matte glazes cover the piece.

The source of Robineau's motif
here was a border design by H. E.
Simson illustrated in *Dekorative Vor-
bilder* from 1901 (volume 12, page
55). The rhythmic design which she

has used is unusual in her excised
work, where she consistently used
rigid vertical and banded, non-
rhythmical designs.[1]

1. Martin Eidelberg, "Robineau's
Early Design," in *Adelaide Alsop Robineau,* ed., Peg Weiss (Syracuse:
Syracuse University Press, 1981), 81,
82.

Exhibitions: Turin Exposition, Turin,
Italy, 1911–Grand Prix and Diploma

della Benemerenza; Paris Salon,
1912; Musée des Arts Décoratifs,
Paris, 1912; "Panama-Pacific Inter-
national Exposition," San Francisco,
1914–Grand Prize; "Robineau Me-
morial Exhibition," Metropolitan
Museum of Art, New York, 1929;
"Arts and Crafts Movement in
America 1876–1916," Princeton
University, Princeton, New Jersey,
1972; "A Century of Ceramics in the
United States, 1878–1978," 1979

99

## 99 Adelaide Robineau

*Poppy Vase,* 1910
Porcelain
H. 6, Diam. 3¾ in. (15 × 9.3 cm.)
Marks: conjoined *AR* in a circle excised; *O, U, C,* and *1910* incised–all on bottom
Museum purchase   P.C. 16.4.3

Ovoid porcelain vase tapers at shoulder to a short rimmed mouth. A design of two decorative poppies is incised on both sides with a linear decoration surrounding the vase at the shoulder. The design was created by the use of inlaid slip in the incised area. The poppies are an orangish pink slip with dark and light green slip in the leaves, stems, and linear designs. The surface is an ivory iridescent crystalline glaze with a light green area below the rim.

Exhibitions: Turin Exposition, Turin, Italy, 1911–Grand Prix and Diploma della Benemerenza; Paris Salon, 1912; Musée des Arts Décoratifs, Paris, 1912; "Panama-Pacific International Exposition," San Francisco, 1915–Grand Prize; "Robineau Memorial Exhibition," Metropolitan Museum of Art, New York, 1929; "A Century of Ceramics in the United States, 1878–1978," 1979

## 100 Adelaide Robineau

*The Night Has a Thousand Eyes,* 1910

Stoneware
H. 7¾, Diam. 7¾ in.
(19.3 × 19.3 cm.)
Marks: conjoined *AR* in a circle excised on bottom; *The Night Has a Thousand Eyes* incised on bottom
Museum purchase   P.C. 30.4.84

Bulbous, squat, gourd-form vase with wide mouth. The stoneware body has a raised design covered by blue, gray lava, and white matte glazes.

**101 Adelaide Robineau**

*Vase,* 1910
Porcelain
H. 11½, Diam. 2¾ in.
(28.75 × 6.8 cm.)
Marks: conjoined *AR* in a circle excised on bottom; *1910 11 U C* incised on bottom
Museum purchase   P.C. 16.4.9

Tall, slender, bottle-shaped form of porcelain with wide-rimmed mouth. Three incised water lily decorations at the base act as feet for the piece. Incised linear patterns decorate the neck of the vase. The body is in an orange matte glaze with pink-gray crystalline dripping glaze as an overglaze. Green and yellow matte glazes are on the feet. A pearl crystalline glaze is on the rim.

The mark *UC* indicates that this piece was made while Robineau was at University City. Here she has used multiple glazes—first a warm orange, then a crystalline glaze over it. The crystalline glaze was not carried to the bottom, but the resulting rivulets formed as the glaze flowed create a lovely, thick dripping effect. This is a complex piece, involving exquisitely colored glazes, incising, and carving.

Exhibitions: Turin Exposition, Turin, Italy, 1911–Grand Prix and Diploma della Benemerenza; "A Century of Ceramics in the United States, 1878–1978," 1979

**102 Adelaide Robineau**

*Turtle Vase,* 1913
Porcelain
H. 21, Diam. 10½ in.
(52.5 × 26.25 cm.)
Marks: conjoined *AR* in circle excised on bottom; *C* and *1913* incised on bottom
Anonymous gift   P.C. 74.24

Large, cylindrical porcelain vessel, lower half tapering to footed base. An excised and pierced underwater motif, organized into narrow vertical bands, covers the upper half of the vase with flowing seaweed, water, and turtle medallions. Three turtles beneath the foliage create feet, two of which are missing. The cylindrical shape, covered in yellow, light green, blue, and ochre glazes, altered in firing.

This exquisitely carved monumental vase slumped during firing and was never exhibited.

1 0 0

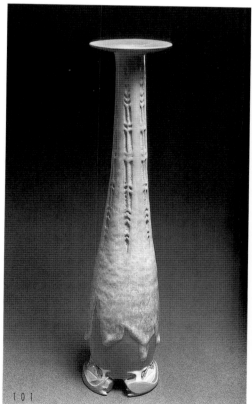

1 0 1

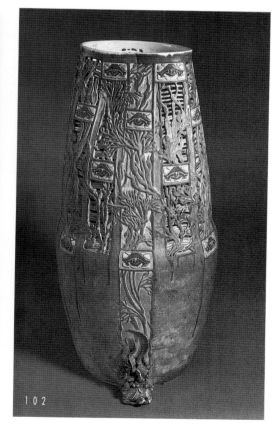

1 0 2

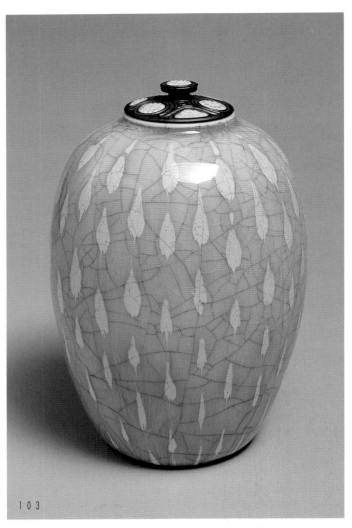

103

### 103 Adelaide Robineau

*Vase with Daisy Cover,* 1914
Porcelain
H. 6½, Diam. 4½ in.
(16.25 × 11.25 cm.)
Marks: *1914,* conjoined *AR* in circle,
and *9*—all incised on bottom
Gift of Dr. Ethel T. Eltinge
P.C. 82.33.2a, b

Porcelain ovoid vase with cover. The body tapers at the shoulder to a rimmed mouth. The round flat cover has a small raised knob in the center decorated with a daisy. Excised daisy designs in relief ornament the cover. The body is covered with a celadon crackle glaze and random spots of light blue. A blue band surrounds the neck.

This vase has the same decorative motif as a Robineau base in the Everson collection, though the coloring is very slightly different.

### 104 Adelaide Robineau

*Jar With Cover,* 1919
Porcelain
H. 7½, Diam. 8 in. (18.75 × 20 cm.)
Marks: conjoined *AR* in circle and *1919* incised on bottom. Old paper sticker reads: *75.00/Art no. 15/79–79*
Gift of Dr. Ethel T. Eltinge
P.C. 82.33.1a, b

Large, porcelain globular jar with cover. The surface is covered with brown and green crystalline glaze. The cover of the jar is incised with a decorative design that suggests a stem. The cover is in a brown metallic glaze.

This exceedingly fine piece is reminiscent of the gourd or squash-like pieces of Taxile Doat. The exquisite cover is deceivingly metal-like.

### 105 Adelaide Robineau

*Snake Bowl,* 1919
Porcelain
H. 4¼, Diam. 4½ in.
(10.6 × 11.25 cm.)
Marks: conjoined *AR* in a circle excised; *1919* incised on bottom
Museum purchase   P.C. 30.4.81

Round, ridged porcelain bowl with coiled snake serving as rim. The modeled snake's head is in relief at front. Blue-gray, green, tan, and cream iridescent glazes are used in a snakeskin motif. The interior is in cream crackle glaze with a golden brown, clear, glassy crystalline burst in the center.

Exhibitions: "Robineau Memorial Exhibition," Metropolitan Museum of Art, New York, 1929; "Art Deco Environment," 1976; "A Century of Ceramics in the United States, 1878–1978," 1979

104

105

## 106 Adelaide Robineau

*Threshold Plate,* 1923
Stoneware
H. 2¾, Diam. 15¼ in.
(6.8 × 38.1 cm.)
Marks: conjoined *AR* in a circle excised; *1923* incised; *Threshold* inscribed in brown—all on bottom
Museum purchase    P.C. 30.4.48

Footed stoneware plate with flat ledge encircled by banded rim. The deep well is incised with concentric circles to the center. Gray-green, ochre, light blue, and dark blue glazes create geometric linear designs and patterns. The well section is dark brown.

Threshold Pottery, a low-fire ware, was produced by Robineau's students at Syracuse University. This particular piece is an anomaly: the well is typical Robineau, carefully incised, with a Mayan-like medallion of a stylized sea monster with forked tongue in the center surrounded by concentric rings. The ledge of the plate, however, is freely decorated with stripes and lozenges, quite out of character with the well treatment and with Robineau's work in general. Perhaps this piece was a collaboration between Robineau and a student, or perhaps it was finished by a student.

107

AR in a circle, which is most often seen as the potter's mark on the bottom of her works. Incised linear patterns concentrated around the monograms serve as framing devices and occupy the bottom half of the vase. The bottom of the vase is covered in beige, tan, brown, and olive matte glazes with a copper crystalline effect near the top. The top section is beige.

This piece originally had a base. The subdued tones, incised vertical linear motif and the restrained form of this vase combine to place it squarely within the Arts and Crafts style which was so much a part of Robineau's aesthetic.

Exhibitions: Turin Exposition, Turin, Italy, 1911–Grand Prix and Diploma della Benemerenza; "A Century of Ceramics in the United States, 1878–1978," 1979

### 109 Adelaide Robineau

*Scarab Vase (The Apotheosis of the Toiler),* 1910
Porcelain
H. 16⅝, Diam 6 in. (41.6 × 15 cm.)
Marks: conjoined *AR* in a circle excised on bottom; *THE APOTHEOSIS OF THE TOILER . 60; 1910' MADE FOR THE U.C. WOMEN'S LEAGUE* incised on bottom; con-

### 107 Adelaide Robineau

*Lantern,* 1908
Porcelain
H. 8, W. 6 in. (20 × 15 cm.)
Marks: conjoined *AR* incised; *1908* and *668* excised—both inside vessel
Museum purchase P.C. 16.4.5

Ovoid-shaped porcelain lantern with tapering neck and flat top captures the spirit of ancient Chinese lanterns. The body is covered with an intricate geometric carving, creating six sections separated by linear frames. In the center of each frame is a flower encircled within its own frame. Pierced sections at the top half of the lantern reveal the interior. The middle section remains unpierced with incised lattice work. The attached cover has six floral carved designs within frames which surround a central hole.

The lantern is decorated in brown, blue, green, yellow, and white glazes.

Porcelain lanterns with elaborate pierced patterns were made in China during the eighteenth century. A six-sided Chinese lantern with similar rectangular and circular patterns was illustrated in *Keramik Studio* in 1913, five years after this piece was produced. But Robineau had undoubtedly seen one earlier, for her piece is strikingly similar to those produced in the Orient, though less flamboyant and more circumscribed.

Exhibitions: Turin Exposition, Turin, Italy, 1911–Grand Prix and Diploma della Benemerenza; "A Century of Ceramics in the United States, 1878–1978," 1979

### 108 Adelaide Robineau

*Monogram Vase,* 1905
Porcelain
H. 12¼, Diam. 5 in. (30.6 × 12.5 cm.)
Marks: conjoined *AR* in a circle excised; *141* incised—both on bottom
Museum purchase P.C. 16.4.17

Tall, ovoid-shaped porcelain vase with raised, tapered neck. The body is decorated with three excised Robineau monograms, the conjoined

108

joined *AR* incised on underside of lid; conjoined *AR* in circle and *1910, U.C.* incised on underside of base
Museum purchase
P.C. 30.4.78a, b, c

Club-shaped porcelain vase with knobbed lid and pedestal base. The vase is intricately carved and pierced with an overall scarab pattern and three center medallions with radiating scarab motifs. Half-medallions are at the shoulder, and a linear design is excised on the neck. The carved lid and six-footed carved and pierced base repeat the scarab motif. White and pale turquoise glazes are used on the relief design, the background is unglazed.

The *Scarab Vase* was produced at University City, and took, it is reputed, over one thousand hours of slow, patient work. Rightly called *The Apotheosis of the Toiler*, the vase is decorated with a scarab motif. The scarab, literally a beetle, is originally an Egyptian symbol and in hieroglyphics meant "to become" or "to create," and also represented a "phenomenon" or "marvel," a most appropriate iconographic motif for this tour de force. The idea of the beetle repeatedly rolling its egg in a ball of dung up hill relates to the theme of the vessel.

The piece endured two firings. At the end of the first firing, there appeared several cracks at the base of the vessel. Robineau patiently filled the cracks with ground porcelain, reglazed the piece, and the second firing resulted in a perfect object with no hint of the earlier damage.

The vase was intended for the American Women's League but was returned to Robineau when the organization floundered. It was purchased by the Museum from Samuel Robineau after her death. It was included in a lot of forty-four objects for which the Museum paid $4,000.

Exhibitions: Turin Exposition, Turin, Italy, 1911–Grand Prix and Diploma della Benemerenza; Paris Salon, 1912; Musée des Arts Décoratifs, Paris, 1912; "Panama-Pacific International Exposition," San Francisco, California, 1915; Grand Prize; "Robineau Memorial Exhibition," Metropolitan Museum of Art, New York, 1929; "A Century of Ceramics in the United States, 1878–1978," 1979

110 **Adelaide Robineau**
*Crab Vase,* 1908
Porcelain
H. 7⅜, Diam. 2½ in.
(18.4 × 6.25 cm.)

109

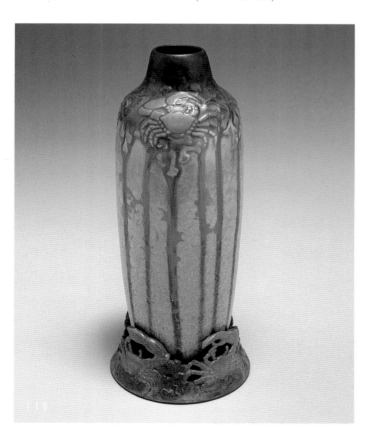

Marks: conjoined *AR* in a circle excised; 571 incised —both on bottom; on inside of base: incised cypher of conjoined *AR*
Museum purchase   P.C. 16.4.2a, b

Tapered, cylindrical porcelain vase, with high shoulder sloping gently into narrow neck. The vase sits in a reticulated ring base. The excised decoration of crabs around the shoulder is repeated on the ring base. Brown and tan flowing matte glaze and aqua, blue, and orange crystalline glazes cover the piece.

The sea served as inspiration for several Robineau pieces, perhaps owing to the suggestions of water inherent in the workings of her glazes. The *Viking Vase* (entry 98), *Water Lily Vase,* c. 1899 (private collec-

tion), and another vase of 1910 (entry 101) with an incised design of water lilies, are concerned with this subject. She also did a matte glaze vase, *The Sea,* in 1927 (entry 111), and her large, but ill-fated, *Turtle Vase* (entry 102), with its undulating seaweed motif, in 1913.

Exhibitions: Turin Exposition, Turin, Italy, 1911–Grand Prix and Diploma della Benemerenza; "A Century of Ceramics in the United States, 1878–1978," 1979; "The Art That Is Life," Museum of Fine Arts, Boston, 1987–1988

112

**111 Adelaide Robineau**

*The Sea,* 1927
Porcelain
H. 8½, Diam. 4¾ in.
(21.25 × 11.8 cm.)
Marks: conjoined *AR* in a circle excised on bottom; *1927/The Sea* incised on bottom
Museum purchase   P.C. 30.4.82

Ovoid porcelain vase tapers to a short neck with flared mouth. Four incised handles surround the vase, connecting at the neck and shoulder. The body is covered with incised lines encircling the vessel. A sea motif is incised on the band near the base of the vessel. Iridescent light brown and green glazes cover the body; thick white crackle glaze covers the rim.

Exhibitions: "Robineau Memorial Exhibition," Metropolitan Museum of Art, New York, 1929; "Art Deco Environment," 1976; "A Century of Ceramics in the United States, 1878–1978," 1979

**112 Adelaide Robineau**

*Gourd Vase,* 1926
Porcelain
H. 7¾, Diam. 5 in.
(19.3 × 12.5 cm.)
Marks: conjoined *AR* excised on bottom; *1926* incised on bottom
Museum purchase   P.C. 30.4.49

Gourd-shaped, footed porcelain vase. The tapering neck with incised bands continues to a small mouth. The exterior is covered in mottled green and brown matte glazes. The neck and mouth are in a black matte glaze.

This vase is reminiscent of the gourd vases of Taxile Doat, though more conventionalized. The reference to its vegetal counterpart is unmistakable.

Exhibitions: "Robineau Memorial Exhibition," Metropolitan Museum of Art, New York, 1929; "A Century of Ceramics in the United States, 1878–1978," 1979

**113 Adelaide Robineau**

*Unfinished Vase,* 1928
Porcelain
H. 14⅛, Diam. 5¼ in. (35.3 × 13 cm.)
Marks: conjoined *AR* in a circle excised; *1928* incised—both on bottom
Museum purchase    P.C. 30.4.87 a-c

Bullet-shaped, lidded porcelain vase with three-footed pedestal base. Excised and incised linear designs decorate the surface. Ridged bands encircle the bottom section of the vase giving way to a flat central portion with incised arc lines and ridges. The cover has an unfinished, flared rim and concentric rings above.

   This unfinished piece was bisque-fired after Robineau's death. It illustrates her creative method, in which she kept the work at the same stage on the entire piece, rather than completing any one part at a time.

**114 Adelaide Robineau**

*Cinerary Urn,* 1928–1929
Porcelain
H. 33, Diam 5½ in.
(82.5 × 13.75 cm.)
Marks: conjoined *AR* in a circle and stylized scarab excised; *"De Profundis "Clamavi", Adelaide Alsop Robineau = Born April 9, 1865 Died February 18, 1929/Samuel Edouard Robineau = Born December 20, 1856 Died* (left unfinished) incised on bottom
Gift of Samuel E. Robineau
P.C. 30.4.79

Tall, tapered porcelain vessel with stopper. Concentric rings run from top to bottom, interrupted by a wide band on the bottom third and a narrow band just above at midsection. The flared mouth has a narrow band around the neck, immediately below the mouth. The stopper is also decorated with rings, and a pointed top. Bronze-black matte glaze covers the body, with bands in white crackle glaze. White glaze runs off the lower band, streaking over the black rings below.

   Robineau's cinerary urn was left unfinished at her death. It was glazed and fired by Carlton Atherton, a former student. The original design called for an incised motif involving human figures passing through tongue-like flames.[1]

   The urn contains the ashes of Adelaide Robineau and those of her husband.

---

1. Peg Weiss, ed. *Adelaide Alsop Robineau* (Syracuse: Syracuse University Press, 1981), 208 n. 42.

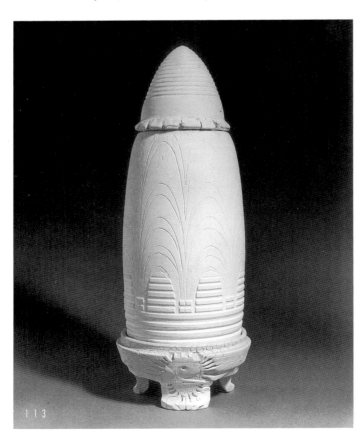

113

114

## ROOKWOOD POTTERY
### 1880–1967
### Cincinnati, Ohio

One of the most important and most productive of the art potteries was Rookwood, begun in 1880 in Cincinnati, Ohio, by Maria Longworth Nichols. Like many other women in the art pottery movement, Nichols began as a china painter and expanded her interests to pottery production. In the beginning the pottery survived mainly because the Nichols family fortune provided financial stability to the venture, but in 1883 Nichols added a manager, William Watts Taylor, who put the pottery on a business-like footing.

The earliest pieces produced at Rookwood reveal the use of a variety of decorating techniques indicative of a firm still seeking an individual style. These early years, 1880 to 1884, saw the use of a great deal of gilding, and a smear-glaze technique was popular. In 1884 Laura Fry discovered that colored slips could be applied with an atomizer and the traditional underglaze slip-decorated ware became a hallmark of the pottery and was designated "Rookwood Standard." This work characterized the period from 1884 to 1898.

In 1889 the future of the pottery was determined. At the Universal Exposition in Paris that year, Rookwood was awarded a Gold Medal for excellence; it was also during this year that Rookwood became financially successful. The following year Nichols, now Mrs. Bellamy Storer, ceased active association with the pottery and Taylor became president of the newly formed corporation.

Rookwood Standard had always incorporated the use of high gloss glazes, but in 1901 matte-glazed pieces were shown at the Buffalo exposition, and later a transparent matte glaze was used over colored slip decorations. In 1915 Rookwood's "Soft Porcelain," with its rich bright glazes, first appeared. These later innovations allowed Rookwood ware to be more easily mass-produced, since they depended less on the use of individual artists. Pieces without artists' signatures appeared in the early 1900s and the number of such unmarked pieces increased through the years.

The pottery had a number of successive presidents and managers,

115

surviving both the Depression and the Second World War, until 1959 when it was sold to the Herschede Clock Company which moved it to Starkville, Mississippi. Production ceased in 1967 and the assets of the company, including molds and glaze formulae, were sold to Briarwood Lamps in Starkville.

### 115 Rookwood Pottery
Decoration attributed to Albert Valentien
*Monumental Vase,* 1883
Earthenware

H. 21, Diam. 12 in. (52.5 × 30 cm.)
Marks: *ROOKWOOD* below kiln mark, *1883* and *G.*—all impressed on bottom
Museum purchase  P.C. 85.25.2

This large, buff earthenware vase is ovoid in shape with wide shoulders, a narrow base, a high cylindrical neck with a band about the center, and a straight-sided, cup-shaped mouth. The body of the vase is divided into three sections by diagonal bands of stamped decoration in gold. One section is decorated with a stormy landscape of trees and a spi-

der, the other with wisteria blossoms in blue-gray, the third with swallows and a large, crescent moon. Except for the blue wisteria blossoms, the colors are earth tones with touches of gold. The neck is covered by a clear gloss glaze.

The decoration of this early piece is attributed to Albert Valentien, who was in charge of the decorating department at Rookwood from 1881 to 1905.[1] He and his wife, Maria Bookprinter Valentien, also a decorator at Rookwood, studied abroad from 1899 to 1900. They moved to

San Diego in 1907, where Albert spent many years painting the wild flowers of California.

1. Herbert Peck, *The Book of Rookwood Pottery* (New York: Crown Publishers, Inc., 1968), 147.

### 116 Rookwood Pottery

Kataro Shirayamadani, decorator
*Vase with Ferns,* 1890
Earthenware
H. 10½, Diam. 9¼ in.
(26.3 × 23.1 cm.)
Marks: Rookwood monogram with four flames, *8, F,* and *Y* incised; decorator's signature incised in Japanese. Two stickers read: *C of C 169* and *SHIRAMADAM #166*
Museum purchase   P.C. 77.46

Classic, baluster-shaped vase with short, wide neck flaring into a wide everted lip. The buff earthenware body has a standard Rookwood glaze of ochre blending to brown at the base. The underglaze decoration of ferns is in green, ochre, and brown tones.

The full volumetric form and the careful nuances of the slip decoration make this an exceptionally fine piece. Kataro Shirayamadani came to Rookwood from Japan in 1887. Except for a ten year period from 1915 to 1925 when he returned to Japan, he remained at Rookwood until his death in 1948.[1]

A Japanese influence was evident at Rookwood from the very beginning. The gentle relief created by slip decoration and the depth of color of Rookwood glazes resemble Japanese lacquer work. The concern with nature and the reverent depiction of flowers, grasses, and birds was also derived in part from Japanese art. The pottery made prints and periodicals dealing with Japan available to decorators, and a wide variety of Japanese objects were on view at the Cincinnati Art Museum. Rookwood decorators had ample opportunity to immerse themselves in things Japanese.

Exhibitions: "A Century of Ceramics in the United States, 1878–1978," 1979

1. Herbert Peck, *The Book of Rookwood Pottery* (New York: Crown Publishers, Inc., 1968), 147.

### 117 Rookwood Pottery

Matthew A. Daly, decorator
*Vase with Japanese Peasant Figures,* 1889
Earthenware
H. 13½, Diam. 10 in.
(33.75 × 25 cm.)
Marks: Rookwood monogram, *488, D, G,* and *MAD/L* incised on bottom
Gift of Todd M. Volpe and Beth

Cathers, Jordan-Volpe Gallery, New York  P.C. 86.22

Plump, ovoid vase of brown earthenware with neck and flaring lip. Two figures of Japanese peasants are painted in slip under the glaze.

Matthew Daly, one of the leading decorators at Rookwood, joined the pottery in 1882. He left Rookwood in 1903. A widower, in 1928 he married Olga Reed Pinney, who had been a decorator at Rookwood.

Floral motifs were the mainstay of Rookwood decoration, but late in the 1880s new decorative subjects, including figures and portraits, were added. An initial interest in Japanese figures was superceded by a variety of others, including American Indians and copies after Old Masters.

## 118 Rookwood Pottery

Elizabeth N. (Lingenfelter) Lincoln, decorator
*Water-lily Vase*, 1900
Earthenware
H. 4½, Diam. 8¼ in.
(11.3 × 20.6 cm.)
Marks: Rookwood monogram and flames, *494, A,* and *LNL* incised on bottom
Gift of Mr. and Mrs. H. Gillis Murray  P.C. 78.5.1

The squat, ovoid vase with slight neck and everted lip has a standard glaze shading from brown to ochre and underglaze slip decoration of two water-lily blossoms, one bud, and leaves.

Elizabeth Lincoln started at Rookwood in 1892 and by 1899 had become a decorator.[1] She was of German descent and during the height of the anti-German sentiment that surrounded the First World War she, like many others of German extraction, changed her name from Lingenfelter to Lincoln. Though she is best known for her decoration in matte glaze, this vase illustrates her exceptional skill in underglaze slip painting as well. The water lily was a traditional motif in Japan, and a popular one at Rookwood. Its use was inspired by the arrival in Cincinnati of Japanese lilies and lotuses for the Japanese pond created on the property of a local horticulture enthusiast.

1. Herbert Peck, *The Book of Rookwood Pottery* (New York: Crown Publishers, Inc., 1968), 145.

117

118

**119 Rookwood Pottery**
Albert Valentien, decorator
*Hydrangea Vase*, 1904
Earthenware
H. 14⅝, Diam. 9½ in.
(36.5 × 23.75 cm.)
Marks: Rookwood monogram *787B*,
and *A Valentien* incised on bottom.

Museum purchase with funds from
the Dorothy and Robert Riester Ceramic Fund   P.C. 86.9.4

Ovoid-shaped vase of light gray
earthenware with neck that rises to
a flared lip. The underglaze slip decoration of hydrangea flowers and

leaves is in tones of grays and greens.
Diffused coloring graduates from
dark green at the top to pale gray at
the base, and is covered overall by a
gloss glaze.

After about 1895 the floral decorations used on Rookwood vases began to follow the form of the vessel.

Earlier designs had been frontal,
meant to be seen from one point of
view only. Here the branches and
leaves, as well as the blossoms, encircle the form and carry the eye
from top to bottom, creating more
of a sense of completeness.

120

**120 Rookwood Pottery**

*Clockwise, beginning at left:*
*Teapot,* 1906
Earthenware
H. 4½, Diam. 6¾ in.
(11.3 × 16.8 cm.)
Marks: Rookwood monogram and flames, *VI,* and *404* incised on bottom
Gift of Hajime and Mitsue Kozuru
P.C. 84.9a, b

The squat, ovoid body of this teapot has a curved spout and a bamboo and brass handle. The white earthenware body has a green matte glaze, shading to yellow-green and ochre. An incised Greek key design bands the shoulder. The slightly domed cover has a butterfly finial.

This teapot shape was produced in a variety of glazes and decorative motifs. There were matching sugars and creamers as well.

*Vase,* 1917
Earthenware
H. 7⅝, Diam. 3½ in.
(19 × 8.75 cm.)
Marks: Rookwood monogram with flames, *XVII* and *2411* incised on bottom
Gift of Helen Checco   P.C. 77.73

Tapered, cylindrical vase with narrow, gently sloping shoulder and short neck. The upper third of the body is decorated in relief, glazed a soft medium green matte with a slight crackle. The lower section is in rose matte glaze.

*Vase,* 1919
Porcelain
H. 9¼, Diam. 3¾ in.
(23.1 × 9.4 cm.)
Marks: Rookwood monogram with flames, *XIX* and *2430* impressed on bottom
Gift of Ronald A. Kuchta
P.C. 76.111

A slightly tapered, cylindrical vase of white porcelain, with narrow shoulder, short neck, and rounded lip. The vase is in a rose matte glaze and decorated in relief with crocus blossoms around the upper third of the body. The remaining section is divided by stems into six sections, creating a leaf pattern.

Cecil A. Duell, decorator
*Mug,* 1909
Earthenware
H. 5½, W. 5¼ in. (13.8 × 13.1 cm.)
Marks: Rookwood monogram with flames, *IX, CAD* incised on bottom; *1071* and an inverted triangle impressed on bottom
Gift of Nancy Farr Fulmer
P.C. 78.34.16

This cylindrical mug with buff clay body has a **C**-shaped handle, which is grooved where it meets the top of the body. The medium green matte glaze accents three yellow-green five-pointed fleurettes in relief around the top.

Cecil A. Duell joined Rookwood in 1907 and left to serve in the First World War.[1] He was a sculptor and had a metal-casting business in Cincinnati.

1. Herbert Peck. *The Book of Rookwood Pottery* (New York: Crown Publishers, Inc., 1968), 144.

*Vase,* 1919
Porcelain
H. 6¼, Diam. 3¾ in.
(15.6 × 9.3 cm.)
Marks: Rookwood monogram with flames, *XIX,* and *231* impressed on bottom
Gift of Ronald A. Kuchta
P.C. 76.110

This tapered, ovoid vase has a gently sloping shoulder and rounded lip. The white porcelain body is covered with a mauve matte glaze. A raised lozenge design forms a band just below the shoulder.

*Sugar Bowl,* 1925
Porcelain
H. 3¼, W. 4½ in. (8.1 × 11.3 cm.)
Marks: Rookwood monogram with flames, *XXV,* and *354* impressed on bottom
Gift of Nancy Farr Fulmer
P.C. 78.34.14

The broad, pear-shaped form with widely flaring mouth has angular handles projecting from the rim to the broadest area of the body. The white porcelain body is covered with mauve matte glaze.

*Sugar Bowl,* 1922
Porcelain
H. 4, W. 4½ in. (10 × 11.3 cm.)
Marks: Rookwood monogram with flames, *XXII,* and *2559* impressed on bottom
Gift of Nancy Farr Fulmer
P.C. 78.34.13

This sugar bowl has a broad, pear-shaped form, truncated, with two **D**-shaped handles. A leaf or gadroon design decorates the lower half and the whole is covered by a mauve matte glaze.

121

**121 Rookwood Pottery**
Sallie E. Coyne, decorator
*Scenic Vase*, 1916
Earthenware
H. 10¾, Diam. 4 in. (26.8 × 10 cm.)
Marks: Rookwood monogram with flames, *XVI, 941C, V,* and *SEC* impressed on bottom
Museum purchase in memory of Edward Beadle with funds from friends   P.C. 84.41

This tapered, cylindrical vase has a sharply defined, concave shoulder rising into the neck. The white earthenware body has an elegant vellum glaze and is decorated with a winter scene of trees and stumps and an evergreen forest in the distance. The scene is in blues and grays with the sky of mauve shading to pale rose and yellow.

The mark indicates the date (XVI), the shape number and size (941C), the glaze (V for vellum), and the decorator (SEC in monogram). Sara (Sallie) Coyne became a decorator at Rookwood in 1892 and remained with the firm until 1931.[1]

1. Herbert Peck, *The Book of Rookwood Pottery* (New York: Crown Publishers, Inc., 1968), 143.

**122 Rookwood Pottery**
Frederick Rothenbusch, decorator
*Scenic Vase*, 1907
Earthenware
H. 9¼, Diam. 5¼ in.
(23.1 × 13.1 cm.)
Marks: Rookwood monogram with flames, *VII, 925CC, A,* and *FR* (monogram of Frederick Rothenbusch) incised on bottom
Museum purchase in memory of Ruth Leonard   P.C. 77.47

This ovoid, cylindrical vase with gently sloping shoulders and low, wide neck has a vellum glaze, slightly crackled. The lower half is gray-green, with the scene above in shades of blue, topped by gray-green. Frederick Rothenbusch, nephew of Rookwood decorator Albert Valentien, came to the pottery in 1896 and remained until 1931.[1]

1. Herbert Peck, *The Book of Rookwood Pottery* (New York: Crown Publishers, Inc., 1968), 146.

122

123

124

### 123 Rookwood Pottery

*Vase*, 1925
Porcelain
H. 6¼, Diam. 3¾ in.
(15.6 × 8.4 cm.)
Marks: Rookwood monogram with
flames, *XXV*, and *2780* impressed on
bottom
Gift of Nancy Farr Fulmer
P.C. 78.34.19

Bottle vase with squat, ovoid body
and long, wide neck flaring into a
trumpet-shaped mouth. The white
porcelain body has a yellow-ochre
matte glaze, with a gadroon decoration, topped by a dotted band. The
neck is decorated overall with diapered scale pattern.

### 124 Rookwood Pottery

Edward T. Hurley, decorator
*Bird of Paradise Vase*, 1928
Earthenware
H. 14⅝, Diam. 9½ in.
(36.5 × 23.75 cm.)
Marks: *E.T.H.*, Rookwood mono-
gram, *224GC* inscribed on bottom
Museum purchase   P.C. 86.9.3

Ovoid vase of buff earthenware with
sloping shoulder and flared lip covered in glossy glaze. The body is decorated in a multi-colored, bird of
paradise motif.

Edward Hurley joined Rookwood
in 1896 and married Irene Bishop,
another Rookwood decorator. A major figure at Rookwood, he remained
with the pottery until 1948. Hurley
had a deep love of nature and was a
master of landscape decoration, particularly of vellum-glazed pieces.

The highly stylized treatment of
the decoration on this vase is indicative of the turn which decoration
took in the early years of the twentieth century, not only at Rookwood,
but throughout the country. The
movement veered steadily away from
naturalism toward flat, stylized, more
general forms. The unusual coloration of this piece is typical of Hurley,
who was intensely interested in glazing and firing.

125

## ROSEVILLE POTTERY
## 1890–1954
## Zanesville, Ohio

Roseville Pottery was organized in 1890 in Roseville, Ohio, under the direction of George F. Young, and incorporated in 1892. In 1898 a second pottery was acquired in Roseville, as well as a plant in Zanesville, Ohio. Another pottery in Zanesville was added in 1901, and in 1910 the two Roseville factories were closed and the two Zanesville locations continued to produce Roseville lines, one concentrating on art pottery, the other on utilitarian wares. Art pottery was never produced at the Roseville locations.

The earliest art pottery line, Rozane, was an imitation of Rookwood Standard, with underglaze slip decoration using portraits, animals, and flowers. Other lines were added, sometimes several each year, but the most unique was probably Della Robbia, designed by Frederick H. Rhead, who was art director from 1904 to 1908. This consisted of stylized designs created by a sgraffito process with colored slips.

Beginning in 1919 Roseville became mainly a producer of industrial artware rather than of art pottery.[1] Individual decoration of artware had for the most part ceased a few years earlier, but Rozane Royal had continued in production until 1919 and

some hand-decorated goods were still produced until the firm's final years.

---

1. Paul Evans, *Art Pottery of the United States* (New York: Charles Scribner's Sons, 1974), 267.

### 125 Roseville Pottery
*Sunflower Jardiniere*, 1925–1930
Earthenware
H. 12, Diam. 17 in. (30 × 42.5 cm.)
Marks: none
Museum purchase with funds from the Dorothy and Robert Riester Ceramic Fund   P.C. 88.9

Large, ovoid, earthenware jardiniere flaring at the shoulder with a raised ledge surrounding the wide mouth.

Large golden sunflower blossoms and green leafy stems in relief surround the vessel. The rough background below is also green. The area above the shoulder is brown with an ochre interior.

### 126 Roseville Pottery
*Clockwise, beginning at left:*
*Imperial Vase*, 1924
Stoneware
H. 8⅝, Diam. 7⅛ in.
(21.5 × 17.8 cm.)
Marks: *481* in crayon on bottom
Gift of Ronald A. Kuchta
P.C. 84.14.1

Ovoid vase with pronounced shoulder gently blending into vertical neck. The buff clay is covered in mauve matte glaze on the body; the blue-purple glaze on the neck streaks into greens which run down over the body. A raised chain design surrounds the neck. The interior glaze is mauve and green.

*Mostique Vase*, 1915
Stoneware
H. 10⅛, Diam 5¼ in.
(25.3 × 13.1 cm.)
Marks: mark on bottom obliterated by glaze
Gift of Ronald A. Kuchta
P.C. 84.14.2

Tapered, beaker-shaped vase with wide flaring mouth. A stylized design of flower buds on stems is incised around the upper body. The gray stoneware body is covered with matte gray glaze on the exterior and a dark green gloss on the interior. The design is yellow, blue, and alligator green.

*Vase*, 1912–1923
Stoneware
H. 6⅛, W. 6¼, D. 1⅞ in. (15.3 × 15.6 × 4.6 cm.)
Marks: *V* within an *R* stamped on bottom
Gift of Nancy Farr Fulmer
P.C. 78.34.10

Rectangular vase of buff earthenware with small foot, narrow shoulder, short neck, and rounded lip. The small inverted Bristol handles bridge the neck and body. The dark green matte glaze on the top section drips down over the lighter green body.

*Bowl*, n.d.
Earthenware
H. 5¼, Diam. 6½ in.
(13.1 × 16.3 cm.)
Marks: Roseville monogram and *238–5* incised on bottom
Gift of Helen Checco   P.C. 77.75

Spherical bowl of white earthenware with foot, concave shoulder, and slightly rising neck. An incised linear design surrounds the upper half, just below the shoulder. The bowl is covered overall in green mottled matte glaze.

*Mostique Bowl*, 1915
Stoneware
H. 2¾, Diam. 7 in. (6.9 × 17.5 cm.)
Marks: *V* within an *R* imprinted on bottom
Gift of Ronald A. Kuchta
P.C. 84.14.3

1 2 6

Squat, ovoid form of buff stoneware with slight rise at the lip. Four indentations on the bottom create four wide feet. The gray, textured matte glaze body is decorated with two stylized, embossed designs in blue, yellow, green, and brown gloss glazes repeated four times each around the body. The interior is in green gloss glaze.

## SATURDAY EVENING GIRLS
## 1906–1908
## PAUL REVERE POTTERY
## 1908–1942
## Boston, Massachusetts

Saturday Evening Girls, or "S.E.G.," was an organization of young immigrant women who met on Saturday evenings for cultural activities. Ceramics was included with the encouragement of Mrs. James J. Storrow, the group's patron. Regular production was begun in 1908 and the name Paul Revere Pottery was adopted (it was also known as "The Bowl Shop"). Miss Edith Brown was the designer and director of the pottery, and the decorators were young women who were expected to learn all the aspects of pottery, including throwing, design, and glaze chemistry.

In 1917, with the financial support of Mrs. Storrow, a new pottery was built in Brighton, Massachusetts.

Production ranged from vases and lamps to open-stock dinnerware and breakfast and tea sets. A child's breakfast set decorated with animals was the most popular item. Both matte and gloss glazes were used for decorated wares, and in some cases designs were incised and outlined in black in the Art Nouveau style.

In spite of the enthusiastic acceptance of its wares, the pottery required continual financial subsidization and it finally closed in January 1942.

127 **Paul Revere Pottery
(Saturday Evening Girls)**
Brighton, Massachusetts
*Vase*, c. 1921
Earthenware
H. 12, Diam. 8 in. (30 × 20 cm.)
Marks: *S.E.G., 12–21, EG,* and *01* painted on bottom
Gift of Leonard Fried   P.C. 81.23.5

Tall, cylindrical vase with gently tapered sides and rounded base, high

1 2 7

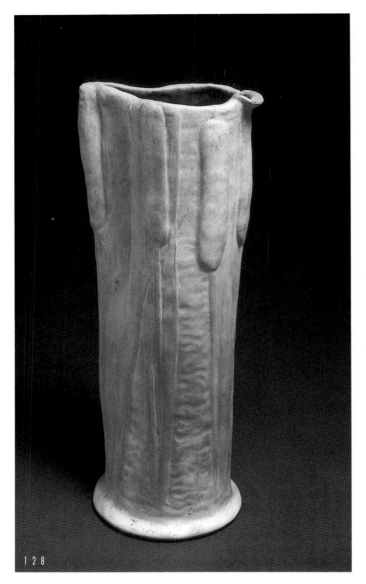

128

129

shoulder, and broad neck. Three applied handles are attached to the neck and body just below the shoulder. Medium blue gloss glaze with tiny lighter blue speckles covers the buff earthenware body.

### TIFFANY POTTERY
### 1898–1920
### Corona, New York

Louis Comfort Tiffany's flirtation with art pottery was short-lived, but during the brief period from 1898 to 1920 some of the most original and sensitive pieces of art pottery in America were produced by his firm. Tiffany pottery was first shown in 1904 at the Louisiana Purchase Ex-

position in St. Louis, and was offered for sale commercially the following year.

Most of the pottery was mold-made and in the Art Nouveau style for which Tiffany became famous. The forms are sophisticated and the decorative motifs, which are incorporated into the forms, are derived from nature. Glazes are subtle and elegant.

Tiffany pottery is relatively scarce for a number of reasons. It was produced for only a brief period, and if pieces did not sell within a certain length of time they were either given to employees or destroyed. By 1914 Louis Comfort Tiffany had begun to lose interest in ceramics and between

1917 and 1920 production ceased.

### 128 Tiffany Pottery
*Cattail Vase*, 1904–1914
Stoneware
H. 12, W. 4⅞ in. (30 × 12.1 cm.)
Marks: LCT monogram incised on bottom
Museum Purchase   P.C. 77.36

Tall, cylindrical vase altered as it rises upward to resemble a handled pitcher with pinched lip. The bottom flares outward abruptly to form a rounded foot. A raised design of cattails and leaves covers the white semi-porcelaneous body, which is unglazed on the exterior, and blue-green on the interior.

### 129 Tiffany Pottery
*Vase with Cover*, c. 1901
Stoneware
H. 8¾, Diam. 3⅞ in.
(21.8 × 9.6 cm.)
Marks: LCT monogram, *LC Tiffany Furnaces*, and *P5111* incised on bottom
Gift of Mr. and Mrs. Bronson Quackenbush   P.C. 78.40.6a, b

Oviform vase with rounded, flat-topped cover that sits inside the mouth of the vase. A raised relief design of milkweed pods and leaves covers the vase which is in a variegated green glaze overall.

Exhibitions: "A Century of Ceramics in the United States, 1878–1978," 1979

130

**130 Tiffany Pottery**
*Vase with Pansies*, c. 1910
Stoneware
H. 10⅜, Diam. 4½ in.
(25.9 × 11.3 cm.)
Marks: LCT monogram incised on bottom
Gift of Mr. and Mrs. Bronson A. Quackenbush   P.C. 78.40.7

Tall, cylindrical vase with wide foot. A raised and perforated decoration of pansy flowers, leaves, and stems decorates the white semi-porcelaneous body, which is covered in a mottled green glaze.

The natural motif and the way it is interpreted are indicative of Tiffany's affinity for the Art Noveau style. Though this piece bears the monogram of Louis Comfort Tiffany, it, like all other Tiffany ceramics, is the product of the studio and was not actually made by Tiffany himself.

Exhibitions: "A Century of Ceramics in the United States, 1878–1978," 1979

**UNION PORCELAIN WORKS**
**1863–c. 1925**
**Greenpoint, New York**

Thomas C. Smith's Union Porcelain Works produced first soft paste porcelain, and then beginning in 1866 hard paste porcelain. In 1874 Karl Müller modeled special commemorative pieces and other wares. The firm made mass-produced objects as well as artwares.

**131 Union Porcelain Works**
*Uncle Sam Pitcher*, c. 1876
Porcelain
H. 9¾, W. 9¾ in. (24.4 × 24.4 cm.)
Marks: *U.P.W.* impressed in barrel on side
Museum purchase with funds from the Dorothy and Robert Riester Ceramic Fund   P.C. 88.11

Large, ovoid pitcher with tusked-walrus-head spout, and handle in the shape of a bear. Relief designs decorate both sides. On one side are a bearded Uncle Sam, a figure of Gambrinus (mythical Flemish king credited with first brewing beer) holding a mug of beer, and a ram atop a barrel, which is impressed with the pottery's initials. The opposite side depicts a man with a large sword grasping a Chinese man at the neck, illustrating the anti-Chinese sentiments of Bret Hart's 1870 poem, "Plain Language from Truthful Jones." This pitcher was probably designed by Karl Müller.

131

132

## VAN BRIGGLE POTTERY
### 1902–present
### Colorado Springs, Colorado

Artus Van Briggle was a decorator at Rookwood Pottery in 1894 when the pottery sent him to study painting at the Académie Julian in Paris. While there he saw Chinese matte glazes on works in museums and upon his return to Rookwood he succeeded in reproducing them. Van Briggle suffered from tuberculosis and in 1899 moved to Colorado. He opened a pottery in Colorado Springs in 1901 and the following year the Van Briggle Pottery Company was founded. Van Briggle died in 1904 but his wife Anne continued production, and was succeeded by several other directors. The company is still in production today.

### 132 Van Briggle Pottery

*Clockwise, beginning at left:*
*Flower Bowl*, 1913
Earthenware
H. 4½, Diam. 7 in.
(11.25 × 17.5 cm.)
Marks: Van Briggle monogram over
*1913* incised on bottom
Gift of Leonard Fried   P.C. 81.23.2

This stoneware form is covered with a dark olive matte glaze. The squat, bulbous bowl tapers toward the base. The stems of nine stylized leaves emerge from the base, with the actual leaves forming a border around the lip. The leaves are slightly accentuated with a light coating of maroon matte glaze.

*Ginger Jar Vase*, after 1920
Earthenware
H. 9, Diam. 9¼ in.
(22.5 × 23 cm.)
Marks: Van Briggle monogram and
*Van Briggle Col. Spgs.* incised on bottom
Gift of Mr. and Mrs. Victor Cole
P.C. 83.30.2

This large, ovoid vase tapers at the neck to produce a very pronounced vertical lip. The body is decorated with four stylized flowers, executed in low-relief. The floral pattern begins at the base and continues up the body until the flowers center and rest on the lip. Decorated overall with a matte glaze of turquoise, the flower forms are slightly accentuated with cobalt matte glaze.

*Vase*, after 1920
Earthenware
H. 8, Diam. 3½ in. (20 × 8.8 cm.)
Marks: Van Briggle monogram and
*Van Briggle Colo. Spgs.* incised on bottom
Gift of Mr. and Mrs. Victor Cole
P.C. 83.30.13

This tapered form begins at a modestly flared base. Four "gothic arch" divisions climb vertically, interceded by four floral/sun motifs. A maroon matte glaze with light blue matte accents covers the piece.

*Bud Vase*, c. 1920
Earthenware
H. 7¾, Diam. 3½ in.
(19.4 × 8.8 cm.)
Marks: Van Briggle monogram and

*Van Briggle* incised on bottom (in script)
Gift of Mr. and Mrs. Victor Cole
P.C. 83.30.17

This bud vase in bottle form tapers slightly toward the rim, which is defined by a shallow incision. The squat, slightly squared base is simply decorated with four equidistant, vertical forms in low relief. The glaze is primarily turquoise matte, but the base has been decorated with a spray of light cobalt blue glaze.

*Flower Bowl*, c. 1920
Stoneware
H. 3¼, Diam. 5 in. (8.1 × 12.5 cm.)
Marks: Van Briggle monogram and
*Van Briggle* incised on bottom
Gift of Mr. and Mrs. Victor Cole
P.C. 83.30.10

This squat form tapers lightly from mid-point to the lip. The slightly recessed area supports a continuous geometric border pattern composed of interlocking diamonds and circles. The base is slightly defined. A light blue matte glaze covers the vessel in an uneven application; the border pattern is accentuated with cobalt matte glaze.

*Bookends of Polar Bears*, n.d.
Earthenware
Each: H. 4, W. 3½, L. 5½ in.
(10 × 8.75 × 13.75 cm.)
Marks: Van Briggle monogram under glaze on back
Gift of Mr. and Mrs. Victor Cole
P.C. 83.11, 12

Pair of bear bookends, with each bear portrayed on all fours, as if walking. The entire bookend is glazed in Ming blue.

*Bowl*, n.d.
Earthenware
H. 2¾, Diam. 3½ in. (6.8 × 8.8 cm.)
Marks: Van Briggle monogram and
Van Briggle/COLO SPGS/80 incised on bottom
Gift of Nancy Farr Fulmer
P.C. 78.34.21

Small, tri-sectioned bowl formed by three stylized leaf sections—each decorated with a butterfly in low relief. There are slight variations in each panel—both in the butterfly and the leaf form. The bowl is decorated with a maroon matte glaze and the butterflies are sprayed with a cobalt matte glaze.

### 133 Van Briggle Pottery

*Lorelei Vase*, designed in 1901
Earthenware
H. 10½, Diam. 4¼ in.
(26.25 × 10.6 cm.)
Marks: Van Briggle monogram and
*Van Briggle Colorado Springs* incised on bottom
Gift of Ronald and Andrew Kuchta in memory of Clara May Kuchta
P.C. 80.2

This ovoid form tapers, then flares slightly at both the lip and the base. The "Lorelei" figure emerges from the body of the vase in various degrees of relief, with her spiraling figure echoing the vase's contours. The

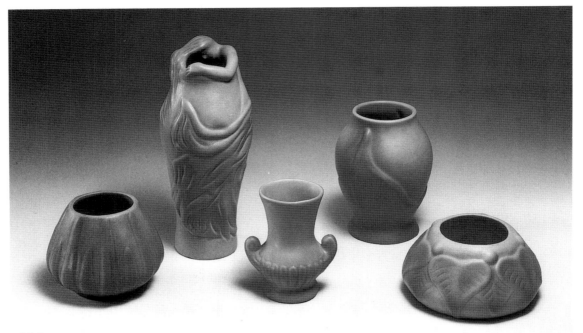

134

figure's head, flowing hair, and left arm form the lip. The vase is decorated with a white matte glaze.

Van Briggle's sojourn in France had introduced him to Art Nouveau and he became one of the most important American proponents of that style. The gracefully flowing lines and feeling of reverie or melancholia of his figures are in keeping with the Art Nouveau aesthetic. The low relief decoration and matte glazes accent the forms on which they are used, becoming an integral part of the piece, rather than appearing to be applied decoration only.

### 134 Van Briggle Pottery

*Clockwise, beginning at left:*
*Vase/Flower Bowl*, n.d.
Earthenware
H. 4½, Diam. 5½ in.
(11.25 × 13.75 cm.)
Marks: Van Briggle monogram and *Van Briggle, Colo. Spgs.* incised on bottom
Gift of Mr. and Mrs. Victor Cole
P.C. 83.30.5

A squat, ovoid form tapering toward the lip. This flower bowl is decorated with sixteen rounded, vertical leaf blades in low relief extending from the base toward the lip. Eight blades meet midway up the bowl, while the remaining eight extend entirely to the lip. A cobalt matte glaze accentuates the decoration while the overall glaze is a turquoise matte.

135

*Lorelei Vase*, designed in 1901
Earthenware
H. 11, Diam. 4½ in.
(27.5 × 11.25 cm.)
Marks: Van Briggle monogram and *Van Briggle/Colorado Springs* incised on bottom
Gift of Mr. and Mrs. Victor Cole in memory of Sirkka Liisa Hodgson
P.C. 83.30.1

This vase is identical to entry 133, but slightly larger, and with a turquoise and light blue matte glaze.

*Vase*, 1904–1920
Earthenware
H. 6¾, Diam. 5½ in.
(16.8 × 13.75 cm.)
Marks: Van Briggle monogram incised on bottom above *ME3* and *Van Briggle Colo Spgs*
Gift of Nancy Farr Fulmer
P.C. 78.34.22

This elegant, baluster-form vase flares slightly at both the lip and the base. Two stylized leaf forms begin at the base, and flow up either side in relief. The buff stoneware body is decorated with a graduated turquoise to light blue matte glaze, with light blue occurring mainly on the base and leaf forms.

*Flower Bowl*, n.d.
Earthenware
H. 3½, Diam. 6½ in.
(8.75 × 16.25 cm.)
Marks: Van Briggle monogram, *Van*

*Briggle Colo. Spgs.* incised on bottom
Gift of Mr. and Mrs. Victor Cole
P.C. 83.30.8

This low, squat form is slightly asymmetrical at both base and lip. Ten stylized leaf shapes surround the body of the bowl, with five heart-shaped leaves shown in full, and five partial leaves appearing behind and between the complete images. Five evenly spaced nodules accent the bowl opening. The overall turquoise matte glaze leaf pattern is accentuated with a light spray of cobalt glaze.

*Vase*, n.d.
Earthenware
H. 5¼, W. 4¼ in. (13.1 × 10.6 cm.)
Marks: Van Briggle monogram, *Van Briggle, Col. Spgs M23* incised on bottom
Gift of Mr. and Mrs. Victor Cole
P.C. 83.30.16

1 3 6

1 3 7

Stoneware vase with gadrooned style lip and upturned handles on both sides covered in a Ming blue glaze.

### 135 Van Briggle Pottery

*Indian Head Vase*, c. 1930
Earthenware
H. 11¼, Diam. 6 in. (28.1 × 15 cm.)
Marks: Van Briggle monogram and *Van Briggle Colo. Sp'gs* incised on bottom
Gift of Ronald A. Kuchta
P.C. 87.100.3

Earthenware vase with large round spread foot tapering to a flared cylindrical form with a round, rimmed mouth. Three high relief Indian heads decorate the shoulder. The Indians' braids continue down the sides of the vase in Ming blue matte glaze becoming one near the base. Aqua matte is applied overall.

### 136 Van Briggle Pottery

*Nymph at Pool Edge with Flower Holder*
Earthenware
H. 9½, W. 15¼, Diam. 11¼ in.
(23.8 × 38 × 28 cm.)
Marks: Van Briggle monogram and *Van Briggle Colo Spring Colo. U.S.A.* incised on bottom
Gift of Mr. and Mrs. Victor Cole
P.C. 83.30.3, 4

Female figure gazes into a low, open pool. Inside rests a movable flower holder decorated with a turtle. The overall glaze is a turquoise matte, but a cobalt matte is used to accentuate the figure's hair, drapery, exterior of pool, flower holder, and stylized flora on flower holder.

### 137 Van Briggle Pottery

*Vase*, c. 1920
Earthenware
H. 10, Diam. 5½ in.
(25 × 13.75 cm.)
Marks: Van Briggle monogram and *Van Briggle Colo. Sp'gs.* incised on bottom
Gift of Ronald A. Kuchta
P.C. 87.100.4

This conical-shaped earthenware vase has a slightly flared base and short, cylindrical neck with rimmed mouth. The interior is brown, with brown at rim and section near the base; the top half of the base is green.

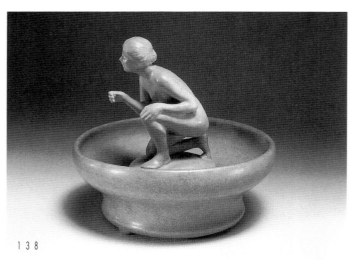

138

## WALRATH POTTERY
## 1908-1918
## Rochester, New York

Frederick E. Walrath studied with Charles Fergus Binns at Alfred University and later was associated with Columbia University, Newcomb Pottery, and the Mechanics Institute in Rochester, New York.

The objects produced by Walrath are in the spirit of the Arts and Crafts movement, with their matte glazes, simple, strong forms, and stylized motifs. The later half of the 1890s saw an interest in sculptural motifs integrated into the vessel form, but Walrath preferred to keep his figures separate, perching them on rims or placing them within low flower bowls.

### 138 Walrath Pottery
Frederick Walrath
*Flower Bowl with Nymph*, n.d.
Earthenware
H. 6½, Diam. 6½ in.
(16.3 × 16.3 cm.)
Marks: *Walrath* incised on bottom
Museum purchase   P.C. 77.51

Flower bowl with high base curving into bowl, three small feet, no lip. A nymph kneels on one knee; her right hand reaches forward and forms a hole for a flower. The figure is placed on a round base in the center of the bowl. The buff clay is covered in matte green glaze.

## WELLER POTTERY
## 1872-1949
## Zanesville, Ohio

Samuel Weller began a pottery business in 1872 in Fultonham, Ohio. In 1888 the manufactory was moved to Zanesville. By 1896 Weller was producing art pottery, which he named Louwelsa, using the same process as Rookwood Standard.

Jacques Sicard, who had worked for many years with Clement Massier at Golfe Juan, France, came to Weller in 1902. Working in secrecy, he made richly decorated pieces with metallic lusters on an iridescent ground. Sicard returned to France in 1907.

Weller was one of the most successful art potteries, producing a variety of lines. It began to decline after the death of Samuel Weller in 1925, and the production of art pottery ceased in 1926, though the manufactory continued in operation until 1948 and was dissolved in 1949.

### 139 Weller Pottery
Albert Wilson, decorator
*Spaniel Vase*, c. 1895
Earthenware
H. 13½, Diam. 9 in.
(33.75 × 22.5 cm.)
Marks: *Louwelsa/Weller* within a circle and *X481* impressed on bottom. *S* incised on bottom. *A. Wilson* brushed under glaze on back
Museum purchase with funds from the Dorothy and Robert Riester Ceramic Fund   P.C. 88.12

Wide, baluster-shaped earthenware vase with neck extending to flaring mouth. The body is covered in predominantly brown glaze with a depiction of a spaniel on the vessel face in olive, golden yellow, and brown underglaze.

### 140 Weller Pottery
Jacques Sicard, decorator
Vase, 1901-1910
Earthenware
H. 22, Diam. 10 in. (55 × 25 cm.)
Marks: none
Museum purchase with funds from the Dorothy and Robert Riester Ceramic Fund   P.C. 88.10

Ovoid earthenware vase with second lobe at shoulder which tapers to narrow mouth. Intricate gold floral decoration covers the vase with blue, green, purple, and red metallic background.

139

140

# AMERICAN CERAMICS
# 1920 – 1950

## BARBARA PERRY

By the 1920s the Arts and Crafts movement and the success of the art potteries had instituted an American ceramics tradition and established clay as an acceptable medium for making art. The easily enjoyed decorative style of art pottery had created a public that was receptive to works made of clay. The technical discoveries made by the art potteries and the establishment of the New York School of Clayworking and Ceramics at Alfred University in 1900 had provided ceramists with a knowledge of materials and techniques. Placing the teaching of ceramics in a university setting had given it prestige and a certain amount of acceptance. Ceramists had gained a modicum of respect and thereby were encouraged to continue exploring this rich medium, not from the point of view of the production potter, but as studio potters, creators of unique objects whose sole raison d'être was aesthetic enjoyment. Thus, by the 1920s the basic factors needed for the development of the studio pottery movement were in place.

Young people eager to work in clay no longer had to become caught up in the production pottery system. There were ceramics courses available in accredited schools and universities that provided the technical expertise previously available only through training in a production pottery. Ohio State, Alfred, the Cleveland Institute of Art, the Art Institute of Chicago, and various museum schools now offered courses for the aspiring ceramist.

Many of these schools were staffed by Alfred graduates, or pupils of Alfred graduates. These teachers perpetuated the "Alfred aesthetic," one which would pervade the American ceramics scene for years to come. Charles Fergus Binns, founder of the School of Clayworking at Alfred, left a

legacy of technical knowledge and a host of inspired students, but more importantly, he established an attitude toward clay which respected the character of the medium and the formal aspects of the vessel. He projected the theory that technical and aesthetic considerations were of equal importance in the production of ceramic art. According to Binns, the ceramist, like any other artist, should be involved in all aspects of ceramic creation, including clay preparation, glaze formulation, shaping, decorating, and firing. Gone was the idea of division of labor associated for so long with the production potteries of the previous century.

### THE VESSEL

Binns's long tenure at Alfred saw the establishment of a strong vessel aesthetic, with a reverence for classic form and strong technical values. "The classic Alfred vessel" came to be the standard by which all was measured. The teachings of Binns were promulgated throughout the country as Alfred graduates found academic positions and opened studios of their own. Beautifully formed, subtly glazed vessels with a formal reticence and quiet elegance were produced—Arthur Baggs's *Cookie Jar* of 1938 (entry 145) is a classic example.

Arthur E. Baggs, a student of Binns's at Alfred, was another important figure in American ceramics during the 1920s and 1930s. Baggs taught at Ohio State University and there propagated Binns's theories, including his important concept of the necessity of unity in the ceramic object. According to Binns, the technical and aesthetic aspects of a piece were of equal importance; shape, decoration, and glaze formed a unified whole. The ideals and energy of these two men helped to set the

standards and goals of American ceramists for some time to come.

This does not mean, however, that there was any amount of conformity among artists working with the vessel. Indeed, the richness of the work produced during the 1930s and 1940s resulted from the disparate approaches taken. The technical assurance and the sense of inquiry that American ceramists had acquired allowed them the freedom to experiment, investigate, and question. They experimented with materials, techniques, and tools. They looked to other cultures and other times for stylistic inspiration, and they questioned the role of the ceramist and the position of ceramics in the hierarchy of the arts.

Glen Lukens searched the mountains and deserts of the West Coast for native materials from which to prepare his clay bodies and glazes (entries 180–182). The unique results of these experiments, combined with a highly original handling of the clay and glazes, produced pieces that were forerunners of the Expressionist style of the late fifties and sixties. Lukens's love of nature led him to use his materials with respect for their origin, and his results were earthy, natural, and unpretentious, but with a wonderful honesty and sensuousness. His vessels evoke the elements of fire and the earth, with their luscious molten glazes, bubbling surfaces, and clay bodies that reveal the processes of their formation.

Henry Varnum Poor, who was not initially trained as a ceramist, looked to the clay surface as a canvas, forming loosely wrought platters and bowls, which would be vehicles for his decorative motifs, sometimes figural, sometimes not, but always confidently conceived (entries 202 and 203). He was interested in the architectural uses of clay and handled the material with more freedom and daring than many of his university-trained colleagues.

Dorothea Warren O'Hara carved the exteriors of her bowls and Viktor Schreckengost, who had been responsible for the creation of the lively *Jazz Bowls* while working at Cowan Studio Pottery, sometimes carved out the entire vessel itself from great lumps of clay (entries 196, 244, and 245).

The sources of influence were as diverse as the ensuing products. The Natzlers—Gertrud and Otto—arrived in the United States in 1938 and immediately began to produce elegant, sensuous vessels in a traditional, classic style, with Gertrud throwing the forms and her husband devising the glazes (entries 192 and 193). They brought from their native Vienna the sparse, astringent, clean-lined vessel aesthetic associated with the Secessionist style of a few years earlier. But Gertrud's genius on the wheel and Otto's continuous experimenting brought forth exquisite vessels that were incredibly thin, sumptuously glazed, and made reference to both eastern and western traditions.

Primitive cultures and styles inspired the husband and wife team of Edwin and Mary Scheier. Mary formed the vessels, which Edwin then decorated with incised and modeled linear figures loosely based on figural forms of exotic, primitive cultures, mostly those of ancient Central America (entries 236–239). The Scheiers also worked in stoneware, a deviation from the preoccupation with earthenware that characterized most of the earlier years of this period.

The influences of the Far East, which were to pervade American ceramics in the ensuing decades, began to appear in the loose, calligraphic decorations of Randolph Webb and Marion Fosdick(entries 256 and 159). Binns, of course, brought with him the baggage of the English arts and crafts tradition, as well as experience gained at the Royal Worcester Porcelain Works. Marguerite Wildenhain (entry 261) was Bauhaus-trained and studied under Kandinsky, Moholy-Nagy, and Marcks. She brought more than the "form follows func-

tion" theory, accenting honesty and reverence for the materials and a subtle sensitivity, which was often misinterpreted as mere simplicity. Some artists revealed Surrealist tendencies, while others clung to Art Deco motifs. Maija Grotell brought from her native Finland a lively interest in all of the arts and looked outside of ceramics and the ceramics tradition for her inspiration (entry 172). She encouraged her students, through both her teaching and her own work, to acquire technical competency and a personal sense of style first, and then begin to experiment—in other words, to allow one's work to take its own direction.

An important figure in American ceramics during the 1940s, but whose influence lasted for a much longer period, was Sam Haile, an Englishman who came to America in 1939. He was invited by Charles Harder to teach at Alfred. There he advocated a return to the basic ingredients of pottery making, spurning the intricate formulations and procedures he found in use there. Haile worked in the vessel genre, but much more freely than was customary at Alfred. His decoration was painterly, related to the Abstract Expressionist style that was currently under way in New York (entry 173).

## THE PUEBLO REVIVAL

The traditional pottery making of the Pueblo cultures of New Mexico and Arizona underwent a revival in this period. During the previous century, the opening of the Santa Fe trail and later the arrival of the railroads had made metal pails and containers and manufactured kitchenware readily available; as a result the Pueblo potters no longer made their traditional everyday vessels, except as souvenir items for the tourist trade. But in the 1920s and 1930s a renewed interest in fine Pueblo wares supported a revival of native American pottery making (entries 206–222).

This revival took different forms in the different pueblos. San Ildefonso pottery was of relatively high quality and during the 1920s the quality improved even more. As in all cultures, change was inevitable, and new forms and designs were added to

the older repertoire. Maria and Julian Martinez of San Ildefonso in northern New Mexico, began to produce their famous black-on-black ware, eventually abandoning completely the polychrome wares they had previously produced. They adopted new shapes as well, adding them to the traditional shapes they still worked with. Zia potters, who had adopted Acoma and Zuni decorative schemes, were re-introduced to their own ancient traditional wares through photographs, drawings, and excavated shards. They turned from the adopted forms and designs and began to produce wares closer to their own heritage. San Juan potters of New Mexico studied the ancient wares made in their pueblo and chose to return to an incised ware, made by their ancestors hundreds of years before. The potters of Santa Clara, a Tewa pueblo near San Ildefonso and San Juan along the Rio Grande, experimented with new forms and techniques, including both black-on-black and polychrome wares. Animalitos, or small, sculptural animal images, were still popular and were refined and upgraded.

One important development in Pueblo pottery production was the emergence of the individual artist. In 1925 Maria Martinez began to sign her work. Pueblo pottery ceased to be anonymous. Other Pueblo potters began to sign their work as well, and soon individual artists began to receive recognition. The works of particular potters were sought after and collected. The Pueblos had joined the art world. In 1933 Maria Martinez sent three entries to the Ceramic National, and other Pueblo artists followed in ensuing years.

The individualism apparent in American ceramics during this period is typical of American art in general. Diversity, expressionism, and a strong interest in materials are characteristics of both American art and American ceramics. American artists have always been pragmatic, dynamic, intuitive, sensuous, and inventive.

These characteristics were in evidence in other areas of ceramics as well. In spite of, or perhaps in reaction to, the vessel aesthetic propagated by Binns, Baggs, and their students and followers (the theories and findings of both men were published widely), there arose in America in the 1920s an interest in clay sculpture. American artists had always used clay as a sculptural medium, but usually masked its properties, making the work assume the appearance of stone, wood, or bronze. A few artists did take advantage of its malleability, as seen in Jonathan Scott Hartley's "The Sunflower" (entry 83), where the texture of the clay is evident, especially in the modeling of the flower itself. But by and large clay had been overlooked, indeed scorned by sculptors intent on producing works imitative of the traditional European style. It continued to be used for molded objects, of course, especially in those art potteries still in production. But young artists were unhappy with these methods and were eager to break out of the worn traditions of the art potteries and the stale nineteenth-century style.

## CLAY SCULPTURE AND THE VIENNESE INFLUENCE

The opportunity for innovation was seized by a group of young ceramists from Cleveland, Ohio. Intrigued by the works of Viennese ceramists, which they had seen in the International Exhibition of Ceramic Art, and encouraged by their teacher, Julius Mihalik, who had taught in Vienna, a number of them went to Vienna to study. Viktor Schreckengost, Russell Barnett Aitken, and Edward Winter, who later would marry the ceramist Thelma Frazier, studied at the Wiener Kunstgewerbeschule and fell under the influence of a group of young Viennese who worked at the Wiener Werkstätte and other workshops in the Austrian city. It was the free, loose handling of the clay that intrigued the Americans. These Austrian ceramists were turning out witty, casually wrought sculpture (and vessels) which spoke blatantly, if not elegantly, of the nature of the medium, with assembled parts, elongated figures, dripping glazes, garish colors, and an irreverence that was totally in keeping with the attitudes of the young Americans. Their sculpture was often created from hollow forms thrown on the wheel, and assembled together. Or their

figures were modeled in the form of long-legged maidens with details of clay added to the surface. At the same time that the Americans were studying in Vienna, Vally Wieselthier and later, fellow Austrian Susi Singer, came to America to exhibit, live, and teach, reinforcing the Viennese influence.

Thus, Vienna became more influential in American ceramics during the 1930s and 1940s than France, which was then the center of Modernism. Taxile Doat and Art Noveau had, of course, influenced Adelaide Robineau and Louis Tiffany at the turn of the century, but during the following years the French influence on American ceramics waned. The style, subject matter, and techniques of many American ceramics sculptors were derived instead from the Austrians' work.

The humor exhibited in the American work of the 1920s and 1930s ranged from the subtle and intellectual approach of Viktor Schreckengost to the raucous good fun of Russell Aitken. Schreckengost, one of the finest ceramists of the time, used his wit as he said "to relieve Depression blues," and also to make critical allusions to the political situation in Europe (entry 247). He was one of the few artists who spoke up about the coming terror in Europe, and dared to do so in spite of opposition from those of influence in the art world. Aitken spoofed everyone, including some of the most admired artists of the time, but was never biting in his attacks (entry 141). His work was widely collected, and he sold as much as he could produce.

Thelma Frazier Winter received the Viennese influence second hand, as did many other ceramists. Winter had the ability to absorb styles and motifs freely from those about her but to turn them into something unique and personal. Her long-legged figures in opaque white glazes are as Viennese as any found in Europe, inspired no doubt by the Austrian work she had seen in exhibitions traveling here in the United States. She also used subject matter popular at the time, such as characters from *Alice in Wonderland*, mythology, and literature—but always giving them a unique

interpretation (entries 263–265).

Ruth Randall, who taught at Syracuse University, had also studied in Vienna and produced portraits in clay as well as animal figures, often with the whimsy typical of the period (entries 224–226).

There was also great interest in the production of large scale sculptural works in clay at this time. The two most prominent figures were Schreckengost and Waylande Gregory—although their working methods varied greatly and their careers took opposite paths. Schreckengost was pragmatic and innovative, while Gregory was intense, idealistic, and, in a sense, unyielding. Government projects, both local and federal, and the New York World's Fair of 1939 gave both of these men opportunities to work on a grand scale. Schreckengost produced works for the Cleveland Zoo and for public buildings as well as for the Fair, and Gregory is noted mainly for his fountains and architectural work. Gregory preferred to work in large scale, but found few patrons to buy such large pieces, which eventually ended up in his storage area or garden.

## THE DEPRESSION

The Depression brought with it a number of government projects aimed at relieving the plight of artists, including ceramists. The most successful of the projects funded by the Works Progress Administration Federal Art Project was that managed by Edris Eckhardt, a Cleveland ceramist who had studied with Alexander Archipenko and who taught at the Cleveland School of Art (now the Cleveland Institute of Art). She organized a workshop which produced limited editions of figurines depicting various characters from children's literature. The workers were given freedom to decorate the mold-made figures in their own fashion, and as a result each was in that sense unique. They were sold to libraries and in shops nationwide and Eckhardt was able to turn the profits into fuel for a new kiln.

Most of the work produced by artists working in clay under the auspices of the government programs was stylistically similar—neoclassic in form and idealistic in concept. This is largely due to the fact that it was public art, usually architectural, and neoclassicism was seen as the appropriate style in such circumstances.

The government programs also commissioned works of art in traditional styles from the Pueblo potters to be placed in the National Park Service Regional Headquarters building in Santa Fe. Maria Martinez of San Ildefonso, as well as artists from other pueblos, participated in this program.

The Depression was also responsible for encouraging artists who normally worked in other materials to turn to clay. Clay was available and it was inexpensive. Thus, many artists looked to this medium when others were beyond their means. Isamu Noguchi, Reuben Nakian, Alexander Archipenko, and Elie Nadelman were only a few of those who worked in clay during the 1930s.

It was during this period that American ceramists also began to assess their roles in the American art scene in general. There was no ceramic sculptural tradition upon which to build, and so these young ceramists began to come to grips with the question of their role in the art world. They saw clay sculpture as an enigma, not appropriately considered a craft, yet not accepted in fine arts circles. They questioned just what position it held in the arts. As Thelma Frazier Winter said, "much of the thinking has been experimental, a search to find out just what ceramic sculpture should be, an effort to make it grow up as a fine art."

## THE CERAMIC NATIONALS

The young sculptors had an ally at the Syracuse Museum of Fine Arts (now Everson Museum). Anna Olmsted, the director of the museum, conceived the idea of a national ceramics exhibition. At that time, there was no museum here in the United States that held such an exhibition; indeed, few museums showed contemporary ceramics at all. Nor were there dealers or galleries who specialized in works of clay. The Ceramic Nationals became a focal point for American ceramists—a place where they could achieve national attention

(the exhibitions traveled to other American museums and abroad), see the most recent works of other artists, and meet other ceramists. From the very outset Olmsted underscored the importance of sculpture; in fact, her correspondence concerning the establishment of the exhibitions emphasizes clay sculpture as a primary interest on the part of the museum.

Olmsted's enthusiasm for sculpture was shared by R. Guy Cowan, who had come to Syracuse as art director for Onondaga Pottery Company, makers of Syracuse China, after the closing of his own Cowan Pottery Studio near Cleveland. Cowan was a constant supporter of the Ceramic Nationals, an advisor to Olmsted, a frequent member of the jury, and eventually a trustee of the museum. Cowan had produced sculptural pieces in his own pottery, and had persuaded the Cleveland Museum of Art to provide a section for clay sculpture in the annual May shows. It was in his pottery that many of the young Cleveland artists who became consistent prizewinners in the Ceramic Nationals got their first start, as designers and decorators.

The Cleveland school, as it has come to be called, dominated the sculpture sections during the early years of the exhibitions. They regularly entered, usually were accepted, often won prizes, and frequently served on juries. And it should be noted that while some Cleveland artists also worked in industry, designing for production potteries, the focus of the exhibitions remained on ceramics as an art form. There was no attempt to include a section for commercial design or production (though there were occasional prizes awarded for works which would lend themselves to mass production). The artists and the museum encouraged the acceptance of ceramics as a fine art, not as a craft or commercial interest. In fact, in the correspondence of Anna Olmsted, ceramics is always referred to as art rather than craft, and the entrants as artists, rather than ceramists or craftsmen.

Though the Cleveland artists were a major presence in the Ceramic Nationals, there were always many other American

sculptors whose works were regularly accepted: Alexander Archipenko, Susi Singer, Vally Wieselthier, Carl Schmitz. Nor was the Viennese style the only one in which sculptors worked. Archipenko, of course, worked in the European modernist mainstream. Others, particularly during the WPA era, worked in a neoclassic style. Nadelman's work was expressionistic, while Carl Walters's forms were solid and firmly modeled (entry 255) much like the sculpture of the Renaissance, especially his horses. Noguchi showed traces of Haniwa influence, and Reuben Nakian's work was earthy and sensual, much like Rodin's. Bernard Frazier's stoneware figures looked more like stone than clay, and had a great strength (entries 160 and 161). Just as there was a bubbling of individuality in the vessel genre, so was there a wide diversity in the kinds of clay sculpture produced in America during this period.

## WOMEN IN THE STUDIO

In 1939 Thelma Frazier Winter won first prize for sculpture in the Ceramic National, the first time the prize had gone to a woman. This was not the signal of a new role to be taken by women in ceramics, but rather an affirmation of an already established fact: that women were now working in the medium without concern for "propriety." Once relegated to the decorating tables, women now were involved in all aspects of production, from wedging the clay to creation of the forms, glaze calculation, and firing. Women had made their own places in the studio, where they were not fettered to an established system overseen by men. They were the heirs of Robineau, Perry, and O'Hara, who had pioneered the studio potter movement, and the independence gained by these women allowed the younger generation occasion to prove that skill, creativity, and sensitivity had nothing to do with sex.

This pertained to those women working in the vessel genre as well. In fact, in team situations, particularly in husband-wife collaborations, it was often the woman who created the forms, with the men handling the glazing or firing. Gertrud Natzler, for

**Vally Wieselthier** (b. Austria, 1895), *Vase,* c. 1923. Earthenware, H. 10, W. 7 inches (25 × 17.5 cm). Museum Purchase with funds from the Dorothy and Robert Riester Ceramic Fund. This vase is indicative of the work being done in Vienna during the first decades of the century when Viktor Schreckengost and other American ceramists were studying in the Austrian city. The plasticity of the clay is apparent in the twists of the handles and the throwing marks on the body. The glaze is loosely applied, and the resulting impression is one of spontaneity and liveliness.

tury, then, one finds that the distinctive character of American ceramics clearly emerged. A studio system replaced the production pottery. The technical knowledge gained during the previous forty years gave artists the freedom to experiment. Individual expression abounded, with work ranging from classic austerity to a sensual, often playful romp with the medium. Vessels and sculpture were equally accepted and equally innovative. One finds in the work of this era the same spirited energy, concern with the physical properties of the medium, sense of experiment, and continual search for the new and the expressive that appears throughout American art in general.

This era came to an end just after the Second World War, as the country focused on a return to normal life, and new influences and attitudes were beginning to be felt. The coming years would be ones of continued change in American ceramics. A totally new aesthetic would find expression in exciting and innovative work produced by young artists who were feeling the same freedom as their predecessors. By the 1950s institutions had been established and a climate created in which ceramics was accepted on its own terms, without apology or pretense.

The seedlings of an American ceramics tradition emerged from 1920 to 1950. When Bernard Leach pronounced that American ceramics lacked a "taproot," he was misinterpreting the genus. This was a plant of a different structure. American ceramics has a wide, fibrous root system, a network which reaches out to absorb a great variety of influences, creating, in the end, a rich amalgam from which each artist can choose to use those elements that are most satisfying to him or her. The result is not a pure, inimitable style, or one which lends itself only to variations on a theme; instead, its themes are endless, constantly evolving and being renewed by the vigor which comes from such variety. In the second half of the century American ceramists continued to explore the possibilities of the medium, search in unexpected places for inspiration, and produce a body of work which was truly expressive of the diversity and energy of their American culture.

instance, produced elegant vessels as vehicles for Otto's glazes. Mary Scheier made bowls which Edwin decorated, and Maria Martinez made vessels for Julian's designs.

Women were working individually as well, successfully operating their own studios or functioning as part of university programs. Marguerite Wildenhain worked at Pond Farm in Guerneville, California. Vally Wieselthier worked in New York, and Maija Grotell headed the ceramics department at Cranbrook Academy in Bloomfield Hills, Michigan. Marion Fosdick

taught with Binns at Alfred University. Edris Eckhardt taught at the Cleveland Institute of Art, and Laura Andreson was in Los Angeles at the University of California. An examination of the archives of the Ceramic National exhibitions reveals that women consistently entered, were accepted, and won prizes in the annual shows, and served on juries as well. Women were making a mark on the ceramics world and were being accepted professionally because of their skills and accomplishments.

During the second quarter of this cen-

141

## RUSSELL BARNETT AITKEN
### (b. 1910)

Russell Barnett Aitken graduated from the Cleveland Institute of Art and did post-graduate work in Vienna and Berlin in 1932 and 1933. Upon his return from Europe he set up a studio called the Pottery Workshop in Cleveland with fellow ceramist Whitney Atchley. He taught in White Sulphur Springs, West Virginia and in 1935 opened a studio in New York.

Aitken's work reveals the early influence of Vienna, both stylistically and iconographically. His subjects included animals and figures, and are nearly always witty and satirical, though never bitingly so. His *Futility of a Well Ordered Life,* now in the collection of the Museum of Modern Art, is a burlesque of a painting by Salvador Dali. He spoofed the myths of Europa and the Bull, as well as the Virgin and the Unicorn. In both of these pieces his female figures have the elongated legs and opaque white glaze typical of Viennese work of the time. He was also fond of horses and did a number of works with western themes. Aitken worked in clay for only about ten years, having never returned to the medium after serving in the Second World War.

Aitken participated in the Ceramic Nationals of 1933, 1934 and from 1936 through 1940.

### 141 Russell Aitken
*Student Singers,* 1933
Earthenware
H. 12, W. 12, D. 5½ in. (30 × 30 × 13.75 cm.)

Marks: *AITKEN / 1933* incised on bottom
Gift of the artist   P.C. 39.317

Earthenware sculpture of three duelists in mid-song, each grasping a frothy mug of beer, arms intertwined. The central and left figures hold swords whose sharp diagonal lines are juxtaposed against opposing diagonals of their legs. The left figure is dressed in gray, while the other two figures wear colorful costumes. The base is pebbled, resembling gray cobblestones.

This work was done upon Aitken's return from his studies in Europe, where he had been made an honorary member of the Corps Hilaritas, a Viennese dueling society. The figure in gray is a student who has just finished his first duel. The figure in blue is the head of the Corps, while the figure in red is the Fuchs Major.

His red cap is decorated with a fox tail which curls around the back.

The figures are unified by the entwined arms and the repetitive lines formed by the angles of the legs and swords. The repetition of the circle of the eyes, mouths, buttons, mugs, and fists also provides a unifying motif.

Exhibitions: "Third Annual Robineau Memorial Ceramic Exhibition," First Prize for Best Piece of Ceramic Sculpture 1934; "An Exhibition of Contemporary American Ceramics," 1936; "A Century of Ceramics in the United States, 1878–1978," 1979; "The Diversions of Keramos, American Clay Sculpture 1925–1950," 1983

## LAURA ANDRESON (b. 1902)

Laura Andreson was born in San Bernardino, California and studied at the University of California in Los Angeles and Columbia University. She returned to UCLA in 1936, where she taught ceramics, using low-fire clays and hand-building techniques. She turned to stoneware after a deposit of clay was found in northern California, and sought equipment and information which allowed her to teach wheel-throwing. Her own forms were hand-built until 1944, when she began to use the wheel. After 1957 she also worked in porcelain—one of the first West Coast ceramists to use this medium. Her retirement from teaching in 1970 has provided her with more time for her own creative work.

Andreson was one of the pioneer ceramists in California. She worked at a time when there were no established programs in ceramics on the West Coast, and little available material or information. She did extensive research in glaze formulae, often shaping her forms as vehicles for the glazes. The glazes usually came first, then she created an appropriate shape on which they were carried. She was influenced by the Bauhaus style and her pieces have clean lines and deceptively simple forms. Andreson was elected to the Academy of Fellows of the American Crafts Council, and was given honorary membership to the National Council on Education in the Ceramic Arts.

### 142 Laura Andreson

*Cookie Jar,* 1946
Earthenware
H. 9, Diam. 7⅛ in. (22.5 × 17.8 cm.)
Marks: *Laura Andreson* incised in script on bottom
Purchase prize given by Haeger Potteries, "11th Ceramic National," 1946   P.C. 47.507a, b

Tall earthenware jar whose sides taper slightly outward. The flat cover has a spiral design on its knob handle. A matte glaze with copper luster is on the exterior, with a lighter speckled glaze at the top. Narrow copper rings surround the body.

Exhibitions: "A Century of Ceramics in the United States, 1878–1978," 1979

143

142

## WHITNEY ATCHLEY (b. 1908)

Whitney Atchley was born in Des Moines, Iowa and studied at the Cleveland Institute of Art, after which he joined the staff of Cowan Pottery in Rocky River, Ohio. Along with Russell Aitken, he organized and operated the Pottery Workshop in Cleveland. Later, Atchley became a freelance advertising artist and headed the ceramics department at the California School of Fine Art in San Francisco. He exhibited in the Ceramic National in 1933, 1937, 1941, 1947, 1949, and 1950, when he won a prize for pottery. In 1952 he served as chairman of the regional jury in San Francisco.

### 143 Whitney Atchley

*Plate,* 1941
Earthenware
H. 3, Diam. 18½ in.
(7.5 × 46.25 cm.)
Marks: *WA 41* incised on face of plate
Gift of IBM Corporation from "Contemporary Ceramics of the Western Hemisphere," 1941
P.C. 63.24

Large, footed earthenware plate with sloping sides and rounded well. An incised, linear design of a female nude covering her face with her arm reveals the dark brown clay body beneath. Gray and beige glazes are loosely brushed overall.

## CARLTON ATHERTON (b. 1900)

Carlton Atherton was a student of Adelaide Alsop Robineau at Syracuse University, and it was to him that Robineau entrusted her glaze formulae before her death in 1929. He also was responsible for the glazing of her unfinished *Cinerary Urn,* for which she left instructions. Atherton went on to teach at Ohio State University.

He exhibited in the Ceramic National in 1933, 1938, 1939, 1940

144

(when he was awarded honorable mention for pottery), and 1941. He also participated in the Golden Gate International Exposition in 1939.

**144 Carlton Atherton**

*Bowl,* 1933
Earthenware
H. 3½, Diam. 14¾ in.
(8.75 × 36.8 cm.)
Marks: *1933* inscribed on bottom
Bequest of Montague Charmin
T.N. 133

Large, round, footed bowl of buff earthenware covered by Persian blue glaze. The pattern around the rim consists of a wide and narrow dark blue stripe running parallel around it. The stripes are repeated in the recess of the bowl, with a figure of a resting antelope in dark blue within the circle.

**ARTHUR EUGENE BAGGS
(1886–1947)**

Arthur Baggs studied at Alfred University under Charles Fergus Binns and at the Art Students League in New York. While a student at Alfred, he went to Marblehead, Massachusetts where he helped set up a pottery in a sanitarium to be used for patient therapy. By 1908 the pottery had become so productive that it was turned into a commercial venture—Marblehead Pottery—which Baggs finally purchased in 1915. He continued work at the pottery during the summers even after he was appointed professor of ceramic arts at Ohio State University in 1928. Marblehead Pottery finally closed in 1936. Baggs was interested in glaze chemistry and was responsible for the rich, velvety glazes that characterize Marblehead pottery. He also worked for a time as a glaze chemist at the Cowan Studio Pottery, where he produced Egyptian blue and Persian green glazes. He later experimented with salt glazes.

Baggs received many ceramics awards and commendations, including the Charles F. Binns Medal given by the American Ceramic Society.

He won first prize in the 1933 and 1938 Ceramic National Exhibitions, and second prize in 1935. He entered every Ceramic National between 1933 and 1946, and was a frequent juror.

Baggs, like Binns, stressed the necessity for technical control in order to have complete artistic freedom. He emphasized the union between science and art in the making of ceramics, and this philosophy, along with his preference for classic, functional forms, reflected his training at Alfred.

**145 Arthur Baggs**

*Cookie Jar,* 1938
Stoneware
H. 13⅛, Diam. 10 in.
(32.8 × 25 cm.)
Marks: *AEB 1938* incised within a circle on bottom
Purchase prize given by Onondaga Pottery Company, "7th Ceramic National," 1938    P.C. 39.342a, b

Often described as one of the masterpieces of American ceramics, "the ultimate cookie jar" of Arthur Baggs has a spherical, salt-glazed, buff stoneware body with a low foot and

a short neck that curves into an everted lip. The lid, which fits on top of the lip, rises in three domed sections, topped by a handle formed by two grooved loops. Two handles with the same grooves are attached opposite each other at the shoulder.

The form is simple, direct, and classic, with throwing marks vitalizing the surface. The handles emphasize the texture and plasticity of the clay.

The *Cookie Jar* won first prize for pottery in the 1938 Ceramic National.

Exhibitions: "Golden Gate International Exposition," Palace of the Legion of Honor, San Francisco, 1939; "Forms from the Earth: 1,000 Years of Pottery in America," Museum of Contemporary Crafts, New York, 1960; "A Century of Ceramics in the United States, 1878–1978," 1979

146

147

148

### 146 Arthur Baggs

*Vase*, 1938
Stoneware
H. 6⅝, Diam. 5½ in.
(16.5 × 13.75 cm.)
Marks: *AEB 1938* incised on bottom
Purchase prize given by Onondaga
Pottery Company, "7th Ceramic National" 1938   P.C. 39.343

Footed, globular vase with slightly
tapered mouth. Several blue bands
surround the form at the mouth and
base. An alternating blue X and dot
pattern in three rows surrounds the
central portion of the body.

### 147 Arthur Baggs

*Punch Bowl*, 1941
Porcelain
H. 6½, Diam. 11½ in. (16.25 ×
28.75 cm.)
Marks: *AEB 1941* incised on bottom
Gift of Richard V. Smith
P.C. 83.5.8

Circular porcelain bowl with everted rim. The sides curve down gently
to double grooves at the base. Heavy,
semicircular handles are attached at
each side just below the rim. Cream-
colored glaze has been applied
overall.

### CARLTON BALL (b. 1910)
### KATHRYN UHL BALL (b. 1911)

A native Californian, Carlton Ball
studied with Glen Lukens at the University of Southern California in Los
Angeles and taught at other schools
in California, Illinois, and Wisconsin, retiring from the University of
Puget Sound in Washington. He was
interested in all of the crafts, and had
a broad education in the field of art.
He collaborated with his wife Kathryn Uhl Ball, whom he met in college. She graduated from Mills
College in Oakland, California and
studied with Lyonel Feininger. Kathryn often did the decorating, while
Carlton did the throwing, glazing,
and firing. They exhibited in the
Golden Gate International Exposition in San Francisco in 1939 and
1940, and in the Ceramic National
Exhibitions in Syracuse.

Carlton Ball was a most influential
teacher, and often produced monumental works with extraordinary
surfaces.

### 148 Carlton Ball
### Kathryn Uhl Ball, decorator

*Incantation Plate,*
Earthenware
H. 2, Diam. 16 in. (5 × 40 cm.)
Marks: *Plate made by F. Carlton Ball.
Decorated by Kathryn Uhl Ball
9.15.41* painted on back. Label
reads: *#12 / 297/5/1 / Carlton +
Kathryn / Mills College*
Gift of IBM Corporation from
"Contemporary Ceramics of the
Western Hemisphere," 1941
P.C. 63.26

Large earthenware plate with white
slip and underglaze painting. The
decoration depicts two seated female
figures with long flowing black hair.
The figure on the right holds cymbals
decorated with spiral patterns. The
left figure plays a small horn out of
which stream many stars. Around
the figures, in a wide border, are six
leafless trees, grass, birds, and animals
in black, blue, and pink.

Exhibitions: "A Century of Ceramics in the United States, 1878–
1978," 1979

### SORCHA BORU (b. 1906)

Born in San Francisco, Sorcha Boru
(the name is Gaelic; she is of Irish
descent) studied at the University of
California and opened an advertising
and commercial art studio in San
Francisco. Influenced by the work of
Carl Walters (whom she had never
met), she turned from commercial
art to pottery, setting up her own
studio in Menlo Park, California.

### 149 Sorcha Boru

*The Dancer*, 1940
Earthenware
H. 4½, W. 3¾, D. 1 in. (11.25 ×
9.25 × 2.5 cm.)
Marks: *Sorcha Boru 1940* incised on
back of base, *The Dancer* incised on
front of base; sticker affixed to bottom reads: *The Dancer-Sorcha Boru-
San Carlos, Cal.*, typewritten
Gift of Richard V. Smith
P.C. 83.57

Small, partially glazed earthenware
figurine depicting a comical female
with body facing forward while feet
face in opposite directions. The figure's profile faces forward with one
arm resting on both chin and outstretched knee, while the other hand
rests awkwardly on the opposite
knee. The figure has long orange hair

149

with a slight lip at the top. The interior is covered in an earth pink matte glaze with similar rim. The exterior dark brown unglazed body is decorated with deeply incised horizontal wavy lines in a wheat-like pattern. The incised lines are filled with earth pink matte glaze.

Exhibitions: "13th Ceramic National," prize for "piece whose decoration is best suited to its form," 1948

151 **Nancy Wickham Boyd**
*Vase,* 1948
Stoneware
H. 16, Diam. 5½ in. (40 × 13.75 cm.)
Marks: *WICKHAM 1948* incised on bottom

Gift of Mr. and Mrs. William Hull
P.C. 66.20.2

Tall, gently tapering, columnar vase. The brown stoneware body is covered with an earth pink and mulberry brown matte glaze. The middle section is predominantly earth pink with ridges forming concentric brown rings around the vase. Mulberry-colored leaning figures with incised white shadow forms behind them surround the vase.

Exhibitions: "13th Ceramic National," shared prize for "piece whose decoration is best suited to its form" with Boyd's *Flowerpot,* 1948

and wears a black and white striped dress. She stands on a rectangular, unglazed base.

Boru participated in the Ceramic National Exhibitions from 1935 through 1941. This piece is from the ninth of the series, held in 1940, and won an honorable mention.

### NANCY WICKHAM BOYD (b. 1923)
Nancy Wickham Boyd studied at Alfred University and later set up a studio and shop in Woodstock, Vermont. There she produced pottery and decorative items, mainly lamp bases, which she successfully mar-

keted to leading decorators in New York. She was a frequent entrant in the Ceramic National Exhibitions, participating in 1947, 1948, 1949, 1950, 1951, 1955, and 1958.

150 **Nancy Wickham Boyd**
*Flowerpot,* c. 1948
Stoneware
H. 8, Diam. 8¾ in. (21.8 × 22.7 cm.)
Marks: *Wickham* barely legible on bottom
Gift of Mr. and Mrs. William Hull
P.C. 66.20.1

Footed, ovoid stoneware flowerpot

150

151

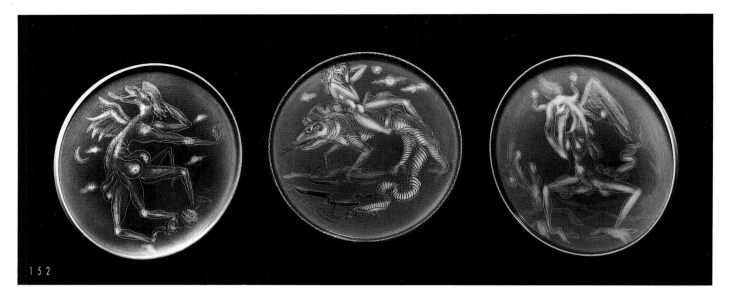

**SASCHA BRASTOFF (b. 1918)**

Sascha Brastoff was born in Cleveland, Ohio and educated at the Cleveland School of Art. He worked in Hollywood as a ceramist and costume designer, and opened his own studio, Brastoff Ceramic Studios. He participated in the Ceramic National Exhibitions in 1939, 1940, 1947, 1948, 1949, 1950, 1951, 1952, and 1958.

**152 Sascha Brastoff**

*Canapé Trays,* c. 1948
Earthenware
Each: H. ⅝, Diam. 11¼ in. (1.5 × 28.1 cm.)
Marks: each tray signed *Sascha Brastoff* on well, under glaze
Purchase prize given by Harper Pottery, "13th Ceramic National," 1948 P.C. 49.560.1–6

Set of six rounded, glazed trays with vertical lips. Each tray is decorated a different color and depicts different scenes.
*From left to right, top to bottom:*
"Night Monster," with a blue speckled background, illustrates a reptilian, winged creature with a moon and landscape in the background.
"Night Rider," with a brown background, illustrates a reptilian monster with a nude balanced on his back, covering her face with her hand. A small gold crescent moon looms beyond. Both the nude and the monster are outlined in gold; the serpentine tongue is especially dominant.
"Sex Monster," with a gray-green background, portrays in white outline a grotesque monster-creature with fins and distorted and elongated limbs. The creature has a long, winding tail.
"Fish Monster," with a green background, depicts a large, multi-tailed fish crowned in gold, a small crescent moon, and minimal landscape.
"Abstract Fruit," with a brown background, differs from the five other trays as it depicts a stylized still life of leaves, cheese, flowers, and fruit rather than imaginary figurative forms.

"Serenade" is also somewhat different from the other works. Although maintaining the fantasy image, the two figures depicted in this piece are more human in form. A seated figure in flowing robes holds a stringed instrument. A ghostlike, headless figure dances nearby wearing decorative gold bracelets, breast and waist decoration, an ornamental shield of sorts, and winged feet.

Together, these six trays present an image of the fantastic world which Brastoff strove to create.

## LYMAN S. CARPENTER (b. 1918)
## VERA TOPPER (b. 1916)

Both Carpenter and Topper studied at the Art Institute of Chicago and exhibited paintings and ceramics at Findlay Galleries there. They also worked at Hull House in Chicago. Carpenter specialized in modeling animals.

### 153 Lyman Carpenter
### Vera Topper

*Mother and Kid,* 1941
Earthenware
H. 7½, W. 8¾, D. 6 in. (18.75 × 21.8 × 15 cm.)
Marks: none
Purchase prize given by Katherine Q. Payne Memorial Fund, "Contemporary Ceramics in the Western Hemisphere," 1941   P.C. 42.523

Earthenware sculpture of mother llama and kid with yellow matte glaze overall. The sculpture sits on a wooden base.

This piece was awarded the Katherine Q. Payne Memorial Award in the 1941 Ceramic National. The award was given "for the sculpture showing unusual humor or whimsy in its conception."

## ROGER D. CORSAW (b. 1913)

A native of Ithaca, New York, Roger Corsaw studied ceramics at Alfred University and received an M.A. in product design from the School of

153

Design in Chicago. He taught at the University of Oklahoma, and participated in the Ceramic Nationals in 1936, when he was awarded first prize, and again in 1937, 1940, 1947, 1948, 1949, 1954, and 1958.

### 154 Roger Corsaw

*From left to right:*
*Bowl,* 1937
Stoneware
H. 2⅜, Diam. 7⅛ in.
(5.9 × 17.8 cm.)

Marks: *Corsaw 1937* incised on bottom, and remains of paper label
Purchase prize given by Onondaga Pottery Company, "6th Ceramic National," 1937   P.C. 38.279.3

Footed bowl of red stoneware with clear crackle glaze on the underside. The interior is glazed in an ochre and purple luster with three narrow rings just under the rim.

*Bowl,* 1937
Stoneware
H. 2, Diam. 6⅞ in. (5 × 17.1 cm.)
Marks: *Corsaw 1937* incised on bottom, and remains of paper label on bottom reads: *3—e corsaw*
Purchase prize given by Onondaga Pottery Company, "6th Ceramic National," 1937   P.C. 38.279.2

Footed bowl of red stoneware with clear crackle glaze on the underside. The inside has a brown fleurette on the bottom against a beige background. Brown and ochre luster glaze covers the sides except for a white band just below the white rim.

*Bowl,* 1937
Stoneware
H. 2½, Diam. 7⅜ in.
(6.3 × 18.4 cm.)
Marks: *Corsaw* incised on bottom; torn paper label on bottom reads: *#51*
Purchase prize given by Onondaga Pottery Company, "6th Ceramic National," 1937   P.C. 38.279.4

Footed bowl of red stoneware with clear crackle glaze on the underside. The interior is covered in a beige-gray crackle glaze with a lighter beige design of leaf shapes interspersed with dots extending to the outer rim.

These three bowls, part of a group of four, won first prize for pottery in the Ceramic National of 1937.

154

### MURRAY DOUGLAS (b. 1915)

Murray Douglas was born in Syracuse, New York, and studied at Wayne State University in Detroit. He received an M.A. and Ph.D. from Ohio State University. He also studied at Cranbrook Academy of Art in Bloomfield, Michigan and eventually returned to Wayne where he taught art education. He participated in the Ceramic National Exhibitions in 1939 and 1940, and from 1946 through 1958.

### 155 Murray Douglas

*Vase,* 1947
Earthenware
H. 12½, Diam. 11¾ in. (31.25 × 29.3 cm.)
Marks: *Murray Douglas* incised on bottom
Purchase prize given by Commercial Decal, Inc., "12th Ceramic National," 1947   P.C. 48.534

Globular earthenware vase with short neck and slight lip. A mottled gray glaze covers the large upper section of the vase and then drips onto the unglazed, dark brown bottom section. Two rows of green linear loop designs surround the vase's central section.

### 156 Murray Douglas

*Vase* and *Plate,* 1947
Earthenware
Vase: H. 8¾, Diam. 4½ in. (21.8 × 11.25 cm.) Plate: H. ¼, Diam. 12⅜ in. (.6 × 30.9 cm.)
Marks: *Murray Douglas* incised on bottom of each
Purchase prize given by Commercial Decal, Inc., "12th Ceramic National," 1947   P.C. 48.535, 48.536

Companion vase and plate covered in yellow glaze with linear and spiraling designs in black.

155

157

158

### KARL DRERUP (b. Germany, 1904)

Karl Drerup was born in Borghorst, Westphalia, West Germany and studied at the Kunstgewerbeschule in Münster, at the Vereinegte Staatsschulen in Berlin, and at the Royal Academy of Fine Arts in Florence. He became a professor of fine arts at New Hampshire State Teacher's College in Plymouth, and worked as a painter, etcher, enamelist, and ceramist. He participated in the Ceramic Nationals from 1938 to 1958, except in 1952.

### 157 Karl Drerup

*Shepherd Vase,* c. 1938
Porcelain
H. 13, Diam. 7⅜ in.
(32.5 × 19.4 cm.)
Marks: *Von Tury, U.S.A.* incised on bottom; *W-9* inscribed on bottom

Purchase prize given by E. I.Dupont NemoursCompany, "8th Ceramic National," 1939   P.C. 40.346

Tall porcelain vase with small bottom swelling to a large mouth. A gray glaze with deep red speckles covers the entire body. A figure of a shepherd holding a lamb is flanked by a ram on the right and a dog on the left, in deep red with black outlines. Arabesques on either side of the shepherd figure suggest organic, vinelike forms.

This vase was designed by Drerup and executed by Drerup and Josef von Tury.

### EDRIS ECKHARDT (b. 1907)

A native of Cleveland, Ohio, Edris Eckhardt was educated at the Cleveland Institute of Art and studied in New York with Alexander Archipenko. She worked at the Cowan Pottery and taught for many years at the Cleveland Institute of Art. She received wide recognition for her work in establishing a successful ceramics program with the Works Progress Administration Federal Art Project in the 1930s. She wrote on ceramic techniques and also conducted a television program on the subject. Unlike the work of her Cleveland colleagues, Eckhardt's ceramic sculpture is intensely personal, reflecting her own life and personality. Eckhardt later became involved in glassmaking and ceased working in clay. She participated in the Ceramic National Exhibitions from 1933 through 1964, except in 1934. She received an honorable mention in 1948 and served as a member of the regional jury in Cleveland in 1949.

### 158 Edris Eckhardt

*Earth,* 1939
Earthenware
H. 13, W. 8, D. 6½ in. (32.5 × 20 × 16.25 cm.)
Marks: *Edris Eckhardt* incised on lower back of neck
Gift of Dr. Paul Nelson   P.C. 84.30

Sculpture of a woman's head in brown earthenware—a self-portrait. The figure is unglazed, except for the green and blue interweaving, leafy organic forms that simulate hair.

Exhibitions: "8th Ceramic National," 1939; "American Art Today," New York World's Fair, 1939; "The Diversions of Keramos, American Clay Sculpture 1925–1950," 1983

159

### MARION LAWRENCE FOSDICK
### (1888–1973)

Marion Lawrence Fosdick was born in Fitchburg, Massachusetts. She studied at the School of Fine Arts in Boston, and at the Kunstgewerbeschule in Berlin from 1912 to 1913. She also studied with Charles Fergus Binns. She taught drawing and design at Alfred University in Alfred, New York from 1915 until 1920, when she became professor of pottery and sculpture. She received the Charles Fergus Binns Medal and was a medalist of the Boston Society of Arts and Crafts. She participated in the Ceramic National Exhibitions from 1933 through 1948, and in 1950 and 1958.

159 **Marion Lawrence Fosdick**

*Carved Stoneware Bowl,* c. 1947
Stoneware
H. 6½, Diam. 18¾ in. (16.5 × 46.8 cm.)
Marks: label affixed to bottom reads: *Artist: Marion Lawrence Fosdick/Address: 100 N. Main St. Alfred, N.Y./ Title: Carved Stoneware Bowl/Medium: Glazed stoneware clay Price: NFS*
Purchase prize given by Homer Laughlin China Company, "12th Ceramic National," 1947   P.C. 48.538

Large, footed stoneware bowl. The turquoise-glazed interior has two incised braid patterns that give way to a ridge-like line surrounding the center. The exterior is unglazed with a large incised pattern circling the bowl.

## BERNARD FRAZIER (1906–1976)

Bernard Frazier was born on a cattle ranch near Athol, Kansas. He studied at Kansas Wesleyan University and graduated from the University of Kansas in 1929. He worked with Lorado Taft and Fred Torrey, and furthered his studies in Chicago at the National Academy of Art, Chicago School of Sculpture, the Art Institute of Chicago, and briefly at László Moholy-Nagy's New Bauhaus. In 1938 he received a grant from the Andrew Carnegie Foundation to serve as sculptor in residence at the University of Kansas, where he remained to establish a department of sculpture. In 1942 Frazier helped organize occupational therapy classes in sculpture. In 1944 he became the director of the Philbrook Art Center in Tulsa, Oklahoma. He returned to the University of Kansas in 1956 to become sculptor-in-residence. He served as a visiting professor at Hindu University in Benares, India, and lectured at other universities in India and Nepal.

Frazier's work reflects his midwestern interests; his subjects are often taken from the plains: horses, deer, cattle, falcons, Plains Indians, and pioneers.

Frazier participated in the Ceramic National Exhibitions in 1941 (prize for ceramic sculpture), 1948 (prize for ceramic sculpture), and 1949, when he was a juror rather than a competitor.

160

160 **Bernard Frazier**

*Prairie Combat*, c. 1940
Stoneware
H. 11½, W. 22, D. 14 in. (28.8 × 55 × 35 cm.)
Marks: none
Purchase prize given by Harshaw Chemical Company, "Contemporary Ceramics of the Western Hemisphere." 1941  P.C. 42.528

Stoneware sculpture of two bison interlocked in a savage battle covered in a glaze of native volcanic ash.

161 **Bernard Frazier**

*Untamed*, c. 1948
H. 26, W. 36½, D. 20 in. (65 × 91.25 × 50 cm.)
Marks: none
Purchase prize given by IBM Corporation, "13th Ceramic National," 1948  P.C. 49.562

Stoneware sculpture of horse with

161

turned head and twisted body, bared ribs, and a wild expression in its eyes. The large tail acts as a point of stability for the piece, which is covered in a native volcanic ash matte glaze.

Exhibitions: "A Century of Ceramics in the United States, 1878–1978," 1979

162

163

## PETER GANINE (b. Russia, 1900)

Peter Ganine came to the United States in 1931. He studied in his native Russia and at the Corcoran School of Art in Washington, D.C. He was a student of Maxwell Müller. Ganine worked in wood, bronze, and pastel in addition to clay. He participated in the Ceramic National Exhibitions continuously from 1938 through 1949, receiving a purchase prize in 1940 and an honorable mention in 1946, both for ceramic sculpture.

162 **Peter Ganine**
*Colt,* 1938
Earthenware
H. 15, W. 6, D. 10 in. (37.5 × 15 × 25 cm.)
Marks: *Ganine* incised on bottom and side near horse's left rear leg
Gift of the artist   P.C. 39.322

Unglazed, stylized sculpture of a young horse with uplifted head.

Exhibitions: "8th Ceramic National," 1939

## THEODORA GOBERIS

Theodora Goberis from Norwich, Connecticut participated in the 1940 and 1941 Ceramic Nationals.

163 **Theodora Goberis**
*Pitcher and Goblet,* c. 1941
Stoneware
Pitcher: H. 8, W. 7½ in. (20 × 18.75 cm.) Goblet: H. 4, Diam. 3¾ in. (10 × 9.3 cm.)
Marks: artist's monogram and cypher incised on bottom
Gift of IBM Corporation
P.C. 63.29

Stoneware set includes pitcher and four goblets (one shown). The ovoid body of the pitcher tapers to a flared mouth with pinched spout and applied handle. Low ridges surround the bottom.

The goblets are mug-shaped and without handles. There are low ridges at the base, similar to those on the pitcher. All five pieces are salt-glazed, with blue brushed floral decoration on two sides of the pitcher. On the goblets, bands of blue surround the top with blue floral decoration brushed on the sides.

Exhibitions: "Contemporary Ceramics of the Western Hemisphere," 1941

## WAYLANDE DESANTIS GREGORY
### (1905–1971)

One of the outstanding ceramists of the period, Waylande Gregory produced a wide variety of works in different styles, techniques, and sizes. His monumental sculptures remain even today among the largest works ever made of clay. He did portraits, fountains, mythological and historic figures, as well as dessert plates, cigarette boxes, and bookends. His style ranged from Beaux-Arts to Art Deco to Realist, and he was as comfortable with architectural ceramics and large scale figures as he was with commercial limited editions.

Gregory was born in Baxter Springs, Kansas and studied at the Kansas City Art Institute and in Chicago with Beaux-Arts sculptor Loredo Taft, who was to give the young Gregory an understanding and appreciation of sculpture of the Renaissance. Taft and Gregory traveled through Europe together in 1928, visiting museums and ceramics centers. A prodigious talent, Gregory achieved success very early in his career, receiving commissions for decorative interiors for the administration building of the University of Kansas, a Masonic temple in Wichita, and the Hotel President in Kansas City, among others.

Gregory returned to the United States to become a designer with the Cowan Pottery Studio in 1928. In 1931 he went to Cranbrook Academy in Bloomfield Hills, Michigan, where he worked for two years. He then set up his own studio in Metuchen, New Jersey. The Atlantic Terra Cotta Company of Perth Amboy had arranged for Gregory to have a work area in one of their plants where he had access to their large kilns. Here he had the opportunity to work on a large scale, experimenting freely with materials and techniques.

Among the large-scale sculptural programs that Gregory created were two fountains: "Light Dispelling Darkness," and "The Fountain of the Atom," the latter created for the New York World's Fair in 1939. He also produced large individual sculptural pieces, some for garden use, but these never proved financially successful for him. His last monumental work was a ceramic mural for the Municipal Center in Washington, D.C., which illustrated the work of

164

165

the city police and fire departments.

Gregory preferred to work on a large scale but since these pieces seldom sold he turned to the production of decorative pieces in limited editions in order to support himself and his wife. These were sold in exclusive stores across the country.

Gregory participated in all the Ceramic National Exhibitions from 1933 through 1946. In 1934 he was given a one-man show during the exhibition.

### 164 Waylande Gregory
*Salome,* 1929
Porcelain
H. 19, W. 11, D. 5 in.
(47.5 × 27.5 × 12.5 cm.)
Marks: none
Museum purchase    P.C. 84.4.12

Porcelain sculpture depicts Salome

holding up the head of John the Baptist, with his halo still intact. Salome wears a long gown and flowing veil draped over her arms and around the back of her body. Red-purple metallic glaze covers the sculpture.

This piece was purchased from the estate of Yolande Gregory, the widow of the artist.

Exhibitions: "The Diversions of Keramos, American Clay Sculpture 1925–1950," 1983

### 165 Waylande Gregory
*Madonna and Child,* n.d.
Earthenware
H. 15½, W. 3½, D. 6 in. (38.8 × 8.75 × 15 cm.)
Marks: *Waylande Gregory* and other illegible markings incised on bottom
Museum purchase    P.C. 84.4.6

Slip-cast Madonna and Child. The seated Madonna holds the Child on her lap. Mary is dressed in a blue gloss-glazed, draped garment with only bare feet, hands, and face exposed. The Child is wrapped in white swaddling clothes from the waist down and has ochre hair and a white halo. The eyes and mouths of both figures are colored. The Madonna sits on an unglazed, rectangular base.

166

**166 Waylande Gregory**
*Europa*, 1938
Earthenware
H. 23¾, L. 27 in. (59.3 × 67.5 cm.)
Marks: none
Museum purchase   P.C. 41.364

Earthenware sculpture of charging bull leaping over waves with nude Europa on his back. A flowing blue veil entwines Europa. The sculpture is unglazed, with stains.

Europa was a popular subject among ceramists during the 1930s and 1940s, particularly with artists of the Cleveland school. Viktor Schreckengost and Russell Barnett Aitken did humorous versions, as did Vally Wieselthier. Gregory's version is more in the Art Deco style than those of his colleagues, whose Europas show more of a Viennese influence.

Exhibitions: "7th Ceramic National," 1938; "The Golden Gate International Exhibition," Palace of the Legion of Honor, San Francisco, 1939; "The Art Deco Environment," 1979; "The Diversions of Keramos, American Clay Sculpture 1925–1950," 1983; "American Art Deco," Renwick Gallery, Smithsonian Institution, Washington, D.C., 1987–1988

**167 Waylande Gregory**

*Woman's Head,* c. 1933
Earthenware
H. 24, W. 9¾, D. 12 in. (60 × 24.4 × 30 cm.)
Marks: *Waylande Gregory* inscribed on bottom of sculpture
Museum purchase   P.C. 84.4.11

Over-lifesize earthenware sculpture of a woman's head with slight downward gaze. The white-glazed head and neck rest atop a circular, black-glazed earthenware base. The woman's features are idealized in the Art Deco style.

Exhibitions: "The Diversions of Keramos, American Clay Sculpture 1925–1950," 1983

**168 Waylande Gregory**

*From left to right:*
*Pink Bird,* n.d.
Porcelain
H. 10¼, W. 13½, D. 6 in. (25.6 × 33.75 × 15 cm.)
Marks: *Waylande Gregory* and copyright mark inscribed on bottom
Museum purchase   P.C. 84.4.7

Slip-cast sculpture of a bird in flight. Figure, including attached base, is

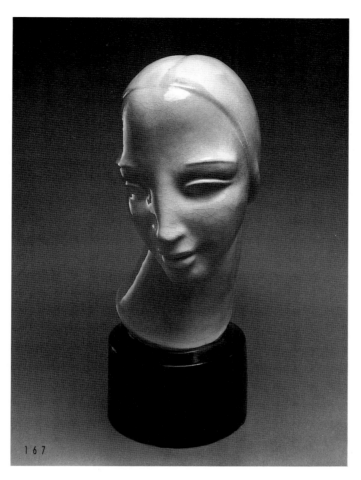

167

covered in a pink matte glaze. Black details highlight the eye, head, and tail; a tear drop design is on the wings.

*Amphora Vase,* n.d.
Porcelain
H. 14, Diam. 6½ in. (35 × 16.25 cm.)
Marks: *Waylande Gregory, New York,* and copyright mark inscribed on bottom
Museum purchase   P.C. 84.4.9

Porcelain oviform vase with flaring base. The central figure of a heron is surrounded by leafy branch forms. The piece is colored in stone gray glaze with white, platinum, and gold.

*Yellow Bird,* n.d.
Porcelain
H. 10¼, W. 13½, D. 6 in. (25.6 × 33.75 × 15 cm.)
Marks: *Waylande Gregory* and copyright mark inscribed on bottom
Museum purchase   P.C. 84.4.8

Slip-cast porcelain sculpture of bird in flight, with yellow body and silver resist decoration on wings with unglazed areas, including base. The eye is picked out in silver resist, and the beak in gold.

168

### 169 Waylande Gregory

*Madonna,* c. 1934
Earthenware
H. 16, W. 8, D. 7½ in. (40 × 20 × 18.75 cm.)
Marks: *Waylande Gregory* incised on back of base
Gift of the artist   P.C. 35.295

Head of Madonna in earthenware, unglazed. The head is tilted downward; the hair, parted in the middle, falls to the base of the work.

Exhibitions: "An Exhibition of Contemporary American Ceramics," 1936; "The Diversions of Keramos, American Clay Sculpture 1925–1950," 1983

### 170 Waylande Gregory

*Clockwise, beginning at top left:*
*Plate,* n.d.
Porcelain
H. 1, Diam. 10½ in.
(2.5 × 26.25 cm.)
Marks: *Waylande Gregory* in script under glaze on bottom
Museum purchase   P.C. 84.4.2

Shallow porcelain plate. The background of the well is brown with a central figure of a stylized deer in silver and white resist and a smaller

169

deer in the distance. Silver and white dots decorate the plate.

*Plate,* n.d.
Porcelain
H. 1¼, Diam. 10½ in.
(3.1 × 26.25 cm.)
Marks: *Waylande Gregory* and copyright mark inscribed on bottom
Museum purchase   P.C. 84.4.10

Flat, footed porcelain plate with wide ledge and shallow well. A tree form with nest and three eggs covers the well. The ground is blue and blue-purple with decoration in white, gold, and black.

*Small Bowl,* n.d.
Porcelain
H. 1½, Diam. 4⅜ in.
(3.8 × 10.9 cm.)
Marks: *Waylande Gregory* inscribed on bottom
Museum purchase   P.C. 84.4.3

Small, thick-walled bowl with black matte glaze and a platinum band on the rim. The center is decorated with a platinum bird in flight. A white linear design highlights the bird; white dots are scattered on the black background.

*Bowl,* n.d.
Porcelain
H. 3¼, Diam. 9½ in
(8.1 × 23.75 cm.)
Marks: none
Museum purchase   P.C. 84.4.5

Bowl with small foot and outwardly curving rim. The exterior is glazed in gold, while the interior is covered overall with a diapered scale design in shades of blue with gold dots.

This bowl was purchased from the estate of Yolande Gregory, the widow of the artist.

*Small Bowl,* n.d.
Porcelain
H. 1½, Diam. 4¼ in. (3.8 × 10.6 cm.)
Marks: *Waylande Gregory* incised on bottom
Museum purchase   P.C. 84.4.4

Small, thick-walled bowl. A green glaze with a gold band on the rim covers the bowl, which is decorated in the center with a leaping deer in gold with white spots. The gold linear design motif on the background suggests grassy leaves.

170

171

172

## CHAIM GROSS (b. Austria, 1904)

Though known primarily for his sculpture in wood, Chaim Gross also works in clay. He was born in Austria and studied at the Kunstgewerbeschule in Vienna before emigrating to the United States in 1921. In New York he studied modeling in clay at the Beaux-Arts Institute of Design with Elie Nadelman, who influenced him greatly. He also studied with Robert Laurent at the Art Students League for a short period.

Though he did some abstract pieces, his main interest throughout his career has been with the human figure. His work is outstanding, though often small in size, and is frequently playful. He did figures of acrobats, children, and circus performers, as well as pieces with religious themes.

Gross lived in New York, where he had a studio, and taught at the Beaux-Arts Institute and at the Art School of the Brooklyn Museum of Art from 1942 to 1959. He received commissions from the United States Treasury Department, the Post Office Department, and the New York World's Fair of 1939, as well as for several synagogues, most notably the International Synagogue at Kennedy Airport in New York.

### 171 Chaim Gross

*Woman and Child*, 1936
Earthenware
H. 2¼, W. 9¾, L. 13⅛ in. (5.6 × 24.3 × 32.8 cm.)
Marks: *Chaim Gross* incised, lower right on front of plate
Museum purchase   P.C. 82.6

Oval earthenware plate with sloping edges. The raised figures of two women hold a child aloft. The colors used are glossy dark blue, gold, and red glazes, with gold highlighting the smaller figure.

## MAIJA GROTELL (b. Finland, 1899–1973)

Maija Grotell was born in Helsinki, Finland, and studied painting, design, and sculpture there at the School of Industrial Art. She then studied for six years with pioneer artist-potter Alfred William Finch. In 1927 she came to the United States, settling in New York, where she taught at the Henry Street Settlement House. In 1936 she taught at Rutgers University, leaving after two years to accept a position as head of the ceramics department at Cranbrook Academy in Bloomfield Hills, Michigan, where she stayed until her retirement in 1966. Under her direction Cranbrook became one of the major American centers for ceramics education.

Grotell was one of the most important figures in the contemporary ceramics scene. Her stature as an artist is equaled by the influence she wielded through her teaching. Her works are monumental and majestic, with strong forms and distinctive glazes. She consistently experimented, yet always held a basic consideration for the unity of the piece, the importance of the relationship between form and decoration.

A spirited teacher, Grotell encouraged individuality and experimentation in her students, while emphasizing the importance of the fundamentality of the medium.

Grotell participated in every Ceramic National Exhibition between 1933 and 1960.

### 172 Maija Grotell

*Vase*, 1945
Stoneware
H. 17, Diam. 9⅞ inches (42.5 × 24.6 cm)
Marks: *MG* incised on bottom
Purchase prize given by Encyclopaedia Brittanica, "11th Ceramic National," 1946   P.C. 47.509

Tall, cylindrical stoneware vase with narrow raised horizontal ridges on the interior and exterior. The rim and interior are in a bluish, opalescent glaze. The decorative pattern on the exterior is created with slip and white glaze on a white and brown surface.

## THOMAS SAMUEL HAILE
### (b. England, 1908–1948)

Although Sam Haile was an Englishman who spent comparatively little time in the United States, he left an indelible mark on American ceramics. He originally studied painting but soon transferred to ceramics and studied at the Royal College of Art in London under the master artist-potter William Staite Murray. He came to the United States in 1939 and was invited by Charles Harder to teach at Alfred University. He later taught at the University of Michigan at Ann Arbor.

Haile brought a new perspective to ceramics, yet never lost sight of the uniqueness of the medium. His approach to surface decoration was influenced by his painterly background and there was always a strong interplay between decoration and form. He also, perhaps as a result of his initial association with painting, advocated a simpler approach to clay, with less emphasis on technical adroitness and more concern for the expressionist qualities of the art form.

Haile was invited to participate in the exhibition "Contemporary Ceramics of the Western Hemisphere, in Celebration of the Tenth Anniversary of the National Ceramic Ex-

hibitions," where he won a prize for pottery. Haile died in a motor car accident in England in 1948.

### 173 Sam Haile
*Orpheus*, c. 1941
Stoneware
H. 29⅝, Diam. 7½ in.
(74 × 18.75 cm.)
Marks: Haile's cypher on side of base
Gift of IBM Corporation
P.C. 63.30

Tall stoneware vase with flared base, undulating, ovoid body, and long, ridged neck. The large cup-shaped mouth resembles a Greek lekythos. Three decorated panels with abstracted linear figures make up the body of the vase. A gray glaze with red, blue, and greenish brown accents covers the piece.

This vase exemplifies Haile's freely executed, decorative techniques and illustrates the influence of Surrealism in his work. These qualities made him a precursor of the Abstract-Expressionist movement in ceramics which surfaced in America in the 1950s.

### JOHN HOWALD

Born in Delaware, Ohio, John Howald attended Ohio Wesleyan University and continued his studies at

173

174

Ohio State University Twilight School. He worked as a commercial artist and industrial designer and was cooperator of Littlefield Kilns. Howald participated in the Ceramic Nationals in 1949 and 1952. He was awarded a prize for pottery in 1949.

## 174 John Howald

*Cookie Jar,* c. 1949
Stoneware
H. 7¾, Diam. 6 in. (19.3 × 15 cm.)
Marks: *John Howald* incised on bottom
Purchase prize given by Homer Laughlin China Company, "14th Ceramic National," 1949
P.C. 50.588a, b

Globular, footed cookie jar with cover. The stoneware body is covered in a flowing translucent gray-green glaze with four brown curving triangular forms at the base. The slightly domed cover, in brown with a green center, is topped by a knob of brown, twisted ribs of clay.

## MARGARET JIPP

Born in Fort Calhoun, Nebraska, Margaret Jipp received her bachelor's and master's degrees from Columbia University. She studied ceramics during summer sessions at Mills College in Oakland, California. She was an elementary school teacher, and participated in the Ceramic Nationals from 1946 through 1950.

## 175 Margaret Jipp

*Vase,* c. 1948
Stoneware
H. 3⅜, Diam. 3⅛ in. (8.4 × 7.8 cm.)
Marks: *M. Jipp* incised on bottom, with *P + oc* beneath signature, also incised
Purchase prize given by Syracuse Branch of American Penwomen, "13th Ceramic National," 1948
P.C. 49.564

Small, barrel-shaped stoneware vase with wide shoulder and short neck. The piece has been salt-glazed and reduction-fired. The design in slip of alternating lines and spirals creates a geometric effect in rust and green. Two circular bands at the top encircle the neck.

This vase was awarded a purchase prize for the best miniature vase suitable for flower arranging in the "Thirteenth Ceramic National" in 1948.

175

## IRENE KOLODZIEJ (MUSICK)

Irene Kolodziej was born in Cleveland, Ohio, and was educated at Western Reserve University. She also studied at the Cleveland School of Art and at Cranbrook Academy in Michigan with Maija Grotell. She was an instructor in ceramics at the University of Missouri, Columbia.

## 176 Irene Kolodziej

*Vase,* c. 1947
Stoneware
H. 7¾, Diam. 10¼ in. (19.3 × 25.6 cm.)
Marks: *IK* incised on bottom
Purchase prize given by O. Hommel Company, "12th Ceramic National," 1947    P.C. 48.543

Stoneware bowl on high straight foot. The interior is glazed in an olive green. The exterior has three vertical blue bands, overlaid with white, amorphous, horizontal shapes, and a buff to olive green glaze on the remaining areas.

176

177

178

### EDGAR F. LITTLEFIELD (b. 1905)

Born in Nashville, Tennessee, Edgar Littlefield studied ceramic engineering at Ohio State University under Arthur Baggs, and later taught there for many years. He did research in copper red and blue glazes and salt glaze, and served as a glaze consultant to the ceramics industry. He was a member of the American Ceramic Society and received many awards. He participated in the Ceramic National Exhibitions from 1933 through 1941 and in 1949, 1951, 1952, and 1962.

### 177 Edgar Littlefield

*Vase,* 1933
Stoneware
H. 11⅛, Diam. 3¾ in.
(27.8 × 9.3 cm.)
Marks: *EL 1933* incised on bottom
Museum purchase    P.C. 35.278

Tall, slim, bottle-shaped vase. The slightly ovoid body tapers to a thin rim. White and dark red glaze with small specks of turquoise covers the exterior, while the mouth and interior are white.

### 178 Edgar Littlefield

*Vase,* 1939
Stoneware
H. 8, Diam. 8¾ in. (20 × 21.8 cm.)
Marks: *EL 1939* incised on bottom
Purchase prize given by Iroquois China Company, "Contemporary Ceramics of the Western Hemisphere," 1941   P.C. 42.527

Short, wide stoneware vase with sides tapering to footed. base. The piece is covered in a gray-green glaze with dark red and chartreuse leaf-like designs between two horizontal bands that circle the body.

Exhibitions: "A Century of Ceramics in the United States, 1878–1978," 1979

**WAYNE LONG**

Wayne Long participated in the Ceramic National Exhibitions from 1947 through 1958, except in 1956. He was a consistent prize winner, and was chairman of the regional jury in Los Angeles in 1952. He taught at the Los Angeles Art Institute.

179 **Wayne Long**
*Plate,* c. 1946
Stoneware

H. 2⅜, Diam. 15⅝ in.
(5.9 × 39 cm.)
Marks: *Wayne* incised on bottom
Purchase prize given by Harker Pottery Company, "12th Ceramic National," 1947   P.C. 48.540

Large, round stoneware plate with slightly sloping sides and small foot. The overall glaze is brown, but an incised fish design on the well reveals the textured clay beneath.

180

### GLEN LUKENS (1887–1967)

Glen Lukens was born in Missouri and first studied agriculture in Oregon. He became interested in art and went to the Art Institute of Chicago, where he studied ceramics under Myrtle French. In 1924 he moved to California and taught in secondary schools. In 1936 he became a professor of ceramics at the University of Southern California and remained there for thirty years. In 1945 Lukens took a leave of absence and went to Haiti, where he set up a training program for native artists under the sponsorship of UNESCO. The purpose of this program was to provide Haitians with a

skill that would supplement their income. The program was highly successful in establishing a home industry, and Lukens received commendations and was made an honorary citizen of Haiti.

Lukens was equally successful as a teacher and artist. He encouraged his students to work directly with the clay rather than from sketches, in order that their work might have more immediacy. His method was to provide his students with solid basic skills and then encourage them to innovate, allowing room for individual growth and creativity.

His own work was sensitive, earthy, and entirely unique at the time. He searched for native mate-

rials, spending time in the deserts and mesas in search of clay and glaze materials. Thus he developed a closeness to the material and a respect for its integrity. He developed original alkaline glazes and used native clay bodies to create simple, almost primal forms covered with thick luscious glazes of deep and brilliant colors.

Lukens won an award in every Ceramic National from 1935 through 1940, and in 1941 he was an invited entrant.

### 180 Glen Lukens

*Bowl*, c. 1936
Earthenware
H. 4, Diam. 11⅜ in. (10 × 29.1 cm.)

Marks: *Glen Lukens* incised on bottom
Gift of the artist  P.C. 40.331.1

Red earthenware, footed bowl with thick, pitted, yellow crackled glaze. The foot is unglazed.

Exhibitions: "5th Ceramic National," First prize for pottery, 1936; "Forms from the Earth: 1,000 Years of Pottery in America," Museum of Contemporary Crafts, New York, 1960; "A Century of Ceramics in the United States, 1878–1978," 1979; "Glen Lukens: Pioneer of the Vessel Aesthetic," American Crafts Museum, New York, 1983

181

182

### 181 Glen Lukens
*Death Valley Plate,* 1941
Earthenware
H. 3¼, Diam. 18¾ in. (8.1 ×
47.7 cm.)
Marks: *Glen Lukens* brushed on
bottom
Gift of IBM Corporation
P.C. 63.32

Large, unglazed tan earthenware
bowl. The wide ledge has three concentric lines of dripped turquoise
glaze.

Exhibitions: "Contemporary Ceramics of the Western Hemisphere,"
1941; "A Century of Ceramics in the
United States, 1878–1978," 1979

### 182 Glen Lukens
*Bowl,* 1936
Earthenware

H. 3⅛, Diam. 6⅛ in. (7.18 ×
15.3 cm.)
Marks: *Glen Lukens* brushed on
bottom
Gift of the artist   P.C. 40.331.2

Small, thick earthenware bowl. The
exterior is rough and unglazed, while
the interior is covered with a thick
blue crackle, alkaline glaze which
drips over the rim in thick globules.

This bowl clearly illustrates Lukens's ability to express the elementary nature of his materials.

Exhibitions: "Forms from the Earth:
1,000 Years of Pottery in America,"
Museum of Contemporary Crafts,
New York, 1960; "Glen Lukens: Pi-
oneer of the Vessel Aesthetic,"
American Crafts Museum, New
York, 1983

183

workshop given at Black Mountain College in North Carolina by Bernard Leach and Shoji Hamada. He participated in the Ceramic National Exhibitions from 1936 through 1947, and from 1950 through 1954, and again in 1958.

### 183 Karl Martz

*Plate,* c. 1940
Stoneware
H. 2½, Diam. 16¼ in.
(6.25 × 40.7 cm.)
Marks: none
Gift of IBM Corporation
P.C. 63.33

Large, deep-footed plate with wide, slightly flared ledge. A raised linear design in the form of an ibis decorates the well. A brown and yellow-green glaze is used overall.

Exhibitions: "Contemporary Ceramics of the Western Hemisphere," Honorable Mention, 1941

### THOMAS McCLURE (b. 1920)

Thomas McClure was born in Pawnee City, Nebraska, and received his B.F.A. at the University of Nebraska and M.F.A. from Cranbrook Academy in Michigan. He taught design at the School for American Craftsmen in Alfred, New York, and became professor of sculpture at the University of Michigan in 1949. He

### KARL MARTZ (b. 1912)

Born in Columbus, Ohio, Karl Martz was educated at Indiana University, where he was granted an A.B. in chemistry, and Ohio State University, where he did graduate work in ceramics. He was an instructor of ceramic art at the Institute of Design in Chicago in 1944, and became a professor of ceramic art at Indiana University in 1945. Martz was greatly influenced by the philosophy of Charles Fergus Binns, and during the 1950s became interested in the ceramics of Japan after attending a

184

185

186

participated in the Ceramic National Exhibitions from 1946 through 1952, and again in 1958.

### 184 Thomas McClure
*Carved Bowl,* 1947
Stoneware
H. 6⅜, Diam. 6⅛ in.
(15.9 × 15.3 cm.)
Marks: *TM* over *47* incised on bottom
Purchase prize given by Homer Laughlin China Company, "13th Ceramic National," 1948   P.C. 49.565

Dark brown, footed stoneware bowl with rounded body tapering to the top. Scenes from the Passion of Christ are excised in continuous relief around the center section, and contained between two incised lines at top and bottom.

### 185 Thomas McClure
*Small Bowl,* 1947
Stoneware
H. 3⅝, Diam. 4½ in. (9 × 11.25 cm.)
Marks: *TM* over *47* incised on bottom
Purchase prize given by Homer Laughlin China Company, "13th Ceramic National," 1948   P.C. 49.566

Brown stoneware, footed bowl with slightly flaring sides. A brown matte glaze covers the exterior, with an abstracted figural motif in white matte glaze surrounding the bowl in a band.

This piece was included in the purchase prize with McClure's Carved Bowl (entry 184).

### HARRISON McINTOSH (b.1914)
Harrison McIntosh was born in Vallejo, California in 1914, and studied at the Art Center School in Los Angeles (1938), the University of Southern California under Glen Lukens (1940), and with Richard Patterson at Claremont Graduate School from 1949 to 1952. He also worked with Bernard Leach at Mills College in Oakland, and at Pond Farm in Guerneville, California with Marguerite Wildenhain.

McIntosh worked briefly as a designer for Metlox Manufacturing Company in California (1955–1956) and taught with Peter Voulkos at the Los Angeles County Art Institute in 1956 and 1957 and again during the summer of 1959. In 1958 he and his wife built a home and pottery studio in the foothills overlooking the San Gabriel valley near Claremont, where he became a full-time potter.

Since his early days at Claremont, McIntosh has used a single stoneware body fired to Cone 5, a low temperature for stoneware. He has concentrated on the vessel, but in the mid-1970s began to expand his production to sculptural forms created from discs, ovoids, and spheres.

Whether vessel or sculpture, his work is always classic, restrained, and subtle, with elegantly refined decoration which has a distinctive hard edge. He has worked extensively in Europe and Japan in both glass and ceramics.

### 186 Harrison McIntosh
*Bowl,* 1948
Earthenware
H. 2½, Diam. 4 in. (6.25 × 10 cm.)
Marks: *McIntosh* incised on bottom
Gift of Richard V. Smith
P.C. 83.5.12

Small, red earthenware, footed bowl, slightly flattened to form four distinct sides. A cream-colored slip is used overall. Alternating dark and light red lines are sgraffitoed vertically through the slip, creating stripes that surround the form. The foot is unglazed.

### WILLIAM McVEY (b. 1905)

William McVey was born in Boston and educated at Rice University in Houston and the Cleveland Institute of Art. He also studied in Paris from 1929 to 1931. Upon his return to the United States he taught in Cleveland and Houston. After service in the Second World War he accepted a position at Cranbrook Academy in Bloomfield Hills, Michigan, where he remained until 1953 when he returned to Cleveland to head the sculpture department at the Institute of Art.

His work is often heroic and monumental. He did many memorial commissions and public works for government buildings and religious organizations. He participated in the Ceramic Nationals from 1949 through 1952, and in 1958, 1960, and 1964. He received awards for sculpture in 1949, 1950, and 1951, and in 1952 served as a member of the regional jury in Cleveland.

### 187 William McVey

*St. Francis,* c. 1949
Earthenware
Figure: H. 28½, W. 18, D. 14½ in.
(71.25 × 45 × 36.25 cm.) Birds: each L. 9½ in. (23.75 cm.)
Marks: none
Gift of IBM Corporation
P.C. 51.593

Unglazed earthenware sculpture depicting St. Francis and two birds. The figure is kneeling with head and hands uplifted and eyes closed. The details on St. Francis and the birds are incised.

Exhibitions: "15th Ceramic National," prize for sculpture, 1950

### 188 William McVey

*Young One,* c. 1950–1951
Stoneware
H. 18, W. 8, D. 6½ in. (45 × 20 × 16.3 cm.)
Marks: tape on bottom reads: *Young One / Wm. McVey*
Gift of IBM Corporation
P.C. 63.48

Stoneware sculpture of seated figure with arms raised and hands held together over head.

Exhibitions: "16th Ceramic National," 1952

189

## CHARLES F. MOSGO

Charles Mosgo worked in Cleveland, and entered the Ceramic Nationals consistently from 1937 through 1956, except in 1948 and 1954. He was a three-time prize winner, and was chairman of the regional jury in Cleveland in 1951.

### 189 Charles Mosgo

*Bowl,* c. 1950
H. 4, Diam. 19 in. (10 × 47.5 cm.)
Marks: *Mosgo* brushed on bottom, with four labels reading: (1) *Bowl / iridescent glaze / Charles F. Mosgo 866 / price 60.00 / c449,* (2) *101151 over 449,* (3) *88,* (4) *PC / 625*
Purchase prize given by Harper Electric Furnace Corporation, "16th Ceramic National," 1951
P.C. 52.625

190

Large footed bowl with wide flared sides. The glaze drips on the exterior, creating a crater effect, in gray and black. The interior rim is black with a spiral design in gray and dark blue, culminating at the center.

### 190 Charles Mosgo

*Bittersweet Jar,* c. 1949
H. 7¾, Diam. 4¾ in.
(19.3 × 11.8 cm.)
Marks: *Mosgo* brushed on bottom
Purchase prize given by U.S. Potters Association, "14th Ceramic National," 1949   P.C. 50.589

Cylindrical, tapering vase with slightly rising neck. Red, white, and black glazes cover the piece in a mottled pattern.

### HAROLD SIEGRIST NASH (b. 1894)

An educator, ceramist, designer, writer, and lecturer, Harold Siegrist Nash was born in Buffalo, New York and studied at Alfred University. He assumed the position of professor of ceramics at the University of Cincinnati in 1927. He participated in the Ceramic National Exhibitions from 1939 through 1941, in 1946, 1948, 1949, and 1956, and was a member of the jury in 1940.

### 191 Harold Nash

*Plate,* 1940–1941
Earthenware
H. 3, Diam. 17 in. (7.5 × 42.5 cm.)
Marks: artist's cypher brushed on bottom
Gift of IBM Corporation
P.C. 63.34

Large, footed plate with coarse-grained cream earthenware body. The wide ledge is deeply modeled with a rhythmic design. A white crackle glaze covers the plate.

Exhibitions: "Contemporary Ceramics of the Western Hemisphere," Honorable Mention, 1941

### GERTRUD NATZLER
### (b. Austria, 1908–1971)
### OTTO NATZLER (b. Austria, 1908)

The husband and wife team of Gertrud and Otto Natzler left their native Vienna in 1938 and settled in Los Angeles. Gertrud studied in Vienna at the Kunstgewerbeschule but Otto had no formal ceramic training. They worked together since they first met in 1933, Gertrud throwing the forms and Otto devising the glazes. They continued this division of labor until Gertrud died, after which Otto began to work with sculptural forms. Their work is in the collections of major museums in the United States and Europe.

Gertrud was an extraordinarily accomplished ceramist, throwing exquisitely elegant forms—simple, sensitive, and classic. She was able to achieve incredibly thin walls in her vessels, yet the forms retained a feeling of strength and vitality, never evolving into artifice or contrivance. They were the perfect vehicles for the unique, textured glazes devised by her husband. Otto constantly experimented with both glaze formulae and firing techniques, achieving remarkable colors and surface qualities.

191

192

Recognition came early to the Natzlers. In 1938 they were awarded a silver medal at the World Exposition in Paris, and in 1939 they won a purchase prize at the "8th Ceramic National" in Syracuse. They participated in every Ceramic National from 1939 through 1966, except 1950 and 1952. They were invited to participate in "Ceramics 70 Plus Woven Forms" at Everson Museum in 1970.

Their earliest works are classic in form and the glazes are dry, earthy, and volcanic. In 1942 Otto began to explore reduction firing. Later the forms had wider cultural references, with subtle oriental and Scandinavian allusions. But always they retained the elegance and sophistication that characterized their work from the very beginning, each piece a masterful combination of the intuitive and intellectual processes that are vital to the creation of any work of art.

### 192 Gertrud and Otto Natzler

*Fruit Bowl,* 1939
Earthenware
H. 2⅜, Diam. 12⅞ in.
(5.9 × 32.1 cm.)
Marks: *Natzler* inscribed on bottom. *1–4* written in pencil below signature

Purchase prize given by Onondaga Pottery Company, "8th Ceramic National," 1939   P.C. 40.347.1

Large, shallow earthenware bowl with Pompeiian turquoise matte glaze on both interior and exterior. The interior is slightly ridged.

The Natzlers had been in the United States for only about a year, and this was their first entry in a Ceramic National Exhibition. The dry texture of the glaze and the subtle turquoise color over the red clay body make this an exceptionally fine piece.

Exhibitions: "Form and Fire: Natzler Ceramics 1939–1972," Renwick Gallery, Smithsonian Institution, Washington, D.C., 1973

### 193 Gertrud and Otto Natzler

*From left to right:*
*Bowl,* c. 1941
Earthenware
H. 3¾, Diam. 13 in. (9.3 × 32.5 cm.)
Marks: *G & O Natzler* inscribed on bottom
Purchase prize given by Ferro Enamel Corporation for group, "Contemporary Ceramics of the Western Hemisphere," 1941
P.C. 42.521

Shallow, footed earthenware bowl.

The interior is covered in a patina glaze with dark green at the center in a star-like diffusion of glaze; the rim has been left unglazed. The patina glaze on the exterior was applied unevenly, creating a dappled effect. The unusual glaze effects, coupled with the extraordinarily thin walls of this bowl, make it a most remarkable piece.

Exhibitions: "Forms from the Earth: 1,000 Years of Pottery in America," Museum of Contemporary Craft, New York, 1960; "Form and Fire: Natzler Ceramics 1939–1972," Renwick Gallery, Smithsonian Institution, Washington, D.C., 1973; "A Century of Ceramics in the United States, 1878–1978," 1979

*Vase,* c. 1946
Earthenware
H. 5, Diam. 3¾ in. (12.5 × 9.3 cm.)
Marks: *Natzler* inscribed on bottom, also *511*
Purchase prize given by Homer Laughlin China Company, for group, "11th Ceramic National," 1946  P.C. 47.511

Ovoid, earthenware vase with rose and sky copper reduction glaze and melt crackle on exterior. The interior is similarly glazed with rose on top near the rim, and sky covering the rest.

Exhibitions: "The Ceramic Work of Gertrud and Otto Natzler: A Retrospective Exhibition," Los Angeles County Museum of Art, 1966; "The Ceramic Work of Gertrud and Otto Natzler," M. H. de Young Memorial Museum, San Francisco, 1971; "Form and Fire: Natzler Ceramics 1939–1972," Renwick Gallery, Smithsonian Institution, Washington, D.C., 1973; "A Century of Ceramics in the United States, 1878–1978," 1979

*Bowl,* c. 1939
Earthenware
H. 4⅝, Diam. 5⅛ in. (11.5 × 12.8 cm.)
Marks: *G & O Natzler* inscribed on bottom, with *347.3* over *9* in pencil, also on bottom
Purchase prize given by Onondaga Pottery Company, "8th Ceramic National," 1939  P.C. 40.347.3

Deep, footed, red earthenware bowl. The body beneath is visible on the rim where the glaze is transparent. The stone-green, glossy glaze is uneven on the interior, giving the illusion of running glaze. The same stone-green glaze covers the exterior with uneven glazing across the body

at intervals. Finger formed ridges are apparent near the rim on the exterior. The foot is unevenly glazed and the red earthenware body shows through.

Exhibitions: "Form and Fire: Natzler Ceramics 1939–1972," Renwick Gallery, Smithsonian Institution, Washington, D.C., 1973

## MINNIE NEGORO

Minnie Negoro was born in Los Angeles and studied there at the University of California. She received her Master of Fine Arts degree from Alfred University, and worked in ceramics under Daniel Rhodes in Wyoming during the Second World War. She taught at the School for American Craftsmen, in Rochester, New York, Chouinard Art Institute in Los Angeles, and at the Rhode Island School of Design. She participated in the Ceramic National Exhibitions from 1946 through 1950, and again in 1958, 1960, and 1962.

194

194 **Minnie Negoro**
*Tea Set,* 1947
Stoneware
Teapot: H. 5½, W. 7⅛ in. (13.75 × 17.8 cm.). Sugar: H. 3⅝, Diam. 3¼ in. (9 × 8.1 cm.). Creamer: H. 3, W. 3½ in. (7.5 × 8.75 cm.)
Marks: *M. Negoro/Alfred/47* painted on bottom
Purchase prize given by Richard B. Gump, "12th Ceramic National," 1947   P.C. 48.544.1–3

Stoneware tea set includes teapot, sugar, and creamer. The footed teapot with cover has a bamboo handle attached with leather strips. A small, footed sugar with cover and a pinched creamer with no handle accompany the pot. All the pieces are covered with gray-green glaze. A line design in dark brown is brushed in the center of each piece.

## ADOLPH ODORFER
### (b. Austria, 1902)

Adolph Odorfer was educated at the Wienerberger Werkstätten Schule für Keramik in his native Vienna and received a B.A. degree from Fresno State College in California. He was an associate professor of ceramics at Fresno State College from 1947 to 1966. He worked as a wheel potter in Lower Austria and Mexico, and as a technician in ceramics factories

195

in São Paulo, Brazil and in Jalisco, Mexico. Odorfer was a consistent participant in the Ceramic National Exhibitions; his works were accepted from 1937 through 1952, and in 1958. In 1948 he served as chairman of the regional jury in San Francisco.

195 **Adolph Odorfer**
*Abraham and Isaac,* c. 1947
Earthenware
H. 20, W. 7 in. (50 × 17.5 cm.)
Marks: encircled *A* with *18* and copyright mark incised on bottom
Purchase prize for religious subject given by Otto L. Spaeth, President Liturgical Arts Society, "12th Ceramic National," 1947   P.C. 48.545

Unglazed, red earthenware sculpture depicting bearded Abraham holding knife above young Isaac's head. Isaac stands with his arms stretched upward to his father. A ram is between Abraham's legs. The figures are stylized, with simple forms and a few incised details.

196

### DOROTHEA WARREN O'HARA
### (1875–1963)

Dorothea Warren O'Hara studied in Munich, at the Royal College of Art in London, at Columbia University, and under Charles Fergus Binns at Alfred University. She had her first exhibition of pottery at the Royal College of Art in London, and exhibited at the Paris Salon. J. Pierpont Morgan was one of her patrons and he helped to create a demand for her work. Upon her return to New York, she opened a studio there, and later established Apple Tree Lane Pottery in Darien, Connecticut. She was especially proficient at glaze calculation and many of her formulae were produced commercially. Unlike many women ceramists of the period, she completed all phases of her work herself.

O'Hara participated in the Ceramic Nationals in 1933 and from 1935 through 1941. She participated by invitation in 1936.

### 196 Dorothea O'Hara

*Bowl,* c. 1940
Earthenware
H. 6⅜, Diam. 10⅜ in.
(16.5 × 25.9 cm.)
Marks: *D* over *W* within a circle incised at bottom
Anonymous gift   P.C. 41.366

Red earthenware carved bowl. The foot and interior are covered with a black glaze. The exterior is decorated with four carved birds, alternating with flowers and leaves.

Exhibitions: "Contemporary Ceramics of the Western Hemisphere," 1941; "Art Deco Environment," 1976; "A Century of Ceramics in the United States, 1878–1978," 1979

197

### LAURA PADDOCK

Laura Paddock worked at Rowantrees Kiln in Bluehill, Maine. She participated in the Ceramic Nationals in 1940 and 1941.

### 197 Laura Paddock

*Duckshead Bowl,* c. 1940
H. 3¼, Diam. 12¾ in.
(8.5 × 31.8 cm.)
Marks: *Laura S. Paddock* incised on bottom. Also on bottom, stamp reading: *R.K. / BLUEHILL / ME.*
Gift of IBM Corporation
P.C. 63.35

Footed bowl with flared sides covered in green on the interior and brown luster on the exterior. A thin band of brown separates the two basic colors at the rim, creating an elegant interplay between them.

Exhibitions: "Contemporary Ceramics of the Western Hemisphere," 1941

## GLIDDEN PARKER (1913–1979)

Glidden Parker was educated at Bates College in his native Maine, and studied German and comparative literature at the University of Vienna. He received his ceramics training at Alfred University. In 1941 Parker set up his own pottery, Glidden Pottery, in Alfred Station, New York. It continued until 1958. Parker participated in the Ceramic Nationals in 1938, 1939, 1947, 1949, 1951, and 1952.

### 198 Glidden Parker

*Covered Casseroles,* c. 1947
Stoneware
Left: H.5⅛, L.11¼, W. 6¾ in. (12.8 × 28.1 × 16.8 cm.) Center:H. 3¾, L. 8¾, W. 5½ in. (9.4 ×21.9 × 13.75 cm.) Right: H. 6, L. 14¼, W. 9½ in.(15 ×35.6 × 23.75 cm.)
Marks: *Glidden 161, Glidden 165, Glidden 163*—impressed, respectively, on the bottom of each
Left and right: Purchase prizes given by Richard B. Gump, "12th Ceramic National," 1947; Center: Gift of Eveleen C. Harrison
Left to right: P.C. 48.546.1a, b; P.C. 48.546.2a, b; P.C. 79.1a, b

A set of three covered stoneware dishes with handles on either end. A plume-like pattern is incised through the white glaze on the exteriors. An identical decoration appears on the interior of the covers, which may also be used as serving dishes.

The two larger pieces received a prize for "best ceramic design suitable for mass production" in the "12th Ceramic National," 1947.

### 199 Glidden Parker

*Covered Casserole,* c. 1949
Stoneware
H. 5¼, L. 11¼, W. 7½ in. (13.1 × 28.1 × 18.75 cm.)
Marks: *Glidden 193* incised on bottom
Purchase prize given by Richard B. Gump, "14th Ceramic National," 1949 P.C. 50.586.2a, b

Square stoneware casserole with handles on opposite diagonals. One handle extends downward to touch the table top. The cover may be used as a serving dish. The exterior has yellow glaze with brown speckles.

This casserole was awarded a purchase prize for "best ceramic design suitable for mass production."

198

199

200

## WINIFRED PHILLIPS (1880–1963)

Born in Claybanks, Wisconsin, Winifred Phillips received her art education at Milwaukee State Teacher's College, Chicago Art Institute, Pratt Art Institute, Alfred University, and Cranbrook Academy of Art. She taught in the art school of Milwaukee State Teachers College, and was a frequent participant in the Ceramic National Exhibitions from 1933 through 1958.

### 200 Winifred Phillips

*Vase,* 1940
Stoneware
H. 12⅞, Diam. 6½ in.
(32.1 × 16.25 cm.)
Marks: *Winifred Phillips B. 60 1940* incised on bottom
Purchase prize given by Hanovia Chemical Company, "9th Ceramic National," 1940  P.C. 41.371

Tall, brown stoneware, beaker-shaped vase. An opalescent glaze covers the interior, while the exterior remains unglazed. Unevenly ridged horizontal incisions cover the vase.

## STEPHEN J. POLCHERT (b. 1920)

Born in Milwaukee, Stephen Polchert studied at the University of Chicago and at Cranbrook Academy of Art. He has taught at Joslyn Art Museum and the University of Omaha. He participated in the Ceramic Nationals from 1949–1952, and again in 1958.

### 201 Stephen J. Polchert

*Left to right:*

*Covered jar,* 1950
Porcelain
H. 6¼, Diam. 6½ in.
(15.6 × 16.25 cm.)
Marks: *S. Polchert 4–50* incised on bottom
Purchase prize given by Jules R. Gulden, "16th Ceramic National," 1951  P.C. 52.632.1

Globular, covered, porcelain jar. A shaded copper reduction glaze on white covers the piece. A faint red, loose band runs around the top, with a heavier, darker red band at the bottom. The convex lid with a knob is also red.

*Sphere,* 1950
Porcelain
H. 9¼, Diam. 7½ in.
(23.1 × 18.75 cm.)
Marks: *S. Polchert 3–50* incised on bottom
Purchase prize given by Jules R. Gulden, "16th Ceramic National," 1951  P.C. 52.632.1

Oviform porcelain vase with small neck and mouth. The body is covered in a shaded copper, crackled reduction red glaze on white. The neck is white with a red band surrounding the upper shoulder.

201

202

## HENRY VARNUM POOR (1888–1971)

Henry Varnum Poor was born in Chapman, Kansas and studied at Stanford University, the Slade School of Art in London, and at the Académie Julian in Paris. Upon his return, he taught at Stanford and at the Mark Hopkins Art Institute in San Francisco. Poor worked in many media, but from 1923 to 1933 he worked mainly in ceramics for reasons of both aesthetics and economy. His interest in ceramics continued, however, and he returned to clay intermittently throughout his life.

Poor was a founder and first president of Skowhegan School of Paint-ing and Sculpture in Maine, and in 1950 he became resident artist at the American Academy in Rome. He received a presidential appointment as a member of the Commission on Fine Arts in 1944 and 1945. In 1954 his book, *A Book of Pottery—From Mud to Immortality* was published.

Poor commented that he had taken up ceramics because it was the only medium in which the artist retained such complete control of the work of art from beginning to end, where both the form and its decoration were equally his.

Poor was a participant in the Ce-ramic National Exhibitions from 1936 through 1948, and in 1954 and 1958.

## 202 Henry Varnum Poor

*Platter with Nude,* 1931
Earthenware
H. 3, L. 17¾, W. 12¾ in. (7.5 × 44.4 × 31.9 cm.)
Marks: *HVP 1931* incised on bottom, remains of labels
Purchase prize given by Ferro Enamel Corporation, "8th Ceramic National," 1939  P.C. 40.348

Deep, oval platter with four strap feet. It has an earthenware body; the underside is unglazed. An interior linear design depicts a standing nude woman with water, boats, and distant landscape in brown, blue, and yellow on an opaque, buff background.

Exhibitions: "Forms from the Earth: 1,000 Years of Pottery in America," Museum of Contemporary Crafts, New York, 1960; "A Century of Ceramics in the United States, 1878–1978," 1979; "Henry Varnum Poor, 1887–1970, A Retrospective Exhibition," Museum of Art, The Pennsylvania State University, 1983–1984

203

204

205

**203 Henry Varnum Poor**
*Two tiles,* c. 1940
Earthenware
Each tile: H. 7½, W. 12⅝, D. ⅝ in.
(18.75 × 31.5 × 1.5 cm)
Marks: none
Gift of IBM Corporation
P.C. 63.36a, b

Two earthenware tiles in relief. One tile depicts two birds in yellow, orange, and blue-gray glazes. The second tile depicts a reptilian figure with a long, curling tail in yellow and black glazes.

These tiles are from the bathing pavillion of Burgess Meredith.

Exhibitions: "Contemporary Ceramics of the Western Hemisphere," 1941

**ANTONIO PRIETO**
**(b. Spain, 1912–1967)**
Born in Valdepenas, Spain, Antonio Prieto studied sculpture at the California School of Fine Arts in San Francisco, and ceramics, painting, and sculpture at Alfred University. He taught at the College of Arts and Crafts in Oakland and at Mills College. During 1963 and 1964 he received a Fulbright Scholarship for study in Spain. Prieto participated in the Ceramic Nationals from 1946 through 1962, except in 1960.

**204 Antonio Prieto**
*Bottle,* 1949
Stoneware
H. 12½, Diam. 5 in.
(31.25 × 12.5 cm.)
Marks: *A. Prieto* brushed on bottom
Gift of Richard V. Smith
P.C. 83.5.3

Stoneware bottle with slightly pinched waist and ribbed neck. The bottle is divided into six sections, alternating blue- and gray-glazed areas. Sgraffito and engobe trailed decoration of birds are on the blue areas, and a repeated **X** design is around the midsection and shoulder. The neck is ribbed.

**205 Antonio Prieto**
*Plate,* c. 1945
Stoneware
H. 1¾, Diam. 13⅜ in.
(4.3 × 33.4 cm.)
Marks: *Antonio Prieto* brushed on bottom
Purchase prize given by Richard B. Gump, "11th Ceramic National," 1946 P.C. 47.512

Black and brown glazed stoneware plate. A linear design of female figures and birds in five rows is incised across the face of the plate; a wavy line is incised around the edge.

## PUEBLO CULTURE

The roots of Pueblo pottery can be traced back to the earliest American cultures. The Mogollon and Anasazi people were probably the ancestors of the present day Pueblos and these prehistoric cultures had a great and unique pottery tradition. This tradition was based on the need for both functional and ceremonial vessels. These vessels were formed and decorated according to the pueblo or village that produced them. With the arrival of the Europeans and early settlers, the age old pottery traditions died as metal and enamel pots and cookware replaced the clay forms.

With the coming of the railroad and tourism, there was a revival of pottery making, but mainly of the curio variety for sale as souvenirs. The quality varied from pueblo to pueblo. During the 1920s the demand for fine wares increased and thus the quality improved and strong efforts were made to rediscover and continue traditional forms and decoration.

During the 1930s and 1940s Pueblo artists participated in the Ceramic National Exhibitions, both as individuals and as a group.

206

### 206 Unknown Pueblo Potter

*At left and far right:*
*Small Birds,* c. 1935
Earthenware
Left: H. 3, W. 3¼, D. 2½ in. (7.5 × 8.1 × 6.25 cm.) Right: H. 3, W. 2½, D. 2½ in. (7.5 × 6.25 × 6.25)
Marks: none
Anonymous gift   P.C. 39.30, 39.34

Two ovoid earthenware birds, one with speckled body and hole at the throat, the other decorated in a geometric feather-and-wing design often seen on Pueblo bowls.

*Center:*
### Hopi Pueblo Potter

*Small Bowl,* 1920–1939
Earthenware
H. 2¾. Diam. 5 in. (6.8 × 12.5 cm.)
Marks: none
Anonymous gift   P.C. 39.1

Small, irregular earthenware bowl. A black, geometric feather-and-wing design has been painted over the tan body.

Bird motifs, including this feather-and-wing design, have been popular among Hopi potters since prehistoric times. A revival of traditional Sikyatki designs was instituted by Nampeyo at the end of the last century when she adapted traditional motifs to contemporary Hopi designs.

### 207 Unknown Pueblo Potter

*Wedding Jar,* c. 1935
Earthenware
H. 6¼, W. 6¾ in. (15.6 × 16.8 cm.)
Marks: none
Anonymous gift   P.C. 39.12

Ovoid vessel of polished blackware, with two flared spouts. The handle is applied on top, connecting the two spouts.

A traditional form, the wedding jar shape was used in many parts of ancient America, both North and South, and is still produced today in the American Southwest, and used at wedding ceremonies—the bride drinking from one side, and the groom from the other.

207

208

## SAN ILDEFONSO PUEBLO
## JULIAN MARTINEZ (d. 1943)
## MARIA MARTINEZ (1884–1980)

Maria Martinez and her husband Julian made traditional polychrome pottery at San Ildefonso before 1918 when Julian discovered how to recreate a traditional blackware which had been unearthed at excavations near the pueblo. Maria formed the vessels, Julian added the decorations and did the firing. After much experimentation, a technique was developed in which the whole background was polished, then matte decoration was painted on and the piece fired. Maria and Julian studied ancient vessels in museums and adapted indigenous designs that had been found in ruins where their ancestors had lived.

After Julian's death in 1943 Maria worked with her daughter-in-law Santana and her son Popovi Da. Maria participated in the Ceramic Nationals in 1933, 1934, 1936, and 1941.

### 208 Maria Martinez

*Plate,* c. 1940 or earlier
Earthenware
H. 2, Diam. 12¾ in. (5 × 31.8 cm.)
Marks: *Marie* inscribed on bottom; label reads: *Martinez #1*; remains of another torn label
Gift of the Pueblo Indian Arts and Crafts Market    P.C. 41.374.8

Large, polished blackware plate. An abstract, geometric, feather-and-wing design with triangular patterning at midsection continues in concentric triangles to the center. The decoration is attributed to Julian Martinez.

Exhibitions: "Contemporary Ceramics of the Western Hemisphere," Special Mention, 1941; "Art Deco Environment," 1976; "A Century of

Ceramics in the United States, 1878–1978," 1979

**209 Maria Martinez, potter**
**Julian Martinez, decorator**
*Bowl,* 1941
Earthenware
H. 3½, Diam. 8½ in.
(8.75 × 21.25 cm.)
Marks: *Marie / + / Julian* inscribed
on bottom, with remains of three labels reading: (1) *(40/8),* (2) *(ST–3 / No Charge / Marie Martinez),* (3) *(M.F.A. / not for sale)*
Gift of Pueblo Indian Arts and Crafts Market   P.C. 41.374.2

Short, hemispherical bowl, in polished blackware with wide mouth. A matte design surrounds the bowl at its shoulder with detailed step and geometric designs.

Exhibitions: "Contemporary Ceramics of the Western Hemisphere," Special Mention, 1941

**210 Maria Martinez, potter**
**Julian Martinez, decorator**
*Vase,* 1934–1943
Earthenware
H. 11½, Diam. 8 in. (28.75 × 20 cm.)
Marks: *Marie / + / Julian* inscribed
on bottom
Gift of John Pentland   P.C. 76.98

Large, polished blackware vase tapering at its rounded shoulder to a long, cylindrical neck which flares slightly at the mouth. A matte black geometric design creates a band surrounding the vase at its shoulder. Matte lines with scallops surround the neck.

Exhibitions: "A Century of Ceramics in the United States, 1878–1978," 1979

**211 Maria Martinez, potter**
**Julian Martinez, decorator**
*Bowl,* 1934–1943
Earthenware
H. 5, Diam. 6½ in.
(12.5 × 16.25 cm.)
Marks: *Marie / + / Julian* inscribed
on bottom
Anonymous gift in memory of Grace Sperry Burns   P.C. 84.23

Squat, bulbous, polished blackware bowl. The section above the waist is decorated in matte with a twisting serpentine *avanyu* figure with an arrow and interspersed geometric shapes.
The *avanyu,* a horned water ser-

210

211

212

213

pent and symbol of thanksgiving for water and rain, is a common motif in Pueblo pottery. Julian first used it on blackware vessels about 1918.

## MARIA MARTINEZ
## SANTANA ROYBAL MARTINEZ

Santana Roybal married Maria's son Adam and decorated Maria's pots after Julian's death in 1943 until 1956, when Maria's son Popovi Da began to decorate them. Santana and Adam made pottery in the style of Maria.

### 212 Maria Martinez, potter
### Santana Martinez, decorator

*Small Bowl,* c. 1950
Earthenware
H. 3½, Diam. 5¼ in. (8.75 × 13.1 cm.)
Marks:  *Maria / + / Santana*  inscribed on bottom
Gift of Mr. and Mrs. Francis P. Maloney  P.C. 78.17

Small, polished blackware bowl. The shoulder is decorated with a band of a repeating geometric feather motif.

The feather design used to decorate this bowl is a modification of a Mimbres black-on-white design from about A.D. 1110.

### 213 Maria Martinez, potter
### Santana Martinez, decorator

*Small Bowl,* c. 1950
Earthenware
H. 3⅜, Diam. 4½ in. (8.4 × 11.25 cm.)
Marks:  *Maria / + / Santana*  inscribed on bottom
Gift of Mr. and Mrs. Edward Beadel  P.C. 82.25.1

Ovoid blackware bowl with shoulder and wide mouth. The top section is decorated in a black matte geometric and scroll design which creates a band surrounding the vessel.

### 214 Maria Martinez, potter
### Santana Martinez, decorator

*Blackware Bowl,* 1943–1956
Earthenware
H. 3½, Diam. 8¼ in. (8.75 × 20.6 cm.)
Marks:  *Marie / + / Santana*  inscribed on bottom
Gift of Richard V. Smith  P.C. 83.5.1

Flat, round polished blackware bowl with wide mouth. A black matte design of *avanyu* and geometric shapes surrounds the bowl and its shoulder.

2 1 4

## JUAN CRUZ (b. 1887)
## TONITA ROYBAL (b. 1887)

Tonita Roybal was a contemporary of Maria Martinez, and Santana's aunt. She and her husband Juan were the last San Ildefonso ceramists to specialize in the old black-on-red style of pottery. Because of its pop-ularity, they also made blackware.

### 215 Juan and Tonita Roybal

*Jar,* 1936
Earthenware
H. 8⅝, Diam. 8¼ in. (21.5 × 20.6 cm.)
Marks: *Tonita* inscribed on bottom, with two labels reading: (1) *Tonita and Juan / Roybal #4 / Lot 54 / San Ildefonso Pueblo / New Mexico,* (2) *$4.00*
Museum purchase  P.C. 36.318

Ovoid, polished blackware jar with wide, high neck and flared mouth. Black matte geometric designs create a band, which surrounds the jar at its shoulder.

---

Exhibitions: "5th Ceramic National," 1936, and traveled to Denmark, Sweden, and Finland in 1939

2 1 5

216

## SAN JUAN PUEBLO
## REGINA CATA

About 1930 Regina Cata began a revival of an ancient type of pottery with incised decoration at San Juan pueblo. She had found shards of ancient vessels with this type of decoration and introduced the technique to the other artists in the pueblo. An incised area is usually accompanied by a polished section below.

## SAN JUAN PUEBLO
## CRUCITA T. CRUZ

Crucita Cruz came from the Tewa Pueblo of San Juan in the Rio Grande valley. She worked in the polychrome style, painting designs in red or white slip and leaving them unpolished.

216 *Left to right:*
**Regina Cata**
*Bowl,* 1941
Earthenware
H. 4½, Diam. 8 in. (11.25 × 20 cm.)
Marks: two labels on bottom reading: (1) *PC 374/9/5 — Jar / Regina Cata,* (2) torn and illegible

Gift of Pueblo Indian Arts and Crafts Market   P.C. 41.374.3

Red earthenware ovoid bowl. Top third of the bowl is polished, while the bottom section is matte. The interior is matte red.

Exhibitions: "Contemporary Ceramics of the Western Hemisphere," Special Mention for Excellence, 1941

**Crucita Cruz**
*Plate,* 1942
Earthenware
H. 1½, Diam. 10¼ inches (3.75 × 25.6 cm)
Marks: *Crucita T. Cruz / San Juan* brushed on bottom. Remains of green label, illegible
Purchase prize, "Contemporary Ceramics of the Western Hemisphere," 1941   P.C. 42.529

Round, shallow earthenware plate with flared rim. The circular area at the center has a linear geometric design with arrows. The outer section has an *avanyu,* the twisting serpentine figure with arrow emanating

from its mouth. The piece is glazed in red, white, and tan.

The *avanyu,* or horned water serpent, is a common motif in Pueblo pottery, though its origins are in Pre-Columbian Mexico. It is a symbol of thanksgiving for water and rain, important in a farming community in an extremely dry climate.

## SANTA CLARA PUEBLO
## PATRUCINO NARANJO

Patrucino Naranjo made the classic polished black pottery that has been a tradition of Santa Clara, a Tewa Pueblo, for over three centuries.

217 **Patrucino Naranjo**
*Vase,* 1941
Earthenware
H. 6¾, Diam. 7½ in.
(16.8 × 18.75 cm.)
Marks: remains of green sticker that reads: *77/40/6 M.F.A.*
Gift of Pueblo Indian Arts and Crafts Market   P.C. 41.374.e

Gourd-shaped vase with raised rim. Vertical ribs surround the body, which is a polished blackware.

Stone-polished blackware has been made at Santa Clara for several hundred years. This form is also a traditional one.

Exhibitions: "Contemporary Ceramics of the Western Hemisphere," Special Mention for Excellence, 1941

## SANTA DOMINGO PUEBLO
## MONICA SILVIN

Monica Silvin worked at the more conservative pueblo of Santa Domingo, where traditional forms and decoration were carefully preserved.

218 **Monica Silvin**
*Jar with Geometric Design,* 1941
Earthenware
H. 7½, Diam. 6½ in.
(18.75 × 16.25 cm.)
Marks: label on bottom reads: *PC374/7/4—jar M/Silvin*
Gift of Pueblo Indian Arts and Crafts Market   P.C. 41.374.4

Bulbous earthenware jar with high neck and flaring rim surrounded by a black band. Black interlocking geo-

217

218

metric designs are painted over the white slip. The base is orange.

Exhibitions: "Contemporary Ceramics of the Western Hemisphere," 1941

## SANTA CLARA PUEBLO
### CATHERINE VIGIL

Catherine Vigil painted her poly-

chrome designs in muted colors directly onto the polished slip surface, a technique that was typical in Santa Clara.

### 219 Catherine Vigil
*Shallow Bowl,* 1941
Earthenware
H. 3¼, Diam. 14½ in.
(8.1 × 36.25 cm.)

Marks: green label on bottom reads:
*111/40/13 / circuit*
Gift of IBM Corporation
P.C. 63.135

Large earthenware bowl with flaring sides. Linear geometric designs in light blue, ochre, and white decorate the brown body.

This particular kind of ware, with

designs in light, muted colors, was an innovation at Santa Clara.

Exhibitions: "Contemporary Ceramics of the Western Hemisphere," Special Mention for Excellence, 1941

219

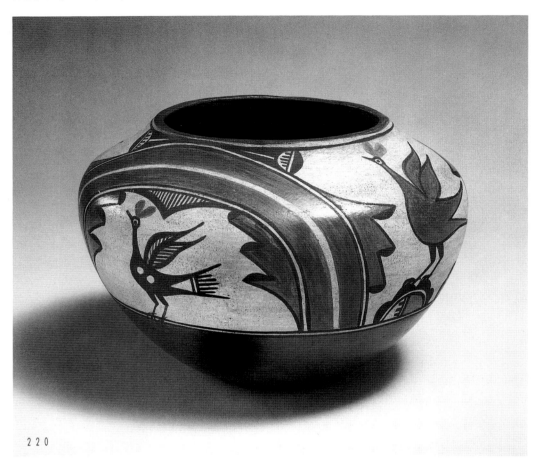

220

221

## ZIA PUEBLO
## HARVIANA TORIBIO

Harviana Toribio was one of many Zia potters who consciously refined earlier pottery traditions. They used white or buff slip with red at the base, and decorations—often bird motifs—in red, black, and occasionally yellow.

### 220 Harviana Toribio

*Jar,* 1941
Earthenware
H. 6, Diam. 8½ in. (15 × 21.25 cm.)
Marks: remains of two labels on bottom. One reads: *177/49/44 S.M.F.A.*
Other illegible
Gift of Pueblo Indian Arts and Crafts Market   P.C. 41.374.3

Ovoid earthenware jar tapering at curved shoulder to a mouth with a raised rim. The bottom third of the jar is polished red with the upper section decorated in geometric and avian designs in red and black over white slip.

Exhibitions: "Contemporary Ceramics of the Western Hemisphere," Special Mention for Excellence, 1941

### 221 Unknown Pueblo Potter
### (pseud., Raymond Watson's Mother)

*Bowl,* 1941
Earthenware
H. 3¼, Diam. 7¼ in. (8.1 × 18.1 cm.)
Marks: none
Gift of Pueblo Indian Arts and Crafts Market   P.C. 41.374.7

Hemispherical earthenware bowl. The exterior top section is white, encircled with brown and red abstract geometric designs. The bottom section is brown. The interior is white with multiple abstract designs in brown and orange, surrounding the sides and well.

Exhibitions: "Contemporary Ceramics of the Western Hemisphere," Special Mention for Excellence, 1941

### 222 Unknown Pueblo Potter
### (pseud., Raymond Watson's Mother)

*Bowl,* 1941
Earthenware
H. 5½, Diam. 13¼ in.
(13.75 × 33.1 cm.)
Marks: *U.S. #130* in pencil on bottom. Three labels read: (1) *circuit,*

(2) *7–2 6.00 / Raymond / Watson's / Mother,* (3) *177/40/35*
Gift of IBM Corporation
P.C. 63.46

Large hemispherical bowl in earthenware. The exterior is dark brown from bottom to shoulder. The bulging shoulder is white, surrounded with brown and red geometric designs and brown lines, and topped by a dark brown rim. The interior is white, with a red geometric pattern and two dark brown bands surrounding the rim. A brown, outlined floral design decorates the center. On the outer well two deer with arrows entering their mouths and leading to their hearts are painted in red and brown. This "entrance trail," as it is called, is a common Pueblo symbol for the breath of life.

Exhibitions: "Contemporary Ceramics of the Western Hemisphere," Honorable Mention, 1941

223

## MYRTON PURKISS (b. Canada)

Myrton Purkiss was born in Victoria, British Columbia and educated at the University of Southern California, and Chouinard Art Institute. He did research in England and France. He participated in the Ceramic National in 1941, and from 1947 through 1952. In 1952 he served as a member of the regional jury in Los Angeles.

### 223 Myrton Purkiss

*Plate,* c. 1941
Stoneware
H. 2¼, Diam. 15¾ in.
(5.6 × 40 cm.)
Marks: *M. Purkiss* brushed on well
Gift of IBM Corporation
P.C. 63.37

Large, footed stoneware plate with flared sides. The well is decorated with a still life of fruit, a vase, a fringed mat, and leaf forms in red, yellow, blue, green, brown, and black crackle glaze.

Exhibitions: "Contemporary Ceramics of the Western Hemisphere," 1941

### RUTH HUNIE RANDALL (1896–1983)

Born in Dayton, Ohio, Ruth Hunie Randall was educated at the Cleveland School of Art and Syracuse University under Montague Charman. She became Charman's assistant in 1930. In 1932 she went to Vienna, where she studied at the Kunstgewerbeschule. She continued to teach at Syracuse University until her retirement in 1962. She traveled widely and exhibited in the Ceramic Nationals from 1932 to 1962. Her works also were shown at the New York and San Francisco World's Fairs and the 1936 Exhibition of Decorative Arts in Paris.

Randall worked with both sculpture and the vessel. Her work was in the mainstream of American clay sculpture during this period.

### 224 Ruth Randall

*Madam Queen,* 1933
Earthenware
H. 11½, W. 8¼, D. 8 in. (28.75 × 20.6 × 20 cm.)
Marks: *Ruth H. Randall* incised on back, at bottom
Museum purchase   P.C. 50.643

Brown earthenware modeled head with semi-matte buff glazes, mounted on a black wood base.

The model for this piece was a Mrs. Shepherd who often sat for students in art classes at Syracuse University. She was one of Randall's favorite models. "Madam Queen" was a character from the Amos and Andy radio shows of the 1930s.

Exhibitions: "5th Ceramic National," 1936; "The Ceramic Art of Ruth Randall," 1960; "Ruth Randall Retrospective," Lowe Art Center, Syracuse University, 1962; "A Century of Ceramics in the United States, 1878–1978," 1979

### 225 Ruth Randall

*Winter Weasel,* 1938
Earthenware
H. 10¾, W. 4¾, D. 9½ in. (26.9 × 11.9 × 23.75 cm.)
Marks: *Ruth Randall* inscribed on bottom; *Winter Weasel* also inscribed on bottom, but partially covered by sticker
Gift of Mrs. Ralph Benedict in memory of her husband Ralph Benedict   P.C. 84.16

Earthenware sculpture of weasel, raised on hind legs, front legs forward and head turned aside. An opaque white matte glaze is used overall, with dark blue accenting the feet, tail, and facial features.

Exhibitions: "7th Ceramic National," 1938; "Golden Gate International Exposition," Palace of the Legion of Honor, San Francisco, 1939; "The Ceramic Art of Ruth Randall," 1960

224

## 226 Ruth Randall

*Tania,* 1947
Earthenware
H. 9¾, W. 8, D. 8½ in. (24.3 ×
20 × 21.25 cm.)
Marks: *Tania Roters Age 5* and *Ruth Randall '47* incised on back of base.
Four labels inside read: (1) *Ramona TANIA/born 3–23–42/died: 10–12–70,* (2) *Ruth Randall/ceramic head,* (3) *MEM. GIFT/Carl & Ramona/Roters '79,* and (4) *"Tania Roters/1947/5 years old*
Gift in memory of Tania Roters from Carl and Ramona Roters
P.C. 79.10.1

Modeled stoneware head of young girl. Opaque white crackle glaze is used overall, with the eyes accented in blue.

Exhibitions: "Ruth Hunie Randall: Ceramics 1923–1981," 1981

225

226

227

### HAROLD EATON RIEGGER (b. 1913)

Hal Riegger was born in Ithaca, New York and received his secondary education at the School of Organic Education, a progressive school in Fairhope, Alabama. He graduated from Alfred University and did graduate work at Ohio State University. He taught at the Philadelphia Museum School of Industrial Art, California School of Fine Arts in San Francisco, the University of Oregon, and Ohio State University. He operated his own studio and taught privately in Mill Valley, California.

Riegger is interested in the use of simple and natural materials, and advocates a return to nature for sources. He was a leading exponent of raku, a firing method in which a pot is removed from the kiln while still red hot and placed in a container of combustible material; the resulting carbonization creates unpredictable surface effects on the vessel.

He participated in the Ceramic Nationals from 1935 through 1951, and in 1958, 1962, 1964, and 1966, winning several prizes and serving as the chairman of the regional jury in San Francisco in 1948.

**227 Hal Riegger**
*Bottle,* 1939
Stoneware
H. 29½, Diam. 7½ inches (73.75 × 18.75 cm)
Marks: *H.E. Riegger* incised on bottom
Purchase prize given by Harshaw Chemical Corporation, "8th Ceramic National," 1939   P.C. 40.349

Large, brown stoneware bottle, unglazed. The amphora-shaped body has a long, thin neck and flared lip. Horizontal rings encircle the body and neck.

**228 Hal Riegger**
*Platter,* 1948
Stoneware
H. 2½, Diam. 17¼ in. (6.25 × 43.1 cm.)
Marks:*Hal* in script incised on bottom, with paper labels reading *Riegger/143* and *C of C/147* also on bottom
Purchase prize given by Harshaw Chemical Corporation, "13th Ceramic National," 1948   P.C. 49.570

Large platter with flared, ridged sides. The well has a spiral design with

solid areas in plum and ochre lusters on olive.

Exhibitions: "13th Ceramic National," Prize for Most Effective Use of Colors, 1948; "A Century of Ceramics in the United States, 1878–1978," 1979

### DOROTHY RIESTER (b. 1916)

Dorothy Riester studied at Carnegie Mellon University in Pittsburgh, where she majored in sculpture and minored in painting. She studied ceramics at the University of Pittsburgh under J. P. Thorley. She received an M.A. in sculpture and design from Syracuse University. Riester taught at Carnegie Mellon University, Syracuse University, and Cazenovia College in Central New York, and participated in the Ceramic National Exhibitions from 1954 through 1966.

A sculptor who works primarily in metal, Riester has received commissions in Syracuse from Temple Adath Yeshurin, Lincoln Bank, and Upstate Medical Center, and most recently Lake Forest, Illinois. Her studio is in Cazenovia, New York, where she resides with her husband Robert. The Riesters have been generous supporters of Everson Museum for many years.

**229 Dorothy Riester**
*County Fair,* 1943
Earthenware
H. 17½, W. 11, D. 7½ in. (43.75 × 27.5 × 18.75 cm.)
Marks: *D. Riester / County Fair / 1943* painted on bottom
Gift of the artist   P.C. 87.75

Earthenware sculpture of large horse, with five attendant figures—three men and two children. The opague glazes are in tans, white, blue, green, and brown. The sculpture rests on a black wood base.

### HENRY ROX (b. Germany, 1899)

Henry Rox was born in Berlin and educated at the Kunstgewerbeschule in Berlin-Charlottenburg, and at the académies Julian and Colarossi in Paris. He came to the United States in 1938 and became a citizen in 1946. He received a Guggenheim Fellowship in 1954, and was a professor of art at Mount Holyoke College and taught advanced sculpture at Worcester Art Museum. He worked on the motion picture *Fantasia* for

Disney Studios. Rox participated in the Ceramic Nationals from 1948 through 1954, and again in 1958. He served as a member of the regional jury in Boston in 1949, 1951, and 1954.

230 **Henry Rox**

*Repose,* c. 1950
Earthenware
H. 12½, W. 5½, L. 9¼ in. (31.25 × 13.75 × 23.1 cm.)
Marks: *HR* cypher incised on back bottom of left leg
Purchase prize given by National Sculpture Society, "15th Ceramic National," 1950 P.C. 51.614

Unglazed earthenware figure on black wooden base. The three-quarter length female nude is bent at hips with her head turned to the side, and her folded arms resting on the vertical section of the base.

228

229

230

231

### ALOYS SACKSTEDER (b. 1911)

Aloys Sacksteder was born in Dayton, Ohio and attended the Cleveland School of Art, Kent State University, and received an M.A. in ceramics from Ohio State University in 1939. Sacksteder taught at Indiana State Teacher's College, Terre Haute, Indiana, and participated in the Ceramic Nationals from 1936 through 1946.

**231** **Aloys Sacksteder**

*Fruit Bowl,* c. 1938
Earthenware
H. 3⅛, Diam. 8½ in.
(7.8 × 21.3 cm.)
Marks: *Aloys Sacksteder* incised on bottom
Purchase prize given by B. F. Drakenfeld, "6th Ceramic National," 1937 P.C. 38.282

Red earthenware, footed, flared bowl with foot covered in beige flecked glaze.

### PAUL ST. GAUDENS (1900–1954)

Born in Flint, Ohio, Paul St. Gaudens, the son of the sculptor Augustus St. Gaudens, was a craftsman, sculptor, writer, lecturer, and teacher. He studied at the Boston Museum of Fine Arts and with Alexander Archipenko and Charles Fergus Binns. He began to make pottery in 1921 in Cornish, New Hampshire. About 1924 he experimented with Mayan designs and became interested in primitive designs of other cultures. In 1936 he married Margaret Perry and set up Panther Hammock Pottery Studio in Coconut Grove, Florida, where they did collaborative work.

St. Gaudens participated in the Ceramic Nationals in 1933, 1934, and 1938.

**232** **Paul St. Gaudens**

*Pitcher,* c. 1933
Earthenware
H. 7, W. 7½ in. (17.5 × 18.75 cm.)
Marks: *P st. G / Cornish* incised on bottom
Museum purchase T.N. 34

Buff earthenware body with mahogany gloss glaze. This baluster-shaped pitcher on a raised foot has been wheel thrown. Its modeled handle is secured with simulated pegs. An applied, oriental motif decorates the shoulder below the pouring lip. Some glaze drips around the mouth. Throwing marks are evident around the body and neck.

Exhibitions: "2nd Robineau Memorial Exhibition," 1933

232

233

234

235

## WILLIAM SALTZMAN (b. 1916)

William Saltzman was born in Minneapolis, Minnesota and educated at the University of Minnesota. He was resident artist and director of the Rochester Art Center in Rochester, Minnesota from 1948 to 1964. In 1966 he took a teaching position at Macalester College in St. Paul.

Saltzman participated in the Ceramic Nationals in 1946.

### 233 William Saltzman

*Horses,* c. 1946
Earthenware
H. 7, W. 7½, D. 7½ in. (17.5 × 18.75 × 18.75 cm.)
Marks: *Horses: William Saltzman* written lightly in pencil on bottom of base
Museum purchase
P.C. 47.555.1, 2

Small, unglazed, stylized earthenware sculpture of two horses, with smoothly modeled surface and applied dots of clay. The manes and tails are roughly incised, with clay dots for eyes.

Exhibitions: "11th Ceramic National," 1946

## HERBERT SANDERS (1909–1988)

Herbert Sanders was born in New Waterford, Ohio and studied with Arthur Baggs at Ohio State University, where he received a Ph.D., the first granted in ceramics in the United States. He was an instructor of ceramics at Ohio State from 1935 to 1938, when he moved to California and established the ceramics department at San José State College. He stayed on as full professor, continuing his research, and later went to Japan as a Fulbright Research Scholar of ceramics from 1958 to

1959. He was awarded the California State Colleges Distinguished Teaching Award in 1966. Sanders was a regular participant in the Ceramic Nationals, exhibiting each year except 1935, 1948, 1951, and 1954. He also was invited to exhibit in "Ceramics 70 Plus Woven Forms" at Everson Museum in 1970.

Herbert Sanders was an important figure in the contemporary ceramics movement for both his teaching and research and for his willingness to share his discoveries and knowledge. He did extensive research in decoration and glazes, especially crystalline and luster glazes. His work is reserved, classic, and refined.

### 234 Herbert Sanders

*Vase,* 1937
Stoneware
H. 11¼, Diam. 7½ in.
(28.1 × 18.8 cm.)
Marks: *H. H. Sanders 1937* incised on bottom
Purchase prize given by E. I. DuPont Nemours Company "7th Ceramic National," 1938   P.C. 39.344

Buff stoneware vase, ovoid shape with short neck and small mouth. Incised bands and black designs decorate the upper half of the vase. Painted bands surround the bottom.

This vase was made prior to Sanders's move to San José State in 1938.

### 235 Herbert Sanders

*Bowl,* 1937
Stoneware
H. 6¾, Diam. 8⅞ in.
(16.9 × 22.1 cm.)
Marks: *H. H. Sanders 1937*
Purchase prize given by E. I. DuPont Nemours Company, "7th Ce-

ramic National," 1938   P.C. 39.345

High, ovoid, footed bowl. The gray-green stoneware body is covered in a brown slip, spatter decoration. Three incised lines circle the body one-half inch from the top, and two

narrow bands are just above the foot.

Exhibitions: "Golden Gate International Exposition," Palace of the Legion of Honor, San Francisco, 1939

236

## EDWIN SCHEIER (b. 1910)
## MARY SCHEIER (b. 1910)

Edwin and Mary Scheier have been working together in clay since their marriage in 1937. Mary studied at the Art Students League and Parsons School of Design, but both of them were largely self-taught in ceramics. During the Depression they taught and worked with the Federal Arts Project in Tennessee, and they set up their first pottery in Glade Spring, Virginia.

As a result of contacts made at a conference they attended at Black Mountain College in North Carolina they took positions at the University of New Hampshire in 1938, Edwin as instructor and Mary as artist-in-residence. During the Second World War Mary assumed Edwin's teaching duties while he was in the army, and she also taught at the Rhode Island School of Design. After the war, the Scheiers participated in Operation Bootstrap, a program in which their role was to set up a production pottery in Puerto Rico. They returned to their positions in New Hampshire, where they remained until their retirement in 1960. They then moved to Oaxaca, Mexico, where they continued to work, Ed-

win expanding his interests to other media. They have lived in Green Valley, Arizona since 1979.

The work of the Scheiers reveals the influences of ancient and primitive art, including that of ancient and contemporary Mexico. Mary made functional pieces, elegant in form and sensitive to the needs of the user. She also threw pots for Edwin to decorate. His use of line, incised or modeled, was graceful, flowing, and full of expression, always suited to the form. He often dealt with narrative subjects, universal themes of birth, regeneration, or ritual, influenced by the primitive art in which he was so interested.

The Scheiers were continuous participants in the Ceramic Nationals from 1940 through 1966, except in 1960, 1962, and 1968, and they won many awards.

### 236 Edwin and Mary Scheier
*From left to right:*
*Vase,* c. 1940
Stoneware
H. 7½, Diam. 4 in. (18.75 × 10 cm.)
Marks: *MADE IN VIRGINIA* incised on bottom, with illegible stamp
Purchase prize given by Onondaga Pottery Company, "Contemporary

Ceramics of the Western Hemisphere," 1941   P.C. 41.361

Brown stoneware, tapered, cylindrical vase with brown glazed interior. The unglazed exterior is encircled with roughly ridged lines, imparting an earthy, primitive look.

*Vase,* c. 1940
Stoneware
H. 9⅜, Diam. 5⅜ in.
(23.4 × 13.4 cm.)
Marks: *Scheier* incised on bottom
Purchase prize given by Onondaga Pottery Company "Contemporary Ceramics of the Western Hemisphere," 1941   P.C. 42.525

Brown stoneware vase, gently gourd-shaped, with low foot. Incised rings run from the top to bottom on the unglazed exterior.

*Bowl,* 1940
Stoneware
H. 4¾, Diam. 7½ in.
(11.8 × 18.75 cm.)
Marks: none
Purchase prize given by Hanovia Chemical Company, "9th Ceramic National," 1940   P.C. 41.362

Brown stoneware bowl, wheel thrown, with brown glazed interior.

The unglazed exterior is encircled with raised stick figures, alternating male, female, and child with halo. An applied blossom is below each child.

### 237 Edwin and Mary Scheier
*Clockwise, beginning at left:*
*Bowl,* c. 1940
Stoneware
H. 5⅛, Diam. 8⅛ in.
(12.8 × 20.3 cm.)
Marks: none
Purchase prize given by Onondaga Pottery Company, "Contemporary Ceramics of the Western Hemisphere," 1941   P.C. 42.524.4

Slightly flared stoneware bowl with incised band of figures. The figures stand with upraised arms, creating a rhythmic pattern around the upper two-thirds of the vessel. The exterior is unglazed, the interior is brown glazed.

*Vase,* c. 1940
Stoneware
H. 9¾, Diam. 6⅛ in.
(24.3 × 15.3 cm.)
Marks: *Scheier* incised on bottom
Purchase prize given by Onondaga Pottery Company, "Contemporary Ceramics of the Western Hemisphere," 1941   P.C. 42.524.5

Tall, stoneware vase which tapers gradually to low foot ring. The piece is narrowly ridged overall, with two bands of incised figures with wide stances and flowing hair. The figures hold hands, creating a rhythmic movement around the body. The interior is glazed in brown, while the exterior remains unglazed.

*Bowl,* c. 1940
Stoneware
H. 4⅛, Diam. 6 in. (10.3 × 15 cm.)
Marks: none
Purchase prize given by Onondaga Pottery Company, "Contemporary Ceramics of the Western Hemisphere," 1941   P.C. 42.524.1

Brown stoneware bowl with low foot and brown glazed interior. Six incised stick figures encircle the unglazed exterior of the bowl in a paper-doll fashion. A small, leafy plant form is below the point where the figures link. The figures' features are roughly incised, with freely flying wavy hair suggested.

*Bowl,* c. 1940
Stoneware
H. 3, Diam. 4½ in. (7.5 × 11.25 cm.)

Marks: *Scheier* incised on bottom
Purchase prize given by Onondaga
Pottery Company, "Contemporary
Ceramics of the Western Hemi-
sphere," 1941  P.C. 42.524.3

Small, footed, brown stoneware
bowl with brown glazed interior.
The unglazed exterior is decorated
with four incised female figures
doing handsprings and creating a
rhythmic, linear pattern that surrounds the form.

Exhibitions: "Forms from the Earth:
1,000 Years of Pottery in America,"
Museum of Contemporary Crafts,
New York, 1960

*Bowl,* c. 1940
Stoneware
H. 3¼, Diam. 4¼ in. (8.1 × 10.6 cm.)
Marks: *Scheier* incised on bottom
Purchase prize given by Onondaga
Pottery Company, "Contemporary
Ceramics of the Western Hemi-
sphere," 1941  P.C. 42.524.2

Small, footed, brown stoneware
bowl with brown-glazed interior.
Five incised female running figures
surround the unglazed exterior.

### 238 Edwin and Mary Scheier

*Coffee Set,* c. 1941
Stoneware
Coffee Pot: H. 8¾, W. 9 in. (21.8 ×
22.5 cm.). Covered sugar: H. 3¾,
Diam. 3 in. (9.3 × 7.5 cm.). Cup:
H. 2¼, Diam. 2½ in. (5.6 × 6.25
cm.). Saucer: H. ½, Diam. 5¼ in.
(1.25 × 13.1 cm.). Creamer (not pictured): H. 3¼, W. 4¼ in. (8.1 ×
10.6 cm.)
Marks: *Scheier* incised on bottoms of
pot and saucers
Purchase prize given by Richard B.
Gump, "12th Ceramic National,"
1948  P.C. 48.551.1–9

Coffee set with red-brown stoneware
body and gray glaze, includes eight
cups and saucers, creamer, covered
sugar, and covered coffee pot. The
oviform coffee pot has low foot, long
thin tapering spout, flat, ridged ear-
shaped handle, and flat lid with tapered knob. The bulbous, footed
sugar has an extended, upturned
rim, and flat cover with tapered knob.
The footed saucer has an upturned
rim. The small cups are also footed,
with bulbous shapes and ridged, tear-
drop handles.
    This group received a Purchase
Prize in the "12th Ceramic National,"
1948, for the best ceramic design

suitable for mass production.

Exhibitions: "Forms from the Earth:
1,000 Years of Pottery in America,"
Museum of Contemporary Crafts,

New York, 1960; "A Century of Ceramics in the United States, 1878–
1978," 1979

237

238

239

**239 Edwin Scheier**

*Bowl,* c. 1949
Stoneware
H. 10¾, Diam. 8 in. (26.8 × 20 cm.)
Marks: *Scheier* incised on bottom
Purchase prize given by Onondaga
Pottery Company, "14th Ceramic
National," 1949   P.C. 50.640

Deep, ovoid stoneware bowl with
wide mouth. The body of the bowl
is treated with sgraffito on brown
slip. A series of incised, primitive figures with raised breasts surrounds
the bowl. Buff and blue tones are
used on the shoulder.

This bowl is a fine example of the
use of primitive motifs in the work
of Edwin Scheier. The figures always
conform to the contours of the vessel, in a rhythmic, graceful, and inventive manner. The design is strong,
sure, and fully realized.

## CARL SCHMITZ
### (b. France, 1900–1967)

Carl Schmitz was educated in his native France and also studied at the State School of Applied Art and the State Academy of Fine Art in Munich. He studied under Jennewein, Milles, and Manship at the Beaux-Arts Institute of Design in New York and established his own studio there in 1930. He taught at Michigan State College and the National Academy of Design. He preferred to work in clay, though he did work in other materials as well.

Schmitz participated in the Ceramic Nationals from 1938 through 1952, and again in 1958, and was a frequent award winner.

### 240 Carl Schmitz

*Seated Woman,* c. 1934
Earthenware
H. 11⅛, W. 7⅞, D. 8⅞ in. (27.8 × 19.6 × 22.1 cm.)
Marks: remains of label which reads: *Pa. Academy of Fine Arts/13th Annual Exhibition of Painting & Sculpture 1935*
Gift of the artist   P.C. 39.325

240

Earthenware sculpture of seated nude girl, left arm resting on her head, which is cast downward. The figure leans on the right leg and arm.

Exhibitions: "Annual Exhibition of Painting and Sculpture," Pennsylvania Academy of Fine Arts, 1935; "8th Ceramic National," 1939

### 241 Carl Schmitz

*Woman With a Lute,* c. 1940
Earthenware
H. 31¾, W. 10, D. 10 in. (79.3 × 25 × 25 cm.)
Marks: none on figure. Metal plate affixed to front reads: *Woman with Lute/Carl J. Schmitz/United States*
Gift of IBM Corporation
P.C. 63.42

Earthenware sculpture in neoclassic style; the female figure is draped mid-waist and holds a lute in her left hand.

Exhibitions: "Contemporary Ceramics of the Western Hemisphere," 1941; "The Art Deco Environment," 1976

241

242

## DON SCHRECKENGOST (b. 1911)

Don Schreckengost was born into a family of potters in Sebring, Ohio. He studied at the Cleveland School of Art, and in Stockholm and Mexico. He became a professor of industrial ceramic design at Alfred University in 1935. He left Alfred in 1945 to become design director of Homer Laughlin China Company, and in 1960 formed his own company, Design for Industry. Schreckengost designed for Hall China Company, Salem China Company, Summitville Tiles, and the Royal China Company, among others.

Don Schreckengost has had a long and varied career in both industrial and studio ceramics. He received the Charles Fergus Binns award and has been recognized by the American Ceramic Society. He participated in the Ceramic National Exhibitions from 1938 through 1946, and again in 1950, when he served as chairman of the national jury of selection and awards.

**242 Don Schreckengost**
*Rodeo,* 1941
Earthenware
H. 2¼, Diam. 19 in. (5.6 × 47.5 cm.)

243

Marks: *D. SCHRECKENGOST + 41 + p* brushed under glaze on back
Gift of IBM Corporation
P.C. 63.43

Large, footed earthenware plate with slightly flared rim and flat well. A linear illustration of a cowboy holding a bull by its horns decorates the well in black. A clear glaze covers the entire piece, including the foot.

Exhibitions: "Contemporary Ceramics of the Western Hemisphere," 1941

**243 Don Schreckengost**
*Decorative Floral Plate,* 1939
Stoneware
H. 1¼, Diam. 19 in. (3.1 × 47.5 cm.)
Marks: *Don Schreckengost 1939* on underside near rim
Gift of IBM Corporation
P.C. 63.141

Large, flat stoneware plate with slightly flared sides. A floral decoration with large central flower surrounded by smaller flowers, leaves, pear and fruit forms in linear design is incised into the plate. A green glaze covers the piece.

## VIKTOR SCHRECKENGOST (b. 1906)

Viktor Schreckengost's great grandfather and grandfather were potters, and his father worked for the Sebring Pottery. His brother, Don, is also a ceramist. Schreckengost was born in Sebring, Ohio, and attended Cleveland Institute of Art, where he was a sculpture student. He also studied with Michael Powolny at the Kunstgewerbeschule in Vienna in 1929. He later returned to Europe and also traveled through Russia, Turkey, and northern Africa.

Schreckengost was a designer at the Cowan Pottery in Rocky River, a suburb of Cleveland, where he produced his famed punch bowls commissioned by Eleanor Roosevelt. He spent a summer in Hollywood, where his work often appeared in movies. He also taught at Western Reserve University, and served as art director and designer for American Limoges China Company, Sebring Pottery Company, and the Salem China Company.

Schreckengost became an industrial designer and has chaired the industrial design department at Cleveland Institute of Art for many years. He has also designed for manufacturers of ceramic, steel, and glass products, among them Murray of Ohio Company. He received the Charles Fergus Binns Medal and was made a Fellow and Honorary Life Member of the American Ceramic Society. He participated in every Ceramic National from 1933 through 1956, was a frequent prize winner, and often served on the juries.

Viktor Schreckengost is an important figure in American ceramics. Early in his career he worked in the Viennese style and helped introduce the Austrian techniques and imagery to his fellow Americans. His sculptural work is witty, sophisticated, and well crafted, and his carved clay vessels are strong and monumental. He has been as effective as a teacher as he has been as an artist.

244

245

## 244 Viktor Schreckengost

*Cacao (Hewn Bowl),* 1947
Earthenware
H. 8¾, L. 16¾, W. 9¼ in. (21.8 × 41.8 × 23.1 cm.)
Marks: *Viktor Schreckengost '47* incised on bottom
Purchase prize given by Hall China Company, "12th Ceramic National," 1947   P.C. 48.552

Hewn, earthenware bowl, oval-shaped with pinched end. The interior is in a beige and gray crackle glaze. The dark brown exterior is incised but unglazed.

Color and shape combine in this piece to form an organic unity. Aptly named, Schreckengost's piece clearly resembles a halved cocoa bean in color and shape.

Exhibitions: "Forms from the Earth: 1,000 Years of Pottery in America," Museum of Contemporary Crafts, New York, 1960; "Viktor Schreck-engost Retrospective Exhibition," Cleveland Institute of Art, 1976

## 245 Viktor Schreckengost

*Oblongata,* c. 1950
Stoneware
H. 16, L. 19, W. 8½ in. (40 × 47.5 × 25 cm.)
Marks: none
Purchase prize given by B. F. Drakenfeld Company, "15th Ceramic National," 1950   P.C. 51.594

Large, hewn stoneware vase. The sides taper to a long, thin ovoid neck. An incised line runs along the rim and one inch below the neck. The gray glaze, with white abstract designs on the sides, fades to darker gray on the lower half of the piece.

Schreckengost ceased to work in clay during the 1950s. This vessel and *Cacao* were formed by carving from a large piece of clay, rather than by modeling and adding pieces, as with his earlier sculptural work. This change in technique was prompted by medical problems with his back which prevented him from lifting

246

heavy lumps of clay. He did continue to work in industrial and commercial ceramics, however.

Exhibitions: "Viktor Schreckengost Retrospective Exhibition," Cleveland Institute of Art, 1976

## 246 Viktor Schreckengost
*Keramos,* 1938
Earthenware
H. 19¼, W. 13½, D. 11½ in. (48.1 × 33.75 × 28.75 cm.)
Marks: none

Gift of the artist  P.C. 42.472

Brown earthenware sculpture, mask-like in form, depicting the head of the bearded Greek god Keramos, patron of ceramists. The head is crowned with leaves and stars. The left hand of the figure holds a vessel. The head is mainly unglazed, with glaze on crown, beard, lips, eyes, lettering, and vessel.

The grapes and garlands in the crown of Keramos refer to his father, Bacchus, while the seven white stars

symbolize Ariadne, his mother, whose crown was thrown into the heavens by Bacchus to become her constellation upon her death. The vessel that Keramos holds was fashioned by the god to hold his mother's ashes. Letters applied to the vessel spell out "Keramos," while similar letters applied to his neck read "Bacchus" and "Ariadne."

This sculpture, done after Schreckengost's return from his second trip abroad, shows a strong

Viennese influence, with its hand-built sections, hollow form, and applied clay decoration.

Exhibitions: "8th Ceramic National," 1939; "Art Deco Environment," 1976; "Viktor Schreckengost Retrospective Exhibition," Cleveland Institute of Art, 1976; "A Century of Ceramics in the United States, 1878–1978," 1979; "The Diversions of Keramos, American Clay Sculpture 1925–1950," 1983

## 247 Viktor Schreckengost

*The Dictator,* 1939
Earthenware
H. 13, W. 12½, D. 10½ in. (32.5 ×
31.25 × 26.25 cm.)
Marks: blue label affixed to bottom
reads: *All Ohio Crafts Cincinnati O
— 1941 /Viktor Schreckengost /2366
Noble Street /Cleveland Ohio / "The
Dictator" 50.00*
Gift of the artist   P.C. 86.13

Glazed earthenware sculpture depicting seated Nero strumming a
lyre. A lion sleeps at his feet, and
putti in the forms of Hitler, Mus-
solini, Stalin, and Hirohito, climb
about the throne. Each figure holds
his attribute: swastika, fasces, ham-
mer and sickle, and flag with rising
sun.

This piece is unusual because of
its political references. Most sculpture produced by studio ceramists
during this period was witty and light-
hearted, but here Schreckengost,
while retaining his sense of humor,
has issued a warning of things to
come. He had just returned from Europe, where he saw the effects of the
Nazi regime and wished to send a
warning to the American people. Be-
lieving that humor would be an effective tool in focusing attention on
the situation, Schreckengost created
this piece, which is technically exceptional and carefully conceived, as
well as witty and provocative.

Exhibitions: "9th Ceramic National," 1940; "A Century of Ceramics in the United States, 1878–
1978," 1979; "The Diversions of
Keramos, American Clay Sculpture
1925–1950," 1983

## 248 Viktor Schreckengost

*Spring,* 1941
Earthenware
H. 15, W. 30, D. 7¾ in. (37.5 ×
75 × 19.3 cm.)
Marks: none
Gift of IBM Corporation
P.C. 63.44

Earthenware sculpture with polychrome matte and high gloss glazes
depicting a leaping lion with a lamb
springing playfully over his back.
The lion has an aqua mane and tail,
with orange mouth and eyes. Other
details are in black and white. The
lamb is white with black details and
an orange flower in his mouth. Aqua
flowers are scattered on base.

This sculptural pun is indicative

247

248

of the humor found in the work of
Schreckengost and other ceramists
during this period. Animals were a
favorite subject of Schreckengost's
and he was always able to accent
those attributes that seemed most expressive of the nature of each animal,
whether with form, color, or texture.

249

250

## DONALD SIEGFRIED

Donald Siegfried lived in San Francisco and participated in the Ceramic National Exhibitions from 1948 through 1950.

### 249 Donald Siegfried

*Tall Jar,* c. 1950
Earthenware
H. 27¾, Diam. 8¾ in.
(69.3 × 21.8 cm.)
Marks: *Don Siegfried* incised on bottom
Purchase prize given by Hanovia Chemical Company, "15th Ceramic National," 1950   P.C. 51.597

Tall, club-shaped earthenware jar with trumpet neck and slight lip. Vertical lines incised from shoulder to base surround the body.

## RICHARD V. SMITH (b. 1912)

Richard Smith was born in Marcellus Falls, New York and studied architecture and design at Syracuse University and ceramics at Alfred University. He worked in the ceramics laboratories at Pass and Seymour in Syracuse, and at the Onondaga Pottery Company. He also taught at Syracuse University. With his wife, painter Betty Wose Smith, he did research to discover the techniques of Greek Attic pottery and of Egyptian faience of the Roman period and earlier.

Smith was active in the organization of the Ceramic National Exhibitions and has been a generous supporter of Everson Museum, serving on the Board of Trustees and on many committees. He participated in the Ceramic Nationals in 1934, 1937 through 1952 except 1941, and in 1960 and 1964.

### 250 Richard Smith

*Bowl,* 1937
Stoneware
H. 2⁷⁄₁₆, Diam. 10⁵⁄₁₆ in. (5.1 × 25.1 cm.)
Marks: artist's cypher, *1937, 1.13* and *190*–all incised on bottom
Purchase prize given by B. F. Drakenfeld Company, "6th Ceramic National," 1937   P.C. 38.283

Buff stoneware, footed bowl with wide, gently sloping rim and deep hemispherical well. A rich blue soda glaze is used overall, with an intense yellow crescent band sweeping along one side of the rim. The crescent band, coupled with the rich blue glaze, implies an eclipse, or other celestial event.

## WILLIAM SWALLOW (b. 1912)

William Swallow was educated in his native Pennsylvania at the Pennsylvania Museum School of Art and the University of Pennsylvania. He taught at the Pennsylvania Museum School in Philadelphia and at Muhlenberg College and was Director of Art at South Whitehall Consolidated Schools in Allentown, Pennsylvania. He participated in the Ceramic Nationals from 1940 through 1958, except in 1954, and won several prizes.

251 **William Swallow**

*The Amish Way,* c. 1941
Earthenware
H. 15, W. 32½, D. 2½ in. (37.5 × 81.25 × 6.25 cm.)
Marks: *W W SWALLOW* incised on bottom left front of right end piece
Gift of IBM Corporation
P.C. 63.45

Four earthenware wall tiles in relief with incising. Each tile depicts a task in everyday Amish life: a woman churning butter, women at market, men tending farm animals, and a man cutting wheat with a scythe.

Exhibitions: "Contemporary Ceramics of the Western Hemisphere," 1941

252 **William Swallow**

*The Cow with the Silver Horns,* c. 1946
Earthenware
H. 14½, L. 23 (36.25 × 57.5 cm.)
Marks: none
Purchase prize given by National Sculpture Society, "11th Ceramic National," 1946  P.C. 47.514

Stained earthenware sculpture of a grazing cow. The black cow has silver horns and incised details on its face and ears. Incised decoration in Pennsylvania German buttermold designs embellishes the cow's back. Incised markings also indicate grass on the area under the cow's belly.

Exhibitions: "11th Ceramic National," Purchase Prize for the work of sculpture possessing highest sculptural quality regardless of production method, 1946; "The Animal Kingdom in American Art," 1978

251

252

## SYRACUSE CHINA CORPORATION

The history of Syracuse China Corporation begins with a small stoneware pottery, Geddes Rockingham Pottery, established in the village of Geddes, now a part of the city of Syracuse, by Williams Farrar (entries 41–43). The Farrar pottery became Empire Pottery Company, which was then reorganized as Onondaga Pottery Company in 1871 (entry 91). Situated on the Erie Canal, the Company had the advantage of easy transportation of both raw materials and the finished product. Onondaga Pottery developed a high-fire tableware that was called Syracuse China. The name of the firm officially became Syracuse China Corporation in 1966.

Syracuse China was one of the finest porcelain tablewares produced in the United States for many years. The Corporation, now a subsidiary of Canadian Pacific (U.S.), Limited, has become one of the world's largest manufacturers of fine commercial dinnerware. (See also entries 540, 541, and page 10.)

### 253 Syracuse China Corporation

Bertram L. Watkin, modeler
*Bust of Charles Lindberg,* 1927
Porcelain
H. 16¼, W. 12¼, D. 8¾ in. (40.6 ×

30.6 × 21.8 cm.)
Marks: *BERTRAM L. WATKIN MODELER 27 7 27* incised on back
Gift of Anna T. Zalewski in Memory of Walter Floyd Zalewski
P.C. 85.72

Unglazed porcelain bust of Charles Lindberg.

Syracuse China Corporation produced seven or eight of these busts of Lindberg, probably in commemoration of his famous flight. Lindberg had visited Syracuse in July of 1927, and had been presented with a gift of Syracuse China.

This bust, which had suffered kiln damage (now repaired), was given to Walter Zalewski, who worked at Syracuse China, by Richard Pass, then president of the company.

### 254 Syracuse China Corporation

*Nature Study, Poppies,* c. 1935
Porcelain
H. ⅞, Diam. 10½ in.
(2.1 × 26.3 cm.)
Marks: *Old Ivory/Syracuse China/O.P. Co.* and *Nature Study, Poppies* stamped under glaze, on back
Gift of Ronald A. Kuchta and anonymous gift    P.C. 87.100.1, 2 and 83.23.1, 2

Flat porcelain plates with wide ledge.

254

The ledges are black with a green stripe and white rim. The green stripe separates the ledge from the white well, on which appears floral motifs.

## CARL WALTERS (1883–1955)

Trained as a painter, Carl Walters brought to ceramics an interest in surface decoration and a sensitivity to color. He studied at the Chase School under Robert Henri and was closely associated with the artists of the Ash Can School. His interest in ceramics led him to Woodstock, where he opened a studio in 1922. Walters's animal forms are not literally descriptive, and he used color and surface ornament for its own sake, rather than for a representational purpose. Animals were his favorite subject, but he also did vessels and "figures in cabinet," or figures set within a box or niche reminiscent of medieval wood carvings.

Walters was mainly self-taught as a ceramist, and was also an accomplished glassmaker and jeweler, as well as a painter. Though he seldom accepted students in his early years, he later established the ceramics department at Norton School of Art in West Palm Beach, Florida. He participated in the Ceramic National Exhibitions from 1935 through 1949, except in 1940 and 1948, serving as a member of the jury in 1935 and 1947.

### 255 Carl Walters

*Cat,* 1938
Earthenware
H. 11½, L. 23, D. 7 in. (29 × 57.5 × 17.5 cm.)
Marks: *Walters 1939* inscribed on bottom, *H* within a circle and a

horse's head incised on bottom
Museum purchase    P.C. 81.26

Earthenware sculpture of crouching cat, tail curled around one side. Black-and-white, zebra-like pattern is used allover.

Exhibitions: "The Animal Kingdom in American Art," 1978; "A Century of Ceramics in the United States, 1878–1978," 1979; "The Diversions of Keramos, American Clay Sculpture 1925–1950," 1983

## RANDOLPH WEBB (b. 1913)

Randolph Webb was born in Burns, New York and had a studio in Alfred, New York. Although legally blind, he worked successfully in earthenware and stoneware from local clay. He participated in the Ceramic Nationals from 1935 through 1938, 1948 through 1950, and in 1958.

### 256 Randolph Webb

*Bowl,* c. 1948
Stoneware
H. 6, Diam. 12½ in. (15 × 31.25 cm.)
Marks: none
Purchase prize given by U. S. Potters Association, "13th Ceramic National," 1948    P.C. 49.571

Stoneware bowl with flared sides. The interior is buff with a wide brown band at top, and a green and brown ring beneath. Two brown and blue rings are on and near the bottom. A rust and green linear design is brushed on the brown ring at the top. The exterior is buff with a rust and green brushed design on two sides.

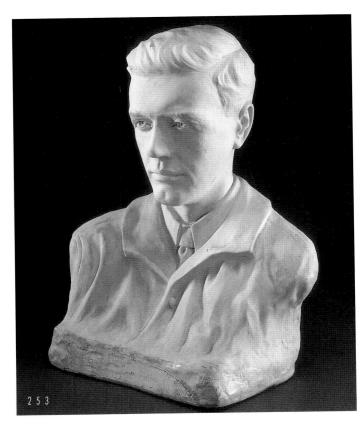

253

255

256

## EGON WEINER (b. Austria, 1906)

Egon Weiner received his art education in his native Vienna, first as a woodcarver's apprentice, then at the School for Arts and Crafts and the Academy of Fine Arts, where he earned an M.F.A. He was a professor of sculpture and life-drawing at the Art Institute of Chicago, where he was named Professor Emeritus in 1971. He served as an educational consultant for the International Film Bureau of Chicago, and received many awards. He participated in the Ceramic Nationals from 1947 through 1952, and in 1958.

### 257 Egon Weiner

*Philosopher,* c. 1948
Earthenware
H. 26¾, W. 10½, D. 12½ in. (66.8 × 26.25 × 31.25 cm.)
Marks: *Weiner* incised on base of sculpture
Purchase prize given by Harper Electric Furnace Corporation, "13th Ceramic National," 1948
P.C. 49.572

Earthenware sculpture of over lifesize head of Nietzsche, mounted on a wooden base. The head tilts forward and the eyes are downcast, with great eyebrows. Weiner's sculpture effectively creates the essence of a man deeply engrossed in thought, with its carefully modeled details and features.

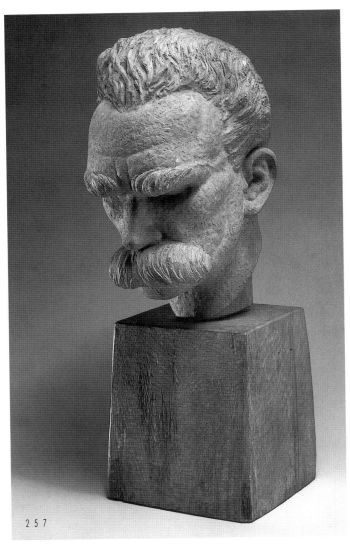

257

258

## DAVID WEINRIB (b. 1924)

Born in New York City, David Weinrib studied at Brooklyn College and Alfred University. He studied painting at the Academmia in Florence and was a potter in residence at Black Mountain College in North Carolina from 1952 to 1954. In 1954, with his wife Karen Karnes, he worked at Stony Point, Long Island. He concentrated on slab-built pieces and eventually gave up clay in favor of other materials. He has become internationally recognized for his sculpture.

Weinrib participated in the Ceramic Nationals from 1949 through 1958. In 1958 he won a Gold Medal at the Second International Congress of Contemporary Ceramics in Ostend, Belgium.

### 258 David Weinrib

*Pair of Vases,* c. 1949
Stoneware
Each: H. 8, Diam. 4¾ in. (20 × 11.8 cm.)
Marks: none
Purchase prize given by Hanovia Chemical Company, "14th Ceramic National," 1949 P.C. 50.585.1, 2

Pair of red stoneware vases, each with slight lip. The first is a footed cylindrical shape with brown, white, and green vertical stripes and an incised linear design. The second is ovoid in shape with brown, white, and orange vertical stripes and an incised linear design.

## VALERIE WIESELTHIER (b. Austria, 1895–1945)

Vally Wieselthier was already a successful artist when she came to the United States from her native Vienna. She had studied at the Kunstgewerbeschule under Michael Powolny and had worked at the Wiener Werkstätte with Josef Hoffmann. She had her own ceramic studio in Vienna, "Keramische Werkstätte Vally Wieselthier," and also worked at Bimini Werkstätte. She visited the United States several times, beginning in 1929 when she was given a solo exhibition in New York. She eventually settled here permanently. She worked at Sebring Pottery, taught at Tulane University, and eventually opened her own studio in New York on East 8th Street. Wieselthier designed wallpaper, jewelry, fabrics, glass, and furniture, while also working in ceramics. She made both sculpture and vessels, and participated in the Ceramic Nationals in 1933, 1938, 1940, and 1941.

Wieselthier was important in American ceramics not only for her own work, which was witty and sophisticated, but also because she brought to the United States a new attitude toward clay that valued the expressive qualities of the medium and recognized the potential of color. She created her sculpture with thrown sections and slabs and coils of clay, which she assembled to create the final object. This carefree style was readily adopted by the Americans, who were eager to break away from the traditional molded ware which was then being produced in America.

259 **Vally Wieselthier**
*Taming the Unicorn,* c. 1941
Earthenware
H. 21, W. 15, D. 15 in. (52.5 × 37.5 × 37.5 cm.)
Marks: none
Gift of IBM Corporation
P.C. 63.47

Hollow earthenware sculpture of maiden riding a unicorn. The maiden is half-length but only the unicorn's head is portrayed. The unicorn is fully modeled, while the maiden has applied ringlets and a veil. Flowing brown, black, blue, and flesh colored gloss glazes are used.

This piece fully illustrates the Viennese style that Wieselthier helped to promulgate in America. The sections are hollow, with details applied and glazes loosely handled. The light-hearted attitude toward the subject is also typical of the Austrians, and became a trademark of American ceramists during this period. The arched eyebrows and wide-set eyes of the maiden are also found in works by other Viennese artists of this time and were seized upon by the Americans who worked in the Austrian style, especially Thelma Frazier Winter and other Cleveland ceramists.

Exhibitions: "Contemporary Ceramics of the Western Hemisphere," Purchase Prize, 1941; "The Animal Kingdom in Art," 1978; "A Century of Ceramics in the United States, 1878–1978," 1979; "The Diversions of Keramos, American Clay Sculpture 1925–1950," 1983

259

260 **Vally Wieselthier**
*Bowl,* n.d.
Earthenware
H. 2⅜, Diam. 8¼ in.
(6.5 × 20.6 cm.)
Marks: *Vally* incised on bottom
Gift of Mr. Howard Lanis
P.C. 84.21

Pinkish-orange earthenware bowl with flared sides and low foot-ring. A turquoise crackle glaze is used overall, except at the foot where the clay body is exposed.

260

261

## MARGUERITE WILDENHAIN
### (b. France, 1896–1985)

Marguerite Wildenhain was educated at the Kunstgewerbeschule in Berlin and at the Bauhaus in Weimar, where she studied with Kandinsky, Feininger, Moholy-Nagy, and Krehan, and earned a master's degree. She taught at the academy in Halle-Saale and designed for the Royal Prussian Manufactory in Berlin from 1929 to 1933, when she opened a studio in Putten, Holland. She came to the United States in 1940, taught at the California College of Arts and Crafts in Oakland, and in 1942 set up a studio and workshop in Guerneville, California, called Pond Farm. She participated in the Ceramic National Exhibitions in 1940 (with her husband Frans), 1946, and 1947.

After settling in California, Wildenhain, who had often designed for commercial potteries, rejected mass-production methods and advocated a return to handcraftsmanship. Through her teaching, writings, and work she has played a major role in bringing the Bauhaus aesthetic to American ceramics. Wildenhain was awarded the Charles Fergus Binns

Medal by the American Ceramic Society.

### 261 Marguerite Wildenhain
*Tea Set,* c. 1946
Stoneware
Pot: H. 5, W. 10 in. (12.5 × 25 cm.). Sugar: H. 2½, Diam. 4½ in. (6.25 × 11.25 cm.). Creamer: H. 3, W. 5½ in. (7.5 × 13.75 cm.). Cups: H. 2¼, Diam. 3¾ in. (5.6 × 9.3 cm.). Saucers: H. 1, Diam. 6 in. (2.5 × 15 cm.)
Marks: *Pond/Farm* over jug shape incised on bottom of pot
Purchase prize given by Richard B. Gump, "11th Ceramic National," 1946   P.C. 47.515.1–13

Hand-thrown, tan stoneware tea set includes covered teapot, sugar, creamer, and five cups with saucers. The footed, squat, globular teapot has a tapered spout and curved ear-shaped handle. The rim is raised and the lid, with knob, is recessed. The pot has gray speckle glaze from top to shoulder and on spout and handle, as well as on lid. The footed, round sugar bowl has the same gray glaze on upper half and interior. The round, footed creamer has a pinched spout

and ear-shaped handle, with the same gray glaze on the upper half and the interior.

This tea set illustrates Wildenhain's ability to unify form and function, and retain the integrity of the material. Her work is spare but fully realized. There is also a sense of the presence of the artist in these pieces, evidence that they were handcrafted,

but with full control of both material and technique. Ironically, this set was awarded a purchase prize for the best ceramic design suitable for mass production in the "11th Ceramic National," 1946.

Exhibitions: "A Century of Ceramics in the United States, 1878–1978," 1979

262

## HELEN WILLIAMS (b. 1907)

Helen Williams was born in Syracuse and studied under Adelaide Robineau at Syracuse University. She became an associate professor of arts and crafts at Syracuse and traveled extensively, especially in Scandinavia, seeking out craft centers. Williams participated in the Ceramic Nationals continuously from 1933 through 1960, except in 1949 and 1954.

262 **Helen Williams**
*Small Vase,* c. 1949
Stoneware
H. 4½, Diam. 5½ in. (11.25 × 13.75 cm.)
Marks: *H W* incised on bottom
Gift of the artist P.C. 50.642

Small, globular vase with wide mouth and yellow gloss glaze. Incised lines create a checkerboard pattern which covers the piece.

This is a duplicate of the piece that was exhibited in the "13th Ceramic National" of Everson in 1948.

## THELMA FRAZIER WINTER (1903–1977)

Though she never studied in Vienna, the work of Thelma Frazier Winter is probably the most Viennese of any produced in America during the 1930s and 1940s. Winter studied at the Cleveland Institute of Art under Julius Mihalik, a ceramist who had taught in Budapest and Vienna before coming to Cleveland. She had close contacts with Viktor Schreckengost, Russell Barnett Aitken, and Edward Winter (whom she later married), all of whom had studied in Vienna and lived and worked in Cleveland. Her work exhibits the gaiety, charm, and humor as well as the same sculptural techniques found in much of the Austrian work of the period.

In 1939 Winter became the first woman to win a first prize for sculpture in the Ceramic Nationals. She was a participant in these exhibitions from 1935 through 1958, except 1936, 1947, 1948, 1951, and 1956. She was a member of the jury in 1950 and 1952. She was also a teacher and writer, intensely interested in ceramics education. She taught in the Cleveland public schools and at the Cleveland Institute of Art and was a frequent contributor to *Design* magazine, an important source book for art teachers. Her book, *The Art and Craft of Ceramic Sculpture*, was published in 1973.

During her student days, Thelma Frazier Winter worked at the Cowan Pottery Studio with Schreckengost, Aitken, Eckhardt, and Gregory, all of whom influenced her in one way or another. She was able to absorb these and other influences and turn them into something uniquely her own.

263 **Thelma Frazier Winter**
*The Performers,* c. 1949
Earthenware
H. 23¼, W. 17, D. 8½ in. (58.1 × 42.5 × 21.25 cm.)
Marks: none
Purchase prize given by IBM Corporation, "14th Ceramic National," 1949 P.C. 50.582.2

Earthenware sculpture of two jesters in multicolored medieval costume. The figure on the right holds two balls, while a third one lies at his feet. The other figure holds a hand of playing cards.

*The Performers* is closely related formally, stylistically, and iconographically to *The Juggler.* The two figures are garbed as the Joker or the Fool—the odd card of the pack in both tarot and playing cards—their headgear is made of ass's ears and bells. They are entertainers, clowns who create a diversion or simply amuse their audience.

The rectangular shape of the piece seems to restrain the figures within it, again evoking the sculptural pieces found in Romanesque and Gothic art. The figures project a vitality and energy which is accented by the constraint of the form. The colors are muted and there is a suggestion of patina, again relating the piece to medieval sculpture.

Exhibitions: "A Century of Ceramics in the United States, 1878–1978," 1979; "The Diversions of Keramos, American Clay Sculpture 1925–1950," 1983

263

264

appeared to be carved rather than modeled. The plasticity of the clay was felt less than in the pieces of Austrian derivation and there was more clarity of form.

Exhibitions: "A Century of Ceramics in the United States, 1878–1978," 1979; "The Diversions of Keramos, American Clay Sculpture 1925–1950," 1983

## 265 Thelma Frazier Winter

*Night with the Young Moon,* 1938
Earthenware
H. 16¾, W. 14, D. 6½ in. (41.8 × 35 × 16.25 cm.)
Marks: none
Purchase prize given by Hanovia Chemical Company, "8th Ceramic National," 1939   P.C. 46.486

Earthenware sculpture of prancing horse with female nude seated backwards on the animal's back. Three cherubs gambol about the legs of the horse, while another, crowned with a crescent moon, is placed near the horse's shoulder. The horse is supported by a large understructure, which serves as the base of the piece. The sculpture is glazed in blue, white, and turquoise.

Selene, the goddess of Night, seated on the back of a horse, rises from the sea to begin her journey across the night sky. She is accompanied by a new moon in the form of a cherub with a halo-like crescent above its head. A sheet of water streams from the back of the horse, under which frolic other cherubs. The glossy flowing glaze gives the impression of shimmering water flowing over the figures.

The Viennese influence is most apparent in the nude figure of Night, with elongated, rather shapeless legs, small hands and head, and wide-set, almond eyes. The opaque white glaze on the figure is also typical of Viennese work during this period. It is interesting that the work of Thelma Frazier Winter illustrates so clearly the Austrian style, though she herself never studied in Vienna. This is an indication of how pervasive this influence was in the United States during this period.

Exhibitions: "A Century of Ceramics in the United States, 1878–1978," 1979; "The Diversions of Keramos, American Clay Sculpture 1925–1950," 1983

## 264 Thelma Frazier Winter

*The Juggler,* c. 1949
Earthenware
H. 19¼, W. 9¾, D. 9½ in. (48.1 × 24.3 × 23.75 cm.)
Marks: none
Purchase prize given by IBM Corporation, "14th Ceramic National," 1949   P.C. 50.582.1

Earthenware figure of a juggler. The figure appears in medieval, multicolored costume and wears a crown. Resting on his forearms, with his feet above his head, he holds one ball in his hands and balances another on his feet.

This figure is contained within the shape of a rectangle and is reminiscent of corbel figures found on Romanesque and Gothic cathedrals. These ancient figures also were usually lighthearted renditions of musicians, acrobats, and grotesques. Winter could have seen these at the Cleveland Museum.

During the late forties and early fifties, Winter took a different approach to her work. Her figures became heavier, more compact, more clearly defined, and more sculptural. Her figures often were contained within this rectangular format, and

266

267

## BEATRICE WOOD (b. 1894)

A native of San Francisco, Beatrice Wood met Marcel Duchamp while studying acting and dancing in Paris in 1916. He encouraged her to draw, and they collaborated, with Pierre Roche, on a publication called *The Blindman*, for which she wrote articles and contributed illustrations.

She discovered the wonders of luster glazes in an antique store in Holland and, determined to make pottery, studied with Glen Lukens, Gertrud and Otto Natzler, and Vivika and Otto Heino. Throughout her career she has explored the variations of luster glazes and works with both the vessel and sculpture. She has a home and studio in Ojai, California, and has traveled extensively while continuing to produce ceramics with rich luster surfaces and elegant forms (often alluding to ancient, even Biblical, vessel forms) that are also frequently highly witty.

Wood participated in the Ceramic Nationals from 1939 to 1946 and in 1950 and 1951. She was recognized by the National Council on Education in the Ceramic Arts in 1987 and has received many honors and awards.

### 266 Beatrice Wood

*Vase*, n.d.
Earthenware
H. 6½, Diam 5 in. (16.25 × 12.5 cm.)
Marks: none
Gift of Mrs. John Williams
P.C. 85.28

Bulging, pear-shaped vase with thin neck and trumpet-shaped rim. A green and gold volcanic glaze covers the piece and suggests an oriental motif on one side.

This piece was probably exhibited in a Ceramic National Exhibition.

## DONALD WOOD

Donald Wood was born in Columbus, Ohio, and studied painting, sculpture, and design at Ohio State University, where he went on to receive a master's degree in ceramics. He taught at Ohio State, and participated in the Ceramic Nationals from 1947 through 1951.

### 267 Donald Wood

*Jar*, 1947
Stoneware
H. 8¼, Diam. 6¼ in.
(20.6 × 15.6 cm.)
Marks: *Don Wood 1947* incised on bottom
Purchase prize given by Onondaga Pottery Company, "13th Ceramic National," 1948   P.C. 49.576

Brown stoneware jar with low foot, ovoid shape, and flat rim. The body is covered in a black slip glaze, except for the rim, which is unglazed. The exterior is excised with simple bull figures, and an undulating line around the base.

268

## RUSSEL WRIGHT (1904–1976)

Born in New York City, Russel Wright studied painting for a short time at Cincinnati Art Academy and took courses at the Art Students League in New York. In 1923 he enrolled in the Columbia School of Architecture, and became a designer of house furnishings, including furniture, wallpaper, textiles, metal ware, and tableware, for leading manufacturers. He designed the food and fashion exhibits at the 1939 World's Fair.

In 1935 Russel and Mary Wright formed a partnership called "Russel Wright Associates." In 1937 he designed American Modern, a sleek, modern dinnerware set which was produced by Steubenville Pottery. It became a great artistic and commercial success. He went on to design other dinnerware, including Casual China and Highlight Dinnerware, but American Modern remained his most successful.

**268 Russel Wright**

*Clockwise, beginning with top left:*
*Steubenville "American Modern" Pitcher,* designed 1937
Stoneware
H. 10½, W. 6 in. (26.25 × 15 cm.)
Marks: *Russel/Wright/MFGT BY/ STEUBENVILLE/U.S.A.* impressed on bottom
Museum purchase   P.C. 84.32

Tall, bulbous, pyriform pitcher. The body tapers upward to form a smoothly curved spout. A granite gray glaze covers the pitcher.

*Steubenville "American Modern" Salad Bowl,* designed 1937
Stoneware
H. 2¼, W. 6¾, L. 9½ in. (5.6 × 16.8 × 23.75 cm.)
Marks: *Russel/Wright/MFGT BY/ STEUBENVILLE* impressed on bottom
Gift of Courtney Spore
P.C. 85.80.1

Rectangular bowl with rim flaring gently towards the center on two

sides and a mottled coral glaze overall.

*Iroquois "Casual China" Carafe,* designed 1946
High-fired commercial body
H. 10, Diam. 4 in. (25 × 10 cm.)
Marks: *IROQUOIS/CASUAL/CHI-NA/by/Russel/Wright/U.S.A.* · impressed on bottom
Museum purchase   P.C. 84.37.47

Carafe with two openings—one at the long, extended neck, the other at the shoulder, which forms a spout.

Casual China was produced by Iroquois China Company in Syracuse, New York. It had a high-fired body, which made it much more durable than American Modern, and was advertised with a guarantee against chipping and breaking in normal use. It was designed for easy stacking during storage.

*Iroquois "Casual China" Creamer,* designed 1946
High-fired commercial body
H. 2½, W. 4½ in. (6.25 × 11.25 cm.)
Marks: *IROQUOIS/CASUAL/CHI-*

*NA/by/Russel/Wright/U.S.A.* impressed on bottom
Museum purchase   P.C. 84.37.43

Creamer with thick, smooth, rounded body covered in tan glaze. A curved, circular handle is opposite the modeled pouring spout.

*Iroquois "Casual China" Party Plate and Cup,* designed 1946
High-fired commercial body
Plate: H. ¾ in., Diam. 10½ in. (1.8 × 26.25 cm.). Cup: H. 2, Diam. 3¾ in. (5 × 9.35 cm.)
Marks: *IROQUOIS/CASUAL/CHI-NA/by/Russel/Wright* stamped on bottom of each
Gift of Courtney Spore
P.C. 85.50a, c

Leaf-shaped plate with raised sections dividing plate into three areas, with a circular section indented to hold the round cup with its curved C-shaped handle. Both plate and cup are glazed in pink.

# A M E R I C A N C E R A M I C S SINCE 1 9 5 0

## G A R T H C L A R K

Revolutions emerge slowly, whether in art or politics. Yet one usually speaks of revolutions as sudden, cataclysmic events because we only acknowledge them at their point of conflagration—when the palaces are burnt down, when the old guard is rudely replaced with the new. But the events that ignite the revolution may simmer for decades, even centuries, before they find revolutionary voice.

While 1950 is generally agreed on as the point of revolution for American ceramics, it was no more than the visible flashpoint. The process actually began in 1878 when the women's art movement began to get under way, producing its first wares—hand-painted china cups and saucers. Ever since, the American ceramics artist has sought an identity that is as unique as the country itself. Propelled along by a lively empiricism and a gift for invention, ceramics has, decade by decade, taken its steps along the road to aesthetic autonomy. Initially the independence of the American ceramist was not evident on an aesthetic level. The art pottery world in particular (with the notable exception of George E. Ohr) was dominated by imitation.

At times ceramists were successful in achieving an American accent, but the language of their art remained steadfastly European. The Danish and French potters were influential at the turn of the century while between the two World Wars, the insouciance of Austria's Wiener Werkstätte and the stylish decadence of France's Art Deco potters set the pace.

### An American Style

One had to look deep beneath the surface to sense the energy and unique spirit that was slowly but inevitably building. American work differed from Europe's in

that it was usually less refined and mannered. Often this was simply the result of artistic naiveté and inadequate skills rather than a deliberate aesthetic view. But gradually American potters became more selective about their European sources, taking what was useful and rejecting the rest. The coarseness of craftsmanship slowly evolved into an aesthetic stance, recognizing that America was a less formal, less structured society than Europe. One can see this directness emerging in pottery during the 1930s, in particular in the work of Maija Grotell, Glen Lukens, and Henry Varnum Poor.

Poor in particular resisted the perfectionist mentality of the Europeans and every one of his plates (except the topmost plate in the kiln) had its image rudely punctuated by three marks—caused by the ceramic stilts that he used to separate the plates during firing. Poor wrote that his work was "not notable for technical perfection. In my first exhibition at the Montross Gallery [in 1922] I enraged potters by showing warped and even kiln-cracked plates because I considered them works of art."[1] This obliged the viewer to explore the spirit of the piece instead of rejoicing in pure technical virtuosity.

Another figure who was important in changing attitudes in America was the British potter and Surrealist painter, T. Samuel ("Sam") Haile. Although his stay in this country was brief—he arrived in 1939 and departed in 1944—his impact was considerable. He taught at Alfred University in New York and in Ann Arbor, Michigan. Those who met him still speak of his energy, his informality, and his insistence on minimizing craft input in order to make art. Haile used just a few simple glazes, threw highly expressionist shapes with exagger-

ated feet, and highlighted throwing rings (those marks left by the potter's fingers). He argued relentlessly and convincingly against the technological bent of education at Alfred University's school of ceramics.

American pottery had several advantages that were not evident in the first half of this century. One was that Americans were (with very few exceptions) not caught up in the confusing issue of utilitarianism. Except for the southern folk potters, there was little interest in making functional wares until the 1950s. As a result, American potters did not suffer the utilitarian/non-utilitarian angst of their counterparts in England. By and large the American ceramists were uncomplicated in their objective—most simply wanted to make art.

After the end of World War II, the dependency of American ceramists on European and British pottery aesthetics briefly increased. The Bauhaus-trained Marguerite and Frans Wildenhain came to the United States, and after their divorce, settled at opposite ends of the nation, both becoming influential teachers—he in Rochester, New York and she in Guerneville, California (entries 261, 567, 568). Gertrud and Otto Natzler, who arrived in the United States just before the outbreak of war, emerged as influential figures as well, winning numerous prizes for their elegant, refined pottery forms and lush glazes (entries 446–450).

In 1950 the British potter Bernard Leach visited the United States and encouraged an interest in Asian pottery, in particular that of China, Korea, and Japan. Leach was then, and remained for many years, the most influential single individual in the ceramics world. In 1940 he published *A Potter's Book* which rapidly became the Bible of the studio potter. Leach converted generations of potters to his Anglicized version of Zen Buddhist aesthetic theory. He also introduced American ceramics to the essentially moral (or moralistic) issue of the useful versus the useless.

Leach, with his tendency to be long on theory and short on intuition, was little impressed with the potential of ceramics in the United States and wrote pessimistically of its ceramic future, stating that it lacked a cultural taproot from which to draw sustenance. In response Marguerite Wildenhain wrote an angry open letter to *Craft Horizons* arguing that "American potters cannot possibly grow roots by implanting Sung pottery or by copying the way of life of the rural population of Japan."[2] Wildenhain argued that the copying of works unrelated to the culture would only produce dilettantes and fakes.

This absence of any single taproot in American ceramics, or any ceramic art of consequence (other than native Indian pottery, which the "modern" potters chose to ignore at the time) was in fact the unique advantage. There was no competition from the past, no intimidation from previous periods of genius. There was no American equivalent to Meissen, Wedgwood, or Sèvres. The American potter was still creatively innocent having not yet reached, in the words of one critic, "a high point from which to decline."[3]

## EASTERN INFLUENCE

Leach returned in 1952 to find his aesthetic—caustically labeled "The Anglo-Oriental Pottery Company" by his detractors—becoming well entrenched in the United States. American potters had belatedly discovered the more rustic wares of the East and quickly became ardent imitators. There were suddenly hundreds of makers of Japanese wares in the early fifties. They became instant converts to Zen and Eastern mysticism. Their kilns flowed with rivers of tenmoku and celadon glaze. But the interest was, in all but a few cases, as ersatz as Wildenhain had feared. Indeed an archaeologist some two thousand years from now, digging through the shard piles of the early 1950s might well deduce that

at this moment Japan and China had banished all their failed potters to the United States.

As with most messiahs, the quality of Leach's mission was obscured by his multitudes of less talented disciples, making it difficult for serious devotees, such as Warren and Alix MacKenzie, to be appreciated. The MacKenzies had studied with Leach in St. Ives, England and returned in 1952 determined to promote and retain a certain classical purism and practical humility in the ceramic arts. Warren MacKenzie, a highly traditional but gifted potter, began to slowly attract like-minded potters to Minnesota and the University of Minnesota where he taught. MacKenzie's influence in fighting for a pure classicism in pottery has been highly beneficial to the field at large. In the eighties MacKenzie's students have been able to reinvigorate the role of the functional potter.

On his second visit Leach was accompanied by two of his closest friends, the craft philosopher Soetsu Yanagi and the potter Shoji Hamada. Their tour, organized by Alix MacKenzie, proved to be a formative event for the rapidly growing ceramics community in the United States. The lectures attracted capacity audiences and provided rare insight into Japanese pottery and its philosophical base.

One of the many ceramists indelibly influenced by the visiting trio was Peter Voulkos (entries 556–563). Voulkos first met Leach, Yanagi, and Hamada when they visited the Archie Bray Foundation in Helena, Montana. Voulkos was then the foundation's first resident potter. Voulkos had studied painting at the University of Montana and then pottery at the California College of Arts and Crafts on the GI Bill.

The Bill had been enacted by Congress to provide ex-servicemen with a college education. Like many ex-servicemen, Voulkos chose the humanities instead of a more conventional and potentially lucrative area of study. In part this was a reaction against the violence and dehumanization of the war years. The GI Bill offered not only Voulkos but a legion of ex-servicemen the unique opportunity to gain an education in the

arts; collectively, they provided the studio arts with a surge of energy and momentum. Expansionist universities and art schools sensed the new needs in this area and rapidly developed the humanities and studio arts programs, of which ceramics was one of the most popular.

Voulkos met up with the trio again as a fellow-participant in a ceramics symposium organized at the Black Mountain School, Asheville, North Carolina, in 1953. Voulkos was impressed by Leach's erudition and scholarship. Described by Michael Cardew as "a perfectly preserved Edwardian," Leach had an impressive old-world authority, which worked well on his American audiences with their Anglophilic tendencies. But it was Hamada who intrigued Voulkos most. He was fascinated by Hamada's quiet communion with clay and his readiness to work wherever he found it. Hamada would speak of "finding the pot" in a piece of clay, meaning that each time he picked up a piece of it, the material would suggest and encourage a slightly different form from the previous one. This was Voulkos's first lesson in trusting the materials to help guide the hand and mind— a lesson that critics ascribed to the "action painting" philosophies of the New York school, with which Voulkos was later to become familiar.

## THE OTIS CIRCLE

In 1954 Voulkos was asked by Millard Sheets to set up a ceramics department at the Otis Art Institute in Los Angeles. Voulkos was then making functional wares for a living, known in particular for his decorated and elegantly thrown bottle vases in the style of Mills College potter Antonio Prieto (entries 476 and 477). Enormously energetic and charismatic, Voulkos soon attracted a group of talented students. The Otis student roster today reads like a holy grail of American pottery; many of these potters were to leave as deep an imprint on contemporary ceramics as their teacher. The students included Ken Price, Billy Al Bengston, Paul Soldner, Mac McClain (McCloud), John Mason, Michael Frimkess, Jerry Rothman, and Henry Takemoto among others. (See entries 283, 423, 475, 494–497, 523–528, and 546.)

However, Voulkos's approach to teaching was not conventional. Voulkos taught by example, infecting his students with his contagious sense of inquiry.[4] They in turn responded by challenging Voulkos and questioning the conventions of pottery. The teacher/student roles were freely exchanged. The atmosphere in the basement of Otis was less that of a pedagogical hierarchy than one composed of "independent contestants."[5]

The pots produced at Otis were an attack on the stultifying mores of western pottery. The forms were aggressively asymmetrical. The surfaces were competitive with the form—not politely subservient as was the tradition. Although we now see beauty in these works and even the underpinning of a classical sensibility, in their day they were considered irredeemably ugly.

Voulkos and company took their inspiration from many sources, primarily the ceramics of Picasso; the Jomon, Shigaraki, and Bizen pottery of Japan; and lastly the painting of the Abstract Expressionist movement. The tradition of Japanese pottery was used differently at Otis than by the Leach school. The Otis group was able to abstract the Japanese influence, excited by what it saw as the radicalism and spontaneity of certain pottery traditions. The encouragement of happenstance in Bizen and Shigaraki wares, the fierceness of their surfaces, and the acceptance of cracks and fissures as part of the aesthetic, all conspired to provide an example (albeit frequently misunderstood and often romanticized) that released the Otis group from the less adventurous, somewhat tentative aesthetics previously dominating American ceramics.

By 1958 Voulkos and his students had succeeded in developing a new language for American ceramic art. The Otis years were the flashpoint, the culmination point of decades of searching for an original voice in ceramic art. The expressive Otis aesthetic was a standard by which all else would be measured until the next revolution. Voulkos and his students had in metaphoric

terms finally stormed the doors of the ceramic Bastille and released American ceramists from their dependency upon European aesthetics.

However, Voulkos must have felt little sense of victory. In 1958 Sheets dismissed Voulkos, no longer able to tolerate what he saw as the increasing eccentricity of the master's ceramics. Sheets was disturbed by the wild happenings in the ceramics department, by the four letter words being "sgraffitoed" onto the vessels, and by the marathon, manic work sessions that lasted until dawn. Voulkos then moved to the University of California at Berkeley where the experiment moved into its second phase.

It was not until 1961 that the ceramics world at large discovered what had taken place at Otis. In that year Rose Slivka, editor of the American Crafts Council's magazine *Craft Horizons*, wrote an article entitled "The New Ceramic Presence."[6] The council's members responded with outrage and disbelief. Slivka had presented evidence of a radical shift in values. The mooring ropes that had once tethered the craft of ceramics so securely to the polite virtues of the *objet d'art* had been severed. Ceramics was quite suddenly cast adrift, tugged and pushed by avant-garde currents that were unfamiliar and profoundly disturbing at the time, at least to the ceramics world.

In 1966 the critic John Coplans organized an exhibition entitled "Abstract Expressionist Ceramics" at the Art Gallery of the University of California at Irvine; it later traveled to the San Francisco Museum of Art. The exhibition and its fine catalogue took up the cudgels where Slivka's article had left off. Coplans's target was not the craft community, but the world of fine arts. The exhibition certainly succeeded in drawing the attention of the fine arts to what was happening in ceramics.

While Slivka and Coplans provided invaluable services to the field, they also planted some of the early seeds of misunderstanding. Both writers related most closely to the traditions of painting. They did not see the ceramics revolution as an

autonomous movement with its own roots and motivations, but as an extension of the genius of American painting. To some extent this was understandable. The New York school of painters had reached its zenith. Pop Art was just emerging. New York was the new center of the painting world. It was logical that the overwhelming achievement of American painting should become not simply *a* standard but *the* standard.

Coplans saw the achievement of Voulkos and company as "the most ingenious regional adaptation yet of Abstract Expressionist painting."[7] This comment was meant to be a heady compliment, but ended up being a paternalistic view that obscured the fact that ceramics was rapidly building a unique expression of its own. This approach was common and ceramists were constantly being praised for having "turned a pot into sculpture" or having "escaped pottery to make art."

This caused an identity crisis for those ceramists who were aware that they were doing significant work and hungered for recognition from the fine arts establishment. The tenor of criticism suggested that acceptance in the art world came from denying ceramic roots of an eight-thousand-year-long tradition. Suddenly the ceramist's past was looked upon with embarrassment because of its unacceptable connections to utilitarianism and the decorative arts.

Many attempts were made to overcome this insecurity. Pots were referred to neutrally as "forms" or more pretentiously as "sculpture." References to ceramic history were avoided. References to fine art connections (no matter how slight) were emphasized. It was not until the late 1970s that the ceramists developed sufficient confidence to again begin to publicly acknowledge and confidently celebrate their roots.

Despite a growing hostility toward the vessel, the early sixties did see continued development of the vessel as an art format. In the early sixties Ron Nagle made superb bottles with wide, spade-like stoppers on which were painted slashes of glaze and brightly colored china paint. At the same time Jim Melchert was exploring the horizontal format of the vessel in his *Leg pot* series. Later in the sixties Michael Frimkess created his extraordinary "melting pots," which employed readily identifiable cultural stereotypes of form—the Chinese ginger jar, the Grecian urn, the Zuni bowl— to engage in a dialogue about political power, discrimination, and third world exploitation. But even though the sixties produced many masterpiece vessels, the interest of this decade focused not on pottery but on sculpture.

## THE FUNK MOVEMENT

Robert Arneson provided ceramic sculpture with the same force of leadership that Voulkos had provided for the vessel. Originally trained as an illustrator and potter, Arneson began to produce gritty, faintly pornographic-looking Surrealist sculpture in the late 1950s and early 1960s. In 1963 he was invited to participate in an exhibition of California sculptors on the rooftop garden of the Kaiser Center in Oakland. In a declaration of independence, Arneson turned his back on the Miro-esque work for which he had become known. He submitted a toilet entitled *Funk John*. The piece was found to be too offensive (it contained ceramic fecal matter—what Arneson politely termed "ceramic emblems") and was removed. With *Funk John* he had broken away, finally making "a Bob Arneson, finally [arriving] at a piece of work which stood firmly on its own ground."[8]

His action has a famous parallel in modern art history. In 1917 Marcel Duchamp sent in a pissoir signed R. Mutt and entitled *The Fountain* to the New York Society of Independent Artists. This work was also removed from the exhibition, but not without igniting the imagination of the Dada movement in New York. The same iconoclasm and irreverence that Dada had excited in the post-war art world was now being felt in the ceramics world of the sixties, and Arneson's *Funk John* gave both title and spirit to a new ceramics movement.

The shock tactics of Arneson and the later Funk ceramists fit the anti-establishment mood of the day. San Francisco's Haight Ashberry district was then the head-

quarters for the counter-culture movement. However it is important to point out that Funk was not Arneson's invention, he simply annexed and reshaped it for his own purposes, and indirectly, for the West Coast ceramics world. The Funk movement had been thriving amongst San Francisco artists since the early 1950s, attracting artists such as Bruce Conner and Joan Brown. The first Funk exhibition, "Common Art Accumulations," took place in 1951 at San Francisco's Place Bar. Funk was diverse in style and materials but common in its rudeness of spirit. As Harold Paris wrote, "In essence, 'It's a groove to stick your finger down your throat and see what comes up,' this is funk."[9]

The "spiritual" center for Funk ceramics developed in Northern California around the University of California at Davis where Arneson was a member of the art department. Arneson inspired and/or taught many ceramists who went on to work in the Funk style, including David Gilhooly, Peter Vandenberge, and Clayton Bailey (entries 350–353, and 554). A second school of Funk ceramics developed around the University of Washington in Seattle in the mid-sixties under the leadership of Howard Kottler and Fred Bauer (entry 280). The Seattle school was somewhat different—less scatological, less raw and visceral. Overall there was a greater stylishness and technical finesse.

The Funk movement was surveyed in 1966 at the Art Museum of the University of California at Berkeley in Peter Selz's excellent exhibition "Funk Art."[10] The exhibition revealed the extent to which ceramics now dominated the Funk movement. Imitations of the Funk style spread across the country and even abroad to Europe. By 1969 there was even a nascent Funk movement underway at the Wolverhampton Polytechnic in England!

Funk was essentially an inversion of Pop Art. In common with Pop Art it used as its icons everyday objects such as Coke bottles, toasters, telephones, toilets, and typewriters. Also it shared Pop's commitment to "commercial" craft (for example, non-art). But Pop artists drew from poster graphics

and advertising design whereas the Funk artists decided to retain an amateur status, deliberately embracing the cheap materials and "clunky" handling of the hobbyist. Glazes were bought from hobby stores and the method of handling the clay was distinctly casual.

The handling of the imagery was also at opposite poles. Pop used its images with an objectivity and detachment. Funk artists used hot color, attached genitals to domestic objects, and rendered their sculptures offensive, subjective, and fetishistic. However, as popular and as widely imitated as ceramic Funk was, it proved resistant to transplantation. The Funk style was rarely convincing outside its two regional centers in Northern California and Seattle. By the early 1970s ceramic Funk was over as a movement. Apart from the work of Arneson and a few others, the movement left behind surprisingly little art of consequence considering the number of ceramists who once claimed membership to Funk art.

Funk had nonetheless served its purpose. It provided ceramics with the seditious genius of Arneson, Kottler's stylish satires, Gilhooly's strange Frog culture, and Bailey's lewd and humorous exploits under the nom de plume, Dr. Gladstone. It acted as a purgative, rescuing ceramic sculpture from its relegation to tasteful, table-top sculpture in the tradition of the figurine or mantelpiece decoration. Ceramic sculpture was no longer a servant to the preciousness of bourgeois taste.

## THE SUPER-OBJECT

By 1970 a new movement, the Super-Object, was already outdistancing Funk in popularity.[11] Even though many of its best known proponents grew out of the Funk movement (notably its leader, Richard Shaw), it was the stylistic opposite of Funk. If Funk can be characterized as art of the dirty, the Super-Object provided the art of the clean. It was meticulous in its craft, a touch nostalgic in its use of imagery, realist in its use of form, and somewhat elegant in its presentation.

Two exhibitions in the early 1970s drew

attention to this new direction in ceramics. The first was Marilyn Levine's New York debut at the "New Realism" exhibitions at the Sidney Janis and O.K. Harris galleries in 1972. Levine exhibited stoneware suitcases and briefcases that appeared to be real leather and required the viewer to literally touch the objects in order to determine that they were in fact hard, fired clay (entry 406).

Harold Rosenberg called her works "translations of objects in a different substance without altering their appearance." Although Levine did produce objects, Rosenberg pointed out that this was "essentially a conceptual art, that brings to the eye nothing not present in nature but instructs the spectators that things may no longer be what they seem."[12] The Super-Object provided a forum where the ceramists could indulge in technical games. It also brought illusionary art back into vogue. As critic Kim Levin noted, "old time illusionist art has collided with the future becoming as literal as minimal forms... form has redissolved into content—Pygmalion is back in business."[13]

In 1973 Richard Shaw and sculptor Robert Hudson collaborated on an exhibition at the San Francisco Museum of Art. The exhibition showed a large group of porcelain objects assembled from several molded elements and painted in the trompe l'oeil tradition, imitating wood surfaces and creating illusory spaces and planes. Hudson and Shaw used a common library of molds and the same techniques, but made individual works. It was a superb exhibition and set off a nation-wide rage for faux surfaces.

In the ceramics schools across the country clay's potential to mimic other materials now became an obsessive odyssey. But without the conceptual intent of Levine's early work or the poetic sensibility of Shaw and Hudson, this imitative technique was little more than a stage for flashy showmanship. Ceramists tried to use Dada and Surrealist references to give the work some depth but for the greater part it came out as a kind of "Hollywood Magritte," high on technical glitz, eccentric imagery, and

claims to familial links with Dada and Surrealism. Yet despite the surface appeal of much of this work it lacked any profound raison d'être. The critic Thomas Albright complained about this direction in American ceramics calling it, "old time ceramic Funk of a decade ago, adapted to the era of high tech.... Eccentricity is not the same as originality. It is a measure of the difference that so much eccentricity can add up to so much sameness."[14]

As always there were those few who rose to the challenge and who managed to use clay's trompe l'oeil propensities to express content. Mark Burns combined this technique with a sharp, punk edge that verged on the sado-masochistic. He created macabre images such as a teapot made of a severed hand and wrapped in a rattlesnake. Kottler used trompe l'oeil with a cooler edge and a sly visual wit as did Patti Warashina and a few others.

While styles were certainly changing, an event in 1972 clearly indicated that fundamental values were also beginning to change. In that year the Everson Museum's Ceramic National, the major showcase for ceramic talent in the United States, was canceled after four decades of serving American ceramics. The decision came from the then director of the museum, James Harithas, and jurors Voulkos, Bob Turner, and Jeff Schlanger. The jurors dismissed the National as being unmanageable and the works submitted as unexhibitable. The bi-annual was replaced with an invitational and a showing of works from past Nationals.

The decision took the ceramics world by surprise and was a considerable shock. Some welcomed the decision as a sign of a new maturity. Others were outraged and accused the jurors of playing God and of cronyism in their selection of a replacement invitational. This decision was a blow for the younger ceramists as they had few alternative platforms that drew national attention to their work.

The reaction of the ceramics world was summed up by Donna Nicolas in her detailed investigation into the demise of the National: "There was excitement, alright.

Incomprehension. Lots of unanswered questions. Mutterings heard from amongst the clay bags. Many felt the jurors' action to be some sort of Olympian hoax, perpetrated by larger-than-life ceramic figures pointing a collective finger and causing the whole show to disappear. A giant power trip? A gesture of courage? Despair? Indifference? Hope?"[15]

Even though the Ceramic National was reinstated in 1987, the decision in 1972 remains as hotly debated today as it was sixteen years ago. Whatever the benefits or damage, the announcement of the decision woke up American ceramists to some tough new realities. It was a dramatic sign that the status quo was changing. The tenor of the jurors' statement made it clear that there were new aesthetic criteria that had to be met.

## NEW EXHIBITIONS

It is arguable that the closing of the National allowed the Everson Museum to take on other important exhibitions. One of the most important and controversial of these was Margie Hughto's "New Works in Clay by Painters and Sculptors." The exhibition brought together a group of major artists who had either not worked with clay before or else had had limited contact with the medium. Included in the project were Anthony Caro, Helen Frankenthaler, Friedel Dzubas, and others (entries 297, 328, 343). The project continued and in "New Works in Clay II" and "New Works in Clay III," non-clay artists such as Kenneth Noland and Miriam Shapiro were joined by ceramists as well (entry 455). The projects, skillfully managed by Hughto, created considerable energy and interchange, and drew further attention to ceramics's growing role in the arts.

If the Everson Museum had inadvertantly contributed a somewhat disturbing beginning to the decade, it more than compensated for this in 1979 when it opened the block-buster exhibition: "A Century of Ceramics in the United States 1878–1978." The museum took on the challenge of producing the first textbook on ceramics history and a 450-object exhibition that traced and defined the last one hundred years of ceramic art.[16]

Sponsored by the Philip Morris Corporation, the exhibition traveled for three years throughout the country. It also spawned a fifty-minute film called *Earth, Fire and Water: One Hundred Years of American Ceramics* (narrated somewhat histrionically by Orson Welles), which was extensively screened on public television. In addition, the Institute for Ceramic History (ICH) was founded in Claremont, California to organize a symposium in conjunction with the exhibition. This was the first conference devoted solely to issues of scholarship and history.[17]

A combination of curatorial sweat, Philip Morris's mighty publicity machine, and fortuitous timing resulted in high attendance and enormous exposure. Quite suddenly American ceramics was transformed from decades of being "a recent phenomena" into a medium with roots, context, and content. Moreover these roots revealed themselves to be surprisingly complex and enriching. The success of the exhibition also had the effect of thrusting ceramics out of its hermetic world into the national art spotlight, drawing enthusiastic critical reviews from John Perreault, Donald Kuspit, John Ashbery, and others.

Writing in *Art in America* Kuspit remarked that the exhibition revealed ceramics as perhaps the "most truly universal art." He added that it was "a rare exhibition that can make us question firmly held aesthetic prejudices and help overthrow fixed, unanalyzed positions... Yet that is precisely what [this exhibition] accomplished... overturning the deeply rooted negative attitude that ceramics is inherently trivial [and] shatters the presumed hierarchy of the arts."[18]

This encouraged a critical re-evaluation both within and without the ceramics world. It also initiated a widespread interest in collecting both contemporary and historical ceramics. The emergence of a new and somewhat affluent marketplace was significant in many ways but primarily because it now shifted the balance of power from the public patron (the educational institu-

tion) to the private patron (the collector).

Until the eighties, the collector had played a relatively small role in the field of ceramics. Most of the successful ceramists in the art world (as compared to the makers of functional wares) sold little or no work and relied upon their teaching salaries to sustain their creative activities. Those who did sell works often did so at prices that were ludicrously low, hardly even covering the material and firing costs.

The majority of public exhibitions of ceramics had, up until this point, taken place in university and college galleries. This dependency upon the educational institutions was not new. It was a relationship that had existed in American ceramics since the turn of the century beginning in 1901 when the New York State School of Clayworking and Ceramics at Alfred University opened its doors under the direction of Charles Fergus Binns. Something of a ceramics evangelist, Binns sent his best students throughout the United States to found ceramics departments at schools, colleges, and universities. By the mid-sixties ceramics departments were opening at a staggering pace and there was a strong demand for teachers.

In 1966 the relationship between the ceramic arts and the educational world was formalized in an organization entitled the National Council on Education for the Ceramic Arts (NCECA). It was composed mainly of ceramics teachers, their students and alumni. By 1979 when the ceramics craze had reached a peak, a combined NCECA/SuperMud conference at Pennsylvania State University, University Park was able to attract a staggering three-thousand delegates. By then there were nearly five hundred institutions offering a B.F.A. or M.F.A. in ceramics in the United States and each year saw thousands of students seeking a place in the ceramics world.

The support of educational institutions was, in common with all dominant forms of patronage, a double-edged sword. Without it many artists—including Voulkos and Arneson—might not have had the freedom to explore their art so radically and noncommercially. On the other hand it set up rules and values that were antithetical to

art. Within the rationalist environment of the university, art was expected to "mean" something so that its worth, effectiveness, and importance could be examined and measured.

All too often exhibitions of ceramics were created to satisfy the narrow political agendas of faculty committees rather than more personal creative concerns. Much of the creative spirit became lost in academic games and in-fighting. In addition, as ceramists could make more money giving guest lectures and leading workshops than by selling their art, personality became a greater asset than technical skill or originality. The values and priorities of ceramists as visual artists were becoming distorted.

By 1980 there was a need for change. This was brought on by a shift in educational emphasis (more students were pursuing legal and engineering degrees, veering away from the humanities) and by a decrease in college enrollments. Art education entered a period of retrenchment and the academic clay "club" began to lose its power. The more talented ceramics graduates could no longer expect a teaching post as a matter of course. Departments were closed, hiring freezes were instituted, and expansion ceased.

As the public sector began to shrink, the private sector began to expand. From the mid-1970s onwards craft shops and galleries had begun to build a following for ceramics—Helen Drutt in Philadelphia and the Hadler/Rodriguez Gallery in New York were among the pioneers. In 1975 Ruth Braunstein, Rena Bransten, and Sylvia Brown opened the Quay Ceramics Gallery in San Francisco, followed in 1979 by Alice Westphal's Exhibit A in Chicago. In 1980 the Okun/Thomas Gallery opened in St. Louis and although short-lived, proved to be highly influential and effective.

While these specialist galleries were attending to ceramic art, several major New York "fine art" galleries became intrigued by the medium and took ceramists into their stables. Allan Frumkin and Allan Stone had for many years showcased ceramic talent. In the 1980s they were joined by a number of other galleries. Blum-Helman launched the British ceramist Andrew Lord into prominence. Charles Cowles took on Voulkos, Ron Nagle, and Michael Lucero. Max Protetch handled Betty Woodman and Richard DeVore; Grace Borgenicht took on John Gill (her first ceramics artist since she showed Kitajao Rosanjin in 1954) and Viola Frey joined Nancy Hoffman. The list is now longer and while ceramics is by no means taking over the art market or even threatening the hegemony of the painter or non-clay sculptor, it is now part of the art marketplace to a degree unimaginable a decade before.

The private sector provided a breath of fresh air allowing the once isolated ceramist a national, and in some cases international, audience. The galleries reinstituted purely visual, aesthetic values after decades of domination by academic politics. Frequent exhibitions at private art galleries throughout the United States have succeeded in engaging the interest of the critics, thus exposing Americans to the nuances and range of contemporary ceramic art. The number of collectors of ceramics has increased dramatically. Significantly, those collecting ceramics today are not the crafts specialists of previous decades. Ceramics is today being purchased across the board by the collector of fine arts.

Museums have become another important client in the ceramics marketplace of the eighties. Survey exhibitions of recent American ceramics at the Whitney Museum in New York, the Boston Museum of Fine Arts, the Los Angeles County Museum of Art, the Stedelijk Museum in Amsterdam, and the Victoria and Albert Museum in London, have greatly increased public awareness of this art form.In addition, the Everson Museum, the United States' most important institution for the ceramic arts, has greatly expanded its activities and collection. In 1986 it founded the Syracuse China Center for the Study of American Ceramics.

Whether the ceramist has now become a member of the fine art or decorative art community is not an issue to be debated in this essay. Of more significance is the fact that ceramics is—whatever its categorization—part of the professional art market and is drawing more and more attention and excitement. This is not to suggest that the marketplace has been a panacea. Much still has to be done to fill the gap left by the retrenching educational support system.

## CERAMICS TODAY

The eighties's most *noticeable* revolution has unquestionably been the transfer of power from the public patron to the private patron. The aesthetic change might seem to have been less dramatic. But in a quiet way, without the frontal attack of the Otis group or the provocativeness of Funk, the aesthetic revolution among American ceramists has continued unabated. There is a new complexity and literacy in ceramic art. This is as much true of the current work of the early revolutionaries such as Arneson—whose banal humor has developed into a complex satire on the nature of art, money, and fame—as it is of young newcomers such as Anne Kraus—who has married personal narrative with the stylistic invention of eighteenth-century Meissen.

The current leaders in ceramic art appear to be less perplexed by their placement within the traditions of the ceramic arts than those who preceded them in the 1950s and 1960s. The acceptance of their rich tradition now fits comfortably within a broad plurality in the fine arts that includes many of the issues of the ceramist. Ceramists today actively mine their past with an engaging freshness of discovery. This is not the grave-robbing superficiality of Postmodernism, nor the faddish mimicry of appropriation.

What is happening in ceramics is infinitely more innocent. The history of painting and architecture has been studied and restudied for centuries. Ceramics history on the other hand has never been part of the art academy studies, and ceramists (unlike painters and sculptors) have discovered their medium's past outside the lecture hall or the didacticism of art surveys. For most contemporary ceramists, the growing inti-

macy with ceramics history has come from highly personal research, from moments of amazement as they stumble onto bodies of historical work which they never imagined to exist. The process is haphazard and naive, without formal analysis, but is proving to be enormously synergistic. Ceramics today is acquiring a sense of historical context without becoming historicist.

What is exciting in the eighties is that the ceramic past of the western world has quite suddenly become a respectable resource. Ceramics suffered a regime through the 1950s and 1960s not unlike that of Modernism's puritanical domination of painting. The omnipresence of Chinese and Japanese wares set the standard for purity and truth in ceramic art. Leach had consistently argued that most western ceramics traditions were irredeemably decadent and this shibboleth was accepted without argument for nearly four decades.

The breaching of this dogma began long before the eighties. In the late sixties and early seventies Michael Frimkess explored the Greek vase as a cultural icon while Jack Earl began his exploration of figurative ceramics enraptured by the beauty of eighteenth-century Meissen figurines (entries 329 and 330). Adrian Saxe first began to explore the political and decorative contexts of Sèvres court porcelains in the mid-sixties (entries 502 and 503). Betty Woodman, who regularly summers in Italy, married both East and West using the polychromatic glazes of the Tang dynasty (A.D. 618–907) with the voluptuary of Mediterranean form (entry 574). However, today the traditions of western pottery have been embraced with new confidence and understanding.

Even within the much beloved eastern pottery traditions there were acceptable and unacceptable styles of work. Sung pottery of the tenth to thirteenth centuries was considered "minimal" and "spiritual" and therefore good in modernist terms. The late Yixing teapots with their careful design and representational tendencies were considered "retinal" and therefore, bad. Yet Richard Notkin was able to cross this borderline of aesthetic moralizing and adopt the Yixing teapot as a starting point for an extraordinary foray into heartfelt political commentary, dealing with the menace of nuclear force, the "gambling" of superpowers, the plight of the urban poor, even using the Yixing teapot to create small, domestic, but immensely moving monuments to man's inhumanity to man (entries 456–459). An opus of heart-shaped teapots comment upon human rights' violations in Vietnam and Afghanistan and pay poignant tribute to those who died in the 1961 South African Sharpeville riots.

The urge to explore the ceramics tradition applies more to the maker of vessels than to those involved in sculpture. Despite the darkly pessimistic pronouncement of some in the 1960s who saw the vessel as an anachronism and banished it from their ceramics departments, the vessel has re-emerged in the eighties fully the equal of sculpture. The eighties have produced what Peter Schjeldahl characterizes as the "smart pot"—an object on the cusp of the fine *and* decorative arts. "The smart pot X-Rays the hoary art/craft distinction to reveal its confusion of values: values of prestige fouling up values of use.... The smart pot accepts the semiotic fate of everything made by human beings, the present wisdom that every such thing is consciously or unconsciously *a sign*. Given the choice the smart pot opts to be conscious. It represses no meaning, however disturbing."[19]

Ceramic sculpture has matured and clarified its role in the eighties. The field can now boast a cadre of mature talents, surprisingly smaller than predicted, but no less arresting: Viola Frey, Robert Arneson, Mary Frank, Stephen DeStaebler, Jack Earl, Robert Brady, and younger artists such as Michael Lucero, Judy Moonelis, Jan Holcomb, and Arthur Gonzalez. (See entries 272, 273, 318, 329, 330, 340–342, 344, 416, and 436.) A characteristic of these artists in the eighties is the extent to which references to the ceramics traditions, once frequent in their early works, have largely disappeared.

An interesting development is that sculp-tural ceramics in this decade is predominantly sculptural in its application. Clay is now being used mainly as modeling material, having been proven poorly suited to the fabricating needs of the minimal and abstract sculptor. The surfaces are sometimes glazed but more and more frequently today they are painted with acrylic or other paint. In the work of certain artists there is no sense of the material at all. Jack Earl's newest works completely cover all sign of clay with meticulous, acrylic-painted surfaces. The same is true of Jan Holcomb, Beverly Mayeri, and Michael Lucero.

Others, such as the masterful Viola Frey, retain the clay/glaze tradition and a loose connection to the ceramics tradition of the figurine. But the surfaces of Frey's towering ten- to twelve-feet-high figures owe more to the styles and syntax of contemporary painting than to any purely ceramic sources. Purists might bemoan this shift in values but it reflects a clear and healthy rendering of priorities. Ceramic sculpture, unlike pottery, is not a genre per se. It is simply a material sub-division within the broader world of sculpture and this is a reality that today's makers of ceramic sculpture have come to acknowledge. Ceramic sculpture has at last reached the point where the medium is decidedly not the message—a major revolution in itself.

The context for the ceramics sculptor is the broader world of contemporary figurative sculpture, a complex world of conceptualism, formalism, and expressionism. This can be seen in the range of issues being addressed. Arneson's work had moved away from his play with banal humor into the frightening realm of the nuclear holocaust. At an exhibition in 1988 at the Carlo Lamagna Gallery in New York, Raymon Elozua presented an exhibition that dealt with the decline of the American steel industry, reflecting upon disturbing and broader issues of economic disintegration and social responsibility within a capitalist society. He combined ceramics with metal and photography.

This exhibition demonstrated both the search among ceramists for more universal content and highlighted a pluralistic trend in use of the media. Viola Frey exhibits paintings and, in common with Arneson, DeStaebler, Michael Lucero, and others, works in bronze as well. Many contemporary ceramists have become involved with printmaking; Andrew Lord and Irvin Tepper have made particularly effective contributions to this field.

So when one speaks of American ceramics today, one is no longer speaking of a simple, cohesive field. Ceramics has lost its homogeneity. Ceramic sculpture and pottery have become two distinct worlds. Stylistically the field is complex. It is no longer simply one or two movements working under a clay umbrella. It comprises many movements that are far removed from each other in their concerns of style and content. The world of the vessel has grown into an artistically credible genre of its own. The sculpture field now has one foot in the ceramics field and the other in painting, printmaking, and the sculpture mainstream itself.

American ceramics overall has grown substantially and successive revolutions have changed its structure, its values, and the content of its art. It is a revolution that is still very much in progress. Changes continue to sweep through the conventions of ceramic art today. In explaining some of the movements I have been obliged, by the brevity of this piece, to resort to certain generalizations which, while true in one sense, obscure contradictory issues that are equally true.

Texts can only fill in the background. And while such a study can be enhanced by exploring a growing body of literature on American ceramics, this book provides a more immediate way of filling in the gaps. The illustrations of the objects themselves speak so clearly of the diversity of the field and its growing sophistication. As Clement Greenberg stated at the 1979 Ceramics Symposium, "results—experienced not discussed or debated—are all that count when it comes to art as art."[20]

# NOTES

1. Henry Varnum Poor, quoted in a letter to Bernard Leach in 1958. See Linda Steigleider, "Ceramics and Design," in *Henry Varnum Poor 1887–1970* (University Park, Pennsylvania: Pennsylvania State University Press, 1983), 41.

2. Marguerite Wildenhain, "An Open Letter to Bernard Leach from Marguerite Wildenhain," *Craft Horizons* 13 (May–June 1953): 12.

3. "The Art with the Inferiority Complex," *Fortune* 16 (December 1937): 114.

4. For a revealing account of Otis and Voulkos's teaching methods see: Mac McCloud, "Otis Clay: 1956–1957," *Ceramic Arts* 1 (Spring 1983).

5. John Coplans, *Abstract Expressionist Ceramics* (Irvine, California: University of California, 1966), 7.

6. Rose Slivka, "The New Ceramic Presence," *Craft Horizons* (July-August 1961).

7. Op. Cit. Coplans, 8.

8. Robert Arneson, quoted in Neal Benezra, *Robert Arneson—A Retrospective* (Des Moines, Iowa: Des Moines Art Center, 1986), 23.

9. Harold Paris, "Sweet Land of Funk," *Art in America* (March-April 1967): 95.

10. See Peter Selz, *Funk Art* (Berkeley, California: University of California, 1967).

11. For an explanation of my term "Super-Object," see Garth Clark's *A Century of Ceramics in the United States 1878–1978* (New York: E.P. Dutton, 1979) and the extensive revision and updating of this work, *American Ceramics: 1876 to the Present* (New York: Abbeville Press, 1988).

12. Harold Rosenberg, "Reality Again," in *Super Realism: A Critical Anthology* (New York: E.P. Dutton, 1975), 139–140.

13. Kim Levin, "The Ersatz Object," *Arts Magazine* (February 1974).

14. Thomas Albright, "The Dividing Line Between Ceramics and Schlock," *San Francisco Chronicle* (August 21, 1979): 41.

15. Donna Nicholas, "The Ceramic Nationals at Syracuse," *Craft Horizons* (December 1972): 33.

16. I co-curated the exhibition and wrote the text to the catalogue, see: Clark, 1979.

17. See Garth Clark, ed., *Transaction of the Ceramics Symposium: 1979* (Los Angeles: Institute for Ceramic History, 1980). ICH also briefly published *The Shards Newsletter* and organized another four international symposia (Waldorf Astoria Hotel, New York, 1981; Nelson Atkins Museum, Kansas City, 1983; Toronto, 1985; and Victoria and Albert Museum, London, 1986). The symposium has now found a permanent home at the Everson Museum of Art's Syracuse China Center for the Study of American Ceramics, where it will be presented every three years.

18. See Donald B. Kuspit, "Elemental Realities," *Art in America* (January 1981): 79.

19. Peter Schjeldahl, "The Smart Pot–Adrian Saxe and Post-Everything Ceramics," in *Adrian Saxe* (Kansas City, Missouri: University of Missouri Gallery, 1987).

20. Clement Greenberg, "The Status of Clay," *The Shards Newsletter* 1 (Winter 1980–81): 1. Also published in Clark, ed., 1980.

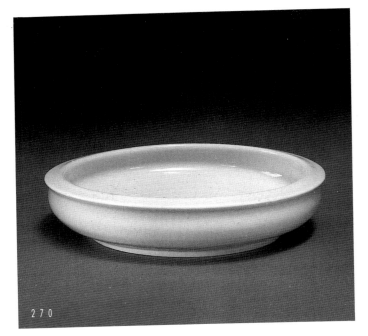

270

271

## R. F. ANDERSON (b. 1935)

Born in Los Angeles, R. F. Anderson was educated at the University of Southern California, and teaches art on the secondary level. He participated in the Ceramic Nationals in 1960 and 1962.

### 269 R. F. Anderson

*Vase*, 1960
Stoneware
H. 7, W. 5½, D. 3½ in. (17.5 × 13.75 × 8.75 cm.)
Marks: *RF Anderson '60* brushed on bottom
Museum purchase from "21st Ceramic National," 1960  P.C. 60.68

Ovoid stoneware form. This wheel-thrown and altered vase is pinched at the sides to form an open, mouth-like slit. It is covered in blue, brown, and gray glazes.

## LAURA ANDRESON (b. 1902)

The pioneer ceramist Laura Andreson retired from academics in 1970, enabling her to devote more time to her own creative work. While her early ceramics were usually hand-built earthenware vessels, she has turned to stoneware, and more

269

recently, wheel-thrown, porcelain pieces. (See also entry 142.)

### 270 Laura Andreson

*Bowl*, after 1975
Porcelain
H. 1⅛, Diam. 5¼ in.
(2.8 × 13.1 cm.)
Marks: *Laura Andreson* incised in script on bottom
Gift of Bryce Holcomb
P.C. 81.51.6

Small, footed porcelain bowl, covered in an off-white crackle glaze. The shallow, curving sides end in a wide, slightly sloping rim.

### 271 Laura Andreson

*Bowl*, 1961
Porcelain
H. 2⅝, Diam. 5¼ in.
(6.5 × 13.1 cm.)
Marks: *Laura Andreson FE 2/61* inscribed on bottom, *T.02/ + 2/FE(A or C)* written in pencil
Gift of Bryce Holcomb
P.C. 81.51.7

Small, footed, circular porcelain bowl. A variegated gold and brown glaze covers the deep form on the interior and exterior.

## ROBERT ARNESON (b. 1930)

Robert Arneson studied in his native California at the College of Marin, Kentfield, the California College of Arts and Crafts, Oakland, and at Mills College, also in Oakland, where he received an M.F.A. in 1958. He worked as an assistant to Tony Prieto at Mills College, and has been head of the ceramics department at the University of California at Davis since 1962. Arneson participated in the Ceramic National Exhibitions in 1960 and 1962, and by invitation in 1987. He also exhibited in "Ceramics 70 Plus Woven Forms," held at Everson Museum of Art in 1970.

In the late 1950s Arneson was influenced by the Expressionist attitudes toward clay which he saw in the work of Peter Voulkos. This led him to investigate the sculptural possibilities of the medium, and in 1961 he threw his famous *No Deposit, No Return* bottle, which became a turning point in his own career and helped to determine the path that American ceramics would take during the next decades. He was an initiator of the Funk movement, in which irreverence, humor, word plays, and eroticism were combined in clay sculpture that amused, offended, shocked, and influenced a generation of young ceramists. Arneson has played an extremely important role in establishing ceramics as a major sculptural medium.

Arneson worked mainly in portraiture throughout the 1970s, creating likenesses of himself and artists who had influenced him. In his recent work, Arneson has used his satirical wit to speak out forcefully against nuclear armament.

272 **Robert Arneson**

*Mountain and Lake*, 1975
Stoneware
Mountain: H. 83¾, W. 175½, D. 38⅛ in. (209.3 × 438.8 × 95.3 cm.). Lake: H. 1, W. 128¼, D. 92 in. (2.5 × 320.6 × 230 cm.)
Marks: none
Museum purchase   P.C. 80.8

Large floor sculpture of free-standing mountain with flat lake in front. Both pieces are composed of modular, interlocking sections. The mountain is pyramidal and has a modeled, ridged surface covered in a tan glaze with blue accents.

The oval lake acts as a reflecting pool for the mountain. Light blue glaze is used in the section that reflects the mountain, and dark blue glaze covers the remainder of the basin. Each of the lake's interlocking pieces is in itself pool-like, with areas of puddled glaze.

Arneson enjoys contrasts, and here he juxtaposes the dry, matte surface of the mountain against the glossy wetness of the pool. During this period he was involved with creating works assembled in sections, and made a number of pieces using bricks. Then he began to form the individual sections himself, creating works that outgrew the gallery scale in which he, and most other ceramists, were working.

Exhibitions: "Nine West Coast Clay Sculptors," 1978; "A Century of Ceramics in the United States, 1878–1978," 1979

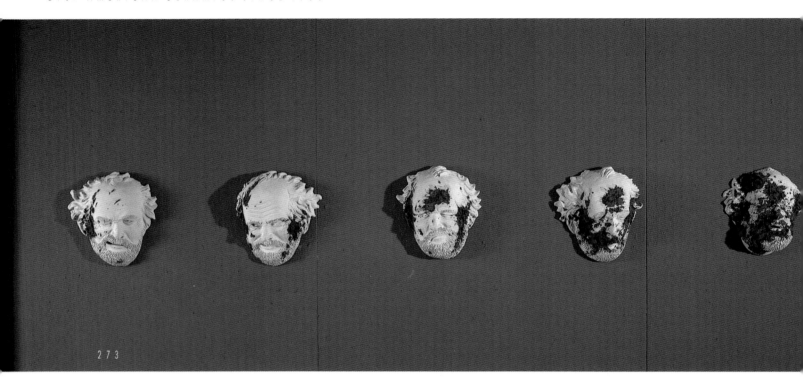

273

**273 Robert Arneson**

*Five Splat*, 1976
Stoneware
Each face: H. 15, W. 12, D. 4¼ in.
(37.5 × 30 × 10.6 cm.)
Museum purchase with matching
funds from the National Endowment
for the Arts   P.C. 80.9

Five-part, white stoneware wall
sculpture consisting of five self-
portraits of the artist, with detailed
facial expressions, hair, and incised
eyebrows, beard, and mustache. To
be viewed in succession, the series
depicts the artist's changing expressions as he is splattered with brown
clay.

Autobiographical references appear throughout Arneson's work. He
wishes to capture a moment of emotion or reaction frozen in time. His
works operate on many levels at once
and their titles can either explain or
disguise their content.

Exhibitions: "Nine West Coast Clay
Sculptors," 1978; "A Century of Ceramics in the United States, 1878–
1978," 1979; "13th Chunichi International Exhibition of Ceramic
Arts," Nagoya, Japan, 1985

**RUDY AUTIO (b. 1926)**

Rudy Autio was born in Butte, Montana, and his native state has figured
predominantly in his art. He studied
at Montana State University in Boze-

274

man, and received an M.F.A. from
Washington State University in
1952. He was resident artist at the
Archie Bray Foundation in Helena
from 1952 to 1956, and then headed
the ceramics and sculpture department at the University of Montana
until 1971. He has received numerous honors and awards. He participated in the Ceramic National
Exhibitions from 1962 through
1968, and was invited to exhibit in
"Ceramics 70 Plus Woven Forms"
at Everson Museum in 1970. His
work was also included in the invitational section of "American Ceramics Now: The 27th Ceramic
National Exhibition," at Everson
Museum in 1987.

Autio has played a major role in
the development of the contemporary idiom in American ceramics.
Early on he worked loosely, contriv-
ing slab-built vessels that were freely
formed and decorated. Construction
methods were obvious on these early
works, but as his interest in the figure
emerged, the vessels became more
finished on the surface and their
shapes began to take on a more human form. The freely applied decoration accented the reference to the
figure but also tended to flatten the
effect of the three-dimensional form.

Though his pieces never lost their
association with the vessel, and indeed became more strongly refer-

ential as his work evolved, Autio grew more and more involved with the figure, both human and animal. His works are containers, but they operate primarily as vehicles for the elegant, gestural paintings that hug their surfaces. The forms also are closely related to the decorative motif, and Autio has, probably more than any other contemporary American ceramist, successfully merged the figurative, sculptural, decorative, and vessel forms. His vision is entirely unique.

**274 Rudy Autio**
*Covered Jar*, c. 1966
Stoneware
H. 28½, W. 14 in. (71.25 × 35 cm.)
Marks: none
Purchase prize given by O. Hommel Company, "24th Ceramic National" 1966   P.C. 66.22

Hand-built, cylindrical stoneware jar with cover and handles. The body is divided into three alternating white-and-green glazed sections and decorated with applied circular forms. The flat, circular top with coil knob is glazed in brown, and a gold band surrounds the neck.

This jar, while primarily referring to the vessel form, also alludes to the figural, with its waisted body and inference to adornment.

Exhibitions: "A Century of Ceramics in the United States, 1878–1978," 1979

**275 Rudy Autio**
*Double Lady Vessel*, 1964
Stoneware
H. 28¼, W. 10½ in.
(71.3 × 26.3 cm.)
Marks: *Autio 64* brushed on side at bottom
Museum purchase from "25th Ceramic National," 1968   P.C. 68.63

Footed, slab-built stoneware vessel. The freely formed, undulating body flares at the top to the opening, although there are side openings as well. White slip is used overall, with black slip, linear decoration portraying a woman on two sides.

This early piece—combining vessel and female form—is more austere and summarily treated than Autio's more recent variations on the theme. It is in this piece, as Garth Clark has pointed out, that Autio's style became fully realized.[1]

Exhibitions: "A Century of Ceramics in the United States, 1878–1978," 1979; "The Eloquent Object," Philbrook Art Center, Tulsa, Oklahoma, 1987

1. Garth Clark. *American Ceramics, 1876 to the Present* (New York: Abbeville Press, 1988), 253.

### RALPH BACERRA (b. 1930)

A native of California, Ralph Bacerra was educated at Chouinard Art Institute in Los Angeles. He later became chairman of the ceramics department at Chouinard, and now has his own studio in Los Angeles. Bacerra participated in the Ceramic Nationals in 1962, 1966, and 1968, and was invited to exhibit in "Ceramics 70 Plus Woven Forms" at Everson Museum in 1970.

Bacerra's work is rich and sophisticated. He often makes references to other cultures, especially those of the Orient. He juxtaposes traditional shapes and decorative styles with contemporary imagery, or uses materials and forms in such a way as to conjure up associations with ancient objects, such as Tang or Imari ceramics.

His colors are rich and often applied in many layers, using both high and low firings. His porcelains have deep and lustrous surfaces, and he uses gold and silver with great surety. He is at ease with the vessel as well as with sculpture, and the results of each are equally highly crafted. In fact, he often combines the two, carving out areas of plates or creating hollow, three-dimensional forms of slabs or thrown sections, which are more sculptural than container-like. Then the result—whether vessel or sculpture—serves as a vehicle for the decoration, which is Bacerra's forte. In his most recent work, while drawing on the imagery of many cultures, he assembles motifs in a collage-like fashion with various patterns, overlapping shapes, and disregard for traditional perspective to create luscious, elegantly designed, and fastidiously crafted objects that offer a sense of luxury and preciousness.

**276 Ralph Bacerra**
*Silver Stripe*, c. 1970
Earthenware
H. 27½, W. 17, D. 5½ in. (68.75 × 42.5 × 13.75 cm.)

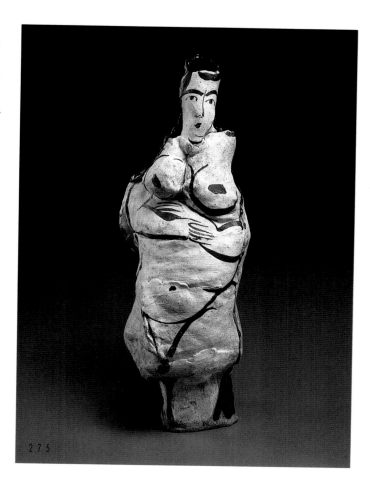

275

276

Marks: none
Purchase prize from "Ceramics 70 Plus Woven Forms," 1970
P.C. 70.26

Slab-built earthenware sculpture resembling a flattened mountain peak.

This monumental, organic piece in deep blue with silver luster striping repeats the massive forms of the hillsides and mountains that surround Bacerra's studio.

## CARLTON BALL (b. 1910)

Carlton Ball was initially trained as a painter but became interested in ceramics through his contacts with Glen Lukens while still a student. He has worked in collaboration with his wife, Kathryn Uhl Ball, and with the painter Aaron Bohrod, who provided the decorative motifs for some of his later work. Ball is particularly interested in the construction of large, wheel-thrown works. (See also entry 148.)

### 277 Carlton Ball

*Night Birds*, c. 1955
Stoneware
H. 17¾, Diam. 11 in.
(44.4 × 27.5 cm.)
Marks: *F. C. Ball* incised on bottom
Museum purchase from "19th Ceramic National," 1955   P.C. 62.9

Ovoid stoneware bottle, tapering at foot and at neck to a flared mouth. A mottled brown and gray glaze and a wax-resist linear bird form decorate the bottle.

Exhibitions: "Forms from the Earth: 1,000 Years of Pottery in America," Museum of Contemporary Crafts, New York, 1960

277

### 278 Carlton Ball

*Vase*, c. 1966
Stoneware
H. 59, Diam. 18 in.
(147.5 × 45 cm.)
Marks: none
Gift of Mr. and Mrs. John D. Williams from "24th Ceramic National," 1966   P.C. 66.64

Tall, wheel-thrown vase with ovoid body tapering to a thin neck and rimmed mouth. A white speckled glaze and wax-resist linear configu-

278

279

Fred Bauer was born in Memphis, Tennessee and studied at the Memphis Academy of Art. He received an M.F.A. from the University of Washington in 1964. Bauer worked at the Archie Bray Foundation in Helena, Montana, and was the recipient of a Louis Comfort Tiffany Foundation grant. He taught at the universities of Wisconsin, Michigan, and Washington.

Bauer worked in the Funk/Super Object idiom in reaction to the preciousness that he felt was associated with ceramics of the European court traditions and the bric-a-brac of mass production. His sculptures are startling for their visceral associations and threatening qualities, and also for their fine craftsmanship.

He participated in the Ceramic Nationals in 1964, 1966, and again in 1968, when he served on the national jury of awards.

280 **Fred Bauer**
*5325-Run Over*, c. 1966
Porcelain
H. 30½, W. 19, D. 9 in. (76.3 × 47.5 × 22.5 cm.)
Marks: none
Museum purchase from "24th Ceramic National," 1966   P.C. 68.27

Porcelain sculptural form, hand-built with applied clay details. Incised words and linear designs on the surface are covered by a gray glaze overall, with red, blue, green, brown, and dark gray details.

**JACQUELINE BELFORT-CHALAT (b. 1930)**
A native of Mt. Vernon, New York, Jacqueline Belfort-Chalat studied at

rations decorate the body. The decorative motif on this monumental vase may have been created by Aaron Bohrod.

**WALTER DARBY BANNARD (b. 1934)**
Walter Darby Bannard was educated at Phillips Exeter Academy and received a B.A. degree from Princeton University in 1956. He is a painter, has been a contributing editor to *Artforum* magazine, and teaches at the School of Visual Arts in New York.

Bannard participated in "New Works in Clay III" at Everson and worked in a relief form that resulted in a clay equivalent of his painting. He first worked in clay at Syracuse Clay Institute in 1978, and has continued to use that medium since then.

279 **Walter Darby Bannard**
*Japan Spring, Number 2*, 1980
Stoneware
H. 20¼, W. 12½, D. 1⅝ in. (50.6 × 31.3 × 4 cm.)
Marks: none
Gift of the artist   P.C. 81.32

Rectangular stoneware plaque with richly textured surface. Abstract curvilinear designs with thick yellow and white glazes accentuate the textural surface. An incised line frames the piece at its edges.

Exhibitions: "New Works in Clay III," 1981

280

Columbia University, the Art Students League, and received an A.B. from the University of Chicago in 1948. She also studied at the Fashion Institute of Technology and at the Royal Academy of Fine Arts in Copenhagen. She has been the director of the fine arts department at Le Moyne College in Syracuse since 1969. Belfort-Chalat is a sculptor who works in a variety of media, including clay.

### 281 Jacqueline Belfort-Chalat

*War*, 1976
Stoneware
H. 18¼, W. 7¾, D. 10½ in.
(45.55 × 19.3 × 26.25 cm.)
Marks: none
Gift of the artist  P.C. 85.65

Stoneware head on wooden base. This hollow, highly textured form of a ravaged victim, with holes in the cheeks and at the top of the head, evokes the horrors and savage destruction of war.

281

### DAVID BENGE (b. 1936)

A ceramist and designer born in Santa Monica, David Benge studied with Laura Andreson at the University of California at Los Angeles and received an M.F.A. from the University of Southern California in 1968. He also studied with Carlton Ball and Susan Peterson. Benge creates functional porcelain pieces, architectural tiles, and ceramic assemblages.

### 282 David Benge

*Magician's Case*, c. 1968
Porcelain
H. 15, W. 26½, D. 18½ in.
(37.5 × 66.25 × 46.25 cm.)
Marks: none
Purchase prize given by Syracuse Society of Architects, "25th Ceramic National," 1968  P.C. 68.64

Slip-cast porcelain sculpture consisting of twenty-seven truncated triangular forms arranged in three equidistant rows of nine, and mounted on a rectangular wooden base. A green with brown glaze is used overall.

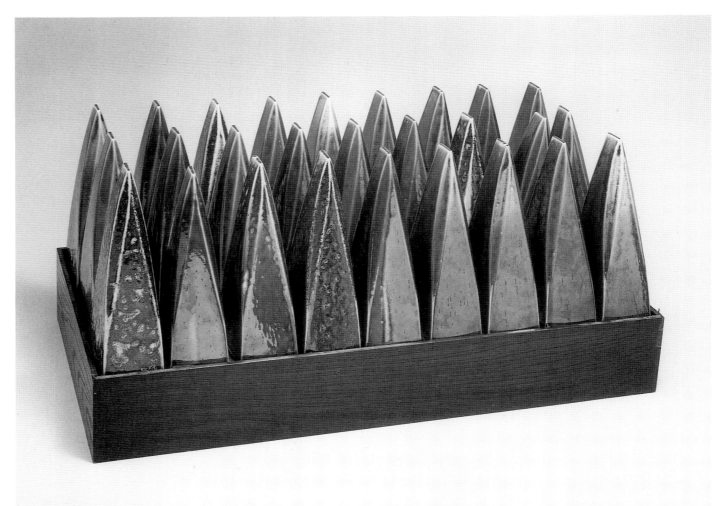

282

## BILLY AL BENGSTON (b. 1934)

Billy Al Bengston was born in Dodge City, Kansas, and studied at Los Angeles City College and at Otis Art Institute. He was part of the experimental group that surrounded Voulkos during those seminal, early years. Bengston had been influenced by Japanese ceramics, especially raku and Oribe, and when he left ceramics and turned to painting these remained as strong undercurrents in his work.

Bengston returned to ceramics in 1975 with the "New Works in Clay by Contemporary Painters and Sculptors" project and ensuing exhibition organized and curated by Margie Hughto at Everson Museum.

### 283 Billy Al Bengston

*Hexagonal Dinnerware*, 1976
Commercial flintware body
Dinner plate: H. 1, L. 12¾, W. 10⅛ in. (2.5 × 31.8 × 25.3 cm.). Small plate: H. 1, L. 10⅜, W. 7¾ in. (2.5 × 25.9 × 19.4 cm.). Dish: H. 1⅞, L. 10¼, W. 7¾ in. (4.6 × 25.6 × 19.4 cm.). Cup: H. 2½, W. 3¼ in. (6.3 × 8.1 cm.). Saucer: H. 1, L. 5⅛, W. 4⅝ in. (2.5 × 12.8 × 11.6 cm.)
Marks: *B.A.B./Syracuse China/1976* brushed in gold on bottom of cup and saucer
Gift of the artist   P.C. 76.56.1–4

*Hexagonal Dinnerware* includes a dinner plate, small plate, dish, cup, and saucer. Hexagonal plates and saucers have deep wells and wide, flat ledges. The footed cup has a straight-sided, cylindrical body with a flat, angled handle. All pieces have black gloss glaze with brown and turquoise sprayed and brushed to create an all-over pattern.

This dinnerware was part of a set created at Syracuse China Corporation as part of the "New Works in Clay" project. Bengston's designs were submitted to Syracuse China, where plaster molds were prepared by Don Foley and the pieces produced in flintware, a Syracuse China body.

The iris motif, which Bengston refers to as "Dracula," was created on these pieces by spraying glazes over a template. The motif is a constant in Bengston's work, often appearing in his paintings as well. He refers to this, and other motifs that he uses, as "signature marks."

Exhibitions: "New Works in Clay by Contemporary Painters and Sculptors," 1976; "A Century of Ceramics in the United States, 1878–1978," 1979

284

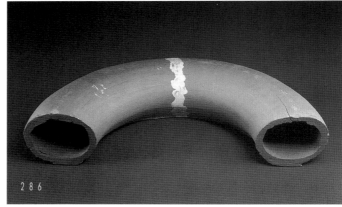

286

285

287

## CURTIS BENZLE (b. 1949)
## SUSAN BENZLE (b. 1950)

Curtis Benzle graduated from Ohio State University, studied at the School for American Craftsmen in Rochester, New York, and received an M.A. from Northern Illinois University. Susan Benzle graduated from Ohio State University and received an M.F.A. from Northern Illinois University.

Susan worked as a weaver before she began to collaborate with her husband in 1979. They now work in porcelain, and have achieved a singular virtuosity with the material. Their delicate forms are elegantly decorated and in the proper light their translucence often reveals decoration hidden between the layers of porcelain.

284 **Curtis and Susan Benzle**

*After You're Gone II*, 1986
Porcelain
H. 7, W. 17 in. (17.5 × 42.5 cm.)
Gift of Frank Sherman and Christopher Darling   P.C. 87.10 a, b

Thin porcelain vessel in narrow, flower form. The petal-like decoration is blue. When light shines through the translucent vessel, swimming fish are revealed painted between layers of the vessel wall. The vessel sits on a sheath-like base.

Exhibitions: "American Ceramics Now: The 27th Ceramic National," 1987

## BROTHER THOMAS BEZANSON

Brother Thomas began to work in clay before he entered the Benedictine order in Weston, Vermont nearly forty years ago. He was born in Halifax, Nova Scotia and graduated from the Nova Scotia College of Art and Design. He also studied philosophy at the University of Ottawa. Since 1985 he has been an artist in residence at Mount St. Benedict in Erie, Pennsylvania. He has traveled widely and his work shows the influences of traditional oriental porcelain.

285 **Brother Thomas**

*Ellipse Vase*, c. 1986
Porcelain
H. 11, W. 16¾, D. 3¼ in.
(27.5 × 41.8 × 8.1 cm.)
Marks: artist's cypher on bottom
Museum purchase with funds from the Dorothy and Robert Riester Ceramic Fund   P.C. 87.50

Wide, thin, elliptical porcelain vase, growing slightly bulbous near the base. A small slit mouth is at the top.

This elegant, finely crafted piece in a blue and purple glaze illustrates Brother Thomas's concern with formal qualities and the influence of the Far East on his work.

## STANLEY BOXER (b. 1926)

A native New Yorker, Stanley Boxer was educated at Brooklyn College and the Art Students League. In 1975 he received a Guggenheim Fellowship. He is an instructor at Vermont Art School and maintains his studio in New York City.

Boxer, a painter and sculptor, had never worked in clay before participating in the "New Works in Clay" project held in Syracuse in 1976. He had worked in stone and wood as a sculptor, producing works that incorporated the column and the arch. He uses these same forms, as well as closed and open forms, in his clay work.

**286 Stanley Boxer**
*Untitled*, 1975
Stoneware
H. 9, W. 36, D. 21 in.
(22.4 × 90 × 52.5 cm.)
Marks: none
Gift of the artist   P.C. 76.49

Hollow, cylindrical, arc-shaped stoneware form with a flat band on top. A wavy line in white slip surrounds the form at the center.

Exhibitions: "New Works in Clay by Contemporary Painters and Sculptors," 1976

## REGIS BRODIE (b. 1942)

A Pittsburgh native, Regis Brodie was educated at Indiana University of Pennsylvania and received an M.F.A. from Tyler School of Art at Temple University in Philadelphia.

Brodie has worked in porcelain, stoneware, and raku. He states that he is mainly interested in the integration of form and surface. His works often contain allusions to landscape.

**287 Regis Brodie**
*Bottle*, 1975
Stoneware
H. 9¼, Diam. 30 in.
(23.1 × 75 cm.)
Marks: *BRODIE* incised on bottom
Gift of the artist   P.C. 76.30

Squat, globular bottle rising from a low, straight foot. The body tapers abruptly to a tiny neck and flared mouth. The shoulder and sides are decorated with incised, circular and linear designs. Gray-blue and dark blue glazes cover the body, with green at the top.

Brodie had an exhibition at Everson Museum in 1976 with Richard Zakin.

Exhibitions: "Two Potters: Regis Brodie and Richard Zakin," 1976

## JO BUFFALO (b. 1948)

Jo Buffalo was born in Cleveland and educated at Syracuse University, receiving an M.F.A. in 1985. She was assistant project director for the "New Works in Clay by Contemporary Painters and Sculptors" project at the Syracuse Clay Institute, Syracuse University, from 1974 to 1976. She taught at Syracuse University and currently teaches at Cazenovia College. She is also a freelance illustrator.

Buffalo has worked as a veterinary assistant and has taught biology in Kenya. Her ceramics reflect both her interest in animals and her African travels. She participated in the "New Works in Clay III" project at Everson, and in those works she created animals, shapes, and surface treatments reminiscent of prehistoric cave paintings. She also collaborates with Christopher Darling at times, producing joint works which Darling forms and she decorates.

**288 Jo Buffalo**
*Chase I*, 1981
Stoneware
H. 19½, W. 22½, D. 2½ in.
(48.8 × 56.3 × 6.3 cm.)
Marks: none
Gift of the artist   P.C. 81.35

Slab-constructed, salt-fired stoneware wall plaque. Linear patterns and a landscape motif with two running deer are incised into the bulging surface. Porcelain slip has been dripped over and inlaid into the surface.

## TOBY BUONAGURIO (b. 1947)

Toby Buonagurio studied at the City College of New York. She initially worked as a painter but changed to ceramics while still a student. Her imagery comes from the mundane world, popular images that anyone can relate to. She has done shoes, automobiles, especially "hot rods," robots, and reliquaries, but transforms them all into funky fantasies

288

289

290

her viewers. Her influences are diverse, from Art Deco, Surrealism, and ancient cultures to the Pop culture of the 1950s and later.

## MARK BURNS (b. 1950)

Mark Burns was born in Springfield, Ohio, and studied at the Dayton Art Institute. He received an M.F.A. in 1974 from the University of Washington, Seattle, where he worked with Howard Kottler and Patti Warashina. He has taught at the Dayton Art Institute, the University of Washington, the State University of New York at Oswego, and Philadelphia College of Art.

Burns combines slip-cast forms with trompe l'oeil imagery to create bizarre, often sado-masochistic imagery, which works symbolically for him on an intensely personal level and intrigues the viewer not only visually but intellectually and emotionally as well. His craftsmanship approaches perfection and this, too,

awes the viewer, adding to the fascination of his exotic pieces.

### 290 Mark Burns

*Vice Squad,* 1985
Earthenware, wood, wire
H. 40, W. 36, D. 22 in. (100 × 90 × 55 cm.)
Marks: none
Purchase prize with funds from the Dorothy and Robert Riester Ceramic Fund, "American Ceramics Now: The 27th Ceramic National," 1987   P.C. 87.37.1

Earthenware trompe l'oeil sculpture of two busts of a devil and a transvestite on a painted wooden platform. The sculpture is assembled from ten separate pieces. The figure on the right is a horned, red devil's head, which rises from a leopard-spotted ashtray. A shoe and skull protrude from the back of the head and multiple stitched scars mark the red face. Two smoking cigarettes and fire surround the neck. The devil

that delight and entertain while also making a serious artistic statement.

### 289 Toby Buonagurio

*Horse Headed Robot #10,* 1981
Earthenware
H. 23, W. 12, D. 12 in. (57.5 × 30 × 30 cm.)
Marks: *toby buonagurio* and copyright mark written on left foot of figure
Gift of Mr. Sidney Wolgin
P.C. 82.40

Colorful earthenware sculpture depicts a futuristic robot with a horse's head. The figure stands with both feet firmly planted and holds in one outstretched hand the bust of a horse with flowing mane, while his other hand brandishes an intricately decorated weapon. The robot is dressed in spectacular armor in a stunning array of colors. Multiple glazes and paints are used in orange, purple, and turquoise with lustrous golds and silvers, flocking, rhinestones, and glitter added.

This piece, like most of Buonagurio's work, is hand-built and cast-constructed with low-fired clay and multiple glazes. She is not a purist, but incorporates an assortment of objects and textures into her sculptures, giving her surfaces great variety. Highly imaginative and inventive, she delights in delighting blows smoke towards the bearded transvestite, who has leopard spotted eyebrows and hair, and two dice protruding from his eyes. Applied flower-pot-like breasts are repeated in the huge, overturned flower pot upon which the figure sits. Tatoo-like decoration of multiple question marks and *"So what?"* appear on his back.

*Vice Squad* exhibits the surreal qualities that permeate the work of Mark Burns. His social commentary, though expressed in very personal, almost secret terms, comes through, while at the same time the viewer is puzzled and even repelled, but completely intrigued.

### 291 Mark Burns
*Magician's Dinnerware*, c. 1974
Earthenware
Hand with cards: H. 11½, W. 9½, D. 6 in. (28.75 × 23.75 × 15 cm.).
Fire with steak: H. 11½, W. 9¾, D. 4½ in. (28.75 × 24.3 × 11.25 cm.).
Bird with crackers: H. 14, W. 10, D. 4¾ in. (35 × 25 × 11.8 cm.)
Marks: *Mark Burns* on bottom of each piece
Gift of Coy Ludwig
P.C. 84.20a, b, c

Set of three sculptures, each decorated on both sides. In the first, a

base representing folded fabric holds upright a plate with checkerboard decoration and a mirror in the center. A hand holding four cards, all aces, appears in front of a mirror, which reflects the back of the hand tatooed with a spade, an eye, and the words "ITS MYSTIC."

The second sculpture has an arch-shaped base covered with painted flames that flare upward toward the dinnerplate, which holds a cooking steak. The plate has a grid and smoke-like decoration. The opposite side portrays flames and smoke in the shape of a question mark.

The third piece has a curved base that supports the plate; both are decorated in a trompe l'oeil motif of crackers. A life-like branch crosses the plate, upon which perches a green and yellow parrot pecking at two crackers. The opposite side depicts similar crackers and a parrot's head and a hand offering a cracker.

Aside from the intriguing imagery, these pieces challenge the viewer to determine the extent to which clay can be manipulated. Burns presents the alternative to the idea that objects should speak of the material from which they are formed.

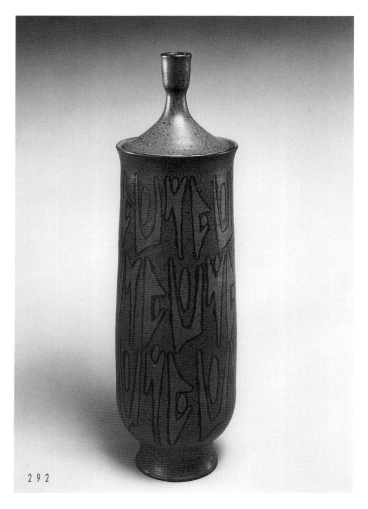

292

293

### CLYDE E. BURT (b. 1922)

Clyde E. Burt was born in Melrose, Ohio and studied at Fort Wayne Art School in Indiana, Cape Cod School of Art in Massachusetts, and at Cranbrook Academy in Michigan under Maija Grotell. He was a ceramics instructor at the Fort Wayne Art School and Museum and has his own studio, Burt and Martker – Designers in Clay. Burt participated in the Ceramic Nationals in 1954, 1956, and 1958.

### 292 Clyde Burt

*Covered Jar*, c. 1956
Stoneware
H. 18, Diam. 5¼ in.
(46.8 × 13.7 cm.)
Marks: *C B* within a circle incised on bottom
Purchase prize given by G. R. Crocker Company, "19th Ceramic National," 1956   P.C. 59.20

Covered stoneware jar with high foot. The slightly tapering, cylindrical form flares slightly at the mouth. The concave lid has a hollow, cylindrical knob. Orange abstract designs in three rows surround the red stoneware body, which is covered with gray matte glaze.

### LIDYA BUZIO (b. Uruguay, 1948)

Born in Montevideo, Lidya Buzio studied drawing and painting with José Montes and Guillermo Fernandez. In 1967 and 1968 she worked with ceramist José Collell. She came to New York in 1972, where she studied with painter Julio Alpuy.

The city has inspired her to paint the skyline on her pots, which she constructs from earthenware slabs. The slabs are formed into complex painted vessels where space is ambiguous and illusory.

### 293 Lidya Buzio

*Gray Roofscape Vessel*, 1984
Earthenware
H. 11½, W. 10¾, D. 9¾ in.
(28.5 × 26.8 × 24.3 cm.)
Marks: none
Gift of Garth Clark Gallery
P.C. 85.57

Tapering, angled, altered cylindrical vessel with stepped rim. A cityscape is painted on the exterior in grays, greens, blues, and yellows. The earthenware has been slip-painted, burnished, fired, and waxed.

In this strong, monumental vessel the form and decoration combine to give a strangely fluctuating sense of space, moving from two to three dimensions, and back again.

## ROSE CABAT

Rose Cabat was born in the Bronx and in 1936 married Erni Cabat, with whom she collaborated in making art during those early years. She began to work in clay after her marriage and worked at Greenwich Settlement House, where she taught herself to use the wheel. She took a five-week course in glaze calculation at the University of Hawaii, but otherwise is mainly self taught. She started in earthenware, then worked up to stoneware and, in the late fifties, to porcelain. She has concentrated on refining a form of vessel that she calls a "feelie." These "feelies" are small ovoid vessels which can be cupped in the hand. The tactility of the piece is of primary importance, and Cabat has devised glazes that are satiny, not glossy, to both the eye and the hand. The form must include a tiny, narrow neck and this tactile surface. Her pots must be held to be enjoyed to their fullest.

The Cabats now live in Tucson. Rose participated in the Ceramic National Exhibition in 1964 and recently was given a retrospective exhibition at the Tucson Museum of Art.

### 294 Rose Cabat

*Turquoise Blue Feelie with Black Runs*, 1985
Porcelain
H. 6½, Diam. 5 in.
(16.25 × 12.5 cm.)
Marks: *Cabat* incised on bottom
Gift of the Mulcahey Foundation   P.C. 88.20

Porcelain, globular form with high shoulder tapering to a tiny raised neck and mouth. A blue luminescent glaze is used overall, and a metallic black glaze at the shoulder drips down over the body. This vessel, from Cabat's "feelie" series, has an unusual, tactile quality.

### ELENA KARINA CANAVIER (b. China)

Elena Karina Canavier was born in Tientsin, China. She studied painting at Jepson Art Institute in Los Angeles, and received a B.A. from the University of Southern California. In 1971 she was granted an M.A. from California State University, Long Beach. She was the Crafts Coordinator for the National Endowment for the Arts from 1974 to 1978, and was arts advisor to Joan Mon-

294

296

dale at the Office of the Vice President, the White House. She has a studio in Washington, D.C.

Canavier's vessels are "tidepool" forms, which she has developed over the years. The interiors are glazed and have a pearly iridescence, reminiscent of deep pools of water. The exteriors are rougher, with bulbous or conical forms, and have a sandy, organic texture. The edges are very thin and fluted or scalloped, like seashells or coral formations. They are rich, undulating, sensual, and exquisite.

### 295 Elena Canavier (*See page 222*)

*Swan III*, 1979
Porcelain
H. 9, W. 12 in. (22.5 × 30 cm.)
Marks: *Elena/8–9–79/B.S.* brushed on bottom
Gift of the artist   P.C. 81.1

Porcelain vessel in shell-like form. The exterior is rough and mostly unglazed, with bulbous forms that flow into a very thin, pleated and fluted shell-like top. The interior has a pale iridescent glaze.

The contrasts of the strong, rough, gnarled exterior with the delicate undulating forms of the top and the watery interior evokes the vast power of the sea, which alternately crumbles rocks and polishes fragile shells.

### J. SHELDON CAREY (b. 1911)

J. Sheldon Carey taught at Columbia University and the University of Kansas. He was a visiting professor at San José State College. From 1953 to 1955 he was an editor of *Ceramics Monthly*. He works in both ceramics and glass.

Carey participated in the Ceramic Nationals intermittently from 1938 through 1958.

### 296 J. Sheldon Carey

*Textured Urn*, c. 1957
Stoneware
H. 20, Diam. 6 in. (50 × 15 cm.)
Marks: typed label taped to bottom reads: *Textured Urn/J. Sheldon Carey/Lawrence, Kansas/$200.00*
Purchase prize given by Homer Laughlin China Company, "20th Ceramic International," 1958
P.C. 60.19

Tall, oviform, footed stoneware urn with cover. The body tapers to a wide, flared mouth, which holds the domed cover. Deep, textural mark-

295

ings on the red body impart a pine-cone-like surface. The cover has a long, cylindrical neck flaring to a trumpet-shaped top. The cover has the same textural motif on the bottom section, with incised bands above. Brown and beige speckled glaze is used overall.

---

Exhibitions: "Forms from the Earth: 1,000 Years of Pottery in America,"

Museum of Contemporary Crafts, New York, 1960

## ANTHONY CARO (b. England, 1925)

Anthony Caro studied at Cambridge and at the Royal Academy Schools in London. He worked with Henry Moore for two years in the early 1950s. Primarily a sculptor in metal, Caro had occasionally worked with

clay before coming to the Syracuse Clay Institute. Here he experimented widely with forms that could be assembled into sculptural pieces similar to those he created in metal.

### 297 Anthony Caro
*Can Company Open*, 1975
Stoneware
H. 10, W. 47, D. 25 in.
(25 × 117.5 × 62.5 cm.)

Marks: none
Gift of the artist   P.C. 76.54a-d

Unglazed, slab-constructed stoneware sculpture consisting of four separate parts. Two curved slabs and a cylindrical form support the large, flattened, curving slab.

---

Exhibitions: "New Works in Clay by Contemporary Painters and Sculptors," 1976

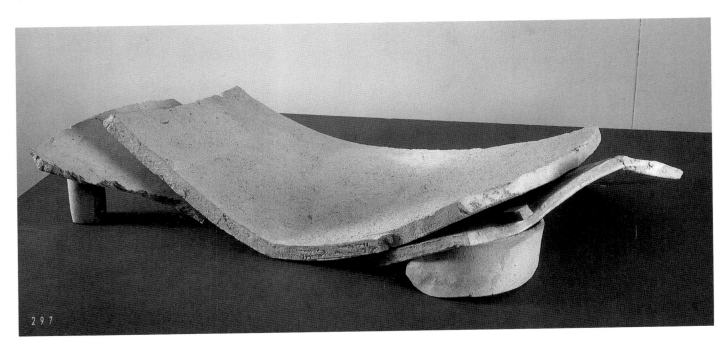

297

## ROY CARTWRIGHT (b. 1937)

Born in Westmoreland, California, Roy Cartwright studied architecture at the California College of Arts and Crafts and received an M.F.A. in ceramics from the Rochester Institute of Technology. He taught at the Cleveland Institute of Art, University of Illinois, and the University of Cincinnati. Cartwright works mainly in stoneware, with attendant muted colors, and concentrates on form and texture.

Cartwright participated in the Ceramic Nationals in 1962 and 1964.

### 298 Roy Cartwright

*Covered Jar*, c. 1970
Stoneware
H. 27, Diam. 13 in.
(67.5 × 32.5 cm.)
Marks: none
Museum purchase in the name of Harris Mining Company
P.C. 70.27

Round, bulging form supported by three columns, which stand on a square base. The cover, cut from the vessel, has a rounded loop knob. Gray-green glaze covers the entire jar.

Exhibitions: "Ceramics 70 Plus Woven Forms," 1970

298

## JOHN WILLIAM CAVANAUGH (b. 1921)

John Cavanaugh worked in Columbus, Ohio. He participated in the Ceramic Nationals in 1951, 1952, and 1956.

### 299 John Cavanaugh

*Goose*, 1951
Earthenware
H. 6⅝, W. 18¾, D. 6¾ in. (16.5 × 46.8 × 16.8 cm.)
Marks: none
Purchase prize given by National Sculpture Society, "16th Ceramic National," 1951   P.C. 52.620

Earthenware sculpture of goose. The flat ovoid body extends out into a long, sinuous neck. Small tail feathers and wing details are articulated. The body is incised to give it a feathered texture. The red earthenware body is covered in a manganese glaze and rests on a small wooden base.

## PAUL CHALEFF (b. 1947)

Paul Chaleff went to Japan in 1976 and this experience has had a profound effect on his work. He returned to the United States and built an anagama-style wood kiln in which he fires his stoneware. His work makes reference to ancient and con-

299

temporary Japanese wares, including those of Shigaraki, Bizen, Iga, and Tokoname. His vessels have a quiet strength and richness and honor the material from which they come.

### 300 Paul Chaleff

*Covered Jar*, 1982
Stoneware
H. 7½, Diam. 9¾ in.
(18.75 × 24.3 cm.)
Marks: *Chaleff* incised on bottom
Gift of Dr. Malcolm Nanes
P.C. 83.27a, b

Wood-fired stoneware jar with cover. The squat, bulbous form is topped by a short, cylindrical neck with two inverted, C-shaped handles below the rim. The concave lid with a short, domed handle fits inside the lip. Ash from firing adheres to the surface, but the body is otherwise unglazed.

300

301

Exhibitions: Jordan-Volpe Gallery, New York, 1983; "The Way of Tea: American Art for the Japanese Tea Ceremony," Art Complex Museum, Duxbury, Massachusetts, 1985

### ANNE CHAPMAN

Anne Chapman studied sculpture under William McVey at Cranbrook Academy and at the Cleveland Institute of Art. She participated in the Ceramic Nationals from 1952 through 1968, except in 1960 and 1962.

### 301 Anne Chapman

*Ebony Horse*, c. 1952
Stoneware
H. 24½, W. 19½, D. 9¾ in. (61.25 × 48.75 × 24.3 cm.)
Marks: *Chapman* in script brushed on bottom of hind legs
Purchase prize given by IBM Corporation, "17th Ceramic National," 1952   P.C. 53.658

Stylized, coil-built stoneware horse with modeled and incised decoration. Black engobe has been applied over blue-green engobe on a low-fired clay with grog. Sgraffito decoration indicates a saddle and bridle, and ornaments the whole body.

302a

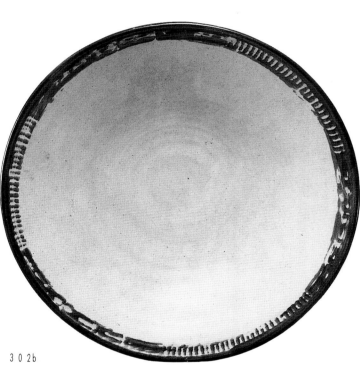

302b

### FONG CHOW (b. China, 1923)

Fong Chow was born in Tientsin, China and educated at Wah Yan College in Hong Kong, at the School of the Museum of Fine Arts in Boston, and at Alfred University. A painter, sculptor, and ceramist, he has his own studio in Alfred and has also designed for industry, particularly Glidden Pottery. He participated in the Ceramic Nationals from 1949 through 1958.

flared mouth is of buff stoneware. The waist flares out from the top and bottom. Vertical panels of alternating charcoal and rice slip cover incised designs on the body. The bottle rests on a black metal ring with triangular feet.

### 303 Fong Chow

*Bowl*, 1951
Stoneware
H. 2⅛, Diam. 4¼ in.
(5.4 × 10.8 cm.)

Marks: artist's cypher incised on bottom, *11P* brushed on bottom
Gift of Richard V. Smith
P.C. 83.5.17

Small, footed stoneware bowl. The gray body is covered in a milky blue crackle glaze. The interior crackle is developed in red.

### ANN CHRISTENSON (b. 1942)

Ann Christenson, a native of Bloomington, Indiana, received a B.A. from the University of California at Berkeley in 1964. She was a studio potter in New York, then managed a studio in Berkeley and taught ceramics in Bay Area schools. She works primarily in porcelain.

303

### 302 Fong Chow

*Ovoid Bowl and Bottle*, 1951
Stoneware
Bottle: H. 13⅝, Diam. 6¾ in. (34 × 16.8 cm.). Bowl: H. 3⅛, Diam. 14¾ in. (7.8 × 36.8 cm.)
Marks: *Glidden* and artist's cypher incised on bottom of each
Purchase prize given by Homer Laughlin China Company, "17th Ceramic National," 1952
P.C. 53.662.1, 2

Shallow stoneware bowl with slightly flared rim, which is decorated with a band of charcoal slip over pressed motifs. The exterior is in charcoal slip, and the interior in rice slip.

The lozenge-shaped bottle with

**304 Ann Christenson**
*Teapot and Two Cups*, 1967
Porcelain
Pot: H. 7, W. 9½ in. (17.5 × 23.75 cm.). Cup: H. 2⅜, W. 5 in. (6 × 12.7 cm.). Cup: H. 2, W. 5 in. (5 × 12.7 cm.)
Marks: none
Purchase prize given by William M. Milliken, "25th Ceramic National," 1968   P.C. 68.86.1–3

Cylindrical, wheel-thrown teapot has high, ear-shaped handle with coiled form at the base. The spout balloons near the pot, then curves upward. The cover has four pinched, raised decorations. The cups are thrown and altered with applied coil handles. White gloss glaze is used overall, with red, blue, green, and brown glazes decorating the handles, cover, and spout of the pot.

## MICHAEL COHEN

Born in Boston, Michael Cohen received a B.F.A. from Massachusetts College of Art in Boston and did graduate work at Cranbrook Academy in Bloomfield Hills, Michigan. He apprenticed with William Wyman in 1956 and 1957, and shared a studio with him—Herring Run Pottery. Cohen is a studio potter who specializes in utilitarian stoneware. Cohen participated in the Ceramic Nationals from 1962 to 1966.

**305 Michael Cohen**
*Left to right:*
*Vessels*, 1962
Stoneware
Left: H. 11, W. 6½, D. 4 in. (27.5 × 16.25 × 10 cm.). Center: H. 15, W. 7, D. 3 in. (37.5 × 17.5 × 7.5 cm.). Right: H. 13, W. 7, D. 3 in. (32.5 × 17.5 × 7.5 cm.)
Marks: artist's stamp and *Mike Cohen* inscribed inside foot
Helen S. Everson Memorial Purchase Prize (for group), "22nd Ceramic National," 1962
P.C. 62.33.1–3

304

305

Slab-constructed stoneware vessels —the one on the right is a branch holder. The interior and rim of the vase on the left are in black gloss glaze, the exterior is washed with yellow-brown and black. Its foot is wheel-thrown, unlike the feet of the other two. The center piece is incised with random marks and textures and washed in yellow-brown and black glaze on the exterior. The branch holder on the far right has applied clay medallion-like designs in blue gloss and irregularly incised markings. The piece is washed overall in yellow-brown and black.

## CLAIR COLQUITT

Clair Colquitt studied with Fred Bauer at the University of Michigan at Ann Arbor and did graduate work at the University of Washington at Seattle. Influenced by Bauer, he creates innovative works, using epoxy and acrylic paints as well as traditional ceramic techniques, adopting whatever method seems appropriate for each piece. His imagery is often taken from mundane sources, such as comic books, movies, and kitsch objects.

**306 Clair Colquitt**
*Mechimantis Cup*, 1968
Earthenware
H. 4, W. 5⅜ in. (10 × 13.4 cm.)
Marks: *Clair Colquitt Mechimantis Cup* incised on bottom
Museum purchase from "25th Ceramic National," 1968   P.C. 68.65

Wheel-thrown earthenware cup. The

306

307

308

flared base is notched to resemble a
gear. The applied handle is a colorful
caricature of a praying mantis. The
interior is glazed in pink, and on the
exterior, light green, silver, black,
yellow, and red, glazes cover the buff
earthenware.

## FRANK A. COLSON
## (b. France, 1931)

Frank Colson was born in Paris and
educated at Scripps College and
Syracuse University. He studied
with Marguerite Wildenhain and
Paul Soldner. His works are hand-
thrown, and he often combines sections to create a work from multiple
parts. Colson participated in the Ceramic Nationals from 1960 through
1964.

307 **Frank Colson**
*Branch Vase*, 1959
Stoneware
H. 10, W. 6, D. 5 in.
(25 × 15 × 13 cm.)
Marks: two stickers on bottom read:
(1) *BRANCH VASE/$50.00* (2)
*Frank Colson/521 Palm Court/
Talaha*[ssee]
Museum purchase from "21st Ce-
ramic National," 1960  P.C. 60.69

Slab-built stoneware branch vase
with one side curving around to create a second wall. Two beaker-shaped
necks extend from the shoulder,
which is decorated with hatch-

ing. Gray and mustard glaze is used
on the piece, with iron brush
decoration.

## CLAUDE CONOVER (b. 1907)

Claude Conover was born in Pittsburgh and studied at the Cleveland
Institute of Art. He regards himself
as a largely self-taught ceramist, de-

vising his own clay bodies, mostly
stoneware, from which he fashions
vessels of classic form with subtle linear surface decoration. He maintains
a studio in Cleveland, Ohio and produces a limited number of works
each year. Conover participated in
the Ceramic Nationals from 1960
through 1966.

308 **Claude Conover**
*Object*, 1963
Stoneware
H. 17½, Diam. 13 in.
(43.75 × 32.5 cm.)
Marks: none
Purchase prize given by B. F. Drak-
enfeld and Company, "23rd Ceramic
National," 1964  P.C. 64.85

309

Hand-built, sculptural stoneware form. The body is bulbous with straight sides and flattened top. Raised linear geometric patterns cover the piece, which is brown with white details.

### ROBERT T. COOKE (b. 1943)

A native of Sunbury, Pennsylvania, Robert Cooke was educated at Newark State College, New Jersey, and received an M.F.A. with honors from Cranbrook Academy. He has taught at Rutgers University since 1971.

**309 Robert Cooke**
*Beast Head,* 1982
Stoneware
H. 27, W. 24, D. 8 in. (67.5 × 60 × 20 cm.)
Marks: none
Gift of John Shafi   P.C. 84.11

Slab-constructed, angular stoneware form. The free form has incised lines and modeled sections. Multi-colored glazes, mainly blue and green, are used overall.

This is one of a series of pieces inspired by the story of Beauty and the Beast, especially as portrayed in the film by Jean Cocteau.

### PHILIP CORNELIUS (b. 1934)

A graduate of San José State University, Philip Cornelius, who was born in San Bernardino, California, also studied with Paul Soldner and received an M.F.A. from Claremont Graduate School in Southern California. He works in earthenware, stoneware, and porcelain. Cornelius participated in the Ceramic Nationals in 1966 and 1968.

**310 Philip Cornelius**
*Lidded Jar,* 1966
Stoneware
H. 20, Diam. 13 in. (50 × 32.5 cm.)
Marks: none
Helen S. Everson Memorial Pur-

chase Prize, "24th Ceramic National Exhibition," 1966  P.C. 66.25

Ovoid, wheel-thrown stoneware jar with flared mouth and domed cover. The blue and tan glazed body is incised with a decoration of a winged, fish-headed figure with two legs.

**311 Philip Cornelius**
*Lidded Jar,* 1966
Stoneware
H. 27, Diam. 18 in. (67.5 × 45 cm.)
Marks: none
Purchase prize given by Hammond

310

311

Lead Products, "24th Ceramic National," 1966 P.C. 66.26

Wheel-thrown, ovoid-shaped jar with high-domed cover. The bulbous body covered in lavender glaze flares to a wide mouth. A fish with wings is incised into the front of the jar.

This jar is quite similar to the preceding entry, but with a higher cover which seems to overpower the smaller body below.

## MOLLY COWGILL (b. 1948)

A native of Rochester, New York, Molly Cowgill was educated at Ohio Wesleyan University and received an M.F.A. from Alfred University in 1974. She has worked mainly in porcelain, and has recently returned to school to study medicine.

312 **Molly Cowgill**
*Bowl,* 1979
Porcelain
H. 3⅝, Diam. 8¾ in.
(9.2 × 21.8 cm.)
Marks: *Molly Cowgill, Richmond Va.* inscribed on bottom
Gift of Mrs. Allen P. Cowgill
P.C. 83.1

Round, footed porcelain bowl. Excised and incised floral designs surround the bowl in low relief. Light gray-green celadon glaze is used overall, except at the unglazed foot.

Cowgill often cuts and carves her vessels, and usually uses celadon glazes. These techniques combine for her, she says, in a way that merges tradition, simplicity, and function.

Exhibitions: "American Porcelain: New Expressions in an Ancient Art," Renwick Gallery, Smithsonian Institution, Washington, D.C., 1981–1984

312

313

314

### VAL MURAT CUSHING (b. 1931)

Val Cushing was born in Rochester, New York and studied at Alfred University, receiving his M.F.A. in 1956. He taught at the University of Illinois at Urbana, and since 1957 has taught at Alfred. He participated in the Ceramic Nationals from 1956 through 1968, except in 1966.

Cushing finds his inspiration in nature and in the clay itself, which he feels has a magical quality. His vessels are clearly enunciated and subtly glazed. Concave and convex shapes are combined in one form, often with lids, which sit within the pot.

### 313 Val Cushing

*Covered Jar I*, 1967
Stoneware
H. 12½, Diam. 9¼ in.
(31.25 × 23.1 cm)

Marks: *Cushing* inscribed on bottom
Purchase prize given by Association of San Francisco
Potters, "25th Ceramic National," 1968   P.C. 68.66

Footed, ovoid stoneware jar with cover. The wheel-thrown vessel is curved at the top with an inverted rim; the dome-shaped cover, with applied loop handle, fits inside the rim. Black and aventurine glazes cover the body. Abstract flower-like forms decorate two sides.

Exhibitions: "A Century of Ceramics in the United States, 1878–1978," 1979

### 314 Val Cushing

*Covered Jar*, c. 1969
Stoneware
H. 18, Diam. 12 in. (45 × 30 cm.)
Marks: three labels on bottom read:
(1) *Val Cushing/Box 792 Alfred/ $70.00* (2) *Cushing/#223* (3) *"Cov-*

*ered Jar" H.18"/Val Cushing Diam. 12"/stoneware/Ceramics 70 Plus Woven Forms*
Museum purchase   P.C. 70.39a, b

Ovoid jar with inverted rim. The domed cover with a flat band handle sits inside the rim. Alternating brown and orange bands with abstract floral designs surround the vessel.

Exhibitions: "Ceramics 70 Plus Woven Forms," 1970. "A Century of Ceramics in the United States, 1878–1978," 1979

### CHRISTOPHER DARLING (b. 1951)

Christopher Darling, a native of Montana, studied at the State University of New York at Geneseo and is a studio potter in Syracuse. He recently has turned to the creation of pit-fired earthenware pieces he calls ritual vessels. After firing, he embellishes them with feathers,

beads, pieces of grapevine, or ties them with linen cord. He also has produced a series of reconstructed vessels, where he breaks the object, then decorates the shards individually and randomly in patterns often referring to various ancient cultures. He then reassembles the vessel and ties it with linen cord. The final effect is that of a centuries old vessel, discovered in fragments and pieced together.

### 315 Christopher Darling
### Jo Buffalo

*Three Civilizations*, 1985
Earthenware
H. 8½, Diam. 7⅛ in.
(21.25 × 17.8 cm.)
Marks: *Buffalo 1985* brushed, *Darling* incised on bottom
Museum purchase   P.C. 85.5

Ovoid earthenware vessel flaring to a wide mouth. This vessel has been fired, broken, and reassembled, with shards decorated before reassembly. A ridge surrounds the pot at its base, with two ridges just below the mouth. A cord is tied around the vessel at these points. The body is decorated in part by geometric and floral designs in orange and green, with brown and white washes on the remaining exterior portions. The decorative motifs allude to those of ancient Greece, Rome, and prehistoric civilizations.

This vessel was created by Christopher Darling and decorated by Jo Buffalo (entry 288), with whom Darling has collaborated on several occasions.

### RUPERT DEESE (b. Guam, 1924)

Rupert Deese received a B. A. from Pomona College and an M.F.A. from Claremont College in California. He has shared a studio with Harrison McIntosh since 1950. Deese taught at Mt. San Antonio College in Walnut, California from 1957 to 1971. He was on the design staff of Interpace Corporation, makers of Franciscan ware, from 1964 to 1983. Since then he has devoted his time to studio work.

315

316 **Rupert Deese**

*Jar*, 1959
Stoneware
H. 8, Diam. 9 in. (20 × 22.5 cm.)
Marks: sticker on bottom reads: *Rupert Deese/stoneware design/Claremont, California*
Purchase prize given by IBM Corporation, "21st Ceramic National," 1960   P.C. 60.85

Bowl-shaped, covered stoneware jar with high, slightly tapered shoulder. The cover is slightly domed, with a flared, hollow knob. A combed, textural design is incised on the lower section. A brown matte glaze, with green and white accents, covers the body.

### ROSELINE DELISLE (b. Canada, 1952)

Roseline Delisle was educated at the College of Old Montreal. She works in porcelain and completes each piece at the wheel, including the decoration. Her vessels are constructed of triangular elements, and are exquisitely wrought.

316

317

### 317 Roseline Delisle

*Triptyque 6*, 1986
Porcelain
H. 21, Diam. 6¾ in.
(52.5 × 16.8 cm.)
Marks: *Roseline Delisle* on bottom
Museum purchase from "American Ceramics Now: The 27th Ceramic National," 1987, with funds from the Dorothy and Robert Riester Ceramic Fund   P.C. 87.80

Porcelain covered jar in three sections, including top. Triangular shapes are stacked upon each other—the conical bottom section is topped by a tapering cylinder with a flat shoulder, which is then topped by a triangular lid with a tiny triangular finial. A black glaze with blue and white accents is applied overall.

### STEPHEN DE STAEBLER (b. 1933)

Stephen De Staebler, a native of St. Louis, studied with Ben Shahn and Robert Motherwell at Black Mountain College in North Carolina. He then received an A.B. in religion (with high honors) from Princeton University, and an M.A. in art history from the University of California at Berkeley. He studied ceramics with Ka Kwong Hui and Peter Voulkos.

He has been a professor of sculpture at San Francisco State University since 1967.

The work of De Staebler is often on a large scale, but ranges from small pieces, such as the one in the Everson collection, to large figural sculptures and architectural settings (he has designed and executed the acoutrements for a chapel on the Berkeley campus). His large figures are modular, allowing for the creation of monumental forms.

The earth, its weathered surface as well as its soil, serves as an inspiration for De Staebler, and his figures express man's relationship to it. Caught in the process of fossilization, they emerge from or dissolve into the earth. His figures appear to have become part of the earth and rock, part of nature itself, and from them emanate references to deeper mysteries of time, place, and purpose.

### 318 Stephen De Staebler

*Untitled*, c. 1976
Earthenware
H. 6¾, W. 4¾, D. 2¾ in. (16.9 × 11.9 × 6.9 cm.)
Marks: *DESTAEBLER 1976* incised under chin

Gift of Mr. and Mrs. Paul Mills
P.C. 77.66

Freely modeled earthenware face with a hollow back. Of all the facial features, only the mouth is fully articulated.

De Staebler uses the earthy qualities of clay to their fullest in this roughly worked piece. The summary treatment leaves the viewer with a sense of mystery.

### RICHARD DEVORE (b. 1933)

Richard DeVore was born in Toledo, Ohio, and educated at the University of Toledo. He received an M.F.A. from Cranbrook Academy, where he studied under Maija Grotell. He succeeded Grotell as head of the ceramics department at Cranbrook, where he stayed until 1978, when he became a professor at the University of Colorado. DeVore was an invited participant in "American Ceramics Now: The 27th Ceramic National Exhibition," held at Everson in 1987.

DeVore's vessels are sensitive, sensuous, and have an aura of the primitive about them. Incredibly thin-walled, they are fragile, yet seem to have withstood the wear of the ages. Sometimes based on ancient American vessels, other times completely contemporary, the vessels are classic in their simplicity, yet visceral in their resolution. The interior is the focal point, usually highlighted with a subtle texture and sometimes a flush of color.

### 319 Richard DeVore

*Untitled # 561*, 1988
Stoneware
H. 8¼, W. 6¼, D. 7 in. (20.6 × 15.6 × 17.5 cm.)
Marks: *Z* incised on bottom
Museum purchase with funds from the Dorothy and Robert Riester Ceramic Fund   P.C. 88.31

Thin-walled stoneware vessel. The cylindrical form has a rounded base. The rim is angled, with a folded corner. Pinkish buff semi-matte glaze covers the exterior, with richer pink shades on the interior. Patches of *craquelleur* appear on both the interior and exterior.

320

321

## KENNETH DIERCK (b. 1927)

Kenneth Dierck studied painting at the University of Washington, his native state, and did postgraduate work in ceramics at California College of Arts and Crafts in Oakland.

Dierck often treats his clay forms like canvases, working with plaques which are sometimes single slabs, and sometimes intricately assembled from many pieces. They are decorated by stamping, modeling, or incising, and the glazes are often applied like paint, creating tensions and spatial qualities. His subject matter is figural and often whimsical.

Dierck participated in the Ceramic Nationals from 1960 through 1968.

### 320 Kenneth Dierck

*From left to right:*
*In Memory of Gussie*, 1959
Stoneware
H. 10¾, W. 12, D. 8 in. (26.9 × 30 × 20 cm.)
Marks: *K U DIERCK* inscribed on bottom
Museum purchase   P.C. 60.70.3

*The Dreamer*, 1959
Stoneware
H. 6¾, W. 7½, D. 6¾ in. (16.9 × 18.8 × 16.9 cm.)
Marks: *DIERCK* incised on bottom
Museum purchase   P.C. 60.70.2

*Sleeping Mime*, 1959
Stoneware
H. 9½, W. 9¼, D. 8 in. (23.8 × 23.2 × 20 cm.)
Marks: *D* incised on bottom
Museum purchase   P.C. 60.70.1

Three stoneware sculptures of egg-shaped heads lying on their sides. The eyes are closed, and the features summarily modeled. One head, *In Memory of Gussie*, has a bird perched on top. The figures are predominantly white and ochre, with accents of blue and lilac.

### 321 Kenneth Dierck

*The Bed*, 1962
Stoneware
H. 18, W. 24, D. 1⅜ in. (45 × 60 × 3.4 cm.)
Marks: *DIERCK* incised on bottom right side
Purchase prize given by Dey Brothers and Company, "22nd Ceramic National," 1962   P.C. 62.43

Stoneware wall relief depicts a woman and bearded man sleeping in a bed. A pot with two flowers lies at the foot of the bed. The details are incised and glazed in green, blue, and white on a brown stoneware body.

322

## 322 Kenneth Dierck

*Innocent City*, 1963
Stoneware
H. 37½, W. 54, D. 3¼ in. (93.75 × 135 × 8.1 cm.)
Marks: none
Helen S. Everson Memorial Purchase Prize, "23rd Ceramic National," 1964   P.C. 64.76

Large, slab-constructed stoneware wall relief depicts street scene of building facades with inhabitants, both human and animal, in doors and windows. The flowers and trees, as well as the figures, are modeled, incised, and applied. Gray glaze is used overall.

## 323 Kenneth Dierck

*Blue Moon*, 1966
Stoneware
H. 23½, W. 13, D. ½ in. (58.75 × 32.5 × 1.3 cm.)
Marks: *K. DIERCK* incised at bottom right
Museum purchase   P.C. 67.10

Rectangular stoneware wall plaque depicts separated forms of a head,

323

arm and hand holding flower, and two birds—one of which rests atop the head, the other on the flower. All are in relief, with incised details. A blue moon shines in the upper left corner. Brown glaze is used overall, with a minor blue detail on the flower and moon.

Exhibitions: "24th Ceramic National," 1967

## JAMES RICHARD DILLINGHAM (b. 1952)

Though he was born in Lake Forest, Illinois, Rick Dillingham has been associated with the Southwest not only because of his schooling, but also because of the nature of his work. Educated at the University of New Mexico in Albuquerque and Claremont Graduate School in Southern California, Dillingham first worked at the Albuquerque Museum restoring pottery. He has also curated several exhibitions on Native American art and is a dealer of contemporary and historical Pueblo pottery and Navajo textiles.

3 2 4

ticed with sculptor Fred Wiesner. He works in a variety of media, often combining them with clay. He often uses porcelain, not for the importance of its traditional concerns, but because of the fitness of the material to his particular needs.

Doell has also worked as a set designer for the theater and recently worked in the Arts/Industry Program at the Kohler Art Center in Sheboygan, Wisconsin.

**325 Glenn Doell**
*The Coquette*, 1979–1981
Porcelain
H. 8½, W. 13 in. (21.25 × 32.5 cm.)
Marks: *g. doell* incised on bottom
Anonymous gift   P.C. 85.63

Footed porcelain bowl with flared rim pinched at intervals. Four relief figures are incised on the sides of the bowl. A male torso within a circle appears on three sides; a partially clothed female figure wearing a large brimmed hat is on the fourth side. Celadon glaze is used overall.

This bowl is one of a series of works that the artist did on the theme of rape.

**324 Rick Dillingham**
*Vase*, 1981
Earthenware
H. 8½, Diam. 8½ in.
(21.3 × 21.3 cm.)
Marks: *Dillingham/Jan 81–10* inscribed on bottom
Gift of Everson Museum Members' Council   P.C. 82.5
Globular earthenware vessel tapers to a slightly raised, altered mouth. This vessel has been broken and reassembled, the resulting cracks are integrated as part of the surface decoration. The buff clay body is covered with black glaze. Orange and white rectangular shapes appear randomly on the body.

This reassembled vessel motif is typical of Dillingham's work and originated in his reconstruction work with Native American ceramics. He uses primitive firing techniques, and sometimes leaves gaps in the forms for visual play.

### GLENN E. DOELL (b. 1951)
Glenn Doell, a native of Huntington, New York, studied philosophy and ceramics at the State University of New York at Potsdam and appren-

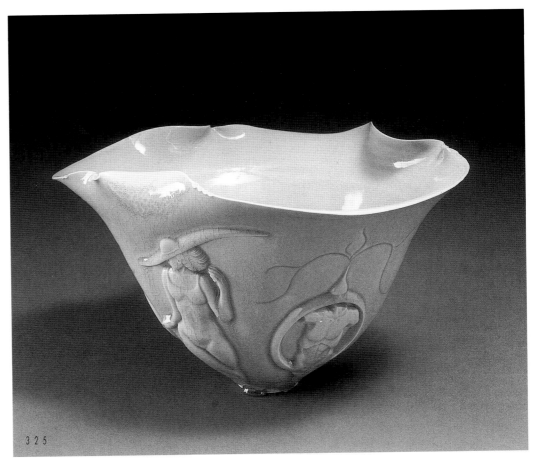

3 2 5

## AMY DONALDSON

The pottery of Amy Donaldson is usually wheel-thrown and functional. She uses wax resist, sgraffito, and glaze on glaze. She participated in the Ceramic Nationals in 1954, 1960, and 1962.

326 **Amy Donaldson**
*Vase*, 1959
Stoneware
H. 18, Diam. 7⅝ in. (45 × 19.9 cm.)
Marks: *Amy Donaldson H 179* written in black on bottom
Museum purchase   P.C. 62.8

Ovoid stoneware vase with sloping shoulder and cup-shaped mouth.

Lines encircle the vase at its shoulder and neck. The body is incised with leafy designs, accented with gray, brown, and blue glazes. A textured band runs around the bottom.

## ELIZABETH DUMANIAN (b. 1917)

Elizabeth Dumanian first began to study ceramics in 1970 at the Syracuse Clay Institute at Syracuse University, having been a public school teacher for many years.

327 **Elizabeth Dumanian**
*Magical Beastie Woodland Fantasy*, 1981
Earthenware

326

327

H. 19, W. 25, D. 2 in. (47.5 × 62.5 × 5 cm.)
Marks: *E. Dumanian* incised on back
Gift of the artist   P.C. 85.7

Unglazed earthenware relief plaque with lattice-like background. A large mythical animal in relief is in the cen-

ter, with three smaller animals surrounding it.

Dumanian's work often involves themes of legendary animals and fairytale figures, with attendant carving and modeling.

## FRIEDEL DZUBAS
## (b. Germany, 1915)

Friedel Dzubas was educated in his native Berlin at the Prussian Academy of Fine Arts and the Kunstgewerbeschule. He left Germany in 1939 and settled in New York in 1949. A painter, he was influenced by Jackson Pollock, and shared a studio with Helen Frankenthaler. His paintings were gestural, and then became more concerned with color. He had had no experience with clay when he was invited to work at the Syracuse Clay Institute. There he did nineteen sculptures, using stoneware clay with oxides added, and firing at different temperatures to achieve different color effects, thus carrying over some of his concerns from painting.

328 **Friedel Dzubas**
*Pink Pile-up*, 1975
Stoneware
H. 16, W. 37, D. 8 in. (40 × 92.5 × 20 cm.)
Marks: none

328

329

Gift of the artist P.C. 76.47a-c

Stoneware sculpture of stacked pile of irregular, pink clay slabs. The irregular widths and lengths of the pieces are accented by Dzubas's use of strong colors—orange-red, yellow-green, turquoise, and brown—on the edges. The clay is pink with gloss glazes.

Exhibitions: "New Works in Clay by Contemporary Painters and Sculptors," 1976; "A Century of Ceramics in the United States, 1878–1978," 1979; "Directions in Contemporary American Ceramics," Museum of Fine Arts, Boston, 1984

## JACK EARL (b. 1934)

Jack Earl attended Bluffton College in his native Ohio, and received an M.A. from Ohio State University in 1964. He taught at the Toledo Museum of Art from 1963 to 1972, then at Virginia Commonwealth University.

Earl was influenced early on by the traditional ceramics he saw at the Toledo Museum—Kandler's figures from Meissen and the Renaissance sculptures of the Della Robbias—works in which craftsmanship reigned supreme. Earl chose the same path, that of the immaculate craftsman, but added to it his own images, those of middle class, midwestern America. His works are curiously unnerving, with their surreal content and seemingly unrelated imagery. His recent works are either sculptural in the traditional sense of three-dimensional figures, or are in the form of a *dos-à-dos*, a two-sided relief sculpture with exquisitely detailed but strange, dream-like subject matter.

Earl participated in the 1968 Ceramic National and was part of the invitational section of "American Ceramics Now: The 27th Ceramic National" held at Everson in 1987.

### 329 Jack Earl

*Ohio Dresser,* 1976
Porcelain
H. 14, W. 12½, D. 6¼ in. (35 × 31.25 × 15.6 cm.)
Marks: *DRESSER Top/by Jack Earl/ 197\*6*
Gift of Thalia and Nathan Cohen P.C. 88.36a, b

Porcelain box in the form of a three-drawer dresser with clothing protuding from the open top drawer. The top lifts off to reveal the inside of the box. Items on top of the bureau include a cap, wallet, coins, book, photo, box, bottle, envelope, radio, lamp, and a sock.

This is one of a series of multiples done while Earl worked at the Kohler Company. The pieces varied, with different objects placed on the top of each.

### 330 Jack Earl

*Untitled,* 1968
Porcelain
H. 17, W. 9¾ in. (42.5 × 24.3 cm.)
Marks: none
Purchase prize given by National Council on Education for the Ceramic Arts, "25th Ceramic National" 1968 P.C. 68.81a, b

Coil-built, baluster-shaped porcelain covered jar. Applied sculptural handles are on two sides—one is a finely crafted female head, the other

330

332

331

a ram's head. Lines and dots surround both figures. The domed cover of the jar has an applied, potted plant knob. Flowers and curved lines are incised on both jar and cover. Celadon glaze is used overall.

This is one of Earl's first pieces in porcelain, and his first entry in the Ceramic Nationals. It won a purchase prize. Here one can see the influence of ancient Chinese ceramics in the form and materials, but the approach to decoration and theme is entirely his own, and typical of Earl's work, both early and late.

### MICHAEL EARNEY

Michael Earney works in Venice, California and entered the Ceramic National in 1968.

### 331 Michael Earney

*Holy Tetractys*, 1968
Earthenware
H. 6⅜, W. 13 in. (15.9 × 32.5 cm.)
Marks: none
Museum purchase   P.C. 68.82

Hand-built, triangular sculpture with ten egg-shaped forms on top.

Opaque white glaze is used on the pink earthenware body.

### KEN FERGUSON (b. 1928)

Ken Ferguson was born in Elwood, Indiana. He studied at Carnegie Institute of Technology and received an M.F.A. from Alfred University.

He was a resident potter at the Archie Bray Foundation in Helena, Montana and has been chairman of the ceramics department at the Kansas City Art Institute since 1964. Ferguson participated in the Ceramic Nationals from 1960 through 1966.

He exhibited in "Ceramics 70 Plus Woven Forms," 1970.

Ferguson has been one of the most influential teachers of ceramics in this country. His own work is honest and forthright, and he cautions his students to achieve the same honesty of purpose and materials. He works with a variety of clays, both porcelain and stoneware, and his forms are both functional and nonfunctional.

### 332 Ken Ferguson

*Storage Jar*, 1962
Stoneware
H. 15, W. 8 in. (37.5 × 20 cm.)
Museum purchase from "22nd Ceramic National," 1962   P.C. 63.22

Tall, cylindrical, covered stoneware storage jar with two applied handles. The straight sides are accented with throwing marks to create a rhythmical motif. The mouth is flared with an inset cover and flat, flared knob. Tan and gray glazes create vertical areas around the jar.

Exhibitions: "A Century of Ceramics in the United States, 1878–1978," 1979

333

334

### 333 Ken Ferguson

*Hare Basket*, 1987–1988
Stoneware
H. 15½, Diam. 16½ in.
(38.75 × 41.25 cm.)
Marks: none
Museum purchase with funds given by friends in memory of Lenore Goldstein   P.C. 88.14

Circular, black stoneware basket form on high pedestal foot. A texture is roughly incised on the foot. A large, freely modeled, leaping rabbit creates the handle of the circular basket form, and smaller playful rabbits decorate the rim.

The two pieces by Ferguson in the Everson collection show the versatility of the artist—each is a monumental example of the directness and the surety with which he works.

### BETTY FEVES (b. 1918)

Betty Feves, born in LaCrosse, Washington, attended Washington State University and received an M.A. in art education from Columbia University. She also studied at the St. Paul School of Art, St. Paul, Minnesota and with Alexander Archipenko, with whom she studied sculpture. Her sculptural figures are semi-abstract, usually with unglazed surfaces. Feves participated in the Ceramic Nationals from 1952 through 1968.

### 334 Betty Feves

*Relief Figure Group*, 1956
Earthenware
H. 13¾, W. 27⅝, D. 2½ in.
(34.3 × 69 × 6.25 cm.)
Marks: none
Purchase prize given by IBM Corporation, "19th Ceramic National," 1956   P.C. 59.23

Earthenware wall relief sculpture in three sections. The six semi-abstract figures stand and sit in various poses; two are female and four male. Each has an incised and/or glazed pattern on his or her body. The figures rest on a base, with a slab back suggesting an architectural structure. Green and yellow matte glaze highlights the details. The three sections are mounted on a wood panel.

### 335 Betty Feves

*Three Figures*, 1954
Stoneware
H. 17¼, W. 7, D. 9 in.
(43.1 × 17.5 × 22.5 cm.)

335

336

337

Marks: *Feves* incised at bottom back
Purchase prize given by Harshaw
Chemical Corporation, "18th Ceramic National," 1954   P.C. 55.698

Stoneware sculpture of three abstract figures. The red stoneware body is covered in a white matte glaze. The figures are seated, with open forms in their centers. The sculpture rests on a single wooden base. United by form and material, these three figures merge into one.

The influences of Archipenko and Henry Moore are obvious here.

### 336 Betty Feves

*Persona*, 1964
Stoneware
H. 16¾, W. 11⅝, D. 7 in. (41.9 × 29 × 17.5 cm.)
Marks: *Feves* on bottom
Purchase prize given by Harris Clay Company, "23rd Ceramic National," 1964   P.C. 64.77

Stoneware sculpture constructed of rectangular slabs. A rectangular slab form with one extended side sits atop another similar form. Primarily unglazed, the slabs are punctured and incised, with gray-green gloss glaze on details.

### JANE FORD (AEBERSOLD) (b. 1941)

Jane Ford first attended Texas Tech University in Lubbock, then studied ceramics and painting at Newcomb Art School at Tulane University in New Orleans, and later received an M.F.A. in ceramics and glass from Alfred University. She currently teaches at Bennington College in Vermont.

Ford's vessels seem to be a complete melding of form and decoration, for the subtle lustrous glazes she uses seem to take their being from the vessel itself.

### 337 Jane Ford

*Sweet Water: Wind River Series*, 1978
Stoneware
H. 16, W. 10½, D. 3 in. (40 × 26.25 × 7.5 cm.)
Marks: none
Gift of the artist   P.C. 81.40

Arch-shaped stoneware vessel with a square opening at the top flanked by strap-like rectangular strips. The piece is slab-constructed and covered in lusters and iridescent glazes in purple, yellow, green, and blue.

Exhibitions: "Jane Ford: Recent Work," 1979; "A Century of Ceramics in the United States, 1878–1978," 1979

## JOHN FOSTER (1900–1980)

John Foster was born in Detroit and educated at the University of Michigan. He was an associate of Charles Harder, Arthur Baggs, and Ross Purdy, whom he met periodically at meetings of the American Ceramic Society. He designed an electrical model of the Revelation Kiln being marketed by Mary Chase Perry Stratton at Pewabic Pottery. Foster worked for Henry Ford, who gave him a studio-laboratory for his own use. In 1950 he created Festivalware, an open-stock dinnerware which he produced with the help of four apprentices.

Foster did consultations and commissions for architects and decorators, and headed the ceramics department at the Detroit Society of Arts and Crafts. He participated in the Ceramic Nationals intermittently from 1934 through 1966.

338

339

**338 John Foster**
*Brussels Bowl*, n.d.
Porcelain
H. 3⅜, Diam. 7⅞ in.
(8.4 × 19.6 cm.)
Marks: *Foster* incised on bottom
Gift of Michigan Potter's Association P.C. 81.2

Footed porcelain bowl with slightly flaring sides. Green and gold crystalline glaze is used overall.

Exhibitions: Brussel's World's Fair, 1958

**339 John Foster**
*Festivalware Bean Pot and Place Setting*, c. 1950
Stoneware
Bean pot: H. 10¾, W. 10½ in. (26.8 × 26.25 cm.) Dinner plate: H.¾, Diam. 8 in. (1.8 × 20 cm.). Small plate: H.¾, Diam. 4¾ in. (1.8 × 11.8 cm.). Cup: H. 2⅞, W. 5 in. (7.1 × 12.5 cm.). Saucers: H.¾, Diam. 6¾ in. (1.8 × 16.8 cm.).

Soup Bowl: H. 3, Diam. 4½ in. (7.4 × 11.25 cm.).
Marks: *Foster Ceramics* painted on bottom of bean pot, dinner plate, small plate, and saucers. *F* incised on bottom of cup and soup bowl.
Gift of Vincent Thomas P.C. 81.9.1–4, 5a, 5b

Single fire stoneware "Festivalware" place setting includes dinner plate, salad plate, cup and saucer, lidded soup bowl, and saucer. Plates and saucers are primarily unglazed with brown and red glaze stripes with abstract fish-like designs encircling them. The cup, with **C**-shaped handle, is glazed dark brown.

The bean pot is footed and has two flared, cylindrical handles. The pot interior is in a dark brown glaze, and like the place setting, the exterior is largely unglazed, with a band of brown glaze around the lower section, along the edge of the cover, and on its handle. Abstract fish designs are on the bands.

Exhibitions: "17th Ceramic National," 1952; Brussels World's Fair, 1968

**MARY FRANK (b. England, 1933)**
Mary Frank was born in London and studied for a short time with sculptor Alfred van Loen. In America she studied modern dance with Martha Graham and drawing at the American Art School in Holland with Max Beckmann. She also studied in New York with Hans Hofmann. She has taught at the New School for Social Research and at Queens College.

Frank works in a variety of media. Her clay work is romantic, sensuous, and celebratory of the material. Her figures are often fragmented, sometimes skeletal, and usually refer to nature in some form. She often makes references to the continuum of time—to things past, present, and to come—and the inevitable tensions that these create.

**340 Mary Frank**
*Sundial*, 1980
Stoneware
H. 8¼, W. 22, D. 17 in. (20.6 × 55 × 42.5 cm.)
Marks: none
Gift of Marvin Schwartz P.C. 82.39.39

Free-formed stoneware sculpture of a sundial. The palette-shaped disk has a round, modeled well with a hole on the bottom. A modeled, applied rod rises from the side of the disk and tapers to a flat, pointed end. Incisions are made on the disk and the well. Three stork-like birds are impressed to the right of the well. Six slab feet support the unglazed piece.

Exhibitions: "13th Chunichi International Exhibition of Ceramic Arts," Nagoya, Japan, 1985

340

341

**341 Mary Frank**

*Double Sundial*, c. 1980
Stoneware
H. 24½, W. 29, D. 17½ in.
(61.25 × 72.5 × 43.75 cm.)
Marks: none
Gift of Marvin Schwartz
P.C. 82.39.38

Unglazed, brown stoneware sculpture with large modeled base. Two
cylindrical stems rise from the base.
One stem is topped by a square slab
with a concave center having a fold-
like section. The other stem is
topped by a round, freely formed
slab with a triangular recession at the
center. A small, part human- part animal figure sits on the base between
the two main configurations.

### 342 Mary Frank

*Horse and Rider*, 1982
Stoneware
H. 23½, W. 48, D. 28 in.
(58.75 × 120 × 70 cm.)
Marks: *R.F.* incised on inside right
of front horse (under front leg)
Museum purchase with funds from
the Stanley Coyne Foundation
P.C. 83.8a h

Slab-constructed, sectioned stoneware sculpture of horse and rider.
The horse is split, creating a wide
chasm over which the rider perches.
The rider grips the mane and expresses fear or horror. Incising and
modeling, including handprints and
small running horses, appear on the
surface of the horse. The sculpture
is unglazed.

The horse is a common theme
throughout the work of Mary Frank,
as is the idea of metamorphosis.
Here, the horse splits and dissolves
beneath the horrified rider, who
struggles to stay astride. The horse-
men of the Apocalypse come immediately to mind, in light of the
terror and destruction implied by the
sectioned figures. The plasticity of
the clay is also used to advantage,
repeating the idea of transformation,
and also accenting the association
with nature.

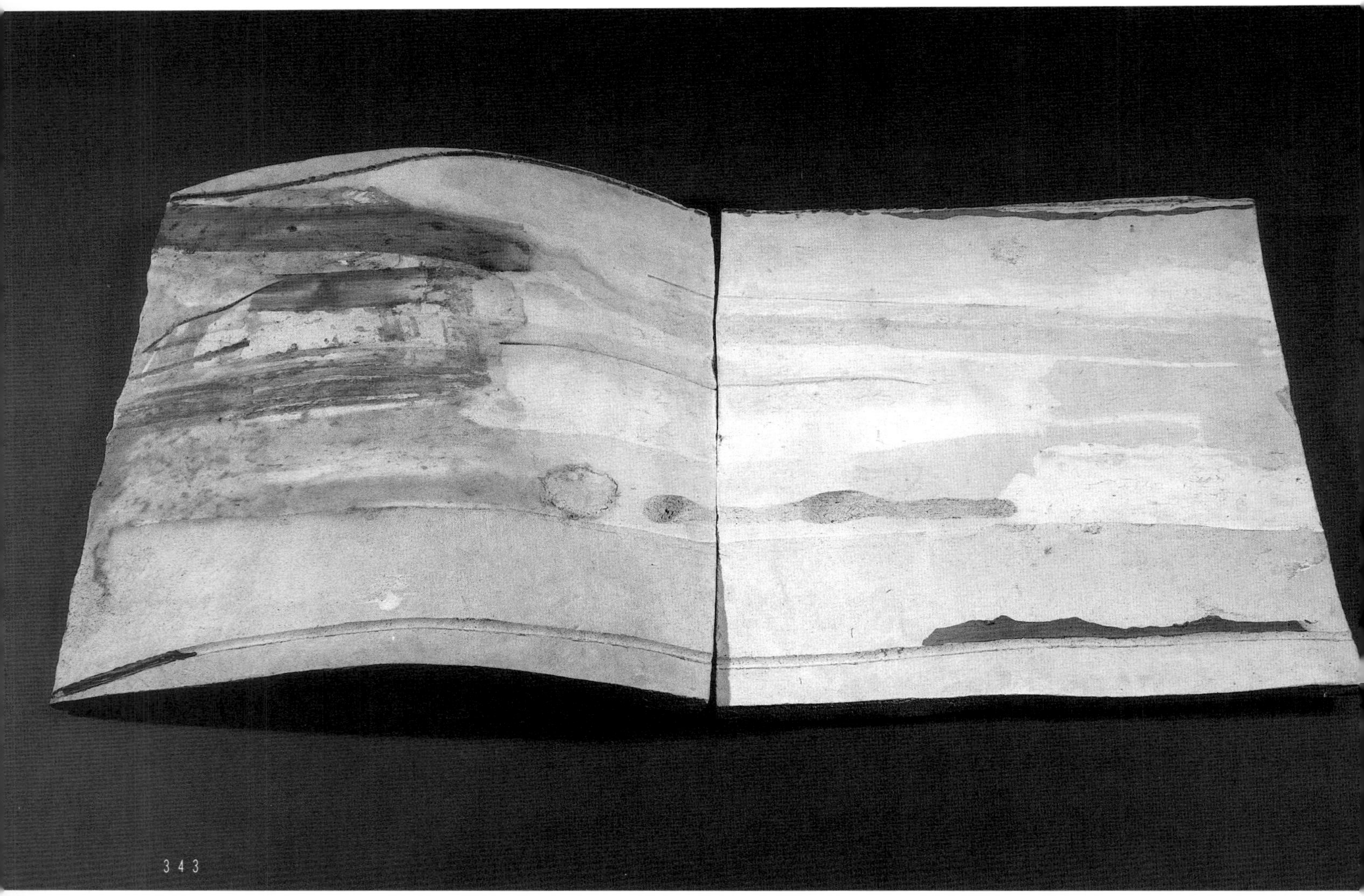

343

## HELEN FRANKENTHALER (b. 1928)

Helen Frankenthaler was born in New York and educated at Bennington College in Vermont. She also studied with Rufino Tamayo and Hans Hofmann. She is primarily a painter, known for the technique of stain-painting. She had already worked in clay, producing a limited edition of plates in 1964, when she came to the Clay Institute in Syracuse.

343 **Helen Frankenthaler**
*Mattress I*, 1975
Stoneware
H. 7, W. 62, D. 34 in. (17.5 × 155 × 85 cm.)
Marks: none
Gift of the artist   P.C. 76.52

Two stoneware slab forms, one with a buckled surface creating a curve. The sides are incised and indented. Underglazes and slips in purple, red, light green, brown, and white cover the piece.

*Mattress I* was created in Syracuse during the project that resulted in the exhibition "New Works in Clay by Contemporary Painters and Sculptors." Frankenthaler applied underglazes directly to wet clay on this piece. She was interested in color and glazes and her pieces were fired at various temperatures to achieve particular color effects. These simple pieces speak not only of color, but also, most eloquently, of the clay from which they are formed.

Exhibitions: "New Works in Clay by Contemporary Painters and Sculptors," 1976; "Helen Frankenthaler Ceramics," André Emmerich Gallery, New York, 1977; "A Century of Ceramics in the United States, 1878–1978," 1979; "Treasure House: Museums of the Empire State," New York State Museum, Albany, 1979–1980

344

## VIOLA FREY (b. 1933)

Viola Frey was born in Lodi, California and studied at the California College of Arts and Crafts in Oakland. She first studied painting, then turned to ceramics. In 1958 she received her M.F.A. from Tulane University in New Orleans. She has taught at the California College of Arts and Crafts since 1965.

Frey's work is mainly figural, involved with massive,life-sized sculptures of men and women up to ten feet in height. These are often menacing figures, intimidating the viewer as they tower above. Frey draws inspiration from bric-a-brac figurines, and her figures sometimes hold smaller figures, both derived from the figurine but given a completely new ethos. Frey also paints and makes ceramic wall forms. Her large plates, meant to be hung on a wall, are collage-like assemblages of cast and modeled objects and forms, often encrusted with thick glazes. Frey refers to these as "bricolages," after the word *bricoleur*, or jack-of-all-trades.

### 344 Viola Frey
*Untitled (Plate)*, 1976
Stoneware
H. 5⅛, Diam. 34 in. (12.8 × 85 cm.)
Marks: none
Museum purchase with funds from the Dorothy and Robert Riester Ceramic Fund  P.C. 86.63

Large stoneware wall plate with flared edges. The high-relief decoration is articulated in multicolor glazes, with yellow predominating. A blue,figural form is at the top and a purple hand print at the bottom, as well as other abstract shapes.

Frey heaps her plates with images and casts from her bric-a-brac collection. She uses concave plates rather than slabs because the depth makes them seem more personal.

345

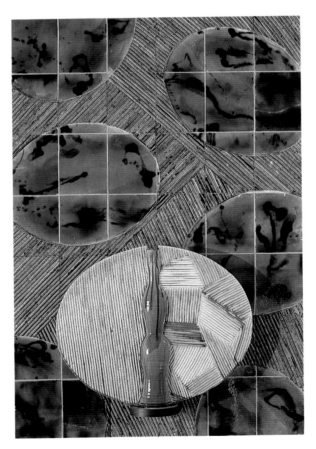

346

## BELINDA GABRYL

Educated at the University of Texas at Austin, where she received an M.F.A. in ceramics in 1977, Belinda Gabryl received Ford Foundation grants in 1975 and 1977. She has taught at the University of Texas at Austin, Brookhaven College in Dallas, Rhode Island College in Providence, and currently teaches at Salve Regina College in Newport, Rhode Island. She participated in the Ceramic National in 1987.

345 **Belinda Gabryl**
*Tornado Teapot and Creamer*, 1986
Earthenware
Teapot: H. 11¼, W. 10½ in. (28.1 × 26.25 cm.). Creamer: H. 5¼, W. 4½ in. (13.1 × 11.25 cm.)
Marks: none
Purchase prize with funds from the Dorothy and Robert Riester Ceramic Fund, "American Ceramics Now: The 27th Ceramic National," 1987 P.C. 87.37.2

Undulating, twisting earthenware teapot and creamer, both multicolored in yellow, black, pink, and aqua. The teapot twists from its flat yellow top to a point at the bottom. The flat cover has a tornado-shaped knob. A curved strap handle and twisted spout project from the body. The pot rests on an undulating saucer with three twisting legs. The creamer twists to a point at the bottom and sits in a saucer with three twisting legs. Both pieces are wheel thrown and altered.

## CLIFF GARTEN (b. 1952)

Cliff Garten, born in Ridgewood, New Jersey, graduated from Alfred University and received an M.F.A. from the Rhode Island School of Design in 1978, where he was a teaching fellow. He is associate professor at Hamline University in St. Paul. Garten has been interested in the relationships between architecture and ceramics, and also in the more general considerations of art: space, color, texture, and light. He participated in "American Ceramics Now: The 27th Ceramic National Exhibition" held at Everson in 1987.

346 **Cliff Garten**
*Hatch, Hatch*, 1984
Earthenware
H. 67½, W. 41½, D. 10¼ in. (168.75 × 103.75 × 25.6 cm.)

Purchase prize with funds from the Dorothy and Robert Riester Ceramic Fund, "American Ceramics Now: The 27th Ceramic National," 1987 P.C. 87.37.3

Two vertical, rectangular earthenware wall pieces. The tiles, interspersed with textured shapes, create oval forms. A shelf with an undulating green vase protrudes from the center of each of the two pieces. Green, lavender, blue, and yellow glazes cover each piece.

Here, Garten makes references to two basic ceramic forms, the tile and the vessel, but uses them to bring into question the relationships between form, color, and space.

## HENRY GERNHARDT (b. 1932)

Born in Salem, Connecticut, Henry Gernhardt was educated at the Norwich Art School in his native state, at the School for American Craftsmen in Rochester, New York, where he studied with Frans Wildenhain, and at Syracuse University, where he received an M.F.A. He was awarded a Fulbright Scholarship in 1958, which enabled him to study at the State School of Applied Arts and the Arabia Factory, both in Helsinki. He has been professor of ceramics at Syracuse University since 1960. Gernhardt participated in the Ceramic Nationals from 1954 through 1968, except in 1958.

347 **Henry Gernhardt**
*Landscape No. 1*, 1969
Stoneware
H. 42½, W. 20, D. 20 in. (106.25 × 50 × 50 cm.)
Marks: none
Museum purchase P.C. 63.140

Tall, straight-sided, rounded forms in stoneware. The two forms are conjoined at the back and have domed tops. Brown glazed band surrounds the central sections, with white glaze overall and olive accents.

The color, form, and surface texture of this piece make reference to landscape, perhaps inspired by the hills that surround Gernhardt's home and studio.

Exhibitions: "Ceramics 70 Plus Woven Forms," 1970

3 4 7

3 4 8

349

University of California at Davis.

Gilhooly's ceramics betray his earlier interest in biology, for he has fashioned a civilization, indeed a culture, of ceramic frogs. An Egyptian symbol of fertility, the frog carries this theme and the attendant ideas of growth and nurture throughout Gilhooly's work. He does not limit himself to Egyptian references, however, and his frog world contains such figures as Frog Victoria, Mao Tse Frog, and the autobiographical Frog Fred. Food plays a prominent role in his frog world and the commentary that Gilhooly makes through this imagery is sometimes pointed, other times oblique.

In 1983 Gilhooly began a series of sculptures on American food in which frogs were excluded as subject matter. In that same year the artist began to work in Plexiglas, attracted by its transparency, and in plastics.

350 **David Gilhooly**
*Boris Frogloff*, 1972
Earthenware
H. 14, W. 13½, D. 12 in. (35 × 33.75 × 30 cm.)
Marks: *Gilhooly, Boris Frogloff, 1972* inscribed inside
Gift of Les Levine   P.C. 84.50.3

Bust of bulging-eyed, frog mummy emerging from wrappings. The green, gnarled face of Boris Frogloff stares ahead with warts, ill-shapen nose, and wide mouth. Multicolored clothing appears beneath the wrappings. The figure wears a black false beard.

This figure reenacts the famous re-

348 **Henry Gernhardt** *(See page 249)*
*It's Out There Somewhere*, 1968
Stoneware
H. 2½, Diam. 15 in.
(6.3 × 37.5 cm.)
Marks: none
Purchase prize given by O. Hommel Company, "25th Ceramic National," 1968   P.C. 68.67

Wheel-thrown and altered, round stoneware bowl with short straight sides. The wide edge flares outward slightly. Two narrow strips lie across the rim and rest on the center of the well, one strip dissipating into the rough surface of the well. The bowl is glazed in brown with gray accents.

349 **Henry Gernhardt**
*Vase*, c. 1964
Stoneware
H. 20, Diam. 20 in. (50 × 50 cm.)
Marks: *Gernhardt* on bottom
Museum purchase from "23rd Ceramic National," 1964   P.C. 64.87

Wheel-thrown and altered bulbous stoneware vase. A raised, round mouth is at the top. Incised and excised designs accented with white glaze create a relief design overall.

## DAVID GILHOOLY (b. 1943)
David Gilhooly studied marine biology at the University of California at Davis before turning to ceramics. He received his M.A. there in 1967 and taught at San José State University, University of Saskatchewan, York University in Toronto, and the

350

turn of the mummy, as played by
Boris Karloff.

## 351 David Gilhooly

*Osiris Canning Factory*, 1973
Earthenware
H. 14½, W. 15, D. 11 in. (36.25 ×
37.5 × 27.5 cm.)
Marks: *Gilhooly* incised on bottom
Gift of Les Levine   P.C. 84.50.5

Earthenware sculpture of frog Osiris
in mummy wrappings lying on his
back in a pile of manure. Three vegetable forms with leafy stalks sprout
through the wrappings on his stom-
ach. Each of the three plant forms
produces a "Frogmans" product—
two cans and a box. An organic form
protrudes from the chin of Osiris
where a false beard would usually
appear. Multicolor glazes are used
on this bizarre sculpture.

Osiris, wrapped in pastry strips
"Frog Wellington style," generates al-
ready processed and packaged food.
While Gilhooly's frogs, according to

351

352

353

his myth, do not eat food (they receive nourishment directly through their skin), they do use food for amusement and art. Through this food motif, the artist makes allusions to consumerism, and also to the shared associations of clay, vegetables, and frogs with the earth.

**352 David Gilhooly** (*See page 251*)
*Osiris Cloning*, c. 1974
Earthenware
H. 36, W. 30½, D. 18 in.
(90 × 76.25 × 45 cm.)
Marks: none
Gift of Les Levine   P.C. 84.50.4

Four-part sculpture of stack of six mummified frogs of graduated sizes. Each frog is wrapped in gray, crosshatched wrappings, and each wears a false beard. The faces are in gold and the hands and feet in black.

Here, with Osiris, the god of fertility, Gilhooly refers to regeneration, a common theme in his work.

**353 David Gilhooly**
*Frog Hell*, 1972
Earthenware
H. 18, Diam. 14 in. (45 × 35 cm.)
Marks: *Gilhooly 1972 T.* incised on bottom
Gift of Les Levine   P.C. 83.17.1

Footed, wheel-thrown, altered, globular earthenware form with large jagged opening. Inside are five large frogs with many small frogs, all appearing to be afire. On the exterior are forms resembling a map of the world in blue, orange, and red, with a red-horned devil frog within a white circle. The orange and red lava-like texture around the opening suggests a raging fire.

Gilhooly's frog civilization had a variety of religions, and here he makes reference to hell, as well as to the source of life (and his art) within the earth.

## JOHN PARKER GLICK (b. 1938)

John Glick was educated in his native Michigan at Wayne State University and at Cranbrook Academy, where he studied with Maija Grotell and received his M.F.A. in 1962. In 1964 Glick established Plum Tree Pottery, where he produces both limited edition and one of a kind functional wares. Dinnerware is produced on a commission basis, and Glick also makes plates, mugs, covered boxes, and bowls.

His surface decoration refers to both Japanese pottery and Abstract Expressionism. He draws on the surface with glazes and slips, creating linear and floral patterns, sometimes in relief. Glick is one of the most important functional potters today, not only for the quality of the work that he produces, but also because of his generosity in sharing information with other ceramists. Glick participated in the Ceramic Nationals in 1960 and 1966.

### 354 John Glick

*Bowl*, 1977
Stoneware
H. 4½, Diam. 18⅝ in.
(11.3 × 46.5 cm.)
Marks: *Glick* incised, Plum Tree Pottery stamp on bottom
Gift of Mr. and Mrs. Robert Eddy   P.C. 78.8

Wheel-thrown, footed stoneware bowl with flared sides. The interior is decorated with multicolored, abstract, linear designs and patterns. Multiple slips and glazes with mineral oxide color washes color the bowl.

Exhibitions: "A Century of Ceramics in the United States, 1878–1978," 1979

### 355 John Glick

*Plate*, 1975
Stoneware
H. 1¾, Diam. 20 in. (4.3 × 50 cm.)
Marks: *Glick* incised, Plum Tree Pottery stamp on bottom
Gift of the artist   P.C. 79.12

Large, wheel-thrown stoneware plate with slightly flared ledge. A multicolored, abstract design has been created on the well and ledge with multiple slips and glazes.

3 5 4

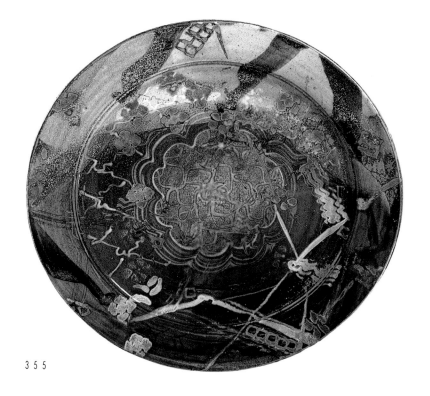

3 5 5

## SCOTT GOEWY (b. 1942)

A native of Fulton, New York, Scott Goewy studied at Wofford College in Spartanburg, South Carolina, at the State University of Iowa's Writer's Workshop, and at the School for American Craftsmen in Rochester, New York under Frans Wildenhain. He established and developed the ceramics department at the Rochester Folk Art Guild in Middlesex, New York, a commune for craftsmen near Rochester, where he has worked for the past twenty years. During this time he has studied crafts through travels to Mexico, Morocco, and Japan. His work has been exhibited under the name of the Rochester Folk Art Guild, where the pieces in the Everson collection were made.

356 **Scott Goewy**
*From left to right:*
*Bowl,* n.d.
Porcelain
H. 3, W. 12½ in. (7.5 × 31.25 cm.)
Marks: none
Gift of Mr. and Mrs. Richard Goewy   P.C. 85.83

Footed porcelain bowl, rounded leaf shape. The rim is curled over on one side with a thick glaze droplet. A vein design is on the well. Green glaze is used overall.

*Vase,* n.d.
Porcelain
H. 7, Diam. 8 in. (17.5 × 20 cm.)
Marks: *RFAG* mark impressed near bottom
Gift of Mr. and Mrs. Richard Goewy   P.C. 84.56.1

Bulbous, ovoid porcelain vase. The flower and stem design in low relief on the front culminates in a flower at the mouth. Celadon crackle glaze is used overall.

*Vase,* n.d.
Porcelain
H. 9½, W. 6½ in.
(23.75 × 16.25 cm.)
Marks: *RFAG* mark impressed near bottom
Gift of the artist   P.C. 84.56.2

Slightly bulbous vase tapering to a cylindrical body with a widely flaring mouth. A floral design in relief covers the surface. Celadon crackle glaze is used overall.

## HARVEY GOLDMAN (b. 1951)

Educated at the University of Illinois

359

Footed stoneware plate with thin, slightly flared rim. Strips of bunched "lace" lie across the center. Black crater glaze is used on the plate, with the imprinted lace pattern in gray.

Griffith says that the Isadora Duncan series blends a circular base, symbolizing the wheel and the pirouettes of the dancer, with two strips of "cloth," which allude to the style of the dancer and her fateful death.

Exhibitions: "Roberta Griffith," Museu de Cerámica de Barcelona, Palau Nacional de Montjuic, Barcelona, 1981

## JAMES GRITTNER (b. 1934)

James Grittner is a native of Westboro, Wisconsin and received an undergraduate degree in art education and an M.S. in art. He participated in the Ceramic Nationals in 1960 and 1964.

### 359 James Grittner

*Bottle*, 1959
Stoneware
H. 10, Diam. 6½ in.
(25 × 16.25 cm.)
Marks: *GRIT* incised on bottom
Museum purchase from "20th Ceramic National," 1960
P.C. 60.71

Footed, ovoid stoneware bottle with wide shoulder tapering to short neck and flared mouth. The brown-grogged stoneware body is tan with a brown, brushed design on the central portion. The rim and mouth are glazed white, and the shoulder is brown.

## ERIK GRONBORG (b. Denmark, 1931)

Erik Gronborg was born in Copenhagen but was educated in the United States, receiving both a B.A. and M.A. from the University of California, Berkeley, in 1962 and 1963. Since then he has become an American citizen and works with mixed media. Gronborg participated in the Ceramic Nationals in 1966 and 1968, and also in "Ceramics 70 Plus Woven Forms" held at Everson in 1970.

### 360 Erik Gronborg

*Stoneware Plate*, 1966
Stoneware
H. 2½, W. 10½, L. 14¾ inches
(6.5 × 26.25 × 36.8 cm)
Marks: *Erik* brushed on bottom in black
Helen S. Everson Memorial Purchase Prize, "Twenty-fourth Ceramic National," 1966  P.C. 66.27

Hand-built, slab-constructed stoneware plate on round foot. The rectangular slab form has layering at the sides and concentric circles at the center. The slab is colored with black metallic glaze with an off-white star at the center and red and white stripes around it; the underlying clay body is revealed in places.

and the University of Massachusetts, where he received an M.F.A. in 1976, Harvey Goldman teaches at Southeastern Massachusetts University in New Dartmouth. In his early work he was concerned with symmetry, centering, and harmony. But in his more recent work he has abandoned this classic approach and altered his forms, creating bulging or dented bodies and off-center, sometimes curled lips and openings.

### 357 Harvey Goldman

*Untitled*, 1985
Earthenware
H. 4½, Diam. 4½ in.
(11.25 × 11.25 cm.)
Marks: none
Gift of Judy Ann Goldman
P.C. 86.55

Small earthenware vessel form. The thick, rounded base supports a sphere-shaped form which tapers to a tiny hole with a slightly raised lip at the top. The base is black, the sphere is black and white, with veining overall.

## ROBERTA GRIFFITH (b. 1938)

Roberta Griffith chairs the art department at Hartwick College in Oneonta, New York. She works in stoneware and porcelain, and has exhibited extensively both here and abroad. Her work is nonfunctional. She also writes on ceramics. Griffith participated in the Ceramic Nationals in 1962 and 1964.

### 358 Roberta Griffith

*Isadora with Black Lace*, 1982
Stoneware
H. 2, Diam. 17 in. (5 × 42.5 in.)
Marks: none
Gift of Ray Schillmoeller
P.C. 82.49

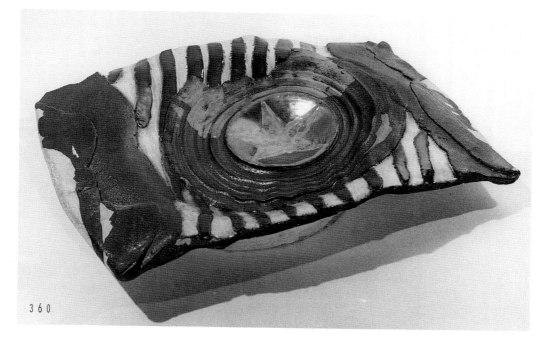

360

362

## CHRIS GUSTIN (b. 1952)

Chris Gustin became interested in clay in 1970 and studied at the University of California at Irvine, the Kansas City Art Institute, and received an M.F.A. from Alfred University in 1977, where he was strongly influenced by visiting Finnish artist Kyllikki Salmenhaara. Gustin taught at Boston University and is now on the faculty of the Swain School of Design in New Bedford, Massachusetts.

361 **Chris Gustin** (*Opposite*)
*Vase*, 1986
Stoneware
H. 21, W. 11, D. 10 in. (52.5 × 27.5 × 25 cm.)
Marks: none
Purchase prize with funds from the Dorothy and Robert Riester Ceramic Fund, "American Ceramics Now: The 27th Ceramic National," 1987   P.C. 87.37.4

Undulating stoneware vase with bulbous appendages, resembles fleshy figure.

The figure has always interested Gustin, and here he has combined it with the vessel, two forms closely allied throughout the history of ceramics. Function is of no significance, except as a limit within which the artist likes to work.

## IRA JOEL HABER (b. 1947)
## GUSTAVO GONZALEZ
## (b. Cuba, 1957)

Ira Joel Haber, born in Brooklyn, is a sculptor and writer. He taught at Fordham University and is an associate professor at the State University of New York at Stonybrook.

Gustavo Gonzalez was born in Cuba and educated at George Washington University, where he earned a B.F.A. with honors and an M.A. in art therapy, and Ohio State University in Columbus, where he received an M.F.A. in ceramics.

362 **Ira Joel Haber, decorator**
**Gustavo Gonzalez, potter**
*Plate*, 1983–1984
Porcelain
H.⅝, W. 12, L. 12 in. (1.5 × 30 × 30 cm.)
Marks: *ira joel haber/1984/g. gonzalez/1983* brushed on back in blue
Gift of John Perreault   P.C. 84.53.2

Chevron-shaped porcelain plate with wide ledge and striped border. The well is decorated with an abstract pattern. The white background is covered with multicolor designs.

The form was made by Gonzalez and decorated by Haber.

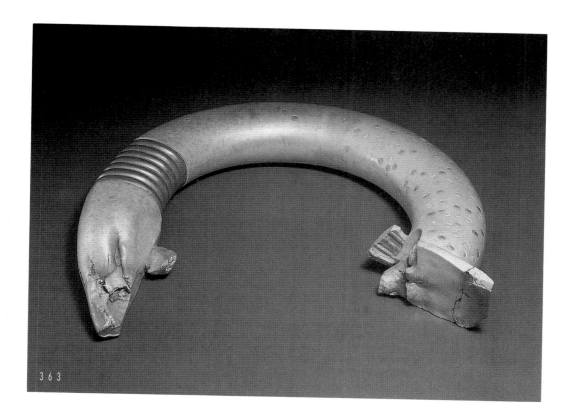

363

## JOSEPH HAWLEY

Joseph Hawley, from California, participated in the Ceramic Nationals in 1964 and 1968.

### 363 Joseph Hawley

*Mary Jane's Turn Again*, 1968
H. 4¾, W. 28, D. 25 in. (11.8 × 71 × 62.5 cm.)
Marks: none
Purchase prize given by A. D. Alpine Company, "25th Ceramic National," 1968  P.C. 68.68

Arc-shaped, yellow, cylindrical form. One end has been altered to a rough point; a rectangular applied section is at the other end. Small, impressed dots appear overall, with a ridged section near one end.

## OTTO HEINO (b. 1915)
## VIVIKA HEINO (b. 1909)

Otto and Vivika met at the League of New Hampshire Arts and Crafts where Vivika was teaching and Otto was a student. Vivika had studied at the California School of Fine Arts in San Francisco, at the University of Southern California under Glen Lukens, and at Alfred University. They were married in 1950 and two years later moved to California where Vivika returned to the University of Southern California to teach for three years, and Otto worked full

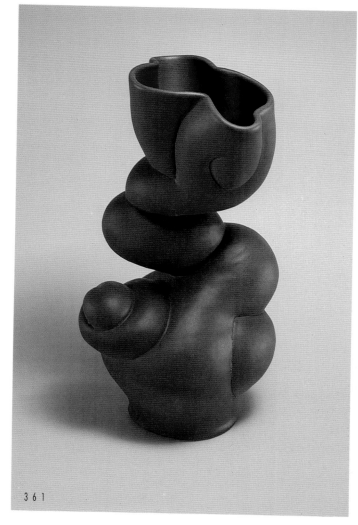

361

time as a studio potter. In 1955 Vivika taught at the Chouinard Art Institute in Los Angeles, where she remained for eight years. She then taught at the Rhode Island School of Design and later operated a studio with Otto in Hopkington, New Hampshire. They now have a pottery in Ojai, California.

The Heino's create architectural wares, as well as vessels—both functional and non-functional. Their forms are classic and often emphasize volume or inner space, as the two vessels from the 1980s in the Everson collection.

### 364 Otto and Vivika Heino *(See page 258)*

*From left to right:*
*Ovoid Vessel*, 1968
Stoneware
H. 15, W. 12, D. 6½ in.
(37.5 × 30 × 16.25 cm.)
Marks: *Otto* brushed on bottom, remainder illegible
Gift of the artists  P.C. 88.44.1

Wheel-thrown and altered stoneware vessel. This large vessel has been flattened and given a pronounced rim which has two pinched projections—one opposite the other. Four wide, vertical grooves—two at either end—are accented with black. Black glaze is splashed and brushed on the exterior, creating a random pattern against the brown-glazed

364

background. The interior has a gray glaze overall.

*Orange Jar*, 1980
Stoneware
H. 10, Diam. 13 in. (25 × 32.5 cm.)
Marks: *Vivika* and *Otto*, and artists' cypher incised on bottom
Gift of the artists   P.C. 88.44.2

Wide, bulbous stoneware jar with low, black foot, ovoid body, and pronounced rim accenting the small black mouth. The orange body is accented by rhythmic throwing marks and black spots.

*Black and White Jar*, 1987
Porcelain
H. 9½, Diam. 11 in.
(23.75 × 27.5 cm.)
Marks: *Vivika* and *Otto*, and artists' cypher incised on bottom
Gift of the artists   P.C. 88.44.3

Bulbous jar of unglazed porcelain. The body rises from a low, black foot to a small, slightly raised rim. The body is accented by rhythmic throwing rings and spots of black glaze. This vessel, and the one to the left, are both full-bodied, and the interior forms are fully realized and clearly expressed.

## CATHERINE HIERSOUX (b. 1938)

Catherine Hiersoux studied with Laura Andreson at the University of California at Los Angeles, and at the University of California at Berkeley. She taught at the College of Arts and Crafts in Oakland, and also did private teaching. Hiersoux works in porcelain, preferring this medium because of the possibilities it provides for detail.

Hiersoux was one of thirteen potters commissioned by Rosalyn Carter to make place settings for the Senate Ladies Luncheon at the White House.

365 **Catherine Hiersoux**
*Plate*, n.d.
Porcelain
H. 2, Diam. 18⅛ in. (5 × 45.3 cm.)
Marks: sticker affixed reads: *Catherine Hiersoux/Porcelain Plate/500.00*

Gift of the Donaldson Family Trust   P.C. 80.32

Large, wheel-thrown porcelain footed plate with slight ledge at edge. A red, brown, and green abstract design decorates the well, with a gloss glaze overall.

365

3 6 7

3 6 8

## WAYNE HIGBY (b. 1943)

Born in Colorado Springs, Wayne Higby studied with Betty Woodman at the University of Colorado and with John Stephenson and Fred Bauer at the University of Michigan, where he received an M.F.A. in 1968. He taught at the University of Nebraska in Omaha, Scripps College, Rhode Island School of Design, and Alfred University, where he has been professor of ceramics since 1973. Higby participated in the 1968 Ceramic National.

Always interested in the vessel, but never in its functional aspects, Higby has used it as a vehicle for imagery, largely inspired by the western landscape he knew as a child. This treatment gives him the opportunity to experiment with the interplay between space, light, and time, both real and illusory.

366 **Wayne Higby** *(See page 260)*
*Tower Mesa*, 1981
Earthenware
H. 8, Diam. 12⅛ in. (20 × 30.3 cm.)
Marks: artist's stamp on side at bottom
Gift of Social Art Club Memorial Fund and museum purchase
P.C. 81.25

Deep, footed earthenware bowl, wheel-thrown and altered. The bowl flares from the foot to its wide mouth. The decoration creates mesa-like forms on both the interior and exterior, which work interchangeably as the bowl is turned, creating illusions of three-dimensional space. Turquoise, black, and gray are used on a crackled white glaze.

Influenced early on by Minoan and Islamic pottery, Higby has chosen to use the vessel form because it involves inner and outer space. On his vessels he creates landscapes that advance and recede, and that change as the vessel is turned. Clouds, rocks, canyons, and mesas appear in his bowls and boxes.

## CHARLES AUSTIN HINDES (b. 1942)

A native of Muskegon, Michigan, Charles Austin Hindes studied at the University of Illinois and received an M.F.A. from Rhode Island School of Design in 1968. He taught at the University of Florida at Gainesville, Rhode Island School of Design, and is chairman of the ceramics department at the University of Iowa.

367 **Charles Austin Hindes**
*Saggar Pot No. 2*, 1977
Stoneware
H. 20¼, Diam. 8¾ in.
(50.6 × 21.8 cm.)
Marks: *Hindes* (illegible) and *12/77* incised on bottom
Gift of the artist   P.C. 79.18

Slab-built, vase-like form, slightly curved at base. The top section is slightly twisted, creating a ledge. A slash at the top creates an extended mouth. The form has been saggar-fired and left unglazed.

Hindes's works betray Japanese influences and are usually hand-built. He specializes in saggar-firing, preferring the colorations that result from this rather than from glazes.

## RICHARD A. HIRSCH (b. 1944)

Rick Hirsch was born in New York and studied at the Art Students League, at the State University of New York at New Paltz, and with Frans Wildenhain at the School for American Craftsmen, where he received an M.F.A. in ceramics in 1971. He taught at Nazareth College in Rochester, New York, Sault College of Applied Arts and Technology, in Sault Sainte Marie, Ontario, Boston University, and now teaches at the School for American Craftsmen in Rochester, New York.

Hirsch is interested in the vessel tradition, but seeks to expand its definition to include form, color, composition, and balance. He specializes in raku, which he studied in Japan, and has achieved remarkably subtle variations of color, tone, and value with this technique.

368 **Rick Hirsch**
*Stoneware Bowl*, 1978
Stoneware
H. 3, Diam. 4¾ in. (7.5 × 11.8 cm.)
Marks: *Hirsch 78* incised on bottom
Gift of Bryce Holcombe
P.C. 81.51.28

Small, footed stoneware tea bowl. The piece is oval, with slightly curved sides and flared base. Luster glaze is used overall, with incising near the base on two sides.

369

**369 Rick Hirsch**

*Ceremonial Cup No. 15*, 1983
Earthenware
H. 16, W. 18 in. (40 × 45 cm.)
Marks: *Hirsch 83* incised on bottom
Gift of Robert and Marguerite
Antell   P.C. 84.6

Wheel-thrown, tripod earthenware
vessel in cylindrical, cup form. A
point protrudes from the side of the
cup. The cup flares to a wide mouth.
The vessel is made of raku-fired *terra
sigillata*.

Hirsch's tripod vessels make reference to ancient traditions of the
Far East and Pre-Columbian America and are only secondarily containers. Their ritual connotations are not
clear but they make manifest the importance of the vessel in past cultures, and for Hirsch this historical
connection is critical.

370

**SIRKKA LIISA HODGSON
(b. Finland, 1926–1983)**

Liisa Hodgson was born in Finland
and was skilled in traditional Finnish
needlework and weaving, as well as
ceramics. She created finely crafted
vessels with elegant and sensuous
forms.

**370 Sirkka Liisa Hodgson**

*Owls,* 1976
Stoneware
H. 3½, Diam. 30½ in.
(8.75 × 76.25 cm.)
Marks: *Hodgson - 76* incised lower
right front
Gift of the Social Art Club in mem-
ory of Liisa Hodgson   P.C. 84.1

Unglazed, round stoneware wall relief plaque with nine owls, each with
applied and incised features. The
background is sectioned with modeling and incising.

Liisa Hodgson was a member of
the Social Art Club, the donor of this
piece.

## PAUL D. HOLLEMAN

Paul Holleman of Arlington, Massachusetts worked in a variety of media. He participated in the Ceramic Nationals from 1949 through 1954 and was a a member of the regional jury in Boston.

### 371 Paul Holleman

*Bottles*, 1951
Stoneware
Left: H. 15½, Diam. 4⅛ in. (38.75 × 10.3 cm.). Right: H. 13½, Diam. 5 in. (33.75 × 12.5 cm.)
Marks: left: 31/*/*Holleman*; right: 32/*/*Holleman*, —both incised on bottom
Purchase prizes given by G.R. Crocker Company, "16th Ceramic National," 1951 P.C. 52.622.1, 2

Companion stoneware bottles with short necks and flared mouths. Linear designs of crusaders, swords, armor, fish, and other motifs decorate both pieces. Blue bond and leopard-spot glazes cover the bottle at the left, while blue bond and celadon are used on the bottle at the right.

Exhibitions: "Forms from the East: 1,000 Years of Pottery in America," Museum of Contemporary Crafts, New York, 1968

### DOROTHY HOOD (b. 1919)

Born in Bryan, Texas, Dorothy Hood studied at the Rhode Island School of Design and the Art Students League in New York. She taught at the Houston Museum of

371

Fine Arts School from 1960 to 1972. She is a painter who worked in clay for the first time in the "New Works in Clay" project, for which she executed eleven slab pieces in a raku-like firing process. Along with these she completed three other sculptures

consisting of slabs using colored clays.

### 372 Dorothy Hood

*Tiara Way*, 1975
Stoneware
H. 24, W. 24, D. 31 in.

(60 × 60 × 77.5 cm.)
Marks: none
Gift of the artist P.C. 76.48

Two large slab forms of low-fire stoneware. The rough textured surfaces with cracking have blue, pink, and gray-brown coloring.

Exhibitions: "New Works in Clay by Contemporary Painters and Sculptors," 1976

### LORRAINE HOOGS (b. 1941)

Born in Hasbrouck Heights, New Jersey, Lorraine Hoogs received a degree in chemistry from Fairleigh Dickinson University and a B.F.A. in ceramics from Syracuse University. Initially she was a functional potter, but while at Syracuse she slowly adopted a more personal style. She now works with porcelain, colored with oxides and ceramic stains.

### 373 Lorraine Hoogs

*Untitled, Weave A*, 1984
Porcelain
H. 18½, W. 21½, D. 1½ in. (46.25 × 53.75 × 3.75 cm.)
Marks: none
Gift of the artist P.C. 85.4

Wall piece of interwoven strips of slate blue, beige, black, and white porcelain.

### MARGIE HUGHTO (b. 1944)

Margie Hughto, a native of Endicott, New York, has been involved in many aspects of ceramics. Having studied under Richard DeVore at

372

373

374

Cranbrook Academy, where she received an M.F.A. in ceramics, she went on to teach at Syracuse University, where she was project director and curator for "New Works in Clay by Contemporary Painters and Sculptors." She became adjunct curator of ceramics at Everson Museum of Art, where she curated the groundbreaking exhibition "A Century of Ceramics in the United States, 1878–1978" with Garth Clark. She also curated "Nine West Coast Clay Sculptors: 1978" at Everson. She has received numerous commissions, most recently for a ceramic mural in a Buffalo subway station.

Hughto was first a painter and her clay work reveals that influence. Her works are generally flat and she uses colored clays, allowing her, as she puts it, to "cut into great chunks of color." She combines slabs of col-

ored clay to form pieces which may be either mounted on a wall or set on a stand. Recently she has been working with handmade paper.

### 374 Margie Hughto

*Fandango*, 1977
Stoneware
H. 26, W. 33, D. ¾ in.
(65 × 82.5 × 1.8 cm.)
Marks: *Margie Hughto 77* incised front lower right. *Margiê Hughto 1977 "Fandango"* on back in black.
Gift of the artist   P.C. 78.38

Square, slab-constructed stoneware piece. Triangular colored clay pieces are pressed into the slab to create a fan shape. The clay is unglazed but colored with blue-gray, orange, and yellow.

Hughto did a series of works on the fan motif, all created from colored clays pressed together.

376

375 **Margie Hughto**
*Orange Blossoms*, 1984
Stoneware
H. 20¼, W. 31, D. 3½ in. (50.6 × 77.5 × 8.75 cm.)
Marks: *Margie Hughto* incised lower right corner
Gift of the artist   P.C. 85.58

Stoneware, slab-like sculpture. Colored clays are pressed together in strips into a fan motif with folded outer edges. The clays are pink, green, and blue, with spots of intensely colored glazes.

Here Hughto is still working with the fan shape but she is beginning to crush the edges, giving the piece more dimension and a less restricting edge.

Exhibitions: "13th Chunichi International Exhibition of Ceramic Arts," Nagoya, Japan, 1985

376 **Margie Hughto**
*Ancient Myth*, 1986
Stoneware
H. 24, W. 42, D. 4½ in. (60 × 105 × 11.25 cm.)
Marks: none
Museum purchase   P.C. 86.62

Slab-constructed, colored clay wall sculpture. Layered shards and slabs are made into a collage, with the edges rolled and curved. Multicolored, light pastel tones with lusters, slip, and glaze cover the assembly.

Most recently Hughto has worked with collaged pieces, each part individually formed and fired, then assembled into rich, shimmering constructions which evoke suggestions of nature, minerals, gem stones, and precious metals.

### KA KWONG HUI
### (b. Hong Kong, 1922)
Ka Kwong Hui was educated in China and worked with Marguerite Wildenhain at Pond Farm in Guerneville, California. He received an M.F.A. from Alfred University in 1952. Hui then worked in New York, and now teaches at Rutgers University. He participated in the Ceramic Nationals from 1949 through 1968, except in 1952 and 1962. He was also invited to exhibit in "Ceramics 70 Plus Woven Forms" at Everson in 1970.

375

378

His early training in sculpture is evident in his ceramic work. His first clay pieces were earthy, with soft, subtle brushwork. More recently he has used simplified, yet unique forms with bright colors, which are clearly stated and finely crafted.

**377 Ka Kwong Hui**
*Untitled*, 1966
Earthenware
H. 18, W. 17, D. 12 in.
(45 × 42.5 × 30 cm.)
Marks: *K. K. Hui* brushed inside foot
Museum purchase from "24th Ceramic National," 1966 P.C. 68.28

Wheel-thrown earthenware sculpture. The tall base tapers to a thick, wheel shape from each side of which protrudes an ovoid shape with a small hole in the end. Black and white glaze in a linear design is used overall.

377

**378 Ka Kwong Hui**
*Ceramic Form*, 1968
Stoneware
H. 22, W. 30, D. 14 in.
(55 × 75 × 35 cm.)
Marks: none
Purchase prize given by Dansk Designs, "25th Ceramic National," 1968 P.C. 68.69

Wheel-thrown, footed stoneware form. The foot tapers to a round, central form with four smaller auxiliary forms, two on each side. Red, black, and white stripes run along the piece, with gold bands accenting the junctures where the sections meet.

These two pieces by Hui place him in the tradition of those artists described as working in the "Super-Object" school of the 1960s. The work of these artists is distinguished by its fine craftsmanship, clear enunciation, and often slick appearance.

Exhibitions: "A Century of Ceramics in the United States, 1878–1978," 1979

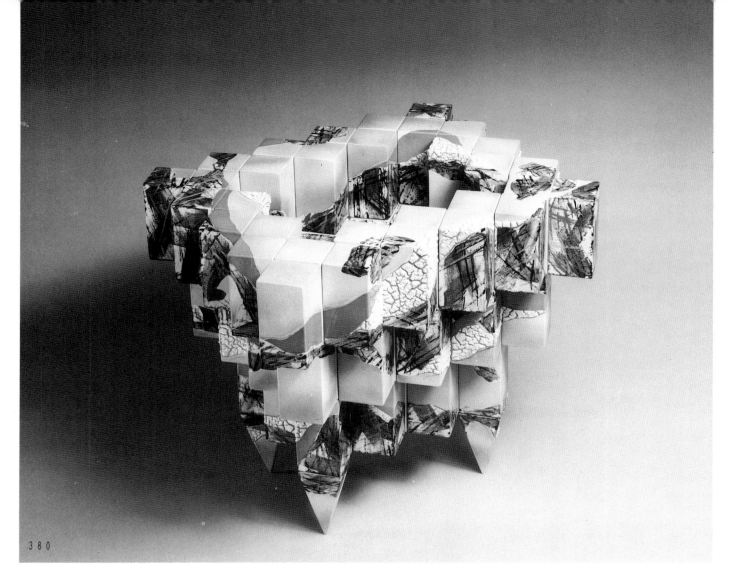

380

## JOSEPH HYSONG (b. 1925)

Born in Derry, Pennsylvania, Joseph Hysong studied at San José State College and taught at the University of Hawaii. He is interested in experimental, wheel-thrown forms and the glaze effects on stoneware and porcelain. He participated in the Ceramic Nationals from 1956 through 1966, except in 1958.

### 379 Joseph Hysong

*Bottle*, 1961
Stoneware
H. 13, Diam. 9 in. (32.5 × 22.5 cm.)
Marks: *HYSONG* incised on bottom
Purchase prize given by Pemco Division of Glidden Company, "22nd Ceramic National," 1962
P.C. 62.38

Large, ovoid stoneware bottle. The piece tapers to a very thin, extended neck with a small mouth. The brown, grogged clay body is colored with brown, blue, tan, and gray glazes.

379

## ITSUE ITO (b. Japan)

Itsue Ito studied at Osaka University of Arts and received an M.A. in ceramics from Mankato State University in Minnesota in 1981. She also received an M.F.A. in ceramics from Louisiana State University at Baton Rouge in 1983. She has taught at Mankato State University and at Louisiana State University and was a technical assistant at the University of Minnesota.

### 380 Itsue Ito

*Shutoh*, 1986
Earthenware
H. 15, W. 18, D. 19 in. (37.5 × 45 × 47.5 cm.)
Marks: none
Purchase prize with funds given by the Hancock Foundation, "American Ceramics Now: The 27th Ceramic National," 1987
P.C. 87.37.5

Earthenware vessel form constructed of interlocking rectangular

381

cubes and supported by four sharply pointed legs. The glazes, in varying shades of blue, purple, white, and black, create an abstract landscape on both the interior and exterior.

## PETER B. JONES (b. 1947)

Peter Jones, an Onondaga/Seneca nation artist, was born on the Cattaraugus Reservation in western New York. He studied at the Institute of American Indian Art in Santa Fe with Hopi artist Otellie Loloma. He also studied at Alfred University, the College of Santa Fe, Bacone College in Muskogee, Oklahoma, and the Archie Bray Foundation in Helena, Montana. In 1977 he returned to the Cattaraugus Reservation, where he researched Iroquois pottery. He now makes vessels in the traditional Iroquois forms, and also contemporary pottery using traditional decorative motifs.

### 381 Peter Jones

*Vases*, 1985–1986
Stoneware
Left to right: H. 5, Diam. 3½ in.
(12.5 × 18.75 cm.); H. 7½, Diam.

382

3¾ in. (18.75 × 9.3 cm.); H. 3¾, Diam. 3¼ in. (9.3 × 8.1 cm.); H. 5¾, Diam. 5¼ in. (14.3 × 13.1 cm.)
Marks: left to right: *P B Jones '86; P B Jones '85; P B Jones '86; P B Jones '86*—all incised on bottom
Museum purchase   P.C. 86.50.2–5

Wheel-thrown stoneware jars with flared mouths. The jars are covered in bright glazes—whites, reds, yellows, greens—with white incised designs based on traditional Iroquois motifs.

### 382 Peter Jones

*Iroquois Square Top Vessel*, 1986
Earthenware
H. 6½, Diam. 5⅞ in.
(16.25 × 14.6 cm.)
Marks: *P B Jones '86* incised on bottom
Museum purchase   P.C. 86.50.1

Pit-fired, coil-built earthenware jar with globular body tapering to cylindrical neck, which flares to a square mouth. Incised, linear, geometric designs are above the center of the body, and four small heads are modeled at the rim with roughly incised features. The unglazed body is orange with black fire clouds.

384

## JUGTOWN POTTERY
### (established 1917)

Jacques Busbee was a portrait painter who studied at the National Academy of Design, the Art Students League, and the Chase School. He and his wife, Julianna, both of whom were born in Raleigh, North Carolina, also collected and studied old pottery. Prohibition laws had driven a fatal blow into the old southern pottery industry, and Busbee determined to save the dying traditions. He located a few remaining potters in Moore County, North Carolina, and established Jugtown Pottery, which produced traditional, utilitarian wares, marketed by Busbee and his wife in New York at their tea room and shop at Washington Square. Later, decorative wares based on classic oriental examples were added to the production.

The pottery floundered for several years after Busbee's death in 1947, but finally stabilized in 1958 and became a non-stock, not for profit corporation with the purpose of continuing the pottery traditions of the county and state. It closed briefly during this transition period, but reopened in 1960 with a new facility.

383 **Jugtown Pottery** (*Opposite*)
*Teapot, Cups, and Saucers*, 1970s
Earthenware
Teapot: H. 5½, W. 10½ in. (13.8 × 26.3 cm.) P.C. 77.90.1a, b. Large cup: H. 2¾, W. 5½ in. (6.9 × 13.75 cm.) P.C. 77.90.3. Large plate: H.⅞, Diam. 8½ in. (2.1 × 21.3 cm.) P.C. 77.90.5. Small cup: H. 2¼, W. 4 (5.6 × 10 cm.) P.C. 77.90a. Small saucer: H.¾, Diam. 5¼ in. (1.8 × 13.1 cm.) P.C. 77.90b
Marks: Jugtown stamp impressed on the bottom of each piece
Gift of Dr. and Mrs. Bertram Merserau

Traditionally shaped teapot, cups, and saucers of red and orange earthenware, covered in tobacco-spit glaze, except for the bottom of the large cup which remains unglazed. The teapot is also of orange clay, but with a clear glaze; and the large plate is of red earthenware with a clear glaze.

The Everson collection also includes five other Jugtown pieces : three cups, a saucer, and a plate. P.C. 77.90.2, 4, 6, 8, 9

## JUN KANEKO (b. Japan, 1942)

Jun Kaneko studied at the Chouinard Art Institute with Ralph Bacerra, at the California Institute of Art, Los Angeles, and at the University of California at Berkeley under Peter Voulkos. He received an M.F.A. in ceramics from Claremont Graduate School, where he studied under Paul Soldner, and he also studied with Jerry Rothman. He taught at Cranbrook Academy from 1979 to 1986, when he established a studio in Omaha.

Kaneko is a highly innovative artist. First trained as a painter, he brings to clay an interest in color and surface treatment as well as a respect for form. His work is entirely personal, and though he is a major figure in American ceramics, his work is not easily categorized.

Kaneko participated in the Ceramic Nationals from 1964 through 1968, and was included in the invitational section in 1987. He was invited to exhibit in "Ceramics 70 Plus Woven Forms" at Everson in 1970.

384 **Jun Kaneko**
*Tegata*, 1966
Stoneware
H. 19, W. 20, D. 5 in.
(47.5 × 50 × 12.5 cm.)
Marks: none
Purchase prize given by Arcadian Landscaping Company, "24th Ceramic National," 1966  P.C. 68.29

Large, hand-built stoneware sculpture. The curved base and slab-like sides taper to a flat top. A decoration of lines, circles, and rectangles is incised and painted on the surface. Light blue glaze is used overall, with decoration in pink, blue, and black.

The decorative motifs on this piece recur throughout the work of Kaneko.

Exhibitions: "A Century of Ceramics in the United States, 1878–1978," 1979

## KAREN KARNES (b. 1925)

Born in New York, Karen Karnes was educated at Brooklyn College and Alfred University. She and her husband David Weinrib headed the ceramics department at Black Mountain College, where, in 1953, she invited Soetsu Yanagi, Shoji Hamada, Bernard Leach, and Marguerite Wildenhain to participate in a ten day symposium. She and Weinrib established their own pottery in Stony Point, New York the following year. Karnes now works in her own studio in Morgan, Vermont. She partici-

383

pated in the Ceramic Nationals from 1951 through 1962, and was invited to exhibit in "Ceramics 70 Plus Woven Forms," 1970.

Karnes has always been a functional potter, and one of the most successful production potters in the country. Her pieces have a quiet but dignified simplicity.

### 385 Karen Karnes

*Demitasse Set*, 1957
Stoneware
Pot: H. 8½, W. 6 in. (21.25 × 15 cm.). Cups: H. from 2¹/₁₆ to 2⅜, W. from 2 to 2¼ in. (5.15–6 × 5–5.6 cm.). Saucers: H.½, Diam. 4⅜ in. (1.25 × 11.3 cm.)
Marks: sticker on bottom of pot reads: *Karnes, Karen (N.Y.)/Lot*

*122/2/1/$70.00 set*
Purchase prize given by Thomas P. Thompson Company, "20th Ceramic International," 1958
P.C. 60.16.1–17

Buff, grogged stoneware demitasse set includes covered pot, eight cups and eight saucers. The baluster-shaped pot is wheel-thrown with a short, curved spout and wide, C-shaped, banded handle. The lid is slightly raised. The cups are straight-sided with ear-shaped handles and slight lips. The saucers are flat with low feet. An orange-brown matte glaze is used overall except on the bottom section of the pot which is unglazed.

385

386

387

**386 Karen Karnes**

*From left to right:*
*Vase*, 1951
Earthenware
H. 15¼, W. 5¾ in. (38.1 × 14.4 cm.)
Marks: none. Tape on bottom from "16th Ceramic National" reads: *Karen Karnes #40*
Purchase prize given by Lord and Taylor, "16th Ceramic National," 1951   P.C. 52.624.1

Free-form earthenware vase. The wide, ovoid base twists and tapers to its cylindrical neck and mouth. The body is decorated in olive green and brown with rows of incised vertical lines and dots.

*Double Vase*, 1951
Earthenware
H. 9½, W. 13⅞ in.
(23.75 × 34.6 cm.)
Marks: *Karnes* inscribed on bottom
Purchase prize given by Lord and Taylor, "16th Ceramic National," 1951   P.C. 52.624.2

Free-form earthenware double vase. Two indentations are on the top between the two mouths. The buff body is incised with a linear pattern. The interior is glazed in brown, and the exterior in brown with an orange glaze accenting the textured areas.

**387 Karen Karnes**

*Covered Jar*, 1983
Stoneware
H. 11¾, Diam. 15 in.
(29.3 × 37.5 cm.)
Marks: none
Given by friends in memory of Lenore Goldstein   P.C. 87.83a,b

Stoneware covered jar with narrow ledge on shoulder and slightly domed cover. A trowled effect is used on top of the cover. Dark blue

388

389

glaze is on the exterior, and blue-green on the interior.

This monumental jar with its unusually large lid is deceptive in its simplicity; its quiet strength lends dignity to the material.

## SUSAN KEMENYFFY
### (b. 1941)
## STEVEN KEMENYFFY
### (b. Hungary, 1943)

Susan Kemenyffy was born in Springfield, Massachusetts and studied at Syracuse University, the Art Students League, the University of Illinois in Champaign, and received an M.A. and M.F.A. from the University of Iowa. She has taught at the University of Wisconsin and was an assistant professor of art at Mercyhurst College in Erie, Pennsylvania from 1974 to 1978.

Steven Kemenyffy studied at Augustana College in Illinois and received an M.A. and M.F.A. from the University of Iowa. He taught at the universities of Iowa and Wisconsin, and has been professor of art at Edinboro University of Pennsylvania since 1969.

Though the Kemenyffys collaborate on their work, they have their own areas of concentration and there is no exchange of ideas between the two while at work. Steven is responsible for the production of the dimensional clay forms, and for the firing. Susan does the decorating and applies the glazes.

388 **Steven Kemenyffy, sculptor**
**Susan Kemenyffy, decorator**
*The Last Lady of Spring*, 1987
Earthenware
H. 46, W. 22¾, D. 17⅜ in. (115 × 56.8 × 43.4 cm.)
Marks: *Kemenyffy (Steven and Su-san) McKean Pa May 1987* incised at top left on back
Gift of Genelle Altmann
P.C. 87.62

Tall, slab-constructed, raku-fired earthenware vessel. The flat body has curved and pointed edges, and is decorated with incised and applied designs. A female figure with striking green eyes and red lips has a bird on her shoulder on one side; the same figure is repeated on the other side holding a bird in her outstretched hand. Intricately detailed, incised linear patterns and designs decorate the figure's clothing, with gold, silver, and pinkish lusters overall.

This subject matter, mostly female figures in romantically fashionable dress, has remained a constant in the work of the Kemenyffys, though it has evolved over the years.

## ERNIE KIM (b. 1918)

A native Californian, Ernie Kim had no formal art education, though he studied privately with Marian Hartwell in San Francisco. He headed the ceramics department of California School of Fine Arts and has maintained a studio for ceramics and commercial design. He participated in the Ceramic Nationals from 1960 through 1968.

389 **Ernie Kim**
*Bowl*, c. 1955
Stoneware
H. 8¾, Diam. 11 in.
(22.2 × 27.7 cm.)
Marks: *KIM* on bottom in white
Anonymous gift T.N. 31

Large, footed stoneware bowl. The slightly curving sides end in a rim accented by two slight ridges. Abstract designs decorate the exterior in orange, brown, and blue glazes.

390

391

392

393

**390 Ernie Kim**

*Covered Jar*, 1955
Stoneware
H. 12½, Diam. 7¼ in.
(31.25 × 18.1 cm.)
Marks: *Kim* incised on bottom
Museum Purchase from "19th Ceramic National," 1956   P.C. 62.14

Large, footed, grogged stoneware jar with cover. The cover sits within the rim and has a knob that tapers to the cup-shaped top. A curvilinear, abstract design in red and brown glazes covers the ovoid jar.

This jar was accepted in the "19th Ceramic National," but sustained damages and was not exhibited.

**391 Ernie Kim**

*Branch Bottle*, 1959
Stoneware
H. 16, Diam. 10½ in.
(40 × 26.25 cm.)
Marks: *KIM* incised on bottom
Museum purchase   P.C. 60.72

Ovoid bottle of grogged stoneware, tapering to short neck and flared mouth. Sections of impressed dots decorate the exterior. Gray-green and brown glazes are used overall.

**JIM KNECHT**

Jim Knecht worked in Greensboro, North Carolina, and participated in the "25th Ceramic National" in 1968.

**392 Jim Knecht**

*Fecundity*, 1967
Earthenware
H. 5¾, Diam. 7 in.
(14.9 × 18.2 cm.)
Marks: *KNECHT* incised on bottom
Purchase prize given by Hammond Lead Products, "25th Ceramic National," 1968   P.C. 68.70

Wheel-thrown earthenware pot with flat bottom, straight sides, and curved rim. Off-white glaze is used overall, with red luster and black slip decoration.

**JOSEPH KONZAL (b. 1905)**

Joseph Konzal, born in Milwaukee, studied at the Beaux-Arts Institute in New York and with Max Weber and Robert Laurent at the Art Students League. He taught at Queens College and Adelphi University in New York and at Kent State University in Ohio.

**393 Joseph Konzal**

*Architectural Direction*, 1955
Stoneware
H. 11⅛, W. 19¼, D. 3¾ in.
(22.9 × 50.1 × 9.8 cm.)
Marks: *KONZAL* incised on lower left side
Museum purchase from "19th Ceramic National," 1956   P.C. 62.10

Abstract stoneware sculpture of brown, grogged stoneware with incised lines.

394

## ANNE KRAUS (b. 1956)

Born in Short Hills, New Jersey, Anne Kraus studied painting at the University of Pennsylvania and ceramics at Greenwich House Pottery in New York and Alfred University.

Kraus's work is loosely based on eighteenth-century porcelains such as Meissen and Sèvres. She uses traditional vessel forms but decorates them in underglaze colors with intensely personal motifs which sometimes border on the surreal, but always seem dreamlike and mysterious.

### 394 Anne Kraus

*Peaceable Kingdom*, 1985
Porcelain
H. 2¼, W. 12½, L. 11½ in. (5.6 × 31.25 × 28.75 cm.)
Marks: *Anne Kraus* on bottom
Gift of Garth Clark   P.C. 85.74

Hexagonal porcelain bowl with upward curving sides and everted rim. The well contains an underglaze painting of a landscape with a girl who looks back over her shoulder at a monkey and dog in a fight. The sides of the bowl have geometric

395

decorations in blue, green, and brown underglaze.

While Kraus's work pays tribute to traditional porcelain styles, her decoration is original, contemporary, and narrative. Her forms are often constructed of separate, slip-cast elements which are combined in many different ways.

### 395 Anne Kraus

*Wind Chime Motel*, 1984
Porcelain
H. 8, W. 7½, D. 4 in.
(20 × 18.75 × 10 cm.)
Marks: *ANNE/KRAUS* within a square, also artist's mark within a square, on bottom
Museum purchase   P.C. 85.14

Porcelain vase, footed, with flattened circular body and curved, scroll-shaped mouth. One side has a central circle enclosing a picture of a motel in a wooded landscape and the inscription: *Souvenir* and *The Wind Chime Motel*. On the opposite side a similar circle encloses wind chimes hanging from a branch. The underglaze decoration is multicolored.

396

397

398

## J. ROLAND LAFFERTY

J. Roland Lafferty, from Meadville, Pennsylvania, participated in the "23rd Ceramic National" in 1964.

### 396 J. Roland Lafferty

*Stoneware Vase*, 1965
Stoneware
H. 12½, W. 13¾, D. 4 in.
(31.25 × 34.3 × 10 cm.)
Marks: *J R Lafferty* incised in script on bottom
Museum purchase from "23rd Ceramic National," 1964  P.C. 66.12

Hand-built, canteen-shaped stoneware vase with three openings at top with slightly raised mouths. The surface is textured with hatching and incising, applied patches and a band. The vase is glazed in tan with orange slip.

## CHARLES LAKOFSKY (b. 1922)

A native of Cleveland, Ohio, Charles Lakofsky studied at the Cleveland Institute of Art, graduated magna cum laude from Alfred University, and received an M.A. from Ohio State University. He was, for many years, chairman of the Art Department at Bowling Green University. He participated in numerous exhi-

bitions and his work is in the collections of the Cleveland Museum of Art, the Butler Institute of Art in Youngstown, Ohio, the universities of Illinois and Wisconsin, and many others. His work was shown in every Ceramic National Exhibition from 1946 to 1966, except that of 1962.

### 397 Charles Lakofsky

*Melon Vase*, c. 1950
Stoneware
H. 6⅝, Diam. 5 in.
(16.5 × 12.5 cm.)
Marks: *Lakofsky* incised on bottom
Purchase prize given by Homer Laughlin China Company, "15th Ceramic National," 1950
P.C. 51.596.3

Footed stoneware vase with melon-shaped body tapering to a small, raised mouth. Four narrow vertical indentations on the sides create its melon shape. Gray celadon glaze is used overall.

### 398 Charles Lakofsky

*Flattened Vase*, 1950
Stoneware
H. 8⅝, W. 5½ in.
(21.5 × 13.75 cm.)
Marks: *LAKOFSKY* brushed on bottom

Museum purchase   P.C. 51.596.2

Flattened stoneware bottle vase with slip decoration and celadon glaze.

### 399 Charles Lakofsky

*Stoneware Bowl*, c. 1950
Stoneware
H. 5¼, Diam. 6¾ in.
(13.1 × 16.8 cm.)
Marks: none
Purchase prize given by Homer Laughlin China Company, "15th Ceramic National," 1950
P.C. 51.596.4

Footed stoneware bowl. A brown slip leaf motif with incising decorates the exterior of the bowl. The whole piece is covered in a buff glaze.

### 400 Charles Lakofsky

*From left to right:*
*Square Bowl*, 1952
Stoneware
H. 5⅝, W. 5⅜ in. (14 × 13.4 cm.)
Marks: *C. LAKOFSKY* incised on bottom
Purchase prize given by G. R. Crocker Company, "17th Ceramic National," 1952   P.C. 53.677.1

Footed, square stoneware bowl. The dark buff body is covered with white slip in the interior. The exterior is white with blue, green, and yellow decoration and an incised textural design.

Exhibitions: "Ceramics by Charles Lakofsky," Art Institute of Chicago, 1960

*Bowl*, 1952
Stoneware
H. 2⅝, Diam. 11⅝ in.
(6.5 × 29 cm.)
Marks: *CHAS. LAKOFSKY* incised on bottom, sticker reads *1969 /exhibited at/The Art Institute/of Chicago/no. 11*
Purchase prize given by G. R. Crocker Company, "17th Ceramic National," 1952   P.C. 53.677.2

Shallow stoneware bowl. The interior has a linear, leaf-like pattern in white, blue, green, and brown. The exterior is white, except for the foot which is unglazed.

Exhibitions: "Ceramics by Charles Lakofsky," Art Institute of Chicago, 1960

399

400

401

**MICK LAMONT**

Mick Lamont entered the "25th Ceramic National" from San Francisco.

### 401 Mick Lamont

*J-Pot*, 1968
Stoneware
H. 12¼, Diam. 9¾ in.
(30.6 × 24.3 cm.)
Marks: none
Purchase prize given by Syracuse China Corporation, "25th Ceramic National," 1968   P.C. 68.71

Wheel-thrown, ovoid stoneware pot with short neck and flared lip. Ash glaze drips over the shoulder.

**WILLIAM LAU (1939–1973)**

William Lau studied at Alfred University, where he received an M.F.A. in 1966. He taught at the University of Michigan, State University of New York at Cortland, and at Greenwich House Pottery in New York.

### 402 William Lau

*Rings*, 1971
Earthenware
Rings: H. 17, Diam. 21 in., (42.5 × 52.5 cm.). Balls: Diam. 3 in. (7.5 cm.) each
Marks: none
Museum purchase from "Regional Exhibition," 1971   P.C. 71.5.3–6

Sculpture of stacked rings with three balls and curved, extruded form in the center. The bottom ring is iridescent white, the center ring blue, and the top ring red, with a purple, extruding form. The balls inside the rings are light green, orange, and violet.

Lau created a series of ring forms. He also created large, whimsical, sculptural pieces, such as a huge set of jacks and ring-toss games.

402

4 0 4

straight sides, flat shoulder, and short neck with wide-rimmed mouth. A loosely textured area at midpoint divides the vessel into two sections. The top section is blue-gray, the bottom section is gray.

This vase illustrates the influence of Japanese ceramics on the Americans during this period. The water-jar form and deliberate rustic quality link it to the wares of Bizen and Iga.

## BRUCE LENORE (b. 1955)

Educated at the Hartford Art School in Connecticut and Rhode Island School of Design, where he received an M.F.A. in ceramics, Bruce Lenore also studied at Sun Valley Center for the Arts in Idaho with Paul Soldner, Robert Turner, and Robert and Paula Winokur during a summer session. He is now an independent studio artist.

### 405 Bruce Lenore

*Space Face*, 1986
Earthenware
H. 13½, W. 6¼ in.
(33.75 × 15.6 cm.)
Marks: *B L 86* on bottom
Museum purchase with funds from the Dorothy and Robert Riester Ceramic Fund   P.C. 86.27

Covered, ovoid earthenware vessel. The body is decorated with a view of the earth from space, and various multicolored elements arranged to resemble a face. The flat cover has geometric objects arranged on top to create a handle.

Lenore says he sees these pieces as puzzles or riddles, providing clues, but allowing each viewer his or her own solution.

## BRUNO LA VERDIERE (b. 1937)

Born in Waterville, Maine, Bruno La Verdiere was educated at St. Martin's College in Washington, St. John's University in Minnesota, and studied under Henry Takemoto at the University of Washington. He also studied at the Art Students League in New York. He has taught at Greenwich House Pottery in New York and at Penland School of Crafts in North Carolina. He participated in the Ceramic National in 1966.

La Verdiere's work has been both functional and nonfunctional, figurative and abstract. He has worked with both wheel-thrown and hand-constructed pieces in a variety of forms, and his work has moved from small, functional objects to large, monumental works which sometimes act as a canvas for his decorations.

### 403 Bruno La Verdiere

*Blue Garden Bottle*, 1970
Stoneware
H. 33, W. 18, D. 8 in. (82.5 × 45 × 20 cm.)
Marks: *Bruno* brushed on lower edge

Museum purchase with funds provided by the Central New York Chapter of Architects and the Syracuse Society of Architects, "Ceramics 70 Plus Woven Forms," 1970   P.C. 70.30

Large, arch-shaped, coil-built stoneware bottle. The shoulders slope to a short neck and slightly rimmed mouth. Incised, textural patterns cover the surface. The exterior is blue-glazed with white and blue linear design.

## DOUG LAWRIE

Doug Lawrie participated in the "21st Ceramic National," 1960, from Claremont, California.

### 404 Doug Lawrie

*Vase*, 1960
Stoneware
H. 7½, W. 5, D. 4 in. (18.75 × 12.5 × 10 cm.)
Marks: sticker on bottom reads: *DOUG LAWRIE/$20.00*
Museum purchase from "21st Ceramic National," 1960   P.C. 60.73

Stoneware paddled vase with

4 0 5

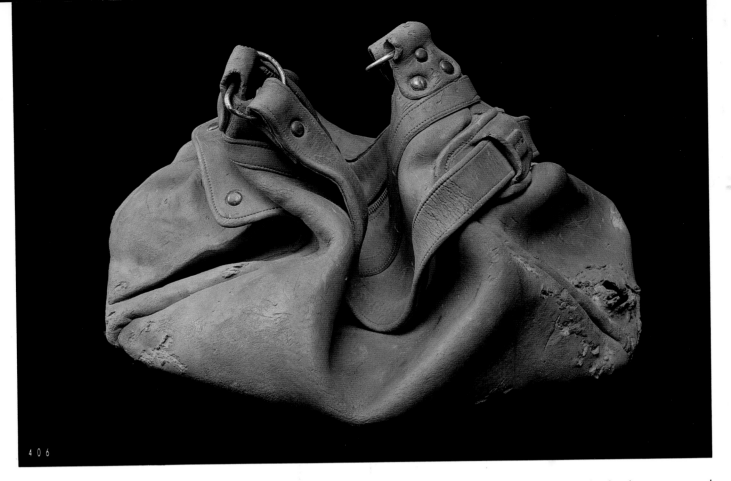

**MARILYN LEVINE (b. Canada, 1935)**

Marilyn Levine was born in Medicine Hat, Alberta, and educated at the University of Alberta, the University of Regina, and the University of California at Berkeley, where she received both an M.A. and an M.F.A. She has exhibited widely and received international recognition for her work. She has lived and worked in the United States since 1971.

Levine works with clay in a trompe l'oeil manner, making leather handbags, suitcases, shoes, and other mundane objects with all of their indications of wear and tear. These "traces" relate the objects to their owners, to time, and to reality. Levine's aim is to evoke a compassion through these associations.

**406 Marilyn Levine**
*Maki's Shoulder Bag*, 1975
Stoneware
H. 7, W. 14, D. 13 in.
(17.5 × 35 × 32.5 cm.)
Marks: none
Museum purchase with matching funds from the National Endowment for the Arts   P.C. 80.10

Stoneware, trompe l'oeil sculpture of a soft leather handbag with a zipper and a strap handle attached by metal rings.

The contrast between the rigidity of fired clay and the suppleness of the represented leather adds an additional element of interest to this piece.

**ROY LICHTENSTEIN (b. 1925)**

A native New Yorker, Roy Lichtenstein studied painting under Reginald Marsh at the Art Students League, and received a B.F.A. and M.F.A. from Ohio State University. He taught at Ohio State, the State University of New York at Oswego, and Rutgers University. He has painted full time since 1964.

Interested in putting two dimensional symbols on three dimensional objects, Lichtenstein collaborated with New York ceramist Ka Kwong Hui to create heads and dinnerware sculptures constructed to give the appearance of having been mass-produced. Having both the reality of three-dimensional form and the illusion of painting, these objects are created in the Pop Art idiom for which Lichtenstein is well known.

**407 Roy Lichtenstein**
*From left to right:*
*Dinnerware*, 1967
Earthenware
H. 10, W. 12¾, D. 8½ in. (25 × 31.8 × 21.25 cm.)

Marks: none
Gift of Ka Kwong Hui
P.C. 88.21.1

Slip-cast, molded earthenware sculpture. A mug, bowl, sugar, and creamer are stacked precariously on the ledged oval platter. A spoon rests on the platter beside the stacked dinnerware. White crackle glaze is used overall with red and metallic silver striped decoration.

*Pitcher on Stand*, c. 1967
Earthenware
H. 10, W. 11½, D. 7 in. (25 × 28.1 × 17.5 cm.)
Marks: none
Gift of Ka Kwong Hui
P.C. 88.21.4

Slip-cast, molded earthenware sculpture. The bulbous pitcher is tipped to pouring position and rests on a rectangular slab base. Bright red, yellow, and blue striped accents cover the piece.

*Dinnerware*, c. 1967
Earthenware
H. 11¼, W. 13½, D. 8½ in. (28.1 × 33.75 × 21.25 cm.)
Marks: none
Gift of Ka Kwong Hui
P.C. 88.21.3

Slip-cast, molded earthenware sculp-

ture. A bowl and saucer, mug, and two cups balance precariously on a large, footed platter with an additional saucer and spoon. The sculpture is glazed white overall with red and blue highlights.

These piles of dinnerware were made from molds taken from the actual objects, then carefully assembled and decorated. The areas of color represent shadows and highlights, but in actuality become compositional motifs in their own right. Even more fascinating is the fact that this is a sculpture done in the size and material of the objects themselves, thus creating an ambiguity in terms of reality.

**408 Roy Lichtenstein**
*Dinnerware*, c. 1967
Earthenware
H. 12, W. 14¾, D. 10 in. (30 × 36.8 × 25 cm.)
Marks: none
Gift of Ka Kwong Hui
P.C. 88.21.2

Slip-cast, molded earthenware sculpture. Three stacked mugs, a spoon, and a small pitcher sit on a ledged, oval platter. White crackle glaze, with vivid red and yellow accents, covers the piece.

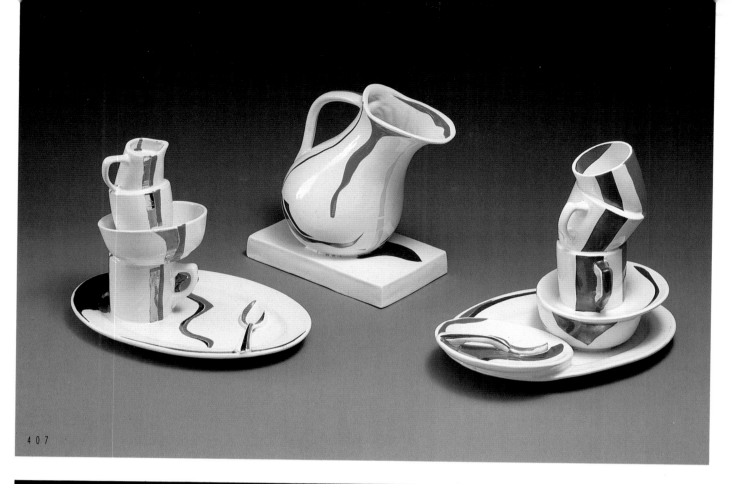

407

408

409

Museum purchase from "19th Ceramic National," 1956   P.C. 63.63

Tall, ovoid stoneware vase tapering to small base. The interior is gray-white. Leaf formations in light brown with thick white outlines cover the exterior of the vase.

### STUART LISSON (b. 1947)

A graduate of Miami University in Ohio, Stuart Lisson returned to his native city and received an M.S. in art education from Syracuse University. He is a free-lance photographer, video producer, and sculptor. He was project photographer for the "New Works in Clay" project at Everson in 1976.

Much of his work has a satirical edge to it.

411 **Stuart Lisson**
*A Little Niche in the Bronx*, 1985
Earthenware

### HENRY W. LIN (b. China)

Henry Lin was influenced by the early ceramic forms of his native China. He produces mainly functional wares. Lin participated in the Ceramic Nationals from 1956 through 1966, except in 1958.

409 **Henry Lin**
*Stoneware Bowl*, 1959
Stoneware
H. 4, Diam. 14¼ in. (10 × 35.6 cm.)
Marks: artist's mark and '59 incised on bottom
Museum purchase from "21st Ceramic National," 1960   P.C. 60.75

Large, wheel-thrown, footed stoneware bowl with flat bottom and straight sides. The interior is in gray and tan glaze with brown speckles. The exterior wall has small, rectangular indentations in rows of three, filled with blue and green gloss glazes in jewel-like tones.

### RICHARD MATHER LINCOLN (b. 1929)

Richard Lincoln participated in the Ceramic National Exhibitions from 1956 through 1968.

410 **Richard Lincoln**
*Vase*, 1956
Stoneware
H. 12¼, Diam. 11⅜ in.
(30.6 × 28.4 cm.)
Marks: *RML Gs* incised on bottom

410

H. 20, W. 14, D. 10 in. (50 × 35 × 25 cm.)
Marks: copyright mark and *1985 Stuart Lisson* on back at base
Gift of the artist   P.C. 87.45

Earthenware sculpture of Babe Ruth within an arch-shaped niche, greatly resembling bathtub shrines often seen during the 1950s and 1960s. The figure looks straight ahead, and holds a baseball bat across his chest. He wears the blue and white Yankee uniform and a detail of the structure of Yankee Stadium appears in the background. The word "Bronx" and eight baseballs are painted silver and sculpted in relief around the arch, framing the player. The arch and base are covered with graffiti.

Exhibitions: "Everson Biennial," 1986; "National Council on Education in the Ceramic Arts Exhibition," Syracuse University, 1987

## KEN LITTLE (b. 1947)
Ken Little attended Texas Tech University in his native state, and received an M.F.A. from the University of Utah. He taught at the University of Montana in the 1970s. During this period he explored various treatments of clay and arrived at some unorthodox uses of the material. He is particularly interested in breaking with the historical concept of ceramics.

412

412 **Ken Little**
*Hat House*, 1978
Stoneware
H. 8¾, W. 8¾ in. (21.9 × 21.9 cm.)
Marks: none
Gift of the artist   P.C. 79.19

Stoneware sculpture of house. The rough surface is covered with incised configurations. Small, multicolored shards are pressed into the surface. A brown, lustrous glaze is applied overall.

Exhibitions: "13th Chunichi International Exhibition of Ceramic Arts," Nagoya, Japan, 1985

411

413

417

**WAYNE LONG**

A Californian, Wayne Long participated in the Ceramic Nationals from 1947 through 1958, except in 1956. He was a frequent prize winner and twice served as chairman of the regional jury in Los Angeles.

**413 Wayne Long**

*Big Catch*, 1958
Stoneware
H. 13, L. 35½, D. 3½ in. (32.5 × 88.75 × 9 cm.)
Marks: *Wayne* incised on bottom right corner
Purchase prize given by IBM Corporation, "20th Ceramic International," 1958    P.C. 60.31

High relief stoneware wall plaque in four sections. A line of ten figures carries large fish. The plaque is incised and partially glazed in green and blue.

**LAURANCE LONGLEY (1906–1976)**

Laurance Longley was born in Des Plaines, Illinois, and studied at the Chicago Art Institute. He was an epigraphic artist for the Oriental Institute of Chicago University and an artist/draughtsman at the Metropolitan Museum of Art. He taught at the Chicago Art Institute and Syracuse University.

**414 Laurance Longley** *(See page 286)*

*Vase*, n.d.
Stoneware
H. 10⅛, Diam. 4¾ in.
(25.3 × 11.8 cm.)
Marks: artist's cypher incised on bottom
Gift of Julia Dietz    P.C. 76.43

Irregularly shaped stoneware vase. The foot flares to a ledge just below midsection. The body tapers to a flat shoulder, straight short neck, and deeply lobed rim. Protrusions are at the shoulder and above the foot. Dark green glaze is used overall.

**JAMES LOVERA**

A native of California, James Lovera studied at the California School of Fine Arts in San Francisco. He is a ceramics designer and participated in the Ceramic Nationals almost continuously from 1946 through 1966.

**415 James Lovera** *(See page 286)*

*Bottle*, 1960
Earthenware
H. 8, Diam. 7 in. (20 × 17.5 cm.)
Marks: *lovera* incised on bottom
Purchase prize given by Canadian Guild of Potters, "21st Ceramic National," 1960    P.C. 60.86

Bulbous earthenware bottle with

small, flared neck and mouth. The interior is in white gloss, the exterior in orange matte glaze with black specks, and the rim is black.

Exhibition: "Forms from the Earth: 1,000 Years of Pottery in America," Museum of Contemporary Crafts, New York, 1960

### MICHAEL LUCERO (b. 1953)

Michael Lucero studied at Humboldt State University in his native California, and received an M.F.A. from the University of Washington in Seattle. Early in his career he constructed skeletal figures from shards and wire, hanging men with pots for heads. After a trip to the Adirondacks he fashioned fish, animals, and insects on which he painted surreal, dreamlike landscapes. His work is both unsettling and reassuring.

416 **Michael Lucero** *(See page 285)*
*The Emperor Moth*, 1986
Stoneware and wood
H. 59, W. 105, D. 11 in. (147.5 × 262.5 × 27.5 cm.)
Marks: *1986 Michael Lucero N.Y.C.* on base
Gift of the Board of Trustees of Everson Museum of Art   P.C. 86.29

Large stoneware and wood sculpture depicts upright moth with outstretched wings. The cylindrical, sectioned stoneware body has three pairs of legs, antennae, and a spiral proboscis which protrudes from the top of the body. The body and wings are decorated with scenes from a dreamlike environment, with natural forms such as trees and clouds juxtaposed with craggy rock surfaces, machine-like parts, and barren landscapes.

This monumental work gives a first impression of doom and destruction. However, upon closer study, one finds that the artist does not present a world without hope, for in the barren, wasted landscape there are green shoots that signal rebirth, and a pink sunset that offers hope of another day.

*The Emperor Moth* was a gift of the Board of Trustees of Everson Museum on the occasion of the opening of the Syracuse China Center for the Study of American Ceramics.

4 1 4

4 1 5

### PHILLIP MABERRY (b. 1951)

A Texan by birth, Phillip Maberry received a B.F.A. in ceramics from East Texas State University and did graduate work at Wesleyan University in Middletown, Connecticut. He was a ceramics technician at the Brooklyn Museum Art School and a visiting artist at the Fabric Workshop in Philadelphia. Maberry uses multiple layers of glaze and simple forms to achieve dazzling, colored vessels and sculpture with powerfully energetic designs that are entirely contemporary.

417 **Phillip Maberry** *(See page 284)*
*Untitled*, 1983
Porcelain
H. 7¾, Diam. 12¾ in.
(19.4 × 31.9 cm.)
Marks: none
Gift of Helene Margolies Rosenbloom in memory of Leon Rosenbloom   P.C. 83.22a, b

Cone-shaped, cast-porcelain bowl supported by a three-legged stand. The interior has brightly glazed, abstract designs in multicolors. The exterior is decorated with vase-shaped designs with black tendrils.

Exhibitions: "13th Chunichi International Exhibition of Ceramic Arts," Nagoya, Japan, 1985

### DAVID MacDONALD (b. 1945)

David MacDonald, a native of Hackensack, New Jersey, received a B.S. from Hampton Institute in Virginia, where he studied with Joseph Gilliard. He also studied at the University of Massachusetts and received an M.F.A. from the University of Michigan at Ann Arbor. MacDonald is now an associate professor of ceramics at Syracuse University.

418 **David MacDonald**
*Untitled Plate*, 1984
Stoneware
H. 4¼, Diam. 27⅞ in.
(10.6 × 69.7 cm.)
Marks: *David MacDonald* on bottom of plate
Museum purchase with funds from Mr. and Mrs. Mark Harwood
P.C. 84.25

Large, deep, footed stoneware plate with widely flaring sides. A deeply carved, geometric design covers the

well. The foot remains unglazed, but red-brown gloss glaze is used on the underside and rim.

MacDonald has been influenced by African art of all kinds. His primary interest is in the vessel form, but he uses it for expressive purposes. In this monumental plate the rim provides a frame for the controlled energy exuded by the carved design within it.

418

419

### RODGER MACK (b. 1938)

Rodger Mack was born in Barberton, Ohio, and studied at the Cleveland Institute of Art, received an M.F.A. from Cranbrook Academy, and studied in Italy on a Fulbright grant. Mack works in many media, including stone, wood, and bronze, as well as in clay. He is a professor of sculpture at Syracuse University.

### 419 Rodger Mack

*Sculptural Bowl*, 1961
Stoneware
H. 3¼, Diam. 16⅛ in.
(8.1 × 40.3 cm.)
Marks: *Rodger Mack 61* incised on bottom
Gift of the artist   P.C. 86.67

Large, footed sculptural bowl with flared sides. An abstract pattern is incised and modeled on the well. Black, green, and yellow glazes are used overall.

420

**JIM MAKINS (b. 1946)**

Born in Johnstown, Pennsylvania, Jim Makins studied at the Philadelphia College of Art, the Brooklyn Museum Art School, and received an M.F.A. from Cranbrook Academy in 1973. Makins works with the vessel, mainly in porcelain.

420 **Jim Makins**
*Porcelain Bowls* n.d.
Porcelain
Left: H. 3¼, Diam. 6½ in. (8.1 × 16.25 cm.). Right: H. 4, Diam. 6½ in. (10 × 16.25 cm.)
Marks: none
Gift of Bryce Holcombe
P.C. 81.51.16, 17

Porcelain bowls on raised feet. Throwing marks on the flared sides create three distinct sections on each bowl.

Makin's forms are controlled and formal, yet the throwing marks, which for him are an integral part of the piece, give a sense of the touch of the artist.

**GRAHAM MARKS (b. 1951)**

Graham Marks was born in New York, studied at the Philadelphia College of Art, and received an M.F.A. from Alfred University. He taught at Kansas State University in Manhattan, Kansas and the School

422

421

for American Craftsmen in Rochester, New York before chairing the ceramics department at Cranbrook Academy.

### 421 Graham Marks

*Untitled No. 3*, 1986
Earthenware
H. 32, W. 32, D. 32 in. (80 × 80 × 80 cm.)
Marks: none
Museum purchase  P.C. 87.5

Large, cone-shaped earthenware sculpture. Knob-like mounds protrude from the surface of this coil construction. Cracks on the flat face allow a dim view of the hollow interior. Metallic shavings have been added to the surface. The rough, other-worldly quality of this piece gives it a meteor-like appearance.

Marks is interested in the interplay between inside and outside space, and provides access to the inner sections of his forms, sometimes through just a crack, as in this piece. The textures of the exterior are achieved by the addition of metal pieces, sandblasting the surface, or repeated firings until the right surface and color are achieved.

Exhibitions: "Graham Marks," Everson Museum of Art and Cranbrook Academy of Art, 1986–1987

### GEORGE MASON (b. 1951)

George Mason, born in Salem, Massachusetts, studied at Occidental College in California, the University of Grenoble, France, and at Cranbrook Academy of Art. He received an M.F.A. from Alfred University in 1976 and also taught there. Mason has worked in architectural ceramics, with tiles and flat sections which he often combines to create collage-like constructions.

### 422 George Mason

*Terra Cotta Vase*, 1981
Earthenware and vitreous china
H. 23, W. 23, D. 3½ in. (57.5 × 57.5 × 8.75 cm.)
Marks: none
Gift of the artist  P.C. 81.33

Earthenware and vitreous china wall plaque with multiple parts arranged on different levels. A vase form in multicolored glazes decorates the center.

Exhibitions: "13th Chunichi International Exhibition of Ceramic Arts," Nagoya, Japan, 1985

### JOHN MASON (b. 1927)

John Mason, a native of Madrid, Nebraska, studied at Otis Art Institute in Los Angeles with Peter Voulkos and at Chouinard Art Institute with Susan Peterson. He taught at Pomona College in Claremont, California, at the universities of California at Berkeley and Irvine, and at Hunter College in New York.

Mason was part of the group at Otis which gathered about Peter Voulkos and initiated the radically new conception of the role of clay as a medium of expression. His style and working methods have changed over the years from an interest in the vessel to architectural forms, mod-

424

425

428

ular constructions, and back again to the vessel, and from Expressionist through Serialist and Minimalist, to a Formalist attitude.

### 423 John Mason *(See page 292)*
*Vase*, 1986
Stoneware
H. 22, W. 13⅞, D. 14 in. (55 × 34.3 × 35 cm.)
Marks: copyright mark and *MASON 2–86* incised on side at bottom
Museum purchase with funds from the Dorothy and Robert Riester Ceramic Fund   P.C. 87.105

Tall, slab-built stoneware vase with flat, square base and twisted form. The straight sides lead up to a flat shoulder and short square neck. Blue and silver-gray glazed areas create a rectangular, checkered pattern on the sides. The base, shoulder, and neck are silver-gray. Random, incised lines appear on the sides.

This monumental vase with its Baroque twist is indicative of the sensibility found in much of the work produced by American ceramists in the past few years, characterized by a revival of interest in finely crafted works which have a certain energy that is contained, yet agitated.

### DONALD MAVROS (b. 1927)
Donald Mavros was born in New York and studied chemistry and ceramics at the Universal School in New York. He works with the vessel form as well as with sculpture. His pieces often have a tactile quality which demands that they be touched. Mavros participated in the Ceramic Nationals in 1950, 1951, 1952, and 1958.

### 424 Donald Mavros
*Primal Scape*, 1958
Earthenware
H. 29¾, W. 8¾, D. 11¾ in. (74.3 × 21.8 × 29.3 cm.)

Marks: none
Gift of the artist   P.C. 87.55

Tall, abstract earthenware form with spiraling wing shape, wooden base, and black, mottled surface.

Exhibitions: "20th Ceramic International," 1958

### 425 Donald Mavros
*Sappho*, 1951
Stoneware
H. 7½, W. 9, D. 12 in. (18.75 × 22.5 × 30 cm.)
Marks: none
Gift of the artist   P.C. 87.54

Stoneware sculpture of reclining female nude. The figure rests on her left hip and elbows, with knees and arms bent as she smooths her hair. The sculpture is highly stylized, with the surface carefully tooled to produce a subtle, allover texture.

Exhibitions: "16th Ceramic National," 1951

### HARRISON McINTOSH (b. 1914)
Harrison McIntosh was born in Vallejo, California, and studied under Glen Lukens at the University of Southern California. He also studied at Claremont Graduate School and worked with Marguerite Wildenhain at Pond Farm in Guerneville, California. He taught with Peter Voulkos at Otis Art Institute in Los Angeles and now maintains his own studio in California. He has worked in Europe and Japan, and designs in both glass and ceramics. His pieces are classically conceived, carefully wrought, and highly crafted.

426 **Harrison McIntosh** *(See page 293)*
*Vase*, 1960
Stoneware
H. 13½, Diam. 15½ in. (33.75 × 38.75 cm.)
Marks: artist's stamp on bottom
Museum purchase from "21st Ceramic National," 1960   P.C. 60.76

Large, squat, globular, footed stoneware vase. The wide shoulder tapers to a short neck, which flares to a cup-

427

429

shaped mouth. The brown body is covered with blue-green matte glaze. White, leaf forms enclose the vase from base to shoulder, creating a precise repetitive motif around the body.

Exhibitions: "A Century of Ceramics in the United States, 1878–1978," 1979

### CHARLES McKEE
Charles McKee entered the "21st Ceramic National" from San Francisco State College where he was teaching.

427 **Charles McKee**
*Footed Branch Vase*, c. 1960
Stoneware
H. 21, W. 21, D. 11½ in. (52.5 × 52.5 × 28.75 cm.)
Marks: *McKee* incised on bottom.

Two labels: One reads *133*, the other *Charles McKee/Mills College/Oakland, California*
Museum purchase from "21st Ceramic International," 1960; O. Hommel Company prize
P.C. 60.77

Stoneware sculptural form with bulbous, elliptical shape on high foot. The neck tapers to a small mouth. Gray glaze with brown specks is used overall. The central section is decorated with brushwork in blue with pink, gray, and black, creating an abstract design.

### LEE McKEOWN
Born in New York, Lee McKeown was educated at Hunter College and studied at the New York School of Interior Design. She studied ceramics at Mendocino Art Center,

Mills College, and San José State University, all in California. Initially interested in functional vessels, McKeown has turned more recently to these rounded forms which convey a sense of unfolding or birth and growth.

428 **Lee McKeown** *(See page 290)*
*Urban Image,* c. 1978
Stoneware
H. 5¾, Diam. 7½ in. (14.4 × 18.8 cm.)
Marks: *M* deeply incised on bottom, *909u1/LeeMcKeown/*copyright mark *1979/M* brushed on bottom
Gift of the artist   P.C. 80.11

Footed, globular stoneware sculptural form, thrown and carved, with an inner section enclosed by outer skin-like form. The inner section is carved with an abstracted cityscape. The outer carved layers overlap. The orange-buff body is covered with a metallic black glaze on the outer shell-like section, which seems to protect the embryonic form inside.

Exhibitions: "13th Chunichi International Exhibition of Ceramic Arts," Nagoya, Japan, 1985

**RUTH GOWDY McKINLEY (b. 1931)**
Ruth Gowdy McKinley was born in Brooklyn and studied at Alfred University with Charles Harder, Daniel Rhodes, and Marion Fosdick. She was a partner in the Ossipee Pottery in New Hampshire from 1955 to 1957, then worked as a studio potter in stoneware and porcelain in Wayland, New York until 1967, when she moved to Ontario. Her pottery is functional and is wheel-thrown, slab-built, or press-molded. She participated in the Ceramic Nationals from 1958 through 1964.

429 **Ruth Gowdy McKinley** *(See page 291)*
*Drambute Jug,* 1960
Stoneware
H. 6½, W. 5⅞ in.
(16.25 × 14.6 cm.)
Marks: *R G M* incised on bottom
Museum purchase   P.C. 60.78a, b

Stoneware jug with squat, bulbous body and wide shoulder that tapers to high neck and flared mouth. The flat lid has a slight point at the center. The small, **C**-shaped handle is attached at the midsection and the shoulder where it forms a ridge that surrounds the jug. Opposite is the small, tapering spout.

## JAMES McKINNEL, JR.

James McKinnel was born in Nitro, West Virginia, and studied ceramic engineering at the University of Washington in Seattle, where he received an M.S. degree. He also studied at the Ecole Metiers d'Art in Paris, Penzance School of Art in Cornwall, and Edinburgh College of Art in Scotland. He has taught at the University of New Hampshire and has a studio in Deerfield, Massachusetts, where he makes stoneware. McKinnel participated in the Ceramic Nationals from 1954 through 1966.

430 **James McKinnel**

*Covered Jar*, 1958
Stoneware
H. 17½, Diam. 8¼ in.
(43.75 × 20.6 cm.)
Marks: *McKinnel* incised on bottom
Purchase prize given by American Art Clay Company, "20th Ceramic International," 1958 P.C. 60.14a, b

Tall stoneware jar with body tapering gently to a flared mouth. The slightly domed top has a high, bulbous, hollow knob. The orange, grogged stoneware body is covered with a sunflower decoration in wax resist. Light gray and brown glazes are used on the jar.

431 **James McKinnel**

*Vase*, n.d.
Earthenware
H. 13½, Diam. 10 in.
(33.75 × 25 cm.)
Marks: *McKinnel* incised on bottom
Anonymous gift   T.N. 32

Oviform stoneware vase with the shoulder sloping gently to a low neck and a wide, everted rim. Throwing rings form a motif on the top half of the vase. It is brushed and dripped with light and dark green glaze over a gray body.

## LEZA McVEY (b. 1907)

Leza McVey was born in Cleveland and educated at the Cleveland School of Art and at Cranbrook Academy. She taught at museums in San Antonio and Houston, at Cranbrook, and the Akron Art Institute. She participated in the Ceramic Nationals continuously from 1948 through 1964.

Form is paramount in McVey's work, with glazes or surface detail

4 3 0

4 3 1

intended only to enhance form. Her shapes are often zoomorphic, asymmetrical, and subtle.

432 **Leza McVey** *(See page 296)*

*Ceramic Form No. 33, 34*, 1951
Left: H. 10⅜, W. 7, D. 5 in. (25.9 × 17.5 × 12.5 cm.)
Right: H. 16, W. 6, D. 5 in. (40 × 15 × 12.5 cm.)
Marks: none
Purchase prizes given by Harshaw Chemical Company, "16th Ceramic National," 1951 P.C. 62.635.2, 62.635.1

Two stoneware vessels in abstracted animal forms, covered in gunmetal glaze. Three legs protrude from each body—one squat and rounded, the other oval and tapering to a long, thin neck. Both stoppers resemble animal heads. These two pieces in the collection show the influence of Surrealism, particularly the amorphous shapes of Paul Klee and Jean Arp, on McVey's work.

Exhibitions: "Forms from the Earth: 1,000 Years of Pottery in America," Museum of Contemporary Crafts, New York, 1960; "Leza McVey: Ceramics and Weaving," Cleveland Institute of Art, 1965; "Design in America: the Cranbrook Vision 1925–1950," Detroit Institute of Arts and traveled to Metropolitan Museum of Art, New York, 1984, and other museums

## ROBERT MEINHARDT

Robert Meinhardt taught at the art school of the Boston Museum of Fine Arts and participated in the Ceramic Nationals in 1951, 1954, and 1956, when he was a member of the regional jury.

433 **Robert Meinhardt**

*Tea Set*, 1954
Stoneware
Pot: H. 5, W. 8½ in. (12.5 × 21.25 cm.). Sugar: H. 2⅜, Diam. 3¾ in. (5.9 × 9.3 cm.). Creamer: H. 2⅛, W. 4 in. (5.3 × 10 cm.)
Marks: artist's mark incised on bottom of sugar and creamer only
Purchase prize given by Iroquois China Company, "19th Ceramic National," 1954   P.C. 55.687.1–3

Brown stoneware tea set includes lidded teapot, creamer, and sugar. A white mottled glaze is used overall, leaving dark brown edges and rims.

433

434

The squat, globular pot has a tapered base and spout and C-shaped handle. Its concave lid has a triangular knob. The sugar and creamer are both deep, footed, and bowl-shaped. The creamer has a pinched pouring lip.

## FRED MEYER (b. 1922)

Fred Meyer was born in Oshkosh, Wisconsin, and attended Wisconsin State Teacher's College. He also studied at the University of Wisconsin, Harvard Graduate School, and received both a B.F.A. and an M.F.A. from Cranbrook Academy. He was professor and chairman of the graduate program in the College of Fine and Applied Arts at Rochester Institute of Technology. Meyer is a painter as well as a sculptor, working mainly with the figure.

434 **Fred Meyer**
*Man with a Corncob Pipe*, 1963
Stoneware
H. 25¾, W. 13, D. 13¼ in. (64.3 × 33 × 33.6 cm.)
Marks: none
Purchase prize given by the Hancock Foundation, "11th Syracuse Regional Art Exhibition," 1963
P.C. 63.3

Stoneware bust of a man wearing a hat and smoking a corncob pipe. The bowl of the pipe is actually made of corncob. The slab-built figure wears a modeled shirt with a jacket over one shoulder. The details are incised.

436

## BRENDA MINISCI (b. 1939)

Brenda Minisci was born in Gowanda, New York, studied at the Rhode Island School of Design and received an M.F.A. from Cranbrook Academy. She taught ceramics and sculpture at the University of Massachusetts at Amherst, Williston-Northampton School in East Hampton, and at Wesleyan University. She works in stoneware, polyester resin and fiberglass, and bronze. Minisci participated in the Ceramic Nationals in 1964 and 1968.

435 **Brenda Minisci** *(See page 298)*
*Memory of a Dark Flower*, 1963
Stoneware
H. 34¾, W. 15 in. (86.9 × 37.5 cm.)

Marks: *BREN* brushed on side at bottom
Museum purchase P.C. 64.27

Stoneware sculpture with bulged square form surmounting the high, cylindrical foot. Applied and incised abstract forms decorate the surface. Black and brown glazes have been applied over the gray body.

This piece was accepted for exhibition in the "23rd Ceramic National Exhibition," 1964, but not exhibited due to damages sustained in shipment.

## JUDY MOONELIS (b. 1953)

Born in Jackson Heights, New York, Judy Moonelis received a B.F.A. cum laude from Tyler School of Art at Temple University in Philadelphia, and an M.F.A. from Alfred University. She received a National Endowment for the Arts fellowship in 1980 and 1986. She has taught at Rockford College in Illinois, Greenwich House Pottery in New York, and New York University, and presently teaches at the New School, Parsons School of Design, in New York.

Moonelis is a sculptor who uses slab-like forms to create what are in reality two-sided paintings. The back does not necessarily reiterate the theme on the front, however. The clay is curved to create freestanding pieces which are scarified, gouged, and roughened so that the surfaces are textured and distressed. Her figural forms are distinctive, often iso-lated, with tortured expressions. Color is applied as if to a painting, but worked in such a way that it seems to come from within the clay.

436 **Judy Moonelis**
*Curving Head*, 1984–1985
Earthenware
H. 44, W. 45, D. 22 in. (110 × 112.5 × 55 cm.)
Marks: none
Purchase prize with funds from the Dorothy and Robert Riester Ceramic Fund, "American Ceramics Now: The 27th Ceramic National," 1987 P.C. 87.37.6

Earthenware floor sculpture, slab-built, curving, with head on each side. Relief and incising depicts long hair, facial features, including open mouth, and ear. The piece is multi-colored, with black and blue predominating.

## MORAVIAN POTTERY AND TILE WORKS

Founded in 1898 by Henry Chapman Mercer, the Moravian Pottery and Tile Works in Doylestown, Pennsylvania has been revived and restored as a pottery which still produces reproductions of Mercer's original designs. (See also entries 85 and 86.)

### 437 Moravian Pottery and Tile Works

Cleota Reed, designer
*Peaceable Kingdom Tile*, 1977
Earthenware
H. 4½, W 4½, D. ½ in. (11.25 × 11.25 × 1.25 cm.)
Marks: *MR/1977* impressed on bottom
Museum purchase P.C. 78.19.2

Red earthenware tile with blue glaze. The figures of a lion and lamb from Edward Hick's *Peaceable Kingdom* are carved in relief in the center. The one inch border contains the inscription "Peaceable Kingdom, Everson, E. Hicks" in raised letters.

This tile, one of a group, was designed by Cleota Reed to commemorate the purchase of Edward Hick's painting *The Peaceable Kingdom* by Everson Museum of Art in 1977.

### 438 Moravian Pottery and Tile Works

*Clockwise, beginning with top left*:
*Untitled (Animal)*, 1981
Earthenware
H. 6, W. 6, D. ½ in. (15 × 15 × 1.25 cm.)
Marks: Moravian Pottery cypher and *1981* impressed
Gift of Dr. Eve Menger from collection of Dr. Karl Menger
P.C. 87.42.36

Earthenware tile, shaped as animal with surrounding leafy growth. Green turquoise glaze embellishes the brown unglazed body.

*Picking Grapes*, 1983
Earthenware
H. 4½, W. 4, D. ½ in. (11.25 × 10 × 1.25 cm.)
Marks: Moravian Pottery cypher and *1983* impressed

4 3 5

4 3 7

Gift of Dr. Eve Menger from collection of Dr. Karl Menger
P.C. 87.42.34

Earthenware tile depicts man with basket picking grapes from the vine. Gold, brown, green, and black gloss glazes are used; some sections have been left unglazed.

*Bird*, 1982
Earthenware
H. 3⅛, W. 4, D. ½ in. (7.8 × 10 × 1.25 cm.)
Marks: Moravian Pottery cypher and *1982* impressed
Gift of Dr. Eve Menger from collection of Dr. Karl Menger
P.C. 87.42.35

Small earthenware tile with dark blue gloss glaze, shaped as (toucan) bird with surface detail.

*Dragon of Castle Acre*, 1980
Earthenware
H. 3½, W. 3¾, D. ½ in. (8.75 × 9.3 × 1.25 cm.)
Marks: Moravian Pottery cypher and *1980* impressed
Gift of Dr. Eve Menger from collection of Dr. Karl Menger
P.C. 87.42.33

Square earthenware tile depicts winged dragon in relief. The raised section is brown unglazed clay, with a glossy, blue glaze background.

This tile is based on a fourteenth-century tile made for Castle Acre Priory in England, which Mercer had seen in the British Museum.

*Penn's Tree Tile*, n.d.
Earthenware
H. 4½, W. 4½, D. ½ in. (11.25 × 11.25 × 1.25 cm.)
Marks: *MR* impressed on back with illegible date
Gift of Dr. Eve Menger from collection of Dr. Karl Menger
P.C. 87.42.32

Square earthenware tile with relief design depicting decorative border in four corners, and circles surrounding a leafy tree design in the center. The background is in brown gloss glaze and the raised section in yellow.

This is a reproduction of MT 520 in Cleota Reed's *Henry Chapman Mercer and the Moravian Pottery and Tile Works* (Philadelphia: University of Pennsylvania Press, 1987).

439

440

## DAVID MORRIS

David Morris studied at the Institute of Contemporary Art in Washington, D.C., and was influenced by Bernard Leach. He also studied at the University of Guadalajara, writing his M.F.A. thesis on the pottery of Jalisco. In the early 1950s he moved to Mill Valley, California, where he set up La Paz Pottery, which he still operates, now in nearby Larkspur Hills, with his son Nicholas.

David Morris was influenced by oriental and Mexican ceramics, and these styles are evident in the functional vessels that he produces.

### 439 David Morris

*Vase*, 1976
Stoneware
H. 15¼, Diam. 9 in.
(38.1 × 22.5 cm.)
Marks: *LAPAZ 1970*, each letter within a rectangle, stamped on bottom
Gift of Bryce Holcombe
P.C. 81.51.11

Orange stoneware, baluster-shaped vase tapers to low neck with flared, wide rim. Four small fluted knobs protrude at equal intervals around the shoulder. The piece is covered in a celadon glaze.

Exhibitions: "13th Chunichi International Exhibition of Ceramic Art," Nagoya, Japan, 1985

### 440 David Morris

*Vase*, n.d.
Stoneware
H. 8½, Diam. 4 in. (21.25 × 10 cm.)
Marks: *PAC* within rectangle stamped on bottom
Gift of Bryce Holcombe
P.C. 81.51.13

Cylindrical stoneware vase with bulbous bottom, long wide neck, and everted lip. Rose glaze is used overall except on an unglazed vertical band at one side. Green edges show through on the glazed area.

441

## 441 David Morris

*Vases*, n.d.
Left: Porcelain, H. 8, Diam. 4½ in. (20 × 11.25 cm.) Center: Stoneware, H. 10, Diam. 6 in. (25 × 15 cm.). Right: Porcelain, H. 9, Diam. 5 in. (22.5 × 12.5 cm.)
Marks: *K* and *W/ PAZ/ PAL* stamped respectively on the bottom of each
Gift of Bryce Holcombe
P.C. 81.51.9, 10, 14

Three double-gourd-shaped vases. The bottom section of each has been left unglazed; the bodies are glazed overall in rose (left), purple (center), and light tan (right).

## 442 David Morris

*Porcelain Vase*, n.d.
Porcelain
H. 8½, Diam. 9 in.
(21.25 × 22.5 cm.)
Marks: artist's stamp on bottom
Gift of Bryce Holcombe
P.C. 81.51.12

Ovoid, footed porcelain vase with gently sloping shoulder and wide

442

rim. The throwing marks are faintly visible over the vessel's surface. Gray celadon (Kuan-type) crackle glaze is used overall, except at the unglazed foot.

### DEAN M. MULLAVEY

Dean Mullavey participated in the Ceramic Nationals in 1951 and 1954.

### 443 Dean Mullavey

*Bowl*, 1952
Stoneware
H. 4, Diam. 5¼ in. (10 × 13.1 cm.)
Marks: *Mullavey, 1 + 2* incised in script on bottom
Gift of the artist   P.C. 52.590

Straight-sided, footed bowl of buff

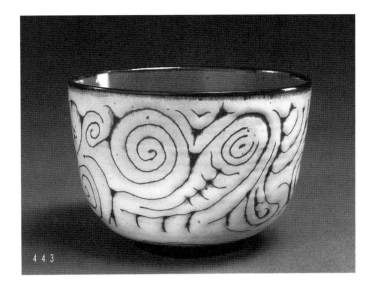

443

444

stoneware. The interior is glazed in light brown with a dark brown rim. The exterior is white with brown sgraffito arabesques, scrolls, and spirals. The foot is dark brown.

### RON NAGLE (b. 1939)

Ron Nagle studied at San Francisco State College in his native city, and taught at the San Francisco Art Institute, the University of California at Berkeley, California College of Arts and Crafts, and Mills College in Oakland.

Nagle has, since the late 1960s, concentrated on the cup form, not the functional utilitarian aspects of the cup, but on the concept of the cup as an open vessel that has both inner and outer form and carries references to man, tradition, and ceremony. He creates the forms, which are then slip-cast, painted, and fired, often dozens of times, until the right color and texture are achieved. He is able to achieve a deep saturation of color which, accompanied by texture and the diminutive size of some of his works, creates a sense of exquisite preciousness which the most traditional of porcelain makers seldom achieved. Yet his work is entirely contemporary and distinctly American.

Most recently Nagle has produced small, sculptural pieces that are only referentially cup-like.

### 444 Ron Nagle

*Untitled XI*, 1982
Earthenware
H. 7, W. 4, D. 4 in. (17.5 × 10 × 10 cm.)
Marks: none
Museum purchase   P.C. 83.7

Geometric earthenware vessel. An angular foot provides the base for this slightly askew, angular form with one rounded, offset edge. A small round opening is at the top. Pink glaze is used overall, except at the offset section, which is yellow with black speckles and a red outline. Pink glaze droplets are around the bottom.

Here Nagle makes reference to Art Deco forms of the 1920s and thirties and to the speckled paint and ice cream colors of the 1950s.

Exhibitions: "13th Chunichi International Exhibition of Ceramic Arts," Nagoya, Japan, 1985

445

### REUBEN NAKIAN (1897–1986)

Reuben Nakian was born in Queens and studied at the Beaux-Arts Institute of Design in New York. He also apprenticed with Paul Manship and shared studio space with Gaston Lachaise.

Nakian worked in metal, plaster, and other materials besides clay. His themes involve classical mythology and it was in his terracotta works that he first explored this subject matter. His work is highly sensual, both iconographically and in his manipulation of the material. His incisive gestures furrow into the clay, imparting a sense of energy and emotion totally in keeping with the subject matter. His terracotta works are both sculptural and flat, with linear forms so deeply carved that at times they seem three dimensional.

### 445 Reuben Nakian

*Nymph and Goat*, 1978
Earthenware
H. 14, W. 18, D. 6 in. (35 × 45 × 15 cm.)
Marks: *Reuben Nakian* and copyright mark at center top, on back
Gift of Mr. and Mrs. Paul A. Brunner   P.C. 80.75

Freestanding earthenware plaque of unglazed buff clay. The incised representation is of a nymph and goat; the nymph runs while glancing back at the pursuing goat.

Exhibitions: "13th Chunichi International Exhibition of Ceramic Arts," Nagoya, Japan, 1985

447

**447 Gertrud and Otto Natzler**
*Bowl*, 1951
Earthenware
H. 4, Diam. 7¾ in. (10 × 19.3 cm.)
Marks: *Natzler* inscribed on bottom
Gift of the artists    P.C. 52.712

Footed, red earthenware bowl, slightly flared. The interior glaze is of deep, golden buff, with a brown wavy line encircling the bottom. The rim is brown and the exterior is in a golden buff, celadon reduction glaze with smoke traces.

Exhibitions: "16th Ceramic National," 1951; "The Ceramic Work of Gertrud and Otto Natzler, A Retrospective Exhibition," Los Angeles County Museum of Art, 1966; "A Century of Ceramics in the United States, 1878–1978," 1979

**GERTRUD NATZLER**
**(b. Austria, 1908–1971)**
**OTTO NATZLER (b. Austria, 1908)**
The lengthy collaboration of Gertrud and Otto Natzler—nearly forty years—has resulted in a body of work that displays a perfect harmony between form and glaze. The Natzler's work constantly evolved, as experimentation was a vital part of their process. In their later vessels, Otto began to explore reduction firing and Gertrud's forms took on some characteristics of oriental and northern European ceramics, becoming more closed and acquiring a certain crispness at times. (See also entries 192 and 193.)

**446 Gertrud and Otto Natzler**
*Vase*, 1958
H. 11, Diam. 10 in. (27.5 × 25 cm.)
Marks: *Natzler* brushed on bottom
Guy Cowan Memorial purchase prize, "20th Ceramic International," 1958    P.C. 60.12

Footed, earthenware, cylindrical vase with straight sides tapering to a wide neck and rimmed mouth. The turquoise copper glaze used overall gathers in droplets at the foot.

Exhibitions: Exhibited in the Vice-Presidential house, Washington, D.C., 1977–1978

446

### 448 Gertrud and Otto Natzler

*Earth Crater Bowl*, 1956
Earthenware
H. 8½, Diam. 12½ in.
(21.25 × 31.25 cm.)
Marks: *Natzler* inscribed on bottom
Purchase prize given by United
States Potters Association, "19th Ce-
ramic National," 1956   P.C. 59.26

Large, deep hemispherical bowl with
low foot. The gray earth crater glaze
creates a deeply pitted surface,
which is surprisingly smooth to the
touch. Rings of gray, blue, white, and
yellow appear on the exterior of the
bowl.

This majestic bowl, with its evenly
textured, highly unusual surface, has
subtle, elegant coloration.

Exhibitions: "Forms from the Earth:
1,000 Years of Pottery in America,"
Museum of Contemporary Crafts,
New York, 1960; "The Ceramic
Work of Gertrud and Otto Natzler,
A Retrospective Exhibition," Los
Angeles County Museum of Art,
1966; "The Ceramic Work of Ger-
trud and Otto Natzler," M. H. de
Young Memorial Museum, San
Francisco, 1973; "A Century of Ce-
ramics in the United States, 1878–
1978," 1979

**449 Gertrud and Otto Natzler**
*Vase*, n.d.
Earthenware
H. 9, Diam. 3½ in.
(22.5 × 8.75 cm.)
Marks: *NATZLER* brushed on
bottom
Gift of Mrs. John Williams
P.C. 85.29

Inverted, conical earthenware vase, tapering to a flat, wide mouth. The dark, orange-red glaze becomes brown at the base, and has an intermittent smoke pattern overall.

This exquisite form complements perfectly the unique, elusive red glaze—each enhancing the other.

**450 Gertrud and Otto Natzler**
*Bottle*, 1960
Earthenware
H. 16, Diam. 11½ in.
(40 × 28.75 cm.)
Marks: *Natzler* inscribed on bottom center
Museum purchase   P.C. 66.21

Footed, globular earthenware bottle tapering to a high sloping neck with a flared mouth. The dark blue and green crystalline glaze creates a running, melting effect on the body.

Exhibitions: "21st Ceramic National," 1960; "Forms from the Earth: 1,000 Years of Pottery in America," Museum of Contemporary Crafts, New York, 1960; "Ceramic Work of Gertrud and Otto Natzler," M. H. de Young Memorial Museum, San Francisco, 1973; "A Century of Ceramics in the United States, 1878–1978," 1979

## IAIN M. NELSON
Iain Nelson entered the "23rd Ceramic National" from Iowa City in 1964.

451 **Iain Nelson**
*Stoneware Bottle*, 1964
Stoneware
H. 11½, Diam. 10 in.
(28.75 × 25 cm.)
Marks: none
Museum purchase from "23rd Ceramic National," 1964   P.C. 67.22

Wheel-thrown, footed, bulbous stoneware bottle. The unglazed, flat shoulder tapers to a neck with a small round mouth. The body and neck are in mottled ochre and brown glaze, with dark red areas.

## ELENA M. NETHERBY
Elena Netherby from Mills College, Oakland, California, participated in the Ceramic Nationals each year from 1946 through 1966.

452 **Elena M. Netherby**
*Bottle Vase*, 1956
Porcelain
H. 5, Diam. 4¾ in.
(12.5 × 11.8 cm.)
Marks: none
Purchase prize given by Pemco Corporation, "14th Ceramic National," 1956   P.C. 59.40

Small, ovoid porcelain bottle vase with a small, raised neck. Concentric rings are incised around the shoulder. A reduced copper coral glaze, which is slightly iridescent, covers the body.

Exhibitions: "Forms from the Earth: 1,000 Years of Pottery in America," Museum of Contemporary Crafts, New York, 1960

## WIN NG (b. 1936)
Win Ng was educated in his native city at San Francisco City College and San Francisco Art Institute, where he received a B.A. He also studied at Mills College. His work is sculptural and highly intuitive. He has been influenced by nature, especially by natural textures.

Ng participated in the Ceramic

451

452

454

Nationals in 1960, 1962, and 1964, winning prizes each year.

### 453 Win Ng

*Directions,* 1959
Stoneware
H. 36, W. 23, D. 4 in. (90 × 57.5 × 10 cm.)
Marks: none
Purchase prize given by E. W. Edwards and Sons, "21st Ceramic National," 1960   P.C. 62.20

Slab-constructed stoneware sculpture made up of three stacked rectangular forms. The vertical form serves as a base; the two horizontal rectangular blocks rest on top. White, tan, blue, and brown glazes cover the piece.

During this period Ng worked mainly with rectangular and circular shapes, exploring his interest in the ancient idea of the positive and negative forces in nature. The rectangular form for him represented the idea of form in space, while the curvilinear expressed the idea of fluidity of movement.

Exhibitions: "Forms from the Earth: 1,000 Years of Pottery in America,"

Museum of Contemporary Crafts, New York, 1960; "A Century of Ceramics in the United States, 1878–1978," 1979

### 454 Win Ng

*Retreat No. 5,* 1964
Stoneware
H. 35, W. 21, D. 14½ in. (87.5 × 52.5 × 36.3 cm.)
Marks: *Win Ng* brushed on back
William H. Milliken Purchase prize given by O. Hommel Company, "23rd Ceramic National," 1964
P.C. 64.79

Slab-constructed stoneware sculpture. This geometric piece is made up of open box configurations and decorated with incised lines and muted polychrome glazes.

*Retreat No. 5* also received the Syracuse Society of Architects prize in the "23rd Ceramic National."

456

## KENNETH NOLAND (b. 1924)

A native of North Carolina, Kenneth Noland studied at Black Mountain College in Asheville, North Carolina, and with Ossip Zadkine in Paris. He has taught at the Institute of Contemporary Art and at Catholic University, both in Washington, D.C. He is one of the most important colorists in contemporary painting. His work at the Syracuse Clay Institute was his first experience with clay. He used both stoneware and porcelain, colored strips or wedges of clay, glaze bits, and glazes to create in all, over one hundred ceramic pieces. He handles the clay in a painterly fashion, often creating large color fields with clearly defined boundaries and embedded specks of brilliant, colored glaze bits.

**455 Kenneth Noland**
*Wall Relief*, 1980
Porcelain, glaze bits
H. 28, W. 21½, D. 3 in. (70 × 53.75 × 7.5 cm.)
Marks: none
Gift of the artist   P.C. 81.53

Rectangular wall-relief with applied colored clay pieces. The basic slab form, with both straight and rough edges, folds near the bottom; strips are applied along the fold. Multicolored glaze bits are set into the surface. The colors are predominantly pink, blue, and tan on white clay.

Exhibitions: "New Works in Clay III," 1981

455

## RICHARD NOTKIN (b. 1948)

Richard Notkin was born in Chicago and educated at the Kansas City Art Institute and the University of California at Davis, where he earned an M.F.A. He has been a visiting professor at several universities, including the University of Utah, Maryland Institute College of Art, and Montana State University, and was recently visiting artist at the Kansas City Art Institute.

Though Notkin's current work is derived to a certain degree from Yixing wares, it is of an entirely different cultural milieu and expresses contemporary concerns, both in imagery and message. Concerned with social commentary, Notkin's works are small in scale and finely detailed, inviting close scrutiny, and thus introspection. He explores environ-mental, economic, and social problems, and their effects upon the quality of our lives.

**456 Richard Notkin** *(See page 309)*
*Cube Skull Teapot* (Variation #6), *Yixing Series*, 1985
Stoneware
H. 5¼, W. 6, D. 2¾ in. (13 × 15 × 6.75 cm.)
Marks: *Notkin/1985* inscribed on bottom
Purchase prize with funds from the Dorothy and Robert Riester Ceramic Fund, "27th Ceramic National" 1987   P.C. 87.37.7

Square, skull-shaped stoneware teapot. A curved lightning bolt creates the handle and spout. Four dice serve as legs to support the teapot. A mushroom-cloud knob rises from the checkerboard lid scattered with checkers. The teapot is unglazed.

Based on the meticulously crafted Yixing wares of Ming China, this teapot nevertheless speaks of contemporary issues.

Exhibitions: "American Ceramics Now: The 27th Ceramic National," 1987; "East-West Contemporary Ceramics Exhibition," Korean Culture and Arts Foundation, Seoul, Korea, 1988

**457 Richard Notkin**
*And They Beat Their Swords into Plowshares*, 1974
Stoneware
H. 23, Diam. 14½ in. including base (57.5 × 36.25 cm.)
Marks: *Notkin* incised on brick, *And They Beat Their Swords into Plowshares* written on bottom of base
Gift of Les Levine   P.C. 84.33

Stoneware sculpture encased within a glass dome with a circular, wooden base. The bottom section of the sculpture is made up of a slab with societal rubbish heaped upon it: a bomb, part of a marble column, wood, and bricks among them. Balanced upon this section and on top of one another are rocks, a cannon, a skull, and a capital of a column. At the top is a cone-shaped plot of earth with a plow. Each object is carefully wrought, with fine detailing, in a miniature trompe l'oeil fashion.

This piece comments on the destructiveness of war and is shaped like an hourglass, warning that the element of time is essential in curbing the world's destructive forces. Notkin considers this piece among his finest.

**458 Richard Notkin**
*The Human Cannonball*, n.d.
Stoneware and string

457

458

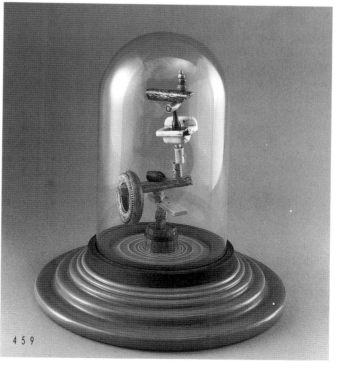

459

From top to bottom: H. 6½, W. 5½, D. 2¼ in. (16.25 × 13.75 × 5.6 cm.); H. 4½, W. 19, D. 15½ in. (11.3 × 47.5 × 38.75) H. 6, W. 10, D. 12 in. (15 × 25 × 30 cm.)
Marks: *Richard Notkin The Human Cannonball* on bottom of cannon Gift of Les Levine   P.C. 84.50.6

Three piece stoneware and string sculpture. The miniature, trompe l'oeil cannon has a stand, barrel, and loading tamper. Smoke drifts from the cannon. The wide flat base with string net is supported by poles set into the base. The insides erupt from the human cannonball figure on the wall, with its limbs extended.

### 459 Richard Notkin

*Capturing the Essence of the Twentieth Century,* 1973
Stoneware
H. 11¾, Diam. 11½ in. including

base (29.3 × 28.75 cm.)
Marks: *"Capturing the Essence of the Twentieth Century"* and *Richard J. Notkin 1973* written on bottom. Central brick incised with *Notkin.*
Gift of Les Levine   P.C. 84.50.8

Stoneware sculpture encased within a glass dome with a circular, wooden base. A miniature trompe l'oeil sculpture consists of items precariously balanced atop a barrel: bricks, stones, pieces of lumber, tire, bottles, cans, and a sink. The barrel is half submerged in water with surrounding ripples.

This unlikely combination acts as an ode of sorts, mocking the remains of the twentieth century.

Exhibitions: "13th Chunichi International Exhibition of Ceramic Arts," Nagoya, Japan, 1985

**ADOLPH ODORFER (b. Austria, 1902)**

Adolph Odorfer came from Vienna to California, where he went to school and later taught for many years. He uses clay as a medium for sculpting, and his forms are largely figurative. (See also entry 195.)

**460 Adolph Odorfer**

*Jungle Witch*, 1951
Earthenware
H. 13¾, W. 6, Diam. 4¾ in. (34.3 × 15 × 11.8 cm.)
Marks: *12, 29, c1*, triangle within a circle, and *A* within a circle, incised, *F51* painted, all on bottom.
Purchase prize given by Hanovia Chemical Company, "16th Ceramic National," 1951   P.C. 52.621

Glazed earthenware sculpture on a round base. The primitive, long-haired figure is shown in three-quarter length, arms clasping two stylized birds. Multicolor glazes are used overall.

**JEFF OESTREICH (b. 1947)**

Born in Minnesota, Jeff Oestreich was educated at Bemidji State University and at the University of Minnesota, where he studied with Warrren MacKenzie. He also apprenticed at the Bernard Leach pottery at St. Ives in Cornwall. He concentrates on the vessel form, in both stoneware and porcelain, inspired by oriental traditions and the quiet harmony of eastern wares.

**461 Jeff Oestreich**

*Compound Vase*, 1986
Stoneware
H. 16⅝, W. 5¼, D. 5¼ in. (41.5 × 13.1 × 13.1 cm.)
Marks: *JO*, and artist's cypher, on side at bottom
Gift of Mr. and Mrs. William Schiever   P.C. 86.88

Tall ovoid stoneware vase with vertical facets top to bottom. The flat shoulder has a high wide neck and mouth. Two small applied handles run from the shoulder to the lower part of the neck. The tan glaze darkens at the facet edges.

461

460

## JULES OLITSKI (b. Russia, 1922)

Jules Olitski came to the United States as a young child. He was educated at the National Academy of Design, the Beaux-Arts Institute, Ossip Zadkine School, and received both B.A. and M.A. degrees from New York University. He also studied at the Académie de la Grande Chaumière in Paris. He taught at New York University, C. W. Post College, and Bennington College.

Olitski is primarily a painter and had limited experience in clay before participating in the "New Works in Clay" project at the Syracuse Clay Institute in 1976.

**462 Jules Olitski**
*Iron Cone 02-3*, 1975
Stoneware
H. 12, Diam. 120 in.
(30 × 300 cm.)

Marks: none
Gift of the artist   P.C. 76.51

Large stoneware floor sculpture in sections. The heavily grogged stoneware body in angling and curved sections is arranged in concentric circles. The pink-buff color is achieved with iron oxide and varied firing temperatures.

The staff for the project worked from the artist's sketches and model, preparing the clay and making slabs. Olitski then finished the sections and surface and decided where to make the cuts that divided the sculpture. He also made the decision to fire the pieces at varying temperatures, allowing for the different pinkish tones in the finished piece.

Exhibitions: "New Works in Clay by Contemporary Painters and Sculptors," 1976

462

463

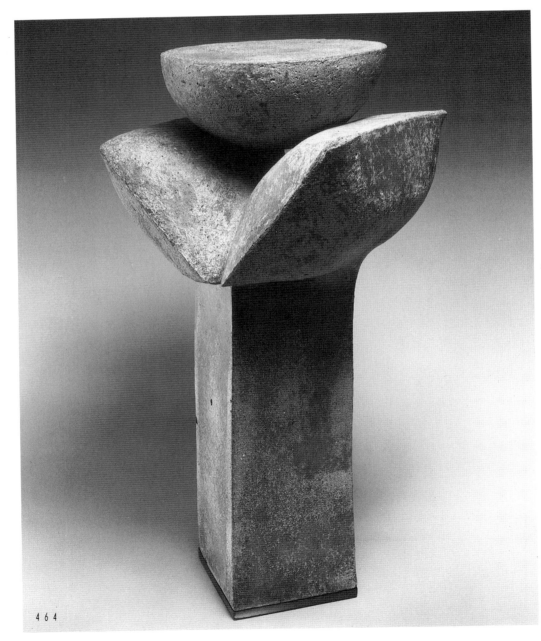

464

**GLIDDEN PARKER (1913–1979)**

In 1941 the Alfred-trained ceramist Glidden Parker set up his own pottery in western New York. (See also entries 198 and 199.)

463 **Glidden Parker**
*Boat (#4034)*, c. 1955
Stoneware
H. 3¼, L. 9⅞, D. 3⅛ in. (8.1 × 24.6 × 7.8 cm.)
Marks: *4034 Glidden USA* inscribed on bottom
Gift of Ronald Kransler   P.C. 87.8

Boat-shaped stoneware dish in "sandstone" glaze. The interior is gray with a white area, the exterior is blue-gray with white and brown striped glaze.

This piece was produced at Glidden Pottery using the RAM process—a means of efficiently pressing clay into a two-part mold and thus reducing the possibility of technical flaws—invented by Richard Steele. The "sandstone" glaze was created by Fong Chow.

**WILLIAM D. PARRY (b. 1918)**

Born in Lexington, Pennsylvania, William Parry studied at Alfred University. He taught at the Philadelphia College of Art and the College of Design at Alfred University. He participated in the Ceramic Nationals in 1960, 1964, 1966, 1968.

464 **William Parry**
*Flower Form*, 1966
Stoneware
H. 25, W. 15½, D. 13½ in. (62.5 × 38.75 × 33.75 cm.)
Marks: none
Museum purchase from "24th Ceramic National," 1966; Syracuse Society of Architects Prize   P.C. 66.30

Hand-built, tan stoneware flower form. Two pillow forms extend like leaves from the tall, rectangular stem. On top of the leaves, a hemisphere form represents a flower. The sculpture is unglazed and rests on a metal base.

465 **William Parry**
*Untitled*, 1968
Stoneware and bronze
H. 6, W. 6, D. 5 in. (15 × 15 × 12.5 cm.)
Marks: artist's cypher on top of bottom bronze section
Museum purchase from "25th Ce-

465

466

467

ramic National," 1968   P.C. 68.84

Bronze and stoneware muffin-shaped sculpture. The domed top of the cylindrical base is lifted up on one side to reveal the bronze inner section and spike-like protrusion. Incised lines create a deep valley on the top.

### LYLE N. PERKINS

Lyle Perkins taught at the University of Massachusetts and participated in the Ceramic Nationals in 1947, 1948, 1952, and from 1960 through 1968.

466 **Lyle Perkins**

*Crown's Guard*, 1963
Stoneware
H. 31, W. 14, D. 12 in. (77.5 × 35 × 30 cm.)
Marks: none
Museum purchase from "22nd Ceramic National," 1963   P.C. 63.23

Multi-footed, multi-necked, ovoid stoneware vase with flat top. One neck flares to a reticulated, circular cup form. Opposite are three necks, each topped with a rectangular form. An abstracted linear pattern covers the body. Manganese turquoise matte glaze is used overall.

### WINIFRED PHILLIPS (1880–1963)

Winifred Phillips was a ceramist, designer, painter, and teacher. She was born in Claybanks, Wisconsin and educated at Milwaukee State Teachers' College. She also studied at the Chicago Art Institute, Pratt Institute in Brooklyn, Alfred University, and Cranbrook Academy of Art in Bloomfield Hills, Michigan. She taught art at Milwaukee State Teachers' College and participated almost continuously in the Ceramic Nationals from 1933 to 1958.

467 **Winifred Phillips**

*Bowl*, 1951
Stoneware
H. 2¾, Diam. 7⅞ in. (6.8 × 18.4 cm.)
Marks: *Winifred Phillips 1951* incised on bottom
Gift of the artist   P.C. 52.630

Footed bowl of gray stoneware. The interior has a crackle glaze mottled with red; the exterior is unglazed. Three deep, incised ridges on the exterior form bands around the bowl.

Exhibitions: "16th Ceramic National," 1951

468

**DONALD PILCHER (b. 1942)**
Born in Los Angeles, Donald Pilcher studied at Chouinard Art Institute and received an M.F.A. from the Rhode Island School of Design. He is a professor of art at the University of Illinois, Champaign-Urbana. He participated in the "25th Ceramic National Exhibition" in 1968.

468 **Donald Pilcher**
*Bowl*, 1968
Stoneware
H. 15, Diam. 18 in.
(37.5 × 45 cm.)

Marks: none
Purchase prize given by American Art Clay Company, "25th Ceramic National," 1968   P.C. 68.73

Deep, wheel-thrown and altered, footed stoneware bowl with an irregular, ridged mouth. Punctures and bulges appear just below the rim. The tan glaze creates rivulets down the sides.

Exhibitions: "A Century of Ceramics in the United States, 1878–1978," 1979

## POLIA PILLIN (b. Poland, 1909)

Polia Pillin was educated at the Jewish People's Institute and at Hull House in Chicago, but she was mainly self taught in ceramics. She was a painter before working in clay, and she uses color decoratively on her clay pieces, much like a painter. She wished to transfer some of the qualities of a painting to her clay work, rather like a new painting medium which had the permanence of ceramics.

Pillin participated in the Ceramic Nationals from 1949 through 1960. She lives and works in Los Angeles.

### 469 Polia Pillin

*Plate*, 1952
Earthenware
H. 1 ¼, Diam. 14 in.
(3.1 × 35 cm.)
Marks: *Pillin* inscribed on bottom
Gift of the artist   P.C. 53.666

Flat earthenware plate with high rim. The well is decorated with multicolored, abstract linear designs, with female figures (one holding an umbrella) and birds. The underside is glazed in brown.

Exhibitions: "17th Ceramic National," 1952

### 470 Polia Pillin

*April*, 1956
Earthenware
H. 1¼, Diam. 21 in.
(3.1 × 52.5 cm.)
Marks: *Polia Pillin* on right front, near bottom
Gift of the artist   P.C. 59.41

Flat plate with high rim. The well is decorated with lively figures, animals, dancers, and trees in a light sweeping style using many colors, predominantly blue. The underside is glazed in glossy, burnished orange.

Exhibitions: "19th Ceramic National," 1956

## STEPHEN J. POLCHERT (b. 1920)

Born in Milwaukee, Stephen Polchert studied at the University of Chicago and at Cranbrook Academy of Art. He has taught at Joslyn Art Museum and the University of Omaha. He participated in the Ceramic Nationals from 1949–1952, and again in 1958. (See also entry 201.)

469

470

471

### 471 Stephen Polchert

*Bottle*, 1958
Stoneware
H. 21½, Diam. 10¾ in.
(53.75 × 26.8 cm.)
Marks: none
Museum purchase   P.C. 60.44

Large, ovoid stoneware bottle tapers to a thin neck and flared mouth. Concentric circles surround the body from mouth to base. Dark glaze patches appear at random around the body and neck. Lithium blue glaze is used overall.

Exhibitions: "20th Ceramic National," 1958; "Forms from the Earth: 1,000 Years of Pottery in America," Museum of Contemporary Crafts, New York, 1960

### LARRY POONS (b. Japan, 1937)

Larry Poons, born in Tokyo, studied painting at the New England Conservatory and at the Boston Museum of Fine Arts School. He carried his love for color into the "New Works in Clay" project at the Syracuse Clay Institute, where he created an eight-by-sixteen-foot wall of clay. He splashed and tossed hundreds of pounds of slip onto this wall, creating a brightly colored surface similar to an abstract expressionist painting. He then cut the wall into squares to dry and be fired, some at higher temperatures than others, thus affecting the resultant coloration. At the conclusion of the project, Poons chose not to reassemble the wall, but rather to let each piece stand as an individual work.

### 472 Larry Poons

*Untitled Wall Tiles*, 1975
Stoneware
Each: H. 17½, W. 19½, D. 1 in.
(43.75 × 48.75 × 2.5 cm.)
Marks: none
Gift of the artist   P.C. 76.53.1, 2

Stoneware wall tiles from "New Works in Clay" series. Two tiles with dripped surfaces of pink, gray, light green, and light blue slip on colored stoneware.

### HENRY VARNUM POOR (1880–1971)

Henry Varnum Poor went to Stanford, and then continued his studies in London and Paris. Many years later, he returned to Europe as artist-in-residence at the American Academy in Rome. While Poor used clay a great deal, working in it nearly continuously for ten years, his ceramics are heavily decorated and reflect his interest in sculpture and painting. His plates and platters were more successful than his vessel forms. (See also entries 202 and 203.)

### 473 Henry Varnum Poor

*Bowl*, 1952
Stoneware
H. 5⅞, Diam. 6⅛ in.
(14.6 × 15.3 cm.)
Marks: *HP 52* incised on bottom, *HVP* in cypher incised just above foot

472

473

Purchase prize given by United States Potters Association, "18th Ceramic National," 1954   P.C. 55.690

Wheel-thrown stoneware bowl on raised foot. The interior is predominantly red with yellow dripping from the rim. Blue, green, red, and yellow glazes are on the exterior, with two black, stylized tree decorations, one on each side.

Exhibitions: "Forms from the Earth: 1,000 Years of Pottery in America," Museum of Contemporary Crafts, New York, 1960; "A Century of Ceramics in the United States, 1878–1978," 1979

## SALLY BOWEN PRANGE (b. 1927)

Sally Bowen Prange was born in Valparaiso, Indiana and studied at the University of Michigan. She has taught independently and also at Stoney Hill Pottery in Chapel Hill, North Carolina.

Prange cuts, pierces, or reshapes the rims of her vessels, which have organic references. She has been influenced by oriental ceramics and prefers working in porcelain.

### 474 Sally Bowen Prange

*Treasure Bowl,* from *Pathfinder* series, 1985
Porcelain
H. 6½, Diam. 9 in. (16.25 × 22.5 cm.)
Marks: *SBP* on bottom
Gift of the artist   P.C. 86.23

Deep porcelain bowl. The rim is slightly flared, altered, and excised. A band is incised on one side. Raspberry volcanic carbide slip is used overall with gold luster detail.

474

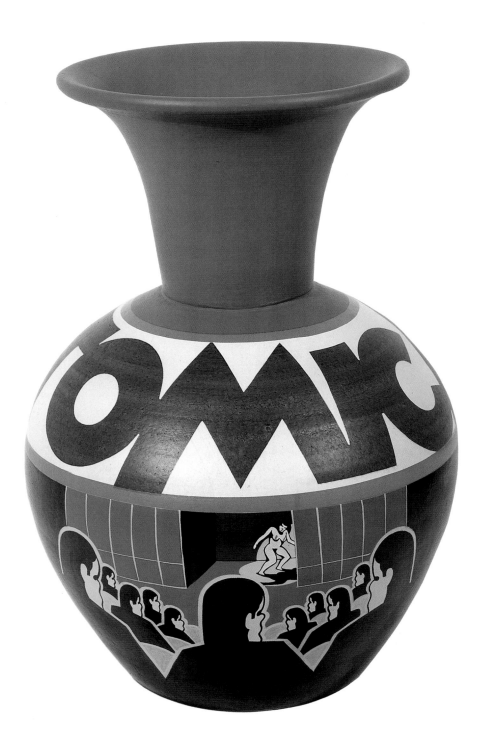

## KEN PRICE (b. 1935)

Born in Los Angeles, Ken Price was educated at Chouinard Art Institute, the University of Southern California, and Alfred University, where he received an M.F.A. He was an important participant in the experimental Los Angeles circle that surrounded Peter Voulkos at Otis Art Institute and has remained one of the most innovative of American artists today.

Early on, Price worked with the vessel form. He then turned to a more sculptural style loosely related to the works of Brancusi and Arp. Color has always been of primary importance in the work of Price, and his later cups and "Happy Curios" pieces were rich and bright. He uses color to both define and dissolve form, to strengthen planar relationships, and impart emotion to his work. He has often abandoned traditional, glazed surfaces for the quicker, brighter effects of enamel and lacquer paint.

### 475 Ken Price

*Club Atomica*, 1986
Earthenware
H. 15, Diam. 9½ in.
(37.5 × 23.75 cm.)
Marks: none
Museum purchase with funds from Syracuse China Corporation
P.C. 86.72

Ovoid earthenware vase with high flaring neck and rim. The vase is predominantly green, with a wide, pinkish-white band at the shoulder and "CLUB ATOMICA" lettered in blue. Below is a scene in a theater-like setting, with a female nude spotlit on a stage before a crowd of anonymous men in black with yellow auras around them.

This is a strong, fully formed vessel with brilliant, almost garish coloring and interesting iconographic references interplaying between the words, the scene, and the form of the vessel.

Exhibitions: "American Ceramics Now: The 27th Ceramic National Exhibition," 1987; "East-West Contemporary Ceramics Exhibition," Korean Culture and Arts Foundation, Seoul, Korea, 1988

476

477

## ANTONIO PRIETO
### (b. Spain, 1912–1967)

Born in Valdepenas, Spain, Antonio Prieto studied sculpture at the California School of Fine Arts in San Francisco, and ceramics, painting, and sculpture at Alfred University. He taught at the College of Arts and Crafts in Oakland and at Mills College. During 1963 and 1964 he received a Fulbright Scholarship for study in Spain. Prieto participated in the Ceramic Nationals from 1946 through 1962, except in 1960. (See also entries 204 and 205.)

**476 Antonio Prieto**
*Bottle*, 1950
Stoneware
H. 9½, Diam. 5⅞ in.
(23.75 × 14.6 cm.)
Marks: *A / Prieto* brushed on bottom
Purchase prize given by Onondaga Pottery Company, "15th Ceramic National," 1950   P.C. 51.595.1

Square, salt-glazed stoneware bottle with narrow neck and slightly flared, everted rim. The wide, gray midsection divides the brown top and bottom and has lines sweeping vertically at the center.

Exhibitions: "15th Ceramic National," 1950; "A Century of Ceramics in the United States, 1878–1978," 1979

**477 Antonio Prieto**
*Tall Vase*, 1950
Stoneware
H. 14, Diam. 6 in. (35 × 15 cm.)
Marks: *A / PRIETO* brushed on bottom
Purchase prize given by Onondaga Pottery Company, "15th Ceramic National," 1950   P.C. 51.595.2

Tall, tapering vase with flared mouth over very short neck. A black vertical linear design runs in three sections down the sides, over the brown and gray reduction glaze.

Exhibitions: "A Century of Ceramics in the United States, 1878–1978," 1979

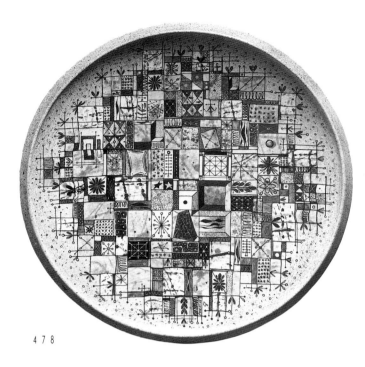

478

## MYRTON PURKISS (b. Canada)

Myrton Purkiss was born in Victoria, British Columbia and educated at the University of Southern California and Chouinard Art Institute. He did research in England and France. He participated in the Ceramic National in 1941, and from 1947 through 1952. In 1952 he served as a member of the regional jury in Los Angeles. (See also entry 223.)

### 478 Myrton Purkiss

*Plate*, 1951
Stoneware
H. 2⅝, Diam. 16½ in.
(6.5 × 41.25 cm.)
Marks: *M. PURKISS* brushed on bottom, with rectangle and star. *PURKISS* incised on bottom. Sticker reads: *designed and made by/M. Purkiss/no/duplicates/U.S.A.*
Purchase prize given by Homer Laughlin China Company, "16th Ceramic National," 1951    P.C. 52.629

Large stoneware plate with everted flat rim. The rounded well has a quilt-

like, interlocking geometric pattern in black, brown, tan, green, and blue.

Exhibitions: "Forms from the Earth: 1,000 Years of Pottery in America," Museum of Contemporary Crafts, 1960

## ELSA RADY (b. 1943)

Elsa Rady was born in New York and studied at Chouinard Art Institute under Ralph Bacerra. She works mainly in porcelain, with precise, geometric forms that are extremely thin-walled and almost metallic in appearance. She participated in the Ceramic National Exhibition in 1968, and now maintains a studio in Venice, California.

### 479 Elsa Rady

*Clipped Wings*, 1984
Porcelain
H. 5½, W. 14⅞, D. 11½ in. (13.75 × 37.1 × 28.75 cm.)
Marks: *ELSA '84* and copyright

479

480

mark incised on bottom of foot.
Gift of Jill and Marion Cole
P.C. 84.17

Thin-walled porcelain bowl. The sleek, angled sides flare from the small foot to the stepped rim with two sections clipped out. Black glaze is used overall, except at the foot which is unglazed.

Exhibitions: "13th Chunichi International Exhibition of Ceramic Arts," Nagoya, Japan, 1985

## ROBERT WARD RAMSEY (b. 1928)
Robert Ramsey entered the Ceramic Nationals in 1960 and 1966 from Long Beach, California.

### 480 Robert Ramsey
*Bowl*, 1960
Stoneware
H. 3¾, Diam. 16½ in.
(9.8 × 41.75 cm.)
Marks: *Ramsey* incised on bottom
Museum purchase from "21st Ceramic National," 1960   P.C. 60.80

Grogged, orange stoneware bowl with straight sides and slightly flared lip. The green gloss glaze in the interior extends over the lip. The exterior modeling creates a texture, with a band of finger-formed indentations on the top half of the bowl. Gray glaze covers the top of the bowl while the bottom half is unglazed.

## RUTH RANDALL (1896–1983)
Ruth Randall taught at Syracuse University and retired in 1962, at which time she was given a retrospective exhibition at the university's Lowe Art Gallery. She remained active professionally, teaching adult classes in Florida for the next fifteen years. Of her later work Randall said, "I've simplified in a lot of ways, and I think my design will become even more abstract as time goes on." She was given an exhibition at Everson Museum, "Ruth Hunie Randall Ceramics 1923–1981," in 1981. (See also entries 224–226.)

### 481 Ruth Randall
*Bird on a Nest*, 1955
Stoneware
H. 12, W. 17½, D. 6½ in. (30 × 43.8 × 16.3 cm.)
Marks: none
Gift of Dr. and Mrs. W. L. Schiffman   P.C. 77.102.3

Sculpture of stylized bird on nest made of red stoneware with slip, glaze, and incising.

Exhibitions: "The Ceramic Art of Ruth H. Randall," 1960; "Ruth Hunie Randall Ceramics," 1981

### 482 Ruth Randall
*Rhythm*, 1983
Earthenware
H. 9½, W. 15¾, D. 3½ in. (23.75 × 39.3 × 8.75 cm.)
Marks: none
Gift of the artist   P.C. 81.14

Slab-built, stylized earthenware sculpture of a swan. The body is hollow with the neck outline incised. The upper neck and head rest on the body. Piercings, suggesting feathers, reveal the inner space.

481

482

483

484

### 484 Ted Randall

*Tall Vase*, 1960
Stoneware
H. 18, W. 14, D. 5 in. (45 × 35 × 12.5 cm.)
Marks: *T. Randall* incised inside foot
Purchase prize given by Mr. and Mrs. Emil Jessen, Arcadian Landscaping, "21st Ceramic National," 1960  P.C. 64.14

Tall stoneware slab vase with high, flared foot. The top of the rectangular slab body is entirely open. The ridged foot flares at the base. Boss and strip relief decorate the exterior; the interior is iron glazed.

### THEODORE RANDALL
### (1914–1985)

Ted Randall was born in Indianapolis, studied at Yale University, and received an M.F.A. from Alfred University, which also granted him an honorary doctoral degree in 1983. He was chairman of the department of design there from 1958 until his retirement in 1981. Randall was important as an artist, teacher, and writer. He participated in the Ceramic Nationals from 1950 through 1960, except in 1953, 1954, and 1956.

Randall produced both functional and sculptural vessels. He had a stong interest in form and his vessels are architectonic and forceful. They are heavy and rich, with a sense of ancient tradition about them.

### 483 Ted Randall

*Wine Bottle*, 1952
Stoneware
H. 11⅝, Diam. 5⅝ in.
(30.3 × 14.7 cm.)
Marks: *T. Randall* incised on exterior just above foot
Purchase prize given by Onondaga Pottery Company, "17th Ceramic National," 1952  P.C. 53.659

Ovoid, footed stoneware bottle with stopper. The piece is coil-built and reduced. The bottom half and foot are smooth, while the top half is incised with concentric rings, dashes, and indentations. The neck tapers to a mouth with an extended lip. The stopper is tear-shaped with an extended knob. Gray glaze covers the interior and edge of the rim.

4 8 5

## LOUIS RAYNOR (b. 1917)

Louis Raynor studied at Alfred University, where he was granted an M.F.A. in 1946. He has taught at Michigan State University and is a production potter. He participated in the Ceramic Nationals from 1946 through 1964, except in 1950 and 1962.

### 485 Louis Raynor

*Planter*, 1964
Stoneware
H. 7½, L. 25½, D. 6⅜ in. (18.75 × 63.75 × 15.9 cm.)
Marks: none
Museum purchase   P.C. 64.30
Footed, slab-constructed, rectangular stoneware planter. The orange-buff, grogged body has one large and five smaller openings on top. The piece has blue and ochre glazes.

This piece was accepted for exhibition in the "23rd Ceramic National Exhibition" but because of damages, it was not shown. It has since been repaired.

## DANIEL RHODES (b. 1911)

Daniel Rhodes, born in Fort Dodge, Iowa, studied painting and sculpture at the School of the Art Institute of Chicago. He received a B.A. in art history from the University of Chicago. He also studied at the Art Students League, with Marguerite Wildenhain, and at Alfred University with Charles Harder and Sam Haile.

He received a Fulbright Research Grant to study in Japan from 1962 to 1963. He has written widely on ceramics and participated in the Ceramic Nationals from 1949 through 1968, except in 1960.

Rhodes began as a painter, but his primary work is in clay. He first worked in the vessel tradition but turned to hand-built forms of high temperature reduction stoneware. He prefers unglazed, textured surfaces, using glazes mainly on interiors or for detailing. He has experimented with clay and fiberglass, fired together to create extremely strong forms.

### 486 Daniel Rhodes

*Form*, 1962
Stoneware
H. 47, W. 18, D. 6 in. (117.5 × 45 × 15 cm.)
Marks: none
Helen S. Everson Memorial Purchase Prize, "22nd Ceramic National," 1962   P.C. 62.3.4

Tall stoneware sculpture, thrown and slab-built. The high cylindrical foot with flared base supports a large rectangular form. Decorations are applied and incised to the body and to the top, which is modeled with a raised mouth.

Exhibitions: "A Century of Ceramics in the United States, 1878–1978," 1979

4 8 6

487

488

### DOROTHY RIESTER (b. 1916)

Dorothy Riester is a sculptor in Cazenovia, New York. While her primary medium is metal, she also works in clay. Her work ranges from small, satirical figures to large, outdoor sculpture. (See also entry 229.)

### 487 Dorothy Riester

*Audience*, 1963
Earthenware
H. 19, L. 30¼, D. 5½ in. (47.5 × 75.6 × 13.75 cm.)
Marks: *D. RIESTER AUDIENCE III 1963* incised on back
Gift of the artist   P.C. 87.76

*Terra sigillata* earthenware sculpture of row of eight seated, elongated figures. Each has incised facial features and strikes a diferent gestural pose, creating individuals within the group. The figures are seated on benches, which rest on a single rectangular base that is mounted on wood.

Exhibitions: "23rd Ceramic National" 1964

### JOHN HOLLISTER RISLEY (b. 1919)

John Risley was born in Brookline, Massachusetts, studied at Malvern College, England, and received a B.A. from Amherst College. He was granted a B.F.A. from Rhode Island School of Design, and an M.F.A. from Cranbrook Academy, where he studied with William McVey. A sculptor and educator, he has taught at Wesleyan University in Middletown, Connecticut. He participated in the Ceramic Nationals in 1948, 1954, and 1958.

### 488 John Risley

*Impasse*, 1958
Stoneware
H. 20¼, W. 8, D. 4½ in. (50.6 × 20 × 11.25 cm.)
Marks: none
Museum purchase from "20th Ceramic International," 1958
P.C. 62.32

Vertical, abstract stoneware sculpture. The niches contain metal rods which skew small stoneware forms to a central section. The unglazed sculpture rests on four black metal legs.

489

**GEORGE ROBY**
George Roby teaches in the Cleveland area. He entered the Ceramic National in 1964.

489 *Bottle*, 1964
H. 22½, Diam. 15 in.
(56.25 × 37.5 cm.)
Marks: none

Purchase prize given by Dansk Designs, "23rd Ceramic National," 1964   P.C. 64.80

Hand-built, pear-shaped stoneware bottle. The bulging form tapers to a short neck and small rimmed mouth. The body is marked with incising and covered in tan and black glaze.

491

492

## ROCHESTER FOLK ART GUILD
### (established 1957)

The Rochester Folk Art Guild is a community of craftsmen, established in 1957 in Middlesex, New York by Louise March. The members live and work on a 318-acre farm. The community was formed to help counteract the specialization of contemporary life. The crafts—including pottery, glassmaking, iron forging, printing, and bookbinding —are seen as a means of mastering oneself. The objects produced by the members bear the mark of the guild rather than individual signatures.

### 490 Rochester Folk Art Guild

*Ceramic Vase*, 1975
Stoneware
H. 10⅜, Diam. 7¼ in.
(25.9 × 18.1 cm.)
Marks: guild stamp on exterior, just above foot
Gift of Dr. and Mrs. Stephen Marshall   P.C. 77.1

Ovoid, salt-glazed stoneware vase with high shoulder and small, slightly raised mouth. A ridge surrounds the vase at its shoulder. Incised fluting on the body is divided into two sections.

### 491 Rochester Folk Art Guild

*Ceramic Jar,* 1975
Stoneware
H. 9⅛, Diam. 10 in. (23 × 25 cm.)
Marks: *RFAG* stamped just above base
Gift of Mr. and Mrs. Robert Farrel   P.C. 77.4

Globular stoneware jar with handles and raised, flared neck. The loop handles have rings attached, one of which hangs freely, the other is attached to the body. The jar is wood-fired and is marked with ash deposits and brown tones.

### 492 Rochester Folk Art Guild

*Porcelain Bottle*, 1976
Porcelain
H. 8, Diam. 6½ in. (20 × 16.3 cm.)
Marks: guild stamp on side at bottom
Gift of Mrs. Louise March
P.C. 77.3

Globular porcelain vessel in the form of an opening bud. Incised lines curve from the base to the small mouth. The body is blue and white with clear gloss glaze overall.

Exhibitions: "13th Chunichi International Exhibition of Ceramic Arts," Nagoya, Japan, 1985

## MONONA ROSSOL

Monona Rossol entered the Ceramic National in 1964 from Madison, Wisconsin.

493 **Monona Rossol**
*Vase*, 1964
Stoneware
H. 7, Diam. 10½ in.
(17.5 × 26.3 cm.)
Marks: none
Purchase prize given by Association of San Francisco Potters, "23rd Ceramic National," 1964   P.C. 64.81

Hand-built stoneware vase with squat bulbous form. The neck flares to a torn mouth. The ribbed body is striped with black glaze; tan glaze is used overall. Roughly organic in form, the piece resembles a squash.

493

494

## JERRY ROTHMAN (b. 1933)

Jerry Rothman was born in Brooklyn, studied at Los Angeles City College and recieved an M.F.A. from Otis Art Institute in 1961. He participated in the Ceramic Nationals from 1962 through 1968.

Rothman was a part of the group that worked with Peter Voulkos at Otis Art Institute. He works in both vessel and sculptural forms, and has been involved both in studio work and commercial ceramics. The term "Bauhaus Baroque" has been associated with his work, for he combines the extravagantly decorative elements of Baroque art with the functional, adding a good measure of contemporary sensibility, creating vessels which are alternately regarded as witty, garish, monumental, and mannered. They are rich, sensual, fully formed and realized works.

494 **Jerry Rothman**
*Not in Central Park #3*, 1964
Stoneware
H. 27, W. 20, D. 16 in. (67.5 × 50 × 40 cm.)

Marks: none
Purchase prize given by A. D. Alpine Company, "23rd Ceramic National," 1964   P.C. 64.82

Organic, twisted stoneware sculpture on a high foot. *"Trees meet the sky / birds fly / men cry / where's the sky / not in Central Park"* is incised on the foot.

495 **Jerry Rothman**
*Bicentennial Tureen*, 1976
Stoneware
H. 15, W. 10¾ in.
(37.5 × 26.75 cm.)
Marks: none
Gift of Garth Clark   P.C. 79.13.2a, b

Bulbous, wheel-thrown soup tureen with a high-domed cover. Modeled configurations on top and at the sides create handles. The piece is dark brown with a luster glaze.

Exhibitions: "13th Chunichi International Exhibition of Ceramic Arts," Nagoya, Japan, 1985

496

**496 Jerry Rothman**
*Ritual #1*, 1978
Earthenware
H. 15½, W. 20 in.
(38.75 × 50 cm.)
Marks: none
Gift of the artist   P.C. 79.14

Large, footed vessel with large curving handles and a bulbous dome-
shaped cover. Four curved legs support the vessel, which is covered in
silver-black luster glaze.

This Baroque tureen is witty, monumental, and functional.

Exhibitions: "Jerry Rothman: Bau-
haus-Baroque," Vanguard Gallery,
Los Angeles, 1978

497

**497 Jerry Rothman**
*Pot*, 1968
Stoneware
H. 22, W. 18, D. 7 in. (55 × 45 ×
17.5 cm.)
Marks: none
Helen S. Everson Memorial Pur-
chase Prize, "25th Ceramic Na-
tional," 1968   P.C. 68.74

Hand-built, footed stoneware pot
with two rounded forms on the sides.
White glaze is overall with abstract,
incised designs in pink, yellow,
green, blue, and tan.

Exhibitions: "A Century of Ceramics in the United States, 1878–
1978," 1979

498

### RENÉ SALZMAN

René Salzman participated in the "23rd Ceramic National" from Brooklyn, New York.

### 498 René Salzman

*Stoneware Pot*, 1965
Stoneware
H. 15½, Diam. 14½ in.
(38.8 × 36.3 cm.)
Marks: none

Museum purchase from "23rd Ceramic National, "1965   P.C. 66.13

Wheel-thrown, irregularly shaped, bulbous stoneware vessel. The high shoulder tapers to a double-rimmed mouth, the lower rim projects like a ledge. Throwing marks are apparent, as are incisions on the sides. The pot is orange, yellow-green, and black.

499

500

### HERBERT SANDERS (1909–1988)

Herbert Sanders made great contributions to the contemporary ceramics movement, particularly through his extensive research in glazes, as these two splendid crystalline vessels demonstrate. (See also entries 234 and 235.)

#### 499 Herbert Sanders

*Globular Vase*, 1966
Porcelain
H. 5, Diam. 5 in. (12.5 × 12.5 cm.)
Marks: *Sanders* incised on bottom
Gift of Mrs. John Williams, purchased from "24th Ceramic National," 1966   P.C. 85.44

Wheel-thrown, globular porcelain vase with short neck and double rim in high gloss gray and ivory crystalline glaze.

#### 500 Herbert Sanders

*Paddled Bottle*, 1966
Porcelain
H. 6½, Diam. 5 in.
(16.25 × 12.50 cm.)
Marks: *Sanders* incised on bottom
Purchase Prize given by Syracuse China Co., "24th Ceramic National," 1966   P.C. 66.31

Wheel-thrown, ovoid porcelain vase. The high shoulder tapers to a small short neck and flared mouth. The interior has light blue glaze at the mouth; the exterior has gold and blue crystalline glaze.

Exhibitions: "24th Ceramic National," 1966; "A Century of Ceramics in the United States, 1878–1978," 1979

#### 501 Herbert Sanders

*Jar*, 1962
Porcelain
H. 10, Diam. 5½ in.
(25 × 13.75 cm.)
Marks: none
Purchase prize given by Canadian Guild of Potters, "23rd Ceramic National," 1962   P.C. 62.42

Porcelain covered jar. The cover tapers to a long, cylindrical handle with a flared top. Green-blue glaze is used overall with brown on the cylindrical handle.

501

502

## ADRIAN SAXE (b. 1943)

Born in Glendale, California, Adrian Saxe studied at the California Institute of the Arts and has been a professor of art at the University of California, Los Angeles since 1973.

Saxe uses both earthenware and porcelain, often in the same work. His works contain an intriguing combination of disparate elements: traditional materials with unconventional or personal iconography, or lava-like earthy forms coupled with exquisitely wrought porcelain. His vessels are often conceived in a hierarchical fashion, with earthy bases that seem to have a primal quality topped by incredibly refined vessel forms. These are often finished with golden stoppers that add a final flourish of elegance.

The porcelains of the eighteenth and nineteenth centuries, especially those of Sèvres, were influential in the development of Saxe's style. These too often disparaged pieces, which evoke so eloquently the Rococo style, represented for him technical achievement as well as a complete reflection of the culture that created them. He values their eccentricities, their complexities, and their refinement.

502 **Adrian Saxe**

*Untitled*, 1980
Porcelain
H. 12½, Diam. 8½ in. (31.25 × 21.25 cm.)
Marks: *SAXE* (underlined) incised, with artist's cypher, which incorporates date: *CMLXXX*—all on bottom
Gift of Social Art Club Memorial Fund in memory of Anna Wetherill Olmsted   P.C. 81.24

Large, cylindrical porcelain vessel with short flared base. The exterior is covered with an excised graphic design of scrolls, circles, bars, and arabesques. A circular shape resembling a gear balances on top of the toothed rim. A celadon crackle glaze is used overall.

This vessel was given to the museum in memory of Anna Wetherill Olmsted, long-time director of the Museum, and initiator of the Ceramic National Exhibitions. Ms. Olmsted was a member of the Social Art Club.

Exhibitions: "The 13th Chunichi International Exhibition of Ceramic Arts," Nagoya, Japan, 1985

503

**503 Adrian Saxe**
*Untitled Jar (Golden Arches)*, 1986
H. 21½, W. 10, D. 6 in. (53.75 ×
25 × 15 cm.)
Marks: none
Gift of Mr. and Mrs. John
Dietz   P.C. 87.9

Porcelain vessel on raku-fired earthenware base. The body flares widely
to the flat shoulder and short neck.
The small, domed lid has a double-
looped handle which forms two
golden arches. The body of the vessel
is covered with beading, applied di-
agonally. Four golden, curved feet

support the piece.
The elegance of this vessel form
contrasts interestingly with the ear-
thier, lava-like base upon which it
sits. Saxe frequently uses these contrasts of carefully wrought objects
with rock-like structures, each ex-
pressing its origins in the earth.

Exhibitions: "The Object as Art,"
Sotheby's, New York, 1987; "East-
West Contemporary Ceramics," Ko-
rean Culture and Arts Foundation,
Seoul, Korea, 1988

**EDWIN SCHEIER (b. 1910)**
**MARY SCHEIER (b. 1910)**
Edwin and Mary Scheier taught ceramics at the University of New Hampshire until their retirement in 1960. They now live in Arizona and continue to work in clay and other media. (See also entries 236–239.)

504 **Edwin Scheier**

*Bowl*, 1958
Stoneware
H. 9½, Diam. 9 in.
(23.75 × 22.5 cm.)
Marks: *Scheier* incised on bottom
Purchase prize given by United States Potters Association, "20th Ceramic International," 1958
P.C. 60.13

Deep stoneware bowl with slightly tapering sides. An incised design of male and female figures rings the bowl. The female figures are upright; the male bodies are inverted, but their heads are upright. Details of facial features, breasts, and feet are in low relief. The interior is in buff glaze, and the exterior in brown.

505 **Mary Scheier**

*Coffee Set,* 1951
Earthenware
Pot: H. 8⅝, W. 9¾ in. (21.5 × 24.3 cm.). Sugar: H. 2⅞, Diam. 3¾ in. (7.1 × 9.3 cm.). Creamer (not pictured): H. 2⅝, W. 4⅝ in. (6.5 × 11.5 cm.). Cup: H. 2⅜, W. 3½ in. (6 × 8.8 cm.). Saucer: H. ¾, Diam. 5⅜ in. (2 × 13.3 cm.)
Marks: *Scheier* incised on bottom of pot, saucer, and creamer. *S* incised on bottom of sugar and cups.
Gift of Richard V. Smith
P.C. 83.5.10a-e

Earthenware coffee set includes four cups, four saucers, sugar, creamer and coffee pot with lid—all round, footed, and in gray-green gloss glaze. The ovoid pot has a long, tapering spout; flat, ear-shaped handle; and flat top with a triangular knob. The creamer has a pinched spout and the same flat, ear-shaped handle as the cups and pot. The rim of the saucer is slightly flared.

5 0 4

5 0 5

506

## JAMES SECREST

James Secrest studied at the Tyler School of Fine Arts at Temple University and received an M.F.A. at Alfred University, where he studied with Daniel Rhodes. He and his brother Philip (entry 509) share a studio in the Bristol Hills Region near Honeoye, New York, where they produce functional wares.

James Secrest taught at the School for American Craftsmen in Rochester, New York, and participated in the Ceramic Nationals from 1948 to 1950, and again in 1956 and 1958.

### 507 James Secrest

*Bowl*, 1956
Stoneware
H. 9½, Diam. 10¾ in.
(23.75 × 26.8 cm.)
Marks: *SECREST* within a rectangle incised on bottom
Purchase prize given by Syracuse China Company, "19th Ceramic National," 1956   P.C. 59.27

Deep bowl with tapering sides. The pink-buff stoneware body is covered in celadon glaze, except at the foot which is unglazed. Vertical, raised lines, closely spaced, surround the bowl.

## MARLIS SCHRATTER

Marlis Schratter participated in the "22nd Ceramic National" from Lexington, Massachusetts.

### 506 Marlis Schratter

*Stoneware Jar with Cover*, 1962
Stoneware
H. 9¼, Diam. 9½ in.
(23.1 × 23.75 cm.)
Marks: *Marlis 88* incised on bottom
Museum purchase from "22nd Ceramic National," 1962   P.C. 63.7

Globular, footed stoneware jar with cover. The flat cover has a hollow, flared knob. The surface of the body has been modeled with an uneven, ribbed texture. Yellow to brown striated slip glaze covers the body. The cover is predominantly brown with yellow highlights.

Exhibitions: "22nd Ceramic National," 1962

507

## 508 James Secrest

*Small Bowl*, c. 1960
Stoneware
H. 3¾, Diam. 4⅜ in.
(9.5 × 10.9 cm.)
Marks: *SECREST* within a rectangle
incised on bottom
Museum purchase   P.C. 61.71

Small, footed earthenware bowl with
slight tapering to the rim. A mottled
green-brown glaze is used overall,
except at the unglazed foot and base.
Glazed S-shapes decorate the exterior of the bowl.

## PHILIP SECREST

Like his brother James, Philip Secrest studied at Alfred University under Daniel Rhodes. The Secrests share a studio near Honeoye, New York. Philip Secrest participated in the Ceramic Nationals in 1949, 1950, 1952, from 1956 to 1960, and again in 1964.

## 509 Philip Secrest

*Fish Casserole*, 1952
Stoneware
H. 1⅞, W. 6⅝, L. 14⅛ in. (4.6 ×
17.2 × 35.3 cm.)
Marks: *Glidden 412* incised on bot-

508

tom, paper sticker which reads:
*Philip/Secrest/#1 $8.80* and *120/1
cat. 130*
Purchase prize given by Homer
Laughlin China Company, "17th Ceramic National," 1952   P.C. 53.663

Buff stoneware casserole. The oval body has a curved rim with handles on each end—one curved and rectangular, the other notched and curved. Together with the body, which is decorated on the interior with a whimsical, linear design of a skeleton, they suggest a fish shape. The casserole is covered in a gray, semi-matte glaze.

509

510

## THOMAS SHAFER (b. 1938)

Thomas Shafer was educated at the University of Iowa, where he studied under James McKinnel. He has found inspiration in Medieval and Renaissance ceramics and in Spanish majolica and luster wares. During the 1960s he made both functional and nonfunctional pieces, slab or wheel-thrown, or sometimes a combination of the two.

Shafer participated in the Ceramic Nationals from 1964 through 1968.

511 **Thomas Shafer**
*Globe*, 1964
Stoneware
Diam. 18 in. (45 cm.)
Marks: none
Purchase prize given by Hammond Lead Products, "23rd Ceramic National," 1964   P.C. 64.83

Hand-built, stoneware, globular form. Incising creates a random surface texture. Cracks appear on the surface of the form where the sections overlap. The openings at the top have jagged edges. Iron oxide slip is used overall.

## MAYER SHACTER

Mayer Shacter is a studio potter who works in Oakland, California. He also operates a production pottery which produces functional wares. While his own work is mainly concerned with the vessel form, his objects are essentially non-functional, although they include sculptural accents which make reference to function.

Mayer Shacter participated in the Ceramic National in 1966 from Venice, California.

510 **Mayer Shacter**
*Purple Heart*, 1968
Stoneware
H. 11, W. 11½, D. 12½ in. (27.5 × 28.75 × 31.25 cm.)
Marks: none
Gift of the artist   P.C. 86.15

Polychrome stoneware sculpture of a heart with interior organs and arteries, all enclosed within a hinged wooden box.

Exhibitions: "24th Ceramic National," 1966

511

512

513

## FLOY SHAFFER

A Bowling Green, Ohio potter, Floy Shaffer entered the "23rd Ceramic National" in 1964.

512 **Floy Shaffer**

*Bowl,* 1964
Stoneware
H. 8¾, Diam. 17 in.
(21.8 × 42.5 cm.)
Marks: label affixed reads: *Floy Shafer/Bowling Green, Ohio/Bowl, 85.00*
Purchase prize given by Mayco Colors, "23rd Ceramic National," 1964  P.C. 64.84

Wheel-thrown, hemispherical stoneware bowl with foot, curved sides, and slight lip. Orange glaze is used overall, with gray-brown accents.

## DAVID SHANER (b. 1934)

Born in Kutztown, Pennsylvania, David Shaner studied at the State College at Kutztown and at Alfred University, where he was granted an M.F.A. in ceramic design. He taught at the University of Illinois until 1963, when he became director of the Archie Bray Foundation in Helena, Montana. He produces functional wares at his own pottery near Big Fork, Montana, which he established in 1970.

Shaner participated in the Ceramic Nationals from 1960 through 1968.

513 **David Shaner**

*Garden Slab,* 1966
Stoneware
H. 3⅝, W. 14½ in. (9 × 36.25 cm.)
Marks: *Shaner* incised on bottom
Purchase prize given by Mayco Colors, "24th Ceramic National," 1966  P.C. 66.32

Hand-built, freely modeled plate form. Brown and gray glaze with white slip cover the piece.

Exhibitions: "A Century of Ceramics in the United States, 1878–1978," 1979

## ANNE SHATTUCK (b. 1953)

Anne Shattuck was born in Salem, Massachusetts and studied in England at the Sir John Cass School of Art and the Harrow School of Art in London, and apprenticed with Bryan Newman in Somerset. She owned and operated her own pottery in Eastham, Massachusetts from 1975 to 1977, and in 1978 opened a studio in Kingston, New York.

Shattuck is a functional potter and specializes in salt glaze. She was chosen as one of fifteen American potters of excellence to display twelve place settings at the White House in 1977.

### 514 Anne Shattuck
*Place Setting*, 1977
Porcelain
Dinner plate: H. 1½, Diam. 11 in. (3.8 × 27.5 cm.). Side plate: H. 1, Diam. 7⅝ in. (2.5 × 19 cm.). Goblet: H. 7⅝, Diam. 3⅓ in. (19 × 8.8 cm.). Bowl: H. 2½, Diam. 5⅝ in. (6.3 × 14 cm.)
Marks: *Anne Shattuck* incised on bottom of each. *1977* incised on bottom of plates.
Gift of the artist   P.C. 80.31a-d

Porcelain place setting includes dinner plate, side plate, bowl, and goblet. Every piece is incised with a linear motif and covered in yellow and iridescent white glazes.

This place setting was made for the White House.

Exhibitions: "American Craftsmen in the White House," 1977

## RICHARD SHAW (b. 1941)

Born in Hollywood, Richard Shaw attended Orange Coast College, Costa Mesa, California, San Francisco Art Institute, Alfred University, and University of California at Davis, where he was granted an M.F.A. He teaches at the San Francisco Art Institute.

Shaw is one of the most important figures in the "Super-object" school which has been so influential in American ceramics during the past decade. He uses porcelain to achieve a trompe l'oeil effect. Shaw has perfected a method of transfer printing whereby the image is burned into the clay. With this he can create incredibly life-like images which are both whimsical and narrative.

514

### 515 Richard Shaw
*Open Book II*, 1978
Porcelain
H. 3¼, W. 12⅞, D, 11⅛ in. (8.3 × 32.1 × 27.8 cm.)
Marks: *Shaw* inscribed on spine
Museum purchase   P.C. 80.23a, b

Porcelain sculpture which is, in fact, a lidded box, made of two trompe l'oeil figures of books. An envelope, a notepad, and scraps of paper, all in clay, rest on top of the closed book. The bottom book has a light green cover and imitated printing. The closed book has a blue cover with tan spine on which appear "Shaw" and "Hog Eye Pr." The envelope is the artist's best deceit, incredibly thin and complete with stamp and postmark.

Exhibitions: "Nine West Coast Clay Sculptors," 1978; "A Century of Ceramics in the United States, 1878–1978," 1979; "13th Chunichi International Exhibition of Ceramic Arts," Nagoya, Japan, 1985

515

516

**516 Richard Shaw**
*Whiplash!*, 1978
Porcelain
H. 12¾, W. 10, D. 7⅜ in. (31.8 × 25 × 18.4 cm.)
Marks: *Richard Shaw* on spine of book

Museum purchase with matching funds from the National Endowment for the Arts   P.C. 80.22

Multicolored, porcelain, trompe l'oeil sculpture of a closed book with vertically stacked "house of cards" upon it. The titles "Whiplash!" and

"Richard Shaw" are on the spine of the book.

The playing cards are a triumph in thinness, perfection of size, and appearance. Photo silkscreen images create exact blue bicycle playing card reproductions.

Exhibitions: "Nine West Coast Clay Sculptors," 1978; "A Century of Ceramics in the United States, 1878–1978," 1979; "13th Chunichi International Exhibition of Ceramic Arts," Nagoya, Japan, 1985

**LARRY SHEP (b. 1931)**

Larry Shep, a native of San Francisco, received a B.A. in architecture from the University of California at Berkeley and studied at the Los Angeles County Art Institute under Peter Voulkos. He participated in the Ceramic Nationals in 1960, 1962, and 1966.

517 **Larry Shep**

*Terrace Vase*, 1960
Stoneware
H. 35, W. 14, D. 12 in. (87.5 × 35 × 30 cm.)
Marks: *Larry Shep* on exterior in black slip
Museum purchase from "21st Ceramic National," 1960   P.C. 60.81

Tall, irregularly shaped stoneware vase with rounded rim. The rough surface is marked with incisions and impressed textures. Two central openings are made below a large blue spot of glaze. Other additional glaze marks are scattered around the body and small clay "pebbles" are applied at the base.

Exhibitions: "21st Ceramic National," 1960; "Forms from the Earth: 1,000 Years of Pottery in America," Museum of Contemporary Crafts, New York, 1960

517

518

### WILLIAM SHINN (b. 1932)

William Shinn was born in Santa Ana, California, and studied initially at Ventura College. After serving in the Air Force he went to the Académie Julian and the Sorbonne in Paris. He received a B.A. in painting and an M.A. in ceramic design from the University of California, Los Angeles. Shinn was a designer of ceramic tiles with Interpace in Los Angeles and now teaches at Allan Hancock College in Santa Maria, California.

518 **William Shinn**
*#2*, 1966
Stoneware
H. 17, W. 24, D. 21 in. (42.5 × 60 × 52.5 cm.)
Marks: none
Gift of Richard V. Smith, purchased from "24th Ceramic National," 1966   P.C. 83.5.4

Egg-shaped, hollow stoneware form with five feet. The fluted surface is covered in iron slip. Three openings are at the top, one large and two smaller.

This large form has a fine sense of volume and an interesting surface treatment.

520

### PETER SHIRE (b. 1947)

Peter Shire studied at Chouinard Art Institute in his native Los Angeles. He is a sculptor and furniture maker and has been working with the prestigious avant-garde Italian design group Memphis/Milano. His ceramic work is stylistically akin to his furniture. He pays lip service to functionalism in his teapots, but they exist more as sculpture than as utilitarian objects. His work is whimsical, with brilliant colors and playfully combined geometrical shapes.

519 **Peter Shire** *(See page 346)*
*Accordion Donut Teapot*, 1984
Porcelain
H. 15¾, W. 15¾, D. 5½ in. (39.3 × 39.3 × 13.75 cm.)
Marks: none
Museum purchased   P.C. 85.6

Geometric porcelain teapot with cover. The low, cylindrical, purple base supports the black, accordion-like, cylindrical body. The lid is composed of a light blue disk and large orange sphere. The triangular black spout is attached to the body with a yellow disk form. The square yellow handle with small diamond cutout is attached to the body by a black circular form.

Shire has used a traditional ceramic form, disregarding its attendant cultural and ceremonial baggage, and given it a thoroughly contemporary expression.

Exhibitions: "Peter Shire Ceramics," Modernism: Art of the Twentieth Century, San Francisco, 1985; "13th Chunichi International Exhibition of Ceramic Arts," Nagoya, Japan, 1985

## JOAN HANG SMITH

Joan Hang Smith lived in Cleveland and Redwood City, California. She participated in the Ceramic National Exhibitions in 1952, 1954, and 1958.

520 **Joan Hang Smith** *(See page 345)*
*Racoon*, 1952
Earthenware
H. 9½, W. 18, D. 7¾ in. (23.75 × 45 × 19.3 cm.)
Marks: *Hang* incised on right, front leg. Paper label reads: *Joan Hang Smith / #1 price $45.00*
Gift of Richard V. Smith, purchased from "17th Ceramic National," 1952
P.C. 83.5.9

Earthenware sculpture of a racoon. The orange clay body has a textured effect to indicate fur, and is glazed in brown, with darker brown accents. The animal seems to be in motion, with its head turned.

*Racoon* was awarded an honorable mention for ceramic sculpture in the "17th Ceramic National," 1952.

## RICHARD V. SMITH (b. 1912)

Richard Smith built Syracuse University's first high-fire kiln while teaching there part time. From that time he worked mainly in stoneware and porcelain. He continued to work in ceramics until 1971. (See also entry 250.)

521 **Richard V. Smith**
*Decanter Set*, 1964
Porcelain
Decanter: H. 7⅜, Diam. 3⅝ in. (19 × 9 cm.). Cup: H. 1½, Diam. 1½ in. (4 × 4 cm.)
Marks: artist's cypher, *20/1/64* incised on bottom of decanter. Cypher only incised on bottom of cups

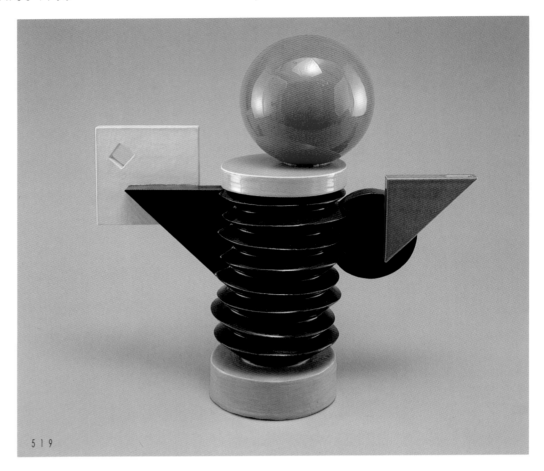

519

521

522

Purchase prize given by Syracuse Allied Arts, and Syracuse Ceramic Guild, "12th Syracuse Regional Art Exhibition," 1964   P.C. 64.8.1–7

Porcelain decanter set includes decanter with stopper and six matching cups. The ovoid decanter has an overhanging shoulder that tapers to a flared mouth with a hollow, flared stopper. The cups are truncated, ovoid forms. Clear glaze is used over the delicately incised double-lined tulip petal design.

### EVERETT O. SNOWDEN

From Oakland California, Everett Snowden participated in the Ceramic Nationals in 1968.

522 **Everett Snowden**
*Pool*, 1968
Stoneware
H. 8½, W. 9, L. 20 in. (21.3 × 22.9 × 50 cm.)
Marks: none
Purchase prize given by *Ceramics Monthly*, "25th Ceramic National," 1968   P.C. 68.75

Slab-built stoneware sculpture. The roofed, temple-like structure with three undulating columns holds a chair inside it, visible through the front. The slab-built base extends forward to create two pools. The sculpture is green, orange, and off-white.

5 2 3

## PAUL SOLDNER (b. 1921)

Paul Soldner was born in Summerfield, Illinois and educated at Bluffton College in Ohio, the University of Colorado, and Otis Art Institute in Los Angeles, where he worked with Peter Voulkos. He has taught at Scripps College in Claremont, California, the University of Colorado, and the University of Iowa. Soldner participated in the Ceramic Nationals in 1956, and from 1960 through 1968.

Soldner pioneered oil-fired kilns and designed fuel efficient burners. He also perfected his own type of kick and electric wheels and clay mixers, which he markets.

A major figure in contemporary American ceramics, Soldner has made raku a major means of expression, giving it a distinctly American flavor. In the late 1960s and early 1970s he explored Japanese philosophy and raku techniques, developing what is now called American raku. Earlier in his career he investigated "extended throwing," creating tall (seven to eight feet) forms. Recently Soldner has investigated new possibilities of salt-firing.

5 2 4

Throughout his work, there has always been an element of chance; he allows the material and the technology to interact independent of artistic control, and has a special reverence for the natural qualities of clay.

523 **Paul Soldner**
*Raku Pot*, 1962
Earthenware
H. 9¾, W. 19½, D. 7¾ in. (24.3 × 48.75 × 19.3 cm.)

Marks: artist's stamp on side of foot
Gift of Louis Cabot   P.C. 83.4

Large, raku-fired, free-form earthenware vessel. The oval shape extends to pointed ends. Slab additions to the top create a roughly shaped mouth. Incised lines, ridges, and applied slabs of clay decorate the body.

### 524 Paul Soldner

*Pot*, 1970
Earthenware
H. 8¾, W. 17¼, D. 4¾ in. (21.9 × 43.1 × 11.9 cm.)
Marks: artists's stamp on side and bottom of foot
Museum purchase from "Ceramics 70 Plus Woven Forms," 1970
P.C. 70.31.2

Free-form, oblong, slab-built earthenware vessel on high foot. The top section is curved and rolled, with two crack-like openings. Striations mark the top and foot. The top is gray, with tan, gray, and black below and on the foot.

### 525 Paul Soldner

*Platter*, 1970
Earthenware
H. 15½ W. 23, D. 3½ in. (38.8 × 57.5 × 8.8 cm.)
Marks: *Soldner* incised on bottom, artist's stamp on face, lower right
Museum purchase from "Ceramics 70 Plus Woven Forms," 1970
P.C. 70.31.1

Freely formed earthenware platter with curving sides and textured overlapping slabs. Burlap and athletic shoe impressions, ridges, and impressed overlapping figural forms have all been stamped into the surface. The platter is beige, pink, and tan, with some parts unglazed.

### 526 Paul Soldner

*Raku Pot*, 1970
Earthenware
H. 13¼, W. 13¾, D. 13¼ in. (33.1 × 34.4 × 33.1 cm.)
Marks: artist's stamp on side of foot
Museum purchase from "Ceramics 70 Plus Woven Forms," 1970
P.C. 70.31.3

Large, footed, free-form earthenware pot. Clay has been applied to the roundish body, and textures incised into it. A hole is on one side. Folds in the clay give way to a small, circular mouth near the top.

525

526

527

527 **Paul Soldner**
*Earthenware Bowl*, n.d.
H. 3½, Diam. 11 in. (8.75 × 27.5 cm.)
Marks: none
Gift of Bryce Holcombe
P.C. 81.51.8

Raku-fired, deep, footed stoneware bowl. Gray linear designs flow freely over the white-glazed surface.

Exhibitions: "13th Chunichi International Exhibition of Ceramic Arts," Nagoya, Japan, 1985

528 **Paul Soldner**
Bottle, 1964
Earthenware
H. 9, Diam. 7 in. (22.5 × 17.5 cm.)
Marks: none
Museum purchase from "23rd Ceramic National," 1964   P.C. 64.86

Raku bottle, wheel-thrown and altered. The ovoid body rests on a high foot. The small mouth is surrounded by a closely fitting, collar-like piece. The body is gray with black and brown brushed decoration.

528

**ALBERT SPENCER (b. 1914)**

Born in Towanda, Pennsylvania, Albert Spencer is now a studio ceramist in St. Petersburg, Florida. He participated in the Ceramic Nationals in 1952, 1958, and 1960.

529 **Albert Spencer**

*Bowl*, 1952
Stoneware
H. 4, Diam. 5½ in. (10 × 13.75 cm.)
Marks: illegible mark on bottom
Gift of the artist   P.C. 53.665

Deep stoneware bowl with red clay body. Red gloss glaze is used overall (except at the unglazed foot), with some brown speckles on the interior.

Exhibitions: "17th Ceramic National," 1952– honorable mention

**ALICE SPERRY**

Alice Sperry was educated at Mount Holyoke College and studied art at Cooper Union, Rhode Island School of Design, and Cranbrook Academy.

5 2 9

She worked at Greenwich House Sculpture Center in New York, and participated in the Ceramic Nationals in 1956 and 1958, winning awards both times.

530 **Alice Sperry**

*Children*, 1956
Earthenware
H. 13½, W. 9, D. 6½ in. (33.75 × 22.5 × 16.25 cm.)

Marks: none
Purchase prize given by IBM Corporation, "19th Ceramic National," 1956
P.C. 59.28

Earthenware sculpture of two young children embracing. The gray-brown body is grogged, with modeling and incising.

**ROBERT SPERRY (b. 1927)**

Robert Sperry, a native of Bushnell, Illinois, studied at the University of Saskatchewan in Canada, the Art Institute of Chicago, and was granted an M.F.A. from the University of Washington in Seattle. He is professor of ceramics at the University of Washington.

Sperry has worked with the vessel and slab wall pieces. He spent time in Japan and was influenced by raku and other eastern ceramics traditions. His work is as much concerned with surface qualities as with form. He participated in the Ceramic Na-

5 3 0

5 3 1

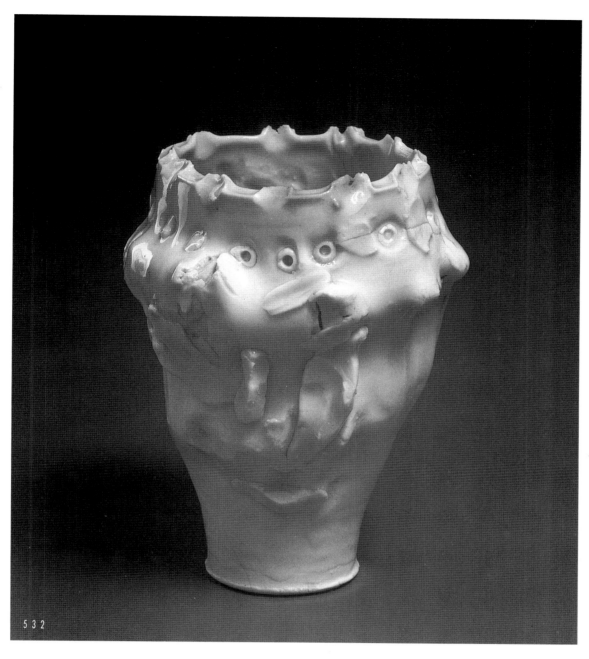

532

tionals in 1954, 1956, and from 1960 to 1964.

### 531 Robert Sperry

*Slab Bottle*, 1961
Stoneware
H. 14, W. 8, D. 4 in. (35 × 20 × 10 cm.)
Marks: *Sperry 61* brushed on bottom
Museum purchase from "22nd Ceramic National," 1962   P.C. 64.15

Slab-built, rectangular stoneware bottle with tapering neck and flat, rectangular rim. Incised and applied clay textural designs have been made on the front and back of the bottle, while the sides remain smooth and undecorated. Tan slip with touches of brown are used over the orange clay body.

### RUDOLF STAFFEL (b. 1911)

Born in San Antonio, Texas, Rudolf Staffel studied under Hans Hofmann in New York, and at the Art Institute of Chicago. He taught at the Tyler School of Art until his retirement in 1978. He participated in the Ceramic Nationals from 1950 through 1960.

Staffel began to work in porcelain in the 1950s when he was invited to create a dinnerware set. The translucence of the material fascinated him and he experimented in creating a porcelain form that would transmit light. His vessels, called "Light Gatherers," are a juxtaposition of thick and thin slabs of porcelain arranged to create a tension or "push-pull" (a term used by Hofmann to describe the action of his own paintings) between dark and light areas. Staffel's vessels are both sculpture and container; the play of light involved in their structures is of primary importance.

### 532 Rudolf Staffel

*Vase*, 1970
Porcelain
H. 8½, Diam. 6½ in.
(21.3 × 16.3 cm.)
Marks: *Rudolf Staffel* incised on bottom
Museum purchase in the name of William M. Milliken, "Ceramics 70 Plus Woven Forms," 1970
P.C. 70.32

Porcelain vase, freely formed. A series of alternating stamped and applied rings surrounds the vase at its top. The rim is pinched at intervals, and bulges protrude in a ring around the vase just below the rim. Some sections are translucent. The interior is in a pale, blue-green glaze; the glaze on the exterior is clear, except for some patches of blue-green.

Exhibitions: "13th Chunichi International Exhibition of Ceramic Arts," Nagoya, Japan, 1985

533

534

## DOROTHY STALLER (b. 1926)

Dorothy Staller is a native of Boston and received a B.A. in art history from Syracuse University. She also studied painting and ceramics at Syracuse. She now works mainly in raku. She has studios in Fayetteville, New York where she works on the wheel, and in Colorado, where she does hand building. Nature is a primary influence in her work.

### 533 Dorothy Staller

*Tree Ghosts*, 1982
Earthenware
H. 13¼, W. 9, D. 8½ in. (33.1 × 22.5 × 21.25 cm.)
Marks: *Staller* inscribed on base
Gift of the artist   P.C. 86.3

Rectangular earthenware jar with flat shoulder and double-rimmed mouth. Abstract landscape scenes in multicolors decorate the sides. This landscape motif was inspired by the hills of central New York, where the artist lives.

## GEORGE STARK (b. 1923)

George Stark, born in Schenectady, New York, studied at Syracuse University, New York State College for Teachers at Buffalo, Columbia University, and received a doctorate in education from the University of Buffalo. He also studied at the Albright Art School in Buffalo and is now a professor of art at the State University of New York at Buffalo. He participated in the Ceramic Nationals from 1952 through 1958.

### 534 George Stark

*Orator*, 1957
Stoneware
H. 7¾, W. 10¾, D. 5½ in. (19.3 × 26.8 × 13.75 cm.)
Marks: none
Purchase prize given by IBM Corporation, "19th Ceramic National," 1957   P.C. 59.29

Unglazed stoneware sculpture of buff, grogged, Jordan clay. The interconnecting, web-like construction has airy, mouth-shaped negative spaces. At top are three tapered sections with mouth-like forms.

## HELENE STARR (b. 1943)

Helene Starr, a native of New York, studied painting at the State University of New York at Buffalo and ceramics at Syracuse University, where she received an M.F.A. She also studied at the Art Students League, Columbia University, Parsons School of Design, and New York University.

Starr became interested in ceramics in 1977 through the Syracuse Clay Institute. She assisted in the "New Works in Clay II" and "III" projects. Her work is done mainly in white earthenware, unglazed; she captures the plastic, sensuous qualities of wet clay. She often incorporates other materials into her sculptures, especially welded metal, which she uses as a support system for the clay forms.

535 **Helene Starr**
*Transition in Motion*, 1981
Earthenware and steel
H. 26, W. 23, D. 8 in. (65 × 57.5 × 20 cm.)
Marks: *Transition in Motion/Helene Starr* on upper back
Gift of the artist   P.C. 81.52

White earthenware sculpture with black steel support. The freely formed slab of clay with folds and creases is set atop a steel understruc-

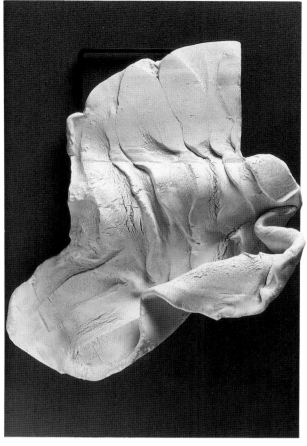

5 3 5

ture, part of which is visible at the top; the entire piece is then mounted on a board. The cracked, variegated surface is unglazed.

### JOHN STEPHENSON (b. 1929)
John Stephenson was educated first in his native Iowa, at the University of Iowa. He received an M.F.A. from Cranbrook Academy in 1958. He taught at the Cleveland Institute of Art, and has been professor of ceramics at the University of Michigan since 1975. He participated in the Ceramic Nationals in 1962, 1964, and 1968.

Stephenson studied in Japan in 1962 and 1963, interested mainly in glaze techniques and in wood firing. He has gradually moved away from the traditional vessel form.

536 **John Stephenson**
*N is for Neko*, 1964
Stoneware
H. 6, W. 14, D. 12 in. (15.6 × 38.8 × 30 cm.)
Marks: illegible mark incised on bottom
Gift of Mr. and Mrs. Emil Jessen   P.C. 73.29

5 3 6

537

Hand-built stoneware sculpture. The shallow circular bowl form is completely covered by its overhanging slab cover, which has an opening in the center. The buff clay body has yellow and brown glazes and incised and stamped decoration. The form has the appearance of a turtle shell.

Exhibitions: "23rd Ceramic National," 1964–prize for best garden sculpture

537 **John Stephenson**
*Vase*, 1962
Stoneware
H. 14, Diam. 12 in. (35 × 30 cm.)
Marks: none
Purchase prize given by B. F. Drakenfeld and Company, "22nd Ceramic National," 1962   P.C. 62.36

Large, globular stoneware vase with raised foot and uneven double rim. Textures have been modeled, incised, and applied to the vase. The piece is green, brown, and yellow.

This vase, with its rustic shape and earthy tones, illustrates the Japanese influence in Stephenson's work.

538

**DEAN STRAWN**

Strawn participated in the Ceramic Nationals in 1952, 1954, and 1958.

539 **Dean Strawn**
*Bottle*, 1954
Stoneware
H. 12¼, Diam. 11½ in. (30.6 × 28.75 cm.)
Marks: *Dean Strawn/1954* incised on bottom
Purchase prize given by Harker Chemical Company, "18th Ceramic National," 1954  P.C. 55.694

Globular, brown stoneware body with short neck and flared mouth. Gray reduction glaze with brown speckles is used overall.

## SUZANNE STEPHENSON (b. 1935)

Suzanne Stephenson was born in Canton, Ohio, and studied at Carnegie-Mellon University and at Cranbrook Academy with Maija Grotell. She taught at the University of Michigan and has been professor of art at Eastern Michigan University since 1963. She has studied woodfiring and ash-glazing in Japan, and luster decoration in Spain. She participated in the Ceramic Nationals from 1960 through 1968.

Stephenson went to Japan in 1962 (her husband, John, had received a grant to study there) and she was profoundly influenced by the earthiness and intuitive approach of Japanese ceramics. This, coupled with her experiences in Spain, brought about a change in her work, and she began to bring a more tactile, gestural, spontaneous approach to the medium.

538 **Suzanne Stephenson**
*Water Rock Vase*, 1986
Earthenware
H. 17, W. 14, D. 12 in. (42.5 × 35 × 30 cm.)
Marks: none
Museum purchase with funds from the Dorothy and Robert Riester Ceramic Fund  P.C. 86.65

Ovoid earthenware vase with high neck and flared, altered mouth. White, gray, yellow, green, blue, and purple glazes have been heavily applied and incised. The thick, tactile quality of the surface invites one to touch it.

539

540

Gift of Syracuse China Corporation   P.C. 86.60a-d

Place setting consisting of service plate, plate, cup, and saucer. The service plate and saucer have flared black ledges rimmed in gold, with white wells. The plate is black overall, with a gold rim and gold and red phoenix motif in the well. The cup is black with a gold rim and white interior.

### 541 Syracuse China Corporation

*Untitled Custom Design Place Setting*, c. 1983
Syralite (commercial body)
Service plate: H. 7/8, Diam. 10 3/8 in. (2.1 × 25.9 cm.). Plate: H. 7/8, Diam. 8 1/8 in. (2.1 × 20.3 cm.). Cup: H. 3, W. 3 3/8 in. (7.5 × 8.4 cm.). Saucer: H. 7/8, Diam. 6 inches (2.1 × 15 cm.)
Marks: Syracuse China Corporation stamp on bottom of each piece
Gift of Syracuse China Corporation   P.C. 86.60.2a–d

Place setting consisting of service plate, plate, cup, and saucer. The service plate and saucer have flared lilac ledges rimmed in gold, with white wells. The plate is rimmed in gold with an abstract floral design overall. The cup is lilac with a gold rim and white interior.

### SYRACUSE CHINA CORPORATION

One of the first china manufacturing companies in America, Syracuse China Corporation—founded in 1856, but known by this name since 1966—is still in operation today, and has become one of the world's larg-est producers of commercial dinnerware. (See also entries 253, 254, and page 10.)

### 540 Syracuse China Corporation

*Phoenix Place Setting*, c. 1982
Syralite (commerical body)
Service plate: H. 7/8, Diam. 10 3/8 in. (2.1 × 25.9 cm.). Plate: H. 7/8, Diam. 8 1/8 in. (2.1 × 20.3 cm.). Cup: H. 3, W. 3 3/8 in. (7.5 × 8.4 cm.) Saucer: H. 7/8, Diam. 6 in. (2.1 × 15 cm.)
Marks: Syracuse China Corporation stamp on bottom of each piece.

541

542

## TOSHIKO TAKAEZU (b. 1929)

Toshiko Takaezu was born in Pepeekeo, Hawaii. She studied ceramics and weaving at the Honolulu School of Art and ceramics at Cranbrook Academy of Art under Maija Grotell. She has taught at Cranbrook, the University of Michigan, the University of Wisconsin, and the Cleveland Institute of Art. She gave up teaching in 1968 to concentrate on studio work.

Takaezu's work has been influenced by Zen Buddhism, nature (particularly landscapes), Abstract Expressionism, and by her native Hawaii, where there is a blend of East and West. She unites form, design, texture, and color in her pieces, and all these elements work together to compose the whole. Her works range from small, closed forms containing a pebble for a rattle-like effect, to "tree" forms, tall structures which seem to fit naturally into the surrounding landscape.

Takaezu participated in the Ceramic Nationals in 1949 and each year from 1952 through 1968. She curated "Ceramics 70 Plus Woven Forms" at Everson Museum in 1970.

### 542 Toshiko Takaezu

*Painted Bowl*, 1962
Stoneware
H. 1⅞, Diam. 13½ in.
(4.6 × 33.75 cm.)
Marks: artists's cypher incised on bottom
Purchase prize given by Pemco Division of Glidden Company, "22nd Ceramic National," 1962
P.C. 62.39

Large, shallow stoneware bowl with small foot. The underside is black with the foot left unglazed. The upper side has an abstract design in flowing glazes in ash, copper, black, pink, and white, with a black rim.

Exhibitions: "A Century of Ceramics in the United States, 1878–1978," 1979; "13th Chunichi International Exhibition of Ceramic Arts," Nagoya, Japan, 1985

543

**543 Toshiko Takaezu**
*Form*, 1967
Stoneware
H. 11½, Diam. 15 in.
(28.75 × 37.5 cm.)
Marks: none
Museum purchase   P.C. 68.76

Squat, rounded, closed stoneware form with slight bulging band surrounding the center. Incising appears on the band and body. Silver and black glazes are used overall and light green is on the central area.

Exhibitions: Exhibited at the Vice-Presidential house, Washington, D.C., 1977–1978; "A Century of Ceramics in the United States, 1878–1978," 1979

**544 Toshiko Takaezu**
*Porcelain Globular Vase*, n.d.
H. 4½, Diam. 5½ in.
(11.25 × 13.75 cm.)
Marks: none
Gift of Bryce Holcombe
P.C. 81.51.23

544

Small, globular porcelain vase with tiny neck and rim. The top half is glazed in dark brown, and the underside in dark green.

**545 Toshiko Takaezu**
*Stoneware Bowl*, 1962
Stoneware
H. 11¼, Diam. 15¾ in.
(28.1 × 39.4 cm.)
Marks: artist's cypher inscribed on bottom
Museum purchase from "22nd Ceramic National," 1962   P.C. 64.21

Large, wheel-thrown bowl with buff stoneware body and slightly flared rim. Throwing marks surround the upper section of the exterior. The interior and rim are in black Albany slip; the exterior is in pink, purple, and blue glazes creating abstract shapes.

Exhibitions: "A Century of Ceramics in the United States, 1878–1978," 1979

545

## HENRY TAKEMOTO (b. 1930)

Henry Takemoto, born in Honolulu, is a sculptor and ceramist. He studied at the University of Hawaii and received an M.F.A. from the Los Angeles County Art Institute. He has taught at Scripps College in Claremont, California, Montana State University, and Otis Art Institute in Los Angeles. He participated in the Ceramic Nationals in 1962 and 1966.

Takemoto treated the clay form as a canvas, largely interested in its decoration with lively calligraphic motifs based mainly on nature. In the 1960s, Takemoto turned from ceramics to design, working with Interpace Corporation.

546 **Henry Takemoto**
*Plate*, 1959
Stoneware
H. 2½, Diam. 16 in. (6.25 × 40 cm.)
Marks: *Takemoto 59* incised on bottom, with brushed linear design
Museum purchase   P.C. 64.23

Large, footed stoneware plate with flared edge. Linear, animal-like figures with stars and spirals decorate the face of the plate in brown and black over a white glaze background.

Exhibitions: "22nd Ceramic National," 1962; "A Century of Ceramics in the United States, 1878–1978," 1979

546

547

**WILLIAM TERSTEEG (b. 1941)**

William Tersteeg received both B.S. and M.F.A. degrees from Southern Illinois University.

547 **William Tersteeg**
*Earth Image*, 1971
Earthenware
H. 19, L. 18¼, D. 9 in. (47.5 × 45.6 × 22.5 cm.)

Marks: none
Museum purchase   P.C. 72.3
Multicolored, earthenware sculpture of stylized earth form with rainbow, clouds, rain, lighting, and sun overhead.

Exhibitions: "Susquehanna Regional Exhibition," Binghamton, New York, 1971–First Prize

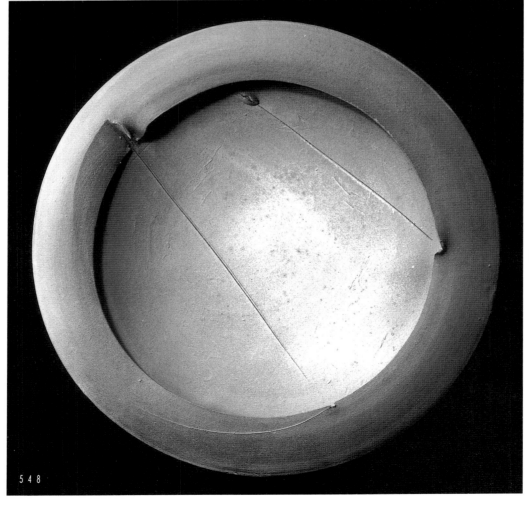

548

**NEIL TETKOWSKI (b. 1955)**

Neil Tetkowski studied at Alfred University and received an M.F.A. from Illinois State University in 1980. He has taught at Denison University and the State University of New York at Buffalo.

Tetkowski works with wheel-thrown earthenware vessels in which the form and surface are equally important. His discs, some extremely large and others plate-size, are sprayed with *terra sigillata* and then fired in a salt kiln at a low temperature. He has recently begun to imbed metal objects such as bolts and gears in his clay forms.

548 **Neil Tetkowski**
*Untitled Plate*, 1985
Earthenware
H. 2¼, Diam. 17½ in.
(5.6 × 43.75 cm.)
Marks: *Tetkowski* incised on bottom
Anonymous donor   P.C. 85.25

Footed, red earthenware plate with wide, curved ledge, altered at points to create an uneven rim. One line is incised on the ledge, and two on the interior.

This disc form is simple yet it has a certain lushness about it.

550

## ROBERT TURNER (b. 1913)

Robert Turner was born in Port Washington, New York, and was educated at Swarthmore College. He studied painting at the Pennsylvania Academy of Fine Arts and ceramics at Alfred University under Charles Harder, Marion Fosdick, and Daniel Rhodes. He set up the ceramics studio and taught at Black Mountain College in North Carolina and in 1958 became a professor of ceramics at Alfred University. He participated in the Ceramic Nationals continuously from 1947 through 1968, except in 1950 and 1964.

Turner has a studio in Alfred, New York, where he works in stoneware. Over the years he has consistently used the vessel format, concentrating on a few forms which he has refined and synthesized. His vessels are volumetric, with a strong sense of inner form. They do not seem constrained by the clay form, but rather the clay seems to take its shape from within.

### 549 Robert Turner

*Bottle*, 1951
Stoneware
H. 9½, Diam. 5½ in.
(23.75 × 13.75 cm.)
Marks: *Turner* incised on bottom.
Sticker on bottom which reads: *R.C.*

*Turner / #1 20.00*
Purchase prize given by United Clay Mines Corporation, "16th Ceramic National," 1951   P.C. 53.626.1

Ovoid stoneware bottle with small flared mouth. Four oval areas of gray reduction glaze are on the sides of the vessel with a spiral decoration in sgraffito. Gray reduction glaze is also used at the mouth; the rest of the body is unglazed brown clay.

### 550 Robert Turner

*Covered Jar*, 1954
Stoneware
H. 7⅛, Diam. 8⅜ in.
(17.8 × 20.9 cm.)
Marks: *TURNER* incised on bottom
Purchase prize given by Homer Laughlin China Company, "18th Ceramic National," 1954
P.C. 55.692a, b

Covered stoneware jar with straight sides and slightly flared lip. The cover is concave with a high, flared knob. Throwing ridges surround the body. Six red circles decorate the gray-green glazed body.

Exhibitions: "Forms from the Earth: 1,000 Years of Pottery in America," Museum of Contemporary Crafts, New York, 1960; "Robert Turner Retrospective," Alfred University, Alfred, New York 1980

549

### TOM TURNER (b. 1945)

Tom Turner is a full time studio potter who works in Delaware, Ohio. He uses porcelain and has experimented widely with that material and with ash glazes. Turner has also written on ceramic techniques.

**551 Tom Turner**
*Covered Jar*, c. 1984
Porcelain
H. 19½, Diam. 14 in.
(48.75 × 35 cm.)
Marks: *Tom Turner/195* within 2 circles incised on bottom
Gift of Christopher Darling and Frank Sherman   P.C. 85.17

Tall, porcelain, covered jar. The small base flares to a body which is composed of two bulbous forms, pinched together at the waist. Three shapes, vestiges of handles, are applied at the shoulder. The raised and flared rim has a slightly domed lid with a knob that matches the applied shapes on the shoulder. The lid and top half of the form are decorated with shapes repeating the bulbous form of the vessel itself in green, rust,

yellow, and white glazes. The bottom section of the jar is gray-green. Turner has used ash and simulated ash glazes on this jar.

### RICHARD USREY (b. 1959)

Richard Usrey was born in Washington, D.C., studied at the University of Colorado, and received an M.F.A. from Syracuse University. He had a residency fellowship at the Banff Centre School of Fine Arts in Alberta, Canada and is a sculptor working in Colorado.

**552 Richard Usrey**
*Lift,* from *Gorgon* series, 1984
Stoneware
H. 24¾, W. 13, D. 7½ in. (61.8 × 32.5 × 18.75 cm.)
Marks: none
Gift of the artist   P.C. 87.68

Sculptural form of interlocking stacked clay forms in shape of a cross. The surface is incised and covered with pale green volcanic glazes.

Exhibitions: "Numen's Last," Syracuse Stage, Syracuse 1987

552

551

### JAYNE VAN ALSTYNE

Jayne Van Alstyne studied at Pratt Institute and Alfred University. She was a product designer for Frigidaire. She also initiated programs of industrial design at Michigan State University and Montana State College at Bozeman. She participated in the Ceramic Nationals in 1950 and 1954.

**553 Jayne Van Alstyne**
*Jar*, 1954
Stoneware
H. 9, Diam. 8 in. (22.5 × 20 cm.)
Marks: *Jayne* incised on bottom
Purchase prize given by O. Hommel Company, "18th Ceramic National," 1954   P.C. 59.16

Ovoid, footed stoneware jar. Gray and brown reduction glazes cover the buff, speckled body in calligraphic decoration, except at the foot, which remains unglazed.

554

555

### PETER VANDENBERGE
### (b. Holland, 1935)

Peter Vandenberge studied at Sacramento State College and received an M.A. from the University of California at Santa Barbara. He also studied with Robert Arneson. He taught at San Francisco State College, and presently teaches at California State University at Sacramento, where he has been since 1973.

Vandenberge worked in the Pop Art tradition during the 1970s, when he produced his studies of vegetables, inspired by the abundance he saw at farmers' markets. He has since gone on to do figural pieces in larger than life sizes, often representing acquaintances or figures from his childhood.

### 554 Peter Vandenberge

*Carrot on a Divan,* c. 1971
Earthenware
H. 13, W. 15¼, D. 12¼ in. (32.5 × 38.2 × 30.5 cm.)
Marks: none
Gift of Les Levine   P.C. 83.17.2

Earthenware sculpture of a female

carrot figure seated on a bed with pillow. The orange carrot is marked with incisions, and a green, leafy form sprouts from the top like a head, with pink and yellow accents. The pillow is multicolored, but the bed is unglazed

Exhibitions: "13th Chunichi International Exhibition of Ceramic Arts," Nagoya, Japan, 1985

### PAUL VOLCKENING (b. 1928)

Born in Minneola, New York, Paul Volckening graduated from the California College of Arts and Crafts in Oakland and received an M.A. from Mills College. He won a Fulbright Scholarship to study ceramics in Helsinki from 1958 to 1959. He taught at New Mexico Highlands University and worked in stoneware, mainly wheel-thrown. He participated in the Ceramic Nationals in 1954 and 1956.

### 555 Paul Volckening

*Bottle Vase,* 1956
Stoneware
H. 12½, Diam. 9½ in.

(31.25 × 23.75 cm.)
Marks: *Paul Volckening* brushed on bottom, also tape which reads: *Paul Volckening $75 / Mills College*
Purchase prize given by Harper Electric Furnace Company, "19th Ceramic National," 1956
P.C. 59.30

Footed, ovoid stoneware bottle vase with tapering shoulder. The low neck flares to a trumpet mouth. A calligraphic design is made overall, in white, rust, and yellow, except at the foot, which is unglazed.

## PETER VOULKOS (b. 1924)

Born in Bozeman, Montana, Peter Voulkos first studied painting at Montana State University. He became interested in ceramics there and went on to the California College of Arts and Crafts, where he received an M.F.A. He worked at the Archie Bray Foundation in Montana and taught at the Otis Art Institute in Los Angeles and the University of California at Berkeley. He participated in the Ceramic Nationals from 1950 through 1962, winning awards each year, except in 1956 when he was an invited member of the jury and in 1960.

Peter Voulkos is one of the most

5 5 6

5 5 7

influential figures in contemporary American ceramics, having revolutionized the whole concept of the art form. Voulkos and those who surrounded him at Otis, artists and students alike, handled the clay loosely, in an expressionist manner, using the material to express itself, as did the Abstract Expressionist painters of the period. An expert on the wheel, Voulkos began to assemble his thrown forms into sculpture, stepping beyond the idea of vessel or container. The experimental nature of his work and of the program at Otis stimulated many other young artists to reach out beyond tradition and explore their own individual styles.

In 1973 Voulkos began a series of plates, in which he punctured, tore, and gouged the forms, creating not only visually assertive pieces, but also thereby making a statement about the role of the vessel and of traditional ceramic forms. He later abandoned clay for a period, working in metal, but recently has returned to the medium.

556 **Peter Voulkos**
*Jug,* 1950
Stoneware
H. 10⅛, Diam. 8¾ in.
(25.3 × 21.8 cm.)
Marks: *Voulkos* inscribed on bottom
Purchase prize given by United States Potters Association, "15th Ceramic National," 1950
P.C. 51.598.1

Bulbous stoneware jug tapering to a small neck with flared mouth. A wax-resist, linear design encircles the top half of the jug. The ochre glaze on the body blends to green.

Exhibitions: "Forms from the Earth: 1,000 Years of Pottery in America," Museum of Contemporary Crafts, New York, 1960

557 **Peter Voulkos**
*Cookie Jar,* 1950
Earthenware
H. 13¾, Diam. 8⅝ in.
(34.3 × 21.5 cm.)
Marks: *Voulkos* and *B* inscribed on bottom
Purchase prize given by United

558

States Potters Association, "15th Ceramic National," 1950
P.C. 51.598.2

Large, footed, ovoid cookie jar. The concave lid flares to a hollow, bowl-shaped knob. Wax-resist, linear designs of whimsical creatures emerge from the glaze on the body.

Exhibitions: "A Century of Ceramics in the United States, 1878–1978," 1979

558 **Peter Voulkos**
*Rice Bottle*, 1951
Stoneware
H. 13¾, Diam. 10 in.
(34.3 × 25 cm.)
Marks: *Voulkos* incised on bottom
Purchase prize given by United States Potters Association, "16th Ceramic National," 1951
P.C. 52.623.2

Large, footed stoneware rice bottle. The ovoid body has a wide shoulder which tapers to a small neck and flared mouth. Voulkos has used local clay and greenish matte glaze with ochre tones. Black linear figures in wax resist cover the bottle.

Exhibitions: "Forms from the Earth: 1,000 Years of Pottery in America," Museum of Contemporary Crafts, New York, 1960; "A Century of Ceramics in the United States, 1878–1978," 1979

559 **Peter Voulkos**
*Covered Bowl*, 1951
Earthenware
H. 11⅜, Diam. 13⅞ in.
(28.4 × 34.6 cm.)
Marks: *Voulkos* incised on bottom
Purchase prize given by United States Potters Association, "16th Ceramic National," 1951
P.C. 52.623.1

Large, footed, hemispherical stoneware bowl with cover. The domed

559

cover sits within the rim and tapers to a flared knob. Dark green glaze covers the body, except where a wax-resist, linear pattern surrounds the upper half of the bowl and cover.

The full, elegant form of this bowl attests to Voulkos's skill on the wheel. The subtle wax-resist decoration enhances and emphasizes the form without competing with it.

Exhibitions: "Forms from the Earth: 1,000 Years of Pottery in America," Museum of Contemporary Crafts, New York, 1960; "A Century of Ceramics in the United States, 1878–1978," 1979

**561 Peter Voulkos**

*Tall Covered Jar*, 1956
Stoneware
H. 25½, Diam. 18½ in.
(63.75 × 46.25 cm.)
Marks: *Voulkos* brushed on base
Museum purchase from "19th Ceramic National," 1956   P.C. 59.14

Exceptionally fine, large, covered stoneware jar with tapering base, bulbous body, and rimmed mouth. The wide cover tapers to a bowl-shaped knob. Broad brush strokes create an abstract design on the body and foot. The jar is light gray overall, with blue, gray, brown, and black decoration.

This monumental jar, a masterwork of wheel-thrown form, illustrates the influence of Japanese ceramics on Voulkos. He had met Shoji Hamada and Soetsu Yanagi in 1952 and 1953, and got to know some of the leading Abstract Expressionists in New York. The influence of both the Japanese and the American Expressionists merge in the form and decoration of this exceedingly fine jar.

Exhibitions: "19th Ceramic National," 1956; "A Century of Ceramics in the United States, 1878–1978," 1979

**562 Peter Voulkos**

*Untitled Plate*, 1978
Stoneware
H. 4¾, Diam. 23 in.

560

**560 Peter Voulkos**

*Covered Jar*, 1954
Stoneware
H. 23, Diam. 9 in. (57.5 × 22.5 cm.)
Marks: *Voulkos* incised on bottom
Purchase prize given by Onondaga Pottery Company, "18th Ceramic National," 1954   P.C. 55.691

Tall, cylindrical stoneware jar with foot and cover. The flat cover, with its raised, cup-shaped knob, sits inside the ledged rim. Incised, curvilinear designs of faces and birds' heads cover the body, which is glazed in blue, gray, and brown.

The decoration on this jar illustrates the influence of Picasso on Voulkos. The incising is carried easily by the strong form.

Exhibitions: "A Century of Ceramics in the United States, 1878–1978," 1979

561

(4.3 × 57.5 cm.)
Marks: *V.O.U.L.K.O.S. 78* brushed
on bottom of foot, five dots brushed
in center
Museum purchase with matching
funds from the National Endowment
for the Arts   P.C. 80.21

Large, footed stoneware plate,
thrown and altered. An incision
across the plate creates an offset section. The small adjoining piece is
lifted inward. Four punctured areas
are on the well, next to the everted
rim.

The plates of the late 1970s are
usually considered the most important that Voulkos produced. This
monumental piece bears the em-
phatic rim, gouges, and holes typical
of the platters of this period. The
underside and large foot of this plate
project the same strength and certainty of concept that the upper face
does.

Exhibitions: "Nine West Coast Clay
Sculptors: 1978," 1978; "A Century
of Ceramics in the United States,
1878–1978," 1979; "13th Chunichi
International Exhibition of Ceramic
Arts," Nagoya, Japan, 1985

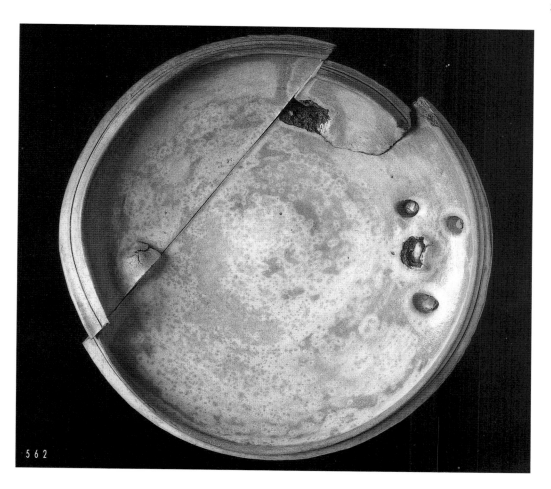

562

### 563 Peter Voulkos

*Plate #1*, 1962
Stoneware
H. 3, Diam. 15 in. (7.5 × 37.5)
Marks: *VOULKOS* brushed on bot-
tom of foot rim
Purchase prize given by O. Hommel
Company, "22nd Ceramic Na-
tional," 1962   P.C. 62.37

Freely formed, footed stoneware
plate. The foot is uneven and the rim
has been altered with a rupture on
one side which continues to the center. The brown stoneware body is
glazed in brown and orange. Semicircular ridges have been formed at
the center, creating a rippling effect.

Though the plates produced by
Voulkos in the 1970s usually receive
the most attention, this plate from
the early 1960s shows that his interest in this ceramic form was piqued
much earlier.

Exhibitions: "Peter Voulkos Retro-
spective," San Francisco Museum of
Art and Museum of Contemporary
Crafts, New York, 1978–1979; "A
Century of Ceramics in the United
States, 1878–1978," 1979

563

564

### ROSE WASSERSTROM (b. 1922)

Rose Wasserstrom studied art at the University of Michigan and art history at Syracuse University. She began working in ceramics at the Rockland Foundation in Nyack, New York, and studied with William Ehrich at the Rochester Memorial Art Gallery.

Wasserstrom has a studio in De-witt, New York, where she works in stoneware and earthenware. She works mainly on the wheel, but also does some slab work. She prefers to use clay slips in her decoration.

**564 Rose Wasserstrom**
*Sgraffito Bottle*, 1986
Stoneware
H. 6, Diam. 5 in. (15 × 12.5 cm.)
Marks: *Wasserstrom* written on bottom
Gift of the artist     P.C. 86.69

Gloubular stoneware bottle with tapering neck and small mouth. Sgraffito ribbing in sets of four vertical lines surrounds the vase from the top to just above the bottom. Gray glaze is on the mouth; the exterior is brown with orange sgraffito.

Exhibitions: "Everson Biennial," 1986

### DAVID WEINRIB (b. 1924)

David Weinrib studied painting, sculpture, and ceramics at Alfred University and became artist-in-residence at Black Mountain College with his wife, Karen Karnes. In 1954 they established a studio in Stony Point, Long Island in an artists' community. Weinrib worked mainly with slab forms, but later abandoned clay to concentrate on other media. (See also entry 258.)

**565 David Weinrib**
*Slab Pot*, 1956
Stoneware
H. 9½, W. 11, D. 5½ in. (23.75 × 27.5 × 13.75 cm.)
Marks: none

565

Purchase prize given by Homer Laughlin China Company, "19th Ceramic National," 1956  P.C. 59.31

Rectangular, slab pot with slightly bulged sides, two slab feet, and a slab "handle" on top. Two circular openings reveal the brown glazed interior. The exterior ends are glazed dark gray-green.

Exhibitions: "Forms from the Earth: 1,000 Years of Pottery in America," Museum of Contemporary Crafts, New York 1960; "A Century of Ceramics in America, 1878–1978," 1979

## LONDA WEISMAN

Londa Weisman worked at Bennington Pottery and now has her own studio in Bennington, Vermont. She participated in the "25th Ceramic National" in 1968.

### 566 Londa Weisman
*Floor Pot #2*, 1969.
Stoneware
H. 20, W. 14¾, D. 16 in. (50 × 36.8 × 40 cm.)
Marks: *BENNINGTON POTTERS, VT (LONDA) / JAN. 24, 1968 / TOO BAD REGRESSION IS SOMETIMES NECESSARY FOR PROGRESS* stamped on bottom
Museum purchase from "25th Ceramic National," 1968  P.C. 70.41

Stoneware vessel constructed of interlocked slabs to form rectangular shape. The slabs are gradually staggered to create a flare at the mouth. The interior is in black slip, the exterior is unglazed.

## FRANS WILDENHAIN
## (b. Germany, 1905–1980)

Frans Wildenhain was born in Leipzig, East Germany and studied at the Bauhaus with Klee, Albers, Gerhard Marcks and the master ceramist Max Krehan. He earned a master of crafts certificate from the State School of Applied Art at Halle in East Germany, where he taught until 1933, when he opened his own studio in Putten, Holland. He came to the United States in 1947, joining his wife Marguerite at Pond Farm in Guerneville, California. In 1950 he joined the faculty of the School for American Craftsmen in Rochester, New York, where he remained until his retirement. He participated in the

Ceramic Nationals in 1948, and from 1951 through 1968.

Wildenhain was important both as an artist and as a teacher. The influences on his work were myriad, but always at the basis was his reverence for nature—plants, rocks and shale, fossils, the sea, and even the "dirt" from which he produced his art. He had visited Japan, where he painted and studied Zen Buddhism. He worked in both vessel and sculptural forms.

### 567 Frans Wildenhain
*Mushroom Pot*, 1969
Stoneware
H. 14½, W. 14½, D. 18½ in. (36.25 × 36.25 × 46.25 cm.)
Marks: none
Museum purchase from "Ceramics 70 Plus Woven Forms," 1970
P.C. 70.33

Stoneware sculpture comprising four stylized, mushroom-shaped forms. Gray, orange-brown, and

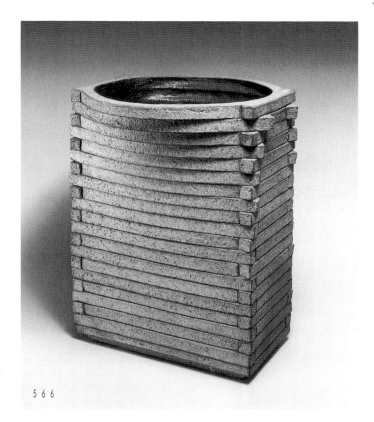

566

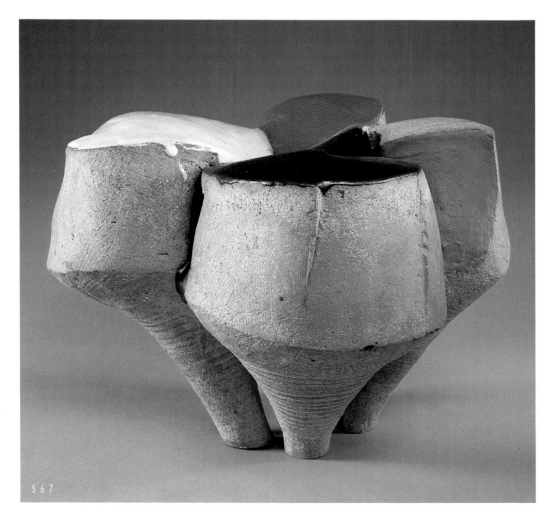

567

white glazes are on top of the forms.

### 568 Frans Wildenhain

*Solanum Tuberosum*, 1977
Stoneware
H. 25, Diam. 27 in.
(62.5 × 67.5 cm.)
Marks: none
Gift of Henry Gernhardt and others affiliated with Hanover Gallery
P.C. 79.35

Large, bulbous, potato-shaped stoneware sculpture. The surface is incised and punctured; there are also raised sections and areas of glaze. The sculpture is capped in white glaze which drips down the sides.

5 6 8

5 6 9

### WILLIAM WILHELMI

William Wilhelmi was born in Iowa and studied at San Diego State University. He received an M.F.A. from the University of California at Los Angeles. His technical knowledge is broad and he has worked in wax-resist, underglaze pencil, luster glazes, and a variety of textures and added materials. He participated in the "25th Ceramic National."

### 569 William Wilhelmi

*Untitled*, 1968
Earthenware
H. 10½, W. 13⅞, D. 5½ in. (26.25 × 34.6 × 13.75 cm.)
Marks: none
Purchase prize given by Harris Clay Company, "25th Ceramic National" 1968 P.C. 68.77

Slab-built, white earthenware sculpture composed of cubes, slabs, and circular forms. The architectonic form is covered with transparent glaze over a penciled, underglaze, perspective drawing.

570

**FRED WOLLSCHLAGER**
Fred Wollschlager studied with
Rudy Autio at the University of Montana and went on to teach in San
Francisco. He participated in the Ceramic Nationals from 1960 through
1968, except in 1964.

570 **Fred Wollschlager**
*Triangle Jar*, 1966
Stoneware
H. 29, W. 16 in. (72.5 × 40 cm.)
Marks: none
Purchase prize given by Harris Clay
Company, "24th Ceramic National,"
1966   P.C. 66.33

Slab-constructed, three-sided stoneware jar with closed top. The sides
are decorated with geometric linear
designs—clouds, dots, spirals, and
striped patterns—in blue, yellow,
white, and black glazes.

571

## MARIE WOO

Marie Woo studied at the University of Washington and received an M.F.A. from Cranbrook Academy in Michigan. She also studied at the California College of Arts and Crafts in Oakland. She teaches at the University of Michigan. Woo participated in the Ceramic Nationals in 1956 and 1958.

### 571 Marie Woo
*Covered Jar*, 1956
Stoneware
H. 8¼, Diam. 7½ in.
(20.6 × 18.75 cm.)
Marks: paper sticker on bottom reads: *MARIE WOO NFS*
Purchase prize given by American Clay Company, "19th Ceramic National," 1956   P.C. 59.33

Bulbous, covered stoneware jar. The body flares at the mouth. Its concave cover tapers to a raised, flared knob. The buff body is covered with iron red glaze, except where a wax-resist, calligraphic design has been brushed on both the jar and cover in black with yellow specks.

## BEATRICE WOOD (b. 1894)

Beatrice Wood, in her ninety-fifth year, lives and continues to work in Ojai, California. Her unconventional forms have become more and more complex, and her lusters have softened into a more subtle richness. (See also entry 266.)

### 572 Beatrice Wood
*"AH!"*, 1967
Stoneware
H. 39, W. 9, D. 8½ in. (97.5 × 22.5 × 21.25 cm.)
Marks: *Beato* on back base in applied clay
Gift of the artist   P.C. 87.64

Stoneware figure on a base. The woman has incised, pink hair, upward turning eyes, and an O-shaped, open mouth. The green dress, which flares at the floor, is decorated with applied pink floral and vine decorations. Her hands are clasped in front. The brown stoneware base has "AH!" applied in clay on the front.

This brightly colored caricature represents a singer in mid-song.

### 573 Beatrice Wood
*Jar with Fish*, 1977
Stoneware
H. 14, Diam. 10¼ in.
(35 × 25.6 cm.)
Marks: none
Gift of the artist   P.C. 87.63

Footed and lidded stoneware jar. The hemispherical body has a narrow, flat shoulder and high tapering neck. The slightly domed lid overhangs the mouth and has a small gold knob on top. Six small incised fish relief forms are applied to the body and neck. Rough volcanic glazes cover the jar in gray-greens with black overall.

---

Exhibitions: "Beatrice Wood: Ceramics and Drawings," 1978; "13th Chunichi International Exhibition of Ceramic Arts," Nagoya, Japan, 1985; "Beato: Homage to Beatrice Wood," 1987

## BETTY WOODMAN (b. 1930)

Betty Woodman was born in Norwalk, Connecticut and studied at the School for American Craftsmen at Alfred University from 1948 to 1950. She also studied painting and sculpture in Italy with Giorgio Ferrer and Leonello Fallacari. She is a professor in the fine arts department at the University of Colorado, and divides her time between Boulder, New York, and Italy. She participated in the Ceramic National of 1964, and was an invited artist in "American Ceramics Now: The 27th Ceramic National," 1987.

Woodman has been influenced by both Chinese and Mediterranean traditions, and she combines these with a truly American spirit to produce containers that are sensual and brilliant, and emphasize volume, form, and space.

572

573

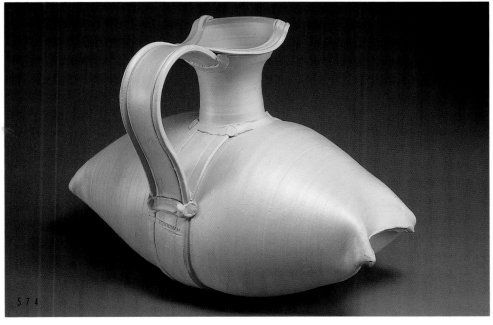

574

**574 Betty Woodman**
*Pillow Pitcher*, 1979
Earthenware
H. 16, W. 22, D. 12 in. (40 × 56 × 30 cm.)
Marks: *WOODMAN* impressed below handle
Gift of Mr. and Mrs. Lester Goldstein P.C. 79.25

Unglazed earthenware pitcher in a bulbous, pillow form with pinched sides. A wide band surrounds the body on either side of the high neck, which flares to a wide spout. The wide strap handle is applied just below the rim and at midsection.

Exhibitions: "A Century of Ceramics in the United States, 1878–1978," 1979; "13th Chunichi International Exhibition of Ceramic Arts," Nagoya, Japan, 1985

## WILLIAM WYMAN (1922–1980)

A native of Boston, William Wyman studied at the Massachusetts College of Art and at Alfred University. He received an M.A. from Columbia University and taught at Drake University in Des Moines, the DeCordova Museum in Lincoln, Massachusetts, Massachusetts College of Art in Boston, and the School of the Museum of Fine Arts, Boston. He operated his own Herring Run Pottery in East Weymouth, Massachusetts, which produced both functional and nonfunctional stoneware objects.

Wyman worked mainly with slab forms, creating vessels with sgraffitoed surfaces, crosses, and elegant architectonic forms he called "Temples." He participated in the Ceramic Nationals from 1952 through 1966.

### 575 William Wyman

*Terrace Bottle*, 1960
Stoneware
H. 20, Diam. 20 in. (50 × 50 cm.)
Marks: none
Purchase prize given by Harshaw Chemical Company, "21st Ceramic National," 1960   P.C. 60.89

Thrown and coil-built stoneware bottle. The rounded form has a short neck and slightly flared mouth. Blue, gray, black, and orange bands surround the vessel in the center. Sand and gravel have been applied to the surface for texture.

Exhibitions: "Forms from the Earth: 1,000 Years of Pottery in America," Museum of Contemporary Crafts, New York, 1960; "A Century of Ceramics in the United States, 1878–1978," 1979

### 576 William Wyman

*Untitled, Slab Vase*, 1962
Stoneware
H. 25½, W. 24, D. 4½ in. (63.75 × 60 × 11.25 cm.)
Marks: artist's stamp and *Wyman 62* incised lower left
Museum purchase   P.C. 62.48

Slab-constructed stoneware vase. Multiple slabs are layered about a rectangular form. Gray glaze with rough diagonal sheeting gives the effect of slate.

### 577 William Wyman

*Homage to Robert Frost*, 1962
Stoneware

576

H. 27, W. 16, D. 3½ in. (67.5 × 40 × 8.75 cm.)
Marks: *W. Wyman* stamped, '62 incised on back lower right corner
Purchase prize given by Syracuse China Corporation, "22nd Ceramic National," 1962   P.C. 62.40

Large, slab-constructed stoneware vessel with flat sides, small neck, and flat square rim. Gouges, incisions, and imbedded pebbles cover the surface. The slips and glaze are mixed with gravel and glass.

The following poem by Robert Frost is incised in a variety of types and scripts: *SOME SAY / THE WORLD WILL END / IN FIRE / SOME SAY IN ICE / FROM WHAT I'VE TASTED OF DESIRE / I HOLD WITH THOSE / WHO FAVOR FIRE * / BUT IF IT HAD TO PERISH TWICE / I THINK I KNOW ENOUGH HATE / TO SAY THAT FOR DESTRUCTION ICE / IS ALSO GREAT AND / WOULD SUFFICE / *ROBERT FROST.*

Exhibitions: "22nd Ceramic National," 1962

575

SOME SAY
THE WORLD WILL END
IN FIRE
SOME SAY IN ICE
from what I've tasted of desire
I HOLD WITH THOSE
WHO FAVOR FIRE

BUT IF IT HAD TO PERISH TWICE
I think I know enough of HATE
to say that for DESTRUCTION ICE

AND
WOULD
SUFFICE

577

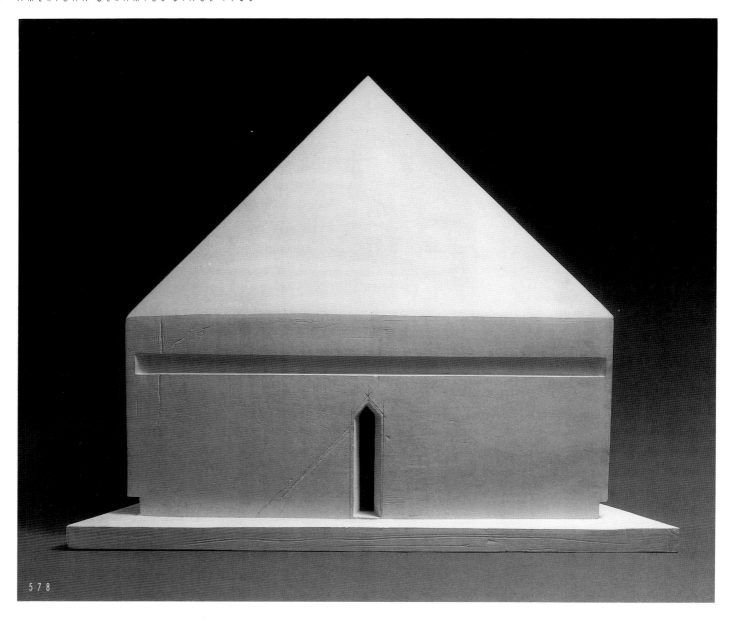

578

578 **William Wyman**
*Temple #8*, 1977
Earthenware
Marks: None
H. 24½, L. 32½, D. 14¾ in. (61.3
× 81.3 × 36.9).
Gift of the friends and students of
William Wyman, Boston
P.C. 80.16

Pyramidal, temple form of unglazed
white earthenware. The sculpture is
sleek and angular, with a slab base.
A narrow door-like opening on one
side leads to the hollow interior. A
recessed band is set above this door.
A narrow, vertical, window-like
opening with a wide frame on each
side is at the back.

This serene, pristine temple form

has an aura of mystery about it because the invitation to enter (through
open spaces) is accompanied by an
interior darkness and by the monu-
mentality of the outer walls—both of
which impart a sense of foreboding.

**JEAN YATES**
Jean Yates participated in the Ceramic Nationals in 1964 and 1966
from Santa Rosa, California.

579 **Jean Yates**
*Seat Box*, 1966
Stoneware
H. 16, W. 18½, D. 12½ in. (40 ×
46.25 × 31.25 cm.)
Marks: none
Purchase prize given by the Associ-

ation of San Francisco Potters, "24th
Ceramic National," 1966
P.C. 66.34

Hand-built stoneware trunk or box
with cover. Two handles are on the
cover, at opposite ends, and rope
handles pass through holes at opposite ends of the box. The top is flat
with a slight curve in the center; the
sides of the box are straight with uneven edges.

**GEORGE YOKOI**
George Yokoi participated in the
1960 Ceramic National from San
Francisco, California.

580 **George Yokoi**
*Bottle with Six Spouts*, 1960

Stoneware
H. 10, Diam. 8 in. (25 × 20 cm.)
Marks: *YOKOI* incised inside foot
Museum purchase from "21st Ce-
ramic International," 1960
P.C. 60.82

High-footed, mushroom-shaped red
stoneware bottle. Six spouts of varying heights protrude from the top of
the mushroom cap. Small clay circular shapes have been applied between the spouts. The throwing
marks are apparent along the body.
A salt glaze is used overall.

**RICHARD ZAKIN (b. 1937)**
Richard Zakin was born in New
York and studied at Syracuse Uni-
versity. He received an M.F.A. from

579

Alfred University. He is professor of art at the State University of New York at Oswego, and is the author of *Kiln Ceramics: A Potter's Guide to Clay and Glazes*. Zakin has written and lectured widely on the technical aspects of ceramics. He participated in the Ceramic National in 1966.

581 **Richard Zakin**
*Untitled*, 1975
Stoneware
H. 10, W. 10½, D. 7 in. (25 × 26.3 × 17.5 cm.)
Marks: *R. Zakin '75* incised on bottom
Gift of the artist   P.C. 76.67
Slab-built vessel with rounded top. A small circular opening is at the top. A curve creates a small, open space at the bottom. Two sets of two incised lines undulate around the top half of the unglazed vessel.

Exhibitions: "Two Potters: Regis Brodie and Richard Zakin," 1976

580

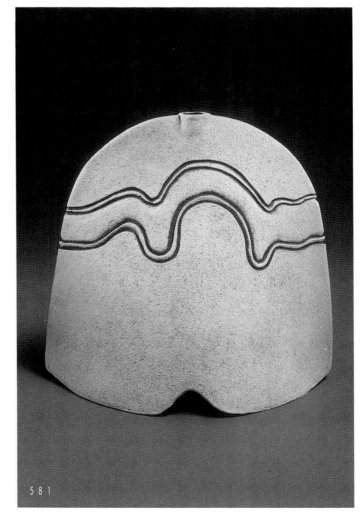

581

582

**ARNOLD ZIMMERMAN (b. 1954)**

Arnold Zimmerman was born in Poughkeepsie, New York, and studied sculpture in La Coste, Provence, where he was a stone carver from 1974 to 1975. He studied ceramics at the Kansas City Art Institute and received an M.F.A. from Alfred University. He also worked at the Archie Bray Foundation in Montana and was resident artist at the Omaha Brickworks Alternative Worksites.

Zimmerman's enormous vessels reveal the influence of Romanesque stone carvings, with their deeply carved surfaces and heavy, massive forms. They twist and turn, often taking on erie human shapes. More recently, Zimmerman has been working on huge gate forms, again deeply carved, with references to even more ancient architectural forms, such as those from Crete or the Middle East.

582 **Arnold Zimmerman**
*Untitled Vessels*, 1982
Earthenware
From left to right: H. 88, Diam. 34 in. (220 × 85 cm.); H. 84½, Diam. 31 in. (211.25 × 77.5 cm.); H. 87¼, Diam. 34½ in. (218.1 × 86.25 cm.) H. 81¼, Diam. 31 in. (201.3 × 77.5 cm.); H. 86½, Diam. 30½ in. (216.25 × 76.25 cm.)
Marks: none
Gift of Lucia Beadel, Edward Beadel, Jr., and Lucia Whisenand in memory of Edward Beadel
P.C. 85.26.1–5

Monumental vessels of blue, pink, green, and tan earthenware. The figures are deeply carved with abstract shapes, ridges, and/or geometric designs reminiscent of Romanesque columns or pilasters. These huge pots, with both ancient and modern references, are monumentally imposing. Their undulating, deeply carved forms are expressive and adamantly physical, emphasized by the reserved, controlled architecture against which they stand.

# CONTRIBUTORS

**William C. Ketchum, Jr.,** is author of numerous books, including *American Folk Art of the Twentieth Century*, published by Rizzoli, and *Potters and Potteries of New York State, 1650–1900*. He has also curated special projects for the Museum of American Folk Art in New York.

**Richard G. Case** is an editor and columnist with the *Syracuse Herald American* and *Herald Journal*. He conducted a study of nineteenth-century potteries in Illinois, and has curated exhibitions of Onondaga county pottery for Everson Museum of Art and the Onondaga Historical Association. Case has an M.A. from the State University of New York and New York State Historical Association at Cooperstown.

**Ulysses G. Dietz** is curator of decorative arts at the Newark Museum. He graduated from Yale University and received an M.A. from the University of Delaware and H.F. Du-Pont Winterthur Museum. He was a curatorial intern at H.F. DuPont Winterthur Museum and a curatorial assistant at Yale University Art Gallery.

**Barbara Perry** is curator of ceramics at Everson Museum of Art. She graduated from Mercyhurst College in Erie, Pennsylvania and received an M.A. and Ph.D. from Syracuse University. She taught at LeMoyne College. Most recently she has curated "American Ceramics Now: The 27th Ceramic National Exhibition."

**Garth Clark** is a ceramic historian and gallery owner. He received an M.A. in modern ceramic history from the Royal College of Art in London. He co-curated and wrote the catalogue for "A Century of Ceramics in the United States, 1878–1978" and has taught and lectured in universities here and abroad. In 1980 he received the Art Critics Award from the National Endowment for the Arts. He founded the Institute for Ceramic History and has written extensively on modern ceramics.

# BIBLIOGRAPHY

## Compiled by Rosemarie Romano, Everson Museum

### BIBLIOGRAPHIES

Campbell, James Edward. *Pottery and Ceramics: A Guide to Information Sources.* Art and Architecture Information Guide Series, vol. 7. Detroit, Mich.: Gale Research Co., 1978.

Strong, Susan R. *History of American Ceramics: An Annotated Bibliography.* Metuchen, N.J.: The Scarecrow Press, 1983.

Weidner, Ruth Irwin. *American Ceramics Before 1930: A Bibliography.* Art Reference Collection, no. 2. Westport, Conn.: Greenwood Press, 1982.

Weinrich, Peter H. *Bibliographic Guide to Books on Ceramics.* Toronto: Canadian Craft Council, 1976.

### DICTIONARIES AND ENCYCLOPEDIAS

Barber, Edwin AtLee. *The Ceramic Collector's Glossary.* New York: Printed for the [Walpole] Society, 1914. Reprint. New York: Da Capo, 1967.

Jervis, William P. *The Encyclopedia of Ceramics.* New York, 1902.

Savage, George, and Harold Newman. *An Illustrated Dictionary of Ceramics.* New York: Van Nostrand Reinhold, 1974.

### AESTHETICS AND CRITICISM

Binns, Charles F. "In Defence of Fire." *Craftsman* 3 (March 1903): 369–372.

"Ceramics in the Art World: NCECA Conference 1987." *NCECA Journal* 8, nos. 1, 2 (1987).

Clark, Garth. "Comment: a Need for Ceramics Criticism." *Ceramics Monthly* 25 (October 1977): 17, 19.

————, ed. *Ceramic Art: Comment and Review 1882–1977.* New York: E. P. Dutton, 1978.

————. "Ceramic Art: Redefinition." *American Ceramics* 1 (Winter 1982): 8–9.

————. "Comment." *American Craft* 46, no. 6 (December 1986/January 1987): 14, 62.

"Clay Criticism: Special Issue." *American Ceramics* 4, no. 4 (1986).

Cushing, Val. "Aesthetics: Aspects of the Vessel in American Ceramics 1900 to 1970: An American Style." *NCECA Journal* 3, no. 1 (1982).

Falk, Lorne. "Will Ceramics Secede from the Art World?" [Fourth International Ceramics Symposium, Toronto] *New Art Examiner* 13 (May 1986): 70–73.

Gombrich, E. H. *The Sense of Order: A Study in the Psychology of Decorative Art.* Ithaca, N.Y.: Cornell University Press, 1979.

Hepburn, Tony. "Art Press Review: Ceramics." *New Art Examiner* 13 (September 1985): 16–18.

Higby, Wayne. "The Vessel: Overcoming the Tyranny of Modern Art." *NCECA Journal* 3, no. 1 (1982): 11–12.

————. "The Vessel is Like a Pot." *American Ceramics* 3, no. 4 (1985): 38–41.

————. "The Vessel: Denying Function." *Ceramics Monthly* 34 (December 1986).

Kangas, Matthew. "Towards a Bicameral Aesthetic of Clay." *American Ceramics* 1 (Winter 1982): 14–15.

Klemperer, Louise. "Critical Dimensions: How Shall We Judge?" *American Ceramics* 1 (Summer 1982): 38–43.

Leach, Bernard. *A Potter's Book.* London: Faber & Faber, 1940.

McTwigan, Michael. "First Things First: Some Second Thoughts on How We View Clay Today." *American Ceramics* 1, no. 1 (1982): 16–17.

Rawson, Philip. *Ceramics.* The Appreciation of the Arts, no. 6. New York: Oxford University Press, 1971.

Ruff, Dale. "Clay Roots and Routes." *American Ceramics* 1 (Summer 1982): 36–37.

Woodman, George. "Ceramic Decoration and the Concept of Ceramics as a Decorative Art." *American Ceramics* 1 (Winter 1982): 30–33.

Woodman, George. "Why (Not) Ceramics?" *New Art Examiner* 13 (September 1985): 35–37.

Yanagi, Soetsu. *The Unknown Craftsman.* Tokyo: Kodansha International, 1972.

### GENERAL HISTORIES

Barber, Edwin AtLee. *Catalogue of American Potteries and Porcelains.* Philadelphia: Pennsylvania Museum and School of Industrial Art, 1893.

————. *The Pottery and Porcelain of the United States: An Historical Review of American Ceramic Art from the Earliest Times to the Present Day.* 3d ed. rev. and enl. 1909. . . . *Combined with Marks of American Potters.* 1904. Reprint. New York: Feingold & Lewis, 1976.

Bernstein, Melvin H. *Art and Design at Alfred: Chronicle of a Ceramics College.* Philadelphia: Art Alliance Press, 1986.

Bray, Hazel V. *The Potter's Art in California: 1885 to 1955.* Oakland, Calif.: Oakland Museum, 1980.

California State University, Art Gallery, Fullerton. *Overglaze Imagery: Cone 019–016.* Essays by Garth Clark, Judy Chicago, and Richard Shaw. Fullerton: California State University, Art Gallery, 1977.

Clark, Garth. *American Ceramics: 1876 to the Present.* New York: Abbeville, 1988.

————, ed. *Transactions of the Ceramics Symposium 1979.* Los Angeles: Institute for Ceramic History, 1980.

Clark, Garth, and Margie Hughto. *A Century of Ceramics in the United States, 1878–1978: A Study of Its Development.* New York: E.P. Dutton in association with Everson Museum of Art, 1979.

Cox, Warren E. *The Book of Pottery and Porcelain.* Vol. 2. New York: Crown, 1944.

Denker, Ellen, and Bert Denker. *North American Pottery & Porcelain.* Pittstown, N.J.: Main Street Press, 1985.

Donhauser, Paul S. *History of American Ceramics: The Studio Potter.* Dubuque, Iowa: Kendall/Hunt, 1978.

"Double Issue." *Design Quarterly* 42, 43 (1958).

Harrington, LaMar: *Ceramics in the Pacific Northwest: A History.* Seattle: University of Washington Press for the Henry Art Gallery, 1978.

Hillier, Bevis. *Pottery and Porcelain 1700–1914: England, Europe, and North America.* New York: Meredith Press, 1968.

Museum of Contemporary Crafts. *Forms from the Earth: 1,000 Years of Pottery in America.* New York: Museum of Contemporary Crafts, 1962.

Norwood, John Nelson. *Fifty Years of Ceramic Education at State College of Ceramics, Alfred.* Alfred, N.Y.: New York State College of Ceramics, 1950.

Phillips, Lisa, ed. *High Styles: Twentieth Century American Design.* New York: Whitney Museum of American Art, 1985.

Preaud, Tamara, and Serge Gauthier. *Ceramics of the Twentieth Century.* New York: Rizzoli, 1982.

R. W. Norton Art Gallery. *The American Porcelain Tradition.* Trenton, N.J.: New Jersey State Museum, 1972.

Ramsay, John. *American Potters and Pottery.* Boston: Hale, Cushman & Flint, 1939. Reprint. Ann Arbor, Mich.: Ars Ceramica, 1976.

Schwartz, Marvin D., and Richard Wolfe. *A History of American Art Porcelain.* New York: Renaissance Editions, 1967.

Stiles, Helen E. *Pottery in the United States.* New York: E.P. Dutton, 1941.

Whitney Museum of American Art. *200 Years of American Sculpture.* New York: Godine, 1976.

Young, Jennie J. "United States." In *The Ceramic Art: A Compendium of the History and Manufacture of Pottery and Porcelain,* 442–487. New York: Harper, 1878.

### CERAMIC NATIONAL EXHIBITION CATALOGUES

Titles and dates are as they appear on the title page of the Ceramic National catalogues which are housed in the Everson Museum archives. The dates given are for the initial showing at the Syracuse Museum of Fine Arts which became Everson Museum of Art in 1951. The first exhibition, the Robineau Memorial Ceramic Exhibition, was not a national show, but open to ceramists of New York State only.

*Second Annual Robineau Memorial Ceramic Exhibition* (National), 1933.

*Third Annual Robineau Memorial Ceramic Exhibition* (National), 1934.

*Fourth Annual Robineau Memorial Ceramic Exhibition* (National), 1935.

*The Fifth National Ceramic Exhibition* (The Robineau Memorial), 1936.

*The Sixth National Ceramic Exhibition* (The Robineau Memorial), 1937.

*The Seventh National Ceramic Exhibition,* 1938.

*The Eighth Annual National Ceramic Exhibition,* 1939.

*The Ninth National Ceramic Exhibition,* 1940.

*Contemporary Ceramics of the Western Hemisphere. In Celebration of the Tenth Anniversary of the National Ceramic Exhibition,* 1941.

*Eleventh National Ceramic Exhibition,* 1946.

*Twelfth National Ceramic Exhibition,* 1947.

*Thirteenth National Ceramic Exhibition,* 1948.

*Fourteenth National Ceramic Exhibition,* 1949.

*Fifteenth National Ceramic Exhibition,* 1950.

*16th Ceramic National,* 1951.

*17th Ceramic National,* 1952.

*18th Ceramic National,* 1954.

*19th Ceramic National,* 1956.

*XX Ceramic International,* 1958.

*XXI Ceramic International,* 1960.

*22nd Ceramic National Exhibition,* 1962.

*23rd Ceramic National Exhibition,* 1964.

*24th Ceramic National Exhibition,* 1966.

*25th Ceramic National Exhibition,* 1968.

*American Ceramics Now: The 27th Ceramic National Exhibition,* 1987.

## ANCIENT AMERICAN POTTERY

Brody, J. J. *Mimbres Painted Pottery.* Santa Fe: School of American Research; Albuquerque: University of New Mexico Press, 1977.

Bushnell, G. H. S., and Adrian Digby. *Ancient American Pottery: Faber Monographs on Pottery and Porcelain.* London: Faber and Faber, 1955.

Giammattei, Victor Michael, and Nanci Greer Reichert. *Art of a Vanished Race: The Mimbres Classic Black-on-White.* Woodland, Calif.: Dillon-Tyler, 1975.

Lister, Robert H., and Florence C. Lister. *Anasazi Pottery.* Albuquerque: University of New Mexico Press in association with the Maxwell Museum of Anthropology, 1978.

Martin, Paul Sidney. *Anasazi Painted Pottery: Collection of the Field Museum of Natural History.* Chicago: Field Museum Press, 1940.

Museum of the American Indian. *Naked Clay: 3000*

*Years of Unadorned Pottery of the American Indian.* New York: Heye Foundation, 1972.

Shepard, Anna O. *Ceramics for the Archaeologist.* Carnegie Institution of Washington, Publication 609. Washington, D.C.: Carnegie Institution of Washington, 1954.

## PUEBLO POTTERY

Babcock, Barbara, Guy Monthan, and Doris Monthan. *The Pueblo Storyteller.* Tucson, Ariz.: University of Arizona Press, 1986.

Bunzel, Ruth Leah. *The Pueblo Potter: A Study of Creative Imagination in Primitive Art.* New York: Columbia University Press, 1929. Reprint. New York: Dover, 1972.

Chapman, Kenneth. *Pueblo Indian Pottery.* 2 vols. Nice: C. Szwedzicki, 1936.

Chapman, Kenneth, and Francis H. Harlow. *The Pottery of San Ildefonso Pueblo.* Albuquerque, N. Mex.: University of New Mexico Press for the School of American Research, 1970.

Dittert, Alfred E., Jr., and Fred Plog. *Generations in Clay: Pueblo Pottery of the American Southwest.* Flagstaff, Ariz.: Northland Press, 1980.

Frank, Larry, and Francis H. Harlow. *Historic Pottery of the Pueblo Indians, 1600–1880.* Boston: New York Graphic Society, 1974.

Harlow, Francis H. *Contemporary Pueblo Indian Pottery.* Albuquerque, N. Mex.: Museum of New Mexico Press, 1965.

———. *Matte-Paint Pottery of the Tewa, Keres, and Zuni Pueblos.* Sante Fe, N. Mex.: Museum of New Mexico, 1973.

———. *Modern Pueblo Pottery: 1880–1960.* Flagstaff, Ariz.: Northland Press, 1977.

Maxwell Museum of Anthropology. *Seven Families in Pueblo Pottery.* Albuquerque, N. Mex.: University of New Mexico Press, 1974.

Trimble, Stephen. *Talking With the Clay: The Art of Pueblo Pottery.* Santa Fe, N. Mex.: School of American Research Press, 1987.

## EARLY AMERICAN POTTERY

Amanda, Suzanne. "Early New England Potters." *Ceramics Monthly* 23 (October 1975): 48–51.

Barber, Edwin AtLee. *Tulipware of the Pennsylvania German Potters: An Historical Sketch of the Art of Slip-Decoration in the United States.* Art Handbook of the Pennsylvania Museum and School of Industrial Art. Philadelphia: Pennsylvania Museum and School of Industrial Art, 1903.

Christenson, Edwin O. *Early American Designs: Ceramics.* New York: Pitman Publishing Co., 1952.

Clement, Arthur W. *Our Pioneer Potters.* York, Penn.: Maple Press, 1947.

———. *Pottery and Porcelain of New Jersey 1688–1900.* Newark, N.J.: Newark Museum, 1947.

Freeman, John Crosby. *Blue-Decorated Stoneware of New York State.* Watkins Glen, N.Y.: American Life Foundation, 1966.

Fryatt, F. E. "Pottery in the United States" *Harper's New Monthly Magazine* 62 (February 1881): 357–369.

Gallo, John. *Nineteenth and Twentieth Century Yellowware.* Richfield Springs, N.Y.: Heritage Press, 1985.

Gates, William C., Jr., and Dana E. Ormerod. "The East Liverpool Pottery District: Identification of Manufacturers and Marks." *Historical Archaelogy* 16, nos. 1, 2 (1982).

Greer, Georgeanna H. *American Stonewares: the Art and Craft of Utilitarian Potters.* Exton, Penn.: Schiffer Publishing Co., 1981.

Guilland, Harold F. *Early American Folk Pottery.* Philadelphia: Chilton Book Co., 1971.

Ketchum, William C., Jr. *The Pottery and Porcelain Collector's Handbook: a Guide to Early American Ceramics from Maine to California.* New York: Funk & Wagnalls, 1971.

———. "Decorative Techniques in American Stoneware." *Antiques Journal* 34 (April 1979): 22–24, 51.

———. *Pottery and Porcelain: The Knopf Collectors' Guides to American Antiques.* New York: Alfred A. Knopf, 1982.

———. *American Country Pottery: Yellowware and Spongeware.* New York: Alfred A. Knopf, 1987.

———. *Potters and Potteries of New York State, 1650–1900.* Rev. 2d ed. Syracuse, N.Y.: Syracuse University Press, 1987.

"Pre-Industrial Salt-Glazed Ware." *Ceramics Monthly* 28 (February 1980): 44–47.

Quimby, Ian M.G., ed. *Ceramics in America.* Winterthur Conference Report, 1972. Charlottesville, Va.: University Press of Virginia for the Henry Francis du Pont Winterthur Museum, 1973.

Ries, Heinrich. *Clay Industries of New York.* Albany: University of the State of New York, 1895.

Ries, Heinrich, and Henry Leighton. *History of the Clay-Working Industry in the United States.* New York: John Wiley & Sons, 1909.

Robacker, Earl F., and Ada F. Robacker. *Spatterware and Sponge.* South Brunswick, N.J.: A.S. Barnes, 1978.

Schwartz, Marvin D. *Collector's Guide to Antique American Pottery.* Garden City, N.Y.: Doubleday, 1969.

Smith, Joseph J. *Regional Aspects of American Folk Pottery.* York, Penn.: Historical Society of York County, 1979.

Spargo, John. *Early American Pottery and China.* New York: Century, 1926. Reprint. Rutland, Vt.: C.E. Tuttle, 1974.

Watkins, Lura Woodside. *Early New England Potters and Their Wares.* Cambridge, Mass.: Harvard University Press, 1950.

Webster, Donald Blake. *Decorated Stoneware Pottery of North America.* Rutland, Vt.: Charles E. Tuttle, 1971.

Weidner, Ruth Irwin. "The Early Literature of Ceramics." *American Ceramics* 1 (Fall 1982): 42–45.

### Bennett Pottery

Barber, Edwin AtLee. "Early Ceramic Printing and Modeling in the United States. I: The Origin of Some Well-Known Game Jugs. II: The Beginning of Ceramic

Printing in America." *Old China* 3 (December 1903):50–55.

*Edwin Bennett and the Products of His Baltimore Pottery.* Baltimore: Maryland Historical Society, 1973.

"A Pioneering American Pottery: Approaching the Century Mark." *Ceramic Age* 25 (March 1935):89.

## Bennington Potteries

Barret, Richard Carter. *Bennington Pottery and Porcelain: A Guide to Identification.* New York: Bonanza Books, 1958.

———. *How to Identify Bennington Pottery.* Brattleboro, Vt.: Stephen Greene Press, 1964.

———. "Little-Known Ceramic Treasures from the Bennington Potteries." *Antiques* 98 (July 1970): 100–109.

Spargo, John. *The A.B.C. of Bennington Pottery Wares: A Manual for Collectors and Dealers.* New and rev. ed. Bennington, Vt.: Bennington Historical Museum, 1948.

———. *The Potters and Potteries of Bennington.* Boston: Houghton Mifflin and Antiques, 1926. Reprint. Southhampton, N.Y.: Cracker Barrel Press, 1969.

Vozar, Linda. "Early Bennington Potteries." *Ceramics Monthly* 25 (October 1977): 54–57.

## Dedham Pottery

Evans, Paul F. "The Robertson Saga. I. The Creative Years, 1866–1889." *Western Collector* 5 (April 1967): 7–12.

———. "The Robertson Saga. II. The Commercial Years, 1891–1943." *Western Collector* 5 (May 1967): 7–12.

Hawes, Lloyd E. "Hugh Cornwall Robertson and the Chelsea Period." *Antiques* 89 (March 1966): 409–413.

———. *The Dedham Pottery and the Earlier Robertson's Chelsea Potteries.* Dedham, Mass.: Dedham Historical Society, 1968.

Hecht, Eugene. "The East Coast Robertsons." *Ceramics Monthly* 35 (February 1987): 22–25.

"Hugh C. Robertson." *Glass and Pottery World* 16 (November 1908): 16.

## Onondaga Pottery (Syracuse China)

Case, Richard G. *Onondaga Pottery.* Syracuse, N.Y.: Everson Museum of Art, 1973.

———. *Jugs and Jugtowns.* Syracuse, N.Y.: Onondaga Historical Association, 1987.

Davison, Mary E. "Williams H. Farrar, Potter." *Antiques* 35 (March 1939): 122–123.

Ketchum, William C., Jr. "Potters of Onondaga County: Geddes-Syracuse." In *Potters and Potteries of New York State, 1650–1900.* 2d ed., 303–311. Syracuse, N.Y.: Syracuse University Press, 1987.

Onondaga Pottery Company. *Little Romances of China.* Syracuse, N.Y.: Privately Printed for Onondaga Pottery Company, 1919.

Onondaga Pottery Company. *Onondaga Pottery Co.: Seventy-Five Years of American Craftsmanship, 1871–*

*1946.* Syracuse, N.Y.: Onondaga Pottery Company, 1946.

Pass, R. H. "Vocational and Apprenticeship School at Onondaga Pottery." *American Ceramic Society Bulletin* 4 (October 1925): 560–561.

## ART POTTERY

Anscombe, Isabelle, and Charlotte Gere. *Arts & Crafts in Britain and America.* New York: Rizzoli, 1978.

Bolger, Doreen, et al. *In Pursuit of Beauty: Americans and the Aesthetic Movement.* New York: Rizzoli with the Metropolitan Museum of Art, 1987.

Bray, Hazel V. "Art Pottery : 1885–1930." Part I of *The Potter's Art in California: 1885–1955,* 1–21. Oakland, Calif.: Oakland Museum, 1978.

Bruhn, Thomas P. *American Decorative Tiles 1870–1930.* Storrs, Conn.: University of Connecticut. William Benton Museum of Art, 1979.

*California Design 1910.* Edited by Timothy J. Anderson, Eudorah M. Moore, and Robert W. Winter. Pasadena, Calif.: California Design Pubs., 1974.

Callen, Anthea. "Ceramics." In *Women Artists of the Arts and Crafts Movement 1870–1914,* 51–93. New York: Pantheon, 1978.

Cincinnati Art Museum. *The Ladies, God Bless 'Em: The Women's Art Movement in Cincinnati in the Nineteenth Century.* Cincinnati: Cincinati Art Museum, 1976.

Clark, Garth. "The Liberation of Clay: The Roots of Modern Ceramic Art." *Studio Potter* 6, no. 2 (1978): 63–70.

Darling, Sharon S. *Chicago Ceramics and Glass: An Illustrated History from 1871 to 1933.* Chicago: Chicago Historical Society; distributed by University of Chicago Press, 1979.

Dietz, Ulysses G. *The Newark Museum Collection of American Art Pottery.* Newark, N.J.: The Newark Museum, 1984.

Eidelberg, Martin. "Art Pottery." In *The Arts and Crafts Movement in America, 1876–1916,* edited by Robert Judson Clark, 119–186. Princeton, N.J.: Princeton University Press, 1972.

———. "American Ceramics and International Styles, 1876–1916." *Princeton University Art Museum Record* 34, no. 2 (1975): 13–19.

———. "The American Pottery Movement: A Critical Analysis [Abstract]." In *Transactions of the Ceramics Symposium, 1979,* edited by Garth Clark, 30–32. Los Angeles: Institute for Ceramic History, 1980.

———, ed. *From Our Native Clay: Art Pottery from the Collections of the American Ceramic Arts Society.* New York: Turn of the Century Editions, 1987.

Evans, Paul. "Art Pottery in California: An American Era in Microcosm." In *Transactions of the Ceramics Symposium, 1979,* edited by Garth Clark, 33–37. Los Angeles: Institute for Ceramic History, 1980.

———. *Art Pottery of the United States: An Encyclopedia of Producers and Their Marks.* 2d ed. New York: Feingold & Lewis, 1987.

Henzke, Lucile. *American Art Pottery.* Rev. ed. Exton, Penn: Schiffer, 1982.

Kaplan, Wendy, ed. *"The Art That is Life": The Arts & Crafts Movement in America, 1875–1920.* Boston: Museum of Fine Arts, 1987.

Keen, Kirsten Hoving. *American Art Pottery, 1875–1930.* Wilmington: Delaware Art Museum, 1978.

———. "Art Pottery in Context [Abstract]." In *Transactions of the Ceramics Symposium, 1979,* edited by Garth Clark, 44–45. Los Angeles: Institute for Ceramic History, 1980.

Kovel, Ralph, and Terry Kovel. *Kovel's Collector's Guide to American Art Pottery.* New York: Crown, 1974.

Ludwig, Coy L. *The Arts & Crafts Movement in New York State, 1890's – 1920's.* Hamilton, N.Y.: Gallery Association of New York State, 1983.

Perry, Elizabeth W. "The Work of Cincinnati Women in Decorated Pottery." In *Art and Handicraft in the Woman's Building of the World's Columbian Exposition, Chicago, 1893,* edited by Maud Howe Elliott. Chicago: Rand, McNally, 1894.

Perry, [Mrs.] Aaron F. "Decorative Pottery of Cincinnati." *Harper's New Monthly Magazine* 62 (May 1881): 834–845.

## CHINA PAINTING

Binns, Charles F. "The Use of American Wares by American Ceramic Decorators." *Keramic Studio* 1 (August 1899): 81–82.

California State University Art Gallery, Fullerton. *Overglaze Imagery: Cone 019–016.* Essays by Garth Clark, Judy Chicago, and Richard Shaw. Fullerton: California State University, Art Gallery, 1977.

Chicago, Judy. "Judy Chicago: World of the China Painter." *Ceramics Monthly* 26 (May 1978): 40–45.

Cross, Nellie A. "National League of Mineral Painters." *Keramic Studio* 10 (August 1908): 79–80.

Darling, Sharon S. "Handpainted China." In *Chicago Ceramics and Glass: An Illustrated History from 1871 to 1933,* 7–12. Chicago: Chicago Historical Society; distributed by University of Chicago Press, 1979.

Frackleton, Susan Stuart. *Tried by Fire: A Work on China Painting.* New York: Appleton, 1886. 3d ed. enl. and rev., 1895.

Keramic Studio. *The Book of Roses: Studies for the China Painter and the Student of Watercolors.* Syracuse, N.Y.: Keramic Studio, 1903.

Keramic Studio. *The Fruit Book: Studies for the Painter of China and the Student of Water Colors.* Syracuse, N.Y.: Keramic Studio, 1906.

Keramic Studio. *The Second Rose Book: Studies for the Painter of China and the Student of Water Colors.* Syracuse, N.Y.: Keramic Studio, 1907.

Keramic Studio. *Flower Painting on Porcelain.* The Class Room, No. 2. Syracuse, N.Y.: Keramic Studio, 1908.

Keramic Studio. *The Art of Teaching a Color Palette and Its Use; Ground Laying; Lustres.* The Class Room, No. 1. Syracuse, N.Y.: Keramic Studio, 1909.

Keramic Studio. *Figure Painting on Porcelain; Firing.* The Class Room, No. 3. Syracuse, N.Y.: Keramic Studio, 1910.

Keramic Studio. *The Conventional Decoration of Porcelain*. The Class Room, No. 4. Syracuse, N.Y.: Keramic Studio, 1911.

Keramic Studio. *Cups and Saucers from Keramic Studio*. Syracuse, N.Y.: Keramic Studio, 1913.

*Keramic Studio* (a journal published in Syracuse, N.Y. from 1899 to 1924) regularly printed information concerning techniques, designs, and exhibitions as well as illustrations of works decorated by prominent china painters.

McClinton, Katharine Morrison. "American Hand-painted China." *Spinning Wheel* 23 (April 1967): 10–12, 43.

McLaughlin, Mary Louise. *Pottery Decoration Under the Glaze*. 3d ed, rev. Cincinnati: Robert Clarke, 1880.

———. *Suggestions to China Painters*. Cincinnati: Robert Clarke, 1883.

———. *China Painting: A Practical Manual for the Use of Ama eurs in the Decoration of Hard Porcelain*. New ed. Cincinnati: Robert Clarke Co., 1904.

———. *The China Painter's Handbook*. Cincinnati, 1917.

National League of Mineral Painters. *Exhibition… From October 24 to November 1, 1896*. Cincinnati: Cincinnati Art Museum, 1896.

Nichols, George Ward. *Pottery: How It Is Made, Its Shape and Decoration: Practical Instructions for Painting on Porcelain and All Kinds of Pottery with Vitrifiable and Common Oil Colors, with a Full Bibliography of Standard Works upon the Ceramic Art*. New York: G. P. Putnam's Sons, 1878.

Paist, Henrietta Barclay. *Design and the Decoration of Porcelain*. Syracuse, N.Y.: Keramic Studio, 1916.

Piton, Camille. *A Complete Practical Treatise on China-Painting in America, with Some Suggestions as to Decorative Art*. New York: J. Wiley, 1878–80.

Weidner, Ruth Irwin. "The Early Literature of China Decorating." *American Ceramics* 2 (Spring 1983): 28–33.

## Arthur Eugene Baggs

Baggs, Arthur. "The Story of a Potter." *The Handicrafter* 1 (April/May 1929): 8–10.

Hall, Herbert J. "Marblehead Pottery." *Keramic Studio* 10 (June 1908): 30–31.

Levin, Elaine. "Pioneers of Contemporary American Ceramics: Arthur Baggs, Glen Lukens." *Ceramics Monthly* 24 (January 1976): 24–30.

Persick, Roberta Stoles. *Arthur Eugene Baggs, American Potter*. Ph.D. dissertation, Ohio State University, 1963.

## Charles Fergus Binns

Alfred University. *Charles Fergus Binns, Memorial, 1857–1934*. University Bulletin no. 3. University Bulletin 11 (November 1935). Alfred, N.Y., 1935.

Avery, C. Louise. " A Memorial Exhibition of the Works of Charles F. Binns." *Metropolitan Museum of Art Bulletin* 30 (May 1935): 106–108.

Bernstein, Melvin H. "University Impact on Ceramics: Charles Fergus Binns at Alfred University." *NCECA Journal* 5 (1984): 38–43.

———. "The Applied Art Years of Charles F. Binns: 1900–1931." Part I, of *Art and Design at Alfred: Chronicle of a Ceramics College*, 11–94. Philadelphia: Associated University Presses, 1986.

Binns, Charles F. "American Clays for Grand Feu Wares." In *Grand Feu Ceramics*, by Taxile Doat. Syracuse, N.Y.: Keramic Studio, 1905.

Binns, Charles F. *The Potter's Craft: A Practical Guide for the Studio and Workshop*. New York: D. Van Nostrand, 1910.

Binns, Charles F. "The Art of Manufacture and the Manufacture of Art." *American Ceramic Society Bulletin* 2 (April 1923): 55–59.

Blasberg, Robert. "Eternity in a Ball of Clay: Reminiscences of Dr. Charles Binns." Edited by Dr. Eugene Hecht. *Arts and Crafts Quarterly* 2 (Winter 1988): 11–12, passim.

Levin, Elaine. "Pioneers of Contemporary American Ceramics: Charles Binns, Adelaide Robineau." *Ceramics Monthly* 23 (November 1975): 22–27.

Norwood, John Nelson. *Fifty Years of Ceramic Education: New York State College of Ceramics at Alfred*. Alfred, N.Y.: New York State College of Ceramics, 1950.

Strong, Susan R. "Charles Fergus Binns 1857–1934, A Chronological Bibliography." Alfred, N.Y.: Scholes Library, 1980.

———. "The Searching Flame: Charles Fergus Binns." *American Ceramics* 1 (Summer 1982): 44–49.

## Taxile Doat (see also University City)

Doat, Taxile. *Grand Feu Ceramics: A Practical Treatise on the Making of Fine Porcelain and Gres*. Translated from the French by Samuel E. Robineau. Syracuse, N.Y.: Keramic Studio, 1905.

Jervis, William Percival. "Taxile Doat." *Keramic Studio* 4 (July 1902): 54–55.

Sargent, Irene. "Taxile Doat." *Keramic Studio* 8 (December 1906): 171–173, 193.

## Fulper Pottery

Blasberg, Robert W., and Carol L. Bohdan. *Fulper Art Pottery: An Aesthetic Appreciation, 1909–1929*. New York: Jordan-Volpe Gallery, 1979.

"Fulper Art Pottery." *Ceramics Monthly* 28 (May 1980): 47–49.

Volpe, Todd M., and Robert W. Blasberg. "Fulper Art Pottery: Amazing Glazes." *American Art and Antiques* 1 (July/August 1978): 76–83.

"W. H. Fulper." [Obituary] *American Ceramic Society Bulletin* 7 (December 1928): 380–381.

## Griffen Smith & Co.

Ball, Berenice M. "Etruscan Majolica." *Antiques Journal* 19 (September 1964): 24–25.

Griffen Smith & Co. *Majolica; Catalogue*. Phoenixville, Penn.: Brooke Weidner, 1960.

Rebert, M. Charles. *American Majolica, 1850–1900*. Des Moines, Iowa: Wallace-Homestead Book Co., 1981.

Weidner, Ruth Irwin. "The Majolica Wares of Griffen Smith & Company. Part I. History and Manufacture." *Spinning Wheel* 36 (January/February 1980): 13–17.

———. "The Majolica Wares of Griffen Smith & Company. Part II. The Designs and Their Sources." *Spinning Wheel* 36 (March/April 1980): 14–19.

## William H. Grueby

Blasberg, Robert W. "Grueby Art Pottery." *Antiques* 100 (August 1971): 246–249.

Eidelberg, Martin. "The Ceramic Art of William H. Grueby." *Connoisseur* 184 (September 1973): 47–54.

Everson Museum of Art. *Grueby*. Essay by Robert W. Blasberg. Syracuse, N.Y.: Everson Museum of Art, 1981.

Perry, Mary Chase. "Grueby Potteries." *Keramic Studio* 2 (April 1901): 250–252.

Russell, Arthur. "Grueby Pottery." *The House Beautiful* 5 (December 1898): 3–9.

## Hampshire Pottery

Pappas, Joan, and Harold Kendall. *Hampshire Pottery Manufactured by J. S. Taft & Company, Keene, N. H.*. Manchester, Vt.: Forward's Color Productions, 1971.

## Jugtown Pottery

Busbee, Jacques. "Jugtown Pottery." *Ceramic Age* 14 (October 1929): 127–130.

Crawford, Jean. *Jugtown Pottery: History and Design*. Winston-Salem, N.C.: John F. Blair, 1964.

Fields, Mary Durland. "Portfolio: Jugtown Pottery." *Ceramics Monthly* 31 (March 1983): 53–60.

## Mary Louise McLaughlin (see also China Painting)

Denker, Ellen Paul, and Bert Randall Denker. "Mary Louise McLaughlin." In *"The Art That is Life": The Arts and Crafts Movement in America, 1875–1920*, edited by Wendy Kaplan, 249–250. Boston: Museum of Fine Arts, 1987.

Levin, Elaine. "Mary Louise McLaughlin and the Cincinnati Art Pottery Movement." *American Craft* 42 (December 1982/January 1983): 28–31, 82–83.

McLaughlin Mary Louise. "Losanti Ware." *Keramic Studio* 3 (December 1901): 178–179.

———. "Miss McLaughlin Tells Her Own Story." *American Ceramic Society Bulletin* 17 (May 1938): 217–225.

Peck, Herbert. "The Amateur Antecedents of Rookwood Pottery." *Cincinnati Historical Society Bulletin* 26 (October 1968): 317–337.

## Henry Chapman Mercer

Barnes, Benjamin H. *The Moravian Pottery: Memories of Forty-Six Years*. Doylestown, Penn.: Bucks County Historical Society, 1970.

Goldner, Steven. "The Moravian Pottery and Tile Works." *Ceramics Monthly* 26 (December 1978): 45–55.

Reed, Cleota. "Henry Chapman Mercer." *American Ceramics* 4, no. 3 (1985): 46–51.

———. *Henry Chapman Mercer and the Moravian Pottery and Tile Works*. Philadelphia: University of Pennsylvania Press, 1987.

## Newcomb Pottery

Evans, Paul F. "Newcomb Pottery Decorators." *Spinning Wheel* 30 (April 1974): 54–55.

Frackleton, Susan Stuart. "Our American Potteries: Newcomb College." *Sketch Book* 5 (July 1906): 430–433.

Ormond, Suzanne, and Mary E. Irvine. *Louisiana's Art Nouveau: The Crafts of the Newcomb Style*. Gretna, La.: Pelican Publishing Co., 1976.

Poesch, Jessie. *Newcomb Pottery: An Enterprise for Southern Women, 1895–1940*. Exton, Penn.: Schiffer Publishing Co., 1984.

Sheerer, Mary G. "Newcomb Pottery." *Keramic Studio* 1 (November 1899): 151–152.

———. "History of Newcomb Pottery." *American Ceramic Society Journal* 1 (August 1918): 518–521.

———. "The Development of Decorative Processes at Newcomb." *American Ceramic Society Journal* 7 (August 1924): 645–649.

## Maria Longworth Nichols (Storer) (see also Rookwood)

"Individual Exhibits at the Paris Exhibition." *Keramic Studio* 2 (September 1900): 95.

"Mrs. Bellamy Storer." [Obituary] *American Ceramic Society Bulletin* 11 (June 1932): 157–159.

Newton, Clara Chipman. "The Porcelain League of Cincinnati." *American Ceramic Society Bulletin* 18 (November 1939): 445–446.

Peck, Herbert. "The Amateur Antecedents of Rookwood Pottery." *Cincinnati Historical Society Bulletin* 26 (October 1968): 317–337.

Storer, Maria Longworth [Nichols]. *History of the Cincinnati Musical Festivals and of the Rookwood Pottery*. Paris: Herbert Clark, Printer, 1919.

## Dorothea Warren O'Hara

"Enameling by Dorothea Warren O'Hara." *Keramic Studio* 14 (February 1913): 204–208.

O'Hara, Dorothea Warren. *The Art of Enameling on Porcelain*. New York: Madison Square Press, 1912.

Robineau, Adelaide Alsop. "Mrs. Dorothea Warren O'Hara." *Keramic Studio* 18 (January 1917): 143.

## George E. Ohr

Clark, Garth R. "George Ohr: Clay Prophet." *Craft Horizons* 38 (October 1978): 44–49, 65.

———. "Robineau and Ohr: A Study in Polarities." In *Transactions of the Ceramics Symposium 1979*, edited by Garth R. Clark, 15–22. Los Angeles: Institute for Ceramic History, 1980.

———. "George E. Ohr: Avant Garde Volumes." *Studio Potter* 12 (December 1983): 8–19.

———. *George E. Ohr*. University, Miss.: University of Mississippi, 1983.

———. "George E. Ohr." *American Ceramics* 4, no. 1 (1985): 44–51.

———. "George E. Ohr." *Antiques* 128 (September 1985): 490–497.

Mississippi State Historical Museum. *The Biloxi Art Pottery of George Ohr*. Text by Garth R. Clark. Jackson, Miss.: Mississippi Department of Archives and History, 1978.

## Pewabic Pottery

Bleicher, Fred, William C. Hu, and Marjorie E. Uren. *Pewabic Pottery: An Offical History*. Ann Arbor, Mich.: Ars Ceramica, 1977.

Brunk, Thomas W. "Pewabic Pottery." In *Arts and Crafts in Detroit 1906–1976*, 141–148. Detroit: Detroit Institute of Arts, 1976.

———. *Pewabic Pottery: Marks and Labels*. Detroit: Historic Indian Village Press, 1978.

Garwood, Dorothy. "Mary Chase Stratton." *Ceramics Monthly* 31 (September 1983): 29–33.

"Louisiana Purchase Exposition Ceramics, Continued." *Keramic Studio* 6 (February 1905): 216–219.

Pear, Lillian Myers. *The Pewabic Pottery: A History of Its Products and Its People*. Des Moines, Iowa: Wallace-Homestead Book Co., 1976.

Robineau, Adelaide Alsop. "Mary Chase Perry: the Potter." *Keramic Studio* 6 (October 1905): 217–219.

## Frederick Hurten Rhead

Bumpus, Bernard. *The Rheads: Artists and Potters 1870–1950*. London: Geffrye Museum, 1986.

Dale, Sharon. "An Englishman in America: Frederick Hurten Rhead." *American Ceramics* 5, no. 2 (1986): 40–45.

———. *Frederick Hurten Rhead: An English Potter in America*. Erie, Penn.: Erie Art Museum, 1986.

———. "Frederick Rhead." *Ceramics Monthly* 35 (May 1987): 27–36.

Rhead, Frederick Hurten. "America as a Ceramic Art Center. Chapter I." *Fine Arts Journal* 22 (April 1910): 183–193.

———. *Studio Pottery*. University City, Mo.: People's University Press, 1910.

## Adelaide Alsop Robineau

Clark, Garth R. "Robineau and Ohr: A Study in Polarities." In *Transactions of the Ceramics Symposium 1979*, edited by Garth R. Clark, 15–22. Los Angeles: Institute for Ceramic History, 1980.

Eidelberg, Martin. "Apotheosis of the Toiler." *American Craft* 41 (December 1981/January 1982): 2–5.

Hull, William. "Some Notes on Early Robineau Porcelains." *Everson Museum of Art Bulletin* 22, no. 2 (1960): 1–6.

*Keramic Studio*. Edited by Adelaide Alsop Robineau. Syracuse, N.Y.: Keramic Studio Publishing Company, 1899–1924.

Levin, Elaine. "Pioneers of Contemporary American Ceramics: Charles Binns, Adelaide Robineau." *Ceramics Monthly* 23 (November 1975): 22–27.

*A Memorial Exhibition of Porcelain and Stoneware by Adelaide Alsop Robineau 1865–1929*. Essay by Joseph Breck. New York: Metropolitan Museum of Art, 1929.

Olmsted, Anna Wetherill. "The Ceramic National Founded in Memory of Adelaide Alsop Robineau." Manuscript. Robineau Archives. Everson Museum of Art, Syracuse, N.Y.

Robineau, Samuel E. "The Robineau Porcelains." *Keramic Studio* 13 (August 1911): 80–84.

———. "Adelaide Alsop Robineau." *Design* 30 (April 1929): 201–209.

"Syracuse Gets Robineau Memorial Group." *Art Digest* 5 (January 15, 1931): 19.

Weiss, Peg., ed. *Adelaide Alsop Robineau: Glory in Porcelain*. Syracuse, N.Y.: Syracuse University Press with Everson Museum of Art, 1981.

## Rookwood Pottery

Hasselle, Bob: "Rookwood: An American Art Pottery." *Ceramics Monthly* 26 (June 1978): 27–37.

"An Historical Collection of the Rookwood Pottery." *Keramic Studio* 8 (April 1907): 274.

Jordan-Volpe Gallery. *Ode to Nature: Flowers and Landscapes of the Rookwood Pottery, 1880–1940*. Text by Kenneth R. Trapp. New York: Jordan-Volpe Gallery, 1980.

———. *Toward the Modern Style: Rookwood Pottery, The Later Years, 1915–1950*. Text by Kenneth R. Trapp. New York: Jordan-Volpe Gallery, 1983.

Keen, Kirsten Hoving. "Rookwood Pottery at the Turn of the Century: Continuity and Change." In *Celebrate Cincinnati Art*, edited by Kenneth R. Trapp, 71–89. Cincinnati: Cincinnati Art Museum, 1982.

Kircher, Edwin J., Barbara Agranoff, and Joseph Agranoff. *Rookwood: Its Golden Era of Art Pottery, 1880–1929*. Cincinnati, 1969.

Peck, Herbert. *The Book of Rookwood Pottery*. New York: Bonanza Books, 1968.

———. *Catalog of Rookwood Art Pottery Shapes*. 2 vols. Kingston, N.Y.: P-B Enterprises, 1971–1973.

———. *The Second Book of Rookwood Pottery*. Tucson, Ariz.: Privately Printed, 1985.

Taylor, William Watts. "The Rookwood Pottery." *Faenza* 3 (January/March 1915): 10–15.

———. "The Rookwood Pottery (Continuazione e Fine)." *Faenza* 3 (July/September 1915): 81–88.

Trapp, Kenneth R. "Japanese Influence in Early Rookwood Pottery." *Antiques* 103 (January 1973): 193–197.

———. "Rookwood and the Japanese Mania in Cincinnati." *The Cincinnati Historical Society Bulletin* 39 (Spring 1981): 51.

Volpe, Todd M. "Rookwood Landscape Vases and Placques." *Antiques* 117 (April 1980): 838–846.

Weidner, Ruth Irwin. "Toward the Modern Style: Late Rookwood." *American Ceramics* 3, no. 3 (1984): 38–41.

## Roseville Pottery

Huxford, Sharon, and Bob Huxford. *The Collectors Encyclopedia of Roseville Pottery*. First Series. Paducah, Ky.: Collector Books, 1976.

———. *The Collectors Encyclopedia of Roseville Pottery*. Second Series. Paducah, Ky.: Collector Books, 1980.

Snook, Josh, and Anna Snook. *Roseville Donatello Pottery*. Lebanon, Penn.: Privately Printed, 1975.

"George F. Young: A Story of Roseville Pottery." *American Ceramic Society Bulletin* 23 (July 1944): 219–222.

## Louis Comfort Tiffany

DeKay, Charles. *The Art Work of Louis C. Tiffany*. Privately Published, 1914. Reprint. Poughkeepsie, N.Y.: Apollo, 1989.

Doros, Paul E. *The Tiffany Collection of the Chrysler Museum at Norfolk*. Norfolk, Va.: The Chrysler Museum, 1977.

Eidelberg, Martin P. "Tiffany Favrile Pottery: A New Study of a Few Known Facts." *Connoisseur* 169 (September 1968): 57–61.

## University City Pottery

Evans, Paul F. "American Art Porcelain, Two: The Work of the University City Pottery." *Spinning Wheel* 27 (December 1971): 24–26.

Kohlenberger, Lois H. "Ceramics at the People's University." *Ceramics Monthly* 24 (November 1976): 33–37.

"Pottery at University City." *Keramic Studio* 11 (January 1910): 185.

Rhead, Frederick H. "The University City Venture." In *Adelaide Alsop Robineau: Glory in Porcelain*, edited by Peg Weiss. Syracuse, N.Y.: Syracuse University Press with Everson Museum of Art, 1981.

## Artus Van Briggle

Arnest, Barbara M., ed. *Van Briggle Pottery: The Early Years*. Colorado Springs: Colorado Springs Fine Arts Center, 1975.

Bane, Reynolds. "Artus Van Briggle: Man and Artist." *Antiques Journal* 30 (August 1975): 30–33.

Bogue, Dorothy McGraw. *The Van Briggle Story*. Colorado Springs: Century One Press, 1968.

Hecht, Eugene. "Artus Van Briggle: The Formative Years." *Arts and Crafts Quarterly* 1 (January 1987): 1, 7, 12.

## Weller Pottery

Henzke, Lucile. "Weller's Dickens Ware." *Spinning Wheel* 24 (October 1968): 16–18.

———. "Weller's Sicardo." *Spinning Wheel* 25 (September 1969): 26–28, 67.

Markham, Kenneth H. "Weller Sicardo Art Pottery." *Antiques Journal* 19 (September 1964): 18.

## 1920–1950

American Federation of Arts. *Critical Comments on the International Exhibition of Ceramic Art*, by Elizabeth Luther Cary, Royal Cortissoz [and] Helen Appleton Read; reprinted, through the Courtesy of The New York Times, New York Herald-Tribune, [and] The Brooklyn Daily Eagle, for the American Federation of Arts.... [New York], 1928.

American Federation of Arts. *International Exhibition of Ceramic Art*. Washington, D.C.: American Federation of Arts, 1928, 1929. [Portland, Maine: The Southworth Press, 1928].

Anderson, Ross, and Barbara Perry. *The Diversions of Keramos: American Clay Sculpture 1925–1950*. Syracuse, N.Y.: Everson Museum of Art, 1983.

Avery, Louise C. "International Exhibition of Contemporary Ceramic Art." *Metropolitan Museum of Art Bulletin* 23 (October 1928): 232–238.

Bray, Hazel V. "Modern Studio Pottery: 1930–1955." In *The Potter's Art in California: 1885 to 1955*, 23–76. Oakland, Calif.: Oakland Museum, 1978.

Clark, Garth, ed. *Ceramics and Modernism: Response of Artist, Designer, Craftsman and Architect*. Los Angeles: Institute for Ceramic History, 1982.

Clark, Robert Judson, et al. *Design in America: The Cranbrook Vision 1925–1950*. New York: Abrams with The Detroit Institute of Arts and Metropolitan Museum of Art, 1983.

Cowan, R. Guy. "A Potter's View of American Potters." *Art News* 35 (October 24, 1936): 15–16.

———. "The Fine Art of Ceramics as Exemplified in the 1936 Exhibition of Ceramic Art at the Syracuse Museum." *Design* 38 (November 1936): 2–7.

Davies, Karen. *At Home In Manhattan: Modern Decorative Arts, 1925 to the Depression*. New Haven, Conn.: Yale University Art Gallery, 1983.

Duncan, Alastair. "Ceramics." In *American Art Deco*, 104–121. New York: Abrams, 1986.

Hoffman, Jay, Dee Driscole, and Mary Clare Zahler. *A Study in Regional Taste: The May Show 1919–1975*. Cleveland, 1977.

Leach, Bernard. "American Impressions." *Craft Horizons* 10 (Winter 1950): 18–20.

Milliken, William M. "Ohio Ceramics." *Design* 38 (November 1936): 17,41.

Museum of Modern Art. *Machine Art*. Essay by Philip Johnson. New York: Museum of Modern Art, 1934.

Olmsted, Anna Wetherill. "Modern Ceramics." In *Decorative Arts, Official Catalog, Division of Decorative Arts, Golden Gate International Exposition, San Francisco, 1939*, 32–41. San Francisco: San Francisco Bay Exposition Company; H. S. Crocker Company; Schwabacher Frey Company, 1939.

Perry, Barbara. "The Figure Emerges: American Clay Sculpture: 1925–1950." *American Ceramics* 3, no. 1 (1984): 34–41.

Richards, Charles R. "The International Ceramic Exhibition." *Creative Art* 3 (October 1928): xlii–xlvii.

Robineau, Adelaide A. "Report of the Ceramics of the International Exposition at Paris, 1925." *American Ceramic Society Bulletin* 5 (1926): 185–190.

Siple, Ella S. "The International Exhibition of Ceramic Art." *American Magazine of Art* 19 (November 1928): 602–619.

Sprackling, Helen. "Some Contemporary American Potters." *House Beautiful* 72 (November 1932): 310–314, 346.

[Treacy, Eleanor?]. "Ceramics: The Art with the Inferiority Complex." *Fortune* 16 (December 1937): 114–122.

Turnquist, Tom. "Studio Pottery: the Movement After Arts & Crafts." *Arts & Crafts Quarterly* 2 (Winter 1988): 14–15.

Weiss, Peg. *The Art Deco Environment*. Syracuse, N.Y.: Everson Museum of Art, 1976.

———. *The Animal Kingdom in American Art*. Syracuse, N.Y.: Everson Museum of Art, 1978.

## Russel Barnett Aitken

"Aitken, Ceramic Sculptor, Has New York Debut, Walker Galleries." *Art Digest* 10 (December 15, 1935): 20.

Anderson, Ross, and Barbara Perry. *The Diversions of Keramos: American Clay Sculpture 1925–1950*. Syracuse, N.Y.: Everson Museum of Art, 1983.

Archbold, G. "Ceramic Sculpture of Russell Aitken." *Design* 36 (December 1934): 17–19.

"Lackwinni Mangoon." *Time* 25 (May 13, 1935): 34,35.

"Russell Barnett Aitken." *Design* 39 (November 1937): 42–43.

## Laura Andreson

Cox, George. "Laura Andreson." *California Arts and Architecture* 58 (January 1941): 20ff.

Levin, Elaine. "Pioneers of Contemporary American Ceramics: Laura Andreson, Edwin and Mary Scheier." *Ceramics Monthly* 24 (May 1976): 30–36.

Mingei International Museum of World Folk Art. *Laura Andreson: A Retrospective in Clay*. Texts by Bernard Kester and Martha Longenecker. La Jolla, Calif.: Mingei International Museum of World Folk Art, 1982.

Petterson, Richard B. "Timeless Vessels: The Porcelains of Laura Andreson." *American Craft* 42 (August/September 1982): 28–38.

Rico, Diana. "Laura Andreson: An Interview." *American Ceramics* 3, no. 2 (1984): 12–19.

University of California, Art Galleries. *Laura Andreson: Ceramics: Form and Technique*. Essay by J. Bernard Kester. Los Angeles: University of California, Art Galleries, 1970.

## F. Carlton Ball

Ball, F. Carlton. *Decorating Pottery With Clay, Slip and Glaze*. Columbus, Ohio: Professional Publications, 1967.

———. "F. Carlton Ball: Autobiographical Notes, Part 1." *Ceramics Monthly* 29 (March 1981): 48–51.

——. "F. Carlton Ball: Autobiographical Notes, Part 2." *Ceramics Monthly* 29 (April 1981): 32–34.

Lovoos, Janice. "F. Carlton Ball, Master Potter." *Ceramics Monthly* 13 (September 1965): 13–16.

Mowry, LaVerne. "A Ceramic Guild at Mills." *Design* 48 (December 1946): 6–8.

"Profile: A Potter & Painter Collaborate." *Ceramics Monthly* 1 (May 1953): 12–14.

### R. Guy Cowan (Cowan Pottery Studio)

Barbero, Kathleen Hill. "Portfolio: Cowan Pottery." *Ceramics Monthly* 33 (October 1985): 45–50.

Brodbeck, John. "Cowan Pottery." *Spinning Wheel* 29 (March 1973): 24–27.

Cowan Pottery Studio. *Cowan Pottery*. Lakewood, Ohio: Donald H. Calkins, n.d.

Cowan, R. Guy. "What Is Art?" *American Ceramic Society Bulletin* 5 (November 1926): 416–421.

Davis, Elrick B. "Ceramic Sculpture is City's Unique Industry." *Cleveland Press*, July 26, 1928.

Rocky River Public Library. *Cowan Pottery Museum*. Rocky River, Ohio: Rocky River Public Library, 1978.

Scherma, George W. "R. Guy Cowan and His Associates." In *Transactions of the Ceramics Symposium 1979*, edited by Garth R. Clark, 77–82. Los Angeles: Institute for Ceramic History, 1980.

### Edris Eckhardt

Anderson, Ross, and Barbara Perry. *The Diversions of Keramos; American Clay Sculpture 1925–1950*. Syracuse, N.Y.: Everson Museum of Art, 1983.

Eckhardt, Edris. "A Chat With Eckhardt on Hollow-Built Sculpture." *Ceramics Monthly* 7 (September 1959): 16–21.

——. "WPA Ceramics." In *Transactions of the Ceramics Symposium 1979*, edited by Garth R. Clark. Los Angeles: Institute for Ceramic History, 1980.

Marling, Karal Ann. *Federal Art in Cleveland 1933–1943*. Cleveland: Cleveland Public Library, 1974.

——. "New Deal Ceramics: The Cleveland Workshop." *Ceramics Monthly* 25 (June 1977): 25–31.

### Waylande Desantis Gregory

Anderson, Ross, and Barbara Perry. *The Diversions of Keramos; American Clay Sculpture 1925–1950*. Syracuse, N.Y.: Everson Museum of Art, 1983.

Gregory, Waylande. "Ceramic Sculpture." *Design* 43 (December 1941): 12–13.

Harrison, Helen, et al. *Dawn of a New Day: The New York World's Fair 1939/40*. New York: New York University Press, 1980.

Levin, Elaine. "Monumental Ambitions: Waylande Gregory." *American Ceramics* 5, no. 4 (1987): 40–49.

Roberts, Mary Fanton. "What's New in American Ceramics." *Arts and Decoration* 47 (December 1937): 26ff.

Watson, Ernest W. "Waylande Gregory's Ceramic Art: Interview." *American Artist* 8 (September 1944): 12–14, 34, 39.

### Maija Grotell

Cranbrook Academy of Art. *Maija Grotell*. Bloomfield Hills, Mich.: Cranbrook Academy of Art, 1967.

Levin, Elaine. "Pioneers of Contemporary American Ceramic Art: Maija Grotell, Herbert Sanders." *Ceramics Monthly* 24 (November 1976): 48–54.

——. "Pioneers of the Vessel Aesthetic: Glen Lukens and Maija Grotell." In *Transactions of the Ceramics Symposium 1979*, edited by Garth R. Clark. Los Angeles: Institute for Ceramic History, 1980.

——. "Maija Grotell." *American Ceramics* 1 (Winter 1982): 42–45.

Schlanger, Jeff. "Maija Grotell." *Craft Horizons* 29 (November/December 1969): 14–23.

### Thomas Samuel Haile

Clark, Garth. "Sam Haile 1909–1948: A Memorial." *Studio Potter* 7, no. 1 (1978): 4–9.

De Trey, Marianne. "Sam Haile: Recollections by Marianne Haile." *Studio Potter* 7, no. 1 (1978): 10–11.

Haile, T. S. "English and American Ceramic Design Problems." *American Ceramic Society Bulletin* 21 (1942): 317–320.

Sewter, A. C. "T. S. Haile, Potter and Painter." *Apollo* 44 (December 1946): 160–163.

——. *T. S. Haile 1908–1948: Memorial Exhibition*. London: Craft Centre of Great Britain, 1951.

### Maria Martinez

Marriott, Alice. *Maria: The Potter of San Ildefonso*. Norman, Okla.: University of Oklahoma Press, 1948.

Peterson, Susan. "Maria Martinez Pueblo Potter." *Craft Horizons* 36 (February 1976): 44–47.

——. *The Living Tradition of Maria Martinez*. Tokyo: Kodansha International, 1977.

——. *Maria Martinez: Five Generations of Potters*. Washington, D.C.: Smithsonian Institution Press, 1978.

Rubinstein, Charlotte Streifer. *American Women Artists From Early Indian Times to the Present*. Boston: G. K. Hall, 1981.

### Gertrud and Otto Natzler

Andreson, Laura. "The Natzlers." *California Arts and Architecture* 58 (July 1941): 14ff.

Barnard, Rob. "Otto Natzler." *New Art Examiner* 13 (September 1985): 60–61.

Craft and Folk Art Museum. *Natzler*. Intro. by Laura Andreson. Los Angeles: Craft and Folk Art Museum, 1977.

Henderson, Rose. "Gertrud and Otto Natzler." *Design* 49 (January 1948): 14.

Levin, Elaine. "An Interview with Otto Natzler." *Ceramics Monthly* 30 (Summer 1982): 64–67.

Los Angeles County Museum of Art. *The Ceramic Work of Gertrud and Otto Natzler: A Retrospective Exhibition*. Los Angeles: Los Angeles County Museum of Art, 1966.

——. *Gertrud and Otto Natzler: Ceramics*. Catalog of the Collection of Mrs. Leonard M. Sperry and a Monograph by Otto Natzler. Los Angeles: Los Angeles County Museum of Art, 1968.

M. H. DeYoung Memorial Museum. *The Ceramic Work of Gertrud and Otto Natzler: A Retrospective Exhibition*. San Francisco: M. H. DeYoung Memorial Museum, 1971.

Natzler, Otto. "The Natzler Glazes." *Craft Horizons* 24 (July/August 1964): 24–27, 39–41.

Renwick Gallery. National Collection of Fine Arts. *Form and Fire: Natzler Ceramics 1939–1972*. Washington, D.C.: Smithsonian Institution Press, 1973.

Rubenfeld, Florence. "Otto Natzler: Solo." *American Craft* 42 (February/March 1982): 2–5.

### Henry Varnum Poor

Lebow, Edward. "Henry Varnum Poor." *American Ceramics* 3, no. 3 (1984): 52–59.

Pennsylvania State University, Museum of Art. *Henry Varnum Poor 1887–1970: A Retrospective Exhibition*. University Park, Penn.: Pennsylvania State University, Museum of Art. 1983.

Poor, Henry V. "Design: A Common Language." *Craft Horizons* 11 (November 1951): 19–21.

——. "Tile Mural." *Craft Horizons* 14 (November/December 1954): 28–30.

——. *A Book of Pottery: From Mud to Immortality*. Englewood Cliffs, N.J.: Prentice-Hall, 1958.

——. "Henry Varnum Poor: A Ceramics Monthly Portfolio." *Ceramics Monthly* 32 (March 1984): 31–41.

Soyer, Raphael, et al. *Henry Varnum Poor: 1887–1970*. University Park, Penn.: Museum of Art, Pennsylvania State University, 1984.

Steigleder, Linda. "Henry Varnum Poor: The Effect of the Hudson River Valley. . . ." *Studio Potter* 12 (December 1983): 53–57.

——. "Henry Varnum Poor 1887–1970." *American Craft* 44 (February/March 1984): 22–27.

### Ted Randall

Bernstein, Melvin H. "The Art and Design Years of Theodore A. Randall: 1958–1973." Part III of *Art and Design at Alfred: Chronicle of a Ceramics College*, 161–216. Philadelphia: Associated University Presses, 1986.

Higby, Wayne. "Ted Randall 1914–1985." *American Craft* 46 (February/March 1986): 95.

Joe and Emily Lowe Art Gallery. Syracuse University. *Ted Randall (1914–1985): A Retrospective*. Texts by Melvin H. Bernstein and Val Cushing. Syracuse, N.Y.: Joe and Emily Lowe Art Gallery, 1987.

Lebow, Edward. "Ted Randall 1914–1985." *American Ceramics* 4, no. 4 (1986): 7.

Randall, Ted. "Notions About the Usefulness of Pottery." *Pottery Quarterly* 7, no. 25 (1961).

——. "The University Impact on Ceramics: A Personal Perspective of the Last Five Decades." *NCECA Journal* 5 (1984): 44–48.

——. "Being and Meaning." *Ceramics Monthly* 34 (January 1986): 55.

Wechsler, Susan. "Ted Randall: An Interview." *Amer-

*ican Ceramics* 3, no. 2 (1984): 48–57.

## Herbert Sanders

Ball, Fred. "Herbert Sanders." *Ceramics Monthly* 19 (November 1971): 14–17.

Levin, Elaine. "Pioneers of Contemporary American Ceramics: Maija Grotell, Herbert Sanders." *Ceramics Monthly* 24 (November 1976): 48–54.

Sanders, Herbert H. *Glazes for Special Effects.* New York: Watson-Guptill, 1974.

Sanders, Herbert H., and K. Tomimoto. *The World of Japanese Ceramics: Historical and Modern Techniques.* Tokyo: Kodansha International, 1967.

## Edwin and Mary Scheier

Lebow, Edward. "A Sense of Line." *American Craft* 48 (February/March 1988): 24–31.

Levin, Elaine. "Pioneers of Contemporary American Ceramics: Laura Andreson, Edwin and Mary Scheier." *Ceramic Monthly* 24 (May 1976): 30–36.

## Viktor Schreckengost

Anderson, Ross, and Barbara Perry. *The Diversions of Keramos: American Clay Sculpture 1925–1950.* Syracuse, N.Y.: Everson Museum of Art, 1983.

Cleveland Institute of Art. *Viktor Schreckengost: Retrospective Exhibition.* Essays by Laurence Schmeckebier and Joseph McCullough. Cleveland: Cleveland Institute of Art, 1976.

Grafly, Dorothy. "Viktor Schreckengost." *American Artist* 13 (May 1949): 48–56.

"New Designs for Mass Production: Four Sets of Tableware Designed by V. Schreckengost." *Design* 37 (November 1935): 14–15.

Schreckengost, Viktor. "Viktor Schreckengost of Ohio." *Studio Potter* 11 (December 1982): 74–79.

Stubblebine, James, and Martin Eidelberg. "Viktor Schreckengost and the Cleveland School." *Craft Horizons* 35 (June 1975): 34–35, 52–53.

"Viktor Schreckengost." *The Studio* 1 (1933).

## Carl Walters

Anderson, Ross, and Barbara Perry. *The Diversions of Keramos: American Clay Sculpture 1925–1950.* Syracuse, N.Y.: Everson Museum of Art, 1983.

Brace, Ernest. "Carl Walters." *Creative Art* 10 (June 1932): 431–436.

"Carl Walters: Sculptor of Ceramics." *Index of Twentieth Century Artists* 3 (June 1936): 305–6.

Homer, William I. "Carl Walters, Ceramic Sculptor." *Art in America* 44 (Fall 1956): 42–47, 64–65.

Museum of Art of Ogunquit. *A Catalogue of the Ceramic Sculpture of Carl Walters, 1883–1955.* Publications on American Art, 1. Compiled by William I. Homer. Ogunquit, Maine: Museum of Art of Ogunquit. Printed by Princeton University Press, 1958.

Walters, Carl. "Tools and Materials: Ceramic Sculpture." *American Magazine of Art* 28 (August/September 1935): 500–502, 561–563.

## Vally Wieselthier

Anderson, Ross, and Barbara Perry. *The Diversions of Keramos: American Clay Sculpture 1925–1950.* Syracuse, N.Y.: Everson Museum of Art, 1983.

Canfield, Ruth. "The Pottery of Vally Wieselthier." *Design* 31 (November 1929): 103–105.

Levin, Elaine. "Vally Wieselthier/Susi Singer." *American Craft* 46 (December 1986/January 1987): 46–51.

Neuwirth, Waltrand. *Wiener Keramik.* Brunswick, West Germany: Klinkhardt and Biermann, 1975.

———. *Wiener Werkstatte: Avantgarde, Art Deco, Industrial Design.* Vienna: The Author, 1984.

"Vally Wieselthier." *Design* 39 (November 1937): 46–47.

"Vally Wieselthier's Austellung in New-York." *Deutsche Kunst und Dekoration* (1929): 39–43.

Wieselthier, Vally. "Ceramics." *Design* 31 (November 1929): 101–2.

———. "Studying Art in Vienna: A Brief Autobiography." *Arts and Decoration* 44 (February 1936): 28ff.

## Frans Wildenhain

Cowles, Barbara, ed. *Frans Remembered.* New York: Fishers, 1980.

Herdle, Isabel. "Frans Wildenhain 1905–1980." *American Craft* 40 (April/May 1980): 34–37.

Johnston, R. H. *Frans Wildenhain: A Chronology of a Master Potter.* Rochester, N.Y.: Rochester Institute of Technology. College of Fine and Applied Arts. Bevier Gallery, 1975.

Levin, Elaine. *Frans Wildenhain.* Rochester, N.Y.: University of Rochester, Memorial Art Gallery, 1980.

———. "Portfolio: Frans Wildenhain." *Ceramics Monthly* 33 (February 1985): 23–30.

Norton, Deborah. "Frans Wildenhain." *American Ceramics* 4, no. 2 (1985): 48–55.

Richards, M. C. "Frans Wildenhain." *Craft Horizons* 35 (February 1975): 28–29.

State University of New York, University Art Gallery, Binghamton, *Frans Wildenhain Retrospective.* Binghamton, N.Y.: SUNY, University Art Gallery, 1975.

University of Rochester, Memorial Art Gallery. *Paley/Castle/Wildenhain.* Rochester, N.Y.: University of Rochester, Memorial Art Gallery, 1979.

## Marguerite Wildenhain

Press, Nancy, and Terry F. A. Weihs. *Marguerite: A Retrospective Exhibition of the Work of a Master Potter.* Ithaca, N.Y.: Cornell University, Herbert F. Johnson Museum of Art, 1980.

Prothro, Hunt. "Sustained Presence: Marguerite Wildenhain." *American Craft* 40 (August/September 1980): 28–31, 76.

Wildenhain, Marguerite. "Pottery as a Creative Craft." *Craft Horizons* 10 (Summer 1950): 27–29.

———. "An Open Letter to Bernard Leach from Marguerite Wildenhain." *Craft Horizons* 13 (May/June 1953): 43–44.

———. *Pottery: Form and Expression.* New York: American Craftsmen's Council, 1962.

———. *The Invisible Core: A Potter's Life and Thoughts.* Palo Alto, Calif.: Pacific Books, 1973.

———. *. . . That We Look and See: An Admirer Looks at the Indians.* Seguin, Tex.: South Bear Press, 1980.

## Thelma Frazier Winter

Anderson, Ross, and Barbara Perry. *The Diversions of Keramos: American Clay Sculpture 1925–1950.* Syracuse, N.Y.: Everson Museum of Art, 1983.

Watson, Ernest W. "The Ceramic Sculpture of Thelma Frazier Winter." *American Artist* 16 (May 1952): 20–23, 52–53.

Winter, Thelma Frazier. *The Art and Craft of Ceramic Sculpture.* London: Applied Science Publishers, 1973.

## Beatrice Wood

Bryan, Robert. "The Ceramics of Beatrice Wood." *Craft Horizons* 30 (March/April 1970): 28–33.

California State University, Main Gallery, Fullerton. *Beatrice Wood Retrospective.* Essays by Dextra Frankel, Garth R. Clark, and Francis M. Naumann. Fullerton, Calif.: California State University, Main Gallery. 1983.

Clark, Garth, and Francis M. Naumann. "Beatrice Wood." *American Craft* 43 (August/September 1983): 24–27, 80.

Handley, Richard, and Jim Danisch. "Beatrice Wood." *Ceramics Monthly* 31 (April 1983): 32–37.

Hapgood, Elizabeth R. "All the Cataclysms: A Brief Survey of the Life of Beatrice Wood." *Arts Magazine* 52 (March 1978): 107–109.

Naumann, Francis M. "Beatrice Wood." *American Craft* 43 (August/September 1983): 24–26, 80.

Phoenix Museum of Art. *Beatrice Wood: A Retrospective.* Essay by Robert H. Frankel. Phoenix, Ariz.: Phoenix Museum of Art, 1973.

Wood, Beatrice. *I Shock Myself: The Autobiography of Beatrice Wood.* Edited by Lindsay Smith. Ojai, Calif.: Dillingham Press, 1985.

## Russel Wright

Hennessey, William J. *Russel Wright: American Designer.* Cambridge, Mass.: MIT Press, 1983.

Pulos, Arthur. "Russel Wright: American Designer." *American Craft* 43 (October/November 1983): 10–13.

Wright, Russel. Archive. George Arents Research Library. Syracuse University, Syracuse, N.Y.

# 1950–1988

Albright, Thomas. *Art in the San Francisco Bay Area, 1945–1980: An Illustrated History.* Berkeley, Calif.: University of California Press, 1985.

American Craft Museum. *The Clay Figure.* New York: American Craft Museum, 1981.

———. *Craft Today: Poetry of the Physical.* Essays by Paul J. Smith and Edward Lucie-Smith. New York: American Craft Museum, 1986.

Axel, Jan, and Karen McCready. *Porcelain: Traditions and New Visions*. New York: Watson-Guptill, 1981.

Brody, Harvey. *The Book of Low–Fire Ceramics*. New York: Holt, Rinehart and Winston, 1980.

Brooklyn Museum. *Designer Craftsmen U. S. A.*. Essay by Anna Wetherill Olmsted. Brooklyn, N.Y.: Brooklyn Museum, 1953.

"California Crafts and Craftsmen." *Craft Horizons* 16 (September 1956): 11–20, 30–33.

Campbell Museum. *Soup Tureens: 1976*. Text by Ralph Collier and Helen Drutt. Camden, N.J.: Campbell Museum, 1976.

———. *Soup, Soup, Beautiful Soup*. Text by Helen Drutt. Campbell Place, N.J.: Campbell Museum, 1983.

Canavier, Elena Karina. "Kohler Conference: Art/Industry Alliance." *Ceramics Monthly* 21 (November 1973): 24–27.

"Ceramics East Coast." *Craft Horizons* 26 (June 1966): 20–24, 98.

Chalke, John. "The Ceramic Identity Scandal of the '70s." *Ceramics Monthly* 28 (December 1980): 25, 27, 29.

Claremont Colleges, Galleries. *Earth and Fire: The Fred Marer Collection of Contemporary Ceramics*. Claremont, Calif.: Galleries of the Claremont Colleges, 1984.

Clark, Garth. *American Potters: the Work of Twenty Modern Masters*. New York: Watson-Guptill, 1981.

———, ed. *Ceramic Echoes: Historical References in Contemporary Ceramic Art*. Kansas City: Mo.: Nelson Atkins Museum of Art, 1983.

———. "Leach in America: 1950's." *Ceramic Arts* 1, no. 2 (1984).

———. "The Pictorialization of the Vessel: American Ceramics." *Crafts* 80 (May/June 1986): 40–47.

Clark, Garth, and Sanford S. Shaman. *The Contemporary American Potter: Recent Vessels*. Cedar Falls, Iowa: Art Gallery, University of Northern Iowa, 1980.

Clark, Garth, and Oliver Watson. *American Potters Today*. London: Victoria and Albert Museum, 1986.

Clark, Garth, et al. *Who's Afraid of American Pottery*. 'sHertogenbosch, The Netherlands: Dienst voor Beeldende Kunst, 1983.

Cochran, Malcolm. *Contemporary Clay: Ten Approaches*. Hanover, N.H.: Dartmouth College, 1976.

Coplans, John. "Sculpture in California." *Artforum* 2 (August 1963): 3–6.

———. "Out of Clay: West Coast Sculpture Emerges as a Strong Regional Trend." *Art in America* 51 (December 1963): 40–43.

———. *Abstract Expressionist Ceramics*. Irvine, Calif.: Art Gallery, University of California, 1966.

Cranbrook Academy of Art. *Cranbrook Ceramics 1950–1980*. Text by Linda Parks. Bloomfield Hills, Mich.: Cranbrook Academy of Art, 1983.

DeCordova Museum. *A Passionate Vision: Contemporary Ceramics From the Daniel Jacobs Collection*. Lincoln, Mass.: DeCordova Museum, 1984.

Depew, Dave. "The Archie Bray Foundation." *Ceramics Monthly* 20 (May 1972): 18–23.

Dormer, Peter. *The New Ceramics: Trends & Traditions*. New York: Thames and Hudson, 1986.

Drutt, Helen. *Robert L. Pfannebecker Collection: A Selection of Contemporary Crafts*. Philadelphia: Moore College of Art, 1980.

———. *American Clay Artists '83*. Philadelphia: Clay Studio Gallery, 1983.

Drutt, Helen, and Wayne Higby. *Contemporary Arts: An Expanding View*. Princeton, N.J.: The Squibb Gallery, 1986.

Duberman, Martin. *Black Mountain College: An Exploration in Community*. New York: E. P. Dutton, 1972.

Evanston Art Center. *The Ceramic Vessel as Metaphor*. Evanston, Ill.: Evanston Art Center, 1977.

Everson Museum of Art. *New Works in Clay by Contemporary Painters and Sculptors*. Text by Margie Hughto. Syracuse, N.Y.: Everson Museum of Art, 1976.

———. *Nine West Coast Clay Sculptors*. Texts by Margie Hughto and Judy S. Schwartz. Syracuse, N.Y.: Everson Museum of Art, 1978.

———. *New Works in Clay III*. Text by Margie Hughto and Brad Benson. Syracuse, N.Y.: Everson Museum of Art, 1981.

Fairbanks, Jonathan L., and Kenworth W. Moffett. *Directions in Contemporary American Ceramics*. Boston: Museum of Fine Arts, 1984.

Falk, Lorne. "The Omaha Brickworks." *American Ceramics* 2, no. 4 (1984): 44–47.

*Functional Glamour: Utility in Contemporary American Ceramics*. Essays by Garth Clark and Gert Staal. 'sHertogenbosch, The Netherlands: Museum het Kruithuis, 1987.

Grossmont College. *Viewpoint: Ceramics 1977*. Essay by Erik Gronborg. El Cajon, Calif.: Grossmont College Art Gallery, 1977.

———. *Viewpoint: Ceramics 1979*. Essay by Garth Clark. El Cajon, Calif.: Grossmont College Art Gallery, 1979.

———. *Viewpoint: Ceramics 1980*. Essay by Sandy Ballatore. El Cajon, Calif.: Grossmont College, 1983.

Hall, Julie. *Tradition and Change: The New American Craftsman*. New York: E. P. Dutton, 1977.

Harris, Mary Emma. *The Arts at Black Mountain College*. Cambridge, Mass.: MIT Press, 1987.

Hayward Art Gallery. *Nut Art*. Hayward, Calif.: Hayward Art Gallery, California State University, 1972.

Hepburn, Tony. "American Ceramics 1970." *Ceramic Review* 7 (1970).

Hopkins, Henry T. *50 West Coast Artists*. San Francisco: Chronicle Books, 1981.

J. B. Speed Museum. *What's New? American Ceramics Since 1980: the Alfred and Mary Shands Collection*. Essays by Peter Morrin and the Reverend Alfred Shands. Louisville, Ky.: J. B. Speed Museum, 1987.

Joe and Emily Lowe Art Gallery, Syracuse University. *New Works in Clay II*. Text by Margie Hughto. Syracuse, N.Y.: Joe and Emily Lowe Art Gallery, Syracuse University, 1978.

Jones, Mady. *Figurative Clay Sculpture: Northern California*. San Francisco: Quay Gallery, 1982.

Kalamazoo Institute of Art. *Contemporary Ceramics: the Artist's Viewpoint*. Kalamazoo, Mich.: Kalamazoo Institute of Art, 1977.

Kansas City Art Institute. *Eight Independent Production Potters*. Kansas City, Mo.: Kansas City Art Institute, 1976.

Knight, Christopher. "Otis Clay: A Revolution in the Tradition of Pottery." *Los Angeles Herald Examiner*, September 29, 1982.

Laguna Beach Museum of Art. *Illusionistic Realism as Defined in Contemporary Ceramic Sculpture*. Essay by Lukman Glasgow. Laguna Beach, Calif.: Laguna Beach Museum of Art, 1977.

Lane, Peter. *Studio Ceramics*. Radnor, Penn.: Chilton, 1980.

———. *Studio Porcelain*. Radnor, Penn.: Chilton, 1980.

Los Angeles Institute of Contemporary Art. *Pacific Connections*. Los Angeles, Calif.: Los Angeles Institute of Contemporary Art, 1985.

Los Angeles Municipal Art Gallery. *Art in Clay: 1950's to 1980's in Southern California*. Exhibition by Betty Warner Sheinbaum. Essays by Susan Peterson, Gerald Nordland, and Eudorah M. Moore. Los Angeles: Los Angeles Municipal Art Gallery, 1984.

McCloud, Mac. "Otis Clay: 1956–1957." *Ceramic Arts* 1, no. 1 (1983).

Maryland Institute, College of Art. *Clay Bodies: Autio–DeStaebler–Frey*. Essay by Ron Lang. Baltimore: Maryland Institute, College of Art, 1982.

Museum of Contemporary Crafts. *Clayworks: 20 Americans*. New York: Museum of Contemporary Crafts, 1971.

———. *Young Americans: Clay/Glass*. New York: American Crafts Council, 1978.

National Council for Education in the Ceramic Arts. *NCECA: San José '82*. Edited by, Marcia Chamberlain, Judith Bettleheim, and Jay Kvapil. San José, Calif.: NCECA, 1982.

New Gallery. State University of Iowa. *Clay Today*. Text by J. McKinnell and Abner Jonas. Ames, Iowa: New Gallery, State University of Iowa, 1962.

Newport Harbor Art Museum. *Contemporary American Ceramics: Twenty Artists*. Text by Karen McCready. Newport Harbor, Calif.: Newport Harbor Art Museum, 1985.

Nordness, Lee. *Objects: U.S.A.*. New York: Viking Press, 1970.

Peterson, Susan. "Exhibitions: Scripps Annual." [25 Year Retrospective] *Craft Horizons* 29 (September/October 1969): 62–63.

Petterson, Richard B. *Ceramic Art in America*. Columbus, Ohio: Professional Publications, 1969.

Philbrook Art Center. *The Eloquent Object: The Evolution of American Art in Craft Media Since 1945*. Text by Marcia Manhart and Tom Manhart. Tulsa, Okla.: Philbrook Art Center, 1987.

Plagens, Peter. *Sunshine Muse: Contemporary Art on the West Coast*. New York: Praeger, 1974.

Pugliese, Joseph. "Ceramics from Davis." *Craft Horizons* 26 (November/December 1966): 26–29.

———. "The Decade: Ceramics." *Craft Horizons* 33 (February 1973): 46–53, 76–77.

Pyron, Bernard. "The Tao and Dada of Recent American Ceramic Art." *Artforum* 2 (March 1964): 41–43.

Renwick Gallery. *The Object as Poet.* Essay by Rose Slivka. Washington, D.C.: Smithsonian Institution Press, 1977.

———. *American Porcelain: New Expressions in an Ancient Art.* Essay by Lloyd E. Herman. Forest Grove, Oreg.: Timber Press for the Renwick Gallery of the National Collection of Fine Arts, Smithsonian Institution, 1980.

Richards, M. C. "Black Mountain College: A Golden Seed." *Craft Horizons* 37 (June 1977): 21–22, 70.

Richardson, Brenda. "California Ceramics." *Art in America* 57 (May/June 1969): 104–105.

Rubenfeld, Florence. "Bay Area Clay: Forerunner to Postmodernism." *New Art Examiner* 13 (September 1985): 44–47.

San Diego Museum of Art. *Sculpture in California, 1975–1980.* Text by Richard Armstrong. San Diego: San Diego Museum of Art, 1980.

San Francisco Museum of Modern Art. *A Decade of Ceramic Art: 1962–1972: From the Collection of Professor and Mrs. R. Joseph Monsen.* Text by Suzanne Foley. San Francisco: San Francisco Museum of Modern Art, 1972.

Scripps College, Art Gallery. *The Fred and Mary Marer Collection: 30th Annual Ceramics Exhibition.* Texts by Jim Melchert and Paul Soldner. Claremont, Calif.: Scripps College, Art Gallery, 1974.

Selz, Peter. *Funk.* Berkeley, Calif.: University of California, Art Museum, Berkeley, 1967.

Senska, Frances. "Pottery in a Brickyard." *American Craft* 42 (February/March 1982): 32–35.

Shapiro, Howard-Yana, and James Yood. "Ceramic Art: Wading Into the Mainstream? *New Art Examiner* 13 (September 1985): 44–47.

Slivka, Rose. "The New Ceramic Presence." *Craft Horizons* 21 (July/August 1961): 30–37.

———. "The American Craftsman/1964." *Craft Horizons* 24 (May/June 1964): 10–11, 32–68, 112–113, 126.

———. *West Coast Ceramics.* Amsterdam: Stedelijk Museum, 1979.

Soldner, Paul, and Peter Voulkos. "Ceramics West Coast." *Craft Horizons* 26 (June 1966): 24, 28, 97.

Southern Illinois University, Edwardsville. *Surface/Function/Shape: Selections from the Earl Millard Collection.* Exhibition by James Ropiequet Schmidt. Essays by Jeff Perrone and Earl Millard. Edwardsville, Ill.: Southern Illinois University, Edwardsville, 1985.

———. *Figurative Clay '87.* Text by James Ropiequet Schmidt. Edwardsville, Ill.: Southern Illinois University, Edwardsville, 1987.

University of Iowa Museum of Art. *Centering on Contemporary Clay: American Ceramics from the Joan Mannheimer Collection.* Text by Jim Melchert. Iowa City: University of Iowa Museum of Art, 1981.

Victoria and Albert Museum. *20 American Studio Potters.* London: Victoria and Albert Museum, 1966.

———. *International Ceramics 72.* London: Victoria and Albert Museum, 1972.

Wechsler, Susan. *Low-Fire Ceramics: A New Direction in American Clay.* New York: Watson-Guptill, 1981.

———. *The Raw Edge: Ceramics of the '80s.* Greenvale, N.Y.: C. W. Post Center, Long Island University, 1983.

———. "Views on the Figure." *American Ceramics* 3, no. 1(1984):16–25.

Whitney Museum of American Art. *Ceramic Sculpture: Six Artists.* Essays by Richard Marshall and Suzanne Foley. New York: Whitney Museum of American Art with the University of Washington Press, 1981.

William Hayes Ackland Memorial Art Center. *Contemporary Ceramic Sculpture.* Essay by Louise Hobbs. Chapel Hill, N.C.: William Hayes Ackland Memorial Art Center, University of North Carloina, 1977.

## Robert Arneson

Arneson, Robert. *My Head in Ceramics.* Benicia, Calif.: Privately Published, 1972.

Chicago. Museum of Contemporary Art. *Robert Arneson.* Text by Suzanne Foley and Stephen Prokopoff. Chicago: Museum of Contemporary Art, 1974.

Cleveland Museum of Art. *Robert Arneson: Portrait Sculptures.* Essay by Tom E. Hinson. Cleveland: Cleveland Museum of Art, 1987.

Des Moines Art Center. *Robert Arneson: A Retrospective.* Text by Neal Benezra. Des Moines, Iowa: Des Moines Art Center, 1985. Biblio., 100–101.

Doubet, Ward. "Robert Arneson: Portrait of the Artist as a Popular Iconoclast." *American Ceramics* 6, no. 1 (1987): 22–31.

Kuspit, Donald. "Robert Arneson's Sense of Self: Squirming in Procrustrean Place." *American Craft* 46 (October/November 1986): 36–45, 64–68.

State University of New York, Art Gallery, New Paltz. *In the Eye of The Beholder: A Portrait of Our Time.* Text by Michael McTwigan. New Paltz, N.Y.: SUNY, Art Gallery, 1985.

## Rudy Autio

Autio, Rudy. "About Drawing." *Studio Potter* 14 (December 1985): 49–50.

———. "My Development as an Artist: Working in Ceramics from 1950–1985." *Fusion* 10 (Winter 1987): 31.

Kangas, Matthew. "Rudy Autio: Massive Narrations." *American Craft* 40 (October/November 1980): 12–17.

———. *Rudy Autio: A Retrospective.* Missoula, Mont.: University of Montana, 1983.

———. "Rudy Autio." *American Ceramics* 3, no. 4 (1985): 64–65.

Lebow, Edward. "The Flesh Pots of Rudy Autio." *American Ceramics* 4, no. 1 (1985): 32–35.

## Ralph Bacerra

Bodine, Sarah. "Ralph Bacerra." *American Ceramics* 2, no. 3 (1983): 48.

Levin, Elaine. "Ralph Bacerra." *Ceramics Monthly* 25 (April 1977): 21–27.

McCloud, Mac. "Deliberately Decorative: The Ceramics of Ralph Bacerra." *American Craft* 47 (June/July 1987): 50–55.

## Toby Buonagurio

Klein, Ellen Lee. "Toby Buonagurio: More Optical Bounce to the Ounce." *Arts Magazine* 60 (March 1986): 55–57.

Mackin, Jeanne. "Toby Buonagurio." *Ceramics Monthly* 30 (December 1982): 36–38.

Piche, Thomas. "Toby Buonagurio." *American Ceramics* 1 (Summer 1982): 10–13.

Shannon, Mark: "Toby Buonagurio." *American Ceramics* 6, no. 1 (1987): 46.

Wechsler, Susan. *Ceramics Today: T. Buonagurio U. S. A.* Geneva: Editions Olizane, 1984.

## Mark Burns

Sachs, Sid. "Mark Burns: Saints and Sinners." *American Ceramics* 3, no. 1 (1984): 58–64.

## Elena Karina Canavier

Everson Museum of Art. *Elena Karina: New Porcelain Vessels and Drawings.* Syracuse, N.Y.: Everson Museum of Art, 1979.

Huntsville Museum of Art. *Karina: New Works in Porcelain.* Huntsville, Ala.: Huntsville Museum of Art, 1982.

## Val Cushing

Bodine, Sarah, and Ed Lebow. "Point Counterpoint: Val Cushing." *American Ceramics* 1 (Summer 1982): 14–17.

"Val Cushing: New Work." *Ceramics Monthly* 30 (October 1982): 27–29.

"Val Cushing." *Ceramics Monthly* 30 (April 1982): 79, 81, 83.

## Stephen De Staebler

Burstein, Joanne. "Stephen De Staebler." *American Ceramics* 3, no. 1 (1984): 42–51.

De Staebler, Stephen. "The Inside of the Outside." *Ceramics Monthly* 34 (September 1986): 36–38.

Edwards, Sharon. "A Conversation with Stephen De Staebler." *Ceramics Monthly* 24 (April 1981): 60–62.

Levin, Elaine. "Stephen De Staebler." *Ceramics Monthly* 29 (April 1981): 54–59.

San Francisco Museum of Modern Art. *Stephen De Staebler: The Figure.* Exhibition by Lynn Gamwell. Essay by Donald Kuspit. San Francisco: Chronicle Books, 1987.

## Richard Devore

Artner, Alan G. "Richard Devore." *American Ceramics* 1 (Winter 1982): 47.

Milwaukee Art Museum. *Richard Devore: 1972–1982.* Text by Gerald Nordland. Milwaukee, Wis.: Milwaukee Art Museum, 1983.

"Richard Devore." *Ceramics Monthly* 29 (October 1981): 38–42.

Rubenfeld, Florence. "The Pottery of Richard Devore." *American Craft* 43 (October/November 1983): 34–38.

## Rick Dillingham

Kane, Sid. "Patchwork Pots." *American Craft* 41 (October/November 1981): 36–39.

Roberts, Dave. "American Raku." *Ceramic Review* 76 (July/August 1982): 22–25.

Zwinger, Susan. "Rick Dillingham." *American Ceramics* 3, no. 1 (1984): 66–67.

## Jack Earl

Cohen, Ronny H. "Jack Earl." *American Craft* 45 (August/September 1985): 18–23.

John Michael Kohler Arts Center. *Ohio Boy: The Ceramic Sculpture of Jack Earl.* Essay by Jack Earl. Sheboygan, Wis.: John Michael Kohler Arts Center, 1987.

Klassen, John. "A Conversation with Jack Earl." *Ceramics Monthly* 29 (October 1981): 68–70.

Museum of Contemporary Crafts. *Porcelains by Jack Earl.* Intro. by Karl F. Cohen. New York: American Crafts Council, 1971.

Nordness, Lee. "Jack Earl." *American Ceramics* 4, no. 1 (1985): 20–31.

———. *Jack Earl: The Genesis and Triumphant Survival of an Underground Ohio Artist.* Racine, Wis.: Perimeter Press, 1985.

## Ken Ferguson

Ferguson, Kenneth. "Starting at the Ears." *Studio Potter* 14 (December 1985): 52–53.

Melcher, Victoria Kirsch. "Tradition and Vitality: The Ceramics of Ken Ferguson." *American Craft* 39 (December 1979/January 1980): 2–7.

Rubin, Michael G. "Kenneth Ferguson." *American Ceramics* 2, no. 3 (1983): 42–47.

Sewalt, Charlotte. "An Interview with Ken Ferguson." *Ceramics Monthly* 26 (February 1978): 25–31.

## Mary Frank

De Cordova and Dana Museum. *Natural Histories: Mary Frank's Sculpture, Prints, and Drawings.* Essays by Hayden Herrera and Stella Kramrisch. Lincoln, Mass: De Cordova and Dana Museum and Park, 1988.

Hays, Johanna Burstein. "Mary Frank." *American Ceramics* 3, no. 3 (1984): 60–61.

Herrera, Hayden. *Mary Frank: Sculpture and Monotypes 1981/1982.* New York: Zabriskie Gallery, 1983.

Kramer, Hilton. "The Sculpture of Mary Frank: Poetical, Metaphorical, Interior." *The New York Times,* February 22, 1970.

———. "Art: Sensual, Serene Sculpture." *The New York Times,* January 25, 1975.

Neuberger Museum. State University of New York, Purchase. *Mary Frank: Sculpture/Drawings/Prints.* Essay by Hayden Herrera. Purchase, NY: Neuberger Museum, 1978.

## Helen Frankenthaler

Gray, C. "Ceramics by Twelve Artists." *Art in America* 52 (December 1964): 27–41.

*Helen Frankenthaler: Clay Sculpture.* New York: André Emmerich Gallery, 1977.

Lafean, Richard. "Ceramics by Twelve Artists." *Craft Horizons* 25 (January/February 1965): 30–33.

*Painters and Clay: A Study in Collaboration 1930–1982.* Los Angeles: Garth Clark Gallery, 1982.

## Viola Frey

Crocker Art Museum. *Viola Frey: Retrospective.* Essay by Garth Clark. Sacramento, Calif.: Crocker Art Museum, 1981.

Dunham, Judith L. "Ceramic Bricolage: The Protean Art of Viola Frey." *American Craft* 41 (August/September 1981): 29–33.

Kelley, Jeff. "Viola Frey." *American Ceramics* 3, no. 1 (1984): 26–33.

Moore College of Art. *It's All Part of the Clay: Viola Frey.* Essay by Patterson Sims. Philadelphia: Moore College of Art, 1984.

## Cliff Garten

Mitchell, Robb. "Cliff Garten." *American Ceramics* 1 (Winter 1982): 48.

Roth, Nancy. "The Vessel in Context: Cliff Garten's Paired Vases." *American Ceramics* 4, no. 3 (1985): 16–23.

## David Gilhooly

Chicago. Museum of Contemporary Art. *David Gilhooly.* Essays by Judith Russi Kirshner and Stephen Prokopoff. Chicago: Museum of Contemporary Art, ·1976.

McConathy, Dale. "David Gilhooly's Mythanthropy, or, From the Slime to the Ridiculous." *Artscanada* 32 (June 1975): 1–11.

Shuebrook, Ron. "Regina Funk." *Art and Artists* 8 (August 1973): 38–41.

Whitney Museum of American Art. *Ceramic Sculpture: Six Artists.* New York: Whitney Museum of American Art with the University of Washington Press, 1981.

## John Glick

Glick, John. "Studio Dinnerware: A Ceramics Monthly Portfolio." *Ceramics Monthly* 27 (December 1979): 43–62.

———. "Renewal." *Studio Potter* 12 (December 1983): 20–29.

Shafer, Tom. "John Glick: The Plum Tree Pottery." *Ceramics Monthly* 20 (September 1972): 20–25.

## Chris Gustin

Bodine, Sarah. "Mocking the Strongman Image: The Vessels of Christopher Gustin." *American Ceramics* 1 (Spring 1982): 16–19.

Gustin, Chris. "Potter's Journey: A Portfolio." *Ceramics Monthly* 30 (December 1982): 45–55.

"Portfolio: Chris Gustin." *American Craft* 47 (April/May 1987): 60–61.

## Wayne Higby

"Ancient Inspirations/Contemporary Interpretations." *Ceramics Monthly* 31 (February 1983): 62–68.

Higby, Wayne. "Drawing as Intelligence." *Studio Potter* 14 (December 1985): 36–37.

Jarmusch, Ann. "From Mesas Through Canyons to the Sea and Back." *American Craft* 41 (April/May 1981): 10–13.

Klemperer, Louise. "Wayne Higby." *American Ceramics* 3, no. 4 (1985): 32–37.

## Rick Hirsch

Hirsch, Rick. "The Raku Family Tradition." *Studio Potter* 7, no. 2 (1979): 28–33.

Hirsch, Richard A., and Chris Tyler. *Raku.* New York: Watson- Guptill, 1975.

"Richard Hirsch." *Ceramics Monthly* 28 (January 1980): 85, 86.

Wechsler, Susan. "The Tripod Vessels of Rick Hirsch." *American Ceramics* 1 (Spring 1982): 8–11.

## Margie Hughto

Barrie, Robert. "Syracuse University." *Ceramics Monthly* 27 (October 1979): 59–65.

Butera, Virginia Fabbri. "The Fan as Form and Image in Contemporary Art." *Arts Magazine* 55 (May 1981): 88–92.

Chayat, Sherry. "The Ceramic Fans of Margie Hughto." *Ceramics Monthly* 28 (May 1980): 40–46.

Everson Museum of Art. *Margie Hughto: Works in Clay.* Syracuse, N.Y.: Everson Museum of Art, 1972.

McFadden, David Revere. "Margie Hughto." *American Ceramics* 1 (Winter 1982): 49.

## Ka Kwong Hui

Crumrine, James, and Hui Ka Kwong. "Dialogue in a Museum." *Craft Horizons* 27 (July/August 1967): 19–21, 42.

Hendricks, Bici. "Hui Ka Kwong." *Craft Horizons* 27 (May/June 1967): 40–43, 73.

Smith, Dido. "Three Potters from China." *Craft Horizons* 17 (March/April 1957): 23–32.

## Jun Kaneko

Cathcart, Linda. "Space in Clay." *Craft Horizons* 35 (August 1975): 29–31.

Falk, Lorne. "Jun Kaneko." *American Ceramics* 3, no. 3 (1984): 42–47.

Griffin, Kit. "Jun Kaneko Workshop." *Ceramics Monthly* 30 (December 1982): 65.

Houston. Contemporary Arts Museum. *Jun Kaneko: Parallel Sounds.* Houston: Contemporary Arts Museum, 1981.

Schonlau, Ree, and Jun Kaneko. "Jun Kaneko: A Ceramics Monthly Portfolio." *Ceramics Monthly* 32 (June/July/August 1984): 49–58.

## Karen Karnes

Hadler Galleries. *Karen Karnes: Works 1964–1977.* Essay by Judith S. Schwartz. New York: Hadler Galleries, 1977.

Hadler/Rodriguez Galleries. *A Potter's Truth: Karen Karnes and Her Wood-Fired Forms of Clay.* Essay by M. C. Richards. New York: Hadler/Rodriguez Galleries, 1981.

"Karen Karnes Retrospective." *Ceramics Monthly* 26 (March 1978): 32–35.

Karnes, Karen. "Karen Karnes: A Conversation." *Studio Potter* 6, no. 1 (1977): 12–17.

Robertson, Seonaid. "Karen Karnes." *Ceramic Review* 50 (March/April 1978): 6–9.

Smith, Dido. "Karen Karnes." *Craft Horizons* 18 (May/June 1958): 10–14.

## Susan and Steven Kemenyffy

Carnegie-Mellon University Art Gallery. *Seventy-Five Years of Pittsburgh Art and Its Influences.* Pittsburgh: Carnegie-Mellon University Art Gallery, 1985.

Nicholas, Donna. "Steven and Susan Kemenyffy." *Craft Horizons* 31 (June 1971): 67.

Vanco, John L. "The Kemenyffys." *Ceramics Monthly* 30 (November 1982): 56–58.

## Anne Kraus

Chayat, Sherry. "There's Comfort in Tea." *American Ceramics* 6, no. 2 (1988): 24–29.

Gardner, Colin. "Reviews: Ferguson and Kraus." *Los Angeles Times*, March 21, 1986.

Malarcher, Patricia. "Storytelling in Clay and Fabric." *The New York Times*, June 1, 1986.

## Marilyn Levine

Battcock, Gregory, ed. *Super Realism: A Critical Anthology.* New York: Dutton, 1975.

Donnell-Kotrozo, C. "Material Illusion: On the Issue of Ersatz Objects." *Arts Magazine* 58 (March 1984): 89.

Foote, Nancy. "The Photo Realists: 12 Interviews." *Art In America* 60 (November/December 1972): 84–85.

Levin, Elaine. "Marilyn Levine: A Ceramics Monthly Portfolio." *Ceramics Monthly* 33 (March 1985): 41–46.

Levin, Kim. "The Ersatz Object." *Arts Magazine* 48 (February 1974): 52–55.

Peterson, Susan. "The Ceramics of Marilyn Levine." *Craft Horizons* 37 (February 1977): 40–43, 63–64.

## Roy Lichtenstein

Glenn, Constance W. *Roy Lichtenstein: Ceramic Sculpture.* Long Beach, Calif.: California State University, Art Galleries, 1977.

Noah, Barbara. "Lichtenstein's Ceramics." *Artweek* 8 (March 1977): 5–6.

"Roy Lichtenstein: Ceramic Sculpture." *Ceramics Monthly* 25 (May 1977): 40–45.

## Ken Little

Caldwell, Susan Havens. *Ken Dawson Little.* San Francisco: Quay Gallery, 1984.

Forde, Ed. "Tall Tales: Ken Little's Portraits of the West." *American Ceramics* 3, no. 3 (1984): 18–25.

John Michael Kohler Art Center. *Ken Little: Shattered Portraits and Unlikely Heroes.* Essay by Joanne Cubbs. Sheboygan, Wis.: John Michael Kohler Art Center, 1983.

## Michael Lucero

Adams, Brooks. "Michael Lucero at Sharpe and Charles Cowles." *Art in America* 73 (March 1985): 157–158.

Fernandes, Joyce. "Michael Lucero." *Arts Magazine* 58 (September 1983): 20.

Morgan, Robert C. "Reconstructing with Shards." *American Ceramics* 2 (Winter 1983): 36–43.

Shannon, Mark. "Michael Lucero: The Unnatural Science of Dreams." *American Ceramics* 5, no. 2 (1986): 28–33.

Zimmer, William. "A New Figure on the Horizon." *American Ceramics* 1 (Winter 1982): 26–29.

## Glen Lukens

Bray, Hazel. "California Pottery in Retrospect." *Studio Potter* 3 (Winter 1974/75): 58.

Keynes, Helen Johnson. "The Pottery of Glen Lukens." *Christian Science Monitor*, April 23, 1940.

Levine, Elaine. "Pioneers of Contemporary American Ceramics: Arthur Baggs, Glen Lukens." *Ceramics Monthly* 24 (January 1976): 24–30.

———. "Pioneers of the Vessel of Aesthetic: Glen Lukens and Maija Grotell." In *Transactions of the Ceramics Symposium 1979*, edited by Garth R. Clark. Los Angeles: Institute for Ceramic History, 1980.

———. *Glen Lukens: Pioneer of the Vessel Aesthetic.* Los Angeles: California State University, 1982.

———. "Glen Lukens: Pioneer of the Vessel Aesthetic." *American Ceramics* 1 (Spring 1982): 40–43.

———. "Glen Lukens." *Ceramics Monthly* 30 (May 1982): 40–44.

Lukens, Glen. "The New Handcraftsman." *California Arts and Architecture* 46 (December 1934): 13.

McCloud, Mac. "Glen Lukens: Pioneer Ceramist." *American Craft* 42 (June/July 1982): 12–15.

Peterson, Susan. "Glen Lukens 1887–1967." *Craft Horizons* 28 (March/April 1968): 22–25.

## Phillip Maberry

Cobb, James B. "Phillip Maberry." *American Ceramics* 3, no. 3 (1984): 66–67.

Schwartz, Judy S. "Phillip Maberry." *American Ceramics* 1 (Winter 1982): 50.

Warren, Ron. "Phillip Maberry." *Arts Magazine* 58 (March 1984): 21.

## Jim Makins

"Jim Makins: Tableware." *Ceramics Monthly* 28 (October 1980): 33.

Makins, Jim. "Jim Makins, Urban Potter: A Conversation." *Studio Potter* 9 (December 1980): 4–10.

"National Design Competition." *Ceramics Monthly* 34 (April 1986): 34–35.

## Graham Marks

Drutt, Matthew. "Graham Marks." *Ceramics Monthly* 32 (June/July/August 1984): 47–48.

Everson Museum of Art. *Graham Marks: New Works.* Essays by C.E. Licka and Wayne Higby. Syracuse, N.Y.: Everson Museum of Art, 1986.

McTwigan, Michael. "The Fruitful Mysteries of Graham Marks." *American Ceramics* 1, no. 2 (1982): 32–39.

Morgan, Robert C. "Graham Marks." *American Ceramics* 3, no. 1 (1984): 70–71.

## John Mason

Giambruni, Helen. "Exhibitions: John Mason." *Craft Horizons* 27 (January/February 1967): 38–40.

Hudson River Museum. *John Mason: Installations From the Hudson River Series.* Yonkers, N.Y.: Hudson River Museum, 1978.

Kelley, Jeff. "In Search of a Transparent Art: John Mason." *American Ceramics* 2 (Winter 1983): 26–31.

Krauss, Rosalind. "John Mason and Post-Modernist Sculpture: New Experiences, New Words." *Art in America* 67 (May/June 1979): 120–127.

Los Angeles County Museum of Art. *John Mason: Sculpture.* Intro. by John Coplans. Los Angeles: Los Angeles County Museum of Art, 1966.

McCloud, Mac. "John Mason." *Ceramics Monthly* 36 (January 1988): 46–48.

Nordland, Gerald. "John Mason." *Craft Horizons* 20 (May/June 1960): 28–33.

Pasadena Museum of Modern Art. *John Mason: Ceramic Sculpture.* Essay by Barbara Haskell. Pasadena, Calif.: Pasadena Museum of Modern Art, 1974.

## Harrison McIntosh

Chaffey Community College. Rex W. Wingall Museum-Gallery. *Harrison McIntosh, Studio Potter: A Retrospective Exhibition.* Essays by Garth Clark and Hazel Bray. Chaffey, Calif.: Rex W. Wingall Museum-Gallery, Chaffey Community College, 1979.

McCloud, Mac. "Harrison McIntosh." *American Craft* 45 (April/May 1985): 22–25.

McIntosh, Catherine. "Harrison McIntosh: Studio Potter." *Ceramics Monthly* 27 (October 1979): 42–48.

Petterson, Richard. "Harrison McIntosh: A Ceramics Monthly Portfolio." *Ceramics Monthly* 17 (June 1969): 19–26.

## Leza McVey

McVey, Leza S. "Leza S. McVey." *Everyday Art Quarterly* no. 27 (1953): 20–25.

"Profile: Leza McVey." *Ceramics Monthly* 1 (June 1953): 22–23.

## Judy Moonelis

Nos, Gnosis. "Crossing the Boundaries of Intimacy." *American Ceramics* 5, no. 2 (1986): 18–27.

Stein, Judith. "Judy Moonelis." *American Ceramics* 1 (Summer 1982): 60–61.

Winter, David. "Judy Moonelis." *Artnews* 85 (January 1986): 111.

## Ron Nagle

Cohen, Ronny. "Ron Nagle." *Artforum* 27 (January 1984): 76–77.

Halverstadt, Hal, Ed Ward, and Joseph Pugliese. "Ron Nagle in Rock and Clay: The Songwriter, The Potter." *Craft Horizons* 31 (June 1971): 34–37, 70–72.

Hays, Jo Anne Burstein. "Beyond Ceramic Traditions." *Artweek*, October 27, 1984: 3.

McTwigan, Michael. "Ron Nagle." *American Ceramics* 2, no. 4 (1984): 62–63.

San Francisco Art Institute. *Ron Nagle: Adaline Kent Award Exhibition*. Essay by Sylvia Brown. San Francisco: San Francisco Art Institute, 1978.

## Reuben Nakian

"Hirshhorn Collection." *Ceramics Monthly* 23 (May 1975): 20–23.

Kiriki, Alain. "Reuben Nakian at the Hirshhorn." *Art in America* 69 (April 1981): 147.

Marks, Claude. *World Artists 1950–1980*. New York: H. W. Wilson, 1984.

Nakian, Reuben. "Apprentice to the Gods." *Studio Potter* 14 (December 1985): 29–31.

## Win Ng

"A Portfolio of California Sculptors: Win Ng." *Artforum* 2 (August 1963): 30.

Riegger, Harold Eaton. "The Pottery of Win Ng." *Ceramics Monthly* 11 (April 1963): 14–17.

Uchida, Yoshiko. "Win Ng." *Craft Horizons* 20 (January/February 1960): 32–35.

## Richard Notkin

Dunas, Michael, and Sarah Bodine. "The Precarious Scale of Justice: Richard Notkin's Precious Protest." *American Ceramics* 5, no. 3 (1987): 16–23.

Eder, Lynn. "Richard Notkin." *Ceramics Monthly* 30 (November 1982): 59–63.

Kansas City Art Institute, Kemper Gallery. *Ceramic Artists: Distinguished Alumni of Kansas City Art Institute*. Edited by Sherry Cromwell-Lacy. Kansas City: Kansas City Art Institute, Kemper Gallery, 1983.

"Richard Notkin/Irene Vonck." *Ceramics Monthly* 35 (May 1987): 65, 67.

## Jeff Oestreich

Crane, Tim. "Speakeasy." *New Art Examiner* 13 (September 1985): 12–14.

MacKenzie, Warren. *Minnesota Pottery: A Potter's View*. Minneapolis: Art Gallery, University of Minnesota, 1981.

Murphy, Terri. "Jeff Oestreich: Potter." *Ceramics Monthly* 29 (September 1981): 50–55.

Oestreich, Jeff. "Some Thoughts on Studio Pottery." *Ceramics Monthly* 31 (October 1983): 52–57.

## Kenneth Price

Hopkins, Henry T. "Kenneth Price." *Artforum* 2 (August 1963): 41.

Los Angeles County Museum of Art. *Robert Irwin/Kenneth Price*. Essay by Lucy Lippard. Los Angeles: Los Angeles County Museum of Art, 1966.

———. *Ken Price: Happy's Curio's*. Intro. by Maurice Tuchman. Los Angeles: Los Angeles County Museum of Art, 1978.

Simon, Joan. "An Interview with Ken Price." *Art in America* 68 (January 1980): 98–104.

## Elsa Rady

Burstein, Joanne. "Elsa Rady." *American Ceramics* 1 (Summer 1982): 52–53.

McCloud, Mac. "Elsa Rady: Porcelain Vessels." *American Ceramics* 3, no. 4 (1985): 58–63.

## Daniel Rhodes

McDonald, Robert. "Daniel Rhodes." *American Craft* 46 (February/March 1986): 18–21.

Rhodes, Daniel. *Clay and Glazes for the Potter*. Philadelphia: Chilton, 1957.

———. *Stoneware and Porcelain: The Art of High-Fired Pottery*. Philadelphia: Chilton, 1959.

———. *Kilns: Design, Construction and Operation*. Philadelphia: Chilton, 1968.

———. *Tamba Pottery: The Timeless Art of a Japanese Village*. Tokyo: Kodansha International, 1970.

———. *Pottery Form*. Radnor, Penn.: Chilton, 1976.

———. "Daniel Rhodes: Pottery and the Person." *Ceramics Monthly* 25 (January 1977): 39–42.

———. "A Clay Life." *Ceramics Monthly* 35 (September 1987): 28–31, 64.

Richards, M. C. "Dan Rhodes." *Craft Horizons* 18 (September/October 1958): 14–19.

## Jerry Rothman

Clark, Garth R. *Jerry Rothman: Bauhaus Baroque*. Claremont, Calif.: Ceramic Arts Library, 1978.

Glasgow, Lukman. "Jerry Rothman." *Ceramics Monthly* 29 (September 1981): 37–41.

"Jerry Rothman." *Ceramics Monthly* 24 (November 1976): 38–39.

## Adrian Saxe

Clark, Garth. "Adrian Saxe: An Interview." *American Ceramics* 1 (Fall 1982): 22–29.

Forde, Ed. "Exhibitions: Adrian Saxe." *American Ceramics* 2, no. 3 (1983): 64–65.

Kansas City Gallery of Art. *Adrian Saxe*. Essays by Jeff Perrone and Peter Scheldahl. Kansas City: Kansas City, Mo.: Kansas City Gallery of Art/ University of Missouri, 1987.

Mays, John Bentley. "Stylistic Ensembles." *American Craft* 47 (October/November 1987): 42–49.

Perrone, Jeff. "Porcelain and Pop." *Arts Magazine* 58 (March 1984): 80–82.

## Richard Shaw

Braunstein Gallery. *Richard Shaw: Illusionism in Clay: 1971–1985*. Essay by Joseph Pugliese. San Francisco: Braunstein Gallery, 1985.

California State University, Main Art Gallery, Fullerton. *Richard Shaw, Ed Blackburn, Tony Costanzo, Redd Ekks, John Roloff*. Essay by Suzanne Foley. Fullerton, Calif.: California State University, Main Art Gallery 1976.

———. *Ten Years Later: Ed Blackburn, Tony Costanzo, Robert Rasmussen,(a.k.a. Redd Ekks), John Roloff, Richard Shaw*. Essay by Elaine Levin. Fullerton, Calif.: California State University, Main Art Gallery, 1987.

Newport Harbor Art Museum. *Richard Shaw/Ceramic Sculpture*. Essay by Jan Butterfield. Newport Beach, Calif.: Newport Harbor Art Museum, 1981.

San Francisco Museum of Modern Art. *Richard Shaw/Robert Hudson: Works in Porcelain*. Essay by Suzanne Foley. San Francisco: San Francisco Museum of Modern Art, 1973.

White, Cheryl. "Master of Illusion: Richard Shaw." *American Ceramics* 6, no. 2 (1988): 30–37.

## Peter Shire

Burstein, Joanne. "Peter Shire." *American Ceramics* 1 (Spring 1982): 52–53.

Glasgow, Lukman. "Peter Shire." *Ceramics Monthly* 28 (December 1980): 66–67.

McCloud, Mac. "Eccentric Juxtapositions." *Artweek* 12 (December 26, 1981): 1.

## Paul Soldner

Burstein, Joanne. "Paul Soldner." *American Ceramics* 1 (Spring 1982): 46–47.

Dunham, Judith. "Paul Soldner." *American Craft* 42 (October/November 1982): 24–28.

Levin, Elaine. "Paul Soldner: A Ceramics Monthly Portfolio." *Ceramics Monthly* 27 (June 1979): 59–69.

Rubin, Michael G. "Paul Soldner." *American Ceramics* 1 (Fall 1982): 38–41.

Soldner, Paul E. "Raku as I Know It." *Ceramic Review* (April 1973).

———. "The Personal Mark." *Studio Potter* 14 (December 1985): 62–64.

## Rudolf Staffel

Clark, Garth R. *Rudolf Staffel.* Philadelphia: Helen Drutt Gallery, 1981.

Sachs, Sid. "Rudolf Staffel: Past and Present." *American Ceramics* 1 , no. 1 (1982): 34–37.

———. "Rudolf Staffel." *New Art Examiner* 13 (September 1985): 63.

Staffel, Megan. "Memory, Process, Material, and Hand: Rudolf Staffel, a Daughter's Perspective." *NCECA Journal* 7, no. 2 (1986): 15–16.

## Toshiko Takaezu

Brown, Conrad. "Toshiko Takaezu." *Craft Horizons* 19 (March/April 1959): 22–26.

Hurley, Joseph. "Toshiko Takaezu: Ceramics of Serenity." *American Craft* 39 (October/November 1979): 2–9.

Tsubota, Anne. "Toshiko Takaezu." *American Ceramics* 2, no. 4 (1984): 64–65.

## Robert Turner

Hays, Johanna Burstein. "Robert Turner." *American Ceramics* 3, no. 4 (1985): 50–57.

Lebow, Edward. "Robert Turner." *American Craft* 46 (June/July 1986): 28–33, 67–69.

Milwaukee Art Museum. *Robert Turner: A Potter's Retrospective.* Essays by Kenneth Westphal and Gerald Nordland. Milwaukee, Wis.: Milwaukee Art Museum, 1986.

Turner, Robert. "Born Remembering." *Studio Potter* 10 (June 1982): 2–10, 12.

## Peter Voulkos

Albright, Thomas. "Peter Voulkos, What Do You Call Yourself?" *Artnews* 77 (October 1978): 118–124.

Brown, Conrad. "Peter Voulkos." *Craft Horizons* 16 (September/October 1956): 12–18.

Burstein, Joanne. "Peter Voulkos." *American Ceramics* 1 (Summer 1982): 50–51.

Coplans, John. "Voulkos: Redemption through Ceramics." *Artnews* 64 (Summer 1965): 38–39, 64–65.

Fischer, Hal. "The Art of Peter Voulkos." *Artforum* 17 (November 1978): 41–47.

Iwabuchi, Junko. "Peter Voulkos in Japan." *Ceramics Monthly* 31 (September 1983): 52–54.

Levin, Elaine. "Peter Voulkos: a Ceramics Monthly Portfolio." *Ceramics Monthly* 26 (June 1978): 59–68.

Los Angeles County Museum of Art. *Peter Voulkos: Sculpture.* Los Angeles: Los Angeles County Museum of Art, 1965.

Museum of Modern Art. *Sculpture and Paintings by Peter Voulkos.* New York: Museum of Modern Art, 1960.

Slivka, Rose. *Peter Voulkos: A Dialogue with Clay.* Greenwich, Conn.: New York Graphic Society, 1978.

## Betty Woodman

Albright College, Freedman Gallery. *The Ceramics of Betty Woodman.* Essay by Jeff Perrone. Reading, Penn.: Albright College, Freedman Gallery, 1985.

Devore, Richard. "Ceramics of Betty Woodman." *Craft Horizons* 38 (February 1978): 28–31, 66–67.

Heartney, Eleanor. "Betty Woodman." *New Art Examiner* 13 (November 1985): 55.

Rochester Art Center. *Betty Woodman: The Storm in a Teacup.* Text by Garth R. Clark. Rochester, Minn.: Rochester Art Center, 1980.

Russell, Ina. "Reversing the Object's Role." *Artweek* 19 (March 19, 1988): 6.

Wechsler, Susan. "Betty Woodman." *American Ceramics* 1 (Winter 1982): 53.

Woodman, Elizabeth, and George Woodman. "Ceramist's Odyssey of Clay: Italy." *Craft Horizons* 30 (May/June 1970): 18–19.

Woodman, Betty. "The Italian Experience." *Studio Potter* 11 (June 1983): 10–12.

## William Wyman

Horovitz, Israel. "William Wyman: the Rebel in the Conservative." *Craft Horizons* 30 (October 1970): 10–15.

Montgomery, Susan J. "Witness the Spirit of William Wyman." *American Ceramics* 4, no. 3 (1985): 30–35.

Pappas, Marilyn R. "The Temples of William Wyman." *American Craft* 40 (February/March 1980): 24–27.

## Arnold Zimmerman

"Arnold Zimmerman." *Ceramics Monthly* 35 (March 1987): 61, 63.

Priest, Ellen. "Arnold Zimmerman." *American Ceramics* 2 (June 1983): 20–23.

# INDEX